The Economics of New Goods

Studies in Income and Wealth
Volume 58

National Bureau of Economic Research
Conference on Research in Income and Wealth

The Economics of New Goods

Edited by
Timothy F. Bresnahan and
Robert J. Gordon

The University of Chicago Press

Chicago and London

TIMOTHY F. BRESNAHAN is professor of economics at Stanford University
and a research associate of the National Bureau of Economic Research.
ROBERT J. GORDON is the Stanley G. Harris Professor in the Social
Sciences at Northwestern University and a research associate of the
National Bureau of Economic Research.

The University of Chicago Press, Chicago 60637
The University of Chicago Press, Ltd., London
© 1997 by the National Bureau of Economic Research
All rights reserved. Published 1997
Printed in the United States of America
06 05 04 03 02 01 00 99 98 97   1 2 3 4 5
ISBN: 0-226-07415-3 (cloth)

1000946095

Copyright is not claimed for "Comment" on chap. 2 by Jack E. Triplett;
chap. 9 by Paul A. Armknecht, Walter F. Lane, and Kenneth J. Stewart;
and chap. 10 by Marshall B. Reinsdorf and Brent R. Moulton.

Library of Congress Cataloging-in-Publication Data

The economics of new goods / edited by Timothy F. Bresnahan and
    Robert J. Gordon.
        p.   cm.—(Studies in income and wealth ; v. 58)
    Includes bibliographical references and index.
    ISBN 0-226-07415-3 (cloth : alk. paper)
        1. Consumer price indexes—Congresses. 2. New products—Con-
gresses. I. Bresnahan, Timothy F. II. Gordon, Robert J. (Robert James),
1940–   . III. Series.
HB225.E3 1997
338.85′28—dc20   96-27822
                                                                             CIP

Since this volume is a record of conference proceedings, it has been exempted from the rules governing critical review of manuscripts by the Board of Directors of the National Bureau (resolution adopted 8 June 1948, as revised 21 November 1949 and 20 April 1968).

Contents

Prefatory Note

This volume contains revised versions of the papers and discussion presented at the Conference on Research in Income and Wealth entitled New Products: History, Theory, Methodology, and Applications, held in Williamsburg, Virginia, on 29–30 April 1994. Conference participants also attended a preconference at the National Bureau of Economic Research in December 1993.

Funds for the Conference on Research in Income and Wealth are provided to the National Bureau of Economic Research by the Bureau of the Census, the Bureau of Economic Analysis, the Bureau of Labor Statistics, the Department of Energy, the Internal Revenue Service, the National Science Foundation, and Statistics Canada; we are indebted to them for their support. The New Products conference was supported under National Science Foundation grants SES93-20826 from the Economics Program and 93-21051 from the Methodology, Measurement, and Statistics Program.

We also thank Timothy F. Bresnahan and Robert J. Gordon, who served as conference organizers and editors of this volume.

Executive Committee, April 1994

Charles R. Hulten, chair	Stanley Engerman
Ernst R. Berndt	Zvi Griliches
Geoffrey Carliner	Marilyn E. Manser
Carol Carson	Robert P. Parker
Rosanne Cole	Sherwin Rosen
W. Erwin Diewert	Charles A. Waite

Volume Editors' Acknowledgments

We are very much indebted to Kirsten Foss Davis and to Rob Shannon for organizing the conference on which this volume is based. We thank two anonymous referees for their helpful comments. We also thank Ernst Berndt, Zvi Griliches, Charles Hulten, and Jack Triplett for invaluable ideas in planning the conference.

Introduction

Timothy F. Bresnahan and Robert J. Gordon

The value of an hour of human life has been immeasurably increased by the successive invention of electric urban transport followed by motor transport on an ever more extensive highway infrastructure; faster trains soon made obsolete by piston and then jet airplanes; primitive local telephone service followed by ever cheaper long-distance service, cellular phones, and spreading data links; a host of durable appliances that greatly reduced household drudgery; and generations of home-entertainment devices, from crackling radios to small, dim, black-and-white televisions to today's color television systems of startling size and clarity to compact-disc players with lifelike fidelity. As we write, this list is being augmented by the spread of multimedia personal computers and the imminent accessibility to many homes of huge amounts of information through CD-ROMs and the World Wide Web. The length of human life, as well as its quality, has likewise been increased by a host of new medical hardware, from x-ray magnetic resonance imaging machines, as well as by an array of pharmaceutical marvels, from penicillin to the latest antidepressants.

Clearly, new goods are at the heart of economic progress. But that realization is only the beginning of an understanding of the economics of new goods. The value created by new goods must somehow be converted into an exact quantitative measure if official data on inflation (like the Consumer Price Index) are to represent accurately the theoretical concept of a true "cost-of-living" index, and if official data are to capture the annual increase in output and productivity contributed by the invention of new goods, as well as by steady improvements in the quality of old goods.

The Economics of New Goods encompasses the history of invention and

Timothy F. Bresnahan is professor of economics at Stanford University and a research associate of the National Bureau of Economic Research. Robert J. Gordon is the Stanley G. Harris Professor in the Social Sciences at Northwestern University and a research associate of the National Bureau of Economic Research.

improvement, exploring the theory that converts the broad notion that new goods improve human welfare into specific, quantitative ideas about measurable improvements in welfare and presenting detailed case studies of the problems encountered in converting theory to practice. This introduction to the volume attempts to advance our understanding of economic innovation and the economics of new goods. In so doing, it places within a broader context the specific contributions within these covers, which include historical treatments of new goods and their diffusion over substantial periods of time, practical exercises in measurement addressed to recent and ongoing innovations, and the real-world methods of adjusting for quality change carried out in official statistical agencies.

Human Welfare, the Cost-of-Living Index, and the Consumer Price Index

Innovations are important if they make a difference in the way human beings live and work. Most people share a set of common values and goals and agree on what it means to realize these objectives more fully. People care about freedom; nourishment; shelter; mobility; the onerousness and duration of work; and the offsetting uplift from family, friends, and entertainment. New goods matter if they improve the quality of life along these lines and/or allow the current quality of life to be maintained at less expense.

The contribution of new goods to consumer welfare is inseparably linked to the concept of the true cost-of-living (COL) index and to the creation of aggregate measures of the price level and national output. The standard definition of a COL index is the ratio in two situations (usually two time periods) of the minimum expenditure required to achieve the same level of well-being. A meaningful consumer price index linked to the notion of consumer welfare should approximate the true COL index, and measures of the output of consumer goods (i.e., real consumption expenditure) should be calculated by deflating current-dollar consumer expenditure by the same consume price index. Yet difficulties in translating the theoretical notion of a COL index into an actual consumer price index are significant. What does "the same level of well-being" mean when products are replaced by new versions embodying different quality attributes? An even more profound difficulty is, what does "the same level of well-being" mean when entirely new products are introduced that were unavailable in the first time period?

The Sears Catalogue Experiment

Many of the new goods we discuss here have made a huge difference in human life, and their invention explains why almost any person living in an advanced economy today would be appalled by the suggestion that they be cast back two centuries and forced to live in an era lacking these goods. The many dimensions of sacrifice suggested by the thought experiment of being cast back two centuries are represented by a more specific conceptual exercise that has been discussed frequently in the literature on price indexes and quality change. If you had one thousand dollars to spend, would you rather order from the first Sears, Roebuck & Co. catalogue of 1893 or from the final catalogue published a century later, in 1993? An entire century's worth of inflation makes your dollars worth much less than in 1893 according to official price indexes: in fact, less than one-tenth as much. Yet the newer catalogue offers a vast array of useful and attractive items not available or even imagined in 1893. The value of these changes is central to an understanding of how much richer society has become over time, in dimensions that are neglected by official measures of inflation.

However, the Sears catalogue exercise involves a subtlety, because most people would want to play the game both ways. They would prefer to spend their first two or three hundred dollars at 1893 prices: on steak at $0.50 per pound, on four-course restaurant meals at $1.29 apiece, or on men's work pants at $2.29 a pair. But they would want to spend their last few hundred dollars on videocassette recorders (VCRs), compact-disc players, and other wonders of modern life. And, going beyond the confines of the catalogue example, they would without question prefer to be treated for disease at today's hospital rather than at its 1893 equivalent. In contrast to official price indexes, which state that more than ten times the income is required to maintain a given standard of living today than in 1893, most people are likely to choose a much lower number—three, five, or seven times, but not more than ten times. This assessment restates the widespread belief, discussed further below, that the official U.S. Consumer Price Index (CPI) is biased upward to a significant degree.

The Sears catalogue example points to some of the difficulties in creating quantitative measures of economic progress. Some goods, particularly raw foodstuffs, have not changed appreciably and have undeniably increased in price manyfold. Yet in many other cases, inventions have greatly reduced the price of fulfilling a particular human need, as in the case of light, discussed in the first paper in this volume, and have also greatly expanded the quantity of the commodity that is available (at any price) to the average household.

The lightbulb example illustrates the power of really important new goods. Little more than a century ago, such activities as evening reading or entertaining were luxuries. A series of new goods, such as whale oil for lamps, gaslight, and then the electric lightbulb, rapidly lowered the costs of using artificial light, a commodity which is complementary to a wide variety of household and workplace activities. Thus, as artificial light grew cheaper, activities which had been economic only for short parts of the day spread to evening, activities confined to summer became year-round, and jobs became easier to perform.

The True COL Index and the CPI

Because of these complementarities, large changes in households' cost of light lowered the true COL index substantially. When artificial light gave people their evenings, it added time to their day. Constraints which made evening time less valuable were removed. A properly calculated COL index should reflect this advance and measure how much better-off consumers are, taking into account all the adjustments consumers make to their new circumstances (Diewert 1990). Thus, the decrease in the COL caused by the electric lightbulb is not confined to the difference in cost between oil lamps and electricity. Instead, it captures as well the value of time saved by consumers in trimming wicks and cleaning lamps, and the value of time freed for them both to pursue leisure activities in the evening and to make more productive their work activities during winter early mornings and late afternoons.

The official CPI in the United States and in most other countries makes no attempt to quantify the value of new products and often introduces them into the index many years after their initial introduction into the marketplace and after the initial phase of quality improvement and cost reduction. Therefore, the CPI has been widely assumed to incorporate a substantial upward bias, that is, to overstate the rate of inflation.[1] Recently this issue has entered the policy debate over the U.S. federal budget deficit. Many federal benefits expenditures are indexed to the CPI, as are parts of the tax code. A reduction in the CPI growth rate of 1 percentage point, or use of an alternative index growing that much more slowly, would reduce the deficit by $634 billion cumulatively between 1996 and 2005 (see U.S. Congress 1995, fig. A-2). The interplay between the economics of new goods and the construction of official price indexes is a major theme of this book.

Major Inventions, Minor Inventions, and Continuous Improvement

Thomas Edison's invention of the lightbulb, Henry Ford's introduction of the Model T, Vladimir Zworykin's television picture tube, and the Wozniak-Jobs innovations in the Apple II computer are all viewed as landmark events, "macro inventions" in the language of Mokyr (1990). These and many other new goods represent an expansion of the productive economy's ability to meet human needs. People have always wanted to extend the hours of daylight, to travel, to be entertained; workplaces have always needed to write and to calculate. Yet these landmark examples point to a complex, ongoing process. With each of these innovations a whole new industry was founded, but that was not the end of the story. In each case there followed subsidiary innovations that created dramatic improvements in performance and quality at substantially lower cost. In each case there followed also the development of related industries, from electricity generation to truck transportation to television and cable broadcasting to computer software production. In each case there was a change in the way people lived and worked, as ever cheaper electricity made possible home appliances that reduced drudgery, as motor transport led to the growth

---

1. The CPI also is subject to other forms of bias, including traditional substitution bias, outlet-substitution bias, and functional form bias, that are beyond the scope of the present volume. For a recent review see Wynne and Sigalla (1996).

of suburbs and a dispersion of economic activity, as television shifted entertainment from vaudeville and movie theaters to the home, and as the personal computer made possible working at home and scores of new service industries. Lowering costs, improving quality and performance, setting off subsidiary innovation processes, and permitting whole new ways of living—these are all part of the new-goods process.

The Household Production Function

The lightbulb example illustrates the value of using the "household production function" approach, introduced by Becker (1965), among others. The basic idea is that the activities that directly produce consumer welfare are indirectly produced by combining household time and purchased market commodities. The introduction of a new good, the lightbulb, is usefully viewed as one of a series of technical advances which lower households' costs of an activity called "making light." The technical advances themselves are very different from one another and are totally unconnected to the daily activities of households. Oil lamps called for improvements in ships, the better to hunt whales. Gaslight called for improvements in mining. The lightbulb was part of Edison's whole cluster of electrical inventions. Its invention stimulated an enormous outpouring of subsidiary inventions in the production and distribution of electricity, which accompanied further improvements in the lightbulb itself. The overall effect of all these different technical advances was to permit changes in the way that households produced light. The resulting fall in the "price of light" was dramatic and hugely valued by every household, regardless of its members' occupations, social class, or level of income.

The scope of the impact of new goods is quite broad. Consider the problem of wearing clean clothing. A century ago, this called for a large commitment of time and money. Technical change in a variety of areas led to new goods which dramatically reduced this cost. Among these were the washer and dryer, classic household labor-saving devices. Together with innovations in materials such as wash-and-wear fabrics and inexpensive detergents, these inventions permitted substantial savings in the household time allocated to the drudgery of creating clean clothes, releasing much of that time for more pleasant activities. The substitution of machines and fabrics for household labor, however, represents only part of the improvement. It also lowers the marginal price of one output of household production, clean and colorful clothing. As a result, households substitute toward this output. Depending on the strength of this substitution, there may actually be little saving of labor. All of the benefits are consumed as higher-quality final consumption, the ultimate aim of household production.

Multiple Dimensions of Wants

When new goods, new kinds of goods, or whole new industries achieve marketplace success, we infer that they satisfy previously unmet, or at the least badly met, needs. The needs for transportation services now met by the automobile always existed, and in order to understand the value of the invention of the automobile, it helps to distinguish at least five attributes of transportation services: cost, speed, production of by-products, comfort, and flexibility in providing transportation at the chosen time and between the desired origin and destination. In this context, predecessor goods like horses and railroads have several disadvantages. Horses are expensive (notably in land), slow, and very dirty, albeit very flexible in providing service between any two desired points. In contrast, railroads are relatively fast, comfortable for longer trips, quite inflexible, and only cost effective when many people desire to make the same journey at the same time. Automobiles combined the low costs and speed of their machine-powered predecessors and the flexibility of their muscle-powered predecessors with by-products (emissions) that seemed to present far fewer problems of health and cleanup expense than did animal waste. This previously unavailable combination of features explains why motor transport was perceived to have such a high value and had such far-reaching indirect consequences.

Clearly, the automobile has been one of the greatest forces for freedom in the whole of human history. It has made affordable to hundreds of millions, and soon billions, of people some of the things that human beings crave the most: autonomy, mobility, and a greater choice about where to live and whom to have as neighbors. As every country in every region of the globe reaches the level of development currently represented by Thailand or Malaysia, the first thing desired by virtually every household is a car.

The attribute described above as "flexibility" explains why the mobility provided by the automobile is so valuable. Cars owned by individual households save time in contrast to common carriers like the bus, train, or airplane. When passengers are "batched" together into large units per departure, there is inevitably an increased waiting time for the next departure for a given destination, and some passengers will leave at a departure time different from the one they originally desired. The increased destination flexibility of the automobile permits a more spread out pattern of residential land use, which in turn fosters privacy and freedom. The value of the suburban single-family house to its inhabitants emerges, at least in part, from the decline in the COL created by the invention and development of the automobile.

Quality Improvements in Existing Products

If a new industry is sufficiently important, demand for improvements in its product will call forth more inventions that lead to a stream of new goods. The early automobile was hard (and dangerous!) to start, cost an arm and a leg, had a rough ride, broke down frequently, and offered little protection from the elements. A series of improvements in a wide variety of components led to automobiles which provided far more value to users. Similarly, early computers were large, slow, required years of training to use, consumed vast amounts of power, failed frequently, and could not store programs or databases large enough to solve many common problems. Improvements in a wide variety of underlying technologies, from photolithography to software engineering, have permitted the development of computers that are vastly superior in all these dimensions.

Health Improvements

When we think about increases in social welfare over time, we focus on objective human needs that were first satisfied by one or more new goods. As we have seen, the long-standing desire for mobility and flexibility was satisfied by the automobile and the complementary capital and services (e.g., highways and service stations) that grew up to support it. Similarly, people have always had headaches and have always been in danger of death from infection. Aspirin and penicillin solved these problems and clearly increased human welfare. Any invention or discovery of new goods of this type raises the ability of the productive sector to meet human needs. The costs of achieving any given level of well-being (the true COL index) fall dramatically when modest expenditures can save previously unsavable lives or assuage previously unavoidable pain. Life expectancies have increased by about one-half during this century. Much of the credit for this tremendous improvement in human welfare goes to public health improvements interacting with technological advances in the medical and pharmaceutical industries.

The founding of new industries and the creation of new goods have promoted freedom and mobility, lengthened lives, virtually eliminated household drudgery, provided new conveniences, created previously unimaginable worlds of entertainment, saved time, and made a wide variety of human wants easier to satisfy. Any previously unmeasured decline in the true COL in comparison with the CPI has as its counterpart a large previously unmeasured increase in real wages. Today's workers obtain more services of greater value in return for less time spent at work and less time spent at household production.

Complementarities

We have already indicated that the full diffusion of a new good may require a host of supplementary inventions and innovations, such as highways and service stations in the case of the automobile. New goods are seen as inputs into economic processes such as household production. Combined with other inputs, some new themselves, the new goods produce useful services. There are at least three different types of complements to new goods. First, there are market-supplied complements: gasoline for automobiles, software for computers, or programs for television. Second, there are public or external complements: roads, the Internet, or the electromagnetic spectrum in the three examples above. Finally, there is information capital or changes in practices that come from using the new goods: consider the driver at the wheel, the travel agent at the computer screen, or the parents sleeping while their children watch cartoons. All of these complementary relationships are part of the process by which new goods are integrated into the fabric of everyday life.

The absence of the complement when the new good is first introduced may slow the rate at which it produces social gain. Individual consumers or businesses examining the new good may find it initially unattractive because of the absence of crucial complements. Creating the complements is often itself as technological an activity as creating the new good (Bresnahan and Trajtenberg 1995) and thus subject to the problems of incentives for innovation. The pace of creation of potential social gains from the new good is then determined by the pace of invention of complements. As the literature on the diffusion of new technologies emphasizes, the process of adaptation may proceed far more slowly than the process of invention. The pace then depends on the cost and difficulty perceived by the adapter in making complementary changes.

Yet complementarities have another side, which is leverage. New goods which establish a system or platform for complements can set off a train of complementary innovation. Thus the invention of computer hardware has led to generations of software development. The motion picture camera and projector have led to the production of thousands of films. Record, cassette, and compact-disc players have led to a vast multitude of sound recordings and a huge increase in the demand for performing artists. This leverage is a powerful force for creating a wide variety of new follow-on products. Typically, these are in the relationship of hardware to software. The leverage comes from a variety of uses or contents delivered over a general and reusable system.

Complementarities and Consumer's Surplus

The existence of complementarities to new goods leads to two other conceptual areas. Suppose that automobiles are only valuable with gasoline and roads, and that to achieve the full social value of automobiles we need to reorganize urban and suburban land use. Since many of those things in fact occurred, we might draw figure 1. In the figure, we draw two demand curves, D_0 and D_1. D_0 represents the demand for automobiles before the complementary investments have been made, and D_1, the demand curve afterward. Clearly D_1 will be farther from the origin as long as the introduction of complements increases the demand for automobiles.

In figure 1 we have also drawn the consumer's surplus that would be gained by lowering the price of automobiles from its initial value to the level represented by the horizontal line. Note that the social value of the invention of the automobile is conditional on the existence of the complements. The "before" consumer's surplus is smaller because automobiles are hard to use if gasoline cannot be purchased readily, and because without supermarkets or suburban houses automobiles confer fewer benefits. The large "after" consumer's surplus triangle is at least in part the result of investing in the complements as well as inventing and improving the automobile.

While figure 1 shows a large consumer's surplus triangle associated with

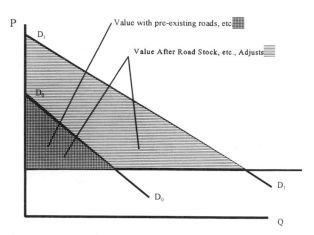

Fig. 1   Value of cars with and without complements

complementary investments, the distinction may be exaggerated from the perspective of today's consumer. The process of investing in the new good and its
complements brought with it a whole new set of habits, tastes, and knowledge;
eliminating the automobile would apparently leave us very badly off. Yet were
our grandparents that badly off? They did not have the modern tastes and habits; they lived in communities where shopping was within walking distance at
a time when walking down the street brought its own benefits of greetings from
neighbors and of close social contact.

This distinction is closely related to the traditional concerns of index number
theory. It is well known that a consumer price index based on the Laspeyres
formula (i.e., using the expenditure weights of the first year of an interval of,
say, a decade) exaggerates the true change in the COL by ignoring shifts in the
expenditure patterns of consumers in response to changes in relative prices. In
the classic example, using initial weights for expenditures on beef and chicken
exaggerates the increase in the COL when the relative price of beef increases
and consumers shift toward chicken. And in parallel, the use of a Paasche formula (i.e, using the expenditure weights of the last year of the interval) understates the true change of the COL.

In the same way, assessing the value of an invention like the automobile
from today's perspective, with its highly dispersed suburbs, jobs, and other
aspects of land use, surely overstates the value of automobiles as a new good.
The favorable aspects of denser neighborhoods cited above may simply be unfamiliar to today's suburban residents, who therefore place no value on them.
Similarly, the old-fashioned general store may have charged higher prices than
succeeding forms of retailing like the supermarket, but it provided a community center, information, and gossip that many lonely individuals would value
today if they knew where to find them.

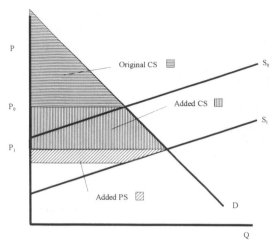

Fig. 2   Effects of a supply shift

Price Measurement and Consumer Value

Our introduction of the consumer's surplus triangles in figure 1 suggests a way of illustrating how intimately the measurement of changes in the true COL is related to the concept of consumer's surplus (or value). Let us consider a new good that reduces the cost of an hour of viewing recent movies, namely the VCR. The invention is represented in figure 2 by a downward shift in the supply curve for "entertainment services" from S_0 to S_1. The demand curve D is unchanged, since we assume no change in income, tastes, or the prices of other related goods. The market for entertainment services shifts from an equilibrium with price P_0 to one with larger quantity and lower price, P_1.

However, the true change in the cost of making the services is measured by the vertical downward shift in the supply curve S_0 to S_1, not the observed difference in price $(P_0 - P_1)$. These two concepts differ because of the upward-sloping supply curve. The job of the official price measurement agency is to measure the marginal cost of an increase in output, so that the true change in cost can be disentangled from the observed change in price. At present this task is not adequately carried out by the statistical agencies in most countries, except in special cases, including that of automobiles in the United States where a considerable effort is made to obtain from manufacturers an estimate of the added cost of new equipment. The hedonic price technique is an alternative method that uses statistical regression to obtain an estimate of the added price (and implicitly cost) contributed by an extra quantity of an output "characteristic" (e.g., speed and memory size for a personal computer); in figure 2 this is analogous to measuring the slope of the supply curve S_1.

In figure 2, consumer's surplus prior to the invention is the triangle labeled "Original CS." The invention adds the "Added CS" area. The remaining area, labeled "Added PS," represents the increase in producer's surplus associated with the invention. Thus, the one-dimensional representation of the decline in price corresponds to a two-dimensional gain received by consumers and producers together.

Distinguishing New Goods from New Varieties of Existing Goods

Thus far we have emphasized the long-run impact of major new goods. But not every trivial difference between one good and another warrants the label "new good." We know that consumers exhibit strong tastes for certain goods as a result of fads, fashion, and the influence of advertising (which may simultaneously serve as a valuable conduit of information and as an influence on consumer tastes for particular products and brand names). How can we distinguish between the "fad and fashion" type of consumer preference and the preferences revealed by the "objective unmet needs" criterion that we have previously employed to identify genuinely new goods?

The Taste for Variety

A central theme of this section is that we cannot always trust consumer behavior to reveal the true value of goods and services. To see this, consider "low hemlines" as a new good. We see consumers switching to low hemlines, refusing to treat low hemlines as a perfect substitute for higher ones. Are we then correct in calculating a consumer's surplus associated with low hemlines as a new good? A few years later, we would be forced by this precedent to treat high hemlines as a new good creating consumer's surplus. Obviously, an error has been made. The error lies in modeling this as a stable taste for variety. Each time, the demand for the switch to the other length is a demand for novelty, not for variety. To complete the welfare calculation, we would need to "age" the older product type, that is, to remove surplus from it because it had become nonnovel. The switch would then be explained as escaping from the old, and we would correctly conclude that welfare has remained constant over time. A complementary way to approach this problem is to admit that anything novel is inherently subject to depreciation. Below we return to the role of depreciation in assessing the gains from new goods.

Welfare Gains within Product Categories

Is acetaminophen as much a new good as aspirin? If we continue to use the ability to satisfy objective previously unmet human needs as our criterion for assigning the terminology "new good" to a new product, we would stress the advantages of acetaminophen over aspirin: some people are allergic to aspirin, many people's stomachs are irritated by it, and so on. Similarly, a dramatic expansion in the number and kind of antibiotics offers physicians the opportunity to avoid adverse side effects and to deal with bacteria resistant to penicillin (the first antibiotic). The increasing variety of both painkillers and antibiotics, arising from an ongoing process of new-goods introductions, allow the product category "pharmaceuticals" to meet objective human needs in an ever more satisfactory way. Thus we distinguish between new goods which open up whole new product categories and other new goods which increase quality or variety within product categories. As long as there are diminishing returns to quality and variety, new goods that establish entire new categories (like the automobile) will be economically more important than improvements that occur within categories.[2]

The last observation calls for methodologies that measure the economic importance of new goods. By how much *has* the true COL been lowered by the invention of aspirin? by the further development of acetaminophen? As with all COL-measurement approaches, the authors in this volume use demand-based assessments of willingness to pay. The effort is to assess the amount by which consumers would have to be compensated for their headaches if aspirin (or acetaminophen but not aspirin) were prohibitively expensive. The wide variety of available measurement tools—price indexes, hedonic price indexes, and demand-system measurement—are all attempts to make this assessment. All use demand behavior to reveal value in use.

For consumer goods, the objective unmet needs approach to defining new goods has limitations. If we return to the example of painkillers, we note that many of the new products in this category are (it seems) trivial recombinations of existing ingredients. With some marketing magic, however, they nonetheless sometimes succeed in gaining substantial market share. A research approach which seeks to name the previously unmet need will be likely to fail. Indeed, many analysts are tempted to conclude that the value of these new varieties is basically zero. Implicitly or explicitly, they find that the consumers who switch to these new varieties are making a mistake. At least in this example, there seems to be blatant contradiction between the "objective unmet needs" approach and the actual behavior of consumers.

Many of the same analytical problems arise throughout the consumer goods economy where advertising, marketing, and, more generally, image matter a great deal. Is the motion picture *Rocky IV* a new good? Is its relationship to *Rocky* to be understood as embodying diminishing returns in the same way as the relationship of tetracycline to penicillin? The importance of image, reputation, and marketability suggests that the two relationships are fundamentally different.

Marginal Value versus Inframarginal Value

In evaluating the latest new goods from Hollywood, it is important not to fall into errors associated with the diamond/water paradox. We may find that many current motion pictures or music albums are tawdry or cheap. Dramatic

---

2. The literature on product quality and product variety contains a great deal of analysis of the extent of diminishing returns. See Eaton and Lipsey (1989).

declines in the costs of making and disseminating entertainment products are the result of many new types of high-tech equipment used in the entertainment and communications industries, and of such new household goods as the radio, record player, cassette player, compact-disc player, and VCR. This lower cost of producing entertainment services, as in figure 2, naturally leads to a lowered threshold for introducing a new motion picture or album. That the marginal entertainment product is, well, marginal, does not show that there is no contribution to economic welfare from the totality of new entertainment products. Stated another way, inframarginal consumers receive a huge gain in consumer's surplus from the lower quality-adjusted price of entertainment.

Similarly, our great-grandparents would probably find most modern uses of such basic commodities as light or clean water extremely wasteful. These commodities are so much cheaper than they were a few generations ago that rational consumers put the marginal lumen and liter to much lower-value uses. The total contribution of the new goods in permitting this "waste" is not to be discounted, however. Many inframarginal uses are far more valuable than those at the margin, and again the gain in consumer's surplus can be enormous.

Current controversies over the wasteful use of water and energy should remind us that the perspective of stable preferences is not always the right approach. Between different people now, and within the same group over time, values, tastes, knowledge, and assumptions about the world may all change in response to changing relative prices made possible by technological advances. The very process of long-term economic growth, and especially of changes in style of life and work, contributes to these changes in values, tastes, knowledge, and assumptions. As a result, to assume that tastes remain fixed over a long period of time—decades or centuries—is surely an analytical error.

The Measurement of Value

The economic importance of new goods ultimately lies in their contributions to consumer welfare. Measuring that contribution reliably is therefore an important aspect of constructing a true COL index. Since much technical progress in modern societies is embedded in new goods, any quantitative assessment of long-run economic success also calls for these measures.

Measuring the Novelty of New Goods

Does a new good provide fundamentally different value to a user, or can it be viewed as embodying different quantities of particular "characteristics" that already existed? The first antibiotic might be viewed as a fundamentally new good, since the characteristics of having bacteria-killing capabilities did not exist in previous drugs. In contrast, an electronic calculator might be viewed as a "repackaging" of characteristics previously embodied in slide rules and rotary-electric calculating machines. This distinction between fundamental novelty and repackaging brings together some of the basic modeling and measurement questions that lie at the heart of this book. Should we think of the automobile as just another transportation mode with somewhat different characteristics than the railroad or horse and buggy?

There are advantages to taking this view. One can think of the underlying consumer need of fast, flexible transportation as being fundamental. The costs of meeting that need fell with the introduction and development of the automobile. The researcher's task is to quantify the extent of that fall in cost, which can be represented by the downward shift between supply curves S_0 and S_1 in figure 2 above. This task is not trivial, for it involves thinking through such diverse issues as the availability of gasoline and roads, the crankiness of early starters, and the external (unpriced) cost of streets previously made filthy by horse droppings. Having solved those problems, however, the researcher has the somewhat easier task of putting the new good in overall context. A particular need was badly met and now is better met. A useful quantification of *how much* better is the carefully researched total social cost of meeting the need. This is the characteristics approach of Lancaster (1979) or the household production function approach of Becker (1965).

An alternative view stresses the differences rather than the similarities of the new good. Automobiles and horses, or automobiles and railroads, are such poor substitutes that we should think of a new item in the utility function—automobile services. Raff and Trajtenberg discuss this distinction in their paper on the early automobile industry (chap. 2 in this volume). They note that some new automobiles have "new item in the utility function" features, for example, those that embody dramatic changes in product characteristics. Others seem instead to offer cheaper versions of existing characteristics. Raff and Trajtenberg link this distinction about the economic role of the new vehicle to the difference between product and process innovation. At its most valuable, product innovation adds new items to the utility function, rather than lowering the prices of existing goods. In contrast, process innovation reduces the cost of existing goods.

One can probably take either side of this debate on any of a wide variety of groundbreaking new goods. The radio receiver can be thought of as a wholly new good or, together with the broadcast, as a combination of a more rapidly delivered newspaper, a more versatile player piano, and a cheaper, though lower sound quality, concert hall. The computer can be thought of as a revolutionary invention or as a much cheaper calculator, bookkeeper's binder, and typewriter rolled into one. This volume contains interesting examples of each approach, both of which have their strengths and weaknesses.

At the other extreme, we can probably assume that an incremental automobile product—say a light blue rather than a dark blue 1995 Ford Escort—has a single product demand curve well approximated by the horizontal line $dd(-\infty)$ in figure 3. That is, the light blue and dark blue models are perfect substitutes. If the light blue model were priced one hundred dollars more than the dark blue model (and otherwise identical models in other colors), it would sell very few, if any, units.

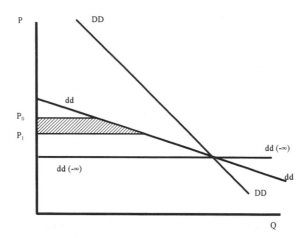

Fig. 3   Consumers' gain from lowering one product's price

Hedonics and Welfare

A closely related issue is the difference between hedonic pricing and the extent of the COL reduction associated with a new good. Hedonic pricing reports the change in quality-adjusted prices for goods that are changing in quality. If newly introduced goods are nearly perfect substitutes (after quality adjustment) for existing products, linking them into a hedonic index will capture their value. That near perfect substitution goes under at least three alternative names: (1) "repackaging," (2) high substitution elasticities across products, and (3) the absence of market power for single sellers. However, if the new goods are close but not nearly perfect substitutes for existing ones, hedonic pricing will miss part of the COL reduction associated with the new good.

Recently, Trajtenberg (1989) has offered an analysis of these intermediate cases. One ingredient in his theory is a product's uniqueness, determined by its distance from other products in the product space. The farther any particular product is from others, the more it tends to have product-specific demand curves like dd and not $dd(-\infty)$. Examples are products which extend the product space or which fill in important gaps in the product space. Such new products will (1) have economic value through product-specific consumer's surplus, not just by lowering the hedonic price line for the whole industry, (2) have moderate substitution elasticities with other products, and (3) provide some market power for sellers.

In figure 3 we offer a simple illustration of this point. In it we quality-adjust the prices of all goods in the same market so that they may all be shown along the same vertical axis. For convenience in graphing we assume that at the same quality-adjusted prices all the goods sell the same quantity, although this assumption is irrelevant. In figure 3, the demand curve labeled DD shows how the demand for a typical single good changes when the prices of all goods in the market are altered together. DD has slope because it is a market, not a single-product, demand curve. We also show two alternative single-product demand curves. The one labeled $dd(-\infty)$ is horizontal and corresponds to products that are perfect substitutes. When products are perfect substitutes, any seller raising the price of its product above other sellers' prices instantly experiences a decline in its demand to zero. There is no area under demand curve $dd(-\infty)$: removing a product from the marketplace, leaving the price of perfect (quality-adjusted) substitutes in place, does not lower welfare.

By contrast, the alternative single-product demand curve labeled dd is sloped. This corresponds to the case of close but not perfect substitutes. A reduction in the price of this product from P_0 to P_1 increases consumer welfare. Ignoring income effects, the increase in welfare is the consumer's surplus, the shaded area under dd between P_0 and P_1.

Following from the important contribution by Trajtenberg, two of the papers in this volume attempt a calculation of this sort: Hausman's paper on cereals and Greenstein's paper on computers. This measurement exercise is difficult because the slope of dd depends on the degree to which preexisting goods are (after quality adjustment) substitutes for the new good.

The Depletion Hypothesis, Diminishing Returns, and Other Qualifications

In most advanced industrial countries, the growth rate of productivity slowed significantly in the past two decades in contrast to the half century prior to 1973. This much-discussed "productivity slowdown" was addressed by Nordhaus (1982) who proposed his "depletion hypothesis." The world is running out of new ideas just as Texas has run out of oil. Most new goods now, compared with those of a century ago, are not founding whole new product categories or meeting whole new classes of needs. Is it merely a coincidence that the period of most rapid productivity growth in U.S. history corresponded to the interval between roughly 1920 and 1965, when such fundamental inventions as motor cars, airplanes, electric machines, light, appliances, radio and television, chemicals, plastics, antibiotics, together with their complementary and subsidiary inventions, were spreading through the country? Slow productivity growth since the early 1970s may be a result of diminishing returns, which in our framework can be interpreted as a predominance of innovations that take the form of repackaging rather than the introduction of truly new products.

Diminishing Returns: Too Much Complexity, Variety?

Surely, some might respond, the ever spreading personal computer and its associated software have created a revolution as profound as the great inventions of the late nineteenth and early twentieth centuries. But there is room for doubt. It is hard to find much evidence of productivity growth created by personal computers (see Baily and Gordon 1988). Much of the increase in the output of computers captured by the official computer price index (based on the hedonic technique) measures increases in speed and memory size that are consumed by the requirements of ever more complex software. The benefits to the average user of marginal refinements in software sophistication and graphical interfaces are minor compared to the benefits of the invention of the original spreadsheet and word processing software. Many computer users and administrators are dismayed by the current cycle of upgrades and obsolescence with its attendant need to buy new hardware, install new programs, and retrain staff, all in the name of benefits that provide dubious value.

Along the same line, modern innovations may be coming up against inherent limits in the availability of time and the size of the human "stomach." Some inventions in the home entertainment industry, such as the replacement of the cassette player by the compact-disc player, provide alternative uses of a fixed amount of time with a marginal improvement in the quality of that time. Supermarkets are crammed with new food products, but each new product replaces the "stomach space" previously available for older products. Has the level of satisfaction actually increased, or do we have here another example of illusory benefits created by marketing and advertising? Those taking this approach would view with some skepticism the benefits of the development of Apple-Cinnamon Cheerios estimated by Hausman in this volume.

Negative Developments in Modern Society

We have already stressed that new inventions breed changes in tastes. Today's suburbanite places a higher value on the automobile, out of necessity, than a resident of a dense community in the late nineteenth century where home and work were close together and where nearby shops provided information services for which today's resident is dependent on electronic media. If we could transport the family of 1895 to today, it might marvel at many inventions but lament the passing of some of its favorite pastimes, including the dance hall, player piano, and burlesque.

The danger of exaggerating the importance of new goods comes not just from the change in tastes over time, but also from developments that are objectively negative from the perspective of either 1895 or 1995. Not just crime but the fear of crime has increased greatly in most areas of the country, leading to expenditures on guards, security systems, and even walled-in communities with security checkpoints. The investment in "security services" increases the gross domestic product without causing a corresponding increase in consumer welfare.

We refrain from placing environmental pollution on the list of modern negatives, because pollution in most American cities has been greatly reduced since World War II, primarily by a shift from coal to natural gas for heating but also by a series of government regulations that have added devices to automobiles, electric generating stations, steel mills, and other facilities, and have measurably cleaned up the air. Pollution surely got worse between the dawn of the industrial revolution and some point in the twentieth century, but then this process was reversed by the benign development of facilities for the widespread distribution of natural gas together with compulsion from government regulations.

This introduction has emphasized the many dimensions in which new goods improve economic welfare and the reasons much of this improvement in economic well-being has been omitted from official statistics that measure economic progress. This section has introduced three types of qualifications. First, the pace of introduction of truly new goods, contrasted with "repackaging" innovations, may have slowed down. Second, our tendency to place a value on new goods from our modern perspective introduces a classic index number problem, since new goods may appear to be less valuable to hypothetical observers from a century ago with different values and tastes for community, mobility, and adventure. Finally, some new developments are objectively negative, including crime and pollution.

Our summaries of the papers in this volume are grouped into three categories: "Historical Reassessments of Economic Progress," "Contemporary Product Studies," and "Measurement Practice in Official Price Indexes." In discussing the major findings of these papers, we will return to many of the themes advanced so far and point to links between the papers and our previous analysis. Could the qualifications introduced in this last section qualify in a substantial way our presumption that official statistics have substantially understated the rate of economic growth? The dramatic findings of our first paper on the history of light force us to confront this issue head on.

The Papers in This Volume

Historical Reassessments of Economic Progress

The lead paper in the volume is by William D. Nordhaus. This highly original paper breaks new ground by creating a quantitative history of light from the open fire of cave dwellers to the modern compact fluorescent lamp. Data are developed for the whole historical range of lighting devices, including data on light output in lumens and on energy consumption in Btus, allowing the calculation of improvements in lighting efficiency through time. Today's compact fluorescent lamp produces a ratio of lumen-hours per thousand Btu that is thirty thousand times higher than the cave dwellers' open fire. Over the shorter period since 1800, the nominal price of light in 1992 is estimated to have fallen to one three-hundredth of its value in the year 1800. By Nordhaus's calculation, the nominal price of light declined by 3.6 per year over the past two hundred years relative to a hypothetical alternative price index based on the price of energy inputs.

The Nordhaus paper illustrates the importance of framing an analysis of new goods in terms of the characteristics they produce (lumens) rather than the goods themselves (whale-oil lamps, electric bulbs). By pricing the characteristic itself, Nordhaus is able to leap across history, linking successive products without missing the consumer's surplus created by, say, the switch from gas to electricity. His paper shows that it is possible to extend the characteristics approach beyond its previous use in defining computer output in terms of two primary characteristics, speed and memory.

Nordhaus enters more speculative territory when he extrapolates from his new evidence on the price of light to consider the magnitude of possible bias in historical data on the aggregate price level and the aggregate real wage. This involves speculating about the annual rate of bias for goods and services classified into three groups, ranging from traditional unchanging goods like food consumed at home to goods like transportation, home entertainment, and medical care that have experienced an enormous amount of technological change. In contrast to official data showing that real wages increased by a factor of 13 from 1800 to 1992, Nordhaus's "low-bias" estimate is for an increase by a factor of 40 and his "high-bias" estimate is by a factor of 190. As shown by discussant Charles Hulten, disposable personal income per capita in the United States in 1991 was approximately $17, 200, and thus 1800 real disposable income in 1991 dollars would be $1,300 by the official estimate, $430 by the low-bias estimate, and $90 by the high-bias estimate. The fact that these estimates strain credulity echoes several themes introduced above, including the need to evaluate changes over long periods not only from the perspective of end-of-period tastes but also from the perspective of beginning-of-period tastes, and the issue of diminishing returns to increases in such modern characteristics as lumens, computer speed, and automotive horsepower.

A new set of historical price indexes is also produced by Daniel M. G. Raff and Manuel Trajtenberg in chapter 2. This pioneering paper develops new data, hedonic price equations, and hedonic price indexes extending back to the dawn of the U.S. automobile industry in 1906. The basic result is that the real (CPI-adjusted) quality-adjusted price of automobiles declined at an average rate of roughly 5 percent per year from 1906 to 1940, thus halving every thirteen years. During the first decade of the interval prices fell even faster, reaching a rate about half as rapid as the rate of price decline reported in the best recent studies of the personal computer. This finding reinforces our previous emphasis on the product cycle, in which prices decline more rapidly in the early years of a product, and on the role of the product cycle in creating a significant bias in official price indexes when products are introduced late (the automobile was not introduced into the CPI until 1935).

Along the way, the authors discuss a number of fundamental issues involved in applying the hedonic methodology. One of these involves the absence of market-share data, since it would be highly desirable to weight the observations for the various models by their sales. To deal with this problem, the authors develop a separate hedonic index for low-priced Ford models and report that there is only a small divergence between the Ford index and their index for the industry as a whole. Another important issue involves the treatment of individual characteristics which, while statistically significant, do not plausibly enter the consumer's utility function and lead to misleading hedonic price indexes when included in the regressions. Their discussion is part of a larger literature on the difficulty of applying the hedonic regression technique to a complex product like the automobile when several of the measurable characteristics (horsepower and especially weight) are ones that the consumer does not care about, while some that the consumer does care about ("ride" and "handling") may be difficult or impossible to measure.

In chapter 3 Walter Y. Oi provides a general analysis of the economics of inventions together with an application to a specific product, the air conditioner. Oi links the problem of defining a new product with that of defining a monopoly, where the operative issue is the lack of a close substitute. A new product is then one for which there is no close substitute available in the market, a definition that admittedly begs the question of what constitutes "close." The social value of an invention is measured, as in figure 2 above, by the sum of producer's and consumer's surpluses generated by the new product. Often this approach will understate the value of the higher quality of a new product like the jet plane, which not only reduced the real price of air travel but also was faster, safer, and quieter than its predecessors. In fact, Oi states that the social returns to a major invention like the telephone, penicillin, the computer, or air-conditioning "far exceed" the sum of consumer's and producer's surpluses by affecting third parties, changing preferences, and opening the way for technical advances in other sectors. The static approach also implies that some socially worthwhile inventions will remain uninvented ("in the womb") because in some cases the profits available to a monopolist inventor protected by the patent system do not cover the cost of the invention. Oi argues that unsuccessful inventions are not like dry holes in oil exploration, because there is no final product which can absorb the costs of the unsuccessful inventions.

Oi discusses numerous other aspects of the general process of invention. The cost of invention is not exogenous; rather, research and development play a dual role, not only increasing the average cost of an innovation but also raising its probability of success and its ultimate value. Oi develops more fully the idea of the product life cycle that we have discussed above and relates it to the speed of adoption or diffusion of a new product. The lag between invention in the laboratory and introduction into the marketplace can be long and variable, exceeding twenty years for fifteen of fifty inventions cited by Oi.

The case study in Oi's paper concerns the air conditioner, the dissemination of which was subject to a long lag between the issuance of the fundamental patent in 1906, the first introduction into movie theaters in 1922, and the mass-market sale of room air conditioners in the early 1950s. Oi's analysis focuses on the air conditioner as a major factor in bringing about convergence of real wages and productivity in the southern and northern United States. He also points to a variety of benefits and costs for households, ranging from better and longer sleep and a reduction in allergies to the disappearance of "front porch society of Dixie" as "more neighbors closed doors and windows." He also examines a wide variety of externalities in the framework of figure 1 above, including the role of air-conditioning in raising the value of land in Manhattan, reducing automobile accident rates, and reducing the price of textiles and cigars.

A very different type of new good is examined by Joel Mokyr and Rebecca Stein in chapter 4. The authors argue that much of the great decline in mortality in the four decades prior to World War I can be attributed to an invention—the discovery and successful diffusion of the germ theory of disease. The analysis is embedded in a model of household decision making within the household production framework developed by Becker and others. In this framework, households combine goods and services purchased on the market ("market goods") with their own time to produce the "final goods" that appear in the household's utility function. For instance, households combine a television set and time to produce the enjoyment of watching a television program. In this interpretation the germ theory of disease offered households a new technology for transforming market consumption and time into better health. As households came to understand the processes that caused disease, they reallocated a certain amount of expenditure toward goods like soap and clean water and changed personal habits, thus shifting the way market goods and time were combined in the household production function toward greater emphasis on hygiene and personal care.

Mokyr and Stein echo Oi's emphasis on the long lag between the invention of the germ theory, its acceptance by doctors, and finally its diffusion into the practice of the ordinary household. Some of the authors' evidence for the diffusion of the theory rests on the rise, despite price increases, in England's per capita consumption of soap, particularly after 1900. They also discuss the role of improvements in the preservation of milk, improvements in the feeding of infants, and the democratization of access to piped water. The paper raises an issue about the allocation of public resources in that it implies that the level of poverty mattered less than the way households used the limited resources they had. In contrast to those who view rising incomes as a prerequisite for reduced mortality, it implies that public health education can have a high payoff even in those less-developed countries where the rate of economic growth is slow.

Contemporary Product Studies

In chapter 5, Jerry A. Hausman expands the theory of the COL index to incorporate new goods. New goods may be used in standard formulas, providing that the "virtual price" assigned to the new good before it is introduced is the one that sets demand to zero. As an example of this analysis, Hausman undertakes to estimate the virtual price for a single new good, Apple-Cinnamon Cheerios, and calculate the surplus resulting from its introduction.

As with many consumer-products industries, ready-to-eat breakfast cereals offer a complex web of substitution possibilities among individual products. The virtual price of any particular new variety can only be higher than prevailing prices if existing varieties are not very good substitutes for the new good. This leads to considerable estimation efforts in order to learn the relevant demand elasticities. Hausman's estimation framework permits different amounts of similarity among cereal varieties. The extrapolation down to zero quantity to calculate the virtual price is also treated in a very flexible way. This flexibility in econometric estimation is, at the present moment, responsible for a gap between one-time COL index calculations in research papers like this one and the production calculations done by the statistical agencies.

Hausman's estimates lead to the conclusion that the virtual price for Apple-Cinnamon Cheerios was approximately twice the prevailing market price after the entry of the product. As a result, the new-good consumer's surplus for its introduction was substantial. Assuming this experience to be representative of the many new-product introductions in the cereal market, Hausman provides a back-of-the-envelope calculation that the CPI for cereal may be overstated by as much as 25 percent.

Finally, Hausman examines imperfect-competition effects. Under perfectly competitive price-setting, we typically assume that the prices of all other products may be held constant in assessing the impact of a new good. With imperfect competition, however, the marginal revenue of substitute products may be shifted in a first-order way. Hausman uses the Apple-Cinnamon Cheerios entry example to show that these effects can be substantial.

In chapter 6 Robert C. Feenstra and Clinton R. Shiells examine a possible upward bias in import price indexes because of the omission of new product varieties. Rapid growth of imports into the U.S. from developing countries over the last several decades provides much of the impetus for this study. The suspected price index bias has direct effects on the measured value (in U.S. consumer's surplus) of this trade. It also has the indirect effect of contaminating estimates of import demand, possibly leading to too-high estimates of income elasticities and too-low estimates of price elasticities.

Feenstra and Shiells use an econometric procedure to correct import price indexes. They build an economic model of preference for variety. The model shows how the demand for a given firm's (or country's) products responds to increased variety. They then show how to correct price indexes for omitted varieties in a way that depends on observable share data and a few unknown parameters. The econometric estimation, performed for all U.S. imports (except petroleum) at the three-digit SITC (Standard International Trade Classification) level, provides the unknown parameter estimates which permit construction of the corrected price index.

In chapter 7, Ernst R. Berndt, Linda T. Bui, David H. Lucking-Reiley, and Glen L. Urban examine product-level demand for antiulcer medications. They concentrate particularly on marketing variables, an important part of the new-good commercialization process in prescription drug markets. The focus is on the determination of sales at the individual product and brand level. The analysis distinguishes between "industry-expanding" and "rivalrous" marketing efforts. They find a smaller industry-expanding effect when more marketers are competing. They also find that rivalrous marketing efforts depreciate much more rapidly than do industry-expanding ones. This investigation into the effects of marketing variables on demand serves as part of a discussion of the competition among drug inventors and producers to introduce new products. The raw technology of a drug, its ability to provide health benefits, can generate no consumer's surplus until the drug is prescribed and used. The marketing efforts studied here provide the information, and perhaps the persuasion, that cause use.

In drug competition, invention of new chemical entities takes a long time. A leading product, such as Tagamet in the antiulcer market studied here, has time to build up considerable first-mover advantages. Berndt et al. show how marketing efforts for the second drug entering the market, Zantac, were important in overcoming these first-mover advantages. The process of informing (physician) customers is important in competition as well as in realizing the consumer's surplus associated with new products.

In chapter 8 Shane M. Greenstein attempts to measure the economic benefits that technological innovation in the computing industry gave to buyers. Covering the period 1968–81, this paper distinguishes between the declining price of computing power and the extension of computing capabilities. Extensions were important throughout the 1970s as computers became capable of performing ever larger tasks. In Greenstein's framework, the computer capable of completing a previously infeasible task is a new good. If two smaller computers cannot perform the tasks a larger one (with the sum of their capacities) is programmed to do, invention of the larger one creates new surplus for buyers, which Greenstein sets out to measure.

Greenstein examines this issue in a vertical product-differentiation model: all computer users value the same index of computer performance, but some value it much more than others. It is the consumer's surplus of the high-performance valuers which will drive the calculation of the social value of extending the product range.

Greenstein finds substantial consumer's surplus of this type. Over and above the benefits of a continuing decline in the price-performance ratio, the extension of the product range provided as much as half of the consumer's surplus enjoyed by computer users in the 1970s. Further, the benefits of extension in the early years of computing arise from the technical benefits of the few dominant computer systems of that era, such as the IBM system 360 and system

370. Finally, it appears that the time lags before buyers achieve the benefits of a new extension are quite long, a finding in common with those of Oi and Mokyr-Stein.

Measurement Practice in Official Price Indexes

In chapter 9, Paul A. Armknecht, Walter F. Lane, and Kenneth J. Stewart review the methods currently used to deal with new products in the best-known official U.S. price index. They distinguish replacement items (new models of previously available items that replace old models), supplemental items (new brands of currently available goods that supplement rather than replace older brands or models), and entirely new items that do not fit within any established CPI item category. Regarding new products, the authors admit that the CPI has no method for comparing totally new products with older products. New products are introduced into the CPI through a process of "sample rotation" in which item and outlet samples are reselected each year for 20 percent of the geographic areas. Thus, on average, it takes five years for a new item to enter the CPI, and even longer for a totally new product type like the VCR, which was introduced into the CPI in 1987, about a decade after it began selling in volume. Month-to-month price changes of new products are included in the CPI only in the months and years subsequent to their introduction. In the month of transition both the old and the new item (or outlet) is priced and all of the price difference is treated as a quality difference. Thus, if the new items or outlets provide consumer satisfaction more efficiently, the CPI will miss that effect. This may have occurred in the shift to newer discount outlets or in the replacement of cassette and record players by compact-disc players.

Because the CPI does not have any procedure for placing a value on the price decline implicit in the introduction of new products, much of this paper concerns the treatment of replacement and supplemental items for existing products. Much of their discussion involves the substitution that is initiated by field agents when an item is discontinued. The field agent introduces a new or updated version if possible, and Bureau of Labor Statistics (BLS) commodity analysts determine the treatment of the newly substituted item. In some cases the new item is considered to be directly comparable, and any quality difference between the old and new item is missed. A problem is created for products like televisions, which often fall in price although their features have improved. Analysts treat the new model as comparable to capture this decline in price but miss the additional improvement in quality built into the new model. The opposite case is when a new model or item is judged to be of dissimilar quality to an old version. Then the weight applied to the model is applied to the average rate of change in the product category of which that model is a part. This method creates problems for classes of goods like automobiles which change little in price except when new models are introduced; recently, new methods have been introduced to distinguish price changes across model years from those within model years. The third treatment occurs when direct quality adjustments are made between old and new models. This has long been done for new cars and trucks, based on production-cost data supplied by manufacturers, and is now done for specific apparel-item groups using the hedonic regression method.

In chapter 10 Marshall B. Reinsdorf and Brent R. Moulton address a bias in the U.S. CPI which has become known as "formula bias." This results from a tendency for sellers' prices to exhibit mean reversion. Prices that are low tend to rise at a rate higher than average, often because items have been on sale and return to the regular price. Prices that are relatively high tend to decline, or at least rise at a rate lower than average, as competition takes effect. A Laspeyres component index gives a large weight to those sellers offering sale prices in the base period and tends to rise rapidly as the heavily weighted sale prices revert to their regular values.

It is known that this type of basis can be avoided through the use of geometric mean indexes. The authors calculate alternative geometric and Laspeyres-type component indexes for the same underlying price data for the period June 1992–June 1993 and reach two findings. First, the geometric mean component indexes almost always exhibit lower rates of price growth than the Laspeyres-type component indexes do. More important, the size of the difference between the two indexes varies substantially between classes of items. For fresh fruits and vegetables and apparel, the Laspeyres indexes showed rates of change 2 to 3 percentage points higher than the geometric mean indexes. For other expenditure categories, however, the differences tended to be smaller, in most cases less than 1 percent a year. Overall, the authors conclude that replacing the Laspeyres-type formula with geometric mean indexes would (for items other than shelter) reduce the inflation rate in the overall CPI by about 0.4 percent per year.

In chapter 10, Andrew Baldwin, Pierre Després, Alice Nakamura, and Masao Nakamura have concentrated on the introduction of new goods in the Industrial Product Price Index (IPPI) in Canada and the Domestic Wholesale Price Index (DWPI) in Japan. They find that many goods newly introduced into the PPI and WPI are not actually new but have been produced for a long time previously. Many of the new goods are simply modifications of deleted goods. As in the United States all of the price differential between deleted and "new" goods is treated as a quality differential.

Much of their focus for both countries is on the treatment of computers. In Canada starting around 1986 the U.S. hedonic price index for computers was used as a proxy for Canadian prices, but in 1990–91 Statistics Canada began to develop its own hedonic price indexes. The Bank of Japan introduced U.S.-made computers into its import price index as long ago as 1965 but first introduced Japanese-made computers into its domestic WPI in 1987. The hedonic regression method for computers was introduced with the 1990 revision of the WPI. This is desirable in itself but has the undesirable side effect of tending to exaggerate differences in the growth rate of computer prices from other prices, as other goods are still priced by the matched-models method. Somewhat surprisingly, the authors find that, despite the delay in introducing computing equipment into the PPI for Canada and WPI for Japan, these omissions had small effects on the overall values of the Canadian and Japanese indexes. This occurred primarily because of the relatively small share of computers within the total of manufacturing output for the two countries.

References

Baily, Martin N., and Robert J. Gordon. 1988. The productivity slowdown, measurement issues, and the explosion of computer power. *Brookings Papers on Economic Activity* 19 (2): 347–420.

Becker, Gary S. 1965. A theory of the allocation of time. *Economic Journal* 75 (September): 493–517.

Bresnahan, Timothy, and Manuel Trajtenberg. 1995. General purpose technologies: "Engines of growth"? *Journal of Econometrics* 65 (1): 83–108.

Diewert, W. Edwin. 1990. The theory of the cost-of-living index and the measurement of welfare change. In *Price level measurement,* ed. W. E. Diewert, 79–147. Contributions to Economic Analysis, vol. 196. Amsterdam: North-Holland.

Eaton, B. Curtis, and Richard G. Lipsey. 1989. Product differentiation. In *Handbook of industrial organization,* vol. 1, no. 10, ed. Richard Schmalensee and Robert D. Willig, 723–68. Amsterdam: North-Holland.

Lancaster, K. J. 1979. A new approach to consumer theory. *Journal of Political Economy* 74:132–57.

Mokyr, Joel. 1990. Punctuated equilibria and technological progress. *American Economic Review* 80 (2): 350–54.

Nordhaus, William D. 1982. Economic policy in the face of declining productivity growth. *European Economic Review* 18 (May/June): 131–58.

Trajtenberg, Manuel. 1989. The welfare analysis of product innovations, with an application to computed tomography scanners. *Journal of Political Economy* 97:444–79.

U.S. Congress. Senate. Advisory Commission to Study the Consumer Price Index. 1995. Toward a more accurate measure of the cost of living. Interim report to the Senate Finance Committee. 15 September.

Wynne, Mark A., and Fiona D. Sigalla. 1996. A survey of measurement biases in price indexes. *Journal of Economic Surveys* 10, no. 1 (March): 55–89.

I   Historical Reassessments of Economic Progress

1   Do Real-Output and Real-Wage Measures Capture Reality? The History of Lighting Suggests Not

William D. Nordhaus

1.1   The Achilles Heel of Real Output and Wage Measures

Studies of the growth of real output or real wages reveal almost two centuries of rapid growth for the United States and western Europe. As figure 1.1 shows, real incomes (measured as either real wages or per capita gross national product [GNP]) have grown by a factor of between thirteen and eighteen since the first half of the nineteenth century. An examination of real wages shows that they grew by about 1 percent annually between 1800 and 1900 and at an accelerated rate between 1900 and 1950.

Quantitative estimates of the growth of real wages or real output have an oft forgotten Achilles heel. While it is relatively easy to calculate nominal wages and outputs, conversion of these into real output or real wages requires calculation of price indexes for the various components of output. The estimates of real income are only as good as the price indexes are accurate.

During periods of major technological change, the construction of accurate price indexes that capture the impact of new technologies on living standards is beyond the practical capability of official statistical agencies. The essential difficulty arises for the obvious but usually overlooked reason that most of the goods we consume today were not produced a century ago. We travel in vehicles that were not yet invented that are powered by fuels not yet produced, communicate through devices not yet manufactured, enjoy cool air on the hot-

William D. Nordhaus is professor of economics at Yale University and a research associate of the National Bureau of Economic Research.

Helpful comments on economics, physics, and index number practices were given by Ernst Berndt, William Brainard, Carole Cooper, William English, Robert J. Gordon, Zvi Griliches, Tim Guinnane, Charles Hulten, Stanley Lebergott, Michael Lovell, Joel Mokyr, Sherwin Rosen, Robert Solow, T. N. Srinivasan, and Jack Triplett. Robert Wheeler brought the diary and experiments of B. Silliman, Jr., to the author's attention. Alice Slotsky generously tutored him on Babylonian history. All errors and flights of fancy are his responsibility.

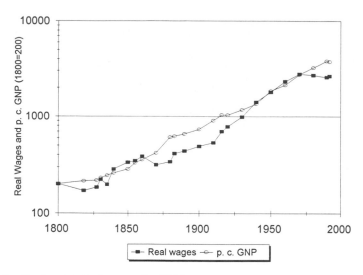

Fig. 1.1   Real wages and per capita GNP

test days,[1] are entertained by electronic wizardry that was not dreamed of, and receive medical treatments that were unheard of. If we are to obtain accurate estimates of the growth of real incomes over the last century, we must somehow construct price indexes that account for the vast changes in the quality and range of goods and services that we consume, that somehow compare the services of horse with automobile, of Pony Express with facsimile machine, of carbon paper with photocopier, of dark and lonely nights with nights spent watching television, and of brain surgery with magnetic resonance imaging.

Making a complete reckoning of the impact of new and improved consumer goods on our living standards is an epic task. The present study takes a small step in that direction by exploring the potential bias in estimating prices and output in a single area—lighting. This sector is one in which the measurement of "true" output is straightforward but where misleading approaches have been followed in the construction of actual price or output indexes. The bottom line is simple: *traditional price indexes of lighting vastly overstate the increase in lighting prices over the last two centuries, and the true rise in living standards in this sector has consequently been vastly understated.*

The plan of this paper is as follows: I begin with an analysis of the history of lighting, focusing particularly on the revolutionary developments in this field. I then use data on lighting efficiency to construct a "true" price of light and compare this with "traditional" price indexes that are constructed using traditional techniques. In the final section I engage in a *Gedankenexperiment* on the extent to which revolutionary changes in technology may lead to similar

---

1. The revolutionary implications of air-conditioning are considered in Oi, chap. 3 in this volume.

biases for other consumer goods and services and the consequent underestimation of the growth of real incomes over the last century.

1.2   Milestones in the History of Light

1.2.1   Basic Measurement Conventions

I begin with some simple conventions. What we call "light" is radiation that stimulates the retina of the human eye. Radiation in the visible spectrum comprises wavelengths between 4×10^{-7} and 7×10^{-7} meter. Light flux or flow is the name for the rate of emission from a source, and the unit of light flux is the lumen. A wax candle emits about 13 lumens, a one-hundred-watt filament bulb about 1200 lumens, and an eighteen-watt compact fluorescent bulb about 1290 lumens. The unit of illuminance (the amount of light per unit area) is the lux; one lux equals one lumen per square meter. Unobstructed daylight provides about ten thousand lux, while the level of illuminance of an ordinary home is about one hundred lux. In the candle age, a room lit by two candles would enjoy about five lux.

The efficiency of a lighting device can be measured in many ways, but for my purposes I am interested in the light output per unit of energy input. This is measured either as *lumen-hours per thousand Btu* (British thermal units), or alternatively today as *lumens per watt*.

1.2.2   Evolution

The first and in some ways most spectacular stage in the development of illumination is the eye itself, which evolved to exploit that part of the spectrum in which the sun (and moon) concentrate the greatest part of their radiated energy. Having adapted to daylight, the next stage for prehistoric humans was to devise means to illuminate the night, or dwellings like caves. The history of lighting reveals primarily the extraordinarily slow evolution in technology for the first few million years of human societies and then the extraordinarily rapid development from about the time of the Industrial Revolution until the early part of this century.

1.2.3   Open Fires

The first use of artificial or produced light probably coincided with the controlled use of fire. The first tool, known as the Oldowan chopper, has been dated from 2.6 million years ago, while the tentative identification of domesticated fire used by *Australopithecus* was discovered in Africa and dates from 1.42 million years ago. More definitive evidence of the controlled use of fire was found in the caves of Peking man (*Homo erectus*) dating from around 500,000 years ago. Presumably, open fires were used partially as illuminants in caves. It seems likely that sticks were used as torches in early times. (See table 1.1 for a brief chronology of the history of lighting.)

Table 1.1	Milestones in the History of Lighting
1,420,000 B.C.	Fire used by *Australopithecus*
500,000 B.C.	Fire used in caves by Peking man
38,000–9000 B.C.	Stone fat-burning lamps with wicks used in southern Europe
3000 B.C.	Candlesticks recovered from Egypt and Crete
2000 B.C.	Babylonian market for lighting fuel (sesame oil)
1292	Paris tax rolls list 72 chandlers (candle makers)
Middle Ages	Tallow candles in wide use in western Europe
1784	Discovery of Argand oil lamp
1792	William Murdock uses coal-gas illumination in his Cornwall home
1798	William Murdock uses coal-gas illumination in Birmingham offices
1800s	Candle technology improved by the use of stearic acid, spermaceti, and paraffin wax
1820	Gas street lighting installed in Pall Mall, London
1855	Benjamin Silliman, Jr., experiments with "rock oil"
1860	Demonstration of electric-discharge lamp by the Royal Society of London
1860s	Development of kerosene lamps
1876	William Wallace's 500-candlepower arc lights, displayed at the Centennial Exposition in Philadelphia
1879	Swan and Edison invent carbon-filament incandescent lamp
1880s	Welsbach gas mantle
1882	Pearl Street station (New York) opens with first electrical service
1920s	High-pressure mercury-vapor-discharge and sodium-discharge lamps
1930s	Development of mercury-vapor-filled fluorescent tube
1931	Development of sodium-vapor lamp
1980s	Marketing of compact fluorescent bulb

Sources: Stotz (1938), de Beaune and White (1993), Doblin (1982), and Encyclopedia Britannica 11th and 15th editions.

1.2.4   Lamps

Open fires are relatively inefficient, and *H. sapiens* not only developed the ability to start fires (dated as early as 7000 B.C.) but also invented capital equipment for illumination. The first known lighting tool was a stone, fat-burning lamp that was used in western Europe and found most abundantly in southern France. According to de Beaune and White (1993), almost two hundred fat-burning Paleolithic lamps dating from 40,000 to 15,000 B.C. have been identified. These lamps were made from limestone or sandstone and can easily be fashioned with shallow depressions to retain the melted fuel. Chemical analyses of residues of the fuel have shown that it was probably animal fat. De Beaune and White estimate that a Paleolithic lamp had the lighting power of a candle. Modern replicas are relatively easy to build, requiring but half an hour, suggesting that, like modern lights, most of the cost of early lighting devices was in the fuel rather than in the capital.

In Greece, lamps (from the Greek *lampas,* meaning torch) fashioned from pottery or bronze began to replace torches about 700 B.C. The Romans manufactured molded terra-cotta lamps, sometimes decorative and elaborate. The earliest markets for lighting fuel arose in early Babylonia around 2000 B.C. According to Dubberstein (1938), Babylonians used sesame oil as an illuminant in temples, although it was too expensive to employ in homes. The wage of a common laborer was approximately one shekel per month, which was also approximately the price of two *sutu* (ten liters) of sesame oil. I have performed a number of experiments with sesame oil and lamps purportedly dating from Roman times (see the appendix). These experiments provide evidence that an hour's work today will buy about 350,000 times as much illumination as could be bought in early Babylonia.[2]

As Europe declined into the Dark Ages, there was a clear deterioration in lighting technology, with lighting returning to the Paleolithic open saucer that performed more poorly than the wicked Roman lamps. Van Benesch (1909) describes the medieval peasant's practice of burning pine splinters. Sometimes the torch was held in the mouth to leave the hands free.[3] Virtually all historical accounts of illumination remark on the feeble progress made in lighting technology in the millennia before the Industrial Revolution.

1.2.5   Candles

Candles appeared on the scene several millennia ago, and candlesticks were recovered from Minoan Crete. From the Greco-Roman period until the nineteenth century, the most advanced and prestigious lighting instrument was the wax candle; indeed, the mark of nobility was to be preceded by a candle in the bedtime procession. Candle making was a respected profession in the Middle Ages, and some of the earliest labor struggles occurred between the wax and tallow chandlers of England in the fourteenth and fifteenth centuries. Students of international trade will recall the famous satirical "Petition of the Candle Makers" of Frédéric Bastiat:

> *To the Chamber of Deputies:*
>   We are subjected to the intolerable competition of a foreign rival, who enjoys such superior facilities for the production of light that he can inundate our national market at reduced price. This rival is no other than the sun. Our petition is to pass a law shutting up all windows, openings and fissures through which the light of the sun is used to penetrate our dwellings, to the prejudice of the profitable manufacture we have been enabled to bestow on the country.
>   *Signed:* Candle Makers. (quoted in Samuelson and Nordhaus 1992, 677)

---

2. I am particularly grateful to Alice Slotsky for tutoring me on the intricacies of Babylonian price and measure data. Analysis of Babylonian wage and price data are contained in Dubberstein (1938), Farber (1978), and Slotsky (1992). During the old Babylonian period of Hammurapi/Samsuiluna (around 1750 B.C.), a common laborer earned about one shekel a month while a *sutu* (a measure equal to six *qa* or five liters) of sesame oil cost about half a shekel. Conversion of these to lighting efficiency and labor costs is discussed in the appendix.

3. Details on the history of lighting are contained in many sources; the "mouth torch" is described in Gaster and Dow (1919).

Tallow gradually replaced wax as the former was much less costly, and in the eighteenth and nineteenth centuries whale-oil candles became the illuminant of choice.

1.2.6   Gas and Petroleum

One of the remarkable features of human history is how slow and meandering was the progress in lighting technology from the earliest age until the Industrial Revolution. There were virtually no new devices and scant improvements from the Babylonian age until the development of town gas in the late eighteenth century. By contrast, the nineteenth century was an age of tremendous progress in developing lighting technologies and reducing their costs (although, as we will see, you would have great difficulty discovering that from the price indexes on light).

A key milestone in illumination was the development of town gas, which was produced from coal and was used both in residences and for street lighting. There were a number of parallel attempts to introduce gas, but William Murdock is usually thought of as the father of gas lighting. As was often the case before the routinization of invention, he experimented on himself and his family in his home in 1792, and when they survived he started a commercial enterprise. The first quarter of the nineteenth century saw the great cities of Europe lit by gas.

The petroleum age was ushered in by the discovery of "rock oil" in Pennsylvania. We are fortunate that the first entrepreneurs had the good sense to hire as a consultant Benjamin Silliman, Jr., professor of general and applied chemistry at Yale and son of the most eminent American scientist of that period, to perform a thorough analysis of the possibilities of rock oil for illumination and other industrial purposes. (A thoroughly underpaid academic, Silliman served as a consultant for industrial interests and later lost his reputation when he predicted, to the contrary opinion and consequent displeasure of the head of the U.S. Geological Survey, that great quantities of oil were to be found in southern California.) For his report to the Pennsylvania oilmen, Silliman distilled the oil, ran a series of tests, and developed an apparatus he called a "photometer" to measure the relative illuminance of different devices. Silliman's 1855 report was suppressed on commercial grounds until 1870, but it is probably the best single source of data on both prices and efficiency available before this century (see his results in table 1.2).

Although energy consumption is the bête noire of today's environmental movement, it is interesting to contemplate how history would have unfolded if in 1850 technology had been frozen, by risk analysts or environmental impact statements, at the stage of coal gas and whale oil. One happy environmental effect of these new technologies, as Louis Stotz reminds us, was that "the discovery of petroleum in Pennsylvania gave kerosene to the world, and life to the few remaining whales" (1938, 6). After the development of the petroleum industry, kerosene became a strong competitor of gas, and the declining prices

Table 1.2   **Silliman's Lighting Experiments, 1855**

				Efficiency		Price of Illumination	
Fuel	Apparatus	Fuel Rate (per hour)	Fuel Price (cents per volume)	(candle-hours per hour)	(lumen-hours per 1,000 Btu)	(cents per candle-hour)	(cents per 1,000 lumen-hours)
Town gas (cu. ft.)	Scotch fish tail	4	0.40	5.4	31.9	0.30	22.8
	Scotch fish tail	6	0.40	7.6	29.7	0.32	24.5
	Cornelius fish tail	6	0.40	6.2	24.4	0.39	29.8
	Argand burner	10	0.40	16.0	37.8	0.25	19.2
Sperm oil (fl. oz.)	Carcel's lamp	2	1.95	7.5	23.0	0.52	40.1
Colza oil (fl. oz.)	Carcel's lamp	2	1.56	7.5	23.0	0.42	32.1
Camphene (fl. oz.)	Camphene lamp	4	0.53	11.0	16.9	0.19	14.9
Silvic oil (fl. oz.)	Diamond lamp	4	0.39	8.1	12.4	0.19	14.8
Rock oil (fl. oz.)[a]	Camphene lamp	3.4	0.06	8.1	14.6	0.03	2.0

Source: Silliman (1871).

[a]Price for kerosene refers to 1870.

Table 1.3   **Efficiency of Different Lighting Technologies**

Device	Stage of Technology	Approximate Date	Lighting Efficiency (lumens per watt)	Lighting Efficiency (lumen-hours per 1,000 Btu)
Open fire[a]	Wood	From earliest time	0.00235	0.69
Neolithic lamp[b]	Animal or vegetable fat	38,000–9000 B.C.	0.0151	4.4
Babylonian lamp[a]	Sesame oil	1750 B.C.	0.0597	17.5
Candle[c]	Tallow	1800	0.0757	22.2
	Sperm	1800	0.1009	29.6
	Tallow	1830	0.0757	22.2
	Sperm	1830	0.1009	29.6
Lamp	Whale oil[d]	1815–45	0.1346	39.4
	Silliman's experiment: Sperm oil[e]	1855	0.0784	23.0
	Silliman's experiment: Other oils[f]	1855	0.0575	16.9
Town gas	Early lamp[g]	1827	0.1303	38.2
	Silliman's experiment[e]	1855	0.0833	24.4
	Early lamp[e]	1875–85	0.2464	72.2
	Welsbach mantle[e]	1885–95	0.5914	173.3
	Welsbach mantle[e]	1916	0.8685	254.5
Kerosene lamp	Silliman's experiment[e]	1855	0.0498	14.6
	19th century[h]	1875–85	0.1590	46.6
	Coleman lantern[i]	1993	0.3651	107.0
Electric lamp				
Edison carbon	Filament lamp[j]	1883	2.6000	762.0
Advanced carbon	Filament lamp[j]	1900	3.7143	1,088.6
	Filament lamp[j]	1910	6.5000	1,905.0
Tungsten	Filament lamp[j]	1920	11.8182	3,463.7
	Filament lamp[j]	1930	11.8432	3,471.0
	Filament lamp[j]	1940	11.9000	3,487.7
	Filament lamp[k]	1950	11.9250	3,495.0
	Filament lamp[k]	1960	11.9500	3,502.3
	Filament lamp[k]	1970	11.9750	3,509.7
	Filament lamp[k]	1980	12.0000	3,517.0
	Filament lamp[l]	1990	14.1667	4,152.0
Compact fluorescent	First generation bulb[m]	1992	68.2778	20,011.1

Note: The modern unit of illumination is the lumen which is the amount of light cast by a candle at one foot.

[a]See appendix.

[b]From de Beaune and White (1993), assuming that the device is one-fifth as efficient as a tallow candle.

[c]A candle weighing one-sixth of a pound generates 13 lumens for 7 hours. Tallow candles are assumed to have three-quarters the light output of sperm candles.

[d]Whale oil is assumed to have the efficiency of a candle and one-half the caloric value of petroleum.

[e]See table 1.2.

[f]Other oils tested by Silliman included silvic oil, camphene, and colza oil. Here I choose camphene, largely wood alcohol, as the most cost effective.

Table 1.3   (continued)

gFrom Stotz (1938, 7f). According to Stotz, expenditures of $30 per year on town gas at a price of $2 per 1,000 cubic feet would produce 76,000 candle-hours. After the introduction of the Welsbach mantle, efficiency improved from 3 candles per cubic foot to 20 candles per cubic foot; town gas had 500 Btu per cubic foot.

hAccording to Stotz (1938, 8f), expenditures of $25 per year on kerosene at a price of $0.135 per gallon would yield 90,000 candle-hours per year.

iEstimate on a Coleman kerosene lantern from Coleman Corp. (personal communication).

jGaster and Dow (1919, 75, 79).

kLinear interpolation between 1940 and 1980.

lA standard incandescent bulb tested by *Consumer Reports*.

mAccording to *Consumer Reports*'s first test of compact fluorescent bulbs (Bright ideas in light bulbs 1992).

of both gas and kerosene led to a healthy competition which continues even to this day for heating.

1.2.7   Electric Lighting

The coup de grâce to both oil and gas for illumination came with the twin developments of electric power and Thomas Edison's carbon-filament lamp, discovered in 1879 and introduced commercially in New York in 1882. Although popular American legend elevates Edison above his peers, he did not in fact make any quantum leaps in this technology.

The first lighting by electricity took place with the electric-arc lamp as early as 1845. Michael Faraday's experiments were the decisive point in the development of electricity, and it was at his suggestion that the first trial of an electrically illuminated lighthouse took place at Dungeness in 1857. Electricity was used to light the Tuileries gardens in Paris in 1867. Filament lamps were made by Frederick de Moleyns in England in the 1840s, but the first practical "glow lamps" were simultaneously invented by J. W. Swan in England and Edison in the United States. Edison combined technical inspiration with commercial perspiration when he also generated electricity and distributed it from the Pearl Street substation in New York in 1882.

The first bulbs used carbon filaments that had short lifetimes and produced only 2.6 lumens per watt (see table 1.3). The major improvement in the efficiency of the lightbulb came from metal filaments, particularly tungsten, which raised the efficiency to almost 12 lumens per watt by 1919. Since that time, there has been very little improvement in the technology of the lightbulb itself, which reached an output of only 13–14 lumens per watt by the 1990s. In contrast, since the Edison bulb there have been great improvements in lamp technology for large users, and the efficiency of industrial or street lighting shows an even greater improvement than that of the residential-use lamps that I study here.

Until the last decade, the tungsten-filament lightbulb was both relatively unchanging and unchallenged for home uses. Arc, mercury-vapor, and other types of fluorescent lighting were understood at the beginning of this century, but they were more costly and complicated and made little progress in residential applications. Fluorescent bulbs were developed in the 1930s, but they were suitable only for specially installed fixtures. The most recent phase of the lighting revolution has been the introduction of compact fluorescent bulbs in the late 1980s and 1990s. The early compact fluorescent bulbs were expensive, bulky, and only marginally more efficient than the incandescent variety. The Compax bulb of the mid-1980s generated 47 lumens per watt, compared with 68 lumens per watt by 1992. Only in the last decade, with greatly improved technology and some promotion in poorly designed cross-subsidy schemes by electric utility companies, has the compact fluorescent bulb begun to replace the incandescent lamp in residences. The latest entry in the evolution of lighting has been the E-bulb, announced in 1994, which is the first electronic application and is about as efficient as other compact fluorescent bulbs.

1.2.8   Summary Data on Efficiency and Prices

Table 1.3 provides estimates of the efficiency of different devices back to the fires of Peking man. The estimates for both the Paleolithic lamps and open fires are extremely rough and are based on my measurements (see the appendix). The most reliable measurements are those of Silliman in 1855 and those from the modern era.

The overall improvements in lighting efficiency are nothing short of phenomenal. The first recorded device, the Paleolithic oil lamp, was perhaps a tenfold improvement in efficiency over the open fire of Peking man, which represents a 0.0004 percent per year improvement. Progression from the Paleolithic lamps to the Babylonian lamps represents an improvement rate of 0.01 percent per year; from Babylonian lamps to the candles of the early nineteenth century is an improvement at the more rapid rate of 0.04 percent per year. The Age of Invention showed a dramatic improvement in lighting efficiency, with an increase by a factor of nine hundred, representing a rate of 3.6 percent per year between 1800 and 1992.

Each new lighting technology represented a major improvement over its predecessor. What is striking, as well, is that in each technology there have been dramatic improvements. The Welsbach gas mantle improved the efficiency of gas lamps by a factor of seven, and another 100 percent improvement was seen between the kerosene lantern of the 1880s and today's Coleman lantern. There were marked improvements in the ordinary lightbulb in the four decades after Edison's first carbon-filament lamp, with most of the gain achieved by 1920. Overall, from the Babylonian sesame-oil lamp to today's compact fluorescent bulb, the efficiency of lighting has increased by a factor of about twelve hundred.

So much for the elementary physics. The questions for the economist are, what has happened to the true price of a lumen-hour, and have traditional price indexes captured the true price change?

1.3   Traditional Approaches to Measuring Prices

1.3.1   Introductory Considerations

My major concern here is whether traditional approaches to constructing price indexes capture the major technological changes of the last two centuries. I begin in this section by reviewing alternative approaches to the construction of price indexes and turn in the next section to a superior (if not superlative) technique. The major point will be to show that price indexes miss much of the action during periods of major technological revolution. They overstate price growth for three reasons: first, they may not capture quality changes; second, they measure the price of goods and services but do not capture the changes in efficiency of these goods and services; and, third, they do not capture the enormous changes in the efficiency of delivering services when new products are introduced. The present section begins with a simple analysis of the issue and then reviews the construction of traditional price indexes in practice.

1.3.2   Theoretical Considerations

It will be useful to lay out the fundamental issues.[4] For many practical reasons, traditional price indexes measure the prices of goods that consumers buy rather than the prices of the services that consumers enjoy. For purposes of measuring the true cost of living, we clearly should focus on the outputs rather than on the inputs. More precisely, we must distinguish between a goods price index that measures the price of *inputs* in the form of purchased goods and a characteristics price index that measures the (implicit) price of the *output* in the form of services.

The economics underlying the construction of the true price of light relies on the economics of hedonic prices, or more precisely on the calculation of the price of *service characteristics*. I will describe the theoretical background briefly.[5] Suppose that the underlying utility function is $U(C_1, C_2, \ldots)$, where C_i is the quantity of characteristic i, which might be the number of lumens of light, the temperature of the dwelling, the fidelity of the sound reproduction, and so forth. Service characteristics are produced by purchased goods $(X_1, X_2, \ldots)$, which might be lighting devices, fuel, furnaces, or compact-disc players. Service characteristics are linked to goods by production functions. Generally, goods produce multiple service characteristics, and this often leads to difficulties in determining the implicit hedonic prices. I will simplify the analysis by assuming that each good is associated with a single characteristic, so that

---

4. The theory of index numbers is an ancient art, dating back at least to the Bishop of Ely in 1707 (see Diewert 1988 for an illuminating review). Modern treatments can be found in Deaton and Muellbauer (1980) or Diewert (1990).

5. See Triplett (1987) for an excellent summary of the theory of characteristic prices.

$C_{it} = f_{jit}(X_{jt})$ is the production function by which good j produces characteristic i at time t. In the case of light, the f_{jit} function is taken to be linear, so this means that at any time there will be a dominant technology and a unique implicit hedonic price of each characteristic.[6]

For the exposition I will suppress the time subscript. The consumer faces a budget constraint $I = p_1 X_1 + \cdots + X_m p_m$, where I is nominal income and p_i is the price of good i. We can also associate hedonic prices (or shadow prices) with each of the service characteristics. These are actually the shadow prices of the utility maximization and can be derived as follows: Assuming identical consumers, maximizing utility subject to the production function and budget constraint yields first-order conditions

$$(1) \qquad \lambda = (\partial U/\partial C_i)(\partial C_i/\partial X_j)/p_j$$

for all purchased goods j that deliver characteristic i. Equation (1) shows the consumer's maximization in terms of purchases of goods. At a more fundamental level, however, we are interested in the trend in the characteristic prices. Therefore define the shadow price on characteristic $i(q_i)$ as

$$(2) \qquad q_i = p_j/(\partial C_i/\partial X_j).$$

Substituting equation (2) into equation (1) we get the appropriate first-order condition in terms of service characteristics. In equation (2), q_i is the shadow price of characteristic i (its units for lighting are dollars per lumen-hour). The characteristic price is simply the price of the good (p_j) divided by the efficiency of the good in delivering the characteristic ($\partial C_i/\partial X_j$).

Using this approach, we can distinguish traditional price indexes from true price indexes. A *traditional* price index, P_t, measures (some index of) goods or input prices:

$$(3) \qquad P_t = \sum_{j=1}^{n} p_{j,t} \zeta_{j,t},$$

where $p_{j,t}$ are the prices of the goods and $\zeta_{j,t}$ are the appropriate weights on the goods. By contrast, a *true* price index, Q_t, measures the trend in the prices of the service characteristics:

$$(4) \qquad Q_t = \sum_{i=1}^{m} q_{i,t} \omega_{i,t},$$

where $q_{i,t}$ are the prices of the characteristics and $\omega_{i,t}$ are the appropriate weights on the service characteristics.

How can the traditional prices go wrong? There are three ways. (1) *Incorrect*

---

6. This assumption is oversimplified if the prices of the good or of complementary factors are different for different consumers. The most important exception would be the shadow price of the complementary capital, which would differ depending on whether the consumer had capital embodying an old technology or was buying a new capital good. I resolve this by calculating the "frontier hedonic price," which measures the price assuming that consumers are replacing their capital equipment.

weights. The first source of error arises if traditional price indexes use the wrong weights. This is probably relatively unimportant, for the shares are simply the expenditure weights and these can be directly observed and are not affected by use of traditional rather than true prices. (2) *Improvements in efficiency.* The second source of error comes because of changes in the efficiency of the production function for the service for a given good. If the production function is improving over time, this will lead to a decline in the service-good price ratio, $q_{j,t}/p_{i,t}$, which will be entirely missed by traditional price indexes. (3) *Incorrect linking of new goods.* Traditional price indexes can go astray in a third way if new goods are introduced for which the service-good price ratio is lower at the time that the new good is introduced. Hence, if good $(j+1)$ replaces good j, then a bias for the new good arises if the ratio $q_{j+1,t}/p_{i,t}$ is lower than the ratio $q_{j,t}/p_{i,t}$ at the time of introduction of the new good into the price index.

Two points emerge from this analysis, the first obvious and the second not. First, for the case where the good delivering the service does not change but where there are improvements in the efficiency of the production function $f(\cdot)$, the ratio q_i/p_j will not change much as long as the efficiency does not change much over time. We need to examine a good's efficiency in producing the service to determine whether there is a significant bias in traditional price measures.

The second point relates to new goods. Say that the good delivering a particular characteristic changes: good $(j+1)$ replaces good j in delivering characteristic i, so equation (2) drops out of the consumer equilibrium and is replaced by the equation for the new good, $q_i = p_{j+1} (\partial C_i/\partial X_{j+1})$. *For new products, the price index will be accurate if the shadow price of the service characteristic for the new good, $j + 1$, is the same as that for the old, j, at the date when the new good is introduced into the price index.* Because shadow prices tend to be equal very early in the life cycles of new goods, this suggests that early introduction of new goods is the appropriate treatment.

My procedure in what follows will be to calculate the true price of the service characteristic of lighting (q_i being the lumen-hour) as a replacement for the traditional price index of fuel (q_j being the price of candles, town gas, or electricity).

1.3.3   Treatment of Quality Change in Practice

Before World War II, little attention was paid to the problem of quality change and new products. Since that time, however, it has been increasingly recognized that adjusting for quality change is a major issue in constructing price indexes. The common presumption among most economists is that price indexes fail to deal adequately with quality change and new products; furthermore, it is generally presumed that there is an upward bias of prices (or inflation) over time. It is useful to review the current practices so as to understand the way quality is treated today.

Those who construct price indexes are, of course, quite aware of the quality-change issue (see, e.g., Armknecht, Lane, and Stewart, chap. 9 in this volume). There are three techniques for dealing with quality change or new products. (1) *Direct comparison.* One approach is simply to divide the second-period price by the first-period price. This technique implicitly assumes that the quality change is insignificant and is the technique followed for the preponderance of goods and services. (2) *Linking.* In this approach, prices are adjusted by factoring out price differences in a base time period where prices for both commodities exist. This method assumes that the relative prices in the base period fully reflect quality differences. (3) *Adjusting for quality differences.* A final method is to adjust the price to reflect the estimated value of the quality difference. For example, car prices might be adjusted on the basis of horse-power, fuel economy, and size; computer prices might be adjusted by assuming that the quantity of output is a function of speed and memory. To be accurate, this method requires both reliable estimates of the service characteristics of old and new products and an appropriate imputation of the economic value of the change in service characteristics. As of 1990, only two adjustments were routinely used in the official price indexes of the United States: for computer prices and for housing prices.

In analyzing traditional techniques, it is useful to start with the simplest case, which involves quality improvement of existing products or the introduction of new products for the same service characteristic. For this class of new or improved products, the problems arise primarily in calculating the quantity of service characteristics delivered by old and new products. Typically, the statistician will simply assume that the products deliver the same quantity of service characteristics per dollar of spending at a given date and will then use the method of linking to splice together the prices of the new and old products. Two problems are likely to arise with new products. First, new goods are likely to be introduced into price indexes relatively late in their product cycle; late introduction leads to an upward bias in price indexes because the relative prices of the service characteristics of old and new goods begin to diverge markedly after the introduction of a new good into the market. Second, many new goods experience rapid improvement in efficiency of delivering service characteristics, so the bias from using goods prices rather than service-characteristic prices may be particularly severe for goods in the early stages of the life cycle.

For a relatively small number of products, the services are genuinely new and in essence expand the range of service characteristics spanned by available commodities. For example, when the first artificial lighting was produced half a million years ago, or when anesthetics or space travel were first introduced in the modern age, or if we really could visit Jurassic Park, these service characteristics would be genuinely novel and we could find no market benchmarks for creation of hedonic prices. However, such genuinely novel commodities are quite rare because most new products are in reality new combinations of old wines in redesigned bottles.

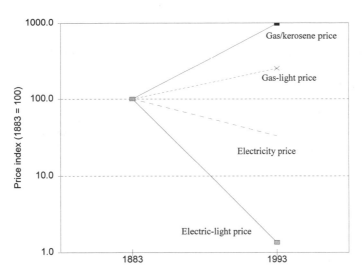

Fig. 1.2   Bias in price indexes

Construction of price indexes for products that represent new service characteristics requires greater knowledge about preferences than the other two cases. Current thinking suggests that the appropriate technique is to estimate the value of the new-characteristic commodity by determining the reservation income at which consumers would be indifferent to the choice between the budget set without the new-characteristic commodity and the actual income with the new-characteristic commodity. In considering the true price of light, this problem does not arise and is not considered further in this study.

1.3.4   An Illuminating Example of the Bias in Lighting Prices

Before I turn to the actual construction of traditional and true price indexes, I can make the point with a simple example of lighting prices over the century from 1883 to 1993. I take this period because Edison priced his first electric light at an equivalent price to gaslight, so the prices per unit of light output for gas and electricity were equal in 1883. Since the 1883 price of kerosene light was also reasonably close to that of town gas during this period, I will compare the prices of electric light with that of gas/kerosene light over the last century.

Figure 1.2 shows the result. Over the last century, the prices of the fuels (which are from traditional price indexes and are shown by the dashed lines) rose by a factor of 10 for kerosene and fell by a factor of 3 for electricity. If an ideal traditional (frontier) price index were constructed, it would use late weights (following electricity prices) since this is the frontier technology. Hence the ideal traditional (frontier) price index using the price of inputs would show a fall in the price of light by a factor of 3 over the last century. If the price index were incorrectly constructed, say using 1883 consumption weights and tracking gas/kerosene prices, it would show a substantial upward increase by a factor of 10.

A true (frontier) price index of output or illumination, by contrast, would track the lowest solid line in figure 1.2, which shows a decline by a factor of 75 over the last century. This shows a steeper decline in price relative to the price of electricity because of the vast improvements in the efficiency of electric lighting.

Hence if we compare the worst traditional price index (the gas/kerosene price) to the true price, we see an overstatement by a factor of 750 in this simple example. The overstatement comes, first, from incorrect weighting of the different fuels and, second, because of the improvements in the efficiency in production of the services. It is instructive to note that even the most superlative price index can only correct for the first of these defects, and I must turn to estimation of characteristic production functions to determine the magnitude of the second bias.

1.3.5 Traditional Price Indexes for Light

The first step in the comparison is to obtain a "traditional" or conventional estimate of the price of light. Actually, the U.S. Bureau of Labor Statistics (BLS) does not currently calculate a price of light or lighting. The closest thing to that concept is the price of energy, which is broken down into different fuels (gas, electricity, and oil). Earlier indexes sometimes did include the price of "fuel and light," either in wholesale or in consumer price indexes. The other component of the price of light is the prices of lighting devices, which are not included as a separate index.

To construct the traditional price of light, I patched together the most closely related series. The earliest data, for the period 1790–1851, was the wholesale price of "fuel and light" from Warren and Pearson (1933). There is a short period, 1851–80 for which I constructed consumer prices using the index of the price of "fuel and light" from Hoover (1960). Then for the period 1880–90, I returned to the Warren and Pearson index of fuel and light. For the period 1890–1940, I used the BLS wholesale price index of fuel and light (U.S. Bureau of the Census 1975). From 1940 on, there are two variants available. The first links the earlier series with the U.S. Consumer Price Index series on gas and electricity, which is the closest component to a price index of lighting costs in the current index; I call this series "Light I."

A second series reflects the fact that since 1940 virtually all lighting has been powered by electricity, so I have constructed a price series for electricity from the composite price of electricity used in residences; this second series is called "Light II" and rises less rapidly than Light I because of the rapid fall in electricity prices over the last half century. For comparative purposes, I also use a consumer price index for all commodities recently prepared by McCusker (1991). All three series are shown in table 1.4.

It is clear that the traditional indexes that have been constructed are only rough proxies for what might have been used as a price of lighting if the official statistical agencies actually had set about trying to measure the price of light. But this traditionally measured price of light is probably representative of the approach taken for most commodities at any particular time. It should be recalled that as of 1990 there were only two hedonic price indexes included in all the price calculations of the U.S. government (these being for housing and computers), so we can think of this audit of the reliability of the traditional price of light as a representative (albeit small) sample of prices.

1.4   *Lux et Veritas:* Construction of the "True Price of Light"

1.4.1   Theoretical Background

In constructing an ideal or true price, we want to employ the price of the service characteristic as defined in equation (2) rather than that of the good (just as we want to measure the price of the output rather than the price of the input). The true price index is then constructed according to the formula in equation (4) rather than by the traditional goods price index defined in equation (3). It is clear that in principle the characteristics approach is superior, but because of the labor involved in constructing characteristics prices, statisticians almost always collect goods prices, and price indexes rely almost entirely on the price of goods.

1.4.2   Implementation

Measurement

In this section I describe the actual calculations of the true price of light. Unlike many estimates of hedonic price indexes, the true price of light is conceptually very simple in that there are laboratory measurements of light flux and illuminance, as discussed above. As with all goods, light has a number of different service characteristics: (1) illumination or light flux (measured in lumens), (2) wavelength (usually proximity to wavelength of sunlight), (3) reliability (in terms of constancy and lack of flicker), (4) convenience (ease of turning off and on, low maintenance), (5) safety (from electrocution, burns, ultraviolet radiation),[7] and (6) durability (lifetime and ease of replacement or fueling).

In practice, the true price of light is constructed with a number of simplifying assumptions. For the present purpose, I restrict the calculation in a number of respects: (1) The only characteristic that I analyze is the first, illumi-

---

7. It is easy for those living in the modern age to overlook the terrifying dangers of earlier technologies. Early lighting devices, especially lamps and candles, were serious threats to life. A number of eminent women, such as Fanny Longfellow and Lady Salisbury, burned to death when their dresses caught fire from candles. One-third of New York tenement fires in 1900 were due to lamps or candles. See Lebergott (1993).

Table 1.4   Basic Data on the True Price of Light

| | True Price of Light | | Index, Real Prices (1800 = 100) | Light Price in Terms of Labor (hours of work per 1,000 lumen-hours) | Official Price Indexes | | | Price Ratio (true to official price) | |
| | Per 1,000 Lumens | | | | | | | | |
Date	(current prices) (1)	(1992 prices) (2)	(3)	(4)	CPI (1800 = 100) (5)	Light I (1800 = 100) (6)	Light II (1800 = 100) (7)	Light I (8)	Light II (9)
ca. 500,000 B.C.				58					
38,000–9000 B.C.				50					
1750 B.C.				41.5					
1800	40.293	429.628	100.000	5.387	100.0	100.00	100.00	1.00	1.00
1818	40.873	430.117	100.114	6.332	101.3	93.71	93.71	0.92	0.92
1827	18.632	249.985	58.186	3.380	79.5	86.16	86.16	1.86	1.86
1830	18.315	265.659	61.835	2.999	73.5	72.96	72.96	1.61	1.61
1835	40.392	596.089	138.745	7.569	72.3	69.81	69.81	0.70	0.70
1840	36.943	626.774	145.888	5.057	62.8	66.04	66.04	0.72	0.72
1850	23.199	397.362	92.490	2.998	62.3	59.75	59.75	1.04	1.04
1855	29.777	460.980	107.298	3.344	68.9	64.15	64.15	0.87	0.87
1860	10.963	176.505	41.083	1.152	66.2	61.64	61.64	2.27	2.27
1870	4.036	41.390	9.634	0.330	104.0	84.28	84.28	8.41	8.41
1880	5.035	65.907	15.340	0.489	81.5	57.86	57.86	4.63	4.63
1883	9.228	122.791	28.581	0.750	80.1	55.97	55.97	2.44	2.44
1890	1.573	23.241	5.410	0.133	72.2	45.28	45.28	11.60	11.60

	(1)	(2)	(3)	(4)	(5)	(6)	(7)	(8)	(9)
1900	2.692	42.906	9.987	0.2204	66.9	55.03	55.03	8.24	8.24
1910	1.384	19.550	4.550	0.0921	75.5	56.57	56.57	16.47	16.47
1916	0.346	4.282	0.997	0.0154	86.1	88.31	88.31	102.92	102.92
1920	0.630	4.228	0.984	0.0135	158.9	194.56	194.56	124.40	124.40
1930	0.509	4.098	0.954	0.0104	132.5	93.30	93.30	73.86	73.86
1940	0.323	3.092	0.720	0.00549	111.3	85.22	65.78	106.44	82.16
1950	0.241	1.350	0.314	0.00188	190.7	84.28	62.61	140.66	104.49
1960	0.207	0.940	0.219	0.00102	234.4	102.28	70.89	199.45	138.24
1970	0.175	0.608	0.142	0.00055	307.3	111.50	75.01	256.26	172.39
1980	0.447	0.730	0.170	0.00068	652.3	313.43	179.34	282.82	161.83
1990	0.600	0.618	0.144	0.00060	1,035.1	479.80	275.57	322.31	185.12
1992	0.124	0.124	0.029	0.00012	1,066.3	503.94	281.09	1,631.55	910.03

(1) From table 1.5.

(2) Col. (1) reflated into 1992 prices using the consumer price index in col. (5).

(3) Index of col. (2) using 1800 = 100.

(4) From table 1.6.

(5) From McCusker (1991).

(6) A chain index was constructed as follows: Warren and Pearson's (1933) index of wholesale prices of fuel and light was used for the period up to 1850. Hoover's (1960) index of consumer prices for fuel and light was used for the period 1850–80. Warren and Pearson (1933) was used for the period 1880–90. BLS's wholesale price index was used for the period 1890–1940 (U.S. Bureau of the Census 1975). The U.S. CPI for the price of gas and electric fuels was used for the period 1940–92.

(7) Same data as col. (6) through 1929. From 1929 to 1992, the Bureau of Economic Analysis implicit deflator for consumer purchases of electricity was used as the price of light (U.S. Dept. of Commerce 1986).

(8) Ratio of the index of Light I to the true price of light.

(9) Ratio of the index of Light II to the true price of light.

nation. For the most part, the other service characteristics are of modest importance and can be tuned to optimal specifications inexpensively. (2) Because of the lack of data on the actual use of different technologies, I construct a frontier price index, which estimates the cost of the best available technology. This obviously would not apply to the backwoods farmer but is likely to apply to city dwellers. (3) I consider only the marginal cost of lighting in terms of fuel. Other costs, including capital, risk, labor, and environmental costs, are omitted primarily because of lack of data. It should be noted, however, that the traditional price indexes also consider only fuel costs.

Data and Reliability

The major contribution of this study is to provide estimates of the price and efficiency of different lighting devices. The procedure begins with estimates of the light output (in lumen-hours) for different lighting devices. A summary of these efficiencies is shown in table 1.3. The data have varying levels of reliability. Estimates from Silliman (1871) and twentieth-century sources are probably quite reliable, while those for other years (particularly for the earliest periods) should be regarded with considerable caution.

Estimates of the prices of fuel come from a variety of sources. Prices for the modern era were drawn either from national data or from local quotations. For the historical periods, Stotz's 1938 history of the gas industry provided most of the data on prices of candles, town gas, kerosene, and electricity. Silliman gathered data on the major fuels for his 1855 experiment. Edison priced electricity in terms of its gas equivalent, writing in 1883: "Our charge for light . . . is at the rate of 1 and 1/5th cents per lamp-hour. . . . A lamp of 16 candlepower was the equivalent of a gas burner supplied with 5 [cubic] feet of gas."[8] This works out to approximately twenty-four cents per kilowatt-hour at the dawn of the electric age, or about three dollars per kilowatt-hour when reflated by McCusker's consumer price index.

Prices in Terms of Goods

The estimates of the true price of lighting are shown in tables 1.4 and 1.5 as well as in figures 1.3 and 1.4. Table 1.4 and figure 1.4 show the nominal price as well as the price in terms of the traditionally measured basket of consumer goods and services.

Prices in Terms of Labor

An alternative measure of the price of light, derived in table 1.6, measures the amount of labor time that would be required to purchase a certain amount of light. This measure is seldom used, so its rationale will be given. It is

---

8. Quoted in Doblin (1982, 20). I am particularly grateful to Clair Doblin for first pointing out many of the sources on lighting efficiency.

Table 1.5　　　　**Price of Lighting for Different Lighting Technologies**

Device	Stage of Technology	Approximate Date	Price (cents per 1,000 lumen-hours)
Open fire	Wood	From earliest time	
Neolithic lamp	Animal or vegetable fat	38,000–9000 B.C.	
Babylonian lamp	Sesame oil	1750 B.C.	
Candle[a]	Tallow	1800	40.293
	Sperm oil	1800	91.575
	Tallow	1830	18.315
	Sperm oil	1830	42.125
Lamp	Whale oil	1815–45	29.886
	Silliman's experiment: Sperm oil[b]	1855	160.256
	Silliman's experiment: Other oils[b]	1855	59.441
Town gas	Early lamp[c]	1827	52.524
	Silliman's experiment[b,d]	1855	29.777
	Early lamp[c]	1875–85	5.035
	Welsbach mantle[c]	1885–95	1.573
	Welsbach mantle[c]	1916	0.346
Kerosene lamp	Silliman's experiment[e]	1855	4.036
	19th century[c]	1875–85	3.479
	Coleman lantern[f]	1993	10.323
Electric lamp	Edison carbon lamp[g]	1883	9.228
	Filament lamp	1900	2.692
	Filament lamp	1910	1.384
	Filament lamp[h]	1920	0.630
	Filament lamp[h]	1930	0.509
	Filament lamp[h]	1940	0.323
	Filament lamp[h]	1950	0.241
	Filament lamp[h]	1960	0.207
	Filament lamp[h]	1970	0.175
	Filament lamp[h]	1980	0.447
	Filament lamp[i]	1990	0.600
	Compact fluorescent bulb[i]	1992	0.124

[a]Price from Bezanson, Gray, and Hussey (1936). Tallow candles generate 0.75 candles; sperm-oil candles generate 1 candle.

[b]See table 1.2. Price from Silliman (1871).

[c]Price from Stotz (1938).

[d]Gas price is in New Haven, Connecticut.

[e]See table 1.2. Price of kerosene is from 1870.

[f]Price in southern Connecticut, November 1993.

[g]See text under *Data and Reliability.*

[h]Average price of residential use from U.S. Bureau of the Census (1975, S116).

[i]Price of electricity as of 1992.

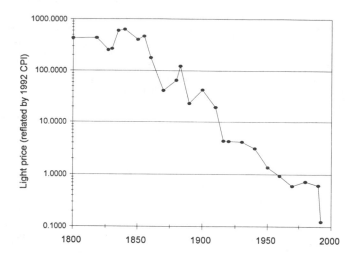

Fig. 1.3   Deflated price of light (cents per 1,000 lumen-hours)

customary to measure the increase in productivity in an industry by the total factor productivity in that industry. This approach is incomplete when we are examining productivity growth of service characteristics. When the service characteristic is produced by a number of different stages (lighting device, fuel, etc.), the impact of all the stages of production must be considered.

In a world where there are k primary factors of production (L_1, L_2, ..., L_k), where all goods and characteristics are produced by constant-returns-to-scale production functions, and where we can invoke the nonsubstitution theorem, we can determine the hedonic prices of the service characteristics (q_1, q_2, ..., q_m) as unique functions of the factor prices (w_1, w_2, ..., w_k). These functions can be written as $q = (q_1, q_2, ..., q_m) = Q(w_1, w_2, ..., w_k; t)$, where t is a time index that represents the various technological changes that are occurring in the different sectors. The labor cost of a service characteristic, q_i/w_1, with labor's price being w_1, is defined as the inverse of the index of overall technological change. If labor is the only primary factor of production, then the ratios of q_i/w_1 are exact measures of the total increase in productivity for the service characteristic C_i. To the extent that there are other primary factors (such as land), the measure used here will misstate the correct input cost index. Given the dominant share of labor in primary input costs, it seems likely that the labor deflation is a reliable measure of total characteristic productivity.

As an example, one modern one-hundred-watt incandescent bulb burning for three hours each night would produce 1.5 million lumen-hours of light per year. At the beginning of the last century, obtaining this amount of light would have required burning seventeen thousand candles, and the average worker would have had to toil almost one thousand hours to earn the dollars to buy the candles.

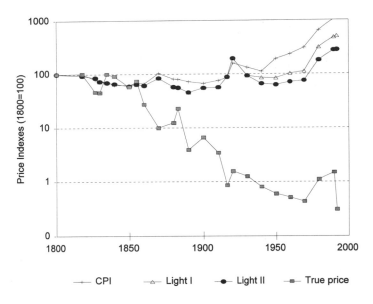

Fig. 1.4   Alternative light prices

In the modern era, with a compact fluorescent bulb, the 1.5 million lumen-hours would need twenty-two kilowatt-hours, which can be bought for about ten minutes' work by the average worker. The trend in the labor requirements to buy our daily light is shown in figure 1.5, where the true index is compared with the trend in the required labor according to a traditional index. Figure 1.6 extends the estimates to the labor time required by a Babylonian to fuel the sesame lamps of that period.

1.5   Comparison of True and Traditional Prices

Figures 1.4 and 1.7 compare the traditional and true price indexes of light as well as the overall consumer price index. The traditional price of light has risen by a factor of between three and five in nominal terms since 1800. This is not bad compared to all consumer prices (again, the traditional version), which have risen tenfold over the same period.

The true price of light bears little resemblance to the traditional indexes. As can be seen in the tables and figures, the traditional price has risen by a factor of between nine hundred and sixteen hundred relative to the true price. The squared correlation coefficient between the changes in the logarithms of the true price and those of either traditional light price is around .07. For Light II, which is probably the more reliable of the traditional indexes, the average annual bias (the rise in the traditional price relative to the true price) is 3.6 percent per year.

Table 1.6   Labor Price of Light

Device	Stage of Technology	Approximate Date	Wage Rate (cents per hour)	Labor Price (hours of work per 1,000 lumen-hours)	Price (cents per 1,000 lumen-hours)
Open fire	Wood	From earliest time		58[a]	
Neolithic lamp	Animal or vegetable fat	38,000–9000 B.C.		50[b]	
Babylonian lamp	Sesame oil	1750 B.C.	1 shekel per month	41.50[a]	
Candle	Tallow	1800	7.5[c]	5.37	40.293
	Sperm	1800	7.5[c]	12.21	91.575
	Tallow	1830	6.1[c]	3.00	18.315
	Sperm	1830	6.1[c]	6.91	42.125
Lamp	Whale oil	1815–45	6.1[c]	4.90	29.886
	Silliman's experiment: Sperm oil	1855	10[d,e]	16.03	160.256
	Silliman's experiment: Other oils	1855	10[d,e]	5.94	59.441
Town gas	Early lamp	1827	7.1[c]	7.398	52.524
	Silliman's experiment	1855	10[d,e]	2.978	29.777
	Early lamp	1875–85	15.4[f]	0.326	5.0345
	Welsbach mantle	1885–95	19.0[g]	0.083	1.573
	Welsbach mantle	1916	28.3[h]	0.012	0.346
Kerosene lamp	Silliman's experiment	1855	17.5[e,i]	0.2306	4.036
	19th century	1875–85	15.4[e]	0.2253	3.479
	Coleman lantern	1993	1,058.0[j]	0.0098	10.323

Electric lamp					
Edison carbon lamp	1883	0.750239	12.3[k]	9.228
Carbon filament	1900	0.220431	12.2[l]	2.692
Carbon filament	1910	0.092096	15.0[l]	1.384
Filament lamp	1920	0.013538	46.6[l]	0.630
Filament lamp	1930	0.010396	49.0[l]	0.509
Filament lamp	1940	0.005490	58.8[l]	0.323
Filament lamp	1950	0.001883	128.2[j]	0.241
Filament lamp	1960	0.001016	203.3[j]	0.207
Filament lamp	1970	0.000551	318.4[j]	0.175
Filament lamp	1980	0.000678	658.6[j]	0.447
Filament lamp	1990	0.000605	992.2[j]	0.600
Compact fluorescent	1992	0.000119	1,049.6[j]	0.124

Source: All data are from earlier tables except wage rates and calculations for the three earliest periods. Sources for wage data are given in specific notes.

[a]See appendix.

[b]The calculation assumes that the Paleolithic lamp is one-third as efficient as the Babylonian lamp. It further assumes that each kilogram (equal to one liter) of animal fat requires 8 hours to catch and prepare (see Pospisil 1963, 227, 254; and Lebergott 1993, 64).

[c]Average monthly earnings of farm workers from U.S. Bureau of the Census (1975, D705) at 250 hours per month. For 1830, this corresponds exactly to the wage rate calculated according to the methodology used in note e.

[d]From table 1.2.

[e]Wages are those paid to a common laborer on the Erie Canal calculated by assuming that the daily work day was 10 hours long. Data are from U.S. Bureau of the Census (1975, D718).

[f]Average annual earnings of nonfarm employees from U.S. Bureau of the Census (1975, D735), assuming 2500 hours per year of work for 1880.

[g]Same as note f for 1890.

[h]Same as note f, but for all workers (U.S. Bureau of the Census 1975, D779).

[i]Wages are from 1870.

[j]Average hourly earnings for private nonfarm industries (Council of Economic Advisers 1993, 396).

[k]Same as note e for 1883.

[l]Same as note f using U.S. Bureau of the Census (1975, D723).

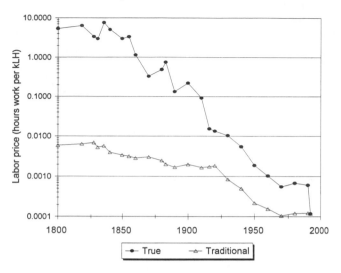

Fig. 1.5   Labor price of light: true and traditional

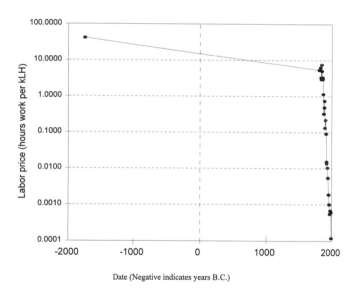

Date (Negative indicates years B.C.)

Fig. 1.6   Labor price of light: 1750 B.C. to present

1.6   Do Real-Wage and -Output Indexes Miss All the Action?

Having seen how far the price of light misses the truth, we might go on to ask whether light might be a representative slice of history. In other words, is it possible that by the very nature of their construction, price indexes miss the most important technological revolutions in economic history? I suggest that

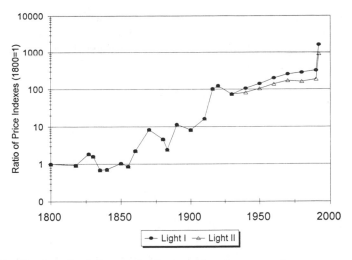

Fig. 1.7   Bias in price index: ratio of conventional to true price

the answer might well be yes. By design, price indexes can capture the small, run-of-the-mill changes in economic activity, but revolutionary jumps in technology are simply ignored by the indexes. What is surprising is how pervasive the range of revolutionary products is. In this section I look at how price indexes treat quality change, examine the treatment of selected inventions, estimate the range of poorly measured consumption, and then hazard an estimate of the potential bias in real wage and real output measures.[9]

1.6.1   Treatment of Quality Change and Inventions in Practice

Traditional Long-Term Estimates of Consumer Prices

In constructing estimates of either real wages or real output, I begin with the relatively firm data of nominal wages or output and deflate them with an estimate of a price index of the consumption bundle or of outputs produced. The measurement of real wages over the last two centuries uses a series of consumer price indexes that have been built by the painstaking research of generations of economic historians including Ethel Hoover, Alvin Hansen, Paul Douglas, Stanley Lebergott, and Paul David.[10] A review of these studies indicates three features: First, most of the early indexes were heavily weighted toward foods. For example, Alvin Hansen's estimates of the cost of living from 1820 to 1840 used prices of twelve foods and three clothing items. Second, most of the early indexes relied upon wholesale prices and assumed that con-

---

9. The question of the bias in traditional price measures and the consequent bias in real incomes has been considered in many studies. See, for example, Baily and Gordon (1988) and Gordon (1990, 1993).

10. See a recent survey in McCusker (1991).

sumer prices changed proportionally with wholesale prices. This is particularly the case for the subject of this study. For example, the Douglas estimates of the cost of living used wholesale prices for "fuel and light" for the period 1890–1926, with the wholesale prices being adjusted to retail prices on the basis of an assumed uniform markup.

The third and most important point is that until the modern age, all "cost-of-living" indexes were in reality indexes of "prices of goods bought by consumers." Collecting goods prices was itself a Herculean task, but we must recognize that these indexes did not measure the trend in the efficiency or *services* delivered by the purchased goods. Hence, the fact that one Btu of gas bought in the nineteenth century delivered a quantity of heat or light quite different from one Btu of electricity bought in the twentieth century never entered into the construction of the price indexes.

The inattention to the services delivered by the purchased good would not matter much if goods changed little or if new products or processes were absent. But during this period, as was seen clearly in the case of lighting and as is suggested below for other goods and serices, there were profound changes in the very nature of virtually all goods and services. Given the inattention to measurement of quality change, it is questionable whether the entire range of qualitative changes is correctly captured today, and there can be no question that it was completely ignored in the period before World War II.

Traditional Treatment of Major Inventions

For revolutionary changes in technology, such as the introduction of major inventions, traditional techniques simply ignore the fact that the new good or service may be significantly more efficient. Consider the case of automobiles. In principle, it would be possible to link automobiles with horses so as to construct a price of travel, but this has not been done in the price statistics for just the reasons that the true price of light was not constructed. Similar problems arise as televisions replace cinemas, air travel replaces ground travel, and modern pharmaceuticals replace snake oil.

The omission of quality change and particularly revolutionary technological change does raise the possibility that most of the action of the Age of Invention was simply missed in our traditional real-product and real-wage measures. Table 1.7 presents a selection from Jewkes, Sawers, and Stillerman's list of the one hundred great inventions (1969). Note how little of the impact of these great inventions was captured in traditional price indexes.

This discussion leads to the thought that the standard methodology of price indexes may be destined to capture the small changes but to miss the revolutionary improvements in economic life. The last century has seen massive changes in transportation, communications, lighting, heating and cooling, and entertainment. Indeed, the tectonic shocks of changing technologies have occurred in virtually every area. Food is perhaps an exception in that the products are superficially the same. Indeed, the relative stability of food products suggests the reason food is the fixed star in all long-term consumer price indexes;

Table 1.7   **Treatment of the Great Inventions**

Invention	Treatment in Price Indexes
Aeronautics, helicopter	Except for lower costs of transportation of intermediate goods, lower prices not reflected in price indexes
Air-conditioning	Outside of refrigerated transportation and productivity increases in the workplace, amenities and health effects not captured in price indexes
Continuous casting of steel	A process innovation that showed up primarily in lower costs of intermediate goods and thus was reflected in price indexes of final goods
DDT and pesticides	Some (now questionable) benefits probably included in higher yields in agriculture and therefore included in price indexes; health benefits and ecological damages largely excluded from price indexes
Diesel-electric railway traction	A process innovation that showed up primarily in the price of goods and services
Insulin, penicillin, streptomycin	Improved health status not captured in price index
Internal combustion engine	Except for lower costs of transportation of intermediate goods, lower prices not reflected in price indexes
Long-playing record, radio, television	Major product inventions that are completely omitted from price indexes
Photo-lithography	Largely reflected in reduced printing costs
Radar	A wide variety of improvements, some of which might have shown up in lower business costs and prices (such as lower transportation costs or improved weather forecasting)
Rockets	A wide variety of implications: major application in telecommunications showed up in consumer prices; improvements in television not captured in price indexes; improved military technology and nuclear-war risk not reflected in prices
Steam locomotive	Reduced transportation costs of businesses reflected in price indexes; expansion of consumer services and nonbusiness uses not reflected
Telegraph, telephone	Improvements over Pony Express or mail largely unreflected in price indexes
Transistor, electronic digital computer	As key inventions of the electronic age, impacts outside business costs largely omitted in price indexes
Xerography	Major process improvement: some impact showed up in reduced clerical costs; expansion of use of copied materials not captured in price index
Zipper	Convenience over buttons omitted from price indexes

Note: Inventions are selected from Jewkes, Sawers, and Stillerman (1969).

in addition, the omnipresence of food is a tip-off that the price indexes are misleading.

A Classification of Consumption Changes

The last section suggested that existing price indexes—and perforce existing measures of real output and real incomes—fail to capture the major shifts in technologies and therefore underestimate long-term economic trends. How pervasive are these major shifts? This is an awesomely difficult question, and in this section I present a *Gedankenexperiment* that suggests the importance of qualitative change in economic life.

The approach taken here is to examine *today's consumption bundle,* and then to divide it into three categories. In each case, the question is how great the change in the good or service has been since the beginning of the nineteenth century:

1. *Run-of-the-mill changes.* This category of good is one where the changes in technology have been relatively small and where price indexes are likely to miss relatively little of the quality change or impact of new goods. This category includes primarily home consumption of food (such as potatoes), most clothing (such as cotton shirts), personal care (such as haircuts), furniture, printed materials (such as books), and religious activities (such as going to mass). In these areas, there are to be sure some categories where life has improved in ways that are not captured, such as more timely news, pasteurized milk, and high-tech running shoes. But the overall underestimate of quality change is likely to be much less than that which we uncovered for light.

2. *Seismically active sectors.* A second category is one where there have been both major changes in the quality of goods and provision of new goods, but where the good or service itself is still recognizably similar to its counterpart at the beginning of the nineteenth century. Examples in this category are housing (such as high-rise apartments), watches (which still tell time but do it much more accurately while simultaneously taking your pulse and waking you up), personal business (including financial services and the information superhighway), space-age toys, and private education and research.

3. *Tectonic shifts.* The final area is the category in which lighting is placed. It is one where the entire nature of the production process has changed radically. In these sectors, the changes in production and consumption are so vast that the price indexes do not attempt to capture the qualitative changes. This category includes household appliances (such as refrigerators and air conditioners), medical care, utilities (including heating, lighting, and other uses of electricity), telecommunications, transportation, and electronic goods (such as radio and television). In each of these cases, there is virtually no resemblance between the consumption activity today and that in the early nineteenth century. Indeed, in many cases, the basic science or engineering that underpins the technology was undiscovered or poorly understood in the earlier age.

Clearly, this categorization is extremely rough, and refinements would probably shift some of the sectors to different categories. It is unlikely, however, that the size of the category experiencing tectonic shifts would shrink. Because of the aggregation, it is likely that many tectonic shifts are buried in run-of-the-mill or seismically active sectors. For example, the lowly toilet is classified as furniture but delivers a service that would delight a medieval prince.

Table 1.8 shows the basic breakdown for 1991. According to this categoriza-

Table 1.8   Consumption by Extent of Qualitative Changes, 1991 ($ billion)

Sector	Run-of-the-Mill Sectors	Seismically Active Sectors	Tectonically Shifting Sectors
Food			
Home consumption	419.2		
Purchased meals		198.5	
Tobacco		47.8	
Clothing			
Apparel	208.9		
Cleaning and services		21.1	
Watches and jewelry		30.6	
Personal care			
Toilet articles		38.2	
Services	24.0		
Housing			
Dwellings		574.0	
Housing operation			
Furniture and utensils	116.3		
Appliances			25.5
Cleaning and polishing		52.8	
Household utilities			143.2
Telephone and telegraph			54.3
Other	49.6		
Medical care			656.0
Personal business			
Legal and funeral	60.3		
Financial and other		257.5	
Transportation			438.2
Recreation			
Printed	42.9		
Toys		32.3	
Electronics and other goods			84.2
Other	51.7	51.2	27.4
Private education and research		92.8	
Religious and welfare	107.7		
Total	1,080.6	1,396.8	1,428.8
Percent of total	27.7	35.8	36.6

Source: Prepared by the author based on U.S. Department of Commerce (1986), with updates from BEA's *Survey of Current Business.*

Note: "Run-of-the-mill" sectors are ones in which the goods or services have changed relatively little or in which price indexes can measure quality change relatively easily. "Seismically active" sectors are ones in which the goods or services are recognizable from the early 19th century but for which there is likely to have been major changes in quality and great difficulty in measuring quality change accurately. Industries subject to "tectonic shifts" are ones in which the nature of the good or service has changed drastically (as in lighting) or for which the good or service did not exist at the beginning of the 19th century (as in antibiotics).

tion, about 28 percent of current consumption has experienced minor changes over the last two centuries, 36 percent has been seismically active, and 37 percent has experienced tectonic shifts. In other words, almost three-quarters of today's consumption is radically different from its counterpart in the nineteenth century. As a result, it is likely that estimates of the growth of real consumption services is hampered by significant errors in the measurement of prices and that for almost two-fifths of consumption the price indexes are virtually useless.

1.6.2   Measuring True Income Growth

Theoretical Background

How badly biased might our measures of real wages and real incomes be? The measurement of true income growth obviously depends crucially on the correct measurement of both nominal incomes and true price indexes. Measurement of nominal incomes is probably subject to relatively modest error for marketed commodities, but the measurement of true prices may be far off the mark. We can obtain an exact estimate of the bias in measurement of real income and real wages as follows.

I assume that the appropriate measure of real income, $R(t)$, is a smooth utility function of the form $U[C_1(t), C_2(t), \ldots]$, where $C_i(t)$ is the flow of service characteristic i at time t. I do not assume any particular form for R. All that is needed is the customary assumption that the utility function is locally constant returns to scale. Under this assumption, I can in principle construct Divisia indexes of real-income changes by taking the weighted average growth of individual components.

It will be more convenient to transform the direct utility function into a *characteristic indirect utility function* of the following form:

$$(5) \qquad\qquad R = V(q_1/I, q_2/I, \ldots, q_n/I).$$

(In this discussion, I suppress the time dimension where it is unnecessary.) This utility function has all the properties of the standard indirect utility function except that the prices are characteristics prices rather than traditional goods prices. R in equation (5) is a measure of real income in that it represents the utility that can be obtained with market prices and income.

I would like to estimate the *bias in the measurement of real income due to the mismeasurement of the prices of service characteristics*. For simplicity, assume that the only price that is incorrectly measured is the first (say, the price of light). Assume that q_1^* is the measured price of the characteristic and q_1 is the true price; then rewrite the utility function as

$$(6) \qquad\qquad R = V[(q_1/q_1^*)(q_1^*/I), q_2/I, \ldots, q_n/I].$$

The ideal measure of real income is the measure of utility in equation (6). Further, the growth in real income can be calculated as the growth in R over time. Let g_Z be the rate of growth of variable Z. Then, because the V function is locally linearly homogeneous, the growth in utility (equal to the growth of real income) is given by

$$(7) \qquad g_R(t) = g_I(t) - [\sigma_1(t)g_{q_1}(t) + \sigma_2(t)g_{q_2}(t) + \dots],$$

where $\sigma_i(t)$ equals the (local) share of spending on service characteristic i in total spending at time t. Note that because the share of income devoted to spending on characteristic i is unaffected by the bias in the calculated price, the calculated share can be estimated without any hedonic correction. This implies that the bias in the calculation of real income or real output, $g_R(t)^* - g_R(t)$, is simply equal to

$$(8) \qquad \text{Bias in measuring real income growth} = g_R(t)^* - g_R(t)$$
$$= \text{Bias from good } 1 = \sigma_1(t) [g_{q_1}(t) - g_{q_1^*}(t)].$$

In words, the bias in the growth rate of real income or real output is equal to the share of the service in total consumption times the bias in the growth rate of the service in question.

Bias for Lighting

I calculate the bias in real income using the data in the tables and the formula in equation (8). According to my calculations, the average annual bias for lighting is 3.6 percent per year. The share of lighting in total consumer expenditures is difficult to estimate (see table 1.9). It probably consisted of slightly above 1 percent of budgets in the last century but has declined to less than 1 percent today; I assume that light's share averaged 1 percent over the last two hundred years. This suggests that the real-wage and -output growth using Light II has been underestimated by 0.036 percent per year because of the misestimate of lighting's price alone.

Using the formula in equation (8), and assuming a constant share, I find the

Table 1.9   **Budget Studies on Lighting**

Period	Household Income ($/year)	Spending on Lighting ($/year)	Spending on Lighting (% of spending)	Total Lighting (1,000 kilolumen-hours)
1760s	£48	£0.45	0.94	28
1815–55	180	22.0	12.2	117
1875	333	2.2	0.7	48
1880	309	30.0	9.7	988
1890	354	25.0	7.1	1,170
1960	7305	23.5	0.3	13,241

Sources: For 1760s, for a Berkshire family, from Burnett (1969, 167); for 1815–55, 1880, and 1890 from Stotz (1938); for 1875 from Hoover (1960, 183) from a survey of 397 families; for 1960 from Darmstadter (1972) for electricity from lighting.

total bias in the growth of real income or real wages for Light II to be 0.01 ×
log(0.036 × 192) = 0.068 (or 0.074 for Light I). In other words, just correcting for light adds 7 percent to the total growth of real wages over the period
1800–1992. In terms of dollar values, the bias in the measurement of the price
of lighting (using Light II) would increase the value of consumption by about
$275 billion in 1992 relative to 1800. This is approximately equal to the con-
sumer's surplus equivalent of the unmeasured quality change in lighting.

A Gedankenexperiment for All Consumption

To calculate the potential bias for all consumption requires assumptions
about how much the bias in the measurement of the true price of different
categories might be. There are few proxies to use. One measure is that for
light, where I determined that the true price of light fell 3.6 percent per year
relative to the traditionally measured price of light. Other hedonic indexes include that for computers, where the estimated bias is close to 15 percent per
year, and that compiled by Robert Gordon for capital goods, where the bias is
estimated to be 3 to 4 percent per year (see Gordon 1990).

For the thought experiment, I assume a "high" and a "low" estimate for the
bias. For the low estimate, I assume that there has been no bias in the run-of-
the-mill sectors, a bias in the seismically active areas that is one-fourth the
estimated bias for light, and a bias in the tectonic sectors that is one-half that
of light. (See table 1.8 for a list of the different industries in each category.)
For the high-bias estimate, I assume a bias of 0.5 percent per year in the run-
of-the-mill category, a bias one-half that of light in the seismically active areas
and a bias equal to that of light in tectonically shifting sectors. More specifically, the bias rates are 0, 0.93, and 1.85 percent annually for sectors 1, 2, and
3 in the low case and 0.5, 1.85, and 3.7 percent annually for the same sectors
in the high case. In addition, I have taken the shares of the different sectors in
1929 from the same sources used for table 1.8 and made rough estimates from
budget studies of the budget shares over the last century. By this reckoning,
the share of the run-of-the-mill sectors has decreased from about 75 percent of
total consumption at the beginning of the last century to 28 percent today.[11]

The base estimate of the rate of growth of real wages from 1800 to 1992 is
1.4 percent per year using traditional price indexes. The estimated growth rate
is 1.9 percent per year with the low assumption about the bias in price indexes
and 2.8 percent per year with the high assumption. In terms of living standards,

---

11. The calculation of the bias for consumption was constructed as follows. I calculated from
the National Income and Product Accounts for 1929 the same breakdown of consumption between
the three innovation categories (run-of-the-mill, seismically active, tectonically shifting) as shown
in table 1.8. For each major consumption sector (food, clothing, etc.), I then estimated for 1929
the share of each of the three innovation categories. The next step was to obtain budget studies for
the years 1874, 1890, 1901, and 1918 (from U.S. Bureau of the Census 1975), with an extrapolation back to 1800 using English data from Burnett (1969), shown in table 1.9. I then constructed
a Törnqvist index of the bias by taking the within-period shares of each of the major consumption
sectors and multiplying them by the estimated bias for each sector, using the estimated low or
high bias as stated above and the proportion of each of the three innovation categories.

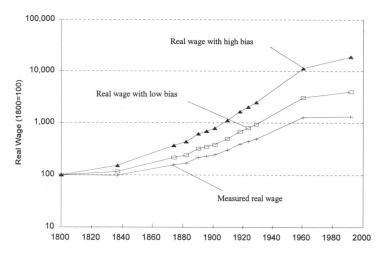

Fig. 1.8   Traditional and true real wages

the conventional growth in real wages has been by a factor of 13 over the 1800–1992 period. For the low-bias case, real wages have grown by a factor of 40, while in the high-bias case real wages have grown by a factor of 190. Figure 1.8 shows the trends in real wages according to the measured real-wage series along with the estimated true real wages with the high and the low estimate of the bias in measuring consumer prices.

Note as well that because the composition of consumption has evolved over the last two centuries from predominantly run-of-the-mill sectors to more technologically active sectors, the degree of bias or underestimate of real-wage increases has probably increased over this period. Under the methodology for estimating bias used here, the bias has more than doubled from 1800 to 1992 according to the low-bias assumption and has slightly less than doubled according to the high-bias assumption.

Clearly, the alternative estimates of real-wage growth provided by the thought experiment are highly speculative. On the other hand, they are consistent with an emerging set of estimates in the literature on hedonic prices that suggests that we have greatly underestimated quality improvements and real-income growth while overestimating inflation and the growth in prices.

1.7   Conclusion

I have shown that for the single but extraordinarily important case of lighting traditional price indexes dramatically overstate the true increase in prices as measured by the frontier price of the service characteristic. This finding implies that the growth in the frontier volume of lighting has been underestimated by a factor of between nine hundred and sixteen hundred since the beginning of the industrial age.

If the case of light is representative of those products that have caused tectonic shifts in output and consumption, then this raises the question of whether the conventional measures of real-output and real-wage growth over the last two centuries come close to capturing the true growth. Of today's consumption, perhaps one-quarter has undergone only modest changes since the mid-nineteenth century (locally grown foods, clothing, some types of personal care). More than one-third of consumption takes place in tectonically shifting industries and in ways that were virtually unimaginable at that time—including medical care, transportation, recreation, and much of household operation. If the half of consumption that takes place in tectonically shifting industries shows even a small fraction of the unmeasured growth that we have uncovered in lighting, then the growth of real wages and real incomes in conventional estimates might be understated by a very large margin.

While this point may get lost in the details of national income accounting, it was obvious to Adam Smith even before the Age of Invention:

> Compared with the extravagant luxury of the great, the accommodation . . . of the most common artificer or day-labourer . . . must no doubt appear extremely simple and easy; and yet it may be true, perhaps, that the accommodation of a European prince does not always so much exceed that of an industrious and frugal peasant, as the accommodation of the latter exceeds that of many an African king, the absolute master of lives and liberties of ten thousand. (1776, 12)

Appendix
Estimates for Babylonian Lamps and Peking-Man Fires

For early technologies, no references were found on either lighting efficiency or costs. To provide rough data on these, I undertook measurements for sesame oil and firewood. All measurements of illumination were taken using a Minolta TL-1 illuminance meter.

For fire, 21 pounds of firewood were burned in a standard home fireplace. This provided measurable illumination for 3.4 hours with an average level of illumination of 2.1 foot-candles. The zone of illumination is less than a candle because of the floor and walls, so the average illumination is assumed to be 5 lumens per foot-candle, for a total illumination of 1.7 lumen-hours per pound. At an energy content of 5 million Btu per ton, this yields 0.69 lumen-hours per thousand Btu. I have no reliable data on prehistoric labor costs of obtaining firewood. It is assumed that 10 pounds of firewood could be foraged, trimmed, and dried in 1 hour. This yields 58 hours of work per one thousand lumen-hours.

For sesame-oil lamps, I purchased a Roman terra-cotta lamp supplied by Spirits, Inc., of Minneapolis, Minnesota. It was certified as dating from Roman times and closely resembled museum artifacts from Roman times that I viewed, but its age could not be independently verified. This lamp was fueled by 100 percent Hunza pure cold-pressed sesame oil with a wick extracted from a modern candle. This proved a remarkably efficient device, with an efficiency very close to that of a modern candle. One-quarter cup (60 ml) burned for 17 hours with an average intensity of 0.17 foot-candles. The zone of illumination is less than a candle's and is estimated to be 10 lumens per foot-candle. The total illumination was therefore 28.6 lumen-hours, for an efficiency of 17.5 lumen-hours per thousand Btu. This represents a major improvement in efficiency over firewood.

To obtain the labor price of Babylonian illumination, I assume that Babylonian lamps are reasonable represented by the Roman terra-cotta lamp and that the measurements are representative. Wages were around 1 shekel per month during the period investigated, while sesame oil sold for approximately 0.1 shekel per liter. Using the data on illumination, this yields 42 hours of work per one thousand lumen-hours. Note that while this is no major improvement over the estimated labor price of firewood, the quality of the light from the lamps is far superior and the lamp is much more easily controlled.

References

Baily, Martin E., and Robert J. Gordon. 1988. The productivity slowdown, measurement issues, and the explosion of computer power. *Brookings Papers on Economic Activity,* no. 2:347–431.

Bezanson, Anne, Robert D. Gray, and Miriam Hussey. 1936. *Wholesale prices in Philadelphia, 1784–1861.* Philadelphia: University of Pennsylvania Press.

Bright ideas in light bulbs. 1992. *Consumer Reports,* October, 664 68.

Burnett, John. 1969. *A history of the cost of living.* Harmondsworth, England: Penguin.

Council of Economic Advisers. 1993. *Economic report of the president and of the council of economic advisers.* Washington, D.C.: Government Printing Office.

Darmstadter, Joel. 1972. Energy consumption: Trends and patterns. In *Energy, economic growth, and the environment,* ed. Sam H. Schurr. Baltimore, Md.: Johns Hopkins University Press.

Deaton, Angus, and John Muellbauer. 1980. *Economics and consumer behavior.* Cambridge: Cambridge University Press.

de Beaune, Sophie, and Randall White. 1993. Ice Age lamps: Fat-burning lamps. *Scientific American* 268, no. 3 (March): 108.

Diewert, W. Erwin. 1988. The early history of price index research. Discussion Paper no. 88-26, Department of Economics, University of British Columbia, Vancouver.

———, ed. 1990. *Price level measurement.* Contributions to Economic Analysis, vol. 196. Amsterdam: North-Holland.

Doblin, Clair. 1982. Historic price data for electricity, town gas or manufactured gas. *IIASA Memorandum* (International Institute for Applied Systems Analysis, Laxembourg, Austria), 13 July.

Dubberstein, Waldo H. 1938. Comparative prices in later Babylonia (625–400 B.C.). *American Journal of Semitic Languages and Literature* 56 no. 1, (January): 20–43.

Farber, Howard. 1978. A price and wage study for northern Babylonia during the old Babylonian period. *Journal of the Economic and Social History of the Orient* 21 (pt. 1): 1–53.

Gaster, Leon, and J. S. Dow. 1919. *Modern illuminants and illuminating engineering.* 2d ed. London: Sir Isaac Pitman & Sons.

Gordon, Robert J. 1990. *The measurement of durable goods prices.* Chicago: University of Chicago Press.

———. 1993. Measuring the aggregate price level: Implications for economic performance and policy. In *Price stabilization in the 1990s: Domestic and international policy requirements,* ed. Kumiharu Shigehara, 233–68. Houndmills, England: Macmillan.

Hoover, Ethel D. 1960. Prices in the 19th century. In *Trends in the American economy in the nineteenth century,* 141–90. NBER Studies in Income and Wealth, vol. 24. Princeton, N.J.: Princeton University Press.

Jewkes, John, David Sawers, and Richard Stillerman. 1969. *The sources of invention.* New York: Norton.

Lebergott, Stanley. 1993. *Pursuing happiness: American consumers in the twentieth century.* Princeton, N.J.: Princeton University Press.

McCusker, John J. 1991. How much is that in real money? A historical price index for use as a deflator of money values in the economy of the United States. *Proceedings of the American Antiquarian Society* 101, pt. 2 (October): 297–373.

Pospisil, Leopold. 1963. *Kapauku Papuan economy.* New Haven, Conn.: Yale University Press.

Samuelson, Paul A., and William D. Nordhaus. 1992. *Economics.* New York: McGraw-Hill.

Silliman, Benjamin, Jr. 1871. Report of the rock oil, or petroleum, from Venango Co., Pennsylvania, with special reference to its use for illumination and other purposes. *American Chemist,* July, 18–23.

Slotsky, Alice Louise. 1992. *The bourse of Babylon: An analysis of the market quotations in the astronomical diaries of Babylonia.* Ph. D. diss., Yale University.

Smith, Adam. 1776. *The wealth of nations.* Modern Library.

Stotz, Louis. 1938. *History of the gas industry.* New York: Stettiner Bros.

Triplett, Jack. 1987. Hedonic functions and hedonic indexes. In *The new Palgrave: A dictionary of economics.* Vol. 2, 630–34. London: Macmillan.

U.S. Bureau of the Census. 1975. *Historical statistics of the United States: Colonial times to 1970.* 2 vols. Washington, D.C.: Government Printing Office.

van Benesch, F. 1909. *Das Beleuctungswesen vom Mittelalter bis zur Mitte des XIX. Jahrhunderts aus Oesterreich-Ungarn.* Vienna: A. Schroll and Co.

Warren, George F., and Frank A. Pearson. 1933. *Prices.* New York: John Wiley and Sons.

U.S. Department of Commerce. 1986. *The national income and product accounts of the United States, 1929–82.* Washington, D.C.: Government Printing Office.

Comment   Charles R. Hulten

It is hard to imagine a more appropriate place than Colonial Williamsburg in which to discuss a paper on historical living standards. Step outside the conference center and you enter the life of the late eighteenth century. Stroll down the main street of Williamsburg and you see the techniques used to make can-

Charles R. Hulten is professor of economics at the University of Maryland, College Park, and a research associate of the National Bureau of Economic Research.

dles, wigs, barrels, and other items of eighteenth-century life. Enter a tavern or private dwelling and you have a window on the daily life of that era. At some point during the visit, you will probably ask yourself, "What would my life have been like had I been born two hundred years earlier?"

According to Bill Nordhaus, you would have been quite a bit poorer—far poorer than indicated by official statistics and very much poorer than the casual experience of Williamsburg would probably suggest. Working with what is undoubtedly the longest time series in econometric history—from Peking man to the present—Nordhaus argues that "traditional price indexes of lighting vastly overstate the increase in lighting prices over the last two centuries, and the true rise in living standards in this sector has consequently been vastly understated." The magnitude is truly remarkable: according to the estimates of this paper, "the traditional price has risen by a factor of between nine hundred and sixteen hundred relative to the true price." This leads to the conclusion that it is possible "that by the very nature of their construction, price indexes miss the most important technological revolutions in economic history."

An attempt to quantify the magnitude of the "miss" is presented in section 1.6. A *Gedankenexperiment* is performed there which leads to the conclusion that, when quality improvements are taken into account, real wages may have increased by a factor that ranges from 40 (the low-bias case) to 190 (the high-bias case) over the period 1800–1992. The conventional (non–Nordhaus corrected) growth of real wages has been a factor of 13–18 over this period. This is clearly a very large miss.

The magnitude of this result may incline some readers to skepticism. However, the size of the quality correction for lighting should evoke no surprise from those familiar with the paper by Cole et al. (1986) on adjusting the price of computers for quality change. That paper implied that quality improvements in computing equipment have proceeded at double-digit rates (10 to 20 percent per year) for several decades. In light of the Cole paper, a major contribution of the current paper is to show that the computer result is not an isolated phenomenon.

Indeed, the two papers together virtually force the debate over appropriateness of the conventional goods approach of standard economic theory. Textbook treatments of supply and demand are based on the market transaction of well-defined goods like candles, oil lamps, and electric lightbulbs. This is the paradigm that is found wanting when improvements in quality take the form of new goods—lamps replacing candles, for example. The alternative offered by Nordhaus, Cole et al., and many others (including Robert Gordon, Zvi Griliches, Robert Hall, Sherwin Rosen, and Jack Triplett) is to organize the analysis by the characteristics delivered by goods, rather than by the goods themselves. In this paradigm, the principal characteristic linking candles, oil lamps, and lightbulbs is the amount of light that they produce.

The two paradigms are not necessarily incompatible. Goods can be seen as "packages" of characteristics, so that statements that apply to one must also apply to the other. Ideally, the issue under consideration should dictate which form of analysis is most useful. For example, when the main issue is about market structure, the goods approach may be preferred, because goods are the unit of market transaction. On the other hand, when new goods that embody old characteristics appear in the market place, the use of the characteristics technique may be a more useful way to measure the contribution to growth or welfare. And, according to Nordhaus, the alternative goods approach in this context can be highly misleading.

It is now clear that economic historians, productivity specialists, and just about everyone else in the economics profession must recognize that quality change is an important source of welfare improvement that is almost certainly missed by conventional measurement techniques. However, it must also be recognized that even if the goods approach does give the wrong answer, it does not follow that the characteristics approach in its current incarnation necessarily gives the right answer. Indeed, the following extension of Nordhaus's *Gedankenexperiment,* which asks what level of per capita income is implied by the Nordhaus results, suggests that the characteristics answer may *overstate* the true amount of welfare gain: When 1991 disposable personal income per capita in the United States (approximately $17,200) is adjusted by the conventionally measured wage-deflation factor of 13 cited by Nordhaus for the period 1800–1992, the result is a real disposable income of around $1,300 in 1800; on the other hand, if Nordhaus's low-bias deflator is used, the resulting 1800 income in the United States is only about $430; the high-bias deflator yields an estimate of 1800 real disposable income of $90.

Taken literally, these comparisons imply that a person possessing the average disposable income in America today should be willing to accept a massive reduction in spending power—from $17,200 to the $90–430 range—in order to avoid being sent back in time to an equivalent status in colonial America. Alternatively, it suggests that the average colonial should prefer living in the America of today, with as little as $90 per year, to staying put in the late eighteenth century. It is hard to imagine anyone wanting to live in modern America with an income of $90; it is only just imaginable that anyone would want to live with an income at the upper end of the Nordhaus range.

This extension of the Nordhaus *Gedankenexperiment* is obviously rather loose. It compares living standards across vastly different cultural and economic milieus, and it does not include other types of purchasing power parity adjustments that tend to narrow income differentials between rich and poor economies (i.e., the PPP corrections that raise real per capita income in Mozambique from $60 to $570). However, while it is certainly possible that the average American colonial was about as well-off as the average resident of the poorest contemporary countries, the size of the Nordhaus adjustment invites the speculation that there may be upward biases in the characteristics approach to valuing new goods.

A full treatment of this issue is beyond the scope of this comment and, since

I agree with the thrust of Nordhaus's results, if not with their magnitude, I will only offer the following illustration of how the characteristics approach might yield misleading results. Consider a characteristic, X, for which the process of innovation is essentially serendipitous and costless. X is packaged with another characteristic, Y, into a good Z. Suppose, now, that a run of good luck and inspiration yields a surge of technical improvements that increases the effective quantity of X, first from an index of 100 to 200, then from 200 to 300; Y remains unchanged. Suppose, finally, that the marginal value of the second increment of 100 units of X is far less than the marginal value of the first increment because Y is fixed, though both exceed the marginal cost, which we take to be zero. Let us also assume that the first improvement in X for fixed Y translates into a marginal change in value in the good Z from an index of 100 to 150, and the second improvement in X yields a change in Z from 150 to 160.

In this scenario, an analysis which focused on the characteristic X in isolation would suggest a threefold improvement in welfare, whereas the effective increase is only 60 percent. In other words, there is an upward bias in the characteristics approach. On the other hand, a purely goods-based approach leads to the opposite bias. Since the improvement in X is essentially costless, the price per unit of Z is unchanged even though it embodies more of the characteristic X. A statistician using conventional goods-oriented techniques would thus attribute a zero effect to the innovation in X.

This is a stylized example, but it may apply in some degree to real-world cases. The replacement of horses by cars, for example, obviously brought on a major revolution in transportation that is certainly understated by a simple comparison of horsepower. However, once the new technology became established, further increases in power were far less significant given the other characteristics of the transportation package (the basic nature of cars, roads, and drivers). The fact that cars can now be propelled to speeds in excess of three hundred miles per hour by hugely powerful engines is important to only a handful of race-car drivers and enthusiasts. A simple characteristics index that focused only on the characteristic "maximum available horsepower" would not pick up these nonlinearities and would assign the same weight to the five fold increase from one hundred to five hundred horsepower that it assigned to the increase from one to five horsepower.

There may be a similar problem with the use of the characteristic "maximum available lumens" to measure the progress in providing light, and with the use of an index like "million instructions per second" (MIPS) to measure increases in computing power. As with horsepower, there is probably some level of both lumens and MIPS at which most users are satiated (particularly when other characteristics are held equal or change gradually).

The example set out above applies to the case in which the costs of innovation are small relative to the benefits. Some attention must also be given to those situations in which the costs and benefits of innovation are fully arbitraged. If, for example, a new type of lightbulb is four times more efficient but also costs four times as much to put in the light socket, then there is no net improvement in welfare ("better" investment is equivalent to more investment in this case). Something like this seems to have happened with the new generation of high-efficiency lightbulbs, which cost a great deal more than their less-efficient predecessors. In this case, a characteristics index based solely on the saving of energy (i.e., one that does not pick up the full cost dimension) will overstate the welfare improvement.

These caveats should not, however, deflect attention from the contribution made by this ingenious and highly original paper. While there is no characteristics index of the value of scientific ideas—no index of *veritas* to match the Nordhaus index of *lux*—the contribution of this paper to the goods versus characteristics debate is undoubtedly very large. Although much more remains to be done on the "technology" of the characteristics approach, Nordhaus, by demonstrating that the Cole et al. finding on computers is not an isolated case, has established the presumption that the chararacteristics approach to new technologies is the most promising way of treating the difficult and important problem of new goods.

Reference

Cole, Rosanne, Y. C. Chen, J. A. Barquin-Stolleman, E. Dullberger, N. Helvacian, and J. H. Hodge. 1986. Quality-adjusted price indexes for computer processors and selected peripheral equipment. *Survey of Current Business* 66 (January): 41–50.

2   Quality-Adjusted Prices for the American Automobile Industry: 1906–1940

Daniel M. G. Raff and Manuel Trajtenberg

2.1   Introduction

The empirical literature on new goods has long shown an interest in the automobile. The hedonic approach was introduced to the profession in Court's 1939 attempt to measure the evolution of automobile prices on a quality-adjusted basis. Griliches (1961), Triplett (1969), Ohta and Griliches (1976), and Gordon (1990, chap. 8), all leading references, continued the study of the industry. Yet each of these, only Court excepted, is focused on developments that took place in the years after the Great Depression, a period when the automobile as an innovation was clearly mature. Recent research suggests that the largest contributions of new goods to welfare changes may well come much earlier on (Trajtenberg 1990). The industry's annual model changes pose the price index question perfectly well in the postwar period. But the most salient questions about new goods necessarily take us further back in time.

Straightforward facts about the history of automobile manufacturing in America support this view. In the first three decades of this century, the indus-

Daniel M. G. Raff is associate professor of management at the Wharton School of the University of Pennsylvania and a faculty research fellow of the National Bureau of Economic Research. Manuel Trajtenberg is associate professor of economics at Tel Aviv University and a research associate of the National Bureau of Economic Research.

The authors are grateful to Timothy Bresnahan, Geoffrey Carliner, Martin Feldstein, Robert Gordon, Zvi Griliches, Thomas Marx, Jeanne Pryce, and Morton Raff for encouragement and practical assistance; to Thomas De Fazio, Jack Triplett, and Daniel Whitney for technical discussions; and to librarians at the Boston Public Library, the Detroit Public Library, the Harvard Business School, the Massachusetts Institute of Technology, and, above all, the Motor Vehicle Manufacturers Association for kind access to their collections. Erik Chuang provided superb research assistance managing a complex data-entry process. Even amid a large group of able and devoted data enterers, Irving Birmingham cannot pass unremarked. Roxanne Jones-Toler and Scott Stern were Spartans at the pass. The authors had useful comments from audiences at the 1994 NBER Summer Institute. This research was supported by the National Bureau of Economic Research and the National Science Foundation. The usual disclaimer applies.

try went from scarcely existing, insofar as Census of Manufacturers enumerators were concerned, to being in terms of the value of products the largest industry in the economy.[1] Over the period we study in this paper, the most casual observer can recognize how much the product changed. Manufacturing methods evolved equally dramatically. So too did market prices. In 1906, for example, there were no new automobiles for sale at a price equal to or below the gross national product (GNP) per capita at the time of $336 (U.S. Bureau of the Census 1976, series F2). In fact, the average price in our database for that year is nearly ten times that amount. By 1940, when our data end, a household with a year's GNP per capita to spend ($754) had a choice of fifty-nine different models, and the average price of cars on the market that year was only about twice that sum.

The industry saw tremendous changes over this period as well. Indeed, contrasted with the tight oligopoly and dull performance of the post–World War II decades, the vibrancy of these early years is almost shocking. There was an early and well-organized attempt at cartelization that failed. Entry eventually proceeded at a breakneck pace. Attracted by the palpably vast opportunities, hundreds of new firms burst onto the scene every year, the total running to well in excess of a thousand. More than ten thousand distinct models were on offer at one time or another. Intense competition in price and quality persistently pushed price-performance ratios to new lows.

The consequences were far reaching. One advertising slogan early in the period ran "One day, one dollar; one year, one Ford." In the very beginning, automobiles were strictly playthings of the rich. But well before 1940, cars were routinely purchased by ordinary working households. The consequences of this for American economic life were themselves pervasive and profound. At the turn of the century, even private urban transportation was often powered by horses. Roads were often dusty when dry and all but impassable when wet. But by 1940, the internal combustion engine ruled the road. Road-construction techniques were recognizably modern. All-weather paved roads existed all over the nation. Bedroom suburbs and even places of work and trade were located in areas where trains and trolleys did not run. The automobile was a new good with important consequences.

There is a vast literature on the industry's history.[2] However, quite surprisingly, it contains no systematic quantitative analysis of the period in which most of the technical change happened. Price indexes would be a useful start. We proceed in steps. The first is simply to complement the existing hedonic literature by pushing the span of its automobile quality-adjusted price calculations backward to 1906, thus closing in on the birth of the industry and the product. These price indexes can be used for a variety of purposes. We propose a crude decomposition of the price change into product- and process-

1. By value-added, it ranked 5th out of 326 in 1929. Combining it with the Census's automotive bodies and parts industry brings that rank to 1st as well.
2. For a recent survey see Flink (1988). His bibliography is extensive.

innovation components, identifying constant-quality price change with manufacturing economies and quality change with design improvement. We also use our indexes for comparisons to hedonic price indexes for other industries at a comparably early stage of the product life cycle and for comparisons to hedonic price indexes for this industry in the later periods previously studied. In particular, we couple our results to those of Gordon's (1990) analogous exercise for the post–World War II period to consider the industry's history in the long view. Finally, we assess several possible sources of bias in our results.

The paper proceeds in six main parts. Section 2.2 is a technical introduction to the product. In section 2.3 we discuss the data. In section 2.4 we give preliminaries to the hedonic analysis and discuss the regressions. In section 2.5 we present the main results in terms of quality-adjusted price indexes and put them in the wider context. In section 2.6 we consider the seriousness of two potential sources of bias in the index numbers. Section 2.7 concludes the paper.

2.2   Cars: A Technical Overview

Automobiles are complex products, arguably the most complex consumer durable at the turn of the century as well as now. This basic fact permeates our approach to measurement and hence to gathering data. We thus begin by recognizing that any design for a self-propelled land vehicle must confront a series of interrelated engineering problems. Any particular design (i.e., any particular vehicle a consumer might buy) represents a particular set of solutions to these problems.

The generic problems are simply stated. The first task is to generate power from the fuel in a sustainable fashion. Gasoline, for example, can be mixed with air and exploded in a controlled way in a confined space.[3] If one wall of the space can move relative to the others, the kinetic energy of the explosion becomes linear motion. This can be converted into rotary motion to turn wheels, and the rotary motion will be smoother if the mixing and exploding go on in several sites in some staggered sequence. All the mechanical elements involved in creating and transforming the linear motions need to be kept lubricated and relatively cool.

Since the car is heavy, especially when loaded with passengers, there is substantial inertia to be overcome in starting forward motion. Connecting the rotating shaft to a device that gears up or down to various degrees the speed of rotation helps in accomplishing this.[4] It is convenient to allow the operator to

---

3. Getting the power generation started poses some problems distinct from those of continuing it. The design of the valves letting the gases into, and eventually out of, the space is also a subject in itself.

4. Early automobile engines had a fairly flat torque curve. As engines became more efficient—in the engineer's sense of generating more power per unit displacement—torque curves became more peaked. The more this was so, the more convenient it was to operate the engine at a relatively steady pace irrespective of the speed at which one wanted the wheels to turn. This too made multiple gears desirable. (Both the phenomenon and the solution will be familiar to bicycle riders.)

engage and disengage the entire gear mechanism from the engine from time to time. When this (clutch) mechanism is engaged, the rotary motion then needs to be transmitted to at least some subset of the wheels, and this in a fashion that allows the vehicle to turn.[5] There must also be a steering mechanism to guide the turns and a braking system to slow or stop the vehicle as required. A body, with seats and upholstery, is essential to make the car useful, and there must be some system between the chassis frame and the wheels to mediate between irregularities in the road's surface and irregularities in the ride. For this latter reason and others, it has also proved convenient to mount tires on the wheels.

This functional description of a car touches on all the main mechanical systems. They are many, and none is simple in itself. In choosing specific solutions to each of the individual problems, general strategies must be adopted (e.g., the gasoline engine rather than, say, the steam engine or the electric motor), as well as detailed specifications for each of them (e.g., the numbers of cylinders and their dimensions, the compression ratio, the operating temperature range, etc.). Overall performance will be sensitive to each solution and often also to the interactions between them.

The potential for such system interaction is elaborate. It is not merely true, for example, that the systems making up the engine must be well adapted to one another: elements of the design of the entire power train and chassis may also be implicated. It is unfortunately very difficult to capture these interactions in summary variables. We thus adopted the second-best procedure of identifying the most important systems (from both engineering and manufacturing perspectives) and seeking data on their attributes. Our data set comprises roughly forty attributes representing the state of the systems.

2.3 Data

Computing quality-adjusted price indexes, even using as undemanding a method as the hedonic, requires large amounts of very detailed data. One needs prices and detailed attribute information for virtually all the different models marketed in each period.[6] Studies such as this thus rest firmly on the breadth of their data.

The primary source of most information about the identities and systems of individual models that covers any wide range of models is the set of specification tables published in the contemporary trade press at the time of the annual

5. When the vehicle turns, the inner and outer wheels cover different distances. They therefore need to rotate at different rates.

6. The more demanding methods, sketched in n. 13 below, are potentially more illuminating— for example, they can be used both to quantify welfare gains and to delineate their timing. The problem is that they require quantity data, that is, information on the quantities sold of each individual model in each year. No such database exists as of this writing. It is possible that one could be put together and coupled to the price and attribute data of this study. But doing this would be a major research enterprise in itself and was utterly beyond the scope of this paper.

Table 2.1   **Manufacturers and Models**

Year	Manufacturers	Mechanical Models	Body Models
1906	≅90	≅100	≅200
1908	61	132	153
1910	224	424	1,006
1912	161	316	977
1914	140	259	871
1916	121	192	495
1918	122	172	681
1920	126	155	569
1922	122	156	780
1924	93	127	696
1926	61	104	603
1928	48	117	784
1930	45	104	874
1932	33	90	752
1934	30	72	420
1936	26	64	460
1938	22	54	387
1940	21	62	414

Notes: The number given here for body models is the number for which we have data on price, wheelbase, and displacement. The number of body models in the underlying database is larger since in some early years data on displacement was not consistently available. The number of observations used in the regressions is slightly smaller since the regressions used only observations that also had complete information on the relevant systems.

New York Auto Show.[7] The trade journals vary in the attributes they report.[8] The attributes reported in each source also change slowly over time. The information given about some attributes is not as revealing as it might be.[9] The tables are nonetheless very detailed and an extremely rich data source.

Each mechanically distinct variant identified in the tables could usually be purchased with any of several different bodies. We call these pairings body models and use them as our unit of observation. We were constrained (by time and finances) to enter body-model data only for alternate years and to go back no further than 1906.[10] Table 2.1 gives some basic descriptive statistics. We have a total of over 11,000 observations (i.e., of body models offered). The number rises sharply in the earliest years, more through entry than through model proliferation. It peaks in 1910 at 1,006. There is a second surge after

7. Kimes and Clark (1985) gives somewhat more comprehensive coverage in its descriptive prose and images but not in its attribute descriptions.

8. This may be sensitive to the balance between consumers, the retail and repair trade, and manufacturers and engineers in each periodical's readership.

9. For example, the tables may report manufacturer rather than design type. Or they may report design types, but in a way that blurs the distinction between minor and major variants. With sufficient background research, however, much of this can be rendered useful.

10. Subsequent to the completion of this paper, we were able to extend the data set back to 1901. We will exploit the new data in future work.

World War I and a third at the end of the 1920s, after which time the number declines considerably. There was a pronounced decline in the number of manufacturers over the whole period and substantial model proliferation in the 1930s.

	Manufacturers	Body Models per Manufacturer
1910–20 average	153	5.1
1920–30	90	7.6
1930–40	30	18.4

After some research, we concluded that the attributes reported by the periodicals *Automotive Industries* and *Motor* together generally spanned the information available. We thus drew the data on attributes and prices from these periodicals.[11] Coverage was then compared against the listings in Kimes and Clark (1985), apparently the most authoritative hobbyist source. Spot checks with other researchers and comparisons with industry histories and other such investigations covering this period, published and otherwise, have revealed no important or systematically unutilized information.[12] It is important to note that our data represent only firms operating above a certain minimal economic threshold, namely ones that were large enough to make advertising at the major annual trade show attractive. We may thus have left out experimentalists and bespoke manufacturers so aloof from commerce that they left customers to find their own way to the factory. We have surely left out some hopeful entrepreneurs who had and possibly even announced bold plans but never in fact made any cars. But we have found no evidence that we have left out any products that were actually easy to buy, and this is the breadth of data that the hedonic method requires.

2.4   Hedonic Analysis: Preliminaries

The main goal of this paper is to construct price indexes that reflect as accurately as possible the vast improvements that took place in the design, manufacturing, and performance of cars during our chosen period. Given the fact that quantity data are unavailable, the only viable approach is to estimate hedonic price regressions and compute on that basis quality-adjusted price indexes. This has been the standard practice for the problem of quality adjustment since Griliches (1961).[13]

11. Our procedure was to code data on the selected attributes from the most comprehensive source of auto show mechanical-attribute tables available to us at the time of initial coding. We then went to that source's body tables to create the fuller row space in the identifier, price, and body-type columns and then copied the mechanical-attribute data appropriately. We then went to the other periodical's tables and augmented as appropriate both the row space of individual manufacturers' body models and the column space of attributes we thought worth recording.

12. The most notable unpublished source is Griliches and Ryan (1971).

13. If we had possessed detailed quantity data, we would have estimated discrete-choice models of demand, retrieved from them the underlying parameters of a utility function (i.e., marginal utilities of the attributes of cars and of income), and computed with the help of these welfare-

The hedonic approach has well-known limitations.[14] The fact that the hedonic surface reflects neither utility nor supply but rather the tangency between the two restricts the extent to which hedonic-based price indexes can be thought to capture fully the effects of quality change. Hedonic methods are particularly ill suited to periods of sharp change in technology (as might be reflected in shifts in the distribution of brands in attribute space). Nevertheless, hedonic quality-adjusted price indexes for cars during the first half of this century can significantly improve our knowledge of the evolution of this industry during its early stages. Moreover, since similar indexes for the post–World War II period are available (e.g., Gordon 1990), we can put together a series of quality-adjusted prices almost a century long for one of the most important sectors of the economy.

In this section we examine first the evolution of automobile prices over time (the dependent variable). We then consider the selection of attributes, that is, our explanatory variables. Finally, we present and discuss the estimates of hedonic price regressions from which our index number calculations derive.

2.4.1 Evolution of Automobile Prices

Since we study a relatively long period, the choice between using product prices stated in current dollars or corrected for changes in the general price level may be an important one. During our period there were two major swings in the general price level, the short but sharp inflation that followed World War I and the more familiar deflation that occurred at the onset of the Great Depression. Prices in the post–World War II period also had a complex history. Deflating raw prices by, for example, the Consumer Price Index (CPI) would control for this. Each series is illuminating in its own way. We present most of our results, here and later in the paper, in both ways.

Figure 2.1 shows the time series of mean prices in our data set, stated in current dollars. The most striking feature is the size of the drop. Automobile prices fell by 51 percent, from $3,290 in 1906 to $1,611 in 1940. The CPI rose during the same period by 59 percent and hence inflation-adjusted car prices dropped by almost 70 percent. To give a better sense of what these numbers mean, figure 2.2 translates them into terms more meaningful to us: in 1993 prices the average car offered in the 1906 market sold for $52,640; whereas by 1940 the mean had dropped to $16,565 (not so far, incidentally, from the average nominal price of cars in 1993). This dramatic fall in prices is one of the single most important facts pertaining to the evolution of the automobile industry in its first half century, reflecting as it does both momentous technological advances and vast expansion of the market for automobiles.

As with most developments in the history of the automobile, the price de-

---

based price indexes. Trajtenberg (1990) and Pakes, Berry, and Levinsohn (1993) illustrate the method. Such procedures obviate most of the thorny problems that arise (see, e.g., section 2.6 below) when using the hedonic method.

14. For a more expansive treatment of these matters, see Trajtenberg (1990, 34–44).

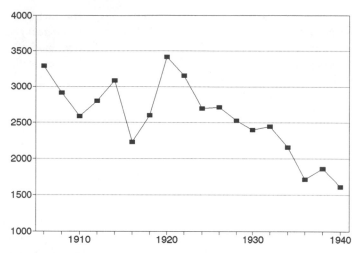

Fig. 2.1   Automobile prices 1906–1940 in current dollars

cline was far from uniform over time. The largest part of the fall in CPI-deflated prices occurred in two installments early in our period: from 1906 through 1910 and from 1914 through 1918. In the course of the latter four years, the CPI-deflated price of cars shrank by almost one-half (from over $44,000 to $25,000 in 1993 dollars).[15] From 1918 on there was for the most part a downward trend, but the overall drop was not nearly as dramatic as that of the earlier period.

The rise in prices from 1910 to 1914 was associated with a large and widespread increase in the size and power of cars. Why precisely the big 1914–18 decline occurred remains to be established. Recalling the dramatic introduction of mass-production methods at Ford at the end of calendar year 1913, it is tempting to attribute the subsequent sharp decline to Ford. Interpretive caution is in order here, however. Ford introduced mass production alone at first. There were very few different Ford models in those years. Ford cars therefore represent a tiny percentage of our sample. If we had weighted prices by sales in calculating the series, then the price drop would be much more dramatic, and a big part of it would be due to Ford. But our series was not generated in that way. It is possible that the course of the actual series owes to cross-price elasticities or to the discovery of new market niches. Tastes may also have shifted downward in time of war. There certainly was a noteworthy downsizing of cars on the market, but what the cause of this was we cannot yet say. The subsequent secular decline of the series presumably has something to do with

15. We see here, for example, how the information conveyed by looking at current prices is greatly distorted by the post–World War I inflationary surge. Nominal prices were actually higher in 1920 than in 1906, but controlling for inflation reveals that prices had dropped by more than one-half!

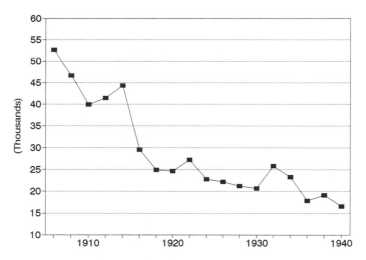

Fig. 2.2   Automobile prices 1906–1940 in constant 1993 dollars

the diffusion of mass-production methods across establishments, but that is a complex subject of its own (see Raff 1991 and Bresnahan and Raff 1991, 1993).

2.4.2   Selection of Attributes

One fundamental difficulty has beset all hedonic car studies from Court (1939) onward. It is that of identifying a set of attributes that can be taken to be the most important performance attributes of cars and that can be measured in a consistent fashion over time. Only if quality in this sense is quite tightly controlled for can we begin to regard as reliable quality-adjusted price indexes based on hedonic regressions.

Any quality-adjustment method requires regressors that would in principle go directly into a consumer's utility function. "Reliability," "smoothness of ride," "safety," "comfort," and so forth, are presumably the sort of attributes in question. But these are extremely hard to quantify in an objective or even consistent manner. Engineering (i.e., technical) attributes are much easier to measure, but they are certainly further removed from the quality dimensions perceived by consumers.

The difficulty in identifying structural relationships between engineering attributes and utility stems from the fact, sketched in section 2.2 above, that for all their pervasiveness and ease of operation, cars are extremely complex machines. Their overall performance depends in a complicated way upon the performance of each of their systems, upon trade-offs made between systems, and upon the extent to which their design is well integrated. All this makes it a formidable challenge to devise variables that will even proxy the performance of individual model designs in an unambiguous and parsimonious way.

We have made some progress in that respect in this study by including (apparently for the first time) actual measures for many of those systems (brakes, clutch, drive mechanism, etc.). Whether our selection of systems and variable definitions is the most appropriate or effective only further investigation will reveal.

In the end, we decided to include three categories of attributes in the hedonic regressions: measures of vehicle size, engine power, and the technology of five major engineering systems. Size and power have been used in virtually all automobile hedonics studies. They are very closely associated with price, and casual empiricism suggests that consumers do care about them. For systems, we initially attempted to cover all the major ones identified in section 2.2. In particular pairs of years, however, we often had to make significant compromises in the face of data limitations of various sorts.[16]

For size we use wheelbase, measured in inches.[17] For power we have available for most years two alternative measures: rated horsepower (HP) and displacement. We opt for the latter whenever it is available because it captures more information (i.e., stroke, bore, and number of cylinders).[18] The five systems we chose are the rear axle, clutch, brakes, drive type, and suspension. The dummy variables are defined in table 2.2 with their names as they appear in the hedonic regression results later in the paper.[19]

Each of these systems underwent dramatic changes over the period studied. Technical innovations, changes in demand, and the shifting interactions with related systems made particular designs emerge and diffuse, only to be superseded later by others. The methods of this project require us to trace and grasp the evolution of system design over time, both in order to define the categories that eventually appear as dummy variables in the hedonic regressions and to form priors as to the likely signs of their coefficients. In addition, we believe that the time paths followed by competing designs are of significant interest in themselves. They show vividly the contest between alternative systems and the speed of diffusion of those that emerged as dominant. We present in the appendix a technical and graphical description of the evolution of the main systems.

If one of the types should become a virtual standard (i.e., if its share among the competing models approaches 100 percent), then it approaches collinearity with the regressions' constant terms. The system can no longer be included in

16. Some systems that clearly are important did not exhibit sufficient variation (because a certain type was universally adopted very quickly). In other cases the qualitative categories reported in our sources were not consistent over time and hence could not be expressed across adjacent years as uniform dummy variables.

17. The results are very similar if one uses weight instead.

18. Rated HP is determined by a formula that is not sensitive to important features of engine design. In general, it is not the same as average or maximum HP. For the years 1906–10 we did not have consistent measures of displacement or its determinants and were obliged to use rated HP faute de mieux. We can observe that for the years for which we had both regressors, the results were not sensitive to which one we chose.

19. In the case of each dummy, of course, there is a residual category. Thus, for example, RAXLE50F = 1 if the rear axle was half floating, RAXLE50F = 0 if it was of a different type.

Table 2.2   **Systems Variable Definitions**

System	Variable
Rear Axle	RAXLEF: rear axle of the fully floating type
	RAXLE50F: rear axle of the half-floating type
Clutch	CLDISC: clutch using disc
	CLPLATE: clutch using plates
	CLSPLATE: clutch using a single plate
Brakes	BRIHYDRA: internal hydraulic brakes
Drive type	DRSBEVEL: drive, spiral bevel
	DRHYPOID: drive, hypoid
Suspension (spring type)	SPHELLIP: spring, half-elliptic

the regression. That is the case for the spring type from 1928 on, for example: the half-elliptical type had been adopted by then in over 95 percent of all cars marketed. In other cases, though, one type became dominant but then differentiated as subvariants appeared. In this case, the system can still be included: it merely requires a different dummy variable. For example, by 1928 the dominant clutch type was plate, but for a few years afterward the market split between single plate and double plate. In the case of the drive type, the spiral bevel acquired absolute dominance by 1922; but from 1926 on it had to compete against the hypoid type. By 1940 the latter was present in 80 percent of all models.

2.4.3   Estimating Hedonic Regressions

We estimate semilog hedonic regressions using both current and CPI-deflated prices for every pair of adjacent years and include a dummy for the later year in the pair.[20] Tables 2.3–2.5 show the results. Since we are interested primarily in computing quality-adjusted price indexes, we content ourselves here with pointing out certain salient features of the regressions without analyzing them in comprehensive detail.

The coefficient of wheelbase is strikingly stable across most of the regressions, and strongly statistically significant throughout. The coefficient of displacement (i.e., power) is also quite steady during the 1920s, though it is less stable both before and after. The systems variables are for the most part significant, but aside from a few relatively short-lived instances (e.g., CLPLATE from 1914 to 1920), their coefficients vary a great deal.[21]

Note that the R^2 values are high and systematically increasing over time, rising from about .70 in the years 1910–20 to about .90 in the years 1930–40.

20. Henceforth we refer to the coefficient on the dummy for the later year as the hedonic coefficient. Recall that adjacent years in our database are in fact two years apart.

21. We will not attempt to interpret the magnitudes of particular coefficients here. The literature appears to be divided on whether this is a useful activity; and it would in any case require a technical discussion not germane to the goals of this section.

Table 2.3   Hedonic Price Regressions for Automobiles (semilog) 1906–1920

	1906–08	1908–10	1910–12	1912–14	1914–16	1916–18	1918–20
D-CURRENT[a]	−0.36	−0.26	−0.09	−0.13	−0.27	0.15	0.31
	(−9.4)	(−8.8)	(−6.1)	(−8.5)	(−8.3)	(6.8)	(17.0)
D-CONSTANT[b]	−0.36	−0.29	−0.13	−0.17	−0.35	−0.17	0.03
	(−9.4)	(−10.0)	(−9.0)	(−11.0)	(−11.0)	(−7.8)	(1.5)
WHEELBASE	0.04	0.03	0.02	0.03	0.046	0.05	0.04
	(16.0)	(19.0)	(14.9)	(20.0)	(45.0)	(45.0)	(21.0)
HP	0.008	0.015					
	(3.3)	(11.0)					
DISPLACE			0.002	0.002	0.00	0.00	0.009
			(18.7)	(18.0)	(0.0)	(0.0)	(5.3)
RAXLEF			0.076	0.002	−0.08	−0.07	−0.04
			(4.9)	(0.1)	(−4.1)	(−3.6)	(−1.9)
CLDISC			0.05	0.08			
			(3.7)	(5.5)			
CLPLATE					−0.14	−0.11	−0.11
					(−3.2)	(−4.5)	(−6.0)
DRSBEVEL					0.099	0.06	0.18
					(2.8)	(2.1)	(5.7)
SPHELLIP			0.097	0.074	−0.046	0.04	0.0005
			(5.7)	(3.7)	(−1.5)	(1.6)	(0.0)
R^2	0.75	0.70	0.70	0.70	0.69	0.73	0.77
MSE	0.119	0.099	0.087	0.087	0.113	0.111	0.089
N	356	1,150	1,798	1,710	1,271	1,115	1,165

Note: Numbers in parentheses are *t*-statistics.

[a]Second-year dummy, current prices.

[b]Second-year dummy, constant (CPI-deflated) prices.

Table 2.4 **Hedonic Price Regressions for Automobiles (semilog) 1920–1930**

Variable	1920–22	1922–24	1924–26	1926–28	1928–30
D-CURRENT[a]	−0.09	−0.15	−0.10	−0.07	−0.13
	(−5.0)	(−8.7)	(−6.3)	(−4.9)	(−11.0)
D-CONSTANT[b]	−0.085	−0.17	−0.14	−0.04	−0.11
	(−4.5)	(−9.8)	(−8.4)	(−2.7)	(−9.0)
WHEELBASE	0.05	0.05	0.05	0.04	0.035
	(25.0)	(30.0)	(36.0)	(39.0)	(37.0)
DISPLACE	0.0007	0.001	0.001	0.002	0.003
	(4.0)	(5.3)	(9.5)	(17.0)	(22.0)
RAXLE50F	0.005	−0.0008	0.008	0.13	0.04
	(0.3)	(−0.5)	(3.9)	(6.2)	(2.5)
CLDISC	0.06	−0.002			
	(2.9)	(−0.09)			
CLPLATE			0.044	0.006	
			(2.5)	(0.3)	
DRSBEVEL	0.16				
	(3.2)				
SPHELLIP	−0.07	−0.05	−0.05	−0.07	
	(−3.6)	(−2.5)	(−2.4)	(−2.8)	
R^2	0.72	0.75	0.80	0.83	0.86
MSE	0.099	0.099	0.079	0.065	0.057
N	1,234	1,403	1,286	1,370	1,649

Note: Numbers in parentheses are *t*-statistics.
[a]Second-year dummy, current prices.
[b]Second-year dummy, constant (CPI-deflated) prices.

Table 2.5 **Hedonic Price Regressions for Automobiles (semilog) 1930–1940**

Variable	1930–32	1932–34	1934–36	1936–38	1938–40
D-CURRENT[a]	−0.2	−0.08	0.01	0.10	−0.05
	(−15.0)	(−4.2)	(0.5)	(9.7)	(−2.4)
D-CONSTANT[b]	−0.003	−0.06	−0.02	0.15	−0.04
	(−0.3)	(−3.1)	(−1.3)	(8.7)	(−2.1)
WHEELBASE	0.04	0.04	0.04	0.03	0.016
	(37.0)	(28.0)	(22.0)	(21.0)	(10.7)
DISPLACE	0.002	0.0003	0.03	0.004	0.005
	(12.0)	(1.2)	(13.0)	(20.0)	(23.0)
RAXLE50F	−0.09	−0.16	0.04		
	(−4.2)	(−5.2)	(1.4)		
BRIHYDRA	0.06	0.02	−0.11		
	(3.8)	(0.8)	(−4.8)		
CLSPLATE	0.05	−0.15	−0.05		
	(2.5)	(−6.1)	(−1.6)		
DRHYPOID		0.22	−0.05	−0.03	−0.095
		(7.0)	(−2.1)	(−1.9)	(−4.2)
R^2	0.87	0.89	0.92	0.89	0.83
MSE	0.066	0.064	0.043	0.052	0.072
N	1,589	958	787	832	800

Note: Numbers in parentheses are *t*-statistics.
[a]Second-year dummy, current prices.
[b]Second-year dummy, constant (CPI-deflated) prices.

Likewise, the mean square error (MSE) of the regressions systematically decreases over time. This pattern may be seen more clearly in the course of the average MSE decade by decade:

Decade	Average MSE
1906–10	0.1100
1910–20	0.0974
1920–30	0.0798
1930–40	0.0594

It is thus quite evident that the fit of the hedonic regressions improves over time. It is not entirely clear why we should observe this pattern. One possible explanation is that the looser fit in the earlier years reflects greater technological heterogeneity and so a greater number of omitted aspects of quality. Subsequent convergence toward standard designs varying principally only in size and power would by itself then lead to improving fit. It is also possible that with the increasing maturity of the market for automobiles, the preferences of consumers became increasingly well defined and the consumers themselves increasingly well informed. Both of these factors would have worked to force prices more and more into line with the observed attributes. It would be interesting to see whether the phenomenon of a tighter fit of the hedonic regression as an industry evolves from infancy to maturity is also found in other markets.

2.5   Quality-Adjusted Price Indexes

In this section we compute quality-adjusted price indexes for automobiles, decompose them into two components corresponding to process and product innovation, and break down the entire period into more homogeneous subperiods. We also compare them to parallel indexes for computers. Finally, we couple our series to Gordon's (1990) for the postwar decades so as to see the industry's history whole.

2.5.1   Simple Quality-Adjusted Price Indexes

On the basis of the hedonic coefficient, denoted hereafter by α, we compute a quality-adjusted percentage price change as follows:

$$\%\Delta\text{QAPrice} = \exp\alpha - 1.$$

Here QA stands for quality-adjusted, $\%\Delta$ for percentage of change.[22] We calculate $\%\Delta$QAPrice both for α's estimated on the basis of current prices and for α's estimated on the basis of CPI-deflated prices. We then construct corresponding quality-adjusted price indexes with the results shown in table 2.6.

---

22. Note that for small values of α, $\%\Delta$QAPrice $\cong \alpha$. But as α grows larger in absolute value, so does the difference between $(\exp\alpha - 1)$ and α.

Table 2.6   **Quality-Adjusted Price Indexes for Automobiles: 1906–1940**

Year	Rate of Change Using		Index Using	
	Current Prices	Constant Prices	Current Prices	Constant Prices
1906	—	—	100.0	100.0
1908	−0.30	−0.30	70.0	70.0
1910	−0.23	−0.25	54.0	52.4
1912	−0.09	−0.12	49.3	46.0
1914	−0.12	−0.16	43.3	38.8
1916	−0.24	−0.30	33.1	27.4
1918	0.16	−0.16	38.4	23.1
1920	0.36	0.03	53.4	23.8
1922	−0.09	0.09	47.9	25.9
1924	−0.14	−0.16	41.2	21.9
1926	−0.10	−0.13	37.3	19.0
1928	−0.07	−0.12	34.8	16.7
1930	−0.04	−0.10	33.4	15.0
1932	−0.18	0.00	27.4	14.9
1934	−0.08	−0.06	25.3	14.0
1936	0.01	−0.02	25.5	13.8
1938	0.19	0.16	30.2	16.0
1940	−0.05	−0.04	28.8	15.4
Annual average 1906–1940	−0.03	−0.05		

Note: Constant prices are CPI-deflated (1993 = 100).

The main findings are as follows. First, quality-adjusted prices (based on CPI-deflated prices) fell at an average rate of slightly more than 5 percent per year from 1906 to 1940, thus halving every thirteen years. This is by absolute standards quite a substantial pace. In terms of constant 1993 dollars, it means that the average price of a car of constant quality was $52,600 in 1906 and fell to just $8,100 by 1940. To put this in perspective, if the industry had continued to innovate at the same rate from 1944 to 1994, a car by then would have cost just $582 on a quality-adjusted basis.

Second, as is to be expected, the rate of change of quality-adjusted prices was generally larger in absolute value when we used CPI-deflated prices than when we used current prices. The exception is periods of marked deflation, during which automobile prices—like the prices of many durables—dropped more slowly than the CPI.[23] Third, we ran different variants of the hedonic regressions and constructed the corresponding indices in order to ascertain the role played by the inclusion of the variables representing the five engineering systems. The results (not shown in the tables) indicate that their inclusion does

23. Thus in 1922 and 1932 the %ΔQAPrice based on current prices shows large declines whereas the %ΔQAPrice based on CPI-deflated prices either increases or shows no decline. The largest discrepancies between the two occurred in 1918 and 1920 because of the post–World War I inflation.

make a difference, but for the most part it is a small one—in the range of 0.5 to 1.5 percentage points per year in the computation of %ΔQAPrice.[24]

2.5.2   Process versus Product Innovation

We next compute a rate of quality change, defined as a residual:

$$\%\Delta\text{Quality} = \%\Delta\text{Price} - \%\Delta\text{QAPrice}.$$

If the attributes of cars remain constant, %ΔPrice is exactly equal to %ΔQA-Price, and %ΔQuality must equal zero. Suppose, on the other hand, that cars improve. Then %ΔQAPrice is strictly less than %ΔPrice. We might call the difference—that is, %ΔQuality—pure quality change. If there is some technical advance then this difference would be positive. (In this case %ΔQAPrice would be negative, since it refers to the quality-adjusted price decline.) Notice that %ΔQuality can take negative values if quality-adjusted prices drop less or rise more than unadjusted prices. That would be the case, for example, if prices did not change but some cars displayed fewer of some attributes that were positively valued (or, more precisely, that show a positive coefficient in the hedonic regression).

The series is displayed in table 2.7. The 5 percent average annual decline of quality-adjusted prices can be decomposed as follows. Prices by themselves (CPI-defaulted) dropped at the rate of 3 percent per year. The residual "quality" therefore increased at a rate of 2 percent. If we identify constant-quality price change with manufacturing economies and quality change, as we have defined it, with design improvements, then these numbers suggest that 60 percent of the decline in quality-adjusted prices was due to process innovation and only 40 percent was due to product innovation or quality change per se.

This partition of the overall quality-adjusted price decline into a product-innovation and a process-innovation component should be regarded cautiously (see also Griliches 1961). Many modern manufacturing economies, for example, come from simplifying designs (see, for example, Whitney 1988), and a reliable decomposition would therefore have to study specific innovations. And prices can certainly fall for a variety of reasons, among them increased competition and lower input prices. But the identification with process innovation seems plausible because of the dramatic economies offered by the development and diffusion of mass-production methods. There can be no doubt that the set of techniques grouped under the umbrella term "mass production" constituted one of the most important innovations in manufacturing methods of all time and had tremendous consequences in terms of unit costs, scale, and

24. The one important exception is 1914–16. During that period there was a big drop in prices (amounting to −33 percent in CPI-deflated prices), but at the same time there was a significant downsizing of cars (i.e., both mean wheelbase and power declined a great deal). As a result, the drop in quality-adjusted prices is less than that of unadjusted prices (−0.30 versus −0.33). If one were to exclude wheelbase and power from the regression, but include the systems, then the quality-adjusted price decline jumps to −54 percent!

Table 2.7   **Price and Quality Indexes for Automobiles (in constant 1993 dollars)**

Year	Mean Price	Mean QAPrice	%ΔPrice	%ΔQAPrice	%ΔQuality
1906	52,640	52,640			
1908	46,640	36,848	−0.11	−0.30	0.19
1910	39,860	27,583	−0.15	−0.25	0.10
1912	41,400	24,214	0.04	−0.12	0.16
1914	44,242	20,424	0.07	−0.16	0.23
1916	29,483	14,423	−0.33	−0.30	−0.03
1918	24,875	12,160	−0.16	−0.16	0.00
1920	24,566	12,528	−0.01	0.03	−0.04
1922	27,146	13,634	0.11	0.09	0.02
1924	22,732	11,528	−0.16	−0.16	0.00
1926	22,082	10,002	−0.03	−0.13	0.10
1928	21,241	8,791	−0.04	−0.12	0.08
1930	20,702	7,896	−0.03	−0.10	0.07
1932	25,803	7,843	0.25	0.00	0.25
1934	23,236	7,370	−0.10	−0.06	−0.04
1936	17,842	7,264	−0.23	−0.02	−0.21
1938	19,036	8,422	0.07	0.16	−0.09
1940	16,565	8,107	−0.13	−0.04	−0.09
Annual			−0.03	−0.05	0.02

production capabilities. The drop from, say, the $2,000–$3,000 cars of the early years to the less-than-$500 Ford Model T would never have been possible with the craftlike production and assembly methods that prevailed early in the century.

It remains to be established, however, precisely how much of the industry's overall price drop can be attributed to the diffusion of mass production and what exactly the causal link was. Casual evidence suggests that the relationship was very nonlinear, perhaps because of the interplay between innovation and competition. Recall that prices dropped a great deal in the immediate aftermath of Ford's introduction of mass production. Recall also that this was a period in which Ford was the only producer to operate in this fashion. We speculated above that the generalized drop was due to competitive pressures brought about by Ford's drastic price reductions. That the downward trend in prices continued along with the diffusion of mass production is certainly consistent with this explanation, but it is not clear how closely synchronized the two processes were.[25] It would also be interesting to see whether the steep and sustained drop in prices experienced by the automobile industry over more than three decades is typical of new industries along their trajectory toward maturity or whether it was unique.

25. Nor can it be at this time. Surprisingly little is actually known about the diffusion of these methods on the firm and establishment levels. See Raff (1991) and Bresnahan and Raff (1993) for a start.

Table 2.8   **Rates of Change of Automobile Prices: Subperiods**

Subperiod	Rate of Change
%ΔQAPrice	
1906–18	−0.22
1918–22	0.06
1922–30	−0.13
1930–40	0.01
1906–40	*−0.10*
%ΔQuality	
1906–14	0.17
1914–24	−0.01
1924–32	0.12
1932–40	−0.11
1906–40	*0.04*

2.5.3   Quality-Adjusted Price Changes over Subperiods

Price changes averaged over the entire period conceal significant and interesting differences across subperiods. In this section we present the bare facts. We leave for future work detailed examination and explanation of the differences.

As table 2.8 reveals, one can clearly distinguish four periods in terms of %ΔQAPrice and %ΔQuality. Note that the partition is not exactly the same for the two measures. Most of the innovation appears to have occurred very early on (i.e., 1906 through either 1914 or 1918, depending on which series one uses). Moreover, the highest rates of quality change occurred at the very beginning (1906–14). This is undoubtedly the portion of our period in which the greatest proportion of entrepreneurs were engineers or mechanics by training, knowledge spillovers were all-pervasive, and design bureaucracies were shallowest. Whatever the mechanisms may have been, the pattern lends further support to the conjecture that it is indeed in the course of the emergence of a new industry that the largest strides in product innovation are made.[26] An important implication of this is that if one leaves out those early stages in computing quality-adjusted price indexes, one is bound to grossly underestimate the welfare effects of product innovation.

In order to gain some perspective on the observed rate of innovation in cars during the initial period, it is worth comparing it to the rate in what might be regarded as the parallel period for personal computers, namely 1982–88. As reported in Berndt and Griliches (1993), the average rate of quality-adjusted price decline in that industry during that period was somewhere between −0.20 and −0.30 percent per year (depending on the sort of estimate used). For cars, our results show a figure of about half that size (−0.11 percent per

26. Trajtenberg (1990) documents this pattern for the case of computerized tomography (CT) scanners.

year for 1906–18, −0.14 percent per year for 1906–14). This is quite remarkable considering that the case of personal computers is widely regarded as extreme in its rate of real-price decline. The decline for personal computers derived primarily from a long and steady series of dramatic improvements in integrated circuit—in particular, microprocessor—design and manufacturing capabilities. No major automobile component experienced such sustained dramatic price/performance declines.[27] Yet the entire choice spectrum of cars displayed 11–14 percent yearly rates of quality-adjusted price drops for roughly a decade!

The biggest discrepancy between the picture presented by %ΔQAPrice and that by %ΔQuality is in the period 1914–18. During those years prices came down steeply, but measured quality stagnated or even worsened a little. As already mentioned, those years saw a substantial downsizing of cars. In the context of hedonic measurement, this registers as quality decline. A similar phenomenon happened in 1936, when a significant price drop (of over 20 percent) was more than offset by downsizing, resulting in a measured quality-change residual of −21 percent.[28] However, it is doubtful that the reduction in the mean of some of the measured attributes during those episodes corresponds to welfare loses of the magnitude suggested by the hedonic computations. We discuss why this is so in section 2.6 below.

Another interesting fact to notice is the dramatic changes from period to period and the cyclical pattern that they follow. This could in principle be a manifestation of economies of scale in production or of competition in the product market driving profit margins. This too is a finding in want of further research and interpretation.

2.5.4.   A Longer Horizon

It is natural to want to place the main findings of this section in the context of a more extended history of the industry. The obvious way to do this is to link the appropriate series of our data to the recent series of Gordon (1990), which runs from just after the war through the early 1980s. Since Gordon's series also derives from unweighted regressions, it is in fact appropriate to link the two directly.[29] The linking can be accomplished using numbers relating 1937 and 1950 cross sections from Griliches (1961). Table 2.9 gives the combined series.[30] Figure 2.3 illustrates.

It would be in the spirit of the literature to give a detailed interpretation to

---

27. T. L. De Fazio, Charles Stark Draper Laboratories, Cambridge, Mass., personal communication.

28. This happened again after 1975 (Gordon 1990). In that instance, the improvement in fuel economy offset the estimated value of the decline in size. It is unfortunate that no broadly based data on model fuel economy exists for the period studied in this paper.

29. His regressions do not incorporate our systems approach, but much of the explanatory power in both is carried by the common variables.

30. The break in the series is ultimately due to the cessation of automobile production during World War II.

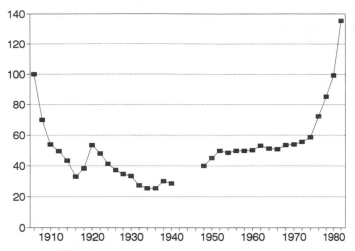

Fig. 2.3   Quality-adjusted price index 1906–1982 from current-dollar data (1906 = 100)

Table 2.9   **Combined Hedonic Price Index**

Year	Index	Year	Index	Year	Index	Year	Index
1906	100.0	1934	25.3	1956	49.7	1970	53.9
1908	70.0	1936	25.5	1957	50.3	1971	57.8
1910	54.0	1938	30.2	1958	49.7	1972	55.6
1912	49.3	1940	28.8	1959	50.8	1973	54.5
1914	43.3			1960	50.3	1974	58.4
1916	33.1	1947	34.7	1961	50.8	1975	68.5
1918	38.4	1948	39.9	1962	52.8	1976	72.0
1920	53.4	1949	46.9	1963	51.8	1977	74.3
1922	47.9	1950	45.0	1964	51.3	1978	85.4
1924	41.2	1951	48.8	1965	50.3	1979	88.9
1926	37.3	1952	49.7	1966	50.8	1980	99.2
1928	34.8	1953	49.7	1967	51.3	1981	124.9
1930	33.4	1954	48.3	1968	53.4	1982	135.3
1932	27.4	1955	50.8	1969	52.3	1983	140.8

Note: The coefficient on the variable D in table 4 of Griliches (1961) was used to splice the third column of our table 2.5 and column 6 of table 8.8 in Gordon (1990).

this figure. But the underlying series are in terms of current prices and the radical changes in the general price level that occurred over this extended period suggest deflating by the CPI first. This yields the series illustrated in figure 2.4. The explosion at the end of the series in figure 2.3—proportionately roughly as large as the declines of the early years—is revealed to be for practical purposes entirely due to inflation. The overwhelming bulk of the quality-adjusted price decline in this industry came in a tremendous burst before the

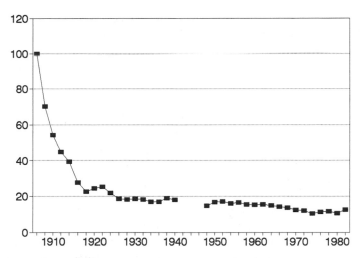

Fig. 2.4   Quality-adjusted price index 1906–1982 deflated by the Consumer Price Index (1906=100)

1920s. By the time the Depression was over, so was most of the story. Computations of growth rates averaged out over very long intervals can indeed miss the most salient details.

2.6   Potential Biases

The fact that our estimates are based on unweighted hedonic regressions may introduce biases in the quality-adjusted price indexes, primarily in those subperiods that experienced pronounced shifts in the structure of the market. The main concern is that our indexes may understate the extent of the real price reduction associated with the introduction and diffusion of mass-production methods and the concomitant ascendancy of low-end models, primarily the Ford Model T. The issues here are interesting and worth exploring.

There are two intertwined but nevertheless distinct aspects to the Model T phenomenon. First, true mass-production methods were deployed in manufacturing it. These methods allowed Ford to realize vast economies of scale and concomitant cost savings which emerged in substantial part as steep price reductions. The low prices sustained the mass market. Second, the Model T was a smaller, simpler, less powerful, and less luxurious car than virtually any other car of its time. These two aspects are intimately connected.

It is quite clear that if the Model T had been produced with the craft methods that were prevalent in the industry at the time, its price would have been much higher. In fact, hedonic regressions including a dummy variable for Ford in the early period show large negative coefficients on the dummy, in some years amounting to a price discount of 40 percent. That is, the Ford Model T was radically cheaper than what was warranted by the mere fact that it was smaller, simpler, and less powerful than other cars in the market. This was the force of mass production.

On the other hand, it seems equally clear that introducing mass-production methods in manufacturing the higher-end models of the time, even if it had been technologically feasible, would have not rendered cars nearly as low-priced as they needed to be to hit the more elastic segments of demand. In fact, the mass market revealed itself only as the price dropped to about $500, about one-sixth of the mean price of cars in preceding years. In other words, the adoption of mass-production methods could be justified only if one could produce in very large quantities, and such cars could find a market only if they were to be very cheap. This, in turn, necessitated the design of a small, stripped-to-the-bone type of car. Similarly, as the mass-production methods spread to other manufacturers, they were applied first (and, for quite a while, only) to cars at the low end or, more precisely, to small, simple cars designed specifically with these demand and production relationships in mind.

What are the implications of these facts for the construction (and interpretation) of our price indexes? There are two, one related to the fact that we do not have quantity data, the other to the inherent limitations of the hedonic methods in these circumstances. We discuss them sequentially in the remainder of this section.

2.6.1   Lack of Quantity Data: Biases and Remedies

Our lack of detailed quantity data, which obliges us to base our calculations on nothing more complex than unweighted hedonic regressions, might cause a serious underestimate of the price fall that took place as mass-production methods were introduced and the Ford Model T captured a large share of the total market. One can think of this as a sampling problem. As the market composition shifted dramatically toward the low end, we keep sampling according to the old frame of reference in which all models received their initial—implicitly, equal—weights. How big a problem is this? To assess the extent of the bias, we bring in two additional sets of numbers. These are a separate index for Ford cars alone, which we have calculated for this purpose, and the automobile component of the Producer Price Index (PPI) of the period, a component which is based primarily on mass-produced cars.

The simplest way to assess the extent of the bias without resorting to unavailable broadly based quantity data is to take the lowest-priced Ford as a reasonable proxy for the mass-market car of each year, create a quality-adjusted price index for Ford, and observe how it compares to our QAPrice index. Figure 2.5 does this. It was convenient to start the Ford series with a figure for 1910, so the comparison runs from 1910 to 1940.

It is important to note that Ford sold just one basic design, with only minor variations, from the beginning of the period shown here through 1927. The first epoch in the Ford series is a long decline, punctuated only by a spike in

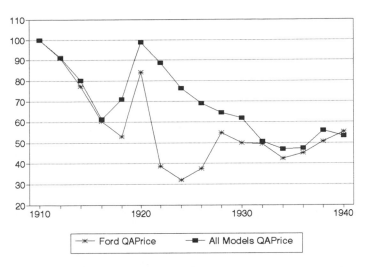

Fig. 2.5   Ford quality-adjusted price versus all models quality-adjusted price (1910=100)

the immediate postwar years which represents the sharp but transitory postwar inflation, the company's financial crisis, and its desperate—if in the end quite effective—measures to avoid insolvency.[31] During this decade and a half, Ford cars were produced with unusually capital-intensive methods.[32] Output exploded and economies of scale were exploited relentlessly. By 1926, the design was unchanged but the market was not. It was in this period that Ford acquired, for the first time, serious competition for the low end of the market.[33] The Model T clearly needed to be replaced, and the late 1920s at Ford were the epoch of the more sophisticated Model A. Production ramped up and costs fell, albeit more slowly than before. By the mid-1930s, bolstered by the Depression-induced shakeout of smaller-scale producers, all three low-end makes were moving upmarket in attribute space, and the final series of Ford numbers reflects this.

Figure 2.5 faithfully depicts these developments. We can see that the divergence between the unweighted series and Ford's starts in 1918 and goes on until 1930, with Ford's showing—as expected—a lower index. But it is in the mid-1920s that the difference becomes very pronounced, with the Ford index reaching a low of less than one-half the level of the unweighted index in 1922–24. The mechanics of this are quite simple. Our unweighted index converges back toward its 1916 level quite slowly from the postwar inflation spike. The Ford series, by contrast, positively vaults back onto the track of the scale-

31. On the company's postwar troubles, see Nevins and Hill (1957).
32. In the 1920s the Ford mother plant was often said to be the largest single industrial establishment in the world.
33. This came from General Motors' Chevrolet (circa 1924) and Chrysler's Plymouth (1928).

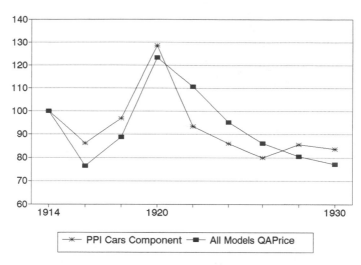

Fig. 2.6   Producer Price Index cars component versus quality-adjusted price 1914–1930 (1914=100)

driven economies. It comes back up mid-decade as consumer tastes shifted toward the less spartan models the rest of the manufacturers were by then making. Two points thus emerge. First, it is when the market is experiencing dramatic changes in the composition of its output that the lack of quantity data proves most awkward for the hedonic method. Second, however, the unweighted index tells quite an accurate story over the long run of our period.

Figure 2.6 presents a similar comparison, but this time with the automobile component of the PPI. This was quantity-weighted average of the prices of specific models of six manufacturers, representing the broad sweep of the market.[34] This is in effect a selective quantity-weighted index uncorrected for changes in quality. The most important feature of the figure is that the two series have the same broad qualitative features. But contrary to Gordon's findings for the post–World War II period, there is no trending bias to the PPI component here. The relative positions of our index and the PPI series change as downsizing or quality-enhancement in the ordinary sense dominate. In this, our index is surely superior. The figure also shows our index to be off in periods of market composition change. This is just what we observed with the Ford series.

2.6.2   Potential Biases due to Downsizing

The second potential source of bias stems from the other aspect of mass production, namely that it involved manufacturing low-end cars. In fact, from

---

34. The manufacturers were Buick, Cadillac, Chevrolet, Dodge, Ford, and Packard. See, e.g., U.S. Bureau of Labor Statistics (1929, 2 and table 9).

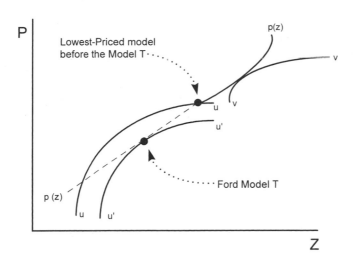

Fig. 2.7   Downsizing bias

the middle of the second decade of the twentieth century to the middle of the third, there was a pronounced downsizing trend in the mix of models offered in the market, with a concomitant reduction in prices. (A second downsizing wave, less pronounced, occurred in the late 1930s.) As we have remarked, it remains to be established how precisely this relates to the advent of mass production since Ford alone introduced those methods to begin with and Ford models constituted only a tiny fraction of the population of models. Clearly, these issues can be properly dealt with if and only if extensive quantity data become available.

But the problem in this context is that the hedonic method cannot (and was never meant to) assess the trade-offs in utility between a reduction in measurable quality (for example, HP) and the price reduction. All it can do is tell whether the prices fell on average more or less than what the reduction in quality would have warranted and translate that measure into a price index. Is such an index an accurate representation of the underlying changes in consumers' welfare as a consequence of the introduction of low-end cars? Without more information it is impossible to say, but there is good reason to suspect not.

Consider the hypothetical situation depicted in figure 2.7. Price is measured on the vertical axis (P), a positively valued attribute such as HP on the horizontal (Z). In the base period, the hedonic function is the solid line $p(z)$. The indifference curve $u-u$ represents consumers who buy the lowest quality-price combination but are not "satisfied": satisfaction requires tangency between the indifference curve and the hedonic surface. (Compare their situation with that of the consumers represented by the indifference curve $v-v$.) In the second period, new low-end models appear. As a consequence, the $u-u$ type of consumers can attain a higher utility level, $u'-u'$. A hedonic quality-adjusted price index might decrease somewhat, show no change at all (as shown in figure 2.6), or even increase. In any case, it will be biased upward: the distance between $u - u$ and $u' - u'$, which is a rough approximation for the welfare gain associated with the change, will always exceed the distance between the old and new hedonic curves. Indeed, the overall bias may be very large if consumers of the $u - u$ type make up a large fraction of the market. This seems likely to have been the case in the late part of the second decade of the twentieth century and the first half of the third decade. Without quantity data and the more demanding computational methods, however, we cannot assess the magnitude of the bias. We can only identify the periods in which this bias is likely to occur and interpret hedonic-based results for those periods as lower bounds for the true quality-adjusted price reductions.

2.7   Conclusion

Most of the change in quality-adjusted prices (based on CPI-deflated prices) of American automobiles between 1906 and 1983 occurred during the period studied in this paper. Between the years 1906 and 1940, quality-adjusted prices fell at an average rate of 5 percent per year, thus halving every thirteen years. That is a very brisk pace. In the first eight to twelve years of the period, the pace was even brisker, about one-half the size of the best recent estimates for the personal computer industry. We find this one-half an intriguingly high fraction for an industry that in its time wrought equally radical changes on society and on the feasibility of other innovations. Methodological reflections suggest that the true fraction may be even higher.

Our measured decline can be divided into price and quality components. Prices themselves (CPI-deflated) dropped at a rate of 3 percent, whereas quality as we measure it increased at a rate of 2 percent per year. This suggests that 60 percent of the decline in quality-adjusted prices was due to process innovation and only 40 percent to product innovation or quality change per se.

One innovation of this study was to include much more detail about the mechanical aspects of the vehicles in the regressors. Regression results, some reported here and some not, indicate that inclusion of systems variables does make a difference. For the most part, however, the difference is a small one (about 1 percentage point in the computation of %ΔQAPrice). This may grow larger as researchers' sophistication about engineering issues grows.

These estimates all derive from unweighted regressions. Comparisons of the unweighted index with an index derived from low-end Ford models, a reasonable proxy throughout the period for the mass market, reveals a significant divergence for a brief (transitional) period but otherwise fairly thoroughgoing conformity. Thus long- and even medium-term measures of the sort discussed above would be unaffected by the choice of index. Comparison of our index with a quantity-weighted Bureau of Labor Statistics index that does not correct

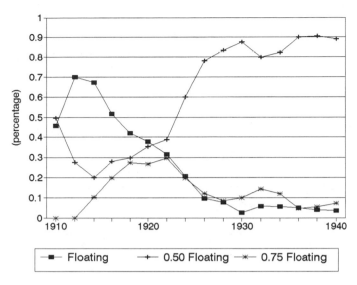

Fig. 2A.1   Rear axle designs 1910–1940

for quality change reinforces this point and also underlines the importance of correcting for quality.

This paper is a first quantitative glimpse into one of the most dynamic and interesting periods in the history of modern industrial sectors. A number of substantive questions clearly worthy of further research have emerged. Pursuing most of them would require a database incorporating quantity data. More light may thus be shed in future work.

Appendix
The Evolution of System Designs

Figure 2A.1 shows the initial division of rear axle designs between the floating and the lighter and cheaper half- (or semi-) floating design. The main design issue here is how the weight of the car is distributed over the axle.[35] Initially, the semifloating approach lost ground to the fully floating, presumably as it became clear that contemporary single bearings were inadequate to carry the loads and stresses involved. As incremental innovations in bearing design emerged, the proportion of semi- and three-quarters-floating designs in the population grew at the fully floating's expense; finally the bearing innovations

35. For details and some drawings, see Newcomb and Spurr (1989, 268–70).

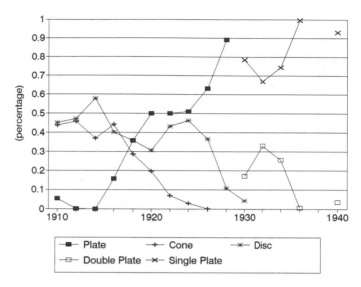

Fig. 2A.2   Clutch designs 1910–1940

seem to have been perfected, the half-floating design itself was perfected, and it essentially drove the others out of the population entirely.

The population of clutch types is displayed in figure 2A.2. There were initially a number of competing approaches (and in principle a number of variants of each). The cone design was familiar to machinists and in that sense accessible. But the mechanism needed regular cleaning and adjustment, engagement was abrupt, and the heaviness of the mechanism made gear changing difficult. The plate family did not have these problems. Initially, inadequacies of the facing materials made single-plate clutches inappropriate for relatively heavy cars. The decline of the multiplate percentage in the 1930s may well represent the declining percentage of heavy automobiles. Improved facing materials probably also play some role.

Figure 2A.3, badly afflicted with missing data, shows a similar sort of rise and fall. Hydraulic brake systems were at first expensive relative to mechanical ones. (There were also engineering reasons for wanting some of the tubing to be flexible and suspicions about the tubing's integrity persisted for some time.) Relative cost may account for the relative decline in hydraulic systems' incidence in the early Depression years. But they were almost completely dominant by the end of the decade.

Drive types are the subject of figure 2A.4. This variable concerns the means by which power was transmitted to the rear axle. Chain drives were mechanically simple and common in the very earliest cars. They contributed to a smooth ride since they involved a relatively high ratio of sprung to unsprung

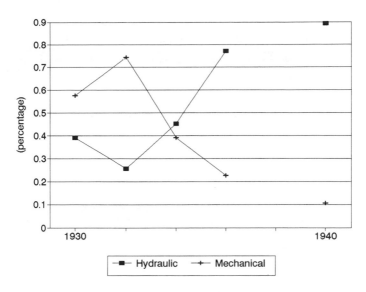

Fig. 2A.3 Brake designs 1930–1940

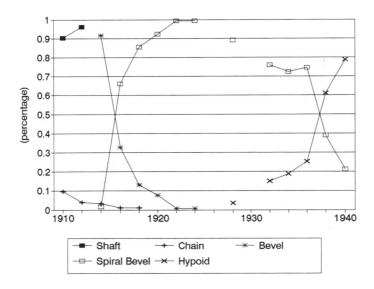

Fig. 2A.4 Drive designs 1910–1940

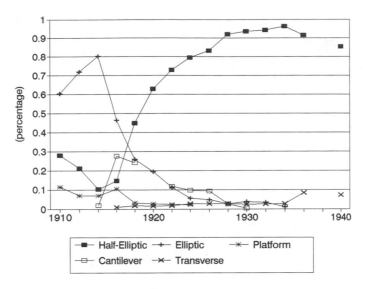

Fig. 2A.5   Spring designs 1910–1940

weight. But they were also noisy and potentially dangerous. They did not last in the population. Ordinary bevel gears had fewer of these faults but were still noisy relative to spiral-beveled gears. The spiral-bevel design emerged as the most desirable for a time but was eventually eclipsed by another innovation, hypoid gearing, that maintained the advantages of the spiral bevel and allowed the driveshaft to be lowered relative to the body.

Figure 2A.5 shows population percentages for types of springs. The transverse design seems to have been effective only for extremely light vehicles. The competition among the other designs for most of our period is best understood as being between the fully elliptic on the one hand and the half-elliptic family on the other.[36] The latter group included the half-elliptic design, the cantilever (a half-elliptic mounted in a slightly different fashion and requiring additional metal parts to constrain the axle), and the platform design (a more complex and heavier variant with no performance advantages). The issue between the full- and half-elliptics concerned how high above the axle the chassis and body had to sit. Presumably due to some combination of improving roads, evolving fashions in body styles, and the desire to take weight out of designs (so as to increase acceleration, improve fuel economy, etc.), the half-elliptic family and the half-elliptic design within it won out. In the graph, one again observes initial heterogeneity and the emergence of a dominant design.

---

36. Toward the end of our period one first begins to see the coil springs that were related to the development of independent front suspension.

References

Berndt, E. R., and Z. Griliches. 1993. Price indexes for microcomputers: An exploratory study. In *Price measurements and their uses,* ed. M. F. Foss, M. E. Manser, and A. H. Young, 63–93. Chicago: University of Chicago Press.

Bresnahan, T. F., and D. M. G. Raff. 1991. Intra-industry heterogeneity and the Great Depression: The American motor vehicle industry 1929–1935. *Journal of Economic History* 51:317–31.

———. 1993. Technological heterogeneity, adjustment costs, and the dynamics of plant shut-down behavior: The American motor vehicle industry in the time of the Great Depression. Working Paper no. FB-93-09. Graduate School of Business, Columbia University, New York.

Court, A. T. 1939. Hedonic price indices with automotive examples. In *The dynamics of automobile demand,* ed. General Motors Corporation. 77–99. Detroit, Mich.: General Motors.

Flink, J. J. 1988. *The automobile age.* Cambridge: MIT Press.

Gordon, R. J. 1990. *The measurement of durable goods prices.* Chicago: University of Chicago Press.

Griliches, Z. 1961. Hedonic price indexes for automobiles: An econometric analysis of quality change. In *Price statistics of the federal government,* ed. NBER Price Statistics Review Committee, general series 73, 137–96. New York: National Bureau of Economic Research.

Griliches, Z., and P. Ryan. 1971. Hedonic price analysis for vintage automobiles. Unpublished.

Kimes, B. R., and H. A. Clark, Jr. 1985. *Standard catalogue of American cars 1805–1942.* 2d ed. Iola, Minn.: Krause.

Nevins, A., and F. E. Hill. 1957. *Ford: Expansion and challenge 1915–1933.* New York: Scribner's.

Newcomb, T. P., and R. T. Spurr. 1989. *A technical history of the motor car.* New York: Adam Hilger.

Ohta, M., and Z. Griliches. 1976. Automobile prices revisited: Extensions of the hedonic hypothesis. In *Household production and consumption,* ed. N. E. Terleckyj, 325–90. New York: National Bureau of Economic Research.

Pakes, A., S. Berry, and J. Levinsohn. 1993. Applications and limitations of some recent advances in empirical industrial organization: Price indices and the analysis of environmental change. *American Economic Review Papers and Proceedings* 83:240–46.

Raff, D. M. G. 1991. Making cars and making money in the interwar automobile industry: Economies of scale, economies of scope, and the manufacturing that stood behind the marketing. *Business History Review* 65:721–53.

Trajtenberg, M. 1990. *Economic analysis of product innovation: The case of CT scanners.* Cambridge, Mass.: Harvard University Press.

Triplett, J. E. 1969. Automobiles and hedonic quality measurement. *Journal of Political Economy* 77:408–17.

U.S. Bureau of Labor Statistics. 1929. Wholesale prices 1913–1927. *Bulletin no. 473.* Washington, D.C.: Government Printing Office.

U.S. Bureau of the Census. 1976. *Historical statistics of the United States.* Washington, D.C.: Government Printing Office.

Whitney, D. E. 1988. Manufacturing by design. *Harvard Business Review* 66 (4): 83–91.

Comment   Jack E. Triplett

Technical change can, it is well known, alter the production process or it can alter the characteristics of the product. Raff and Trajtenberg appropriately and imaginatively employ the hedonic method to explore and illuminate product-oriented technical change in automobiles from 1906 to 1940.

The economics of differentiated products concerns the production, sale, purchase, and use of the bundle of characteristics that are embodied in the product. An empirical hedonic function provides estimates of the prices of the characteristics in the bundle, and also helps, with a priori knowledge, to isolate empirically the characteristics. Because the hedonic function is determined by the technology of producing characteristics and by buyers' preferences for them (Rosen 1974), hedonic prices will be influenced in a predictable way by technical change.

The automobile hedonic model employed by Raff and Trajtenberg derives from Court (1939) and Griliches (1961), and is fundamentally the same as that in studies such as Gordon (1990), Ohta and Griliches (1976), and my own earlier work on automobiles (Triplett 1969). The hedonic functions for automobiles in this literature are primitive in many ways. They portray the complexities of automobile production or use solely through measures of carrying capacity and engine performance, plus the presence or absence of a small number of amenities. The simple automobile hedonic model is undoubtedly a better description of automobile technology in the historical period covered by Raff and Trajtenberg than it would be for more recent periods—the automobile is far more complex now, and what consumers want and expect from it is much harder to model in 1995 than in, say, 1910.[1]

Nevertheless, the simple automobile hedonic model's shortcomings need to be kept in mind in interpreting automobile hedonic measures for any period. My comments on this simple automobile hedonic model represent not so much disagreement with the reservations Raff and Trajtenberg have expressed about it (I endorse their useful discussion of engineering complexity) but, rather, differing empirical points of emphasis.

The major reservation concerns the variables in automobile hedonic functions. The entire theoretical literature on consumer price indexes rests on the implicit assumption that the consumption quantities that appear in index num-

Jack E. Triplett is chief economist at the Bureau of Economic Analysis of the U.S. Department of Commerce.

This paper does not represent an official position of the Bureau of Economic Analysis or of the U.S. Department of Commerce.

1. In Triplett (1990), I argued that the complexity of the modern automobile probably precludes the current use of hedonic methods in constructing automobile price indexes for the U.S. Consumer and Producer Price Indexes (CPI and PPI). In the CPI and PPI cases, alternative methods exist for constructing quality-adjusted automobile price indexes. For the 1906–40 historical period, the same alternatives to hedonic methods do not exist.

ber formulas are arguments of the consumer's utility function. It is sometimes overlooked that hedonic price indexes for consumer goods are based on exactly the same assumption: The characteristics in properly specified hedonic functions are consumption quantities that generate utility; they are arguments of a utility function that is defined on characteristics, rather than simply on goods (see Rosen 1974 for elaboration of this point with respect to hedonic functions, and Triplett 1983, 1987 for its application to hedonic price indexes).

One cannot emphasize too strongly that the simple automobile hedonic model incorporates only the roughest kinds of proxies for the true automotive services that consumers desire. Carrying capacity and performance—the major variables in the simple automobile hedonic model—provide an inadequate representation of what the automobile does for its buyer, and therefore also of what automobile companies and engineers design and produce. Obvious omissions are braking and safety characteristics, as well as comfort and other characteristics of luxuriousness. Yet, even capacity and performance characteristics are described very inadequately by the technical specifications that have been published in industry sources.

The best simple measure of passenger capacity is probably body space: the distance between the car's engine and its rear axle. This is a standard chassis dimension that is used within the industry for body-manufacturing purposes but seldom appears in industry publications. Tables of interior dimensions appear at least as early as 1928 (*Motor* 1928), yet wheelbase and overall length have been, since Court (1939), the primary measures of size in automobile hedonic functions, partly because they are consistently measured over the years and appear in most published compilations of automobile specifications.

Speed and acceleration are desired automobile performance characteristics. They were especially important in the 1906–40 period explored by Raff and Trajtenberg because performance was lower then and increments to performance much more expensive. The engine measure that is most closely related to automobile performance is torque (a measure of engine twisting power), not the horsepower the engine develops. However, torque is almost never published in statistical compilations before 1940, and even horsepower data are fragmentary for much of the period.[2] For most years, we have instead the cylinder capacity (displacement) of the engine and its "rated" horsepower.[3] Neither one is adequate for describing the trend of engine performance over time because actual power rose steadily relative to both engine displacement and rated horsepower.

2. The compilation in Naul (1978) presents, from unspecific original sources, actual horsepower for many U.S. automobile engines back to 1920. For some cars, however, data are incomplete or missing entirely.

3. Rated, or "taxable," horsepower was computed according to a formula that considered only cylinder bore. The formula was developed early in the century but was rapidly made obsolete by developments in engine design. In Great Britain, rated horsepower was used for taxation purposes. A table in *Motor* (1928) presents displacement, rated horsepower, and actual horsepower for most 1928 U.S. cars.

Beyond mere size and engine performance, a host of characteristics generates utility to the consumer of automobile services. From this perspective, it is difficult to understand why publishers selected the particular measures that appear in industry sources.[4] A few of the variables commonly tabulated (e.g., type of lubrication system, type of valves, and number of forward speeds in the transmission) have implications for some property that is important to the buyer (engine reliability, engine efficiency, and driving flexibility and performance, respectively, in the three examples cited) as well as for cost of production. A few others have implications for maintenance; a detachable cylinder head, for example, makes it far easier to grind the valves, a routine maintenance required at frequent intervals in the 1920s and 1930s, though the nondetachable head avoids all problems with cylinder head gaskets, which in the earlier years of the automobile's history were a source of mechanical failure.

No direct statistics in the published data sources measure speed and acceleration, handling ease, cornering ability, reliability, smoothness of engine, controls, and ride, and so forth. The substantial technical innovations to automobile engines, brakes, transmissions, and bodies in the 1930s, for example, vastly improved the quality of the end-of-decade car compared with the one that had been available at the beginning of the decade. All of these changes are more or less ignored in the simple automobile hedonic model, for lack of published specifications on consumer-oriented characteristics. Similar statements can be made about data for earlier decades in the automobile's history.

One can also, it is well known (see Rosen 1974), interpret the independent variables in hedonic functions as outputs of automobile producers, which means they are arguments in producers' cost functions. But the published automobile specifications are also not very closely related to technical changes that engineering departments of automobile companies were working on at the time. Ohta and Griliches (1976) make the valid distinction between what they call technical characteristics and performance characteristics. Unfortunately, the specifications that are published on automobiles are related—a little bit—to both, but do not correspond very well to either. What we have, at best, are variables that are rough proxies for the true characteristics that in a hedonic model are the outputs of producers and the arguments in buyers' utility functions.

The most one can say about the simple automobile hedonic model is (a) one hopes that the variables included in the regressions are functions of the true arguments of consumers' utility functions and producers' cost functions and (b) one hopes additionally that the function that relates the regression variables to the true characteristics is a stable one.[5] If the variables that are put into the

4. Examples of such sources are the National Automobile Chamber of Commerce ([1925] 1970) and *Motor* (1928).
5. This is not a new point. This proxy variable problem was noted in the original hedonic automobile article by Court (1939), and by Griliches (1961), and it was emphasized in Triplett (1969), and Ohta and Griliches (1976).

hedonic model—or for that matter, into the more general welfare model that Trajtenberg (1990) and others have discussed—are not the true characteristics that enter the utility function, or the outputs that define the characteristics-space cost function, empirical results will be misleading. The true utility-generating characteristics and the proxy measures incorporated into empirical hedonic functions may move differently over some periods.

This is not merely a call for better data and more research, though it is that. It has potentially serious implications for the interpretation of the work that has been done so far. Consider Raff and Trajtenberg's discussion of what they call "downsizing" of automobiles in the 1930s. Adoption of independent front suspension systems was the major innovation in automobile suspensions in that decade. In a sense, independent front suspensions are like the other innovations that are omitted from the simple automobile hedonic model: We have no adequate measures of the ride and handling improvements wrought by innovations in suspension design, and accordingly the hedonic measures miss some of the quality improvement that we would like them to measure. But there also was an indirect effect: The independent front suspension permitted moving the engine forward in the body frame, which meant there was more body space available than before for a given wheelbase size. Some designers took advantage of the changed body space–wheelbase ratio to increase passenger space, while others reduced the wheelbase, leaving passenger space unchanged. What the published automobile *specifications* show is a decline in average wheelbase, which one might incorrectly interpret as downsizing. But a good part of the wheelbase decline was not matched by a decline in the average usable carrying capacity of the car. Quite the contrary: a typical car after the introduction of the independent front suspension was more roomy inside, not less roomy.

Similar comments can be made of other periods of apparent downsizing of automobiles. The downsizing period in the U.S. industry in the late 1970s, mentioned by Raff and Trajtenberg in their discussion of the study by Gordon (1990), was striking in that it represented a substantial reduction in the ratio of external to internal automobile volume. U.S. cars within every size class were made smaller on the outside without shrinking the usable interior dimensions. And although I have not studied closely the 1915–18 downsizing period that Raff and Trajtenberg also mention, technical changes in this era reduced the size and weight of engines, especially, and made it possible to produce smaller-engined, lighter cars that gave their owners superior performance in use compared with the older, larger, and less-efficient designs. With the wheelbase and engine-displacement proxy variables used by Raff and Trajtenberg—and by all the rest of us—these technical improvements will be mismeasured.

Bias can also result from the use of either rated horsepower or cubic inches of engine displacement as a measure of automobile performance. Technical changes in the automobile engine continually raised actual developed horsepower relative to displacement and rated horsepower. A contemporary British account (Twist [1934] 1988) compared performance of the 3½-liter Bentley of the 1930s with the Bentley 3-liter model that was introduced at the beginning of the preceding decade (both model designations referred to the displacement of the car's engine). The substantial improvement in performance might have been expected, roughly, from the substantial increase in actual developed horsepower (approximately 110–120 for the later car, compared to approximately 65–70 for the earlier one), but it could not have been predicted from the relatively modest half-liter change in cylinder displacement. The Bentley was by no means unique. Increased engine performance relative to engine size was typical, not unusual, in U.S. cars as well as in those in the United Kingdom.

The examples suggest that hedonic price indexes are upwardly biased because of this proxy variable problem (i.e., they do not pick up enough of the quality changes that have occurred in cars). Empirically, upward-bias cases probably predominate in automobile hedonic studies, but that is not necessarily always the case. The difficulty is not that our proxy measures are biased in a known direction; rather, they are unreliable, so the sign of bias is not always known a priori. For complex products like the automobile, we need better data on characteristics, data that more nearly match the requirements of the theory of hedonic functions and hedonic indexes.

References

Court, Andrew T. 1939. Hedonic price indexes with automotive examples. In *The dynamics of automobile demand,* ed. General Motors Corporation, 99–117. New York: General Motors.

Gordon, Robert J. 1990. *The measurement of durable goods prices.* Chicago: University of Chicago Press.

Griliches, Zvi. 1961. Hedonic price indexes for automobiles: An econometric analysis of quality change. In *The Price Statistics of the Federal Government.* Hearings before the Joint Economic Committee of the U.S. Congress, 173–76. Pt. 1, 87th Cong., 1st. sess. Reprinted in Zvi Griliches, ed. 1971. *Price indexes and quality change: Studies in new methods of measurement.* Cambridge, Mass.: Harvard University Press.

Motor. 1928. Vol. 49, no.1, January. New York: International Magazine Company, Inc.

National Automobile Chamber of Commerce. [1925] 1970. *Handbook of automobiles.* Reprint, New York: Dover Publications.

Naul, G. Marshall, ed. 1978. *The specification book for U.S. cars, 1920–1929.* Osceola, Wis.: Motorbooks International Publishers and Wholesalers.

Ohta, Makota, and Zvi Griliches. 1976. Automobile prices revisited: Extensions of the hedonic hypothesis. In *Household production and consumption,* ed. Nestor E. Terleckyj, 325–90. Studies in Income and Wealth, vol. 40. New York: National Bureau of Economic Research.

Rosen, Sherwin. 1974. Hedonic prices and implicit markets: Product differentiation in pure competition. *Journal of Political Economy* 82 (January-February): 34–55.

Trajtenberg, Manuel. 1990. *Economic analysis of product innovation: The case of CT scanners.* Cambridge, Mass.: Harvard University Press.

Triplett, Jack E. 1969. Automobiles and hedonic quality measurement. *Journal of Political Economy* 77:408–17.

———. 1983. Concepts of quality in input and output measures: A resolution of the user-value resource-cost debate. In *The U.S. national income and product accounts: Selected topics,* ed. Murray F. Foss, 269–311. Chicago: University of Chicago Press.

———. 1987. Hedonic functions and hedonic indexes. In *The new Palgrave: A dictionary of economics,* ed. John Eatwell, Murray Milgate, and Peter Newman. Vol. 2, 630–34. London: Macmillan.

———. 1990. Hedonic methods in statistical agency environments: An intellectual biopsy. In *Fifty years of economic measurement: The jubilee of the Conference on Research in Income and Wealth,* ed. Ernst R. Berndt and Jack E. Triplett, 207–33. Chicago: University of Chicago Press.

Twist, Brian. [1934] 1988. The new and the old. *The Autocar,* 30 March 1934. Reprinted in *Autocar on Bentley, since 1919,* comp. David Hodges. Bideford, England: Bay View Books.

3 The Welfare Implications of Invention

Walter Y. Oi

3.1 New Products and Processes

We welcome novelty, perhaps because we view new things through rose-colored glasses. We recall the new things that survived and forgot the failures: flavored catsup, the Superball, and the DC-4. The importance of new consumer goods and services was emphasized by Stanley Lebergott, who wrote,

> Suppose that automobiles and penicillin disappeared, and electric washing machines, refrigerators, disposable diapers, electricity, and television. Suppose indeed that every economically significant good added since 1900 disappeared. And suppose that the remaining items—salt pork, lard, houses without running water, etc.—were marked down to 1900 prices. Would today's Americans then judge that their economic welfare had improved? Or would they, if anything, conclude that they derive more "welfare" from their material goods than their great-grandparents did from theirs?
>
> Consumers might, of course, have taken no pleasure in books once they saw television. But the array of available goods changes slowly. . . . Twentieth-century consumers could therefore usually choose last year's budget items this year if they desired. Yet real consumer expenditure rose in seventy of the eighty-four years between 1900 and 1984, as consumers continually switched to new goods. Such repetition reveals consumers behaving as if the newer goods did indeed yield more *worthwhile experience*. (1993, 15)

The welfare of the community has clearly been increased by the discovery of new products and new techniques. Inventions are the source of the technical advances which were, according to Denison (1962), responsible for one-third to one-half of the growth of the American economy. However, the upward trend in productivity slowed and nearly stopped in 1973. The Council of Economic Advisers offered four reasons for the slowdown: (1) As more inexperienced

Walter Y. Oi is the Elmer B. Milliman Professor of Economics at the University of Rochester.

women and teenagers entered the labor force, the average quality of the labor input deteriorated. (2) Higher energy prices reduced the demand for a cooperating input. (3) More government regulations impeded the efficient allocation of resources across sectors. (4) There was a decrease in research and development (R&D) expenditures, slowing down the rate of induced technical progress (Council of Economic Advisers 1988). The economy has clearly benefited from the invention of new products and processes. But what is a "new" product?

The task of deciding whether a particular product or service is "new" is similar to the problem of defining a monopoly. A monopoly is ordinarily defined as a firm that is the sole supplier of a good for which there is no close substitute. By analogy, we can define a new product as one for which there is no close substitute available in the market. These definitions beg the question of what constitutes "close." Most of us would probably agree that the telephone, aluminum, penicillin, and xerography were truly new products. Some might quibble about whether the long-playing record, shrink-wrap, or Goody's headache powders should be classified as new products or merely as improvements on existing products. New movies, new books, or new brands of breakfast cereals, soft drinks, and beer ought not to be classified as new products. New movies are always being produced, and each is differentiated from its competitors. The cross elasticity of demand for *ET* with respect to the price of *Pumping Iron* might have been quite small, but both titles were produced to provide movie entertainment. Our theory and statistics would be unduly cluttered if separate product codes had to be set aside for Clear Coke and Special K. Simon Kuznets offered the following definition: "An invention [of a new product or process] is a new combination of available knowledge concerning properties of a known universe designed for production" (1962, 22). He ruled out social inventions and scientific discoveries. To distinguish an invention from an improvement, he argued that there must be an input of "a discernable magnitude of some uncommon mental capacity of a human being." Each invention is somehow unique, which is another way of saying that a new product has no truly close substitute. The discovery of new materials, drugs, and techniques expands the opportunity sets for consumption and production.

3.2   Are There Enough New Products?

The production of knowledge, according to Stigler (1968), differs from the production of goods and services in at least three respects: (1) the outcome is more uncertain; (2) knowledge is easily appropriated; and (3) if the producer is given sole possession, a monopoly position is conferred. Although its consequences were probably recognized, a patent system was embraced to provide inventors with an incentive to engage in the production of knowledge. The inefficiencies of a patent system can be seen with the aid of a static model similar to one examined by Usher (1964). Assume that (1) an invention results

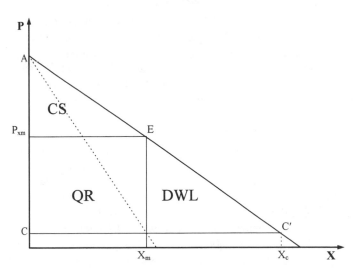

Fig. 3.1   Monopoly pricing of a new good

in the creation of a new product, (2) the invention entails an invention cost of F per period, and (3) the inventor obtains a patent with its associated monopoly power.

Although Usher employed a general equilibrium model, the results can be derived using a simpler partial equilibrium diagram. If income effects can be neglected, the demand curve for the new product, depicted in figure 3.1, is invariant with income and the avoidable fixed cost F.[1] The inventor is presumed to set a monopoly price P_{xm} which equates marginal revenue to the constant marginal cost of production. At this price, the inventor realizes a net profit equal to the quasi-rent over variable costs less the avoidable fixed invention cost, $\pi = QR - F$, and consumers of the new product enjoy a consumer's surplus CS. A commercially profitable invention is one which yields a positive net profit. The value of the utility gain due to the new product is the sum of consumer's and producer's surpluses, $G = (CS + \pi) = (CS + QR) - F$. If knowledge about the new product and the right to produce it were made available to all, its price would fall to C. The output restriction due to the patent system is $(X_C - X_m)$, resulting in the deadweight welfare loss, DWL. An unprofitable invention is one with a negative profit, $\pi < 0$ or $QR < F$, but the invention is still worthwhile to the community if the maximum sum of consumer's and producer's surpluses exceeds F; that is, it is worthwhile to incur the invention cost if the sum of the areas in figure 3.1 exceeds the avoidable fixed

1. If the income elasticity of demand for X is zero, the indifference curves in Usher's diagrams will be vertically parallel. Samuelson (1948) shows that this outcome will arise if utility is linear in Y and separable, $U(X, Y) = v(X) + aY$.

invention cost, $(CS + QR + DWL) > F$. There are surely some unprofitable inventions for which $QR_j < F_j$ that are still socially worthwhile because of the size of the consumer's surplus and deadweight welfare loss.

The preceding analysis presumes that the new product is unrelated to the set of existing goods. Will this same conclusion hold when the new product affects the demands for some related products? Before the invention of electricity, consumers enjoyed a surplus of G_0 from their purchases of gas. Suppose that the invention of electricity, which is sold at marginal cost, yields a consumer's surplus of E_1 in the electricity market. However, the entry of electricity at a price p_E (equal to its marginal cost, which after the invention is below the virtual or threshold price of electricity) shifts the demand for gas, a substitute good, to the left, thereby reducing the consumer's surplus in the gas market to $G_1 < G_0$. Should the decrease in consumer's surplus $(G_0 - G_1)$ be subtracted from E_1 in deciding whether society is better-off by incurring the fixed invention cost for electricity? The answer is *no*. If E_1 is the consumer's surplus when electricity is priced at its marginal cost, the inventive activity is in the public interest if the avoidable fixed invention cost is less than E_1. The reduction in consumer's surplus in the market for the related product, gas, is immaterial.[2]

Fisher and Shell (1968) appealed to the theory of rationing developed by Rothbarth (1941) to handle the problem of new and disappearing goods in the measurement of the cost-of-living index. Imagine a utility function defined over the set of all goods $U = U(X) = U(x_1, x_2, \ldots, x_N)$. A consumer maximizes U subject to an explicit budget constraint, $(M - \Sigma p_i x_i) \geq 0$, and to N implicit nonnegativity constraints, $x_j \geq 0$. No one purchases positive amounts of all goods. The constrained maximum of utility is attained by separating the vector of all goods into a set of I *inside* goods whose marginal utilities are proportional to their market prices and a set of $J = N - I$ *outside* goods whose utility-maximizing demands are determined by binding nonnegativity constraints. If λ and ψ_j are strictly positive Lagrangian multipliers applicable to the binding constraints, the equilibrium of the consumer is described by a system of $N + 1$ equations.

(1) $$\Sigma p_i x_i = M,$$

(2) $$U_i = \lambda p_i, \qquad (i = 1, 2, \ldots, I),$$

(3) $$U_j = \lambda p_j + \psi_j, \qquad (x_j = 0; \psi_j > 0; j = I + 1, \ldots, N),$$

where $\{U_i, U_j\}$ are marginal utilities evaluated at the optimum consumption bundle $\{X_I, 0\}$, including zero demands for the $J = N - I$ outside goods. The

---

2. I assume that the earlier cost of inventing gas is a sunk cost. The generalized consumer's surplus from electricity and gas is the sum $(G_0 + E_1)$. Hicks (1959, 178–79) showed that if electricity was the old product with a consumer's surplus $E_0 > E_1$ and the consumer's surplus of the new product, gas, was G_1, then the generalized surplus would have been $(E_0 + G_1) = (G_0 + E_1)$. The size of the generalized consumer's surplus is independent of the order of integration.

virtual of threshold price of an outside good depends on tastes, income M, and market prices of inside goods P_I.

(4) $$v_j = \frac{U_j}{\lambda} = v_j(M, P_I), \qquad (j = I + 1, I + 2, \ldots, N).$$

When I was a student, I never bought a bottle of Jack Daniel's black-label whiskey (because its virtual price was below the market price), and I rode interurban buses. Now that I am richer, I purchase small amounts of Jack Daniel's and scrupulously avoid bus trips. A binding nonnegativity constraint is equivalent to a zero ration.[3] A new product can be treated as one whose unobserved market price in the base period exceeded its virtual price, $p_{j0} > v_{j0}$, so that it was optimal to demand none of it. A technical advance presumably led to a fall in the current-period market price so that $p_{j1} < v_{j0}$, bringing this product into the inside consumption set. An erstwhile inside good such as a fountain pen could be pushed into the outside consumption set and become a disappearing good because its virtual price falls due to a decrease in the price of a substitute (a ballpoint pen) or a rise in a price of the complement (ink). The analysis by Usher seems to rest on a background model in which utility is defined over a set of *all goods,* past, present and future. Resources have to be allocated to invention to reduce the marginal cost, allowing a market price p_{j1} below the previous virtual price v_{j0}. An advantage of his approach is that it is familar, but is it helpful to imagine that all of the undiscovered new products are enumerated as arguments in a giant utility function?

Innovations often involve the creation of new materials, new techniques of production, and durable capital goods that are only indirectly demanded by final consumers. These are treated in the literature as cost-reducing innovations. The inventor can use her cost advantage to dominate the market for the final product, or she can sell the right to the innovation to existing firms through licensing arrangements. When the idea can be patented, the inventor obtains a monopoly with its associated deadweight welfare loss. Usher's analysis applies to this class of innovations just as it did to new consumer products. However, process innovations are rarely neutral with respect to the final products. Steel from a continuous-casting process has different characteristics than steel produced by the old technique. Numerically controlled machine tools affect not only the demand for labor and materials, but also the quality of the final product. Although the Boeing 707 jet aircraft reduced the cost of air travel per passenger-mile, it was more than just a cost-reducing innovation. It was faster, safer, and quieter than the DC-6 and the Lockheed Electra. The value which consumers attach to higher product quality (safer planes, fewer defec-

---

3. The virtual price of an outside good is below its market price, $(p_j - v_j) = U_j/\lambda > 0$. An increase in income will raise the virtual price of a normal good and lower it for an inferior good. Further, $(\partial v_j/\partial p_i)$ is positive if the outside good x_j and the inside good x_i are substitutes, and negative if they are complements.

tive units, or more durable toys) ought to be reflected in the derived demand for a new producer good. To the extent that it is not, the usual measures of producer's and consumer's surplus understate the social value of the new producer good or process.

The social value of an invention is measured in a static model by the maximum of the sum of producer's and consumer's surpluses generated by the new product. The model invokes at least three assumptions: (1) the profit stream resulting from a patent monopoly constitutes the main incentive for invention, (2) the cost of the invention is exogenous and presumably known, and (3) the inventor's profit and the social value of the new product can be measured from stable preference and opportunity-cost functions.[4] Given these assumptions, the model implies that too few resources will be allocated to inventive activities. Some socially worthwhile inventions will remain in the womb because the patent monopolist's profits will not cover the invention cost.

3.3 Costs of Invention and Innovation

Some discoveries are nearly costless when they are the result of luck and serendipity. Others are, however, the products of intentional research activities, for example, nylon, xerography, Velcro, and many pharmaceuticals. The relationship between the two kinds of discoveries is only slightly different from that described by a familiar production function. A farmer allocates capital, labor, and other resources to produce eggs for profit, while the DuPont Company paid for chemists, buildings, and laboratory facilities to discover nylon. Other inventions, such as the air conditioner and the telephone, probably involved elements of both intentional effort for profit and luck in their discovery. The search for a vaccine or a safer fuel may be motivated by factors other than pecuniary gain. The heterogeneity of inventions and the variety of motives for undertaking inventive activities complicate the problem of estimating an expected cost of an invention.

Invention is surely a risky venture involving a stochastic production function. Finding a new fiber or designing a digital television system are similar to prospecting for an oil or titanium deposit or hunting for a good job. Costs are sequentially incurred until a working well is discovered or the search is abandoned. The probability of success can be increased, and the time to discovery shortened, by allocating more resources to exploration. These same principles seem to apply to the search for an idea. In the case of the Manhattan Project, costs could have been reduced by spreading out the research activities over time. However, the value of the invention, a working nuclear bomb, would have been substantially smaller if the discovery had been postponed five years.

4. I have assumed for analytic ease that income effects can be neglected. Usher (1964) provided a general equilibrium analysis in which preferences for the new product are described by a family of indifference curves, and opportunity costs by a production-possibilities curve, where both are assumed to be stable. The main implications are unaffected by my simplifying assumption.

Inventive activities are, I contend, different from the search activities for oil wells or major league baseball players. The latter activities are undertaken by many similar economic agents and repeated over time. The cost of a dry hole or a barren scouting trip can be allocated to the full cost of producing petroleum or supplying sports entertainment. On the other hand, each invention is unique, a new combination of available knowledge. There is an infinite number of new combinations, which is partially reflected in the wide diversity of inventions and inventors. I cannot identify an industry or final product which can absorb the costs of the "dry holes," the unsuccessful inventions.

The number of patents is observable and is an indicator, albeit an imperfect one, of the output of inventive activities. There is an abundant literature in which the output of patents is related to R&D expenditures, a proxy for the resources allocated to invention. From these relationships, one can estimate the expected marginal and average R&D costs of a patented invention. Several mechanical difficulties surround this approach: (1) the relation is unstable over time; (2) the number of patent awards in any given year may be limited by the availability of patent examiners; (3) goods and research may be jointly produced, posing a problem for allocating costs to each activity; and (4) because over half of the postwar expenditures for R&D were supplied by the government, sometimes on cost-plus contracts, questions may arise about whether patented inventions were produced in an efficient, cost-minimizing fashion.[5] A more serious problem is that inventions are not like oil wells or hockey players. Every new product, even a modest one like the ballpoint pen, is unique. It is inappropriate to aggregate the R&D costs of all inventive activities, even those that do not result in a patent application, to estimate the invention cost for the ballpoint pen, the video camera, the transistor, or superglue.[6] Finally, the cost of discovery alone is often only a small part of the cost of R&D to bring the product to the market.

An invention is defined by Freeman (1991) as the conception of an idea, while an innovation is the commercial application of that idea. In the mundane world of the grocery store, there are thousands of new-product ideas intro-

5. In his excellent survey of the patent literature, Griliches (1990) suggested that the second difficulty could be partially corrected by relating the number of patent applications (rather than awards) to R&D expenditures. However, if inventors anticipate the delays, they may elect to protect the idea through trade secrets rather than by a patent. Estimates of the R&D cost of a patented invention classified by industry and country can be found in Evenson (1993).

6. Spindletop was a unique well. Warren Hacker and Warren Spahn turned out to be very different ball players. An assumption of ex ante homogeneity is useful in allocating resources to exploring for wells, scouting for ballplayers, or producing a movie. *Gone with the Wind* was unique and better than *Getting Gertie's Garter,* but both were produced to entertain moviegoers. The characteristics that distinguish one oil well from another (or one movie from another) are qualitatively different from the attributes that differentiate new products. Nylon might be substituted for rayon, Velcro for a zipper, a snap, or a button. However, an assumption of ex ante homogeneity is surely unreasonable for rayon, Velcro, the Tucker car, or the Spruce Goose. When Scherer (1965) speaks about the output of patented inventions, I get the uncomfortable impression that these inventions are interchangeable.

duced each year, of which a majority never reach the stage of being test-marketed. Of the minority that reach the supermarket shelves, an even smaller number are still on the shelves a year later.[7] Obtaining a patent is only the first step in a long chain. The firm usually has to incur development costs to adapt the idea for commercial use and to establish a distribution channel. Additional research costs may be incurred by the original inventor or by some other party in making improvements to the product which might enhance its chances for commercial success. Although Whitcomb L. Judson patented the zip fastener in 1891, the early zippers had the regrettable feature of popping open at unexpected moments. It remained for Giddian Sundback to patent a superior zip fastener in 1913. These were purchased by the navy during World War I, but the first major commercial adoption was implemented by the B. F. Goodrich Company when zippers were installed in their galoshes in 1923, fully thirty-two years after the Judson patent. In calculating the cost of inventing the zip fastener, the outlays by Judson (properly adjusted for the interest costs) should be added to the costs incurred by Sundback. We are still in the dark about how to allocate the costs of ideas that never get to the patent office or the costs of the stillborn patents which never reach the market. One thing is clear: the assumption that the cost of an invention is exogenous has to be rejected. The probability of success and the value of a successful innovation can both be increased by investing more in R&D, which necessarily increases the average cost of an innovation.

3.4 Diffusion and the Value of an Innovation

Consumers at a given point in time can choose from a list of goods that are available in the market, but that list keeps changing. It is expanded by the introduction of new goods and contracted by the disappearance of other products. I have already noted that a majority of patented ideas are never produced. Additionally, once a good is actually made available to consumers, its acceptance in the marketplace may be excruciatingly slow. The telephone was invented in 1876, but only 40 percent of all American households had a phone in 1940. I can remember owning pants with buttons, but now nearly all pants come with zippers. The adoption or diffusion of a new product frequently follows an S-shaped curve which can be compactly described by three parameters: (1) a starting date when the product is introduced to the market, (2) a speed or rate of adoption, and (3) a saturation level of adoption. Most products will also exhibit a product life cycle whose last phase corresponds to its decline and eventual disappearance from the marketplace.[8] A few products, such as the

---

7. Evidence on the failure rates of new brands and products can be found in Booz, Allen, and Hamilton, Inc. (1971) and in Davidson (1976).

8. The diffusion of a new product or process through its first three phases was nicely described by Griliches (1957). Grossman and Helpman (1991) have developed a model of endogenous product lives.

Table 3.1   **Time Lags between Invention and Innovation**

Lag (years)	Frequency	Cumulative Frequency
0–4	10	10
5–9	14	24
10–14	9	33
15–19	2	35
20–24	10	45
25 or more	5	50

Source: Jewkes, Sawers, and Stillerman (1958).

telephone and radio, may never experience the last phase of a life cycle, at least in our lifetimes. The private and social values of an innovation will be greater, the earlier is the introduction date (following the discovery of the idea), the faster is the speed of adoption, and the higher is the saturation level of demand.

Although an invention only begins to generate benefits after it is made available to users, the data reveal a variable and at times long time lag between invention and innovation. A majority of all patents lie dormant and never reach the innovation stage. Of those that do, the time interval between the date the patent is awarded and the date the innovation enters the market can be long, often longer than the seventeen-year statutory life of the patent. Enos (1962) examined the histories of sixty-two successful inventions and found a mean lag of 14 years. Jewkes, Sawers, and Stillerman (1958) identified fifty-one inventions, and for fifty of them, they prepared capsule case histories. From these histories, I guessed at the dates of invention and innovation.[9] The distribution of these fifty inventions by the length of the lag is shown in table 3.1. The mean lag was 12.5 years, and the lag exceeded 20 years for fifteen of these fifty inventions. In two instances, invention and innovation took place in the same year: Thomas Midgley, Jr., synthesized Freon in 1931, and Peter Goldmark developed the long-playing record in 1948. Cellophane required 12 years to move from the laboratory to the market. We do not have a satisfactory theory to explain the length of the innovation lag.[10]

An inventor can be expected to select a propitious time to introduce her new

9. The dates for the conception of the idea (the invention) and the introduction of that idea to the market (the innovation) were not always obvious from the case histories. Some guesswork was unavoidable. The notes that I took from the case histories are available upon request.

10. Both Freon and the long-playing record were simple inventions that did not require either any special skills on the part of the user or a lot of complementary inputs. Other refrigerants with less-desirable characteristics were available in 1931. Goldmark had to solve problems of rotational speed, finer grooves, the composition of vinyl records, and lightweight pickup. One could argue that Freon and the long-playing record were improvements rather than inventions, in Kuznets's taxonomy. Xerography was patented by Chester Carlson in 1937. The Haloid Company acquired rights to the patent during or shortly after World War II. The timing of the commercial application, that is, the decision to market the copying machine, was evidently made by the president of Haloid and not by the inventor.

invention, a time when incomes are rising, unemployment is falling, and firms are replacing depreciated equipment. Griliches (1990, 1697) reported a procyclical pattern for the growth rate of patent applications. Mansfield (1966) and Freeman (1991) independently reported that the timing of product and process innovations was unrelated to the phase of the business cycle. A contrary, strongly procyclical pattern was exhibited by the sample of 1,101 new products announced in the *Wall Street Journal* over the ten-year period 1975–84. The number of new-product announcements varied from a high of 156 in 1978 to a low of 70 in 1983; they were positively related to the growth rate of gross national product (GNP) and inversely related to the interest rate.[11] The new products in the Chaney, Devinney, and Winer (1991) study differ from the major innovations studied by Mansfield. The first application often involves a primitive version of the innovation which is improved in successive applications; this is the pattern described by Rosenberg (1982). Some products have to be tested by consumers in order for their value to be ascertained. The initial introduction to the market could be part of an experimental development stage. For these products, there is little to be gained by timing the introduction to coincide with a cyclical expansion. The situation is different for an improvement or an imitation where there is less need for experimentation to ascertain consumer acceptance. The new products studied by Chaney et al. appear to contain a larger fraction of "improvements," which may account for the difference in the cyclical timing of introduction dates. The lag between the patent date and the date of introduction to the market is likely to be longer for a truly new product than for an improvement. If the initial patent is the source of the inventor's market power, a long lag not only raises the R&D cost of an innovation but also reduces the size of the deadweight welfare loss.

Once a new product or process has been introduced, information about its properties has to be disseminated. This can be done explicitly by advertising in newspapers, journals, and the media, by distributing samples, or implicitly by word-of-mouth contacts with early consumers. The uncertainty hypothesis advanced by Mansfield (1966) appeals to an epidemic model in which the rate of adoption depends on the ratio of uninformed potential customers to informed incumbent users. As more nonusers become informed customers,

---

11. Chaney, Devinney, and Winer (1991) identified 1,685 new-product announcements in the *Wall Street Journal* from 1975 to 1984. The sample of 1,101 observations included only those products for which they could get stock-price data for the firm. Using an event-study methodology, a new-product announcement was associated with a $26.7 million increase in the market value of the firm. The 100 new products announced in 1975 had an average value of $57.8 million compared to only $3.5 million for each of the 85 new products marketed in 1981. The magazine *Popular Gardening Indoors,* the Asian edition of the *Wall Street Journal,* the Electric Zip Polaroid camera, the Savin 750 plain-paper copier, the Gillette Good News disposable razor for men, the Aqua Flex soft contact lens, the V10 Crawler Tractor from Caterpillar, Kleenex Huggies and Kleenex Super Dry disposable diapers, and the Super King Air F90 corporate prop jet are some of the examples of the new products in the Chaney, Devinney, and Winer sample (609). The authors distinguished between truly new products and updates (similar to the distinction between innovations and improvements made by Kuznets [1962]), but updates are not separately reported in their table 2. The updates may be responsible for the procyclical pattern of new product announcements.

the ratio of nonusers to users declines, sweeping out an S-shaped diffusion curve.[12] In the Griliches (1957) model, the slope of a logistic growth curve will be steeper (implying a faster adoption rate), the lower is the cost of acquiring production information from neighbors or the greater is the relative profitability of the new product. The heterogeneity of potential customers offers an alternative explanation for the diffusion lag. The mainframe computer initially introduced by Sperry Rand required the input of highly skilled technicians. Subsequent design improvements, which reduced the skill requirements of operators, and decreases in price raised the profitability of this computer to a wider range of customers.[13] In the case of a new consumer product such as travel by jet aircraft, there will be a distribution of virtual prices among consumers who are informed about the properties and availability of the innovation. Some knowledgeable consumers may choose to demand none of the new product because their virtual prices are *below* the prevailing market price. The penetration or adoption rate will increase in response to a rightward shift in the distribution of consumers classified by their virtual prices (due possibly to a rise in real incomes, a fall in the price of a complementary good, or a rise in the price of a substitute good) or to a decrease in the price of the new product. Increasing returns will usually generate a declining price profile.[14] Additionally, an innovator may embrace a pricing strategy to practice intertemporal price discrimination. However, an individual's virtual price, which describes his willingness to pay for the new product today, will be smaller, the lower is the anticipated future price. Imperfect foresight, declining unit costs, and improvements in product quality discourage an innovator from establishing a flat price profile for her new product.[15] These arguments, which support the heterogeneity hypothesis, reinforce the uncertainty hypothesis and lead to the

12. The constant of proportionality can vary across products. Bailey (1957) showed that a deterministic model generates a symmetric bell-shaped curve for the infection rate. If, however, the model only yields a constant probability of infection, the infection-rate curve exhibits a positive skew. Coale and McNeil (1972) developed a model for the age distribution at first marriage which better describes the manner in which product information is spread and adopted by a population of potential customers.

13. A formal model in which the optimal time to acquire the innovation varies across firms can be found in Evenson and Kislev (1975). In their model, learning reduces the price of the new capital good. The adoption by more firms reduces the price of the final product, pushing some of the earlier adopters to turn to another new capital good. Similar models of this type have been developed by Grossman and Helpman (1991) and Helpman (1993), who allowed for both innovation and imitation.

14. The fall in the unit costs of producing a new product may be a consequence of (1) the traditional increasing returns to scale which is a property of the production function, (2) learning which raises the efficiency of productive inputs, or (3) the volume effect emphasized by Asher (1956) and Alchian (1959).

15. Coase (1972) posited a model in which a monopoly set a price in the first period to equate the marginal revenue to the marginal cost of producing a durable good. In the next period, the marginal revenue of the residual demand curve was equated to the marginal cost and so on to the following period, thereby sweeping out a price profile that fell over time. Consumers with perfect foresight would refuse to patronize this monopoly in the first period, because by waiting they could obtain the durable good at a lower price. Indeed, with perfect foresight, the equilibrium price would be equal to marginal cost, implying a flat price profile. This implication was challenged by, among others, Stokey (1979).

S-shaped adoption curve which was observed by Griliches (1957) and Mansfield (1966). Further, the relative speed of adoption will be faster, and the saturation level higher, the greater is the degree of homogeneity of potential consumers.[16]

The history of the cable car illustrates an extreme example of a product life cycle. Cable traction was a truly important invention which nearly doubled the speed of urban transportation by horse car. It allowed cities to grow and eliminated the pollution created by horses. According to Hilton (1971), Andrew Smith Hallidie was responsible for the invention when on 1 September 1873, his cable car, the Clay Street Line—all 2,791 feet of it—received its first revenue passengers. No new patent had to be issued; patents were already in place for the essential components: the conduit, the grip, steel cable, and the equipment for the power house.[17] However, it took eight and a half years before C. B. Holmes demonstrated on 28 January 1882 that cable traction could be operated in Chicago and hence in all climates. This is the date which Hilton attaches to the innovation of cable traction: the social application of the idea. Once the superiority of the new technology had been demonstrated, the innovation spread rapidly. However, knowledge can become obsolete, and new information can destroy the value of existing technology. The cable-car line which was made available for revenue service in Chicago on 28 January 1882 established only temporarily the superiority of this mode of urban transportation. "Cable traction was an effort to make a purely mechanical connection between a stationary steam engine and the passenger. We now know that the connection should have been made electrically through attaching the engine to a dynamo and transmitting direct current to motors on electric streetcars" (Hilton 1971, 13).

The electric streetcar that boarded its first passengers in Richmond, Virginia on, 2 February 1888 employed this latter technology, invented by Frank J. Sprague. The new knowledge killed the value of the cable car, whose economic life was ended after six years and five days of unchallenged success. The cable systems scheduled for construction were cancelled, and no new lines were started after the entry of the electric streetcar. Aside from the lines in San Francisco which were retained for their touristic value, the last commercial cable line in Dunedin, New Zealand, ceased operation in 1957. Sprague's electric

16. In his review of the empirical studies of diffusion, Mowery (1988, 487–90) reported the findings of Romeo (1975, 1977), namely that the adoption rates of numerically controlled machine tools were highest in those industries where concentration ratios were low and the size distribution of firms did not exhibit a large positive skew. Firms of similar size probably confront similar technologies and input prices and behave in the same way, including in their timing of entry into the market for a new product or process.

17. The line which climbed the east slope of Knob Hill was tested on 4 August. The one-way trip, up or down a 17 percent slope, took eleven minutes and cost a nickel. By 1876, it handled 150,000 passengers a month, the uphill riders outnumbering the downhill load by a ratio of three to one. The details of this line are reported in Hilton (1971, see especially p. 185). A complete list of all of the cable-car lines that were operated in the United States together with descriptions of each line can be found in Hilton's book.

streetcar had a longer product life, but it was eventually replaced by the motor bus. A majority of all inventions are stillborn, and the economic lives of nearly all products are threatened by the arrival of new and different kinds of knowledge. The uncertain length of a product's life increases the risk to investments in invention.

A patent gives an inventor exclusive rights to her idea for seventeen years. During this period, the inventor can presumably enjoy the supernormal returns of a monopoly protected from direct competition. After the discovery has been made, it is claimed that the marginal cost of making the knowledge available to other firms and economic agents is nearly zero. Welfare can allegedly be enhanced by making the knowledge freely accessible to all through policies that limit the inventor's market power—shortening the patent's life, regulating mandatory licensing arrangements, and so forth. This prescription neglects at least three important factors. First, the patented idea is only a beginning. Costs will be incurred in developing and modifying the basic product before it is in a form suitable to compete with existing products in the market. Most patented inventions never reach the market. Second, instantaneous diffusion of a new product or process is simply uneconomical. It would be prohibitively costly to distribute samples of a new chemical entity to all potential users. The diffusion lags are likely to be efficient ways to disseminate information, to achieve the economies of volume production, and to improve the product's quality during the process of adoption. A higher degree of homogeneity among potential consumers is accompanied by a faster rate of diffusion. Third, the innovator's market power can be threatened by the entry of firms that produce a nearly identical product or by the introduction of a related product. The value of cable traction in Chicago fell not because of the entry of a competing cable car line, but as a consequence of the invention of the elelctric streetcar.[18]

An imitator may be prevented from patenting a product that is nearly identical to one already in the market, but he may be able to enter with a closely related good. The low ratio of innovations to inventions, the long time lags between invention and innovation, and the often slow rate of adoption lead me to the tentative conclusion that we have exaggerated the size of the deadweight welfare loss due to any monopoly power created by a patent system.

3.5   Impact of the Air Conditioner

The telephone and the automobile were major innovations that changed the structure of the economy. The air conditioner had a smaller impact, but it was

18. Domestic sugar producers tried to shield themselves from foreign competition by securing legislation which erected tariff barriers and import quotas. However, the market power of the domestic sugar growers was eroded by the invention of fructose and glucose syrups which are produced by the wet corn milling industry (Standard Industrial Classification [SIC] code number 2064). Over the 1972–88 period, wet corn milling was the second-fastest-growing four-digit manufacturing industry behind semiconductors (SIC 3674).

still an important invention that expanded the production-possibilities frontier and raised the standard of living of consumers. Although the technology for making ice was invented by Dr. John Gorrie in 1851, it was not air-conditioning, which was defined by its inventor as follows: "Air conditioning is the control of the humidity of air by either increasing or decreasing its moisture content. Added to the control of humidity is the control of temperature by either heating or cooling the air, the purification of the air by washing or filtering the air, and the control of air motion and ventilation" (Willis H. Carrier, 28 February 1949, quoted in Ingels 1952, 21). The key resides in the fact that the moisture content of air can be controlled by using a fog nozzle to saturate the air at different temperatures. It was this principle of dew point control which was the basis for Carrier's patent application for "An Apparatus for Treating Air," filed on 16 September 1904. The patent, number 808,897, was issued on 6 January 1906.[19] The invention was a direct response to the Sacket Wilhelm Company's attempts to enhance its profits.

The output of the Sacket Wilhelm Company depended not only on the usual inputs of labor and capital but also on an index of air quality. Although air quality is a function of temperature, humidity, cleanliness, and ventilation, I shall assume for expository ease that it can be described by temperature T yielding a production function $X = f(L, K, T)$. Huntington (1924) observed that labor productivity was systematically related to temperature and climate. The earnings of piece-rate workers were lowest in the winter and summer and highest in the spring and fall. Labor productivity in machine shops was at a maximum at around sixty-five degrees with humidity of 65–75 percent. Productivity and earnings were some 15 percent lower at seventy-five degrees and 28 percent lower when the temperature reached eighty-six degrees.[20] If temperature affects output in a Hicks Neutral fashion, the production function can be written

$$(5) \qquad\qquad X = \phi(T) g(L, K).$$

19. As Ingels (1952, 23) put it, "The use of spray water to humidify air was readily accepted, but Carrier's idea of dehumidifying air by using water was so revolutionary that it was greeted with incredulity and in some cases, with ridicule. However, Carrier proved that air could be dried with water. . . ." The apparatus was refined resulting in his patent application for "Dew Point Control" on 3 February 1914. However, Stuart W. Cramer, a North Carolina textile-mill engineer who patented an air-ventilation system, is given the credit for coining the term "air-conditioning."

20. Huntington assembled data on hourly piece rates by week for workers in three hardware factories in Connecticut, a wire factory in Pittsburgh, and various establishments in the deep South. The hourly piece-rate earnings provide a good measure of net product because the worker was not rewarded for defective units. The time periods varied across sites but were centered around the period 1910–13. The main results are reported in his figures 1, 3, and 8. Differences in climatic conditions between New England and the South were reflected in different seasonal patterns; the summer trough was lower in the South. He claimed that the optimum temperature for physical work was 60 degrees for the Connecticut workers, but it was 65 degrees for the Cuban workers in the South (126). In addition to temperature and humidity, Huntington studied the effects of confinement and variability of climatic conditions on work, mental work, and mortality and morbidity rates.

Let T_M denote the output-maximizing temperature and adopt the normalization that $\phi(T_M) = 1$. Departures in either direction correspond to smaller rates of output, $\phi(T) < 1$ for all $T \neq T_M$. Suppose that a competitive firm operates over a cycle of two periods. Temperatures are, like Meade's atmosphere, exogenous, above the optimum in a hot first period, and below in a cold second, $T_A > T_M > T_B$. Labor is a variable input, but capital has to be the same in the two periods. Each firm maximizes its base case profits:

$$(6) \qquad \pi_0 = p(X_A + X_B) - w(L_A + L_B) - 2rK.$$

Outputs in the two periods are thus given by

$$(5') \qquad\qquad X_A = \phi(T_A)g(L_A, K),$$
$$X_B = \phi(T_B)g(L_B, K).$$

Turn first to a base case in which temperatures, like Meade's atmosphere, are exogenous. Inputs $\{L_A, L_B, K\}$ are chosen to maximize profits. Let $p_A = p\phi(T_A)$ and $p_B = p\phi(T_B)$ define what I call temperature-adjusted product prices in the two periods. In equilibrium, we have

$$(7) \qquad p_A g_{LA} = w, \quad p_B g_{LB} = w, \quad (p_A g_{KA} + p_B g_{KB}) = 2r.$$

The marginal value product (MVP) of labor in each period is equated to the wage, but as in the peak-load pricing problem, the *sum* of the MVP of capital in the two periods is equated to the two-period price.[21] A firm facing unfavorable temperatures is at a disadvantage and consequently supplies less output to the market.

Air-conditioning and central heating are innovations that enabled firms to cool their plants in the first period and to heat them in the second. Productivity is thus increased in both periods by incurring the costs of climate control. It pays to incur these costs if the increments to quasi-rents exceed the total costs of controlling the indoor temperature. The firms that install cooling and heating apparatuses will demand more labor and capital and supply more output to the market. The productivity gains and the returns to the investment will be larger when the initial temperature conditions are more adverse and output is more responsive to temperature changes.[22] The firms that realized the highest returns from controlling air quality were obviously the first to install air-conditioning systems. After the initial wave of installations, Carrier sold his apparatus to movie theaters (the Hollywood Grauman's Chinese in 1922, a Dal-

---

21. Although the capital input K is the same in hot and cold periods, the labor inputs can differ. Thus, if productivity is lower in the first hot period, $\phi(T_A) < \phi(T_B)$, the firm demands less labor in the hot period, $L_A < L_B$, resulting in a lower marginal physical product of capital; i.e., the firm has to employ "too much" capital in the first, hot period.

22. This sensitivity is described by the shape of the $\phi(T)$ function which is amplified in n. 33. Notice that in the examples of the Sacket Wilhelm Company, textile mills, and tobacco factories, the air quality affects total factor productivity. It could be the case that changes in temperature affect only labor productivity in the manner described in n. 34.

las theater in 1924, and the New York City Rivoli in 1925) and to department stores and hotels which profited by enticing customers away from their rivals. Comfort, however, was probably the motive that prompted the federal government to acquire such systems in 1928, first for the House of Representatives and then for the Senate and the White House. Fifty years later, Russell Baker opined,

> Air conditioning has contributed far more to the decline of the republic than unexecuted murderers and unorthodox sex. Until it became universal in Washington after World War II, Congress habitually closed shop around the end of June and did not reopen until the following January. Six months of every year, the nation enjoyed a respite from the promulgation of more laws, the depredations of lobbyists, the hatching of new schemes for Federal expansion, and of course, the cost of maintaining a government running at full blast. Once air conditioning arrived, Congress had twice as much time to exercise its skill at regulating and plucking the population. (1978)

Swollen paper, broken thread, and dry tobacco leaf reduced profits of lithographers, textile mills, and cigar makers, who were among the early adopters of air-conditioning. The innovation involved more than dew point control and had to be adapted to the peculiar needs of the customer: "We simply had to dry more product [macaroni] in an established space which Mr. Carrier guaranteed to do. He accomplished only half as much as he guaranteed, but he cut his bill in half showing high moral principle" (Ingels 1952, 50).

Temperature and humidity exert on ouput not only a direct effect via a static production function like equation (5), but also an indirect effect by affecting labor turnover, absences, and accident rates. Vernon (1921) found that accident rates were at a minimum at sixty-seven degrees, 30 percent higher at seventy-seven degrees, and 18 percent higher at fifty-six degrees.[23] Additionally, hot weather is more injurious to mental productivity; Huntington (1924) concluded that a mean daily temperature of 38 degrees was ideal for mental work, while for physical work, it was 54 degrees. The profitability of climate control thus depends on the firm's location (a proxy for the time over which it experiences adverse weather) and the nature of its production process. Although entrepreneurs were learning about these advantages, the diffusion of air-conditioning was retarded by the Great Depression and World War II.

The development of a more efficient compressor in 1929 and a better refrigerant in 1931, as well as the postwar decline in the price of electricity, reduced the full unit cost of climate control which facilitated the postwar diffusion. Air-conditioning became a profitable investment for a larger number of firms. Air-conditioning systems were installed in factories, stores, and office build-

---

23. Florence (1924) identified six sources of output losses: (1) labor turnover; (2) absences, strikes, and lockouts; (3) output restrictions related to the pace of work; (4) more defective units of output; (5) industrial accidents; and (6) illness. His ideas are extended in a series of productivity studies in Davidson et al. (1958).

Table 3.2   Employment, Payroll, and Value-Added: Manufacturing,
                   1954 and 1987

	Year	United States	South	South (% of U.S.)
1. Number of employees	1954	15,651.3	3,173.6	20.3
	1987	17,716.9	5,590.1	31.6
2. Payroll ($)	1954	245,069.2	40,648.5	16.6
	1987	428,449.3	119,597.4	27.9
3. Value-added ($)	1954	454,837.5	82,013.7	18.0
	1987	1,165,746.8	354,379.5	30.4
4. Annual pay ($)	1954	15,658	12,808	81.8
	1987	24,183	21,395	88.5
5. Value-added per employee	1954	29,061	25,842	88.9
	1987	65,799	63,394	96.3

Source: U.S. Bureau of the Census (1987).
Note: South is defined as the South Atlantic, East South Central, and West South Central divisions.

ings, where the weather adversely affected productivity and sales. The innovation raised labor productivity and enabled adversely situated firms to compete with firms located in temperate zones. The share of manufacturing workers employed in establishments located in the South (bordered by Texas on the west and Maryland on the north) rose from 20.3 percent in 1954 to 31.6 percent in 1987; see table 3.2. Productivity in southern factories climbed relative to plants located in the North and West, as evidenced by the increase in value-added per employee. Indeed, the share of value-added in manufacturing rose from 18.0 to 30.4 percent. The installation of air-conditioning can be expected to raise relative wages of southern workers if (1) southern manufacturing confronts an upward-sloping labor supply curve or (2) more-efficient plants are matched with more-productive workers.[24]

Rows 4 and 5 of table 3.2 show that for the all-manufacturing sector, both annual pay and value-added per employee rose relative to the United States. To see if the same pattern holds within two-digit industries, in table 3.3 I report industry-specific value-added and hourly wages for plants in the South Atlantic division relative to the United States.[25] There is considerable dispersion in the ratios of relative value-added and annual pay (1987 divided by 1954), but on balance, workers in the South Atlantic states were more productive and earned

24. Moore ([1911] 1967) argued that larger firms offered higher piece rates to attract more-productive employees who could more intensively utilize the newer and more expensive capital equipment that they provided. "We have hitherto supposed that it is a matter of indifference to the employer whether he employs few or many people to do a piece of work, provided that his total wages-bill for the work is the same. But that is not the case. Those workers who earn most in a week when paid at a given rate for their work are those who are cheapest to their employers, . . . for they use only the same amount of fixed capital as their slower fellow workers" (149). Oi (1991) appeals to a similar argument to explain the positive association between firm size and wages.

25. The figure of 0.8685 of value-added in 1987 for food is the ratio of value-added per employee in the South Atlantic divided by value-added for all plants in the United States. This relative value-added was lower, 0.8150, in 1954, yielding the growth ratio of 1.0656 = (.8685/.8150).

Table 3.3   Value-Added and Hourly Wages, South Atlantic Division Relative to
                     United States (by two-digit manufacturing industries)

Industry (SIC code)	Value Added			Hourly Wages		
	1987	1954	Ratio	1987	1954	Ratio
Food (20)	0.8685	0.8150	1.0656	0.8668	0.7516	1.1532
Tobacco (21)	1.1748	1.1517	1.0201	1.0319	1.0228	1.0089
Textile mills (22)	0.9212	0.8751	1.0526	0.9741	0.9247	1.0534
Apparel (23)	0.8441	0.8032	1.0510	0.9050	0.8076	1.1207
Lumber (24)	0.8666	0.6468	1.3399	0.8694	0.6794	1.2796
Furniture (25)	0.8399	0.8158	1.0294	0.9015	0.7762	1.1615
Paper (26)	1.1054	1.1706	0.9443	1.0142	0.9616	1.0547
Printing (27)	0.8957	0.8626	1.0384	0.9358	0.8729	1.0721
Chemicals (28)	0.8862	0.8832	1.0034	0.9522	0.9280	1.0260
Petroleum (29)	0.5879	0.8783	0.6694	0.7147	0.9047	0.7900
Rubber (30)	1.0788	0.8945	1.2060	1.0106	0.7730	1.3073
Leather (31)	1.0684	0.9061	1.1790	1.0328	0.9164	1.1270
Stone (32)	0.8975	0.8077	1.1112	0.8976	0.8641	1.0388
Primary metal (33)	1.1586	1.1826	0.9797	0.9814	0.9910	0.9902
Fabricated metal (34)	0.9345	0.9509	0.9827	0.8554	0.8879	0.9634
Machinery (35)	0.9407	0.7713	1.2197	0.8404	0.7849	1.0707
Electrical (36)	1.0687	0.9397	1.1373	0.9362	0.9178	1.0200
Transport (37)	0.8943	1.0037	0.8910	0.8354	0.9557	0.8740
Instruments (38)	0.9303	0.6788	1.3704	0.8822	0.7574	1.1648
Miscellaneous (39)	0.8417	0.8488	0.9916	0.9062	0.8247	1.0989
All manufacturing	0.9217	0.8175	1.1275	0.8584	0.7805	1.0998

Source: U.S. Bureau of the Census (1987).

higher relative wages in 1987 than they did in 1954. The wide dispersion across industries suggests that there are factors in addition to air-conditioning affecting productivity gains. Finally, the log of the hourly wages of manufacturing production workers from the Bureau of Labor Statistics establishment surveys for 1950, 1965, and 1979 were related to the "permanent" mean temperature, heating degree days, and cooling degree days for a sample of forty-one states.[26] The weighted regression results reported in table 3.4 indicate that wages were significantly lower in states with higher temperatures and more cooling degree days. There is a slight tendency for the coefficients to move toward zero between the 1950 and the 1979 samples, but the convergence is negligible

26. The wage data were taken from U.S. Bureau of Labor Statistics (1983, 207, table 92). Temp is the mean temperature averaged over thirty years, while Heat and Cool represent the mean heating degree days and cooling degree days, again averaged over thirty years. Heating degree days are the number of degrees below sixty-five that the average temperature is on a given day. Cooling degree days are the number of degrees above sixty-five (U.S. Bureau of the Census 1993). I averaged the data for the weather stations located in each state. Thus, data for four stations were averaged to get the mean temperature for California, but in Nevada and Alabama, for example, I could get data from only one station each, Reno and Mobile. There is, however, some measurement error in the right-hand-side variables. The sample size was limited by the availability of data for 1950. The observations were weighted by manufacturing employment.

Table 3.4   **Regressions of Log Hourly Wages on Climate Variables**
             (41 states; 1950, 1965, and 1979)

	1950	1965	1979
Hourly Wage (weighted by employment)			
Mean	1.454	2.632	6.665
Standard deviation	0.138	0.377	0.999
Mean (in logs)	0.366	0.957	1.886
Standard deviation	0.132	0.153	0.153
Regressions			
Temp (E-2)	−1.122	−1.093	−1.095
t-value	−4.03	−3.58	−4.00
Heat (E-3)	0.033	0.0033	0.036
t-value	3.22	2.92	3.54
Cool (E-3)	−0.150	−0.131	−0.103
t-value	−5.75	−4.53	−3.84

Sources: Hourly wages of production workers in manufacturing were obtained from U.S. Bureau of Labor Statistics (1993). The climate variables were taken from U.S. Bureau of the Census (1993).

Notes: Temp is annual mean temperature, 1961–90; Heat is mean number of heating degree days, 1961–90; Cool is mean number of cooling degree days, 1961–90.

and probably not statistically significant. The fall in the full unit cost of air-conditioning allowed southern firms to improve their productivity which enebled them the expand their demand for labor and capital. Competitors located in milder climates had less to gain from installing air-conditioning. The output expansion by southern firms must surely have reduced final product prices to the detriment of their northern competitors. The consequence has been a narrowing of the regional differences in real wages. Even though the profitability of air-conditioning had been convincingly demonstrated, it took over sixty years before the adoption rate exceeded 90 percent of all southern establishments.

Although the sales to commercial establishments were important, the residential market held the promise of truly large returns. Carrier recognized this and introduced a room air conditioner in 1931. But sales were disappointing and were discontinued. At the end of World War II, the situation looked good, incomes were high, the costs of producing the apparatus had come down, and electricity was cheap. However, it was not the Carrier Corporation but General Electric, Chrysler, and Frigidaire who introduced room units in 1950. By 1965, 12.8 percent of all households owned an air-conditioning unit. The diffusion was rapid, reaching nearly 70 percent of all households by 1990. The data in table 3.5 reveal some obvious regional differences: 90.7 percent of southern households had air-conditioning compared to only 41.2 percent in the West. Notice that the percentage with a room unit actually declined in the South, where more households installed central air. The rapid diffusion of air-conditioning in both the commercial and the residential sectors shifted the sea-

Table 3.5   Percentage of Households with Air-Conditioning by Region

Year	United States	Northeast	Midwest	South	West
All air-conditioning					
1960	12.8				
1971	43.9	35.1	44.8	58.0	29.8
1974	50.5	42.5	51.3	67.4	30.0
1982	58.0	51.7	57.8	75.8	34.5
1990	69.9	58.9	74.4	90.7	41.2
Room units					
1971	30.9	30.7	33.0	37.1	16.6
1974	31.8	36.2	32.7	37.5	14.8
1982	30.9	40.6	30.5	35.2	13.3
1990	31.0	42.2	34.6	31.9	14.4
Central units					
1971	13.0	4.4	11.8	20.9	13.2
1974	18.7	6.3	18.6	29.9	15.2
1982	27.0	11.1	27.2	40.6	21.2
1990	38.9	16.7	39.8	58.8	26.8

Sources: U.S. Bureau of the Census (1976, table 689; 1993, table 1242).

sonal load curve of electricity use. The peak loads used to occur in the dark, cold winter months, but the brownouts now take place in the steamy summer. The consumer sleeps longer, buys fewer allergy medicines and cold drinks, and probably spends less time at offices and factories that are not air conditioned. As more neighbors closed doors and windows, the front porch society of Dixie disappeared. The holdouts may have decided to acquire a unit to be like the rest of the community. The distinctive character of southern architecture has disappeared from all new construction.[27] One observer claimed that the family tends to stay home and enjoy each other's society; by implication, air-conditioning has strengthened the family as an institution. This claim has not been borne out, perhaps because of the coincidental growth of multicar households.

At the turn of the century and in the immediate postwar years, climatic conditions produced a seasonal pattern on mortality rates, which were highest in the winter and attained a secondary peak in the summer. Additionaly, mortality rates were significantly higher in the hot southern states, a differential attributed to malaria and tropical diseases as well as to heat stress. The amplitude of the seasonal cycle has diminished with a flattening of the winter peak. Sakamoto-Momiyama (1977) attributes the drop in the winter death rate to the spread of central heating. The data on infant mortality rates (IMR) per thousand births classified by region and race are striking (see table 3.6). The IMRs in 1990 were a third to a fourth of what they had been in 1951. The fall in the ratio of mortality rates for whites in the South relative to New England is

27. Arsenault sums it up as follows: "The catalogue of structural techniques developed to tame the hot, humid southern climate . . . transoms placed above bedroom doors . . . are now obsolete." (1984, 623).

Table 3.6   **Infant Mortality Rates (per 1,000 births)**

Race and Region	1951	1967	1990
White			
South	32.77	20.72	7.67
New England	22.63	19.33	6.79
Ratio (South/N.E.)	1.45	1.07	1.13
Nonwhite			
South	47.87	38.51	16.14
New England	41.80	35.04	12.33
Ratio (South/N.E.)	1.15	1.10	1.31

Sources: U.S. Bureau of the Census (1954, 1993).

Notes: South includes South Carolina, Georgia, Alabama, Mississippi, Louisiana, and Texas. New England includes Maine, New Hampshire, Vermont, Massachusetts, Rhode Island, and Connecticut. "Nonwhite" data pertain to all nonwhites in 1951 and 1967, but to blacks only in 1990.

impressive and, I suspect, is due in part to the spread of air-conditioning and central heating. The beneficial effects of climate control on mortality and morbidity rates should have increased the demand for cooler air. If they are not internalized in demand curves, the usual surplus measures understate the social value of the innovation.

Air was demanded by producers because it increased the efficiency of labor and the productivity of other inputs. Room units and central air enabled consumers to reach higher levels of utility. The direct benefits can be approximated by (1) the area between the pre- and postinnovation marginal cost for producers who installed air-conditioning, (2) the size of the consumer's surplus enjoyed by a consumer who can decrease the indoor temperature by D degrees, and (c) the increased profits flowing to the inventor and firms supplying air-conditioning systems. To these, one might want to attach a value to any improvements in the quality of final products from adopting the innovation, climate control in this example.

In addition to these direct benefits, a major innovation generates a variety of external and pecuniary effects. Hirshleifer (1971) pointed out that an inventor has inside information and could supplement his direct profits arising out of his patent protection by speculating in related markets. Eli Whitney obtained a patent for the cotton gin, but he failed to exploit the opportunities for speculative gains in the markets for slaves, cotton-growing land, and sites in the transport network.[28] The effect of air-conditioning on productivity obviously varied across industries and firms. It surely reduced the prices of lithographic print-

28. Hirshleifer writes, "The technological effects . . . include the possible production of new commodities, discovery of new resources, etc. consequent upon the new idea. The pecuniary effects are the wealth shifts due to the price revaluations that take place upon release and/or utilization of the information. Pecuniary effects are purely redistributive" (1971, 271). To the extent that a fixed resource, like land, can be put to a higher-valued use due to the innovation, the price revaluation does more than just redistribute wealth. His distinction between technical and pecuniary effects is similar to but not exactly the same as my definition of direct and induced external effects.

ing, cloth, cigars, and dried macaroni. Since there are economies of scale in cooling air, it favored large firms and stores. Its presence also affected other industries. The construction of high-rise office and apartment buildings and the development of high-speed elevators came after air-conditioning and, I suspect, would not have taken place without it. The early mainframe computers required climate control to be efficiently operated, especially in hot, humid climates. The value of land in Manhattan, Hong Kong, and Chicago would be significantly lower in the absence of air-conditioning. The market demand curves for air-conditioning do not fully capture the external benefits enjoyed by third parties, such as an office in the World Trade Center, an IBM 650 computer to estimate a logistic growth curve, or a movie in August. In the spirit of Russell Baker, it is my understanding that as late as 1970, federal civil servants were allowed to go home if the temperature exceeded 90 degrees, which by the usual presumption should have reduced the output of the government.

The air-conditioning of cars and trucks offers another example of benefits that were not fully anticipated. We knew how to cool a car in 1930 but had to wait until after the war before this improvement to Carrier's basic invention was commercially introduced. In 1965, only 10 percent of all new cars had factory-installed air conditioners, but the penetration rate climbed to 80.6 percent in 1982 and to 91.9 percent in 1990.[29] Driving today is not only more comfortable, but safer. The fatal-accident rate per million vehicle miles fell from 7.59 in 1950 to 1.56 in 1992. When temperature and humidity are high, drivers are less alert, peripheral vision deteriorates, and response rates tend to increase. Theory suggests that when more cars are air conditioned, accident rates ought to fall.[30] In passing, driving is less onerous in an air-contitioned vehicle which may, in part, account for the rapid growth of long-haul trucking.

In 1940, 31.6 percent of all Americans resided in the South. The destruction of employment opportunities, due in large measure to technical advances in agriculture (of which the most significant was probably the mechanical cotton picker), prompted an out-migration to the North and West. The share of the population living in the South fell to 30.7 percent in 1960, reaching a trough around 1965. At least two factors were responsible for the reversal of the out-migration. First, the labor force participation rate of older men decreased, and many chose to retire in the South. The ability to live year-around in a cool, comfortable home must surely have influenced the choice of a retirement site. Second, air-conditioning eliminated the productivity penalty of locating an establishment in the South. The demand for labor expanded, and the per capita income of southerners rose from 76.4 percent of the average for the country as

29. Motor Vehicle Manufacturers Association (1991, 38). The percentage of trucks with factory-installed air conditioners was 52.6 percent in 1982 and 81.4 percent in 1990.

30. The effect of temperature on injury frequency rates at the workplace was established by Vernon (1921). References to other studies that find a positive relation between high temperatures and accident rates in general can be found in Surry (1971, 93). I do not claim that air-conditioning is a major factor in the decline in fatal auto accident rates, but it surely deserves to be studied.

Table 3.7   **Population and Personal Income by Region**

	1950	1970	1990
Population (in thousands)			
East	39,478	49,041	50,809
North	44,460	56,571	59,669
South	47,197	62,795	85,446
West	20,190	34,805	52,786
United States	151,325	203,212	248,710
Per capita personal income (constant 1987 dollars)			
East	8,106	12,072	18,916
North	7,528	10,905	15,876
South	5,384	9,327	14,739
West	7,801	11,490	16,821
United States	7,046	10,799	16,307
Regional per capita income (percentage of U.S.)			
East	115.0	111.8	116.0
North	106.8	101.0	97.4
South	76.4	86.4	90.4
West	110.7	106.4	103.2
United States	100.0	100.0	100.0

Sources: U.S. Bureau of the Census (1995, 461, table 713) and selected issues of the Bureau of Economic Analysis' *Survey of Current Business.*
Notes: North corresponds to Midwest in previous tables, East to Northeast.

a whole to 90.4 percent; see table 3.7. The trend in relative per capita income was in the opposite direction for those residing in the North; per capita income there fell to 97.4 percent of the U.S. average in 1990. It is not surprising that more people are attracted to the South where they can control the indoor climate and command a higher relative income. You can drive to an air-conditioned workplace in an air-conditioned car, shop in an air conditioned mall, and watch a ball game in an air-conditioned dome stadium. A third of the farm tractors have air-conditioned cabs, and in Chalmette, Louisiana, aluminum workers walk around with portable air conditioners strapped to their belts (see Arsenault 1984, 613). Fifteen years ago, Frank Trippett opined that people no longer think of interior coolness as an amenity but as a necessity.[31] The rejuvenation of Dixie could not have taken place without Willis Carrier's invention. The nearly ubiquitous presence of air-conditioning is responsible for higher productivity, more comfortable homes, and longer life expectancies. I initially thought that this innovation would be adopted and imitated in other countries with climates similar to that in the deep South. However, the private

31. Arsenault also reports (1984, 614) that at the 1980 Governors' Conference, Governor Richard W. Riley of South Carolina insisted that the federal assistance program should operate on the assumption that air-conditioning a home in the South was no less essential than heating a home in the North. Energy tax credits should be made available to all.

value of air-conditioning is inversely related to the price of the apparatus and the price of electricity. High energy taxes reduce the demand for air-conditioning. The consequences are lower labor productivity, less work in the hot summer months, uncomfortably hot and humid homes, and poor health.

3.6 Knowledge and Novelty

Invention, defined as "a new combination of available knowledge," can sometimes be produced, but in other instances it is the result of luck. The production of knowledge differs from the relation between output and inputs which is the familiar production function in a neoclassical theory of value. There is more uncertainty in creating a new product. One can point to numerous cases where substantial outlays have failed to solve a problem or to discover a patentable product. Prospecting for an oil well or searching for a job are analogous, in some ways, to searching for a new product or process. But while the cost of a dry hole is part of the full cost of supplying petroleum, each invention is unique, and there is no "knowledge industry" to absorb the costs of unsuccessful inventive activities. In spite of this difference, some have tried to estimate the expected cost by relating R&D expenses to the output of patented inventions. The limitations of these estimates were discussed in section 3.3. Additionally, patented inventions include truly new products and ideas as well as imitations and improvements; that is, patents and patent applications are not homogeneous. Arrow suggests that the cost of an invention (discovering a new idea) is stochastic and depends on the stage of the economy's development: "The set of opportunities for innovation at any one moment are determined by what the physical laws of the world really are and how much has already been learned and is therefore accidental from the viewpoint of economics" (1969, 35). A patent award is only the first step in producing an innovation. A majority of patents are stillborn and never make a debut in the market. The economic lives of the new entrants are threatened by the creation of new knowledge.

A new product may have to be modified and improved before it can be introduced. Information has to be disseminated to potential customers. A distribution channel has to be established. These are some of the components that belong to the "D" in R&D costs. The lag between invention and innovation can be long, often exceeding seventeen years. An inventor can shorten the length of this lag and raise the probability of a successful entry to the market by incurring more R&D costs.

The pace of technical progress can allegedly be stimulated by a policy that subsidizes R&D expenditures, possibly via tax credits. A blanket subsidy cannot differentiate among inventors or types of expenditures. A firm searching for a sugar substitute (when sugar is protected by import quotas) would receive the same rate of subsidy as one incurring R&D costs to discover a biodegradable plastic. Would the same rate of subsidy be granted for test-marketing a new brand of cat food and paying for research scientists? A regulatory agency would have to be created if we wanted to subsidize only the deserving research projects. This agency would have to promulgate something resembling an industrial policy. A subsidy would expand R&D expenditures, resulting in a higher average cost of an invention. Products would be likely to reach the market earlier, more would be spent on unsuccessful ventures, and inventors would have less incentive to cut their losses by stopping dubious projects. It must also be remembered that products are like people and penguins, they have uncertain and finite lives. The discovery of a new alloy could destroy the value of a tin mine along with the R&D capital invested in developing more-efficient tin-mining equipment. The inability to forecast the length of a product's life cycle necessarily increases the risk confronting inventors and innovators. It is not at all obvious that society would realize a positive rate of return on the incremental R&D expenditures attracted by a subsidy program.

The social returns to a major innovation (like the telephone, penicillin, the computer, or even air-conditioning) far exceed the sum of consumer's and producer's surpluses, the private returns accruing to the parties directly involved in the market for the new product or process. A major innovation affects third parties, changes preferences, and opens the way for technical advances in other sectors. The prices of cigars and cloth were lower because of air-conditioning. The diffusion of air-conditioning increased the profitability of engaging in research that led to high-rise office buildings, high-speed elevators, and mainframe computers. Carrier's patent had expired long before air-conditioning was introduced to the residential market. The spread of air-conditioning reversed the outflow of people and jobs from the South. A consumer's surplus measure of the value of driving in an air-conditioned vehicle or shopping in comfort presumes that one can identify a stable demand for the new product, air-conditioning in this example. However, for some new products, experience teaches consumers about additional uses which shift the demand for the new product. The situation for a really successful new good is similar to the *de gustibus* model of Stigler and Becker (1977). As consumers learned more ways to utilize climate control, they demanded more of it, resulting in a larger ex post demand and consumer's surplus. The economic life of a successful innovation will almost certainly exceed the statutory life of the patent. The original inventor may continue to realize supernormal returns because she enjoys any advantages associated with being the first producer and probably has the ability to stay ahead of any competitors in terms of product improvements. A society can encourage more inventive activities by either subsidizing costs or enhancing returns. When we know so little about the costs of invention and innovation (especially the dry ventures), it would seem wiser to consider policies that enhance the returns to inventors. This might be done by extending the patent life for a really novel invention to, say, twenty-five years and shortening it for an improvement or imitation to, say, five years. The patent office would have to make the distinction by reviewing the patent application to see how much it relies on existing knowledge. The merits of renewing patents for a fee should be studied. The objective is to increase the mean, especially the dispersion, of returns to invention. If most inventors exhibit a utility function of wealth with an inflection point of the type posited by Friedman and Savage (1948), a larger dispersion of returns will increase the supply of inventive activity.[32] A policy that operates on incentives stands a better chance of success in promoting a faster pace of technical progress.

Technical progress can occur through the creation of new products or through the discovery of new techniques to produce the old list of products at lower costs. Consider an economy in which all progress takes the form of cost-reducing innovations. The members of this economy can enjoy an ever growing flow of consumption because more goods and services can be produced even with no increase in the quantity or quality of productive inputs. Firms simply acquire the knowledge to produce more corn, tallow, and gingham with the same workers and capital. Alternatively, we can imagine another economy in which progress entails the creation of new goods and services. The people in this economy are forced to adjust to novelty; they confront a continually changing catalogue of goods and services from which they can choose. More time and effort have to be allocated to learning about new foods, places to visit, and whether to buy a new plastic knee rather than to demand traditional medical care to mend a wounded knee. Most of us do not have to choose between these two extreme faces of technical advance; we probably would like to get a mixture. Few of us would opt for the status quo economy. It would be a terribly dull life if innovations only reduced the costs of producing the same menu of goods and services that now populate our markets. People have revealed that they like new things. The uncertainty of what will become available in tomorrow's market surely prompts many of us to put forth more effort today in order to acquire the wherewithal to get a ride on the supersonic jet or the opportunity to influence the outcome of a game via an interactive television set. Hilton noted that "An inventor has an incentive to maximize his claims to novelty" (1971, 21). If the inventor can occasionally deliver on his claims, the welfare of society will continue to grow.

Appendix

Climate and Productivity: A First Approximation

Suppose that output is a function of labor and capital inputs as well as of temperature, T, which is a shorthand term for an index of air quality defined by temperature, humidity, cleanliness, and ventilation.

(A1) $$X = f(L, K, T).$$

---

32. The distribution of prizes in most state lotteries reveals a fairly large number of small prizes (so that a significant number can say that they won something) and a few megaprizes that can be prominently announced on television and in the newspapers. If consumers exhibit a utility function with an inflection point, they will simultaneously purchase insurance and lottery tickets.

Suppose initially that temperature, like Meade's atmosphere, is exogenous and affects output in a Hicks Neutral fashion.

(A1′) $X = \phi(T)g(L, K),$

where $\phi(T)$ is a bell-shaped function attaining a maximum at some ideal, moderate temperature T_M. A competitive firm operates over a cycle of two periods with temperature T_A above the ideal in the first period, and T_B below the ideal in the second period. The capital has to be the same in both periods, but the labor input can be adjusted given the temperature. Ignoring discounting, profits over a cycle of two periods are given by

(A2) $\pi = p(X_A + X_B) - w(L_A + L_B) - 2rK.$

When temperature affects productivity in a Hicks Neutral fashion, its impact can be analyzed by defining what I call temperature-adjusted prices. Let $p_A = p\phi(T_A)$ denote the effective price in the hot period, while $p_B = p\phi(T_B)$ is the effective price in the cold period when the firm is obliged to accept the exogenous temperatures. If we normalize ϕ (T) to equal unity at the ideal temperature, then $p_A < p$, and $p_B < p$. In equilibrium, labor's MVP will be equated to the wage in each period, while the sum of capital's MVP over the two periods is equated to its full-cycle price.

(A3a) $p_A g_{LA} = w, \qquad p_B g_{LB} = w,$

(A3b) $(p_A g_{KA} + p_B g_{KB}) = 2r.$

If hot weather leads to a larger decrement in productivity, $\phi(T_A) < \phi(T_B) < 1$, and $p_A < p_B$. Although labor's MVP is equal to the common wage, g_{LA} will be greater than g_{LB}, an outcome that can only be achieved by hiring fewer workers in hot weather. However, the inability to vary capital over the cycle results in employing "too much" capital in the hot first period. The departures of temperature from the ideal climate, T_M, raise production costs, leading to lower profits. Indeed, profits, π_0 in this base case, will be smaller, the larger are the temperature departures from the ideal.

Suppose that a technological innovation enables the firm to cool the indoor temperature to $T_1 = T_A - D$ at a cost of $(F_A + c_d D)$ and to heat the plant in the cold period to an indoor temperature of $T_2 = (T_B + I)$ at a cost of $(F_B + c_i I)$. The fixed and marginal costs of cooling and heating will depend on the size and insulation of the plant and on the nature of the production process. A bakery is costlier to cool than a warehouse. Profits now are a function of five decision variables $\{L_1, L_2, K^*, D, I\}$, where D and I determine the indoor climates.[33]

---

33. The Sacket Wilhelm Company in Brooklyn wanted temperatures of 70 degrees in the winter and 80 degrees in the summer with a constant humidity of 55 percent. The optimum temperature for worker efficiency is around 67 degrees, but Wilhelm had to consider the effect of temperature on paper and paints.

(A4) $\pi = p(X_1 + X_2) - w(L_1 + L_2) - 2rK^* - F_A - c_dD - F_B - c_iI.$

In equilibrium, the firm will satisfy conditions analogous to equations (A3a) and (A3b), where $p_1 = p\phi(T_1)$ replaces p_A in the hot period, and $p_2 = p\phi(T_2)$ replaces p_B. The optimal decrement in temperature in the hot period, $D = T_A - T_1$, is attained when the marginal benefit is equal to the marginal cooling cost, equation (A5a), provided that the increment to quasi-rent exceeds the total cooling cost, equation (A5b).

(A5a) $p\phi'(T_1)g(L_1, K^*) = c_d,$

(A5b) $p(X_1 - X_A) - \Delta C > (F_A + c_dD),$

where ΔC is the increment in costs of hiring more labor and capital. A similar pair of conditions must hold if it pays the firm to increase the temperature in the cold second period. Remember that the cost parameters $\{F_A, c_d\}$ for cooling depend on the size and insulation of the plant and have declined over time. More importantly, the effect of temperature on productivity, $\phi(T)$, varies across industries. The gain in productivity from cooling and humidifying the air was undoubtedly greater for a textile mill than for a bottling plant. The installation of cooling and heating equipment raises the productivity parameter, $\phi(T)$. As a consequence, the effective product prices climb, ($p_1 > p_A, p_2 > p_B$), prompting the firm to expand output. If a majority of firms in an industry find that controlling the indoor climate is profitable, the price of the product will fall, to the benefit of consumers.

Temperature and Labor Productivity: A Second Approximation

Suppose that the labor input is the product of person hours (H) times the efficiency per hour which is a function of the temperature; $L = E(T)H$, where $E(T)$ attains a maximum at some ideal, moderate temperature. Assume that the exogenous outdoor temperature in the absence of air-conditioning is above this ideal, $T_A > T_M$. A competitive firm chooses labor hours and capital $\{H, K\}$ to maximize profits.

(A6) $\pi = pf[E(T_A)H, K] - wH - rK.$

Let $E = E(T_A)$ denote labor efficiency with the unregulated temperature. Profits π_0 are at a maximum when the MVP of hours and capital are equated to their respective prices.

(A7) $pEf_L = w, \qquad pf_K = r, \qquad \dfrac{f_L}{f_K} = \dfrac{w}{Er}.$

Since $E'(T) < 0$, firms located in hotter places confront a higher "price" per efficiency unit of labor. The capital-to-labor ratio, $K/L = K/EH$, will be higher, but the capital-to-hours ratio, K/H, will be higher if and only if the elasticity of substitution is greater than one. More importantly, if the hourly wage w is the same for all, a firm in a hot place faces a higher price for an efficiency unit of labor and is at a cost disadvantage relative to competitors located in milder climates.

Suppose now that the firm can reduce the temperature by D degrees, to $T^* = (T_A - D)$ at a cost of $(F + cD)$. The firm will install air-conditioning if the increment to quasi-rent exceeds the total cooling cost.

(A8a) $$p(X^* - X) - \Delta C > F + cD,$$

where X^* and D are chosen to equate marginal gains to marginal costs.

(A8b) $$pEf_L = w, \qquad pf_K = r, \qquad -E'(T_A - D)Hpf_L = c.$$

Cooling has an effect similar to a labor-saving innovation. The relative price of labor (w/E^*r) falls, the demand for capital K increases, and the firm supplies more output to the market, $X^* > X$. The increment to labor productivity, $E^* = E(T_A - D)$, depends on the properties of $E(T)$ and on the marginal cost of cooling, c. The model can be extended to demand cooling in a hot period and heating in a cold period, but this extension is not undertaken here.

Household Demands for Heating and Cooling

Comfort is surely a function of the indoor temperature and humidity, which could be included as an argument of the utility function alongside a consumption good, $U(X, T_i)$. Friedman (1987) argued that if heat loss is mainly due to conduction (rather than radiation or convection), the total cost of heating a house is a linear function of the gap between the desired indoor and exogenous outdoor temperatures.

(A9) $$TC = F + c(T_i - T_o),$$

where F is the fixed monthly cost and c is the unit cost of raising the indoor temperature by one degree. Utility is maximized when the marginal rate of substitution of indoor temperature for consumption (taken to be the numeraire) is equated to the marginal cost of raising T_i by one degree.

(A10) $$\frac{U_{Ti}}{U_X} = c(z).$$

Remember that a warmer indoor temperature raises utility, that is, $U_{Ti} > 0$. The heating-cost parameters $\{F, c\}$ depend on the size of the house, the price of energy, and the structure of the home. Specifically, more outlays for insulation z increase the fixed cost F but reduce the marginal heating cost, $c = c(z)$ with $c'(z) < 0$. If consumers in different locations have the same tastes, and if wages adjust to equalize total utilities across locations, persons in colder climates will spend more on insulation and hence confront a lower marginal cost of raising the temperature. They accordingly maintain their homes at a higher indoor temperature. It is a neat model that can parsimoniously explain why houses in Chicago are warmer in the winter than houses in Los Angeles even though the former entail a higher total heating cost. This model has to be extended in at least two directions for a residential demand for cooling to be derived. First, the cost function has to be amplified. Second, the interaction between indoor temperature and home size has to be made explicit in a manner analogous to the household production model of Becker (1965).

The cost of climate control can be decomposed into an avoidable fixed cost plus a variable operating cost that is assumed to be a linear function of the desired temperature decrement, $D = (T_o - T_i)$. The fixed cost is proportional to the price of the apparatus P_a which, in turn, is a function of the volume of air to be chilled and the cost of the compressor, ducts, and other equipment, while the unit cooling cost is a function of the structural charactersitics and the price of electricity P_e.

$$(A11) \quad TC = F + cD = \alpha P_a + c(P_e)(T_o - T_i), \quad \alpha = \frac{r}{1 - e^{-r\tau}}$$

where r is the interest rate and τ is the expected life of the apparatus. Utility is inversely related to the indoor temperature, $U(X, T_i)$, where $U_{Ti} < 0$. The demands for corn and cooling degrees $\{X, D = T_o - T_i\}$ are determined by a budget constraint and the equality of the marginal rate of substitution to the relative price of cooling.

$$(A12a) \qquad\qquad X + F + c(T_o - T_i) = M,$$

$$(A12b) \qquad\qquad -\left(\frac{U_{Ti}}{U_X}\right) = c(P_e).$$

Let $w = w(D)$ denote the marginal offer price that a consumer is prepared to pay for the Dth degree of cooling. The consumer's surplus when D^* is the optimal decrement in temperature is[34]

$$(A13) \qquad\qquad CS = \int_0^{D^*} w(D)dD - c(P_e)D^*.$$

A consumer will incur the avoidable fixed cost if it is less than the consumer's surplus from obtaining a cooler home; that is, he will install air-conditioning if $F < CS$. The fraction of consumers who find that this inequality holds and hence install air-conditioning will climb over time as the price of the apparatus falls, thereby reducing the avoidable fixed cost F, or as the price of electricity declines, thereby increasing the consumer's surplus CS.

---

34. The optimal bundle $\{X^*, D^* = T_o - T_i^*\}$ is obtained by solving equations (A12a) and (A12b). The marginal offer price need not be a strictly declining function of D. The consumer may not be willing to pay much for the first few degrees of cooling from an outdoor temperature of $T_o = 85$ degrees to, say, $T_i = 82$ degrees, but in the neighborhood of equilibrium, it seems safe to assume that $dw/dD < 0$.

The temperature decrement, $D = (T_o - T_i)$, the difference between outdoor and indoor temperatures, tacitly assumes a given volume of air to be chilled by D degrees. If V is the volume of air, the quantity of climatically controlled air demanded by a household can be approximated by $Q = DV$. When air-conditioning was initially introduced to the residential market, most consumers purchased room units which entailed a smaller avoidable fixed cost F but a higher marginal cooling cost $c(P_e)$. These room units also cooled a smaller quantity of air. As incomes rose and as the price of the apparatus P_a and the price of electricity P_e fell, consumers expanded their demand for chilled air, $Q = DV$, by installing central air-conditioning systems. Finally, if the consumption good X is disaggregated, a change in the indoor temperature will differentially affect the demands for particular goods. The ability to reduce the inside temperature from 85 to 65 degrees has to affect the demands for soft drinks, salads, and electric fans. Many of us can remember an occupant of the White House who would turn up the air conditioner in order to enjoy an evening before a crackling wood fire in the summer.

References

Alchian, A. A. 1959. Costs and outputs. In *The allocation of economic resources,* ed. M. Abramovitz, 23–40. Stanford, Calif.: Stanford University Press.

Arrow, K. J. 1969. A classificatory note on the production and transmission of technological knowledge. *American Economic Review, Papers* 29 (May): 29–35.

Arsenault, Raymond. 1984. The end of the long hot summer: The air conditioner and southern culture. *Journal of Southern History* 50, no. 4 (November): 597–628.

Asher, Harold. 1956. *Cost-quantity relationship in the airframe industry.* Santa Monica, Calif.: RAND. 1 July.

Bailey, N. T. J. 1957. *The mathematical theory of epidemics.* New York: Charles Griffin.

Baker, Russell. 1978. No sweat. *New York Times Magazine,* 9 July. Quoted in Arsenault 1984, 605.

Becker, G. S. 1965. A theory of the allocation of time. *Economic Journal* 75 (September): 493–517.

Booz, Allen, and Hamilton. 1971. *Management of new products.* New York: Booz, Allen, and Hamilton, Inc.

Chaney, Paul K., Timothy M. Devinney, and Russell S. Winer. 1991. The impact of new product introduction on the market value of firms. *Journal of Business* 64:573–610.

Coale, Ansley, and Donald McNeil. 1972. The distribution by age of the frequency of first marriage in a female cohort. *Journal of the American Statistical Association* 67 (December): 743–49.

Coase, Ronald H. 1972. Durability and monopoly. *Journal of Law and Economics* 145:143–49.

Council of Economic Advisers. 1988. *Economic report of the president.* Washington, D.C.: Government Printing Office.

Davidson, J. Hugh. 1976. Why most new consumer brands fail. *Harvard Business Review* 54 (March/April): 117–22.

Davidson, J. P., P. S. Florence, B. Gray, and N. Ross. 1958. *Productivity and economic Incentives.* London: Allen and Unwin.

Denison, E. F. 1962. *Sources of economic growth in the United States and the alternatives before us.* New York: Committee for Economic Development.

Enos, J. 1962. Invention and innovation in the petroleum refining industry. In *The rate and direction of inventive activity: Economic and social factors,* 299–322. National Bureau of Economic Research Conference series, vol. 13. Princeton, N.J.: Princeton University Press.

Evenson, Robert. 1993. Patents, R&D, and invention potential: International evidence. *American Economic Review, Papers* 83 (May): 463–68.

Evenson, Robert E., and Yoav Kislev. 1975. *Agricultural research and productivity.* New Haven, Conn.: Yale University Press.

Fisher, F. M., and K. Shell. 1968. Taste and quality change in the pure theory of the true cost of living index. In *Value, capital, and growth,* ed. J. N. Wolfe, 97–139. Chicago: Aldine Publishing.

Florence, P. Sargant. 1924. *The economics of fatigue and unrest: The efficiency of labour in English and American Industry.* New York: Henry Holt.

Freeman, Christopher. 1991. *The economics of industrial innovation.* 2d ed. Cambridge, Mass.: MIT Press.

Friedman, David. 1987. Cold houses and warm climates and vice versa: A paradox of rational heating. *Journal of Political Economy* 95 (October): 1089–97.

Friedman, M., and L. J. Savage. 1948. The utility analysis of choices involving risk. *Journal of Political Economy* 56 (August): 279–304.

Griliches, Zvi. 1957. Hybrid corn: An exploration in the economics of technological change. *Econometrica* 25 (October): 501–22.

———. 1990. Patent statistics as economic indicators: A survey. *Journal of Economic Literature* 28 (December): 1661–707.

Grossman, G. M., and E. Helpman. 1991. Endogenous product cycles. *Economic Journal* 101:1214–29.

Helpman, Elhanan. 1993. Innovation, imitation, and intellectual property rights. *Econometrica* 61 (November): 1247–80.

Hicks, John R. 1959. *Revision of demand theory.* London: Oxford University Press.

Hilton, George W. 1971. *Cable car in America.* Berkeley, Calif.: Howell-North Books.

Hirshleifer, Jack. 1971. The private and social value of information and the rewards for inventive activity. *American Economic Review* 61 (September): 561–74.

Huntington, Ellsworth. 1924. *Civilization and climate.* 3d ed., 13–16, 80–108. New Haven, Conn.: Yale University Press.

Ingels, Margaret. 1952. *Willis Haviland Carrier, father of air conditioning.* Garden City, N.Y.: Country Life Press.

Jewkes, John, David Sawers, and Richard Stillerman. 1958. *The sources of invention.* New York: St. Martin's Press.

Kuznets, Simon. 1962. Inventive activity: Problems of definition and measurement. In *The rate and direction of inventive activity: Economic and social factors,* 19–51. National Bureau of Economic Research Conference series, vol. 13. Princeton, N.J.: Princeton University Press.

Lebergott, Stanley. 1993. *Pursuing happiness.* Princeton, N.J.: Princeton University Press.

Mansfield, E. 1966. Technological change: Measurement, determinants, and diffusion. In *Studies of the employment impact of technological change.* Vol. 2. Washington, D.C.: Government Printing Office.

Moore, Henry Ludwell. [1911] 1967. *Laws of wages, an essay in statistical economics.* Reprint, New York: Augustus M. Kelley Publishers.

Motor Vehicle Manufacturers Association. 1991. *Motor vehicle facts and figures, 1991.* Detroit, Mich.: Motor Vehicle Manufacturers Association of the United States.

Mowery, David C. 1988. The diffusion of new manufacturing technology. In *The impact of technological change on employment and economic growth,* ed. Richard M. Cyert and David C. Mowery, 481–509. Cambridge, Mass.: Ballinger Publishing.

Oi, W. Y. 1991. Low wages and small firms. In *Research in labor economics,* ed. R. Ehrenberg. Vol. 12, 1–39. Greenwich, Conn.: JAI Press.

Romeo, A. A. 1975. Interindustry and interfirm differences in the rate of diffusion of an innovation. *Review of Economics and Statistics* 57:311–19.

———. 1977. The rate of imitation of a capital embodied process innovation. *Economica* 44:63–69.

Rosenberg, Nathan. 1982. *Inside the black box: Technology in economics.* New York: Cambridge University Press.

Rothbarth, E. 1941. The measurement of changes in real income under conditions of rationing. *Review of Economic Studies* 8:100–107.

Sakamoto-Momiyama, Masako. 1977. *Seasonality in human mortality.* Tokyo: University of Tokyo Press.

Samuelson, Paul Anthony. 1948. *Foundations of economic analysis.* Cambridge, Mass.: Harvard University Press.

Scherer, F. M. 1965. Firm size, market structure, opportunity and the output of patented inventions. *American Economic Review* 55 (December): 1097–1123.

Stigler, George J. 1968. A note on patents. In *The organization of industry.* 122–25. Chicago: University of Chicago Press.

Stigler, G. J., and G. S. Becker. 1977. De gustibus non est disputandum. *American Economic Review* 67 (March): 76–90.

Stokey, Nancy L. 1979. Intertemporal price discrimination. *Quarterly Journal of Economics* 94:355–71.

Surry, Jean. 1971. *Industrial accident research.* Toronto: Labor Safety Council. May.

U.S. Bureau of Labor Statistics. 1983. *Handbook of labor statistics.* Washington, D.C.: Government Printing Office.

U.S. Bureau of the Census. 1954. *Statistical abstract of the United States.* Washington, D.C.: Government Printing Office.

———. 1976. *Statistical abstract of the United States.* Washington, D.C.: Government Printing Office.

———. 1987. *Census of manufactures.* Washington, D.C.: U.S. Bureau of the Census.

———. 1993. *Statistical abstract of the United States.* Washington, D.C.: Government Printing Office.

———. 1995. *Statistical abstract of the United States.* Washington, D.C.: Government Printing Office.

Usher, Dan. 1964. The welfare economics of invention. *Economica* 31 (August): 279–87.

Vernon, H. M. 1921. *Industrial fatigue and efficiency.* London: Routledge.

4 Science, Health, and Household Technology: The Effect of the Pasteur Revolution on Consumer Demand

Joel Mokyr and Rebecca Stein

The rise in life expectancy, in particular the decline in infant mortality, remains one of the most impressive achievements of modern technology. Much of this progress was made before 1914 and long before the advent of modern antibiotics. This paper proposes that one key to the decline of the mortality rate is essentially technological in nature. In a simple model of consumer behavior, the household can be viewed as "producing" health for its members, based on a certain set of priors that the household has on what causes disease. These priors changed radically in the closing decades of the nineteenth century as a result of growing knowledge that dictated certain "recipes" to the household regarding food, hygiene, personal and medical care, and so on. The paper discusses the origins of this new knowledge and how households were induced to change their behavior. The central role of changes in the understanding of disease, especially the emergence of the germ theory as the undisputed ruling paradigm, is recognized and some attempt is made to quantify the importance of those changes. We conclude that much of the credit for the increase in life expectancy goes to household decision makers in addition to scientists, physicians, and civil servants.

4.1 Introduction

Consumers purchase goods for two different reasons: because they "enjoy" these goods (i.e., utility *stricto sensu*) and because they believe that these goods are in some way good for their health, that is, that these goods are inputs

Joel Mokyr is professor of economics and history at Northwestern University. Rebecca Stein is a graduate student in economics at Northwestern University.

The financial assistance of National Science Foundation grant SES 9122384 is acknowledged. John Brown, Louis Cain, Deirdre N. McCloskey, the participants in the 1994 Cliometric Conference in Tucson, Arizona, and an anonymous referee made useful comments on earlier versions.

into a household production function which produces, among other things, physical well-being.[1] The health-related component of demand is, however, rarely made explicit and is usually subsumed under "preferences." Thus, if the consumer learns that a certain good that she has been consuming is actually harmful to her health, she may reduce her demand, which would be tantamount to a change in taste. However, no actual change in preferences has occurred; instead, the information available to the consumer has changed. As is widely understood, changes in preferences and changes in information available to the consumer are observationally equivalent.[2]

Although consumer theory typically allows for various kinds of uncertainty, it is unusual for economists to assume that the consumer does not know her own preferences. It is usually assumed that the ordering of preferences is complete and the maximand itself is understood and fully known. In the case of the interaction between consumption and health, however, the information upon which the consumer bases decisions is clearly variable. In the past, consumers have typically been poorly informed about the effects that consumption had on their bodies. As new information became available to them—we shall discuss below how that happened—they changed their behavior. The approach we take in this paper is to define a separate "health" function as a combination of the physical well-being and life expectancy of members of the household, which is being maximized jointly with pure "utility."[3]

The decline in mortality in the West after 1850 is still imperfectly understood. There are at least four explanations in the literature that purport to account for the decline in infectious disease in the industrialized world before 1914. One explanation focuses on the rise in income and living standards, which resulted in improved nutritional status. Improved nutrition enhanced immunity and thus reduced susceptibility to disease and case-specific mortality rates. This hypothesis, associated with McKeown (1977) and Fogel (1991a, 1991b, 1992), has come under heavy criticism (e.g., Szreter 1988 and Ryan Johansson 1994) but has more recently found defenders (Guha 1994). An alternative hypothesis, supported by Szreter (1988) and Brown (1988, forthcoming) gives more credit to public works and local government, especially sani-

---

1. More generally, consumer goods can be inputs into other ultimate goals in the classic Lancaster-Strotz manner. This approach has long been central to the analysis of the household as pioneered by Becker (1976). Historians have expressed the same idea, e.g., De Vries (1993) and Cowan (1983). Empirical studies of such models are reviewed by Strauss and Thomas (1993). For the purpose of this paper, however, we focus exclusively on physical well-being.

2. For a restatement, see Pollak and Watkins (1993). Many of the issues that come up in the economics of fertility and contraception are isomorphic to the issues that come up in the economics of health. The difference, above all, is that it seems reasonable that preferences with respect to health tend to be relatively stable over time, in contrast with the demand for children.

3. A similar approach to the one in this paper can be found in the works of Samuel Preston and his coauthors (Preston 1976; Ewbank and Preston 1990; Preston and Haines 1991), referring primarily to infant mortality decline in the United States after 1900.

tary improvements.[4] These two competing explanations, the protestations of some of their defenders notwithstanding, do not exclude each other. Yet there is some lingering doubt whether, even taken jointly and allowing for synergistic effects between nutrition and infection, they explain the entire phenomenon. If not, there remains an unexplained residual which requires further investigation. One scholar (Fridlizius 1984) feels strongly that there is more to the story and has speculated about exogenous climatic and microbial changes which reduced infectious disease.

Our view is that these stories pay insufficient attention to technology. As in the measurement of total factor productivity, when all inputs have been accounted for, the prime suspect in the residual is changes in knowledge.[5] Technological changes in food preservation, textiles, water supply, transportation, and home appliances have long been mentioned as contributing factors. Even medical treatment did not stand completely still and had a number of major successes to its credit, above all the conquest of smallpox which is still regarded by some as the most important medical success before 1914. Yet there is another aspect of useful knowledge which has not been given sufficient credit, namely the mundane, day-to-day techniques by which homemakers used consumer goods and hard work to keep themselves and their household healthy. In a pioneering paper, Tomes (1990) has termed this "the private side" of the nineteenth-century public health movement. In an age in which an ounce of prevention was worth many pounds of cure, such techniques included domestic sanitation as well as baby care, food quality and composition, proper home heating and ventilation, isolation of patients with contagious afflictions, and care for those with minor sicknesses (e.g., colds, small wounds, and diarrhea) to prevent complications. It should be recognized from the outset that until the twentieth century, the technology employed by households to produce health was highly imperfect by our standards. That is, given incomes, relative prices, and preferences, people could have been healthier and lived longer. Consumers' knowledge about their own bodies, deficient even today, has changed dramatically in the past century; and changes in perceptions about what determines health have been of central importance to changes in demand. Our main argument is that part of the decline in the mortality rate can be interpreted as the result of technological progress at the household level (Mokyr 1993). Such technological progress consisted of course of a supply side, but improved knowledge by households affected their demand for consumer goods as well.

How did households learn about what makes them sick and how to stay

---

4. Serious misgivings about the positive effects of public policy are sounded in the studies collected in Woods and Woodward (1984). Their conclusion is basically that "public health improvements were unlikely to succeed: traditionally control could only be exerted over levels of exposure to food- and waterborne diseases, and the improvements themselves were patchy" (35).

5. This conclusion was also reached recently by Easterlin (1995).

well? The most dramatic change in medical history occurred in the half century before 1914: the understanding and gradual extinction of infectious disease from Western society. This transition was not complete by 1914, but had made enormous progress—decades before the development of effective antibiotics.[6] The most important scientific change in this period, and probably the greatest scientific breakthrough in the history of medicine, was the germ theory of disease, first enunciated by Louis Pasteur in 1864 and subsequently refined and developed by him and by Robert Koch and his followers in the 1870s and beyond.

In what follows, we develop a simple model of consumer demand that explicitly allows for health as part of what is being maximized. This is, of course, hardly new in the demographic literature, in which it has long been recognized that life expectancy is a function of the goods consumed by the individual (of which medical care may be one, though not necessarily one of great importance). What is novel is that we explicitly take into account the difficulty consumers have in understanding their own bodies and the complex interaction of microbes, the external environment, and their immune systems. The understanding of this interaction will never be perfect; unlike mechanical devices or chemicals, the human body is extremely complex and the consumer's control over her body cannot be total. All the same, a lot of progress was made between 1870 and 1914.

4.2   A Simple Model

To distinguish between the alternatives, it is useful to set up the problem formally. As in standard theory, the consumer j maximizes a utility function

$$(1) \qquad U_j = U_j(X_{1j}, \ldots, X_{nj}, L_j),$$

where L is a composite variable of family life expectancy and health, subject to the usual budget constraint $\sum X_i P_i = Y$.[7] Leisure should be regarded as one of the X's (requiring the appropriate reinterpretation of the budget constraint).[8]

---

6. Latour notes wryly that World War I was the first major war in which one could kill immobile masses: "Without the bacteriologists, the generals would never have been able to hold on to millions of men for four years in muddy, rat-infested trenches. These men would have died before gas and machine guns had carried them off " (1988, 112). Following the war, however, the influenza epidemic wiped out tens of millions, and scientists were unable to identify the agent.

7. Whether L measures life expectancy alone, health (the absence of morbidity), or some combination of the two is a difficult issue. The issue seems more perplexing in today's medical environment in which morbidity and mortality are less closely connected. For an age in which infectious diseases were the main causes of death, the distinction seems less acute, although Riley (1991) suggests that while mortality declined during the nineteenth century, morbidity was on the rise.

8. In a more extended version of the model, domestic labor, market work, and leisure are dealt with separately, subject to a time constraint. Presumably all three activities enter the utility function, with domestic and market labor both entering with a negative marginal utility. A critical extension of the model is to include domestic labor explicitly in the L function. We shall treat it here simply as one of the X's.

The special characteristic of this setup is that L is determined by the household production function

$$(2) \qquad\qquad L_j = E + f(X_{ij}, \ldots, X_{nj}).$$

E is a common factor independent of the consumption basket ("environment"), f is the household production function that transforms the goods consumed into longer lives. The function f is an unobserved technical relationship. It converts the X's into a vector of biological characteristics (X) that determines the individual's physical well-being given some level of E. The food component of X takes into account not only caloric intake but also vitamins, minerals, fiber, substances combating free radicals such as antioxidants, and so on. Home heating, cleanliness, medical care, and physical exercise are other examples of X's that enter equation (2). The function f describes not only exposure to harmful microorganisms and chemicals and the effects of consumption on the cardiovascular system, but also the interaction between consumption and the human immune system. Moreover, f is assumed to satisfy the condition that the conversion is *efficient* (i.e., that no X's are wasted in the production process).

The shape of f, however, is not fully known to "best-practice" science, much less to the household. Behavior is therefore determined by the function

$$(2') \qquad\qquad L_j^e = E + (A - \varepsilon_j) f(X_{ij}, \ldots, X_{nj}),$$

where L_j^e is the prior that the consumer has over L, A is a common technology-shift factor that measures improvements in the best-practice priors on household technology, and ε_j is an individual-specific measure of the difference between this individual's technology and the best-practice technology. The disadvantage of a simple formulation like equation ($2'$) is that any changes in the technology of converting X into L are assumed to be Hicks Neutral so that improvements affect all recipes *pari passu*. A more general formulation would allow for separate effects on each good:

$$(3) \qquad\qquad L_j^e = E + \sum_i (A_i - \varepsilon_{ij}) F_i(X_{ij}) \qquad \forall\, j.$$

The term $A_i - \varepsilon_{ij}$ is the *recipe* with which consumer j converts X_i into L. We define it here as a multiplicative deviation from best-practice priors. There is a vector of best-practice recipes associated with the X, but households may not be using the best-practice technique, thus being ε below or above where they would be if they followed the best practice.

A few remarks on equation (3) are in order. First, we can define a level of consumption X^{**}, which is the vector of consumption which maximizes utility by substituting equation (2) into equation (1). This assumes a world of perfect information in which all A's equal unity and all ε's zero, meaning that not only have scientists figured out the exact functional relation between L and every X, but everyone has access to that knowledge, believes it, and uses it flawlessly. In this case the consumer maximizes $U(X, L)$ "correctly" subject only to her budget constraint. Second, we may define $\hat{X}$, a vector of consumption for a consumer who is ignorant of the effect of consumption on health, so that $A - \varepsilon_j = 0$ for all X's, meaning that the consumer disregards the effect of the X's on L. In this case, $L(\hat{X})$ is a purely unintended by-product of consumption. It is possible that by a fluke the completely ignorant consumer will consume just about the "right" amount of X ($\hat{X} = X^{**}$).[9] Even if there are goods for which $F'(\hat{X}) = 0$, so that they have no marginal impact on health, their consumption may not be optimal.[10] This also implies that an increase in any $A - \varepsilon$ (given that $0 < A - \varepsilon < 1$) does not *necessarily* improve L. For a more detailed discussion, see Mokyr (1996). In some historical cases, consumption patterns did lead to high levels of health as an unintended by-product. Perhaps the best-known example is the heavy dependence of the prefamine Irish on potatoes, which produced a comparatively healthy and tall population despite the economy's appallingly low levels of income.

Third, there are few a priori constraints on A and ε and thus on the relation between X and $\hat{X}$. Consequently the effect of changes in A and ε on demand depends on F' as well as on prior levels of A and ε. In principle A could be negative, meaning that best-practice technology believes that a particular good, which is actually harmful, enhances health (e.g., the smoking of tobacco was widely prescribed by seventeenth century doctors; marijuana, in our own age, may be an example of the reverse). It is possible for A to be positive yet $A - \varepsilon$ negative (when folk "wisdom" overrides the knowledge of scientists). The reverse is equally likely: folk wisdom long advocated the use of garlic and red wine as health-enhancing products, and only recently has science begun to catch on. It is thus conceivable that ε is negative, in which case (assuming $A < 1$) consumers are actually doing better than they would be by following the recommendations of best-practice technology. This can also occur when health-enhancing practices are adopted for extraneous reasons (e.g., diet restrictions based on religious considerations). Fourth, this setup shows that health could be improving even without any increase in $A - \varepsilon$, simply because income went up and with it the quantities of health-enhancing goods consumed. This is not necessarily the case, however: rising income does not guarantee an increasing L. For this to occur, we have to assume that

---

9. This would occur if, for all X_i^* which maximize utility, the following condition happened to hold:

$$\frac{\partial U}{\partial L} \frac{\partial L}{\partial X_i} + \frac{\partial U}{\partial X_i} = P_i,$$

where P_i is the full price of X_i (including time cost).

10. This is *not* an "optimum" in the sense that a consumer who consumes the "right" amount of X_i (in that $F'(X_i) = 0$) may still improve her health by shifting consumption from X_i to X_j if $F'(X_j) > 0$.

$$\sum_i \frac{\partial F_i}{\partial X_i} \frac{\partial X_i}{\partial Y} > 0,$$

that is, that the correlation between income elasticity and the health-enhancing effect of all goods together is positive. This is not invariably the case: many goods were desirable but health-impairing (such as alcohol, urban living, prostitution, or tobacco) and others were healthy but had negative income elasticities (potatoes).[11]

The environment variable, E, can similarly be decomposed into a purely exogenous element (such as changes in weather) and a policy-dependent environmental element (changes in local public goods). Converting resources into life-extending public goods itself involves a technology and provides another channel through which changes in knowledge can affect life expectancy. Thus

(4) $$E = E_1 + E_2$$

where E_1 is purely exogenous, and

(5) $$E_2 = \sum_i (B_i - \phi_i) G_i(Z_i)$$

constrained by $\sum P_i Z_i = T$, where the Z's are goods purchased by the government, the G's the "true" function that maps the Z's onto the environment, T the total tax revenues, B the best-practice technology to convert local public good i into improved health for all members of the community, and ϕ the gap between the best-practice technology and the one actually used by the local authority. Equation (5) is thus the public sector analogue of equation (3). Again, quite a number of health-enhancing public works occurred at low levels of B and were by-products of other projects, as in the case where the local government adopted drainage plans (for land reclamation) which had the unintended side effect of eliminating malaria-carrying mosquitoes. Many years before the germ theory, governments had considerable success with health-enhancing public projects, such as the campaign against plague.[12]

There are two sources of market failure in the supply of health-enhancing goods. The public sector has a role in producing the health-enhancing goods Z_i themselves, because the Z's, unlike the X's, cannot be produced efficiently by the single household. This is because of large fixed costs and free-rider problems in public works and because of the inherent problem of externalities

---

11. Furthermore, an increase in wages increases the opportunity cost of time and thus increases the cost of household work, an important input into the L function. The income effect of higher earnings may work in the same direction. It is possible that an increase in income will thus increase the demand for leisure and lead to a withdrawal of household labor from the home and to the purchase of substitutes that are not as effective in maintaining health. Increased use of day-care centers may be a good example of such an effect of a rise in income.

12. During the antiplague campaigns in the sixteenth and seventeenth centuries, physicians were made to wear long tunics to protect themselves against the evil vapors and miasmas that were thought to cause the disease. These coats also happened to protect them against the flea bites that transmitted the disease—an inadvertent by-product of the strategy (Cipolla 1992, 55).

in infectious disease. Furthermore, knowledge as used here is itself a public good, in that it is costly to produce but costless to transfer to another user. In other words, A is a public good because much of the cost of discovering and evaluating new recipes is fixed. Similarly, the public sector has an important function in the diffusion of A. It is not surprising that governments and other public bodies played an important role in supporting health-related research and education. Even if the X's that entered the household production function in equation (3) were purely private goods, the knowledge necessary to transform them into L was not.[13]

This formulation abstracts from the historical reality in a number of obvious respects. First, it makes no distinction between the household and the individual. In actual historical experience, the household made decisions and allocations that affected a collection of individuals in different ways, and complex bargaining may have been involved to determine how the X's would be allocated. This is especially important because the new recipes of cleanliness and good housekeeping tended to be costly in terms of time, and this time cost was disproportionately borne by women (Cowan 1983). Second, it abstracts from interhousehold externalities. In an age of highly contagious disease and shared kitchen and toilet facilities, neighborhood effects were of substantial importance. In effect, these would introduce the X's consumed by one household as arguments in the equation for L of another. Third, when industrialization caused more and more individuals to spend large amounts of time outside their homes, in workplaces, L was affected by the working environment as well, an effect that can be included in the shadow price of leisure. Fourth, by migrating between rural and urban environments, individuals could indirectly choose among different values of E_1 or E_2. Urban environments were, on the whole, far more noisome than rural areas, and the urbanization in this era clearly retarded the mortality decline. Finally, the analysis above abstracts from the often complex dynamic relation between some of the X's and L: while salmonella poisoning occurs within a few hours of exposure, some parasites do not cause symptoms until months later, and resistance to tuberculosis can take years to build up. Eating raw cabbage reduces the probability of developing colon cancer decades later. Such lags may make it difficult for a household decision maker to draw inferences about A and thus may be responsible for the persistence of large ε's. It is tempting to incorporate the dynamic aspects by including a set of different time periods and a discount factor, to weigh the future less than the present and to account for the probability of not surviving the next period. This discount factor itself has an interesting interpretation: as life expectancy improves in society as a whole, each consumer will believe that

13. Insofar as the government produces public goods at the demand of political groups, we may define a third area of knowledge, namely what the individuals in these groups know about the value of B. Changes in their perception of B may lead to growing pressure on the government to produce certain Z's.

she has a greater probability of survival. The discount factor will fall and as a result the consumer may wish to participate more in life-enhancing efforts. Many of the X's are interpreted as investments, as consumption today may affect health many years in the future (Grossman 1972). Yet life expectancy *itself* determines simultaneously the subjective rate of discount, producing positive feedback in the investment in health.

Until about 1750, the pattern of health technology and consumption might be roughly described as long periods in which A fluctuated but in the long haul followed a stationary process with a mean value not much above zero. The complete lack of understanding in premodern society of the nature of disease and the ability of the body to resist it led to an amorphous body of largely erroneous medical knowledge and a huge and highly diverse body of folk wisdom and old wives' sayings about good diet, child care, and other recipes. It is far from obvious whether, in preindustrial Europe, the techniques practiced by official medical science or by folk wisdom should be described as best practice. Formal medicine after 1700 was increasingly subject to radical new approaches that purported to produce a monocausal explanation of disease and suggested cure-all remedies. Such medical messiahs often gained huge followings which melted away as fast as they appeared. Precisely because the medical profession was so severely fractured, it is, in fact, impossible to define best-practice technology, and distinctions between quackery, medicine, and folk wisdom are largely anachronistic.[14] It is quite likely that some traditional herbal treatments and placebo effects gave the knowledge of "wise women" a positive value of A. Yet their ability to fight devastating infections such as pneumonia and diphtheria was obviously limited, and many of the home medicines recommended must have been hard to carry out in addition to having been useless.[15]

The understanding of the nature of disease and the realization of the interaction between consumption and health gradually increased in the nineteenth century, and A and ε started to creep up. Then followed, with long delays, a decline in ε as the new knowledge became accepted. One example of these

14. One example will serve to illustrate this principle: A Scottish physician by the name of John Brown (1735–88) revolutionized the medicine of his age with Brownianism, a system which postulated that all diseases were the result of over- or underexcitement of the neuromuscular system by the environment. Brown was no enthusiast for bleeding; instead he treated all his patients with mixtures of opium, alcohol, and highly seasoned foods. His popularity was international: Benjamin Rush brought his system to America, and in 1802 his controversial views elicited a riot among medical students in Göttingen, requiring troops to quell it. A medical revolutionary in an age of radical changes, his influence is a good example of the difficulty contemporaries had in selecting among alternative techniques and of the enormous possibilities for failure in this area (Brown was asserted to have killed more people than the French Revolution and the Napoleonic Wars combined).

15. One wonders about the recommendation for a cure for whooping cough: drink water from the skull of a bishop, if available. An alternative was to catch a fish, hold its head in the patient's mouth, and return it live to the river so it would take the disease with it. For a list of such examples, see, e.g., Gordon (1993).

changes was the growing realization in Enlightenment Europe that somehow dirt was a cause of disease, an attitude that eventually resulted in the hygienic movement of the Victorian age (Riley 1987). Through much of the eighteenth century, enlightened officials tried to clean up urban environments, "struggling against the thrifty complacency of the inhabitants, unless an epidemic struck" (McManners 1985, 43). Another example is the growing support for breast-feeding by biological mothers instead of artificial feeding or the use of wet nurses; this practice was vociferously advocated by Jean-Jacques Rousseau, among others. It took many decades until the recipes implied by these movements filtered down to the bulk of the population. The slowly changing attitude toward cigarette smoking in the modern Western world is perhaps the best-known example of such diffusion lags in our time.

4.3 Best-Practice Techniques and Their Diffusion

The idea of a best-practice technique in this context can only be defined ex post, with the knowledge and tools now available to us. The definition of equation (2) makes this inevitable, and although even today we do not know exactly the shape of that equation, we certainly know more than people did in the past. The modern scholar must try to sort out what seems in retrospect the "best practice."[16] During much of the nineteenth century, however, it was impossible for contemporaries to identify the best-practice medical knowledge for the purpose of household decisions. As we have seen, there were widely divergent views among scientists and physicians on the nature of disease and therefore on what constituted a healthy lifestyle. Rather than an accepted best-practice technology, there were many different competing recipes, traditions, and fads, and confused consumers often had to make difficult choices on the contradictory recommendations of contagionists and anticontagionists, germ theorists and anti–germ theorists, nurses, midwives, patent medicine salespeople, apothecaries, nutrition "specialists," and quacks.[17] Indeed, the decline in ε can be interpreted not only as the diffusion of knowledge of new recipes and techniques, but also in part as the improved ability to select among these competing alternatives.

16. Thus breast-feeding and aseptic surgery can be defined as best-practice techniques, whereas bloodletting must be regarded as a useless procedure against fever despite its popularity and viability. A good practice in case of diarrhea is to keep up a *high* rather than a *low* level of liquid. Administering laxatives, emetics, and large quantities of opiates were by and large useless or harmful medical practices, and anticontagionist theories of disease were erroneous. It is again only in retrospect that we can determine, similarly, that fresh foods and lemon juice were a good preventive measure against scurvy whereas relieving congestion and ventilating seamen's quarters were not.

17. Certain fads, like Horace Fletcher's theory that health was enhanced by chewing each mouthful at least one hundred times (which was adopted enthusiastically by, among others, economist Irving Fisher and novelist Henry James), survived into the twentieth century despite their scientific uselessness.

There are two major differences between the diffusion of new best-practice technologies among competitive firms and the diffusion of best-practice technology among homemakers.[18] First, households do not compete directly with each other, so the standard mechanism which forces firms to adopt better techniques or risk being competed away does not hold. In fact, even if the information is known to households, there is no guarantee that they will change their behavior. Instead, households will adopt a new recipe if they can be *persuaded* that it works and that it is worth the price and inconvenience. Persuasion, of course, involves theory, evidence, and rhetoric and in that regard the adoption and diffusion of new knowledge is quite different from that in production technology. Second, access to outside information is often more difficult for households than for firms (due to increasing returns in information acquisition and processing), and this is compounded by the inherent complexity of the information at hand.[19] From a statistical point of view, both firms and households need to assess the effect of a factor while holding others constant when evaluating a new technique, adjusting for omitted variables and unobservables and other inference problems. A firm can learn from other firms and from technical literature; when those sources run out it can learn by updating its private information set after each production run and by drawing statistical inferences from production data. By contrast, if the household wishes to make inferences about the effect of certain consumption patterns on survival probabilities, it may not have enough degrees of freedom as long as it learns primarily from its own experience, where it is confined to a small number of observations on mortality.

How did scientists and civil servants determine what the best-practice recipes were, and how did they convey this knowledge to consumers? In this regard, the past two centuries have witnessed a true revolution. Until the end of the eighteenth century, much medical knowledge rested on the obiter dicta of a small number of authorities. Diseases were believed to be caused by chemical imbalances in the human body and health was maintained by moderation. Consequently, even those writers who were genuinely interested in public health often confounded sound medical advice with sanctimonious moralizing and preaching against "intemperance" and "debauchery" (e.g., Frank [1786] 1976, 153–60). The modern mind, with its optimistic belief in learning and rationality, has difficulty understanding how concepts such as the humoral theory of disease survived and were accepted, at least by the practitioners of medicine, for so long despite their contradiction of observation and despite merciless attacks by critics such as Paracelsus. Best-practice science lacked the modern concept of the specific disease with a unique causation, and conse-

---

18. For a theoretical discussion much concerned with this issue of "social learning" see Ellison and Fudenberg (1993).

19. Households may have an incentive to promote others' health awareness if they believe it has positive externalities to their own health status. The idea of contagion should, therefore, enhance public persuasion efforts and it is not surprising that during epidemics such efforts increased.

quently it was not best practice, at least not ex post. The bulk of the population before the nineteenth century wisely ignored what formal medical science had to tell them about the relationship between consumption and health and often relied on traditional folk wisdom, embodied in proverbs and home remedies. The easy accessibility of folk knowledge meant low values of ε but also— with some notable exceptions—low values of A.

The Enlightenment in Europe led to the discovery of a tool that was to overturn this persistent but inefficient system. The collection of *data* and their use in detecting empirical regularities about health gradually became common practice in western Europe during the late eighteenth and early nineteenth centuries (Rosen 1955; Porter 1986). Suddenly large samples of organized and systematic medical information started to become available through "tables of death," or nosologies. Political arithmetic first emerged in the late seventeenth century, and the term "statistics" appears around 1800. At first statistics was a political tool, to chart general economic and social laws with little impact on medical practice narrowly defined (Porter 1986). Yet within a few decades, statistics and numerical methods began to challenge age-old practices in clinical care.[20] The sanitary (or hygienist) movement used statistics as a basis for recommendations about nutrition, cleanliness, housing, water supply, cooking, infant care, and so on. In the 1830s British doctors published a variety of reports on "physical causes of sickness to which the poor are particularly exposed," culminating in the vastly influential summary in the 1842 Chadwick Report. Hygienists regarded statistics as irrefutable facts which demanded action (Wohl 1983, 145). By 1850, for the first time perhaps, something of an amorphous consensus of hygienists began to emerge, and the new Victorian gospel of cleanliness and proper housekeeping took shape.[21] The sanitary movement grew in strength and claimed increasingly that it had found the "correct" levels of private and public consumption. In terms of our model, they raised the values of A and B. In France a parallel movement was spearheaded

20. Rusnock (1990) describes the use of crude statistical methods in evaluating smallpox inoculation during the eighteenth century. The development of statistical methods to test the efficacy of curative technology owed most to Pierre C. A. Louis who developed a "numerical method" for evaluating therapy and in about 1840 provided statistical proof that bloodletting was useless, leading to the gradual demise of this technique (Hudson 1983, 206). A few years later Ignaz Semmelweis observed, on the basis of significant differences in the mortality rate, that puerperal fever was caused by contaminated hands and could be reduced by doctors and attendants washing their hands in antiseptic solution. In Britain the use of statistics in the nineteenth century was pioneered by William Farr, superintendent of the statistical department of the Registrar General (Eyler 1979). After 1850, the use of statistics in public health became almost a rage: between 1853 and 1862 a quarter of all papers read at the Statistical Society of London were on public health and vital statistics (Wohl 1983, 145).

21. The most famous triumph of the "empirical" approach to preventive medicine was the discovery of the waterborne sources of cholera in 1854 by John Snow and William Farr through the quantitative analysis of the addresses of the deceased. At the same time, William Budd demonstrated the contagious nature of typhoid fever and its mode of transmission and successfully stamped out a typhoid epidemic in Bristol.

by the journal *Annales d'hygiène publique et de médecine légale,* edited by René Villermé and his colleagues.[22]

The purely empirical statistical inferences on which these recommendations were based are still a widely used methodology in modern studies of public and private health, even though statistical sophistication has increased a great deal. Whether statistically sophisticated or not, these mid-nineteenth-century methods lacked a model or modus operandi that associated behavior with health effects. Dirt and congestion were known to be correlated with disease, but how and why the causal mechanism operated was unknown. It was an empirical regularity in search of a scientific theory.[23] In that regard, the medical research of Louis and Farr resembled Adolphe Quételet's work on crime and suicide. At times, empirical regularities led science astray, as in the belief (especially widespread in the case of cholera) that the correlation between weather and disease demonstrated the pathogenic character of fog and humidity.

Statistics and probability theory were important because they provided more than observations, they provided a mode of thinking. Especially thanks to the pathbreaking work of Quételet, people slowly learned to think in terms of probability rather than certainty, still largely a novelty in the nineteenth century. After all, the way equation (2) works is through probabilities: if we observe that $F' > 0$, what we really mean is that the conditional probability of contracting a disease given some X_i is higher than the probability given some higher X_i. But these probabilities are not zero nor one, and counterexamples might have obscured the regularities that the sanitarians appealed to.[24] Unlike physics or chemistry, the scientific laws determining private and public health were stochastic, and the implicit statistical models were poorly specified. Health technology was a stochastic science, and empirical work must allow both type I and type II errors. Even a very successful method will normally not work 100 percent of the time. Yet the notion that a few exceptions on either side did not disprove or prove a rule grew as people learned to interpret statistical data.

22. French mathematicians also worked on the theory underlying the use of such statistics. In 1837 Denis Poisson published his celebrated work on the probabilistic properties of jury voting. Three years later his student Jules Gavarret applied these results to public medicine, arguing for rigorous standards for hypothesis testing. Unfortunately, the medical leaders of the hygienic movement were not well trained in mathematics and biostatistics took many decades to develop.

23. Many of the statistical inquiries were undertaken by such freelancers as Henry Rumsey and Henry Mayhew. Another enthusiast for statistics was Florence Nightingale, a member of the Statistical Society of London for fifty years. It seems clear, however, that in the area of data collection the public sector had an advantage, and eventually parliamentary commissions and the Registrar General provided the hygienic movement with the most important pieces of its empirical basis (Hodgkinson 1968).

24. In a famous case, a conservative German doctor, Max Pettenkofer, drank a glass of cholera-infected water to refute the theory that the disease was transmitted through microorganisms in water.

The rhetorical force of statistics was relentless, yet it was ultimately limited. Just as statistical studies without much of a model in our own time have persuaded millions to change smoking and eating habits but have left many more unconvinced, the European household after 1830 was increasingly subject to a barrage of statistics and recommendations based on them that were meant to make civil servants and households see the light and change their consumption bundles to improve their health. This barrage, however, eventually ran into diminishing returns. Nineteenth-century empirical data were deficient in ways fully understood by such contemporary writers as Henry Rumsey (1875). Most of the inferences were based on simple tabulations, had no controls, and almost never recognized the distinction between partial and total effects or worried about statistical significance, let alone endogeneity and simultaneity biases. Consequently the movement ran into the dilemma that although it recognized that a cluster of social problems—poverty, urban congestion, lack of sanitary facilities, bad nutrition—was correlated with high mortality rates and epidemics, it did not know how and why this was the case; consequently it ended up recommending the elimination of poverty and slums as the only possible remedy for disease. Medical statistics turned out to be a more tricky subject than early enthusiasts like Louis had envisaged (Porter 1986, 238).

All the same, the data gathered by the sanitarians changed best-practice thinking about the importance of the environment to health. The historical issue is how these changes in A filtered down to change consumption patterns. In other words, the decline in ε required more than exposure to data, it required inducing people to change their behavior. Persuasion was difficult because by definition any shift in the allocation of the X's involved either an expense or some other kind of adjustment by the consumer, either in terms of time and convenience or in terms of changes in consumption. In interpreting the change in household behavior, it is important to realize that equation (3) reflects *full* prices, including the cost in terms of time. Much of the household production function involved time as much as money: for example, taking a shower today takes no more than ten minutes; a bath in the middle of the nineteenth century, in the absence of indoor plumbing, involved elaborate work in carrying and warming the water and disposing of it later on.[25] The same is true for scores of other household chores, from washing dishes to proper child feeding. In the final analysis, the choices were made by households constrained by budgets and guided by relative prices, but otherwise free to allocate their resources as they saw fit. Short of coercion and the manipulation of relative prices through taxes, the best that those who had seen the light could do was to inform and persuade.

25. Even with bathrooms, however, the amount of work implied by the new household technology was large. As Cowan (1983, 88) remarks, cleaning a bathroom was heavy work and it had to be performed thoroughly and frequently "if the health of the family was to be maintained." Though cleaning technologies improved, the time devoted to cleaning increased, and this time has to be factored into the budget constraint.

How did social reformers, scientists, statisticians, civil servants, teachers, and medical people persuade the population to change its habits?

There were basically three modes of persuasion, then and now. One, as noted, was pure empiricism. A second mode of persuasion was what could be best termed "social control." Without being justified in detail, certain patterns of behavior were turned into social virtues and customs. The tools of this form of social control were the popular press (including such magazines as *Good Housekeeping*), cookbooks, domestic advice books and manuals, schools, the church, exhibitions, and well-meaning organizations run by middle-class ladies such as the Ladies' National Association for the Diffusion of Sanitary Knowledge (founded in 1857).[26] Sanitary missionaries started health campaigns to teach and instruct the ways of good hygiene and child care. Cleanliness was next to godliness, and certain patterns could be imposed on the population by subtle manipulation, falling in the gray area between persuasion and coercion. Furthermore, an effective mode of diffusion was imitation of the social customs of groups that were perceived to be higher up on the social ladder.[27] The social prestige of the early leaders of the hygienic movement helped them gain and persuade audiences almost regardless of the content of their message; the effectiveness of rhetoric is not independent of the social status of the speaker. Later in the century, philanthropists were reinforced by salesmen and advertisers. Commercial interests selling household appliances and cleaning materials used fear, ambition, self-doubt, and every other human weakness to peddle products that were supposed to keep the house clean and its inhabitants healthy.

Yet the most effective weapon in the arsenal of the reformers was a *model*, simple and powerful, that would underpin the empirical regularities discerned by statistics and explain disease as a consequence of household recipes and of the quantities of goods consumed. The importance of such a model was not so much that it could suggest to doctors new medical methods to treat patients (although eventually it did) but that it cleared up the confusion about the best-practice recipes for the household and for the providers of public goods. A model that explained how diseases were caused had immense rhetorical power: it convinced households to choose bundles as similar as possible to the ones recommended by what soon became the undisputedly best practice. It is the argument of this paper that there has been only one macroinvention in

26. Between 1857 and 1881 this association distributed a million and a half tracts loaded with advice on pre- and postnatal care, spreading the gospel of soap and water, and the evidence is that in the late Victorian period the poor were receptive to these volunteers (Wohl 1983, 36–37). For a recent treatment from a feminist perspective, see Williams (1991).

27. One of the poignant documents illustrating indoctrination and social control of housewives by the dogma of cleanliness can be found in the autobiographical notes appended to Cowan (1983). Roberts's (1990) autobiographical book on life in the classic slum of Salford depicts clearly the toil of working-class Edwardian wives and mothers struggling to keep up to the middle-class Victorian standards of cleanliness.

the determination of A and B that has really had that effect: the discovery of the germ theory of disease (see also Spree 1988, 122). Pasteur's model cleared up the confusion, explained the causes of infectious disease, reconciled miasma theory with contagionism, and provided a convincing, and within a short time widely accepted, theory of disease which had far-reaching implications for the best-practice technologies of households and the public sector. It should be stressed that by the term "Pasteur revolution" we really mean a multinational joint effort between 1880 and 1900, led by Germans such as Robert Koch, Albert Neisser, Karl Eberth, Theodor Escherich, and Albert Fränkel, in which pathogenic organisms were discovered at the average rate of one a year. This multinational scientific effort, despite some dead ends, was larger than the germ theory alone and provided a coherent and powerful theory of infectious disease. Moreover, the work of Metchnikoff and Behring on a phagocytosis supplemented the germ theory by showing why in many cases infection and exposure did not lead to symptoms, a favorite argument of the opponents of the germ theory. Similarly, between 1890 and 1900 a series of experiments (most notably by Hallock Park and Alfred Beebe) established the reality of healthy human carriers of infectious diseases, thus filling in another important hole in the logical structure of infectious disease.

In terms of our model, the germ theory has significance in terms of both A and ε. With a few exceptions, such as pasteurization and the methods of antisepsis and asepsis, it did not immediately supply a whole net set of recipes. Nor did it right away provide a cure for any disease, though the diphtheria vaccine came quite early. Above all, it made it possible for households to better select from among existing techniques, reshuffle their resources, and adjust their consumption bundles to reflect the new knowledge. How many households were fully aware of and persuaded by the bacteriological revolution is of course hard to determine.[28] Long before Pasteur, household behavior had been influenced by teachers, journalists, public servants, and physicians calling for improved standards of hygiene in households. Now these admonitions were reinforced by new and powerful rhetorical ammunition. This process of persuasion inevitably moved slowly.[29] The new bacteriology, however, also affected the elite and the role models of the middle class and intelligentsia. As long as these people understood the implications of household choices in terms of the new bacteriology and could translate the new knowledge into advice and social codes of behavior, the positive effects of changes in consumption on life expectancy could be realized. Rather than statistics or admonitions, homemak-

---

28. Compounding the ambiguities of persuasion was the fact that some of the leading sanitarians stubbornly resisted the germ theory (Stevenson 1955).

29. Reading through the *Popular Science Monthly* gives an interesting notion of how the ideas of Pasteur were spread among the educated laymen and of how the old and new paradigms fought over the minds of the public. An article on bacteria was published in 1874 and two public speeches given by Pasteur were translated and published in the magazine in 1875, but in 1877 there was still a lengthy article on spontaneous generation—as if Pasteur had never written.

ers were faced with a clear-cut villain, a concrete if invisible parasite which caused disease, misery, and death. The smoking gun handed over by Pasteur, with its powerful rhetorical image, was as important as a means of propaganda as in its inherent scientific value.

Pasteur was not the first to argue for the microbial explanation of infectious disease.[30] But unlike his predecessors, Pasteur succeeded in changing medical science, public health, and household behavior. The new theories persuaded those who set the tone that microbes caused disease, with all the epidemiological implications thereof. As argued forcefully by Latour (1988), Pasteur told the sanitarians what they wanted to hear by telling them why the recipes they had been recommending all along were by and large correct.[31] We would add that his model, as well as the pioneering experimental techniques that confirmed it and permitted the identification of specific pathogens, vastly augmented the persuasiveness of the sanitary arguments and expanded their domain.

Pasteur's discoveries and their impact on the choices made by households and civil servants also illustrate a pervasive phenomenon in the history of technology. It is commonplace to observe that techniques can be employed by firms and households who do not have the faintest clue *why* they work. As we have seen, in the century before Pasteur, hygienists and sanitarians made many recommendations that were consistent with the germ theory without any understanding of the epidemiological and bacteriological underpinnings. These recommendations made some contribution to the decline in mortality before 1870, though it is hard to know with any precision how large this contribution was. The weakness of recipes without a sound scientific base is that not knowing why something works also means that it is hard to identify what will *not* work. Consequently, the sanitarians often made recommendations that were erroneous and at times downright harmful, thus reducing their credibility.[32] Although

30. The idea of germ-caused infection was first proposed by Girolamo Fracastoro in his *De contagione* in 1546. In 1687 Giovanni Bonomo explicitly proposed that diseases were transmitted because minute living creatures that he had been able to see through a microscope passed from one person to another (Reiser 1978, 72). Bonomo's observations and the microscopy of pioneers like Leeuwenhoek ran into skepticism as they were irreconcilable with accepted humoral doctrine. The great chemist, Justus von Liebig, noted in 1845 that attributing a causal effect to microbes was akin to arguing that the rapid flow of the Rhine was caused by the movement of the water mills of Mainz (Hudson 1983, 154). As late as the 1860s, at least four incompatible "theories" of infection can be discerned (Crellin 1968).

31. Latour (1988) argues that the success of Pasteur's discoveries can be explained by his ideas being coopted by the hygienists, who realized that his discovery underpinned the policies they had been fighting for all along. To a large extent this is an accurate view of Pasteur's amazing scientific success, but Latour does not fully credit the scientific elegance and completeness of the new bacteriology and its unprecedented success in verifying its findings through experimental work. Tomes (1990, 414) and Easterlin (1995, 400) both stress the basic complementarity of the sanitarian movement and the germ theory.

32. Attempts to clean up urban cesspools often led to the dumping of raw sewage into rivers, replacing one set of diseases with another (Mathias 1979, 284 n. 18; Szreter 1988, 20–21). The "miasmatic" theory of disease (which held that infectious disease was spread by bad air) espoused

the post-Pasteur era had its share of mistakes as well, they were discovered quickly and corrected.

Our conclusions are similar to those of Preston and Haines (1991, 209), who note that changes in know-how were the principal factors in twentieth-century advances in survival. Their evidence suggests a somewhat later occurrence, placing most of the effect in the decades after 1895. The differences they detect between the United States and Britain (chap. 5) suggest that this time frame may be peculiar to America. In any event, while they suggest that such know-how may have been important, they do not discuss in detail the technological and conceptual innovations that led to the changes in recipes. It is to those that we now turn.

4.4   Health and Consumption

Below we survey the main changes in recipes brought about by the germ theory of disease.

4.4.1   Food

The changes in recipes regarding food occur in two dimensions: one is the avoidance of disease through a properly germ-free consumption environment and ingredients; the other is a balanced diet containing the proper elements of fresh foods, proteins, and minerals. Pasteur, of course, did not have to teach people not to eat spoiled foods. Some food preservation methods, such as pickling, drying, smoking, and preserving with sugar, were known long before the Industrial Revolution. To that was added in the nineteenth century the technique of vacuum canning (first explored by Appert in 1796). The effects of canned foods on overall health were at first modest because canned food was expensive (the cans were handmade) and of low quality, and it was thus sold largely to ships and the military. Without an understanding of microbiology, killing the bacteria in the cans was largely a matter of trial and error, and it was not until Pasteur that the principles of food canning were understood and its benefits fully appreciated. In 1870, the heated autoclave made by Albert Fryer was based on the explicit idea that heating preserved food by destroying germs (Thorne 1986, 94). The bacteriology of canned foods was further advanced by Americans in the late 1890s when it was realized that vacuum packing was not necessary as long as the air in the can had been properly heated (144–49). Two other inventions are of importance here: dehydration of food (by Gail Borden in 1851) and the gradual introduction of industrial refrigeration.

---

by most hygienists made many positive suggestions but also recommended permanent ventilation, the burning of sulphur, and the dispersing of acids to counteract pathogenic stenches (Riley 1987, 100). The influential German physician Max Pettenkofer fought the microbial theory of disease tooth and nail, yet he was responsible for the implementation of radical public health measures to prevent the spreading of infectious disease in the city of Munich (Goubert 1989, 61).

An important consequence of the acceptance of the germ theory was the fact that food could now be inspected and judged either good or bad by objective and scientific standards. Bermondsey's Medical Officer of Health (Brown 1908) describes in his annual report a case in which five barges of rice tipped into the Thames and lay in the water through three tides. After retrieving and drying the rice, the owner asked to sell it. It was examined and found to be contaminated, and the request was refused. Prior to the discovery of germs it is not clear that such a decision would have been made. Practically every industrialized nation experienced governmental regulation when it assumed responsibility for the purity of its food supply, as exemplified in the Pure Food and Drug Act of 1906.

Of particular interest here are the changing recipes regarding milk, because the groups consuming it (babies and toddlers) were high-risk groups. The information here was complex and choices were often hard. Even after the connection between bad milk and infant mortality was made, without detailed knowledge of the mechanism that led from milk to mortality, attempts to break this linkage often went astray. There was widespread concern about the adulteration of milk, which by being watered down or skimmed could deprive children of much needed nutrients. Second, there was the growing awareness after 1900 that contaminated milk caused infant diarrhea, a major cause of infant mortality. Third, there was a growing suspicion that milk could transmit other diseases, either from the cow or from a variety of sources en route from the dairy to the kitchen. Tuberculosis was identified in milk at an early stage (1888), and the presence of other diseases such as typhoid and scarlet fever was also suspected. For two decades American health organizations saw the adulteration of milk as the source of the problem (Meckel 1990, 62–70). The theory was that watered or skimmed milk lacked some of the necessary chemical components the infant needs, a theory that led to a shower of legislative effort to stop this adulteration. Between 1880 and 1895 twenty-three American municipalities passed ordinances governing the sale of milk, and by 1905 thirty-two states, the District of Columbia, Hawaii, and Puerto Rico had adopted and were enforcing chemical standards (69).[33] This flurry of legislation only helped combat sickness to a limited extent; by prohibiting adulteration of milk it limited contamination of milk that was mixed with contaminated water, but in and of itself it was not enough to ensure a pure milk supply. The various milk acts did have an important impact on future food and milk acts, for they asserted the right of a city to regulate its milk supply even if the milk originated outside city limits. Ambiguities and complexities abound: the effect of legislation and the improvement in the milk supply may have persuaded

33. Adulteration of all foods was feared, and although major efforts were directed against the adulteration of milk, there was legislation regarding other food products too. In 1881 New York passed a state law against food adulteration which was followed by similar laws in Michigan, New Jersey, Illinois, and Massachusetts (Kramer 1948, pt. 1).

some women to switch earlier to cow's milk which, even when improved, remained inferior to breast-feeding.

The Pasteur revolution provided a mechanism to explain how milk was responsible for infant mortality, but it took decades until the exact implications were worked out. Milk preservation has always been a central problem of public health, to the point that fresh milk has been explicitly discouraged as a food for children. Fresh milk ("warm from the cow") was of course unspoiled but could carry the tuberculosis bacilli that spread bovine tuberculosis. Pasteur pointed out in the 1860s that heating milk could eliminate bacteria, effectively destroying mistaken theories of spontaneous generation (Thorne 1986, 138–42), but it took years until these insights were translated into widespread consumption of safe milk. In both the United States and England, books on infant care and infant feeding placed the emphasis on the chemical composition of milk, comparing human milk to that of cows, asses, and goats (Routh 1876; Cheadle 1889; Cautley 1897). Subsequent books did incorporate the new knowledge on fermentation (Cheadle 1896) and even added whole new sections on microorganisms in milk (Cautley 1897). In France, too, the specialists were at odds: while microbiologists recognized the danger of milk serving as a medium for bacteria and the need to sterilize milk by heating and boiling, doctors resisted this recommendation for most of the 1880s (Rollet-Echalier 1990, 173).

Milk could be made safe using a variety of techniques (Rollet-Echalier 1990, 175). The most efficient was "sterilization," an industrial technique which consisted of heating the milk under pressure at a temperature beyond boiling and then rapidly cooling it. Pasteurization, which was cheaper, was little more than a means of preserving fresh milk somewhat longer and was widely felt to harm the flavor. By about 1910 the proportion of pasteurized milk in major American towns was between 15 and 20 percent (Preston and Haines 1991, 23). Finally, households had the option of boiling their own milk for three to four minutes, which in most cases made it safe for use. Yet boiling cow's milk, despite its obvious microbiological advantages, was unpopular. Part of its unpopularity stemmed from the different taste it had (due to the caramelization of the milk sugar), but of equal importance was the belief that boiling milk reduced its nutritional properties.[34] By the 1890s bottled and pasteurized milk were available in London, and even if only the medical profession and a few educated families were aware of the gross bacterial infection of milk which contributed to infant diarrhea and tuberculosis, "this growing inter-

34. For example, sterilized milk was thought to cause scurvy (Apple 1987, 8). This led baby food companies (e.g., Doliber-Goodale) to promote the mixing of their food with fresh milk, which was claimed to be more wholesome. As late as 1912, half the members of the American Pediatric Society still believed that pasteurized milk was harmful to babies because it deprived them of essential nutrients (Meckel 1990, 82). Cheadle writes, "Always have the milk boiled. . . . This is the first grand rule I would lay down. Nurses will fight against it, and mothers object, perhaps, for there is a common prejudice against it; they say it is less nourishing and that it is binding . . . that it is constipating . . . that children don't like it" (1889, 54–55).

est in hygiene encouraged consumers to be suspicious of 'cheap' milk and to favor larger firms with cooling depots in country districts, with steam powered plant for washing churns" (Whetham 1964, 378–79). Vertical imitation and persuasion were the diffusion mechanisms: the knowledge filtered down very slowly from the educated classes to the middle classes and from there through the working classes.[35] The demographic benefits of the Pasteur revolution thus took decades to be realized. Dwork (1987a, 1987b) and Rollet-Echalier (1990) have documented in detail the difficulties in cleaning up the milk supply in Britain and France and have demonstrated how slow and halting progress was in the years prior to the First World War.

From the 1890s on, physicians played an important role in spreading the use of better-quality milk by calling for the establishment of local milk supplies to minimize infection and for regulation of milk production, handling, and transportation (Apple 1987, 57). The movement in the United States was led by Henry Coit, a Newark, N.J., physician, and led to the foundation of medical milk commissions, in which physicians set strict bacterial standards on the milk coming out of dairies. In a number of American towns, milk depots were established to supply mothers with clean milk. The first was founded in New York and was followed by similar institutions in Chicago and Philadelphia (59). Although the number of infants served by this system was small, such institutions helped spread the gospel that clean, pasteurized milk was necessary to ensure healthy babies. Apple surveys other methods by which the importance of clean milk was spread in the United States; these included such journals as *Ladies Home Journal* and *Good Housekeeping,* pamphlets (including the federal government's infant care manual that was circulated among the poor), women's groups and meetings, and more (102–3).

Condensed milk and powdered milk, invented in the 1860s, became widely available in the first decade of the twentieth century. It is therefore tempting to relate qualitative improvements in milk supply to the decline in infant mortality which resumes in Britain after 1900 (Beaver 1973). Such inferences may be rash (Tranter 1985, 80–81; Woods, Watterson, and Woodward 1989, 120). The adoption of safer milk was clearly gradual and was still far from complete in 1900 when the decline in infant mortality started.[36] Furthermore, buying condensed milk was not a sufficient condition for clean baby food. Buchanan (1985) points to the hazards involved in using condensed milk: the high sugar content of condensed milk attracted flies, and tins, often not finished in one feeding, were kept half full, unrefrigerated, and often uncovered until the next meal. Can openers were not available in every household and there is evidence

35. In books on infant care written by doctors and aimed at the professional classes, the boiling of milk was emphasized already in the 1880s (Cheadle 1889; Cautley 1897), but in the more popular books this emphasis is clear only in the early 1900s (Davies 1906; Cradock 1908).

36. A parliamentary commission reported in 1903 that in Finsbury 32 percent of the milk supply contained pus and 40 percent contained dirt. At the same time it was found that 10 percent of all cows produced tubercular milk.

that shopkeepers opened the tins for their customers. The net effect of using condensed milk may have been a higher infant mortality rate rather than a lower one (Ewbank and Preston 1990, 124).

4.4.2   Infant and Child Care

Infant mortality rates have traditionally been a good indicator of the household's ability to convert its consumption into health. Although it would seem at first glance that income would play a central role here, a more careful analysis reveals that the way this income and other household resources, such as the mother's labor and time, were spent was often of much greater importance than the budget constraint itself (Ewbank and Preston 1990, 142). In earlier societies, similarly, the deployment of household resources seems to be the pivotal variable. Imhof (1984) has demonstrated how the variability of infant mortality in Germany depended above all on the socioeconomic structure of society. In regions such as Bavaria where women worked outside the house or were for other reasons incapable of taking care of newborn babies, infant mortality remained high.

Much of our understanding in this area for the United States is due to an important paper by Ewbank and Preston (1990) and by the subsequent work of Preston and Haines (1991). In their view, it was a set of behavioral changes that brought down infant mortality. Whether mothers knew about the germ theory and were persuaded by it or not, they were, during the first years of the twentieth century, exposed to the practical implications of this theory. Mothers were seen as the "first line of defence against childhood disease" (Ewbank and Preston 1990, 119), and the germ theory "focused attention on the transmission of germs from person to person, including transmission within the household." Two components of infant care were stressed in the years 1900–1930: good infant feeding practices and the need for maintaining hygienic conditions in the home. Accompanying these messages was an increase in physical involvement and intervention. By 1906 good child care included such measures as removing children from households containing a person with tuberculosis, if at all possible (122). Infants were to be kept away from children with whooping cough and other infectious diseases. Such efforts were easier in big houses and were probably more common among wealthy households. A cheaper practice was hand washing, and this too was highly recommended during the first decades of the twentieth century. We should note, though, that even such mundane activities as washing hands carried a price before a clean, reliable, and convenient water supply was available.

Advice and education on child care spread through the same sources that promoted the use of sterilized milk: magazines, household books, pamphlets, and milk depots. Ewbank and Preston (1990, 128) note that for the milk depots the distribution of clean subsidized milk may have been only a means to a wider goal of spreading information about hygiene and of changing mothers' day-to-day child-care activities. Other countries had similar organizations:

the Royal New Zealand Society for the Health of Women and Children, Lady Home Visitors, Baby Welcomes, and Infant Consultations in England and *Goutte de Lait* in France. All these organizations aimed to influence intra-household decisions based on the insights of the new bacteriology: choosing breast-feeding over bottle-feeding when possible, heating milk, keeping infant food germ free, spending time and effort in keeping the house clean, and isolating sick household members.

The argument made by Preston and his collaborators about behavioral changes can be interpreted as a change in taste or as one in relative prices or income. In terms of the model presented earlier, a third possibility emerges: that the germ theory constituted a dramatic increase in A which then filtered down to the population through a variety of the mechanisms mentioned above, thus reducing ε. In child care, as in other aspects of household behavior, the new information implicit in an increase in the $(A - \varepsilon)$ term meant a redeployment of household resources. And yet, the remarkable thing about infant mortality is that its decline seems to lag behind that of the rest of mortality and the diffusion of the new knowledge. The year 1900 seems to be the turning point (figs. 4.1 and 4.2). This is most striking in Britain, where infant mortality rates stayed stable and even rose slightly during the last third of the nineteenth century, fell steeply between 1900 and 1914, and underwent an accelerated further decline during the war and its aftermath (Dwork 1987b).[37] Almost identical movements can be observed for Prussia (Spree 1988, 37). The same steep decline in infant mortality in the 1900–1914 period can be observed for *every* country in western Europe, whereas in the previous forty years the movements had been erratic, uneven, and inconsistent even in neighboring countries, with the Netherlands and Sweden experiencing a consistent decline while Belgium and Denmark did not (figure 4.2). The conclusion must be that the germ theory as it emerged in the 1870s and 1880s was not a miracle theory that explained all and instantaneously converted the masses to the true faith of hygiene, but rather marked the beginning of a way of thinking that eventually would lead to further breakthroughs down the road. Pasteur's macroinvention did not attain its full impact until it was complemented by a host of microinventions. The cumulative force of the advances in bacteriology eventually had irresistible persuasive power, but clearly this process was drawn out over decades.

As in the history of technological change, there is a lag of decades between the original macroinvention and its effect on any kind of aggregate statistical data. A striking example of very persistent high levels of ε can be observed with regard to breast-feeding. The advantages that breast-feeding conferred

---

37. The rise in infant mortality at the end of the nineteenth century might have been due to a series of warm summers that increased the breeding of houseflies and therefore the instances of infant diarrhea (Buchanan 1985, 159–60). Woods, Watterson, and Woodward (1989) point out that infant mortality from causes other than diarrhea started to decline around the middle of the nineteenth century. Guha (1994) argues that the temporary increase in diarrhea is due more to a change in diagnosis than to a true change in morbidity patterns.

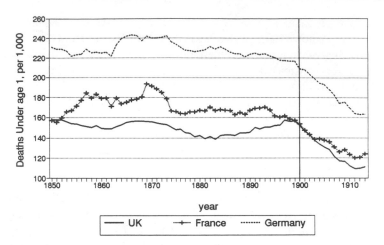

Fig. 4.1   Infant mortality rates, 1850–1914: five-year moving averages
Source: Mitchell (1975, 127–32 table B7).

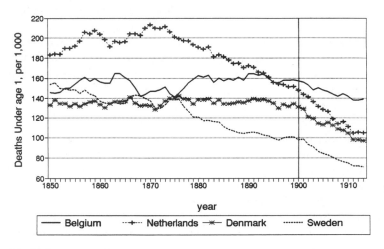

Fig. 4.2   Infant mortality rates, 1850–1914: various countries, five-year moving averages
Source: See fig. 4.1.

upon infants had been known for centuries.[38] Yet its adoption was uneven and halting, and the advantage in monetary cost of breast-feeding seems to have been more of a consideration than health. This is borne out by the German statistics: in the first decade of the twentieth century mothers whose husbands

38. The English physician and follower of Sydenham, Hans Sloane (1660–1753) noted that the ratio of mortality of dry-nursed to wet-nursed children was 3:1. Johann Peter Frank, whose influential book on "medical police" was widely read in the closing decades of the eighteenth century,

earned less than nine hundred Marks were 50 percent more likely to breast-feed their babies than mothers whose husbands made over three thousand Marks. Better-educated families weaned their babies at an earlier age (Spree 1988, app. tables 7, 12). Since in most other respects wealthier and better-educated families were experiencing lower infant mortality rates, this is an unexpected finding. Part of the reason for the long lags in the decline of ε may have been a failure to convince. Dwork maintains that while it had been recognized for many decades that breast-feeding was the most effective preventive measure against lethal attacks of childhood diarrhea, as late as the early twentieth century "the precise reason for this was absolutely unclear" (1987b, 36). The statistical evidence seemed irrefutable, but the mechanisms were poorly understood.[39] It stands to reason that wealthier mothers may have believed that the cause underlying the negative correlation between breast-feeding and infant mortality was the poor hygienic conditions in lower-class kitchens, which created health hazards with artificial feeding that did not apply to more expensive diets.[40] It is also possible, however, that the costs in terms of inconvenience were assessed to be higher among wealthier and better-educated ladies. The proportion of children ever breast-fed was increasing, however, no doubt in part due to the campaigns in favor of the practice. In 1910, about 75 percent of all German babies were ever breast-fed, a proportion which rose to about 95 percent in 1933 (Kintner 1987, 251).[41] Breast-feeding, of course, only reduced the occurrence of certain diseases, but the sudden dramatic decline in infant mortality after 1900 in most Western countries must have been related to the ever-growing propaganda to breast-feed babies.

Many years elapsed between Pasteur's macroinvention and the full understanding of its implications, and more time elapsed before these implications were accepted by those who had the most impact on child care: the mothers. This was understood by English social reformers who came to view the schools as the preferred place for teaching future mothers how to raise their children. Dyhouse (1981) describes a shift in the subjects taught to English working-

---

preached that there was no substitute for mother's milk for a newborn and pointed out that women tended to withdraw from nursing if pregnancies were unwanted (Frank [1786] 1976, 112–13). The most influential proponent of breast-feeding was Jean-Jacques Rousseau, in his *Emile*.

39. One of the most elegant and persuasive rhetorical devices was a bar diagram that showed the startling increase in the death of bottle-fed babies in the summer months, compared to a much smaller increase among breast-fed babies. The diagram was dubbed the "Eiffel Tower" because of its steepness (reproduced in Rollet-Echalier 1990, 465 and Dwork 1987b, 96).

40. The advantages conferred by breast-feeding persist, if in somewhat diminished form, with higher incomes. The average ratio in infant mortality between breast-fed and substitute-fed children for families earning less than 1500 Marks in Düsseldorf between 1905 and 1911 was 1:3.26 and for families earning over 1500 Marks 1:2.58 (Spree 1988, app. table 8).

41. On the basis of cross-sectional regressions for 1910, Kintner suggests that the impact of breast-feeding on infant mortality may have been less than is commonly thought and suggested by the high raw correlations between the two. As she does not control for income, and as income was negatively related to breast-feeding and infant mortality, her coefficients are downward biased and the actual effect of breast-feeding is larger than her equations suggest.

class girls. All through the nineteenth century there was a major emphasis on domestic subjects, but after 1870 the time and effort spent teaching needlework declined and the role of other, more health-related domestic subjects increased (89–90).[42] Originally parents were opposed to such classes being taught in school: mothers felt they could teach cooking just as well at home. As long as knowledge was stable it was possible to rely on mothers to pass household technology on to their daughters, but during periods of scientific advancement mothers were unfamiliar with best-practice technologies, and by having child-care classes in school future mothers were exposed to novel practices and information. After 1870 these classes became an important channel through which knowledge about germ theory and ideas of hygiene and child care were diffused. The teaching of domestic subjects continued to expand through the first decades of the twentieth century, when specific lessons on infant and child care were introduced (Dyhouse 1981, 95).[43] A number of books on infant care were written explicitly to help teachers and students in these new subjects (Davies 1906; Cradock 1908). These included chapters on infant bathing and clothing, infant and child diet, and care in case of accidents and sickness, and stressed cleanliness and hygiene throughout. These books used the persuasive force of the new bacteriology to the fullest.[44]

4.4.3   Water and Energy

Clean water and energy were crucial to the increase in life expectancy. Here, too, the most difficult part of the analysis is to separate supply- and demand-driven changes. Technological changes in water and energy supply were supply-driven factors which reduced the relative prices of clean water, the ability to dispose of waste products, and the means of warming water, food, and air (in terms of financial as well as time costs). A large number of supply-related changes can be listed here, but many of the technological improvements in water and fuel supply depended on known principles of engineering and did not require major breakthroughs in technological knowledge to be discovered.

42. Grants from the department of education for teaching cookery were made available in 1882, and for laundry work in 1890. The number of girls who qualified for the cookery grant rose from 7,597 in 1882–83 to 134,930 in 1895–96. The number of schools teaching laundry work increased from 27 in 1891–92 to over 400 in 1895–96.

43. Following the Boer War there was great concern over the bad health of English men and women. The Inter-Departmental Committee on Physical Deterioration was set up to study this problem and provided many recommendations, including changes in the school curriculum for girls. The education department was quick to expand domestic classes as suggested (Dyhouse 1981, 95–98).

44. A typical passage from one such book reads as follows: "Several ailments and serious diseases from which babies suffer are caused by impure milk. Doctors tell us that there are often things, called 'germs' in the air which are poisonous. We cannot see these 'germs of disease', as we call them, but they really exist. They easily get into milk, and we can see that if a baby drinks milk containing germs the result may be serious. The dust that is blown about the roads on a windy day, or the dust which we can see in a dirty house, often contains some disease germs. That is why it is so important to try to keep our houses and streets clean; it is not only that they may look nice" (Davies 1906, 63).

Like other microinventions, they seem likely to have been brought about when demand for them was perceived. That demand, of course, was coming partially from the public sector, so that changes in φ as well as in ε were of importance. The discovery in the early 1850s that contaminated water was beyond any doubt a carrier of disease, and the realization of why this was so when the typhoid and cholera bacilli were discovered in rapid succession (1880 and 1883, with dysentery to follow in 1898), created a veritable clamor for clean, piped water for the masses. Supply responses to such outcries were to be expected.

Although major improvements in the water supply and the provision of sewer systems came before the age of Pasteur and Koch, the influence of their discoveries was crucial to the decline of waterborne diseases.[45] The idea that water carried pathogens remained controversial for many years.[46] Pasteur himself believed at first that bacterial infection was primarily airborne, and it was not until the discovery of the typhoid and cholera bacilli that water was fully recognized to be a potentially dangerous substance. Even after the link between living microorganisms and disease was confirmed, no fixed standards for water purity could be constructed, and this led to a continued debate over what water should be declared clean enough.[47] After Koch's gelatine process of water examination was introduced in England in 1885, the water could be accurately examined and compared to his standard of one hundred microbes per cubic centimeter. Yet as the recent work of Hamlin (1990) suggests, the discovery that water carried bacteria that could cause diseases was only the beginning. Not until the mid-1890s did bacteriology change the methods of water analysis, and even then many of the bacteria were hard to identify with specific diseases. Bacterial counts could now be carried out, but their interpretation remained in dispute as it was unclear what levels of counts were unsafe. Filtration and sedimentation were widely used, although they were imperfect. To these we should add chlorination, which was found in the late 1890s to be effective against bacterial pathogens. Chlorine had been known since the early 1800s to be an effective and inexpensive disinfectant and deodorant, but the

45. Improvements to water supply and sewage disposal systems centered, in this age, around urban communities and therefore had a comparatively bigger effect on the urban population. It was during these years that urban mortality in England started to decline, and the gap between life expectancy in rural and urban populations decreased sharply. The "urban penalty" of ten years in 1810 declined to seven years in 1861 and to only three years by 1911 (Kearns 1988).

46. In 1836 the French doctor Parent-Duchâtelet realized that water involved some principle of infection that "defied analysis" (Kirby et al. 1990, 427), yet it was not until twenty years later that the link between cholera and contaminated drinking water was established by John Snow's famous discovery, which linked the cholera epidemic in London to the water supply. In 1880, when Koch set his famous microbial standards for drinking water, the war against bacteria in drinking water was seriously begun.

47. Hardy (1984, 276) quotes Dr. Beale of King's College Hospital, who stated that small fragments of dead animal or vegetable matter placed in pure water and left for a few hours would result in the development of simple living organisms which "cannot well be considered prejudicial to health."

idea of using it as an additive to drinking water was not to be seriously considered before the emergence of the germ theory which specified its modus operandi. In 1897 the German bacteriologist Sims Woodhead used bleach solution to disinfect the distribution mains at Maidstone, and the world's first chlorination facility was set up in Middelkerke, Belgium, in 1902.[48] By 1900 it was understood that filtration was essential to rid water of disease-causing germs, and the number of people using filtered water in the United States increased from 1.8 million in 1900 to 10.8 million in 1910 (Preston and Haines 1991, 23).

The period under question here thus witnessed the democratization of access to piped water. In the 1840s, running water was clearly reserved for the rich.[49] By 1914 it was basically universal. Such statistics understate the amount of progress, because they do not take into consideration the improvement in the quality of the water. The same is true for waste disposal. The technology of domestic sanitation improved gradually from open cesspools to the water closets of the twentieth century. In between was a range of intermediate disposal technologies, but it was recognized that despite the higher water costs there was no real alternative to flushing toilets, which had become all but universal in Britain by 1914. Statistical and bacteriological examination revealed to the Medical Officers of Health that other techniques such as middens, pails, and ash closets were associated with typhoid and other diseases and these techniques were gradually abandoned. Without running water, of course, flushing toilets could not work, and thus the change in water technology provided a package deal of improved domestic conditions.

Systems for water supply and sewage disposal needed large capital investments, and before there was full understanding of their necessity both the public and the private sector were inhibited in making such investments. After the 1870s water was no longer seen as a luxury for the rich but as a necessary safety measure to combat disease, and the press, the schools, and the hospitals joined forces to conquer water so that "it was finally water that conquered us by transforming the world and becoming part of our daily life" (Goubert 1989, 25). The need for such large investments made cost-minimizing measures attractive, and before the harmful component in sewage was identified, such measures could not be correctly evaluated and often caused much more harm than was assumed. Thus for example as long as smell was seen as the main indication of a threat, disposing of the smell was the main objective. As the

48. Chlorination is another classic example of bad theory guiding correct policy. Chlorine compounds had been added to water in the 1830s to combat the bad odors of water that were thought by miasma theorists to be the cause of diseases. Although the odor itself did not cause disease, it was a by-product of something that did, even if that agent was still unknown at that time.

49. In London running water was reasonably common even by 1850 (with the faucets usually located in common yards), but in the rest of Britain it was not. For instance, only 4 percent of the population of Bristol had access to piped water in the 1840s, 8 percent in Newcastle (Daunton 1983, 246).

smell would disappear if sewage was mixed with enough water, disposal of sewage in rivers was a natural conclusion. Ideas of the "self-purification powers" of water mentioned by chemists were quickly accepted by water companies eager to avoid the costs of water filtration (46). When such ideas were dropped, towns became more careful, disposing of their sewage downstream. This alleviated the problem for that town but did not solve the health hazard for towns further downstream. Germ theory expanded the public-good problem of sewage disposal from the domain of one town to an issue concerning all the population along one waterway.[50]

Goubert (1989, 50–51) claims that bacteriology caused hygiene to replace cleanliness in water analysis. Cleanliness is closely related to aesthetics and civility and its rules are based on culture. Hygiene, on the other hand, is modern and advanced and based on the laws of science. One of the practical implications of this change from cleanliness to hygiene was the new attention to sewage disposal. It was no longer enough to supply water that looked clear and was therefore assumed to be "innocent"; it had to be scientifically acceptable. From the 1870s London's water closets could no longer be discharged into the water system. This regulation did not come in order to keep the water "clean" but to keep it hygienic. The design of water closets came to address the same problems—many sanitary engineers in England and the United States felt that water for the cleaning of the water closet should not be connected to the rising main of clean water because of the risk of backflow, but only after they understood germ theory did they fully comprehend the threat of backflow and widely implement the separation of the two systems of water supply.

Water-supply issues are usually discussed as public-good questions, but in the nineteenth century, as is the case today, the consumer did have choices to make. One decision the consumer made was the choice of water source. London dwellers could choose between water supplied by the various water companies and water from local wells. These wells were shallow surface wells, and they collected water from drainage as well as from cesspools, slaughterhouses, and graveyards (Hardy 1984, 272).[51] Another decision to be made on the household level was the number of taps and faucets to include in a house. The fewer the taps, the more time and effort involved in fetching water, the more utensils used between collecting the water and consuming it, and the higher the probability that water will be stored, usually uncovered, before use.

50. It was on these grounds, for example, that Missouri, acting on behalf of St. Louis, filed suit against Illinois, demanding that the city of Chicago cease dumping its raw sewage into the Illinois River (Marcus 1979, 193).

51. Hardy (1984) notes that the water from these wells was considered sweet and pure despite warnings to the contrary by medical officers, but it does seem that it was mainly the poor who relied on these sources, which implies that given a choice consumers preferred piped water. Abolishing the surface wells was a slow process, especially before 1891 when the local authorities had no power to compel house owners to supply piped water for domestic purposes unless supplying wells were found to be unfit for use.

Throughout the latter part of the nineteenth century more and more houses had water pipes and water cisterns installed.[52]

Another important question was the reliability of the water supply. Water companies often suffered water shortages and for many years water was not supplied at all on Sundays. On this issue too, however, the consumer had a say.[53] The problem of the Sunday supply was solved in 1870, and over time other shortages and failures were limited too, although it seems that improvements to poor neighborhoods came more slowly. Plumbing was not the only issue in water hygiene. Water suspected to be contaminated could be boiled or filtered by the household; in extreme cases drinking water bought from water carriers or beer could be drunk. By the 1880s, households could buy their own filters, many of them made of carbon, which improved the taste and cleaned away minerals. Goubert (1989, 99) remarks that these filters, which were of course largely ineffective against microbial agents, received a mortal blow when the germ theory became widely accepted. At the same time, the germ theory clearly indicated to rural families, who were not attached to an urban network of filtered water, that private measures to insure a germ-free water supply were crucial. Hand-powered under-the-sink pumps supplemented water carried from nearby wells or rivers, but once the notion that contaminated water could carry infectious disease had sunk in, households could react.

Energy supplies may have been of almost equal importance. Laundry and dishwashing required hot water as did personal hygiene and cooking. The constraint on hot water imposed on most working-class families a strict regime of wash day on Monday and bath night on Saturday (Daunton 1983, 242). Yet the closing two decades of the nineteenth century experienced major changes here too. The large cast-iron coal- or wood-burning ranges or stoves satisfied, through most of the nineteenth century, the need for hot water, cooking, and home heating simultaneously. After 1880, gas, which had primarily been used for lighting until then, came to be used for heating as well. Demand for gas for lighting began to decline as electricity spread, and on both sides of the Atlantic gas for heating and cooking began to spread in the 1890s (Cowan 1983, 90). The slot meter and the gas cooker changed the way homes were being heated, meals cooked, and water boiled (Daunton 1983, 238–41). The price of gas did not decline much (245), but given the much greater convenience of its use the full price was certainly much lower. The changes were thus jointly determined

52. The tenement houses managed by social reformer Octavia Hill were supplied with a communal tap (of cold water) for every floor. This was regarded by her as sufficient and was indeed a great improvement over many of the poorer houses that had only one tap per house, if any at all. The fact that the number of taps supplied to tenants was an issue raised by the Royal Commission on the Housing of the Working Classes in 1884–85 portrays a changing attitude toward the question of water supply.

53. When in January 1866 the local company in Camberwell failed to provide water on a Saturday, a number of gentlemen arrived the next morning at the local turncock's home, threatening to sue the company and the turncock for failing to supply water (Hardy 1984).

by shifts in technology and shifts in demand, the latter motivated in large part by changing notions of the causes of health and disease.

Did the relative price of energy decline during our period? We have noted above that the introduction of gas stoves reduced the time and effort needed to cook food and heat water. For a long time, however, coal remained the main source of energy for both cooking and heating. In figure 4.3 we see that the price of household coal increased until 1900. The price of "best coal," for which we have a longer time series (Mitchell 1988, 748), shows a similar trend, with price increases resuming after 1905. Once again, changes in relative prices do not seem to tell the whole story.

4.4.4   Washing and Hygiene

The importance of the concept of hygiene in connecting consumption and health was not limited to the issue of water supply alone. When hygiene became a scientific term it did not lose its moral connotations. Part of the social-control mode of diffusion was that hygiene would be spread by moral as well as logical persuasion. Thus it is not surprising that in 1882, when religious education was ousted from French lay schools, hygiene became a compulsory subject in primary school curricula (Goubert 1989, 146). The need to keep clean was taught directly through stories and poems and indirectly in dictation passages and grammar books. The school was also a source of practical information: advanced hygienic facilities were often installed earlier there than among the population at large, thereby giving children their first experience with sanitary water closets, baths, and showers (163). The teacher, always

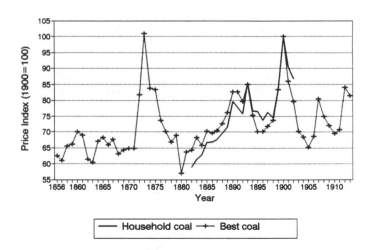

Fig. 4.3   Real price indexes: coal, 1856–1913
Sources: Household coal is the London retail price as given in United Kingdom (1903, 360). Best coal is from Mitchell (1988, 748). General price index is from Feinstein (1972, T140).

viewed as a role model for the future citizens, was required to set an example in cleanliness, and appearance was considered as important as teaching ability.

Education in hygiene was not limited to the children. A cleanliness check was recommended for the beginning of each class, which in effect made the parents involved in this new doctrine. To ensure that a child came to school clean, the parent (or, to be more precise, the mother) had to wash both the child and his or her clothes. Teachers were often also the town clerks, reinforcing the school system in spreading the creed of cleanliness. Consequently, the frequent washing of clothes, like the washing of bodies, became an accepted practice in the latter part of the nineteenth century. Laundry was a strenuous job, carried out mostly by women—either by the female head of the household or by a washerwoman. For washing, a water supply was needed; as cleaning was done by beating and rubbing on boards, there needed to be a working area close to the water supply; and there was also need for lines or fences for drying. To overcome these logistical demands, public and private washhouses were erected. Between 1870 and 1900, more than two hundred washhouses and laundry rooms were opened in Paris (Goubert 1989, 76–77). How much washing was done during this time? Goubert claims that in Paris between 1870 and 1880 three kilograms of clothes and other items were washed per capita per week. This is a vast amount of washing, quite close to our modern standards. The impact on consumption was immediate: the increase in demand for clean clothes led to an increase in demand for water, fuel, and detergents.

An increase in the purchase of health-enhancing goods could, of course, have resulted from a supply-induced change in their relative prices. Table 4.1 shows a large increase in the per capita purchase of soap in Great Britain throughout the second half of the nineteenth century. From a consumption of 8 pounds of soap per year in 1861 it rose to 10.7 pounds in 1871 and 14 pounds in 1881. The increases in soap consumption continued, at a somewhat slower pace, through 1912. Following the technological advances during the Industrial Revolution, the soap industry expanded rapidly, and by 1851 it was a thriving industry. At the Great Exposition of that year, 103 soap manufacturers pre-

Table 4.1   Consumption of All Soap Products

Year	Annual Consumption per Capita (pounds)
1851	7.1
1861	8.0
1871	10.7
1881	14.0
1891	15.4
1901	17.4
1912	18.0

Source: Edwards (1962, 135).

sented an array of products: honey soap, white curd soap, mottled soap, and more (Edwards 1962, 136). With the entrance of William Hesketh Lever into the soap industry in 1885, a new era began (Wilson 1954). Lever's great innovation was packaging the new oil soap Sunlight in separately wrapped bars, thereby breaking the old marketing tradition of producing soap in 3-pound bars that were then cut into smaller pieces by shopkeepers. With a strong marketing campaign that included advertisements and prizes, Lever's market share rose to a peak of 23.1 percent in 1905. But other producers continued to fare well, with total market sales increasing fast enough to accommodate both them and Lever. Edwards (1962, 151) writes that the main element contributing to the increase in soap sales per capita "was undoubtedly the increased consumption of soap among the working classes" due to Lever's advertising that promoted soap to the "factory housewife." This came in conjunction with changes on the demand side, which were spurred by changes in knowledge and a growth of the understanding of soap's role in producing health. It seems likely that the growing awareness of pathogenic microbes created a fertile soil in which the seeds sown by advertisers germinated rapidly.

To what extent was the growth in soap consumption a consequence of supply changes? Figure 4.4 shows the development in the prices of soap and washing soda during this time, deflated by the consumer price index. The real price of soap did fall substantially between the mid-1880s and 1898, but then it rose again until 1908.[54] Changes in prices may explain increased consumption in the late 1880s and 1890s, but they cannot explain the continuous increase in soap consumption throughout the period. It is interesting to note that the period characterized by the sharp decline in infant mortality (post-1900) is one of increasing soap consumption despite price increases. Another important product used in cleaning was washing soda. As figure 4.4 shows, its real price declined through the 1870s but then stabilized and even rose again toward the end of the century.

To return to the issue stated at the outset of this paper, it is hard to believe that a shift in preferences (narrowly defined) occurred that steered households into demanding more goods conveying cleanliness. Nor does it appear to be true that changes in relative prices of the goods associated with cleanliness can by themselves explain the phenomenon. Instead, the information term $A - \varepsilon$ that multiplies the goods in equation (3) increased and changed age-old habits. Statistical evidence on its own would not have brought about a change so drastic; but statistical evidence coupled to a theory that claimed to know why the statistics held true was too powerful to ignore. The full cost of the new recipes consisted of, to a large degree, household time. It is clear from Cowan's (1983) work that households improved their health not only because new, health-enhancing implements and commodities became available or affordable, but

54. The development of the price of primrose soap is almost identical to that of other soaps (yellow, household) and to the prices in other establishments (see United Kingdom 1903, 372–73).

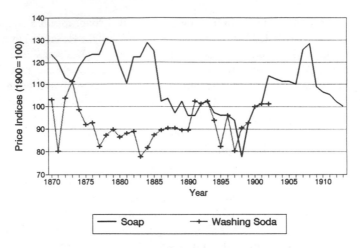

Fig. 4.4   Real price indexes: soap and washing soda, 1870–1913
Sources: Soap prices up to 1902 are the London retail price of primrose soap as given in United Kingdom (1903, 372). Soap prices since 1902 are from Edwards (1962, 156). Washing soda prices are from United Kingdom (1903, 364). General price index is from Feinstein (1972, T140).

also because households devoted more scarce resources—above all, labor—to them. De Vries (1993, 119) notes that after the mid-nineteenth century households increasingly withdrew female labor from the marketplace and allocated it to housework, reversing the effects of what he has felicitously called the "Industrious Revolution" which redeployed labor from housework to the market in the eighteenth century.

What could explain this "industrious counterrevolution"? Housework was not leisure and was often unpleasant and physically exhausting (Cowan 1983, 43–44). A likely explanation is that homemakers were increasingly convinced that such housework was correlated with health and survival. A connection between female labor participation and infant and child mortality has been proposed by Imhof (1984); it should not be assumed that this connection was entirely unconscious.[55] The decision about whether a mother and her children should work was endogenous on the information available to the household. Germ theory showed that preserving children's health is best accomplished by investing more time within the house in cleaning and child feeding. Household labor could not easily be substituted by inputs purchased in the market, so that the effective wage earned by women was lowered. The result was a shift of married women out of the labor force and consequently a decline in child mortality and morbidity.[56]

55. A recent analysis connecting health and domestic labor and making a similar argument from a Marxist perspective is Thomas (1995).
56. The costs were compounded by an excessive zeal for cleaning that often led to practices that were not always necessary. An 1872 article in *Popular Science Monthly* cried out against "careless disinfection" and stated, correctly, that "mere exposure to disinfecting vapors is not enough to

One of the major inputs into the health production function is time, usually women's time. If the relative price of household work, female wages, decreased over this time, it may help to explain an increase in work within the home. Unfortunately, time series of female workers are hard to come by. In figure 4.5 we show the development of real wages for men in the United Kingdom from 1870 to 1913 (Williamson 1995). We also show a series of female laborers' wages on a Northumberland farm (Fox 1903).[57] Both men's and women's wages seem to go up during the later part of the nineteenth century. Thus the opportunity costs of household time did not decline. The gradual decline of female labor force participation in the Victorian era is consistent with information-generated changes in household behavior.

Typhus in England makes an interesting case study of the impact of new standards of cleanliness on morbidity and mortality (Hardy 1988). Typhus was a typical "dirt disease." Until the 1870s the distribution of typhus in London was linked to specific areas within the central, southern, and eastern registration districts. In these areas there were specific places, popularly designated "fever nests," that were recognized by the public health authorities as particular haunts of typhus.[58] Typhus almost disappeared after the late 1870s. Hardy (1993, 204–10) links this disappearance with improvements in the sanitation of housing, improvements in water supplies and hospitals, and the change in the nature of social dislocation. Part of the improvement can be attributed to the construction of the railways and the demolition of houses that stood in the way; some of the poorest and least sanitary houses were destroyed this way. Part of the decline in typhus resulted from public policy aimed at combating disease.[59] Once the connection between cleanliness and health was made, any

thoroughly rid the apartment of danger to future inmates" (Careless disinfection 1872, 122). The recommended procedure was not only to scour the floor and woodwork and to clean the walls and ceiling but also to remove all wallpaper, for "it unquestionably has the power of absorbing and retaining contagious matters, that are not reached by the ordinary processes of disinfection." Works such as *The Woman's Book* (Jack and Strauss 1911) go through pages upon pages of chores to be done around the house. In tersely written prose and in tight print the authors fill 734 pages with "many hints with regards to cleaning etc."

57. We would like to thank Joyce Burnette for providing us with this series.

58. Hardy (1993, 197–98) describes one such house, located in St. Giles. It housed a secondhand clothes shop in the basement, offered rooms to let further up, and housed, among many others, some makers of trinkets for ladies' heads and dresses. An outburst of typhus began with the second-floor family whose daughter, living in nearby Drury Court, had caught the infection from a fellow lodger there. For two months the disease spread from family to family within the house, and all through this time the work within the building did not stop. If such a house was not cleaned and disinfected after an appearance of typhus, infected louse feces might lie undisturbed for years until a new nonimmune occupant arrived. Overcrowding and high turnover of people in such cases as St. Giles only assisted the spread of typhus.

59. Following the passing of the Artisan Dwelling Act of 1875, further houses were demolished under the sponsorship of the Medical Officer of Health. The Nuisance Removal Act helped rectify some specific sanitary defects by encouraging houses to be cleaned and lime washed. In St. Giles, for example, 12,573 improvement orders were issued between 1875 and 1883, and 7,700 houses were cleaned—an average of 971 per year. Out of the 3,968 inhabited houses, therefore, 24.5 percent were cleaned every year.

Fig. 4.5   Real wages for men and women, 1870–1913
Sources: Men's wages are from Williamson (1995, A20–A21 table A1.1). Women's wages are for ordinary women workers from Fox (1903, 323). Price index from Feinstein (1972, T140).

outbreak of disease brought forth a flurry of antisepsis and disinfection that helped eradicate infectious diseases of any kind. Outbreaks of scarlet fever in 1868–70 and smallpox in 1870–73 and 1976–78 brought widespread house-to-house visitations in search of carriers and unvaccinated children. These epidemics also resulted in the widespread disinfection of homes, bedding, and clothing of victims throughout London, eradicating such diseases as typhus at the same time. The disappearance of typhus is especially interesting because it was just as complete in districts whose sanitation caused much contemporary worry, such as Manchester, as it was in relatively well-administered towns, such as Birmingham (Pooley and Pooley 1984; Woods 1984). Other dirt diseases also went on the decline: typhoid fever, cholera, scarlet fever, and food poisoning account for much of the mortality decline after 1870. Prevention, through changed household technology and public goods, was the main cause of the decline in disease after 1870.[60]

4.4.5   Insects

The recognition that insects could serve as vectors of bacteria seems an obvious extension of the germ theory to us, but in fact did not occur for decades after Pasteur's initial breakthroughs. Two discoveries are particularly im-

---

60. Here, too, schools were an important administrative center. Thus, for example, in Bermondsey, one of the poorer boroughs in London, an inspector went around the schools and noted those children unfit to go to school "owing to their verminous condition" (Brown 1908). These 331 children were sent to newly erected baths, where "all received 'a good warm bath' and in the case of vermin in the head a 2 per cent solution of lysol very soon got rid of them." Roberts (1990, 79) describes similar scenes from the viewpoint of a schoolchild remembering the awful shame of children thus disgraced.

portant: the malaria-carrying *Anopheles* mosquitoes, and the yellow fever–carrying *Aedes aegypti* mosquito. Although suspicions that mosquitoes were to blame for disease had been expressed since Carlos Finlay y Barres speculated in 1878 about the sources of yellow fever, the major breakthroughs did not come until the closing years of the nineteenth century. In 1899 the leading bacteriologist in Britain, George Nuttall, codified the best-practice knowledge, saying, "it is certain that under certain conditions insects may play a most important part—both active and passive—in the propagation of bacterial diseases" (quoted in Dwork 1987b, 45). From a European point of view, the most important reinforcement of this view came in 1909 when Charles Nicolle identified the louse as the vector of typhus (the bacterial agent was identified two years later). Typhus and malaria were the most important vector-borne diseases in Europe, but some food-borne diseases like dysentery could also be spread by insects.

The battle against mosquitoes had been, for many years, unintended and indirect. Swamps were associated with fevers and sickness and their ill effect was feared, but the true reason for this connection was not understood, and mosquitoes were not suspected as the villains. All the same, during the eighteenth century, long before Pasteur, a huge amount of private and public effort was invested in swamp drainage. The intention of much of the investment was to clear land for agriculture—not for public health. Yet physicians and agricultural reformers encouraged these efforts, and to facilitate them public authorities offered tax cuts and financial aid (Riley 1986, 840). The effect of the decline of malaria on overall mortality rates is hard to evaluate. The strain of malaria common in the temperate European climate caused more weakness than death, increasing susceptibility to other diseases rather than adding to mortality directly. Such interactive effects make the identification of specific measures hard to pin down. Similar measurement problems face us when we try to evaluate the effect in the decline in the number of fleas, ticks, lice, and so on. The fact that mortality from some diseases (e.g., dysentery) was seasonal, peaking during the warm season when insects thrive, is consistent with the view that insect control played an important part in mortality decline. Warm temperatures, however, would also speed up the division of bacteria, thus accelerating food spoilage and the incidence of food-borne diseases.

Insect control thus was often the unintended beneficial consequence of other efforts. Measures directed at food cleanliness reduced insect contact. So, for example, although covering milk pails was not a good alternative to pasteurization, it reduced contamination by flies. The regular washing of clothes and bed linen got rid of ticks, bedbugs, and lice and reduced insect-borne diseases even though the connection between insects and disease was still unknown. The discovery of the role of insects in disease transmission in the 1890s brought with it a general change of attitude toward insects. From then on they became not just a nuisance, but a menace. The changing attitude toward the common housefly during the first years of this century is an illustrative example: once regarded as an innocent and friendly domestic insect, it was transformed into a "germ with legs" (Rogers 1989), an enemy to the housekeeper and her family.[61] Germs could not be seen, so that even when the knowledge of germ theory spread it was difficult for the housekeeper to fight them. Flies, cockroaches, fleas, and mosquitoes, on the other hand, were an easy and palpable target, and keeping them away from the house was a concrete, practical recommendation that could be followed. Though insects were easy to see and identify, eradicating them took time and effort. To help in this task public baths supplied a disinfection service where poor households could take their beds, linens, and clothes to be disinfected at low or no cost (Brown 1908; Roberts 1990). As insects joined unclean milk and dirty houses as signals of germs to be avoided, some overreaction to the sheer rhetorical power of the anti-insect hysteria was inevitable and relatively harmless creatures such as spiders and cockroaches became victims of the war on germs.

4.4.6   Medical Practices

We finally turn to the consumer good that most directly affects health: medical services. The most significant change brought about by the germ theory was perhaps to transform the status and function of physicians. The impact of the new theories went beyond the demonstration that microorganisms caused infectious disease: the entire concept of disease was clarified and altered. The distinction between cause and symptom, the mechanics of prevention, and a rudimentary notion of immunity, which soon followed drove home the basic idea that the chances of getting sick and the severity of the affliction were determined to a large extent by the action of the household and its allocative decisions. Doctors became the pivotal agents for disseminating this idea. After the emergence of the germ theory and before the emergence of effective antibiotics, the knowledge that infectious diseases were caused by bacterial agents left doctors with a primary function of prevention. In a few cases, the new microbiology found a cure or a vaccine (syphilis and diphtheria). On the whole, however, their role was educational: by realizing the importance of minimizing exposure to bacteria, physicians became agents in the diffusion of the new knowledge. This novel function was a central reason why ε, the lag between best-practice and average technique, declined. In that regard, Pasteur's discovery affected both A and ε in terms of equation (3). While the bacteriological revolution demonstrated that different microorganisms caused different diseases, the effort directed at improvement of hygiene was not disease specific. Changes in consumption patterns and environment affected a range of diseases, and through the complexities of the immune system, diseases interacted with one another in ways that are hard to unravel.

---

61. When the link between diarrhea and flies was established in the second decade of the twentieth century, infant mortality from this disease was still significant. Posters were put up in infant-care centers and local government offices to alert the public to this matter and to advise them on ways to fight flies and protect food and milk from contamination.

Even without antibiotic medication, changes in treatment followed directly from the improved understanding of disease. The treatment of cholera provides a vivid example. When first confronted with the disease in the late 1820s, traditional medicine recommended the use of emetics and purgatives in cholera patients to help the body rid itself of the morbid material there by expediting "natural" diarrhea. The prevailing treatments included bleeding, opium, laudanum, and calomel (mercurous chloride, a powerful laxative prescribed for dozens of diseases). Another popular prescription was tartar emetic (antimony and potassium tartrate) which also was a medication of choice in the eighteenth and nineteenth centuries (Haller 1974). Without a true understanding of disease, the use of harmful "cures" persisted, and potentially beneficial drugs were prescribed in incorrect dosages.[62] By the end of the century, the recommended treatment changed completely, and clinical intervention focused on relieving the symptoms by keeping up high levels of liquids.

Bleeding was revived in the 1820s, along with many practices and doctrines associated with it.[63] It was noted, for example, that a high proportion of patients who could not be bled because their blood was "too thick" died. This led to the conclusion that bleeding was a crucial part of treatment and should be induced as much as possible, especially in difficult cases. The use of statistics and numerical methods finally undermined bleeding practices (Rosen 1955), and after decades of long and often heated debates, it fell into disuse (King 1961). Between 1840 and 1870, a protracted struggle took place between the "old" and the "new" schools of medicine, but the germ theory put an effective end to bleeding as a best-practice technique—although here, too, diffusion was far from immediate. Another clinical practice that fell into disrepute after the bacteriological revolution was the indiscriminate use of panaceas. After 1890, for example, quinine was no longer used against typhus, fluxes, gangrene, cachexias (scrofula, rickets, scurvy), or as a tonic and was restricted to the treatment of malaria (Ackerknecht 1962, 412). The deepest and most revolutionary consequence of the bacteriological revolution, however, was that diseases were demonstrated to be separate entities caused by different agents.

62. One doctor in 1844, perhaps an extreme case, prescribed a tablespoon of calomel (about 250 grains) an hour whereas in 1940 the prescribed dosage was 2 grains (Hudson 1983, 205).

63. François Broussais's career in this regard is telling. His magnum opus, *Examen des doctrines médicales* (1816) made him so influential and popular that his lecture halls at the Val de Grâce medical school had to be changed twice to accommodate his students. His book was translated into many languages, and as late as the 1860s his work was regarded as a milestone in French medicine. The "antiphlogistic" theories invented by Broussais started from the assumptions that nature had no healing power and that the body had to be weakened in order to be rid of disease. He thus recommended depriving the patient of food and administering heavy localized bleeding. His influence raised the imports of leeches from 320,000 in 1823 to an average of 31 million in 1833–34. It is easy to dismiss his work, but his criticism of competing theories and therapeutics was probably helpful, and his basic idea that therapeutics should be directed toward the organ causing the symptoms rather than the symptoms themselves is plausible. All the same, his central doctrine, which designated gastroenteritis as the sole disease that caused all other symptoms, was another attempt to find a holistic approach to the causes of disease and did little to advance clinical treatment.

The holistic approaches of Brown, Broussais, and others were finally abandoned for good by the medical profession.

A major contribution of germ theory to clinical medicine was in surgery: it
provided Joseph Lister with a missing link in his chain of discoveries. With the
insights that the germ theory provided, Lister's recommendation carried a great
deal more conviction than those of his precursors, Holmes and Semmelweis,
who owed their insights purely to empirical regularities. If suppuration of
wounds was due to living organisms, the immediate problem at hand was to
kill these organisms without injuring the living tissues. Lister's discovery of
antisepsis came after a long period of rising hospital mortality. The introduction of anesthesia two decades earlier had made operations easier for both patients and doctors, but prior to antiseptics a rise in operations led directly to a
rise in mortality as postsurgical infection claimed a growing number of victims. By the 1870s hospitals were in dire straits, and there was even talk of
pulling old hospitals down and building new ones in the hope that this would
break the vicious cycle of operations and death (Latour 1988, 48). Pasteur and
Lister focused the issue and gave a concrete solution to the problem: antisepsis.[64] Doctors no longer needed to follow Bouchardat's advice and wait several
days between assigning one maternity patient and another—it was enough to
wash one's hands in carbolic lotion (48).[65] The understanding of germs and
contagion brought a change in the architecture of hospitals: instead of having
one big ward, patients with contagious diseases were placed in smaller areas
linked to the public wards but completely isolated from them (Goubert 1989,
133), and maternity patients were provided with their own area surrounded by
an antiseptic cordon.[66]

As with other medical discoveries, the germ theory did not spread overnight
and the use of antisepsis diffused slowly.[67] Not using the newly acquired

64. The story of Lister's discovery is well known: he heard of Pasteur's discovery by chance and
was, in fact, not the first English doctor to note its significance. Unlike other surgeons, however,
he realized that it provided a theoretical justification for his belief that treatment with carbolic acid
reduced the chances of infection. Lister's own techniques quickly became obsolete when antiseptic
methods were replaced by the aseptic ones of boiling and autoclaving instruments before use.

65. The next step was the use of rubber gloves. These were first used in 1889 by a nurse on the
staff of Dr. William Stewart, Halsted Professor of Surgery at Johns Hopkins Medical School. The
nurse complained that the solution of mercuric chloride produced a dermatitis on her arms and
hands, and Dr. Stewart ordered two pairs of gloves from the Goodyear Rubber Company. The
gloves went into regular use by assistants and were used sporadically by surgeons until finally
entering into general use (Proskauer 1958).

66. The risk of the mother dying at childbirth or during confinement did not decline appreciably
in England during the second half of the nineteenth century. On the other hand, there was a marked
decline in maternal mortality in hospitals over the same period (Loudon 1986). The increasing
gap between maternal mortality in hospitals and in rural homes (where help during labor was given
by "ignorant midwifes") emphasizes how important it is to distinguish between health practices in
different populations and households. The discovery of germs may have enhanced the survival
rates of those women who went to hospitals, but it was another thirty years before all English
women reaped the same benefits.

67. An enlightening anecdote is provided by Fish (1950). When President Garfield was shot,
sixteen years after the introduction of antisepsis, the numerous physicians who saw him did not

knowledge was but one part of the problem; trying to apply it unconditionally was another. The logic of antiseptics was so compelling to some that it was promoted for internal as well as external use (Crellin 1981). Internal antiseptics, for example, were introduced to combat respiratory ailments and were administered by spray or steam. As in so many other examples of new technology, successful and effective use of the macroinvention depended on the supplementary microinventions as much as on the original breakthrough.

Many general physicians, in contrast with hygienists and public-sector physicians (such as the Medical Officers of Health), at first objected to the germ theory and tried to keep its recommendations at arm's length. American physicians in the late nineteenth century were unusually conservative and fought the germ theory of disease tooth and nail. Only the development of the diphtheria antitoxin persuaded American doctors that the old miasmatic theories of disease had to be abandoned and the practice of medicine reformed (Preston and Haines 1991, 8–11). Yet it became clear soon enough that doctors could not turn the Pasteur revolution back, and soon the majority who could not beat the new science joined it (Latour 1988, 129–37) and played a growing role in a transformed medicine. In many ways we should regard physicians in this age as household consultants, advising homemakers how to avoid infectious disease by the proper combination of goods and household work in the kitchen, toilet, and bathroom. Their role was to spread the new knowledge as much as to implement it themselves, a distinction overlooked by McKeown's indictment of the medical profession.

4.4.7 Public Policy

The Pasteur revolution had profound implications for public policy. Above all, new knowledge altered best practices employed by the public sector, that is, it affected the parameter B in equation (5) above. The understanding that there were public-good properties to health was of course an age-old one and had been formulated sharply by Frank in the late eighteenth century in his concept of "medical police." But the lack of a knowledge of what disease was and the uncertainty about transmission mechanisms (resulting in bitter disputes between contagionists and anticontagionists in the nineteenth century) made public policy, with a few important exceptions, rather ineffectual. Policymakers and the citizens whose opinions influenced them had to change their views of public health after Pasteur just as much as homemakers had to account for it in private health.

When households acquired the information about what made them sick and what kept them healthy, they often exerted pressure on the authorities to initiate reforms to produce goods that they could not produce for themselves and that

---

think twice before poking his wound with their fingers. The surgeon general of the navy introduced his finger to its full extent into the wound, as did Dr. J. J. Woodward and Dr. Bliss, two physicians present. A homeopathic physician who rushed into the room added a deep finger of his own. It is not surprising that Garfield died, not of the shot itself, but from infection and complications ten weeks after the incident.

the market would not supply. Consumers were also voters, and in most nations their worries and demands found their way to the politicians' programs, if often in an incomplete and uneven fashion (Brown 1988; Cain and Rotella 1994). It is thus somewhat artificial to separate, as we do in equations (3) and (5), the knowledge of the public servants and the knowledge of the consumers at large. Insofar as policymakers are sensitive to public opinion, public works will be affected by the levels of $A - \varepsilon$, that is, private knowledge.

Nineteenth-century public medicine had increasingly been convinced that many diseases had a profoundly social nature. Epidemiologists in Britain, France, and Germany had established beyond doubt that disease was strongly correlated with poverty and hunger. As no causal model was available, scientists and public reformers leaped to the convenient conclusion that infectious diseases would be eliminated if and when poverty, misery, and hunger disappeared. Public health, therefore, was part and parcel of a wider set of social reforms. To be sure, certain public projects such as a clean water supply and sewage works were understood to have a more direct impact on the incidence of epidemics, but the general feeling was well expressed by the founder of modern physiology, Rudolf Virchow, when he declared in 1849 that "if medicine is really to accomplish its great task, it must intervene in political and social life" (Rosen 1947, 679). His colleague, Salomon Neumann, added that poverty, hunger, and misery were "the inexhaustible sources from which death, disease and chronic suffering originate." Similar positions were espoused at that time in Britain by Edwin Chadwick, Henry Rumsey, John Simon, and others. The nonspecific nature of the causes of disease meant that they could only be fought with a wide array of social-reform measures dealing with housing, sanitation, child labor, education, working conditions, and so on. The masses, the social reformers felt, could not be healthy unless they were at least moderately prosperous. In Rosen's words, medicine was perceived to be social science. Individual health would not be improved until general social conditions were.[68]

The nature of the Pasteur revolution was not to obviate such policies but to sharpen and focus them. Poverty was a correlate of disease but not necessarily its cause. It was no longer necessary to eliminate poverty to combat infectious disease: society could have a class of healthy poor provided they lived a relatively healthy lifestyle. George Newman's important book *Infant Mortality: A Social Problem*, published in 1906, exemplified this change. Writing about infant mortality, he stressed that "poverty is not alone responsible, for in many poor communities the infant mortality is low. Housing and external environment alone do not cause it, for under some of the worst external conditions in the world the evil is absent. It is difficult to escape the conclusion that this loss

---

68. Nineteenth-century socialist thought found this line of reasoning extremely amenable to their cause and often maintained that because the causes of poverty were economic, so were the causes of sickness. By eliminating poverty, socialism would eliminate sickness (Spree 1988, 25).

of infant life is in some way intimately related to the social life of the people." By redeploying existing resources, both in the public sector and in the household, disease among the working classes could be reduced and perhaps eliminated within the existing structures of society. Public health was thus redefined and disease was taken out of the social realm and placed back in the household.[69] The role of the public sector remained important, but it was more carefully circumscribed by market failure. Households could infect each other and shared certain common goods such as sewage and drinking-water supply. Provided, however, that they were properly informed, they could on the whole be held responsible for their own physical well-being.[70] Authorities were to focus on specific diseases which, for one reason or another, could not be controlled by the household. This left a large part for the public sector, from vaccination to the drainage of malaria-causing swamps. Proper child care, domestic and personal cleanliness, and adequate nutrition, on the other hand, were no longer regarded as the essential domain of policy measures since they were not incompatible with poverty and were properly regarded as part of household choice. The poor did not get sick because they were poor, but because germs infected them. Eliminate the germs and you will have healthy poor, as long as they do not fall below a level where their physical well-being cannot be supported—hence the idea of a poverty line.[71] Beyond that, however, the interaction between social problems and medical issues could be defined with some precision. In 1893 the great bacteriologist Emil Behring wrote laconically that thanks to the methods of Robert Koch, the study of infectious disease could be pursued without being sidetracked by social considerations and welfare policies (Rosen 1947, 675).

These policies were most effective in Germany, where, despite lower incomes and lower standards of living, the biggest gains were made in the struggle against infectious disease (Brown 1988, forthcoming). Although there can be no question that until 1914 Germany was a poorer country than Britain, it was more successful in mitigating the worst impact of the urban environment. Brown attributes much of this to public works, yet it must also be possible that German households were more susceptible to the growing pressure from

---

69. As Newman wrote, "Sanitation and preventive medicine have in the past done much to protect the individual from the evil of his environment. The future will lie with the State that is able to protect the individual against himself. And to do that it must build on the family life in the home, for the home is the unit of the State" (1906, 180).

70. Many reformers who doubted the premise called for further education of both adults and children. While mothers were increasingly accused of carelessly promoting infant mortality, Davies defends them, writing, "The fatal mistakes made by mothers in regard to their babies are more often the result of ignorance than of carelessness. It is only by teaching the mothers how to care for babies that we can remove that blot on the home-life of the nation, the alarming mortality of infants under one year old" (1906, 5).

71. The germ theory was not a necessary preamble to this more conservative approach: the leader of the German hygienic movement, Max Pettenkofer, resisted the germ theory yet made it quite clear that in his view health depended first and foremost on consumption choices made by individuals about diet, housing conditions, and so on (Rosen 1947).

authorities to follow a certain set of household rules deemed by them to be healthy, thus allowing households to reduce the gap ε more quickly than elsewhere. It should be added, however, that Germany had much further to go. In the late 1870s, crude death rates in Germany were still around 26.5 as opposed to 21.2 in the United Kingdom, and infant mortality rates, though highly variable within the country, were about 228 per 1,000 in Germany compared to a mere 145 per 1,000 for England and Wales.

4.5   Quantitative Dimensions of the Pasteur Revolution

4.5.1   Aggregate Rates of Income and Mortality

As we have noted, it is hard to discriminate between the different factors that have been argued to have affected general and infant mortality. To test whether rising incomes were a factor in infant mortality decline, we have plotted real wages and infant mortality in the United Kingdom, France, and Germany (fig. 4.6). All three countries show a steady increase in real wages from the mid-1860s, but in all three cases infant mortality did not decrease steadily. Rather, infant mortality seems to vary around a steady plateau until the turn of the century when it suddenly declines sharply. Note also that although France had lower real wages than Germany throughout this period, it had a lower infant mortality. Overall mortality rates do decline steadily, and there can be little doubt that in the long term nutritional status improved, leading to the decline of some nutrition-sensitive adult diseases, especially tuberculosis. This cannot, however, be the whole story.

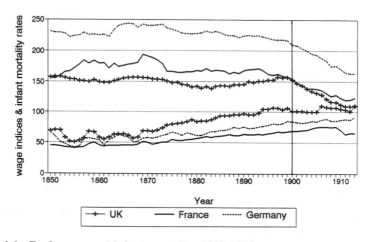

Fig. 4.6   Real wages and infant mortality, 1850–1914
Sources: Infant mortality data, see fig. 4.1. Real wages are from Williamson (1995, A26–A27 table A2.1).
Note: Top three lines are infant mortality rates; bottom three lines are wage indexes.

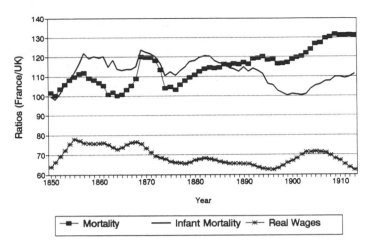

Fig. 4.7   Mortality, infant mortality, and real wages: ratios between France and the United Kingdom
Sources: Infant mortality data, see fig. 4.1. Real wages, see fig. 4.6. Mortality data are from Mitchell (1975, 104–20 table B6).

Comparing the ratios of real wages, overall mortality, and infant mortality in England and France (fig. 4.7) also suggests that income by itself is not a sufficient explanation. As a whole, wages in France were lower than those in England and mortality figures were higher, as the income hypothesis would predict; but closer examination shows that the relative trends were not the same. During the 1890s and the early 1900s, real wages in France were rising relative to those in England, but relative mortality rates in France increased. A similar comparison between Germany and England (fig. 4.8) shows that infant mortality in Germany declined relative to that in England during the 1880s, even though relative wages did not change. After the mid 1890s, real wages in Germany rose relative to those in England, but relative infant mortality increased at the same time. While these data do not prove the income hypothesis to be wrong, they indicate that rising incomes could not be the only factor affecting mortality and infant mortality rates.[72]

4.5.2   Nosologies and Household Perception of Disease

The main argument of this paper is that the Pasteur revolution accelerated a trend that had already begun around the middle of the nineteenth century. This trend consisted of a growing understanding by households of the natural processes that caused disease. The growth in household information and the belief that this information was helpful were spurred on by the germ theory, but evi-

---

72. This finding is wholly consistent with those of Preston and Haines (1991) who conclude that "the growth of income during the twentieth century could not have been the principal factor causing mortality to *decline*" (210, emphasis in original).

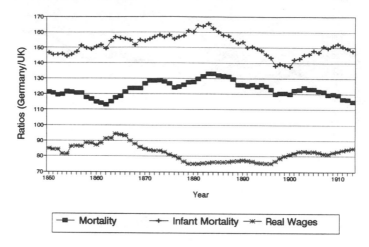

Fig. 4.8   Mortality, infant mortality, and real wages: ratios between Germany and the United Kingdom
Sources: See fig. 4.7.

dence of these changes can be detected earlier. One set of data that bears indirectly on the question of technological change in health is the ideas households had about the causes of death and the relationship of death to disease. This information is not included with most data on death by cause, since the cause of death is often reported by physicians or civil servants. An exception to this is the American census between 1850 and 1880, in which American citizens were asked by the census takers whether somebody had died in the household in the past twelve months and, if so, at what age and of what cause. The causes reported are a very poor indicator of the *actual* causes of death, but that is not what we want to use them for. Instead, they provide some indication of what people *thought* had killed their family members. The classification of these causes provides a clue to the changes in the way the cause of death was perceived in the United States. In particular we are interested in two kinds of issues: (1) whether the reports confused symptoms with disease and (2) to what extent the diseases they identified were real diseases as opposed to more primitive concepts of illness. Of course, these declarations may have reflected the opinions of doctors rather than those of households, but the fact that households had access to doctors, and remembered their verdicts on the causes of death, is in itself an interesting phenomenon.

The sample we used was drawn from three states, Arkansas, Connecticut, and Delaware, for four census years (1850, 1860, 1870, 1880).[73] It included data on 34,113 individuals and provided age at death, gender, place of resi-

73. The data were collected and transcribed from the census manuscript by Accelerated Indexing Systems International, Salt Lake City, Utah. We are deeply indebted to Joseph P. Ferrie for placing the data set at our disposal.

Table 4.2   **Reported Causes of Death in the United States, 1850–1880**

	1850	1860	1870	1880
Diseases of digestive tract	13.65	5.36	5.56	4.87
Diseases of respiratory tract	22.55	29.93	31.66	30.05
Identified infectious diseases	15.93	19.11	20.23	21.18
Unidentified infectious diseases	11.89	11.85	8.90	6.42
Identified noninfectious diseases	5.09	6.53	9.59	8.19
Unidentified noninfectious diseases	14.77	14.95	14.75	20.70
Nondisease	3.96	4.19	4.65	4.00
Other	0.03	0.03	0.05	0.25
Unknown	12.12	8.06	4.61	4.33
Total	100	100	100	100

Source: See text.

dence, place of birth, cause of death, and, in a very small number of individuals, occupation. The transcribed data contain a number of errors, some of which were obvious and could be corrected. These include gender errors (e.g., males declared to have died during childbirth) and misspellings of diseases. To make it amenable to our needs, we divided the declared causes of death into six major categories.[74] The basic findings are presented in table 4.2.

The data clearly show a continuous decline in the proportion of digestive tract diseases, possibly indicating a cleaner food preparation, better food preservation methods, improved urban water supplies, and better basic treatment of patients against dehydration. Equally interesting is the continuous decline in the fourth row, which shows unidentified infectious diseases such as "fever," "chills," "inflammation," "brain congestion," and so on. These are primarily descriptions of symptoms rather than causes, and their decline points to an increase in sophistication. It might appear that this decline is offset by the sharp increase in unidentified noninfectious diseases in 1880, but this result is largely due to an increase of people dying of "old age" and "exhaustion," an increase which was itself perhaps a result of improved medical conditions. Leaving out such questionable categories as well as "debility" and stillborns reduces the difference between 1870 and 1880 from a 6 to a 2 percent gap.

A further analysis of the data reveals some interesting patterns. One is that the two main killers, digestive and respiratory tract diseases, follow the classic premodern seasonal pattern, with high summer mortality for digestive diseases. But the pattern weakens over time. Two crude measures are the coefficient of variation for all twelve months and U, the mean of the months in which mortality exceeded the annual average by more than one standard deviation divided by the annual average. The data for digestive diseases are presented in table 4.3.

74. Because of the nature of the reported causes of death, we could not make use of the International Classification of Diseases prepared by the National Center for Health Statistics.

Table 4.3	Seasonal Variation in Digestive Tract Diseases			
		1850	1860	1870
	Coefficient of Variation	1.15	0.64	0.58
	U	3.34	2.97	2.06

Source: See text.

A third approach to this data set exploits the age distribution reported by the census. As the figures were compiled from reports made by the survivors, the age data reveal something about the population, in that it is well known that age heaping tends to correlate (inversely) with literacy, sophistication, and numeracy.[75] The question is, of course, whether such sophistication also indicates better medical knowledge and understanding. If so, it would provide us with a better clue to how education and rising literacy enhanced people's understanding of disease and reduced mortality. We would therefore expect that lower levels of age heaping would be associated with lower levels of unidentified diseases. The heaping index we use here is rather crude but very easy to calculate; some minor gains can be made by using more sophisticated methods to smooth the age distribution and then computing the deviation of the reported age distribution from the smoothed one. At this stage, we compute a statistic V where

$$V = \frac{\sum a_i/3}{\sum a_j}$$

for $j = 19, 20, 21, 29, 30, 31, 39, 40, 41, 49, 50, 51$ and $i = 20, 30, 40, 50$. In the absence of heaping, assuming approximate linearity of the age distribution, $V \approx 1$.

The value of V declines over time, as might be expected (see table 4.4). More interesting, it tends to be high for poorly defined diseases associated with a primitive knowledge of medicine, and it declines with better-defined knowledge. In other words, our data, however indirect, suggest that education and numeracy were associated with better understanding of the nature of disease and eventually how to avoid it. Much of this chain of inference is still speculative, but we plan to explore it in future work.

4.5.3 The Welfare Impact of Mortality Decline

We have argued that the acceptance of the germ theory fundamentally changed mortality patterns, bringing a decline in death rates at all ages and a

---

75. The technique of age-heaping analysis was first applied to economic history by Mokyr and Ó Gráda (1982) and Mokyr (1985). The principle is that the degree at which populations heap at round ages is strongly and negatively correlated with their ability to compute and their overall degree of mental sophistication.

Table 4.4	Values of V
Cause of Death	V
All causes	
Males 1850–80	1.42
Females 1850–80	1.44
Total	1.43
Both genders	
1850	1.48
1860	1.42
1870	1.43
1880	1.36
By cause (all years)	
Convulsions, chills, fevers	1.65
Dropsy, paralysis, unidentified infectious diseases	1.55
Consumption, cholera	1.32
Identified infectious diseases	1.30
Typhoid	1.38

Source: See text.

sharp decline in infant mortality. In this section we wish to quantify this change and to give some rough estimates of its welfare implications. What we are estimating is the welfare impact of the decline in mortality as a whole, not the net welfare effect of the germ theory of disease. Insofar as the decline in mortality was caused by supply-related factors, the net effect of the Pasteur revolution should be prorated to the contribution of the demand-side factors. At this stage, it is too early to do justice to this complex problem, and what we present below is both incomplete and preliminary.

The welfare losses of a death include two components: the loss to that person and the loss to the person's family and friends. In what follows, we restrict ourselves to one aspect of the mortality decline: the gains in welfare to the consumer himself.

For the first calculation we use the framework suggested by Usher (1973). Usher attempted to find a measure to evaluate the historical decline in mortality rates by expanding the concept of real income to include the fall in mortality rates. In this model the consumer seeks to maximize her own welfare, represented by the function

$$(6) \qquad\qquad U = \sum_{t=0}^{n} P_t U_t,$$

where P_t is the probability of living for exactly t years and U_t is her welfare if she lives for exactly t years. Each possible length of life is therefore represented by a different state of the world and the probabilities are those of being in each state. Given a length of life t the consumer's welfare is an increasing function of her consumption from year zero through year t:

(7)
$$U_t = \sum_{i=0}^{t-1} \frac{C_i^{\beta}}{(1 + r)^i},$$

where r is a rate of discount and β is the elasticity of annual utility with respect to consumption. Two additional mortality variables are useful: D_t is the mortality rate in t years, and S_t is the probability of surviving up to year t. So,

(8)
$$S_t = \prod_{j=0}^{t-1} (1 - D_j),$$

and

(9)
$$P_t = D_t S_t = D_t \left[\prod_{j=0}^{t-1} (1 - D_j) \right].$$

From the equations above one can derive the consumer's willingness to pay for an improvement in the chances of survival. The value of a reduction in the mortality rate at year t becomes

(10)
$$-\frac{\partial C_0}{\partial D_t} = \frac{1}{\beta} C_0 \left[\sum_{j=t}^{n} \frac{(C_j/C_0)^{\beta} S_j}{(1 + r)^j} \right] \frac{1}{(1 - D_0)(1 - D_t)}.$$

Under the further assumption that consumption is constant across all ages so that $C_i = C_j = C_0$, we get the price of an instantaneous reduction in today's mortality rate:

(11)
$$-\frac{\partial C_0}{\partial D_0} = \frac{1}{\beta} C \sum_{j=0}^{n} \frac{S_j}{(1 + r)^j} \frac{1}{(1 - D_0)^2}.$$

If D_0 is very small, so that $1/(1 - D_0)^2$ approaches unity, the right-hand side simplifies even further.

This formulation was chosen for its relative simplicity and its minimal data requirements, but it does rely on numerous assumptions which should be stated clearly. First, one should note that the specified utility function is separable over time and that both consumption and the discount rate are assumed to be constant over the consumer's life. Second, utility here is derived only from consumption—the consumer does not value life independently of the level of consumption. Third, the consumer does not incur any effort in obtaining C_t; loss of utility from work, for example, does not enter the formula independently. Fourth, it is assumed that consumption is independent of the number of people living. If the entire cohort born in 1870 lived to the age of twenty, the wages and consumption would probably be different from those of the 1890 cohort. These externalities between consumers are disregarded in the following calculations.

Subject to these caveats we can proceed to derive an imputation of growth rates. Using the definitions of S_j and P_j we can rewrite the consumer's utility function as

$$(12) \qquad U = \sum_{j=0}^{n} P_j \left[\sum_{i=0}^{j-1} \frac{C_i^\beta}{(1 + r)^i} \right] = \sum_{j=0}^{n} \frac{C_j^\beta S_j}{(1 + r)^j}.$$

Using our assumption that $C_i = C_j = C$ we get

$$(13) \qquad U = C^\beta \left[\sum_{j=0}^{n} \frac{S_{j+1}}{(1 + r)^j} \right],$$

$$U(t) = C(t)^\beta \left[\sum_{j=0}^{n} \frac{S_{j+1}(t)}{(1 + r)^j} \right].$$

One can interpret the term in brackets as a measure of discounted life expectancy. Denoting this expression by $L(t)$ we get

$$(14) \qquad U(t) = C(t)^\beta L(t).$$

We can now define $\hat{C}(t)$ to be the consumption that will leave the consumer indifferent to the choice between two mortality schedules: that of date t and that of the base year (here, 1870). So that

$$(15) \qquad U[\hat{C}(t), D(1870)] = U[C(t), D(t)],$$

and using equation (14), we get

$$(16) \qquad \hat{C}(t) = C(t)[L(t)/L(1870)]^{1/\beta},$$

or, in growth rates

$$(17) \qquad G_{\hat{C}} = G_C + (G_L/\beta).$$

An important aspect of this calculation is that changes in life expectancy are assumed to be independent of the rise in income and consumption. Williamson (1984) objects to this assumption and extends the model to allow changes in life expectancy to be partly endogenous. He assumes that consumption's impact on longevity is best described by a hyperbola, so that the effect of an increase in consumption is bigger at low levels of consumption and then drops off. While this effect may have been important at the early stages of the decline in mortality, during the eighteenth and the early nineteenth centuries, we are not persuaded that it had a comparable impact at this later stage. In the critical post-1890 decline, it was primarily the *composition* of the consumption bundle rather than its *level* that brought about further changes in mortality. Learning about germs implied an awareness of how consumption affected health and this, in turn, brought changes in consumers' allocation of time and resources that led to lower mortality rates. It follows that it is legitimate to count the growth in life expectancy as separate from and in addition to the growth in income, for it was new knowledge, an exogenous change, that brought mortality down.

Two more parameters are needed for the estimation. The discount rate is assumed here to be 5 percent per year. This follows both Usher (1973) and Williamson (1984) and is appealing because it is close to the yield of consols in England during this period; but the discounted life expectancy calculations are somewhat sensitive to this estimate, as both Usher and Williamson show. In choosing the elasticity of utility with respect to consumption, β, we once again followed the suggestions of Usher and Williamson and chose β to equal 0.3. The results are presented in table 4.5.

In table 4.5 we present the annual growth rates in real wages for Sweden, England and Wales, France, and Germany with and without accounting for changes in mortality levels. The first row shows a large growth rate in discounted life expectancy for all four countries, though the estimates range from a 0.1 percent change for Sweden (1871–1911) to a 0.22 percent change in England and Wales during the same period. There is also variation across the different periods. In England the major growth in life expectancy came after 1891 while in Germany and Sweden it is fairly constant across both periods examined.

Converting these annual growth rates in discounted life expectancy to annual growth rates in utility (using the elasticity β = 0.3), we get the annual growth rate in utility due to an increase in life expectancy. These estimates vary from an annual growth rate of 0.72 percent in England (1871–1910) to 0.32 percent in Sweden over the same period. To interpret the impact of these changes, we have computed the annual increase in real wages for the countries

Table 4.5   Welfare Analysis of Mortality Decline, Selected Countries: Annual Growth Rates (%)

	England 1871–1910	England 1871–91	Germany 1871–1901	Germany 1871–91	Sweden 1871–1911	Sweden 1871–91	France 1881–1910
Discounted life expectancy	0.22	0.06	0.2	0.2	0.1	0.13	0.11
*(1/β)	0.72	0.22	0.65	0.67	0.32	0.44	0.35
Real wages	1.12	1.74	1.26	1.24	3.57	2.95	0.7
"True" real wages	1.84	1.95	1.91	1.91	3.89	3.39	1.05
Growth due to increase in life expectancy	39.18	11.03	34.06	34.96	8.25	12.96	33.45

Sources: Mortality data:
England: Williamson (1984).
Germany: *Statistisches Jahrbuch für das Deutsche Reich: Herausgegeben von Kaiserlichen Statistischen Amt.* Berlin: Ferlag von Puttkammer & Fühlbrecht. Population figures are from the 1904 issue, p. 6; survival probabilities are from the 1915 issue, p. 39.
Sweden: *Historisk statistik för Sverige, del 1, befolkning* (Historical statistics of Sweden, part I, population), 2d ed., 1720–1969. Stockholm: Statistiska Centralbyrå, 1969, pp. 16, 112–13.
France: Ministère du Commerce (service de la statistique générale de France), *Annuaire statistique: Statistique de la France.* Paris: Imprimerie Nationale, various issues. 1881 data are from the 1884 volume, pp. 7, 36–43; 1911 data are from the 1914–15 volume, pp. 9, 34.
Wage data: Williamson (1995, A26–A27, table A2.1).

in question, using real-wage data from Williamson (1995). The annual growth in real wages during this period ranged from 3.6 percent in Sweden to 0.7 percent in France. Adding the two together we get an annual increase in "true" real income of 1 percent (in France) to 3.9 percent (in Sweden). The last row of table 4.5 compares the impact of growth in life expectancy to that of the growth of true real wages. In all four countries the share of growth due to increased life expectancy is important. In England, over the period as a whole, nearly 40 percent of real growth is due to increased life expectancy. In Germany almost 35 percent of the annual growth rate is due to the decline in mortality, and in France the figure is 33 percent. It is interesting to compare these figures with those of Sweden (1871–1911 and 1871–91) and England (1871–91). In Sweden, during the half century in question, real wages rose faster than in the other countries, but mortality (already relatively low at the start of the period) did not decline much further. As a consequence, the increase in discounted life expectancy added only 8 to 13 percent of total true growth in income. In England growth in real wages was slightly higher during the first twenty years, while decline in mortality was faster during the later period. As a result the share of annual true growth due to an increase in life expectancy is much lower in the first period: 11 percent versus 39 percent.[76]

These results help address the McKeown-Fogel hypothesis once again. The data do not reveal a consistent relation between increases in income and increases in life expectancy. Some countries had higher income growth than others but smaller changes in mortality. Even for the same country, rises in life expectancy do not necessarily follow growth in income, as the case of England shows. These rough calculations are only a lower bound to the welfare improvements due to overall mortality decline, and yet they are impressive. Even though these forty years were not characterized by technological stagnation, these figures attribute some 8 to 39 percent of all welfare improvements during this time to a decline in mortality. If only, say, a third of this decline is ascribed to the increase in the demand for health-enhancing goods due to changes in consumer information, it no longer seems an exaggeration to place the Pasteur

76. The computations are rather sensitive to the choice of β, which should underline the need for treating them with great caution. The higher β, the lower the contribution of increased life expectancy to welfare increase. The reason for this is that we express the welfare gains of increased life expectancy in terms of consumption equivalents: the lower β, the bigger changes in consumption would have to be to make the consumer indifferent to the choice between two different mortality schedules. The sensitivity of our estimates of the annual growth rate in utility due to increased life expectancy is given below.

β	England 1871–1910	England 1871–91	Germany 1871–1901	Germany 1871–91	Sweden 1871–1911	Sweden 1871–91	France 1881–1910
0.1	2.16	0.65	1.95	2.01	0.96	1.32	1.06
0.3	0.72	0.22	0.65	0.67	0.32	0.44	0.35
0.5	0.43	0.13	0.39	0.40	0.19	0.26	0.21
0.8	0.27	0.08	0.24	0.25	0.12	0.16	0.13

revolution at center stage in the history of economic progress in the half century before 1914.

Although the figures in table 4.5 are in one sense upper bounds of the contribution of growing knowledge to economic welfare through higher values of $A - \varepsilon$, they are also downward biased because they only take into account the loss in consumption of the survivors themselves. A second calculation would add to that the benefits to parents of lower child and infant mortality. This research is still in progress, but its broad outline can be sketched here. The idea is that infant mortality imposes a cost similar to that of "child default" in the emigration literature. The technique involves a life-cycle model in which parents raise their children at a cost that is repaid when children reach maturity and pay society back by maintaining their aged parents and raising their own children. A death that occurs before the break-even point at which the individual has fully paid back his or her debt involves a net cost to society. The estimation of this cost parallels the computation carried out in Mokyr and Ó Gráda (1982).

References

Ackerknecht, Erwin H. 1962. Aspects of the history of therapeutics. *Bulletin of the History of Medicine* 36 (5): 389–419.

Apple, Rima D. 1987. *Mothers and medicine: A social history of infant feeding, 1890–1950.* Madison: University of Wisconsin Press.

Beaver, M. W. 1973. Population, infant mortality and milk. *Population Studies* 27 (2): 243–54.

Becker, Gary. 1976. *The economic approach to human behavior.* Chicago: University of Chicago Press.

Brown, John C. 1988. Coping with crisis? The diffusion of waterworks in late nineteenth century German towns. *Journal of Economic History* 48 (2): 307–18.

———. Forthcoming. Health reform and the decline in urban mortality: The case of Germany, 1876–1912. In *Improving the public's health: Essays in medical history,* ed. Gerald Kearns, W. Robert Lee, Marie C. Nelson, and John Rogers. Liverpool: Liverpool University Press.

Brown, R. K. 1908. *Report on the sanitary condition of the borough of Bermondsey for the year 1907.* London: G. Morrish (Printer).

Buchanan, Ian. 1985. Infant feeding, sanitation and diarrhoea in colliery communities, 1880–1911. In *Diet and health in modern Britain,* ed. Derek J. Oddy and Derek S. Miller. London: Croom Helm.

Cain, Louis, and Elyce Rotella. 1994. Death and spending: Did urban mortality shocks lead to municipal expenditure increases? Paper presented at the Cliometric Society sessions, Allied Social Sciences Association meetings, Boston.

Careless disinfection. 1872. *Popular Science Monthly* 2:122–23.

Cautley, Edmond. 1897. *The natural and artificial methods of feeding infants and young children.* London: J. and A. Churchill.

Cheadle, W. B. 1889. *On the principles and exact conditions to be observed in the arti-*

ficial feeding of infants: The properties of artificial foods and the diseases which arise from faults of diet in early life. London: Smith, Elder and Co.

——. 1896. *On the principles and exact conditions to be observed in the artificial feeding of infants: The properties of artificial foods and the diseases which arise from faults of diet in early life.* 4th ed. London: Smith, Elder and Co.

Cipolla, Carlo M. 1992. *Between two cultures: An introduction to economic history.* New York: W. W. Norton.

Cowan, Ruth Schwartz. 1983. *More work for Mother.* New York: Basic Books.

Cradock, H. C. [Mrs.]. 1908. *The care of the babies: A rearing book for girls.* London: George Bell and Sons.

Crellin, John K. 1968. The dawn of the germ theory: Particles, infection and biology. In *Medicine and science in the 1860s,* ed. F. N. L. Poynter, 57–76. London: Wellcome Institute of the History of Medicine.

——. 1981. Internal antisepsis or the dawn of chemotherapy? *Journal of the History of Medicine* 36:9–19.

Daunton, M. J. 1983. *House and home in the Victorian city.* London: Edward Arnold.

Davies, Crighton [Mrs.]. 1906. *The care of the baby.* London: Blackie and Son.

De Vries, Jan. 1993. Between purchasing power and the world of goods. In *Consumption and the world of goods,* ed. John Brewer and Roy Porter. London: Routledge.

Dwork, Deborah. 1987a. The milk option: An aspect of the history of the infant welfare movement in England 1898–1908. *Medical History* 31 (1): 51–69.

——. 1987b. *War is good for babies and other young children.* London: Tavistock Publications.

Dyhouse, Carol. 1981. *Girls growing up in late Victorian and Edwardian England.* London: Routledge and Kegan Paul.

Easterlin, Richard. 1995. Industrial revolution and mortality revolution: Two of a kind. *Journal of Evolutionary Economics* 5:393–408.

Edwards, H. R. 1962. *Competition and monopoly in the British soap industry.* Oxford: Clarendon Press.

Ellison, Glenn, and Drew Fudenberg. 1993. Rules of thumb for social learning. *Journal of Political Economy* 101, no. 4 (August): 612–43.

Ewbank, Douglas C., and Samuel H. Preston. 1990. Personal health behavior and the decline of infant and child mortality: The United States, 1900–1930. In *What we know about health transition,* ed. John Caldwell, Sally Findley, Patt Caldwell, Gigi Santow, Wendy Cosford, Jennifer Braid, and Daphne Broers-Freeman, 116–48. Health Transition Series. Canberra: Australian National University.

Eyler, John M. 1979. *Victorian social medicine: The ideas and methods of William Farr.* Baltimore, Md.: Johns Hopkins University Press.

Fish, Stewart A. 1950. The death of President Garfield. *Bulletin of the History of Medicine* 24 (4): 378–92.

Feinstein, Charles H. 1972. *Statistical tables of national income, expenditure, and output of the U.K., 1855–1965.* Cambridge: Cambridge University Press.

Fogel, Robert W. 1991a. The conquest of high mortality and hunger in Europe and America: Timing and mechanisms. In *Favorites of fortune: Technology, growth, and economic development since the Industrial Revolution,* ed. Patrice Higonnet, David S. Landes, and Henry Rosovsky. Cambridge, Mass.: Harvard University Press.

——. 1991b. New findings on secular trends in nutrition and mortality: Some implications for population theory. Paper presented at the Nobel Jubilee Symposium, Population, Development, and Welfare, 5–7 December, Lund University, Sweden.

——. 1992. Second thoughts on the European escape from hunger: Famines, price elasticities, entitlements, chronic malnutrition, and mortality rates. In *Nutrition and poverty,* ed. S. R. Osmani, 243–86. Oxford: Clarendon Press.

Fox, A. Wilson. 1903. Agricultural wages in England and Wales in the last fifty years. *Journal of the Royal Statistical Society* 66 (June): 323–59.

Frank, Johann Peter. [1786] 1976. *A system of complete medical police.* Comp. and ed. Erna Lesky. Baltimore, Md.: Johns Hopkins University Press.

Fridlizius, Gunnar. 1984. The mortality decline in the first phase of the demographic transition: Swedish experiences. In *Pre-industrial population change,* ed. Tommy Bengtsson, Gunnar Fridlizius, and Rolf Ohlsson, 71–114. Stockholm: Almqvist and Wiksell.

Gordon, Richard. 1993. *The alarming history of medicine.* New York: St. Martin's Press.

Goubert, Pierre. 1989. *The conquest of water: The advent of health in the Industrial Age.* Princeton, N.J.: Princeton University Press.

Grossman, Michael. 1972. On the concept of health capital and the demand for health. *Journal of Political Economy* 80, no. 2 (March/April): 223–55.

Guha, Sumit. 1994. The importance of social intervention in England's mortality decline: The evidence reviewed. *Social History of Medicine* 7 (1): 89–113.

Haller, John S. 1974. The use and abuse of tartar emetic in the 19th century materia medica. *Bulletin of the History of Medicine* 49, no. 2 (summer): 235–57.

Hamlin, Christopher. 1990. *A science of impurity: Water analysis in nineteenth century Britain.* Berkeley and Los Angeles: University of California Press.

Hardy, Anne. 1984. Water and the search for health in London in the eighteenth and nineteenth centuries. *Medical History* 28 (3): 250–82.

———. 1988. Urban famine or urban crisis? Typhus in the Victorian city. *Medical History* 32 (4): 401–25.

———. 1993. *The epidemic streets: Infectious disease and the rise of preventive medicine 1856–1900.* Oxford: Clarendon Press.

Hodgkinson, Ruth G. 1968. Social medicine and the growth of statistical information. In *Medicine and science in the 1860s,* ed. F. N. L. Poynter, 183–98. London: Wellcome Institute of the History of Medicine.

Hudson, Robert P. 1983. *Disease and its control: The shaping of modern thought.* Westport, Conn.: Greenwood Press.

Imhof, Arthur. 1984. The amazing simultaneousness of the big differences and the boom in the 19th century—some facts and hypotheses about infant and maternal mortality in Germany, 18th to 20th century. In *Pre-industrial population change,* ed. Tommy Bengtsson, Gunnar Fridlizius, and Rolf Ohlsson, 191–222. Stockholm: Almqvist and Wiksell.

Jack, Florence B., and Rita Strauss, eds. 1911. *The woman's book: Contains everything a woman ought to know.* London: T. C. and E. C. Jack.

Kearns, Gerry. 1988. The urban penalty and the population history of England. In *Society, health, and population during the demographic transition,* ed. Anders Brandstrom and Lars-Goran Tedebrand, 213–36. Stockholm: Almqvist and Wiksell.

King, Lester. 1961. The blood-letting controversy: A study in the scientific method. *Bulletin of the History of Medicine* 35 (1): 1–13.

Kintner, Hallie J. 1987. The impact of breastfeeding patterns on the regional differences in infant mortality in Germany, 1910. *European Journal of Population* 3:233–61.

Kirby, Richard Shelton, Sidney Withington, Arthur Burr Darling, and Frederick Gridley Kilgour. 1990. *Engineering in history.* New York: McGraw Hill, 1956. Reprint, New York: Dover Publications.

Kramer, Howard H. 1948. The germ theory and the early health program in the United States. *Bulletin of the History of Medicine* 22 (3): 233–47.

Latour, Bruno. 1988. *The pasteurization of France.* Cambridge, Mass.: Harvard University Press.

Loudon, Irvine. 1986. Deaths in childhood from the eighteenth century to 1935. *Medical History* 30:1–41.

McKeown, Thomas. 1977. *The modern rise of population.* London: Butler and Tanner.

McManners, John. 1985. *Death and the Enlightenment.* Oxford: Oxford University Press.

Marcus, Alan I. 1979. Disease prevention in America: From a local to a national outlook, 1880–1910. *Bulletin of the History of Medicine* 53 (2): 184–203.

Mathias, Peter. 1979. Swords and ploughshares: The armed forces, medicine and health in the late nineteenth century. In *The transformation of England,* ed. Peter Mathias. New York: Columbia University Press.

Meckel, Richard A. 1990. *Save the babies: American health reform and the prevention of infant mortality, 1850–1929.* Baltimore, Md.: Johns Hopkins University Press.

Mitchell, B. R. 1975. *European historical statistics.* London: Macmillan.

———. 1988. *British historical statistics.* Cambridge: Cambridge University Press.

Mokyr, Joel. 1985. *Why Ireland starved: A quantitative and analytical history of the Irish economy, 1800–1850.* Rev. ed. London: Allen and Unwin.

———. 1993. Mortality, technology, and economic growth, 1750–1914: A suggested reinterpretation. Northwestern University, Evanston, Ill. Unpublished.

———. 1996. Technological selection, information, and changing household behavior, 1850–1914. Northwestern University, Evanston, Ill. Unpublished.

Mokyr, Joel, and Cormac Ó Gráda. 1982. Emigration and poverty in prefamine Ireland. *Explorations in Economic History* 19:360–84.

Newman, George. 1906. *Infant mortality: A social problem.* London: Methuen and Co.

Pollak, Robert A., and Susan Cotts Watkins. 1993. Cultural and economic approaches to fertility. *Population and Development Review* 18, no. 3 (September): 467–96.

Pooley, Marilyn E., and Colin G. Pooley. 1984. Health, society and environment in nineteenth-century Manchester. In *Urban disease and mortality in nineteenth century England,* ed. Robert Woods and John Woodward, 148–75. New York: St. Martin's Press.

Porter, Theodore. 1986. *The rise of statistical thinking, 1820–1900.* Princeton, N.J.: Princeton University Press.

Preston, Samuel H. 1976. *Mortality patterns in national populations.* New York: Academic Press.

Preston, Samuel, and Michael Haines. 1991. *Fatal years: Child mortality in late nineteenth century America.* Princeton, N.J.: Princeton University Press.

Proskauer, Curt. 1958. Development and use of the rubber glove in surgery and gynecology. *Journal of the History of Medicine* 13:373–81.

Reiser, Stanley Joel. 1978. *Medicine and the reign of technology.* Cambridge: Cambridge University Press.

Riley, James C. 1986. Insects and the European mortality decline. *American Historical Review* 91:833–58.

———. 1987. *The eighteenth-century campaign to avoid disease.* New York: St. Martin's Press.

———. 1991. Working health time: A comparison of preindustrial, industrial, and postindustrial experience in life and health. *Explorations in Economic History* 28: 169–91.

Roberts, Robert. 1990. *The classic slum.* London: Penguin Books.

Rogers, Naomi. 1989. Germs with legs: Flies, disease and the new health. *Bulletin of the History of Medicine* 63:599–617.

Rollet-Echalier, Catherine. 1990. *La politique à l'égard de la petite enfance sous la IIIe république.* Paris: Presses Universitaires de France.

Rosen, George. 1947. What is social medicine? A genetic analysis of the concept. *Bulletin of the History of Medicine* 21 (5): 674–733.

———. 1955. Problems in the application of statistical analysis to questions of health: 1700–1880. *Bulletin of the History of Medicine* 29 (1): 27–45.

Routh, C. H. F. 1876. *Infant feeding and its influence on life.* 3d ed. London: J. and A. Churchill.

Rumsey, Henry W. 1875. *Essays and papers on some fallacies of statistics concerning life and death, health and disease.* London: Smith, Elder and Co.

Rusnock, Andrea A. 1990. The quantification of things human: Medicine and political arithmetic in Enlightenment England and France. Ph.D. diss., Princeton University.

Ryan Johansson, Sheila. 1994. Food for thought: Rhetoric and reality in modern mortality history. *Historical Methods* 27, no. 3 (summer): 101–25.

Spree, Reinhard. 1988. *Health and social class in Imperial Germany.* Oxford: Berg.

Stevenson, Lloyd G. 1955. Science down the drain: On the hostility of certain sanitarians to animal experimentation, bacteriology, and immunology. *Bulletin of the History of Medicine* 29 (1): 1–26.

Strauss, John, and Duncan Thomas. 1993. Human resources: Empirical modeling of household and family decisions. In *Handbook of development economics.* Vol. 3, ed. T. N. Srinivasan and Jere R. Behrman. Amsterdam: North-Holland.

Szreter, Simon. 1988. The importance of social intervention in Britain's mortality decline, c. 1850–1914: A re-interpretation of the role of health. *Social History of Medicine* 1:1–37.

Thomas, Carol. 1995. Domestic labour and health: Bringing it all back home. *Sociology of Health and Illness* 17 (3): 328–52.

Thorne, Stuart. 1986. *The history of food preservation.* Totowa, N.J.: Barnes and Noble Books.

Tomes, Nancy. 1990. The private side of public health: Sanitary science, domestic hygiene, and the germ theory, 1870–1900. *Bulletin of the History of Medicine* 64 (4): 509–39.

Tranter, N. L. 1985. *Population and society 1750–1940: Contrasts in population growth.* New York: Longman.

United Kingdom. 1903. Report on wholesale and retail prices in the United Kingdom in 1902, with comparative statistical tables for a series of years. Parliamentary Papers, vol. 68.

Usher, Dan. 1973. An imputation to the measure of economic growth for changes in life expectancy. In *The measurement of economic and social performance,* ed. Milton Moss. New York: National Bureau of Economic Research.

Whetham, E. H. 1964. The London milk trade, 1860–1900. *Economic History Review* 17 (May): 369–80.

Williams, Perry. 1991. The laws of health: Women, medicine and sanitary reform, 1850–1890. In *Science and sensibility: Gender and scientific enquiry,* ed. Marina Benjamin, 60–88. Oxford: Basil Blackwell.

Williamson, Jeffrey G. 1984. British mortality and the value of life: 1781–1931. *Population Studies* 38 (March): 157–72.

———. 1995. The evolution of global labor markets since 1830: Background evidence and hypotheses. *Explorations in Economic History* 32, no. 2 (April): 141–96.

Wilson, Charles. 1954. *History of Unilever.* 2 vols. London: Cassell and Co.

Wohl, Anthony S. 1983. *Endangered lives: Health in Victorian Britain.* Cambridge, Mass.: Harvard University Press.

Woods, Robert. 1984. Mortality and sanitary conditions in late nineteenth-century Birmingham. In *Urban disease and mortality in nineteenth century England,* ed. Robert Woods and John Woodward, 176–202. New York: St. Martin's Press.

Woods, Robert I., Patricia A. Watterson, and John H. Woodward. 1989. The causes of rapid infant decline in England and Wales, 1861–1921, part 2. *Population Studies* 43:113–32.

Woods, Robert I., and John Woodward. 1984. Mortality, poverty and the environment. In *Urban disease and mortality in nineteenth century England,* ed. Robert Woods and John Woodward, 19–36. New York: St. Martin's Press.

Comment   John C. Brown

This paper by Joel Mokyr and Rebecca Stein argues that the discovery and successful diffusion of the germ theory of disease—a new technology for household decision making—substantially explains that part of the great mortality decline that ended with the onset of World War I. Two perspectives have generally set the terms of the debate over what prompted the decline in mortality before effective medical treatment became available in the 1930s and 1940s. Nutritionists emphasize that improved resistance to disease resulted from rising living standards. Environmentalists credit enlightened public investments in sewers, waterworks, and other programs with reducing exposure to disease. Both approaches have eschewed developing models of economic behavior that go beyond these medical models of etiology and outcome to interpret mortality as the result of household choices constrained by relative prices, limited resources, and environmental risk.

Mokyr and Stein extend our understanding of the causes behind mortality decline by sketching out just such a model of household decision making within a household production framework. The model focuses upon the importance of household knowledge about what influenced health and diminished the risk of death. The germ theory of disease, developed initially by Pasteur and given strong empirical grounding by Koch's discoveries of the early 1880s, offered households new technologies for transforming consumption and time into better health. Households may have been so far away from best practice that simple reallocation of a limited budget may have had a powerful impact upon reducing mortality. Spending more time on washing and less on work, or more earnings on soap and less in the corner tavern, may have improved the chances that family members, particularly children and infants, survived the risk of infectious disease that characterized late-nineteenth-century living. The germ theory may have provided local officials with important suggestions about best-practice techniques, although most were already convinced by prevailing miasmatic theories that clean and abundant water, fresh air, and effective sewage disposal offered payoffs in reduced mortality. The germ theory's major role was its influence on household behavior. Its logic and consistency with the facts could persuade mothers to replace the treacle-soaked rag with a sterilized pacifier, where decades of carefully tabulated statistical regularities could not. If the germ theory takes on the leading role in the pre-1914 decline that the authors assign it, the welfare payoffs in longer lives from this single innovation rival the fruits of a half century of invention and capital accumulation. While I remain somewhat skeptical about the quantitative estimates of the germ theory's impact, I do not doubt that this paper's provocative thesis will enrich the debate on mortality decline.

The argument requires first winning acceptance for the model. It must then demonstrate that the key insights of bacteriological science of the 1880s had

John C. Brown is associate professor of economics at Clark University.

diffused widely among households and community leaders by 1910. Finally, it requires convincing evidence that the diffusion of this innovation, rather than higher incomes or shifts in relative prices, account for the bulk of declines in mortality that yield such substantial increases in lifetime utility.

The paper achieves the first task with a fascinating historical narrative that casts turn-of-the-century campaigns for infant health, battles against flies, and fights for clean water in terms of exogenous changes in household technologies for improving health. The tales of ignorance of good hygienic practice and the diversity of applications of the germ theory hint at the size of the task that well-informed physicians, social workers, and others faced. The case that the gap was big between the best practice dictated by germ theory and the practice current among households would be strengthened with more evidence that household practices in matters hygienic in the 1880s were significantly different from practices in the 1920s or 1930s.

A more important issue arises from the key role of subjective risk assessment in the model. At the margin, the decision on how much more soap to buy (or whether to rent an apartment with an indoor tap) hinges upon the household's assessment of the payoff: its guess about the likelihood that more soap and accessible water will reduce the prospect of an infant contracting diarrhea. A key result of the literature on risk perception is the difficulty households have in assessing just those kinds of common, everyday risks that are essential to decision making on hygiene. Consumers today generally underestimate the probability of relatively low-risk, but more likely events and overestimate the probability of high-risk, but unlikely events (Slovic, Fischhoff, and Lichtenstein 1985, 246). The same may be true of consumers in 1900. It was not tuberculosis, the ubiquitous but silent killer of the nineteenth century, but the infrequent cholera and typhoid epidemics, with high case-mortality rates, that first attracted the sanitarians' attention. Were the same true of households, we would expect that even when medicine was armed with the germ theory of disease, there would still be slippage between medicine's best (and imperfect) knowledge about the payoff for doing things hygienically and households' own assessments of that payoff. Perhaps for this reason, many turn-of-the-century public health campaigns supplemented educational efforts with efforts to coerce or even bribe households. Housing inspection, regulation of milk supplies, and mandatory inoculations were all designed to enforce appropriate (or even excessive) levels of consumption of goods believed to reduce mortality. Efforts of German cities to increase breast-feeding typically included allowances to nursing mothers (Kintner 1985, 175–77).

While medical historians still debate the question of when the germ theory won out, most evidence points to the 1890s as the decade the best-educated physicians in the United States and Germany accepted the germ theory (Gariepy 1994; Evans 1987, 490–507). The authors acknowledge the potential for a long lag between acceptance by physicians and diffusion into the practice of the poor of Dublin or Hester Street. As in any case of identifying changes in demand for a nonmarketed good, the question of diffusion is difficult to resolve empirically. The authors choose the imaginative strategy of looking for evidence on shifts in the derived demand for inputs into health, holding prices and incomes constant. Thus, the evidence they present on the rise in the per capita consumption of soap in England in the face of price increases (particularly after 1900) offers encouraging support for an outward shift in demand and perhaps diffusion of the germ theory. Evidence that the time and cash price of water did not also fall during this period, as waterworks and indoor plumbing replaced the occasional well and pump in even small towns and villages, would strength this point. More of this kind of indirect information, including a closer examination of the correlates of trends in the labor force participation of married women and of breast-feeding throughout the industrialized West, would buttress the case for diffusion.

Perhaps the most vexing issue raised by this paper is how much of the eventual mortality decline resulted from the advances associated with the germ theory. The problem is straightforward. While this paper emphasizes exposure to infectious disease as an important influence on mortality, mortality also depends on resistance to disease and environmental influences such as weather conditions and pollution of the environment. The evidence on contrary trends in real wages for common labor and infant mortality presented by the authors offers a start at confronting the alternative hypothesis that incomes and prices mattered the most for mortality decline. There are further complications. The declines in child and infant mortality that the paper argues were most responsive to improved household hygiene occurred during a period of declining fertility. Some authors (e.g., Woods, Watterson, and Woodward 1989, 121–26) suggest that fertility decline, by lengthening birth intervals and diminishing the number of higher-parity births, could have contributed to mortality decline. Identifying the separate contribution of the germ theory is also difficult, since miasmatic theories dominant until at least the 1880s recommended many of the same general principles as the new bacteriology: lots of clean water, clean air, and effective disposal of sewage.

A convincing explanation for mortality decline must also be consistent with the observed pattern of change in disease-specific mortality. Some diseases were susceptible to the prophylaxis recommended by the germ theory; others were not. The fall in mortality from tuberculosis contributed substantially to reduced deaths among adults in many industrialized countries, but it is uncertain whether it resulted from a decline in exposure to the disease. Tuberculin testing in England and Germany from 1913 to the 1940s revealed rates of exposure to tuberculosis of up to 90 percent, enough to suggest that other factors also contributed to the decline (Otto, Spree, and Vögele 1990, 301–2; Guha 1994, 104).

These considerations suggest that the lower-bound estimates of welfare gains that can be ascribed to the germ theory, as presented in table 4.5, should be revised downward. The experience of German cities suggests the magnitude of such an adjustment. Confining the period of potential influence to the years after 1880 seems reasonable in view of the historical literature. This adjustment reduces the annual growth in discounted life expectancy over the entire period 1871–1900 to about 0.15 percent. The diseases where application of the germ theory offered the soundest prophylaxis—gastrointestinal disorders, typhoid, and diphtheria—accounted for about 18 percent of the overall mortality decline from the late 1870s until the 1900s (Vögele 1993, table 5). Assuming the same other parameters as the paper, the annual gain to lifetime real wages suggested by this lower-bound calculation is about 0.09 (3.3 * 0.15 * 0.18) percent. As a share of "true" real-wage growth reflecting gains to lifetime consumption, the lower bound is about 7 percent.

Is this lower bound a reasonable estimate of gains from the germ theory? Three things suggest that it is too low and why the Pasteur revolution merits a closer look. Demographic historians emphasize the interrelatedness of morbidity experience and resistance to further infection. In particular, the gastrointestinal diseases that afflicted infants and young children left the survivors weakened and prone to other sources of infection (Preston and Van de Walle 1978). Reducing morbidity from these diseases could have yielded substantial payoffs in reduced mortality from other diseases. More research is needed on how large the payoff from breaking into the gastrointestinal complex may have been. Little is also known about how much households valued reductions in mortality risk. Data from housing markets, labor markets, or episodes of cholera or typhoid may offer some clues. Facing a risk of upward of two in one hundred of dying from the 1892 Hamburg cholera epidemic, over 2 percent of the population—middle and upper classes—fled the city in the few days before a quarantine cut off Hamburg from communication with the outside, and they remained out of the city for about three months (Evans 1987, 348, 408).

Indeed, although the case for substantial benefits before 1914 may need closer examination, World War I and the years following offer potential for substantial gains from the germ theory. The germ theory is widely credited with saving the lives of thousands of combatants who would otherwise have fallen prey to the traditional battlefield killers of typhoid and dysentery. During the subsequent two decades of peace, gains to well-being from continued increases in life expectancy must compare favorably with the anemic growth in real wages of the period.

In the end, this paper raises a key question about the allocation of public resources. The essential hypothesis of the germ theory revolution is that social conditions—poverty, irregular incomes, and poor living conditions—mattered less for household health than how households used what limited resources they had. For this reason, it poses a direct challenge to those who argue that living standards were crucial for improvements in health outcomes during an era when access to medical care made only a minor difference. Did the concern of the social hygienists with the striking correlations between mortality and difficult social conditions distract them from the underlying true cause of ill health of the entire population: ignorance? This question is important for evaluating debates about living standards during the era of industrialization and the success of efforts to reform urban living conditions. It is one of the many issues this thought-provoking paper raises that will likely inform future debates about the great mortality decline.

References

Evans, Richard J. 1987. *Death in Hamburg: Society and politics in the cholera years, 1830–1910.* London: Oxford University Press.

Gariepy, Thomas P. 1994. The introduction and acceptance of Listerian antisepsis in the United States. *Journal of the History of Medicine and Allied Sciences* 49:167–206.

Guha, Sumit. 1994. The importance of social intervention in England's mortality decline: The evidence reviewed. *Social History of Medicine* 7:89–113.

Kintner, Hallie. 1985. Trends and regional differences in breastfeeding in Germany from 1871 to 1937. *Journal of Family History* 10 (summer): 167–82.

Otto, Roland, Reinhard Spree, and Jörg Vögele. 1990. Seuchen und Seuchenbekämpfung in deutschen Städten während des 19. und frühen 20. Jahrhunderts. *Medizinhistorisches Journal* 25:286–304.

Preston, Samuel, and Etienne Van de Walle. 1978. Urban French mortality in the nineteenth century. *Population Studies* 32:275–97.

Slovic, Paul, Baruch Fischhoff, and Sarah Lichtenstein. 1985. Regulation of risk: A psychological perspective. In *Regulatory policy and the social sciences,* ed. Roger Noll, 281–83. Berkeley and Los Angeles: University of California Press.

Vögele, Jörg. 1993. Sanitäre Reformen und der Sterblichkeitsrückgang in deutschen Städten, 1877–1913. *Vierteljahrschrift für Sozial- und Wirtschaftsgeschichte* 80:345–65.

Woods, Robert I., Patricia A. Watterson, and John H. Woodward. 1989. The causes of rapid infant mortality decline in England and Wales, 1861–1921, Part 2. *Population Studies* 43:113–32.

II Contemporary Product Studies

5   Valuation of New Goods under Perfect and Imperfect Competition

Jerry A. Hausman

The economic theory of the Consumer Price Index (CPI) has been well developed (see, e.g., Pollak 1989). The CPI serves as an approximation of an ideal cost-of-living (COL) index. In turn, the COL index answers the question of how much more (or less) income a consumer requires to be as well-off in period 1 as in period 0 given changes in prices, changes in the quality of goods, and the introduction of new goods (or the disappearance of existing goods). The CPI as currently estimated by the Bureau of Labor Statistics (BLS) does a reasonable job of accounting for price changes and has begun to attempt to include quality changes. However, the BLS has not attempted to estimate the effect of the introduction of new goods, despite the recognition of the potential importance of new goods on both a COL index and the CPI (see Fixler 1993).

The omission of the effect of the introduction of new goods seems quite surprising given that most commonly used business strategies can be placed in either of two categories: becoming the low-cost producer of a homogeneous good or differentiating your product from its competitors. The latter strategy has become the hallmark of much of American (and Japanese) business practice. The numbers of cars, beers, cereals, sodas, ice creams and yogurts, appliances such as refrigerators, and cable television programs all demonstrate the ability of firms to differentiate their products successfully. Furthermore, consumers demonstrate a preference for these products by buying them in suffi-

Jerry A. Hausman is the John and Jennie S. MacDonald Professor of Economics at the Massachusetts Institute of Technology.

The author thanks the NSF for research support, Z. Griliches and G. Leonard for useful conversations, and T. Bresnahan, P. Joskow, and W. Nordhaus for helpful comments. Jason Abrevaya provided excellent research assistance. This paper is given in the memory of Sir John Hicks, who first taught the author welfare economics.

cient quantities to make the expected profit positive for the new brands. As the BLS has recognized in its estimation of the CPI: "If the measurement error is systematic, then a systematic difference may exist between the computed CPI and the true [COL index], which would, in turn, affect the measured rate of price change" (Fixler 1993, 3). This paper finds evidence of such a systematic difference which causes the CPI to be overstated by a significant amount due to its neglect of new products.[1]

In this paper I first explain the theory of COL indexes and demonstrate how new goods should be included, using the classical theory of Hicks (1940) and Rothbarth (1941). The correct price to use for the good in the preintroduction period is the "virtual" price which sets demand to zero. Estimation of this virtual price requires estimation of a demand function which in turn provides the expenditure function which allows exact calculation of the COL index. The extensive data requirements and the need to specify and estimate a demand function for a new brand among many existing brands may have proved obstacles to the inclusion of new goods in the CPI up to this point.

As an example I use the introduction of a new cereal brand by General Mills in 1989—Apple-Cinnamon Cheerios. The cereal industry has been among the most prodigious in new-brand introduction. My econometric specification permits differing amounts of similarity among cereal brands, which is quite important given that Apple-Cinnamon Cheerios are closer to other Cheerios brands than to, say, Shredded Wheat. I find that the virtual price is about twice the actual price of Apple-Cinnamon Cheerios and that the increase in consumer's surplus is substantial. Based on some simplifying approximations, I find that the CPI may be overstated for cereal by about 25 percent because of its neglect of the effect of new cereal brands.

I then extend the classical Hicks-Rothbarth theory from its implicit assumption of perfect competition to the more realistic situation of imperfect competition among multiproduct firms. Imperfect competition can be important because introduction of a new brand may allow a multiproduct firm to raise the prices of its existing, closely competing brands. When I take account of the effect of imperfect competition, I find that the increase in consumer welfare is only 85 percent as high as in the perfect competition case. Nevertheless, the CPI for cereal would still be too high by about 20 percent. Thus, I conclude that the introduction of new goods is an important economic occurrence, and the BLS should attempt to develop procedures to incorporate new goods correctly into the CPI. I also find that consumers highly value new goods, which provide significant consumer's surplus despite the existence of other brands which compete closely with the new brand.

1. The BLS does include new goods after they are introduced. However, this procedure misses the additional consumer welfare which arises from the introduction of the new good compared to the welfare in the base period when the good was not being sold.

5.1   Valuation of New Goods under Perfect Competition

Sir John Hicks made one of the first attempts to develop the theory of the evaluation of new goods. In 1940 Hicks considered evaluation of social income and economic welfare, using index number theory to consider the effects of rationing and the introduction of new goods. Hicks correctly saw his approach as the basis for the evaluation of real income under these changes. Without completely working out the mathematics, Hicks stated that for rationed goods the index numbers need to be altered so that the price used would lead to the amount of the ration. This higher price can be considered the "virtual price" which, when inserted into the demand function, leads to the observed amount of rationed demand.[2] For new products Hicks stated that the virtual price for periods in which the goods did not exist would "just make the demands for these commodities (from the whole community) equal to zero" (1940, 144). Modern economists recognize this price as the shadow or reservation price which, used in the demand function, sets demand equal to zero. Of course, new products in a sense are a special case of rationing where the demand for the good is zero. Given the demand function I can solve for the virtual price and for the expenditure (or indirect utility) function and do correct evaluations of social welfare without needing to use the index number formulas discussed by Hicks.[3]

Rothbarth, in a 1941 paper on rationing, put the subject on a firm mathematical footing and introduced the notion that a virtual price arises from the "price system with respect to which the quantities actually consumed are optimum . . . the 'virtual price system'" (100).[4] I use his approach to demonstrate the effect on the price index, or real income, of the introduction of a new good. In period 1 consider the demand for the new good, x_n, as a function of all prices and income, y:

(1) $$x_n = g(p_1, \ldots, p_{n-1}, p_n, y).$$

Now if the good was not available in period 0, I solve for the virtual price, p_n^*, which causes the demand for the new good to be equal to zero:

(2) $$0 = x_n = g(p_1, \ldots, p_{n-1}, p_n^*, y).$$

2. See Neary and Roberts (1980) for a modern treatment of rationing using this approach.
3. See Hausman (1980, 1981) who uses this approach in the context of female labor supply to do welfare calculations.
4. Rothbarth, one of Keynes's last students, faced internment in the United Kingdom during World War II because of his German nationality. Instead, he volunteered for the British army where he died during the war. G. Burtless and I (Burtless and Hausman 1978) were unaware of Rothbarth's paper when we used the term "virtual income" in solving for demands in nonlinear budget set problems. Rothbarth's paper was subsequently pointed out to us by K. Roberts.

The index number approach, used by both Hicks (1940) and Rothbarth (1941), then considers the change in real income to be the ratio $(p_n^*)(x_n)$ / $(p_n)(x_n)$. While this approach is approximately correct, it does not account for the need to change income y as the price is increased in order to stay on the same indifference curve and thus keep the marginal value of income constant. Thus, instead of using the Marshallian demand curve in equations (1) and (2), I use the income-compensated and utility-constant Hicksian demand curve to do an exact welfare evaluation.[5] In terms of the expenditure function I solve the differential equation from Roy's identity, which corresponds to the demand function in equation (1), to find the (partial) expenditure function[6]

$$(3) \qquad y = e(p_1, \ldots, p_{n-1}, p_n, u^1).$$

The expenditure function gives the minimum amount of income, y, to achieve the level of utility, u^1, that arises from the indirect utility function corresponding to the demand function of equation (1) and to the expenditure function of equation (3). To solve for the amount of income needed to achieve utility level u^1 in the absence of the new good, I use the expenditure function from equation (3) to calculate

$$(4) \qquad y^* = e(p_1, \ldots, p_{n-1}, p_n^*, u^1).$$

The exact COL index becomes $P(p, p^*, u^1) = y^* / y$. Note that to use this approach one must estimate a demand curve as in equation (1), which in turn implies the expenditure function and the ability to do the exact welfare calculation of equations (3) and (4). Thus, the only assumption which is required is to specify a parametric (or nonparametric) form of the demand function.

Diewert (1992) reviews the price index literature and calls the use of the expenditure (or cost) function approach the "economic approach," which he relates back to the original paper of Konüs (1939) and compares to the "axiomatic approach," which is more often used in the price index literature. Diewert recognizes the usefulness of the economic approach, but he notes the requirement of knowing the consumer's expenditure function (1992, 18). In the case of new goods the traditional axiomatic approach offers little or no guidance so that demand curve estimation must be undertaken to estimate the virtual or reservation price. Once the demand curve is estimated, the expenditure function comes for "free," since no additional assumptions are required and new

---

5. In equation (2), income, y, is solved in terms of the utility level, u^1, to find the Hicksian demand curve given the Marshallian demand curve specification. Hausman (1981) demonstrates this solution procedure.

6. Hausman (1981) demonstrates how to solve the differential equation which arises from Roy's identity in the case of common parametric specifications of demand. Hausman and Newey (1995) demonstrate how to do the analysis when a nonparametric specification of demand is specified and estimated.

goods can be evaluated.[7] Thus, the economic approach seems to be the only practical approach to the evaluation of new goods.

A potentially more serious problem with the valuation of new goods is the implicit assumption of perfect competition. Indeed, I have not seen this potential problem mentioned in my review of the literature although Robinson's (1933) book on imperfect competition predates Hicks's (1940) paper. The implicit assumption of perfect competition follows from the assumption that prices of other goods remain the same at marginal cost when the new good is introduced. Under imperfect competition with significant fixed costs and free entry which leads to a zero-profit condition, introduction of a new good will lead to somewhat higher prices for existing goods whose demand decreases. This effect will usually be small. A more significant effect arises from the fact that most new products are introduced by multiproduct firms. Introduction of a new good will allow the firm to raise its price because some of the demand for its existing product, which it will lose, will not go to competitors' products, but will instead go to the firm's new product. I will develop the implications of imperfect competition in section 5.6, but first I will apply the classical theory of new products under perfect competition to data from the ready-to-eat cereal industry, perhaps the foremost industry in the introduction of new goods.

5.2   New-Product Introductions in the Ready-to-Eat Cereal Industry

The ready-to-eat (RTE) cereal industry has been among the most prodigious introducers of new brands in U.S. industries.[8] In the period 1980–92 approximately 190 new brands were introduced into a pool of about 160 existing brands. Most new cereal brands, in common with most new-product introductions, do not succeed.[9] Out of the 190 new brands introduced since 1980, over 95 have been discontinued. For instance, of the 27 new brands introduced in 1989, 14 brands had already been discontinued by 1993. Of the 190 new brands introduced during the twelve-year period, only 2 of the 190 brands have a market share (in pounds) of greater than 1 percent. Still, new brands are important in the sense that about 25 percent of all RTE cereal consumption comes from brands introduced within the past ten years. Thus, cereal company executives believe that it is quite important to continue to introduce new brands

7. Confusion sometimes arises over whether the entire expenditure function or all demand curves must be estimated. The answer is no under the usual type of separability assumptions (or Leontief aggregation assumptions) which are commonly used in empirical research and are implicit in statistical agencies' calculations of price indexes. Thus, only the demand curve for the new good needs to be estimated, not the demand curve for all other goods.

8. Recently, the beer industry has also undergone significant new-product introductions with bottled draft beers, dry beers, and ice beers, all introduced within about the past five years.

9. About 80 percent of new-product introductions in consumer goods fail. See, e.g., Urban et al. (1983).

because consumers exhibit a strong preference for continued variety among cereal brands.

Some economists have claimed that this high rate of introduction of new brands is part of an anticompetitive strategy by cereal companies.[10] While both economic theory and the facts of the industry seem contrary to the preemption claim, the RTE cereal industry is highly concentrated with no successful entry by a significant manufacturer in the past fifty years. Six firms have each produced 94 percent or more of all RTE cereals (in dollar sales) over the period 1982–92. Kellogg's share has varied in the range of 37.3–41.5 percent; General Mills' share has varied from 23.0 to 29.0 percent; General Foods' share has varied in the range of 10.4–15.8 percent. Quaker, Ralston, and Nabisco have all been in the range of about 3.0–8.9 percent. Only one other company, Malt-O-Meal, has gained a share above 1 percent.[11] Recently, a move toward further consolidation has occurred. In 1992 General Mills announced a purchase of Nabisco's cereal brands, the largest of which is Nabisco Shredded Wheat. The U.S. government granted permission for this acquisition, and in 1993 General Foods (Post brands) acquired Nabisco's cereal brands. Thus, five major firms are likely to exist, although I would not be surprised if another acquisition occurred soon.[12]

However, while the three largest firms have about 80 percent of the RTE cereal market, it is important to realize that very few individual brands have significant shares. For instance, Kellogg's Frosted Flakes is the largest Kellogg brand, with a share of 5.0 percent (in 1993); Kellogg's Corn Flakes is quite close at 4.99 percent, while Cheerios is the largest General Mills brand, with a share of 5.3 percent. Most brands have quite a small share and the share movement among brands is quite dynamic.

No successful entry by a significant new manufacturer has occurred in the RTE cereal industry in the past fifty years. The RTE industry ha remained highly concentrated during this time period, despite the general perception that investments in the RTE cereal industry earn higher rates of return than in many other industries.[13] During the 1970s, some new entry did occur in the RTE

10. See Schmalensee (1978) and Scherer (1982) who claim that "brand proliferation" served as an entry deterrent in the RTE cereal industry. Both economists testified for the U.S. Federal Trade Commission (FTC) "In the matter of Kellogg Co. et al.," (docket no. 8883, available from the author). The FTC lost this "shared monopoly" case in which it was claimed that a highly concentrated oligopoly deterred entry through the introduction of new brands. Furthermore, Judd (1985) subsequently demonstrated that the preemption story implied by brand proliferation is unlikely to provide credible preemption unless exit costs are high, which is contrary to fact in the RTE cereal industry for a given brand.

11. However, no individual brand of Malt-O-Meal has ever achieved 1 percent. Furthermore, much of Malt-O-Meal's production is for private-label brands.

12. The State of New York is currently challenging General Foods' acquisition of Nabisco, so an extremely small probability exists that Nabisco may become independent again, raising the number of competitors to six.

13. See, e.g., General Mills' 1992 annual report, p. 2, which reports an average after-tax return on capital over five years of 21 percent, "which is among the best in U.S. industry"; Kellogg's 1991 annual report, p. 16, gives an after-tax return on assets of about 15.5 percent for 1991, while

cereals industry for "natural" cereals and by some substantial food-product manufacturers such as Pillsbury, Pet, and Colgate, but these firms did not last long as competitors. Thus, the prospect for actual new entry into the RTE cereal industry is very unlikely, with exit a more likely prospect than new entry. This is despite high growth rates in the 1982–92 period, when average revenue growth was 6.7 percent per year (in real terms).

Since the brand-proliferation models do not yield a credible model of entry deterrence, what is the main reason for the lack of new entry into an industry which otherwise might expect significant new entry? The main impediment to successful new entry into the RTE cereal market is the necessity for an extremely large investment in advertising, all of which is a sunk cost if the new product does not succeed.[14] Industry estimates are that for firms to launch a new brand currently costs $20–40 million for advertising and promotion in the initial year. The investment is typically continued at this level annually for one to two years, unless the brand is discontinued or allowed to decline because of a decision that it will not succeed in the long run. The cumulative investment is expected to be paid off (before any net positive return to the investment is obtained) only after a period of one to two years, although a very few brands do succeed more quickly. This investment is substantial compared to the likely success—a 1 percent share for a new brand is considered to be a great success. Yet almost no new brand achieves 1 percent. Of the approximately 190 new brands which were introduced during 1982–92, only two currently have a pound share of 1 percent or greater.

Thus, the odds of a successful new-brand introduction by an existing RTE manufacturer are daunting; a new entrant would face even longer odds because of start-up costs and the extra cost and difficulty of achieving shelf space for a new brand. An existing manufacturer can transfer shelf space from an old brand to a new brand. However, a new entrant does not have the shelf space to trade. The main "outside" competition which has arisen over the past few years has been the success of "store brands," also called private-label brands.[15] Private-label brands have doubled their market share from about 4 percent to 8 percent over the past five to ten years. For these brands the supermarket provides the shelf space and has the cereal manufactured independently. Indeed, Ralston does the majority of the private-brand manufacturing. Thus private-label corn flakes and other brands seem most successful in providing

---

Kellogg's second-quarter report for the first six months of 1992 yields an annualized return on assets of 17.7 percent (financial reports available from the author). Of course, accounting returns on assets are typically an unreliable guide to economic returns; nevertheless, the cereal industry is widely perceived to be quite profitable.

14. Sutton (1991) analyzes a model where endogenous advertising costs provide the main barrier to entry in the RTE cereal industry.

15. Sutton (1991), in his analysis of competition in the cereal industry, finds only limited competition from private-label brands, which seems contrary to recent developments within the RTE cereal industry.

competition by doing the *opposite* of the brand-proliferation model.[16] The private-label brands do little advertising and position themselves identically to existing brands, while offering a lower price to consumers and a higher profit margin to the stores. This success of the private-label brands provides limited support for the theory that large sunk costs of advertising provide the primary barrier to entry into the cereal industry.

Thus, the high rate of new-brand introduction is not part of an anticompetitive strategy in my view. Still, many economists might well doubt the social value of these new brands, the vast majority of which do not succeed. To concentrate the debate, I consider the value to consumers of the introduction of Apple-Cinnamon Cheerios by General Mills in 1989. I choose this brand because it is close to existing General Mills brands—Cheerios is the largest General Mills brand and Honey-Nut Cheerios are well established in the market. Thus, there is certainly an empirical question of whether consumers place much value on the new brand or whether it is already spanned by existing brands and so creates very little new value to consumers.

5.3   An Empirical Model of Brand Choice in the RTE Cereal Industry

I now proceed to estimate an empirical model of brand choice using a three-level model of demand. The top level is the overall demand for cereal using a price index for cereal relative to other goods. The middle level of the demand system estimates demand among various market segments, for example, the adult or the child segments. The bottom level is the choice of brand, for example, Cheerios, conditional on a given segment's expenditure. Overall price elasticities are then derived from the estimates in all three segments. While this demand structure places restrictions on the overall pattern of substitution across brands, it is considerably less restrictive than other demand approaches typically used to estimate the demand for differentiated products. Clearly, some restrictions are required given the more than one hundred brands of cereal available in the marketplace. The approach also allows for convenient tests of the overall specification of brand segments within the model (see Hausman, Leonard, and Zona 1994 for the testing methodology).

The data used to estimate the model are cash-register data collected on a weekly basis across a sample of stores in major metropolitan areas of the United States over a two-year period. Thus, exact price and quantity data are available, with considerable price variation due to promotions and coupons. The panel structure of the data—approximately 140 time series observations on each brand across seven standard metropolitan statistical areas (SMSAs)—

---

16. Economists for the FTC also claimed that entry was difficult due to the economies of scale in cereal manufacturing which would require an entrant to have several successful brands. They failed to consider contract manufacturing of the type done by Ralston for private-label brands.

allows for quite precise estimation. The panel data also permits identification and instrumental variable (IV) estimation under relatively weak assumptions. Thus, the estimated demand structure should allow a precise estimate of the virtual price for a new cereal brand.

In terms of actual estimation I estimate the model in reverse order, beginning at the lowest level, and then use the theory of price indexes to allow for consistent estimation at the higher (more aggregate) levels of demand. The third (or lowest) stage determines buying behavior within market segments. I use this approach because it accords with segmentation of brand-purchasing behavior, which marketing analysts claim arises with purchasing behavior, and because it limits the number of cross elasticities which will be estimated. My econometric specification at the lowest level is the "almost-ideal demand system" of Deaton and Muellbauer (1980a, 1980b) which allows for a second-order flexible demand system, that is, the price elasticities are unconstrained at the point of approximation, and also allows for a convenient specification for nonhomothetic behavior. However, my experience is that the particular form of the demand specification is not crucial here. Use of a flexible demand system allows for few restrictions on preferences, while decreasing the number of unknown parameters through the use of symmetry and adding up restrictions from consumer theory. For each brand within the market segment the demand specification is

(5) $$s_{int} = \alpha_{in} + \beta_i \log (y_{Gnt}/P_{nt}) + \sum_{j=1}^{J} \gamma_{ij} \log p_{jnt} + \varepsilon_{int};$$
$$i = 1, \ldots, J; \quad n = 1, \ldots, N; \quad t = 1, \ldots, T;$$

where s_{int} is the revenue share of total segment expenditure of the ith brand in city n in period t, y_{Gnt} is overall segment expenditure, P_{nt} is a price index, and p_{jnt} is the price of the jth brand in city n. Note that a test of whether $\beta_i = 0$ allows for a test of segment homotheticity, for example, whether shares are independent of segment expenditure. The estimated γ_{ij} permit a free pattern of cross-price elasticities, and Slutsky symmetry can be imposed, if desired, by setting $\gamma_{ij} = \gamma_{ji}$. This choice of the bottom-level demand specification does not impose any restrictions on competition among brands within a given segment. In particular, no equal cross elasticity–type assumptions restrict the within-segment cross-price elasticities. Since competition among differentiated products is typically "highest" among brands within a given segment, this lack of restrictions can be an important feature of the model. An important econometric consideration is the use of segment expenditure, y_{Gnt}, in the share specification of equation (5), rather than the use of overall expenditure. Use of overall expenditure is inconsistent with the economic theory of multistage budgeting, and it can lead to decidedly inferior econometric results.

Given the estimates from equation (5), I calculate a price index for each segment and proceed to estimate the next level of demand. For exact two-stage budgeting, the Gorman results impose the requirement of additive separability on the next level.[17] To specify the middle-level demand system I use the log-log demand system:[18]

$$(6) \qquad \log q_{mnt} = \beta_m \log y_{Bnt} + \sum_{k=1}^{k} \delta_k \log \tau_{knt} + \alpha_{mn} + \varepsilon_{mnt};$$
$$m = 1, \ldots, M; \quad n = 1, \ldots, N; \quad t = 1, \ldots, T;$$

where the left-hand-side variable q_{mnt} is the log quantity of the mth segment in city n in period t, the expenditure variable y_{Bnt} is total cereal expenditure, and the τ_{knt} are the segment price indexes for city n. The segments that I use are the adult segment which includes brands such as Shredded Wheat and Grape Nuts, the child segment which includes Kix and sugar-coated cereals, and the family segment which includes Cheerios, Corn Flakes, and other similar brands. The price indexes τ_{knt} can be estimated either by using an exact price index corresponding to equation (5), which is constructed from the expenditure function for each segment holding utility constant, or by using a weighted-average price index of the Stone-Laspeyres type. Choice of the exact form of the price index does not typically have much influence on the final model estimates.

Lastly, the top-level equation, which I use to estimate the overall price elasticity of cereal, is specified as

$$(7) \qquad \log u_t = \beta_0 + \beta_1 \log y_t + \beta_2 \log \Pi_t + Z_t \delta + \varepsilon_t,$$

where u_t is the overall consumption of cereal, y_t is deflated disposable income, Π_t is the deflated price index for cereal, and Z_t are variables which account for changes in demographics and monthly (seasonal) factors. To estimate equation (7) I use national (BLS) monthly data over a sixteen-year period with instrumental variables. I have found that a longer time period than may be available from store-level data is often useful to estimate the top-level demand elasticity. The instruments I use in estimation of equation (7) are factors which shift costs such as different ingredients, packaging, and labor.

I now consider the question of identification and consistent estimation of the middle-level and bottom-level equations. The problem is most easily seen in equation (5), the brand-level equation, although an analogous problem arises in equation (6), the segment-level demand equation. Equation (5) for each brand will have a number of prices included for each brand in the segment; for example, I include nine brands in the family segment in the subsequent

17. See Gorman (1971). This subject is also discussed in Blackorby, Primont, and Russell (1978), and in Deaton and Muellbauer (1980b). Note that the almost-ideal demand system is a generalized Gorman polar form (GGPF) so that Gorman's theorem on exact two-stage budgeting applies. Since the additive demand specification at the top level imposes separability restrictions, I have also used a less restrictive specification at the middle level which is not necessarily consistent with exact two-stage budgeting. The results are quite similar.

18. Note that this specification is second-order flexible. However, the Slutsky restrictions have not been imposed on the specification.

estimation. It may be difficult to implement the usual strategy of estimating demand equations where the cost function includes factor-input prices (e.g., material prices), which are excluded from the demand equations to allow for identification and for the application of instrumental variables. There may be an insufficient number of input prices, or they may not be reported with high enough frequency to allow for IV estimation. To help solve this problem, I exploit the panel structure of my data. For instance, suppose $N = 2$, so that weekly or monthly data from two cities is available. Note that I have included brand (or segment) and city fixed effects in the specification of equations (5) and (6). Now suppose I can model the price for a brand i in city n in period t as

$$(8) \qquad \log p_{jnt} = \delta_j \log c_{jt} + \alpha_{jn} + w_{jnt},$$

where p_{jnt} is the price for brand j in city n in period t. The determinants of the brand price for brand j are c_{jt}, the cost which is assumed not to have a city-specific time-shifting component (which is consistent with the national shipments and advertising of most differentiated products); α_{jn}, which is a city-specific brand differential that accounts for transportation costs or local wage differentials; and w_{jnt}, which is a mean zero stochastic disturbance that accounts for sales promotions for brand j in city n in time period t. The specific identifying assumption that I make is that the w_{jnt} are independent across cities.[19] Using fixed effects the city-specific components are eliminated, and I am basically applying the Hausman-Taylor (1981) technique for instrumental variables in panel-data models.[20] The idea is that prices in one city (after elimination of city- and brand-specific effects) are driven by underlying costs, c_{jt}, which provide instrumental variables that are correlated with prices but uncorrelated with stochastic disturbances in the demand equations. For example, w_{jnt} from equation (8) is uncorrelated with ε_{i1t} from equation (5) when the cities are different, $n \neq 1$. Thus, the availability of panel data is a crucial factor which allows for estimation of all the own-price and cross-price brand elasticities.

However, another interpretation can be given to equation (8) and the question of whether w_{jnt} from equation (8) is uncorrelated with ε_{i1t} from equation (5). To the extent that supermarkets set their prices p_{jnt} under an assumption of constant marginal cost (in the short run) and do not alter their prices to equilibrate supply and demand in a given week, prices p_{jnt} may be considered predetermined with respect to equation (5). If prices can be treated as predetermined, then IV methods would not necessarily be needed. IV methods might still be required for the segment-expenditure variable y_{Gnt} in equation (5), however. The need for instruments under these hypotheses can be tested in a

---

19. Note that w_{jnt} are permitted to be correlated within a given city.
20. See also Breusch, Mizon, and Schmidt (1989). With more than two cities, tests of the assumptions can be done along the lines discussed in Hausman and Taylor (1981).

Table 5.1   **Segmentation of the Brands**

Adult	Child	Family
Shredded Wheat Squares	Trix	Cheerios
Special K	Kix	Honey-Nut Cheerios
Fruit Wheats	Frosted Flakes	Apple-Cinnamon Cheerios
Shredded Wheat	Froot Loops	Corn Flakes
Shredded Wheat & Bran		Raisin Bran (Kellogg)
Spoon-Size Shredded Wheat		Rice Krispies
Grape Nuts		Frosted Mini-Wheats
		Frosted Wheat Squares
		Raisin Bran (Post)

standard procedure using specification tests for instruments, as in Hausman (1978).

5.4   Data and Results

The data used to estimate the empirical model of brand choice in the RTE cereal industry are panel data from Nielsen Scantrak. The time series consists of 137 weekly observations from January 1990 to August 1992.[21] The cross section is from seven SMSAs, including Boston, Chicago, Detroit, Los Angeles, New York City, Philadelphia, and San Francisco. In each SMSA Nielsen's sample frame is a stratified random sample of supermarkets which captures the vast majority of all cereal sold. The data are collected on a stock-keeping unit (SKU) basis so that the volume of sales is recorded for each package size of each brand at an average weekly price. I aggregate the data across packages so that the quantity variable is weekly sales, in pounds, for each brand at a weekly average price per pound.

The empirical specification requires specification of brand segments. I choose three brand segments which correspond to the segmentation commonly used in the cereal industry by marketing analysts.[22] Apple-Cinnamon Cheerios is placed in the family segment. The other two segments used are adults' cereals and children's cereals. Some common brands which are placed into the three segments are given in table 5.1. To estimate the model for Apple-Cinnamon Cheerios, I focus on the family segment. The family segment represents about 26.4 percent of sales in the RTE cereal market.

To highlight further the family segment, I include some descriptive statistics

21. Estimation was also undertaken using monthly, rather than weekly, data. The estimated elasticities based on monthly data are quite similar to the weekly-data estimates, although the precision of the estimates is lower.

22. Some choice of segmentation is required to apply the demand system discussed above. However, I have applied the tests of segmentation discussed in the last section with the specification used and it was not rejected by the Hausman specification tests.

Table 5.2   Descriptive Statistics for the Family Segment, 1992

Brand	Company	Average Price ($)	Segment Share (%)
Cheerios	General Mills	2.644	21.62
Honey-Nut Cheerios	General Mills	3.605	15.03
Apple-Cinnamon Cheerios	General Mills	3.480	6.19
Corn Flakes	Kellogg	1.866	14.24
Raisin Bran	Kellogg	3.214	13.11
Rice Krispies	Kellogg	2.475	13.54
Frosted Mini-Wheats	Kellogg	3.420	9.07
Frosted Wheat Squares	Nabisco	3.262	1.48
Raisin Bran	Post	3.046	5.72

for the family segment in table 5.2. This table demonstrates the overall popularity of Cheerios—the three brands have a 42.84 percent share of the family segment, or about an 11.3 percent share of overall cereal sales. However, Apple-Cinnamon Cheerios has a 6.19 percent share of the family segment, or a 1.6 percent share of overall cereal sales. Thus, the introduction of Apple-Cinnamon Cheerios was quite successful by industry standards.

I now turn to estimation of the bottom level of the demand system, which is brand choice for family-segment brands. The results are shown in table 5.3, where fixed effects are used for each SMSA, along with expenditures in this segment, prices for each of the brands, and a display variable. Hausman-Taylor (1981) IV estimation is used along with an unrestricted variance matrix for the stochastic disturbances (seemingly unrelated regression). Note that own-price coefficient estimates are generally precisely estimated. Most of the cross-price effects are also of the expected sign and are generally precisely estimated. Homotheticity of brand choice, which would be a zero coefficient on the expenditure variable, is rejected and not imposed. However, Slutsky symmetry is not rejected so it is imposed on the model specification.

In table 5.4 I now turn to segment estimates with a similar model specification including SMSA effects, overall cereal expenditure, and Stone price indexes for each segment along with a display variable for that segment. Here the dependent variable is sales in pounds, so that I find that adults' cereals have an expenditure elasticity less than unity, children's cereals have an expenditure elasticity which exceeds unity, and family cereals are not different from unity. Segment own-price elasticities are found to be sizable, around −2.0, while segment cross-price elasticities are also found to be large and significant. Thus, overall I find significant competition across cereal brands.

In table 5.5 I calculate the conditional elasticities for the family segment, where I condition on expenditure in this segment. Note that the three brands of Cheerios provide significant brand competition for each other, which is consistent with the "cannibalization" fears of brand managers. In table 5.6 I estimate overall brand elasticities for the family segment after I estimate the top

Table 5.3   Estimates of Demand for Family Segment Brands (seemingly unrelated regression)

	Cheerios (1)	Honey-Nut Cheerios (2)	Apple-Cinnamon Cheerios (3)	Corn Flakes (4)	Kellogg's Raisin Bran (5)	Rice Krispies (6)	Frosted Mini-Wheats (7)	Frosted Wheat Squares (8)
Constant	0.68009	0.38053	0.17563	−0.17958	0.31830	−0.24203	0.25375	0.05343
	(0.07668)	(0.05890)	(0.04212)	(0.07112)	(0.07000)	(0.08851)	(0.05257)	(0.01448)
Time	−0.00038	−0.00024	−0.00001	−0.00002	0.00045	0.00066	−0.00016	−0.00009
	(0.00007)	(0.00005)	(0.00004)	(0.00007)	(0.00007)	(0.00008)	(0.00005)	(0.00001)
$Time^2$	0.00000	0.00000	−0.00000	−0.00000	−0.00000	−0.00000	0.00000	0.00000
	(0.00000)	(0.00000)	(0.00000)	(0.00000)	(0.00000)	(0.00000)	(0.00000)	(0.00000)
Boston	0.06345	−0.00014	0.00872	−0.02327	−0.00377	−0.01844	0.01415	−0.00761
	(0.00417)	(0.00319)	(0.00229)	(0.00389)	(0.00377)	(0.00470)	(0.00282)	(0.00080)
Chicago	0.02883	0.00079	0.01412	−0.00418	−0.01810	0.00546	0.01309	−0.00651
	(0.00398)	(0.00306)	(0.00221)	(0.00367)	(0.00363)	(0.00450)	(0.00278)	(0.00076)
Detroit	0.01412	−0.02172	0.02120	−0.01417	−0.00511	0.00149	0.03371	−0.00042
	(0.00327)	(0.00256)	(0.00186)	(0.00304)	(0.00307)	(0.00374)	(0.00230)	(0.00064)
Los Angeles	0.01962	0.03309	−0.00038	0.01656	0.01923	−0.02906	0.00775	0.00338
	(0.00609)	(0.00468)	(0.00335)	(0.00571)	(0.00555)	(0.00702)	(0.00412)	(0.00113)
New York	0.06180	0.00971	0.01102	−0.00468	−0.00371	−0.02386	0.01465	−0.00379
	(0.00783)	(0.00599)	(0.00430)	(0.00726)	(0.00712)	(0.00898)	(0.00525)	(0.00145)
Philadelphia	0.05204	0.01302	0.01625	−0.02970	−0.02025	−0.01361	0.02708	−0.00122
	(0.00488)	(0.00377)	(0.00272)	(0.00453)	(0.00447)	(0.00558)	(0.00337)	(0.00094)
$\log(Y/P)$	−0.03853	−0.01552	−0.00854	0.02003	−0.01391	0.02685	−0.01258	−0.00246
	(0.00630)	(0.00485)	(0.00346)	(0.00585)	(0.00575)	(0.00726)	(0.00435)	(0.00120)
$\log(DISP + 1)$	0.00313	0.00231	0.00297	0.00579	0.00425	0.00051	0.00261	0.00088
	(0.00052)	(0.00040)	(0.00039)	(0.00059)	(0.00049)	(0.00058)	(0.00043)	(0.00025)

	log(P_1)	log(P_2)	log(P_3)	log(P_4)	log(P_5)	log(P_6)	log(P_7)	log(P_8)
log(P_1)	−0.18855 (0.00736)							
log(P_2)	0.02087 (0.00477)	−0.13165 (0.00756)						
log(P_3)	0.00842 (0.00345)	0.01849 (0.00371)	−0.07070 (0.00446)					
log(P_4)	0.04805 (0.00551)	0.00268 (0.00522)	0.00772 (0.00389)	−0.14438 (0.00825)				
log(P_5)	0.02071 (0.00542)	0.02285 (0.00534)	0.01208 (0.00385)	0.03957 (0.00579)	−0.12861 (0.00873)			
log(P_6)	0.02916 (0.00487)	0.03561 (0.00416)	0.01431 (0.00301)	0.01812 (0.00480)	−0.00791 (0.00494)	−0.14195 (0.00708)		
log(P_7)	0.03010 (0.00465)	0.00239 (0.00569)	−0.00142 (0.00391)	0.01656 (0.00544)	0.03966 (0.00545)	0.02135 (0.00381)	−0.13658 (0.00950)	
log(P_8)	0.00372 (0.00131)	0.00587 (0.00178)	−0.00172 (0.00121)	0.00418 (0.00158)	0.00779 (0.00158)	0.00008 (0.00107)	0.01208 (0.00236)	−0.03206 (0.00202)

Note: Numbers in parentheses are asymptotic standard errors.

Table 5.4   **Estimates for RTE Segment Demand**

	Child (1)	Adult (2)	Family (3)
Constant	−5.17119	3.25706	−0.28328
	(0.57034)	(0.45800)	(0.27096)
Time	−0.00053	−0.00005	0.00008
	(0.00037)	(0.00031)	(0.00018)
$Time^2$	−0.00000	0.00001	0.00000
	(0.00000)	(0.00000)	(0.00000)
Boston	0.00626	−0.24011	0.07987
	(0.03127)	(0.02874)	(0.01517)
Chicago	0.29489	−0.45990	0.01861
	(0.02627)	(0.02352)	(0.01275)
Detroit	0.19954	−0.45975	0.06424
	(0.01948)	(0.01740)	(0.00939)
Los Angeles	0.32056	−0.13663	−0.08183
	(0.03067)	(0.02743)	(0.01514)
New York	0.01482	−0.11560	0.04898
	(0.03350)	(0.02903)	(0.01647)
Philadelphia	0.16905	−0.39635	0.07388
	(0.02317)	(0.02149)	(0.01128)
$\log(Y)$	1.19080	0.72567	0.99868
	(0.03562)	(0.02874)	(0.01700)
$\log(P_1)$	−2.08314	−0.09422	0.38217
	(0.06571)	(0.05058)	(0.02967)
$\log(P_2)$	0.96607	−2.02602	0.20740
	(0.12117)	(0.11479)	(0.05797)
$\log(P_3)$	1.03553	0.33294	−1.82906
	(0.07465)	(0.06014)	(0.03688)
$\log(DISP + 1)$	0.01054	0.04398	−0.00983
	(0.00365)	(0.00401)	(0.00221)

Notes: Dependent variable is segment sales in pounds. Numbers in parentheses are asymptotic standard errors.

level of the demand specification. I estimate the overall price elasticity for RTE cereal from the top-level demand equation to be −0.90 (asymptotic standard error [ASE] = 0.10).

Using these estimates I now calculate the virtual price for Apple-Cinnamon Cheerios as the price at which its market share is zero. I use two methods to calculate the virtual price in which I draw graphs of the conditional demand curves using predicted values from the bottom-level segment of the demand model. The results vary somewhat depending on the aggregation technique chosen.[23] The results are found in figures 5.1 and 5.2. The estimated virtual, or

23. The first method uses the average of the right-hand-side variables for the demand function across all 959 observations to solve for the virtual price. The second method solves for the virtual prices of each of the 959 observations and the average of these prices is used. The results differ because of the nonlinearity of the demand system specification used.

Table 5.5   Conditional Elasticities for Family Segment of RTE Cereal

	Cheerios	Honey-Nut Cheerios	Apple-Cinnamon Cheerios	Corn Flakes	Kellogg's Raisin Bran	Rice Krispies	Frosted Mini-Wheats	Frosted Wheat Squares	Post Raisin Bran
Cheerios	-1.73851	0.16166	0.07110	0.19818	0.15355	0.09268	0.18649	0.02593	0.02716
	(0.04635)	(0.02520)	(0.01759)	(0.02776)	(0.02789)	(0.03008)	(0.02309)	(0.00628)	(0.02951)
Honey-Nut Cheerios	0.21637	-1.83838	0.14169	0.00390	0.18550	0.21253	0.04330	0.04414	0.09425
	(0.03686)	(0.05397)	(0.02562)	(0.03613)	(0.03750)	(0.03263)	(0.03967)	(0.01197)	(0.03863)
Apple-Cinnamon Cheerios	0.23945	0.34899	-2.11677	0.10597	0.23973	0.19848	0.01366	-0.02100	0.12936
	(0.06477)	(0.06330)	(0.07406)	(0.06451)	(0.06614)	(0.05520)	(0.06708)	(0.01993)	(0.06930)
Corn Flakes	0.23185	-0.03254	0.02883	-1.99465	0.23222	0.16056	0.07898	0.02246	0.13165
	(0.04859)	(0.04108)	(0.02952)	(0.06003)	(0.04533)	(0.03831)	(0.04307)	(0.01186)	(0.04444)
Kellogg's Raisin Bran	0.23744	0.21291	0.11121	0.28729	-1.94608	-0.08546	0.33045	0.06454	-0.10626
	(0.04839)	(0.04354)	(0.03084)	(0.04597)	(0.07233)	(0.04318)	(0.04474)	(0.01248)	(0.05031)
Rice Krispies	0.06656	0.19055	0.06997	0.16068	-0.12272	-2.00148	0.10508	-0.00909	0.34211
	(0.05873)	(0.04259)	(0.02824)	(0.04122)	(0.04759)	(0.06512)	(0.03707)	(0.00990)	(0.04614)
Frosted Mini-Wheats	0.43609	0.07708	0.00939	0.16386	0.48235	0.20255	-2.46950	0.14003	0.09692
	(0.05608)	(0.06460)	(0.04498)	(0.06371)	(0.06381)	(0.04921)	(0.11340)	(0.02669)	(0.06562)
Frosted Wheat Squares	0.37740	0.45906	-0.08636	0.26062	0.58179	-0.03396	0.86314	-3.16485	-0.09011
	(0.09617)	(0.12191)	(0.08357)	(0.11035)	(0.11175)	(0.08260)	(0.16566)	(0.13832)	(0.11552)
Post Raisin Bran	-0.10461	0.11474	0.08315	0.23661	-0.35988	0.73072	0.07025	-0.03721	-2.51416
	(0.12414)	(0.10689)	(0.07742)	(0.11177)	(0.12199)	(0.11060)	(0.10844)	(0.03036)	(0.15731)
Mean shares	0.21617	0.15026	0.06193	0.14243	0.13117	0.13539	0.09067	0.01475	0.05722

Note: Numbers in parentheses are asymptotic standard errors.

Table 5.6   Overall Elasticities for Family Segment of RTE Cereal

	Cheerios	Honey-Nut Cheerios	Apple-Cinnamon Cheerios	Corn Flakes	Kellogg's Raisin Bran	Rice Krispies	Frosted Mini-Wheats	Frosted Wheat Squares	Post Raisin Bran
Cheerios	-1.92572 (0.05499)	0.01210 (0.04639)	0.04306 (0.07505)	-0.02798 (0.06123)	0.03380 (0.05836)	-0.20642 (0.07398)	0.23990 (0.06455)	0.18758 (0.10703)	-0.51019 (0.14309)
Honey-Nut Cheerios	0.03154 (0.03080)	-1.98037 (0.05808)	0.21247 (0.06808)	-0.21316 (0.04805)	0.07136 (0.04861)	0.00079 (0.05199)	-0.05929 (0.06752)	0.32712 (0.12496)	-0.16719 (0.11643)
Apple-Cinnamon Cheerios	0.01747 (0.01919)	0.08317 (0.02690)	-2.17304 (0.07525)	-0.04561 (0.03144)	0.05287 (0.03224)	-0.00824 (0.03111)	-0.04682 (0.04591)	-0.14074 (0.08462)	-0.03304 (0.08000)
Corn Flakes	0.07484 (0.03008)	-0.13069 (0.03850)	-0.02343 (0.06503)	-2.16585 (0.06155)	0.15311 (0.04759)	-0.01918 (0.04555)	0.03460 (0.06405)	0.13556 (0.10926)	-0.03062 (0.11573)
Kellogg's Raisin Bran	0.03995 (0.03184)	0.06155 (0.04109)	0.12056 (0.07011)	0.07455 (0.05064)	-2.06965 (0.07614)	-0.28837 (0.05456)	0.36331 (0.06673)	0.46661 (0.11558)	-0.60598 (0.13005)
Rice Krispies	-0.02457 (0.03109)	0.08459 (0.03368)	0.07548 (0.05384)	-0.00219 (0.04071)	-0.21300 (0.04308)	-2.17246 (0.06354)	0.07967 (0.04854)	-0.15285 (0.07886)	0.47670 (0.11284)
Frosted Mini-Wheats	0.10797 (0.02567)	-0.04239 (0.04189)	-0.06872 (0.06978)	-0.03001 (0.04629)	0.24504 (0.04735)	-0.00943 (0.04162)	-2.55178 (0.11603)	0.78352 (0.16839)	-0.09987 (0.11360)
Frosted Wheat Squares	0.01315 (0.00656)	0.03020 (0.01217)	-0.03440 (0.02015)	0.00473 (0.01216)	0.05064 (0.01274)	-0.02772 (0.01045)	0.12664 (0.02682)	-3.17781 (0.13863)	-0.06489 (0.03082)
Post Raisin Bran	-0.02239 (0.02908)	0.04018 (0.03840)	0.07738 (0.06837)	0.06288 (0.04415)	-0.16016 (0.04953)	0.26985 (0.04521)	0.04499 (0.06495)	-0.14035 (0.11447)	-2.62151 (0.15447)

Note: Numbers in parentheses are asymptotic standard errors.

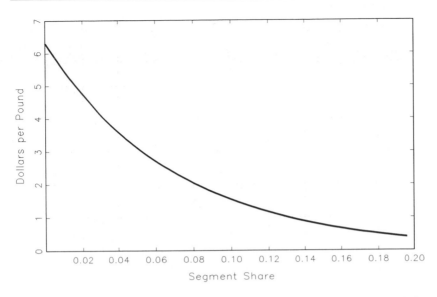

Fig. 5.1   Almost-ideal demand curve for Apple-Cinnamon Cheerios (method 1)

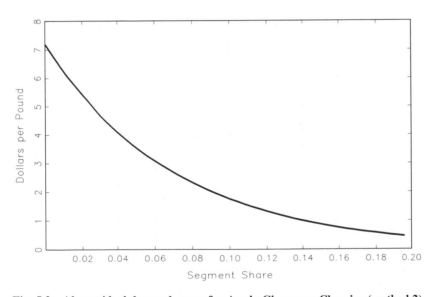

Fig. 5.2   Almost-ideal demand curve for Apple-Cinnamon Cheerios (method 2)

reservation, prices vary across cities from about $6.00 to about $7.50. My best estimate of the aggregate reservation price is $7.14. The ASE of the virtual-price estimate is $1.33, with the lower bound of an (approximate) 95 percent confidence interval estimated at $4.75—35 percent greater than the average price of Apple-Cinnamon Cheerios.

Estimating the (exact) consumer's surplus from the relevant expenditure functions, which is approximately equivalent to calculating the area under the demand curve to the average price of $3.48, yields an estimate of $32,268 on a per city, weekly average. The ASE of the estimate of $32,268 is $3,384, which yields a precise estimate of the consumer-welfare measure.[24] For the United States the annual consumer's surplus is approximately $78.1 million from the introduction of a new brand of cereal. This amount equals about $0.3136 per person per year which is a sizable amount of consumer's surplus. Note that the virtual price of about $7.00 is about twice the actual sales price of $3.50, which seems to be a reasonable estimate. Since the own-price elasticity is about -2.2, the reservation price seems to be in about the correct range.[25]

The estimate of the virtual price of $7.14 depends on the behavior of the estimated demand curve at the vertical axis (zero quantity). While significant price variation is observed in the data, on the order of 50 percent, prices as high as the virtual price are not observed. However, a lower-bound estimate of the virtual price arises from constructing the supporting hyperplane (tangent) to the demand curve in figures 5.1 and 5.2 at the actual average price of $3.48 and observing the implied virtual price. So long as the demand curve is convex, this approach provides a lower-bound estimate to the virtual price. Using this approach I find that the estimated lower-bound virtual price varies between about $5.55 and $5.94 with an ASE of about $0.15. Thus, using the estimated lower bound I find that the average lower-bound reservation price is about 65 percent higher than the average price of $3.48. Thus, a significant amount of consumer's surplus remains, even when a lower-bound estimate is used.

Note that neglecting the effect of the new brand leads to an overstatement of the price index for cereal. If Apple-Cinnamon Cheerios is aggregated with Honey-Nut Cheerios so that they are considered to be a single brand, little effect is found beyond the slightly lower price of the new brand in the estimated average price of the two types of Cheerios. As a simple example, assume contrary to fact that all of Apple-Cinnamon Cheerios' share was taken from that of Honey-Nut Cheerios. Before the introduction of the new brand the price index would be about $4.60, while after its introduction the price index would be about $3.57, for a decrease of about 22 percent—a sizable reduction within the family segment. The decrease in the price index for the family segment is from $3.10 to $2.88, a decrease of 7.1 percent. In the overall price index for cereal the effect would be a reduction of about 0.017 (or $0.052) which is again significant. This estimate of about 1.7 percent would stay approximately

---

24. These exact welfare estimates and ASEs use the method developed by Hausman and Newey (1995).

25. Use of this same estimation technique for other highly differentiated products often leads to significantly higher estimated elasticities. For instance, in Hausman, Leonard, and Zona (1994) we estimate own-price elasticities for brands of beer, e.g., Budweiser, Miller, and Miller Lite, in the range of about -4.0 to -6.2. Thus, the data source and estimation technique do not seem to lead to too-small elasticity estimates.

the same when the assumption is relaxed that Apple-Cinnamon Cheerios takes all its share from Honey-Nut Cheerios. The approximate change in the price index can be calculated by taking Apple-Cinnamon Cheerios' share of about 1.6 percent and multiplying by the difference between the virtual price (about $7.00) and the actual price (about $3.50). The results will differ depending on price differences between Apple-Cinnamon Cheerios and the brands it takes share away from. If all brands had the same price the overall change in the price index would be about 1.5 percent, or approximately the share of the new brand. Thus, to the extent that about 25 percent of cereal demand was from new brands over the past ten years, and under the (perhaps unrealistic) assumptions that the new brands sell for about the same average price as existing brands and that the estimate here would generalize to a reservation price of about two times the actual price, the overall price index for cereals which excludes the effects of new brands would be too high by about the overall share of new brands—25 percent.[26]

5.5 Alternative Model Specifications for New-Brand Introduction

An alternative model of brand choice is the Hotelling-Gorman-Lancaster model of brand choice by attributes. Here a product, such as a car, is described by its attributes, for example, size, weight, and features such as air-conditioning.[27] A discrete-choice model, either a logit model or probit model, is estimated and the demand for new brands is predicted as a function of the attributes. In distinct contrast to these attribute models, I describe each brand uniquely by an indicator (dummy) variable. Indeed, it is difficult to conceive how I would describe Apple-Cinnamon Cheerios in terms of its attributes— perhaps the volume of apples and cinnamon along with other ingredients. Thus, it is readily recognized that for highly differentiated products, the discrete-choice model specification based on product attributes may not be usable.[28] Many economists find appealing the notion of "distance" incorporated in the attribute model. However, it is clear that no reasonable metric exists to describe "how close" attributes are; and, moreover, no aggregator across attributes exists. The commonly used assumptions of linearity seem ad hoc at best. Instead, the appropriate measure of distance between two goods is really

---

26. This estimate is too high to the extent that the exit of existing brands decreases consumer's surplus for consumers still buying those brands. However, cereal brands are typically removed only when their market shares become extremely small because of the significant margins between price and marginal cost. Thus, the loss in consumer's surplus due to exit will be extremely small. However, I cannot estimate this decrease in consumer's surplus due to lack of data.

27. An empirical specification of this model applied to new brands is given by Pakes, Berry, and Levinsohn (1993).

28. While I have often applied probit models to brand choice (see Hausman and Wise 1978), I realized the limitation of these models when I tried applying them to the choices among French champagnes. Somehow, the bubble content could never be made to come in significant in the probit specifications.

their cross-price elasticities, which relate to what extent consumers find the two goods to be close substitutes. Furthermore, the usual discrete-choice model used, the logit model, suffers from the well-known independence of irrelevant alternatives (IIA) problem. The IIA problem typically leads to a vast overestimate of the consumer's surplus from a new good because the model does not incorporate sufficiently the similarities to existing goods. Alternatively, the cross-price elasticities of all goods with a given good are equal; see, for example, Hausman (1975). A more sophisticated specification, the nested logit model, can solve some of these problems but still suffers from the IIA problem at each level of choice. Thus, I consider another continuous demand specification, which bears quite remarkable similarities to the logit model, that has sometimes been used for the estimation of new-product demand.

The most widely used specification in theoretical models of product differentiation is the constant elasticity of substitution (CES) utility function used by Dixit and Stiglitz (1977). The CES utility function takes the form

$$(9) \qquad U(x_1, \ldots, x_n) = \left(\sum_{i=1}^{n} x_i^{\rho} \right)^{1/\rho}$$

The form of the CES utility function makes clear that all goods are treated equally so that the IIA property is still present implicitly in the CES demand function.[29] Economic theorists have found the CES function to be analytically quite useful in studying product differentiation. However, the so-called symmetry property seems a poor guide to empirical reality, where I know that Apple-Cinnamon Cheerios are a much closer substitute to Honey-Nut Cheerios than they are to Nabisco Shredded Wheat or to Total.[30]

Given the implicit IIA property of the CES model, similar to the logit model, it will tend to overvalue variety. This overvaluation arises because the CES demand function does not recognize that some products are closer substitutes to other products. The CES demand function takes the form

$$(10) \qquad x_k = \left[\frac{\sum_{i=1}^{n} x_i^{\rho}}{\sum_{i=1}^{n} p_i^{-\rho/(1-\rho)}} \right]^{1/\rho} p_k^{-1/(1-\rho)} + \varepsilon_k,$$

where the single parameter ρ estimates substitution across goods. Indeed, solving for the cross-price elasticities from equation (10) yields the finding that

$$(11) \qquad \frac{\partial x_i}{\partial p_j} \frac{p_j}{x_i} = \frac{\partial x_k}{\partial p_j} \frac{p_j}{x_k}, \text{ or } e_{ij} = e_{kj} \text{ for all } i, k, j,$$

---

29. See Anderson, de Palma, and Thisse (1992) for an insightful analysis of the similarities of the CES model and the logit model.

30. The CES model has been applied to new-product introduction situations; see, e.g., Feenstra (1994).

which demonstrates the restrictiveness of the CES demand specification. The equality of cross-price elasticities demonstrates that the CES demand function treats all goods similarly (symmetrically), and it cannot provide a reliable basis on which to evaluate new goods. Furthermore, the own-price elasticities depend only on the share of the particular good and the single parameter ρ, a property without any empirical foundation.[31]

I now proceed to estimate the CES demand model of equation (10) using instrumental variables together with nonlinear least squares (NL-2SLS). I estimate $\rho = .580$ (ASE $= .00001$). The estimated CES is $1/(1 - \rho) = 2.13$. The CES demand curve is plotted in figure 5.3. The virtual price is infinite, but I can still calculate the consumer's surplus approximately as the area under the demand curve. The consumer's surplus estimate is about three times as high as my previous estimate of $78.1 million per year. Thus, as I expected, the CES model leads to an unrealistically high estimate of consumer welfare from a new-brand introduction. Neither the CES model nor the logit model distinguish sufficiently the similarities and differences among brands. Thus, a more flexible demand model of the type I estimated above, which allows for an unrestricted pattern of own-price and cross-price elasticities at the segment level, appears to lead to much more realistic estimates of the virtual price and welfare effects of new-brand introduction.

5.6   New-Brand Introduction with Imperfect Competition

Up to this point I have followed the classical Hicks-Rothbarth approach to the evaluation of a new product. However, the implicit assumption in that approach that price equals marginal cost need not hold in most new-product situations. Combined with the fact that most new-brand introductions are undertaken by multiproduct firms with existing competing brands, the introduction of imperfect competition seems necessary for a more realistic evaluation. The basic reason a new product may change other products' prices is that when a firm solves for the profit-maximizing price of its current brands it chooses the price at which marginal revenue from a price increase equals marginal cost. When a multiproduct firm introduces a new brand, some of the demand it would lose if it attempted to raise the price of its existing brands will now be lost to the new brand. Thus, while multibrand firms always worry that a new brand will "cannibalize" the demand for an existing brand, the new brand allows the firm to raise the prices on its existing brands.[32]

---

31. These properties of the own-price and cross-price elasticities are exactly analogous to the properties of the logit demand elasticities, cf. Hausman (1975). Thus, the IIA property holds for both logit models and for CES demand models.

32. A counteracting effect can be that the new brand will cause the price of other firms' brands to decrease because the new brand increases the own-price elasticity of existing brands. The complicated interactions here are currently beyond the scope of economic theory to solve, although Tirole (1988) discusses many interesting examples which appear in the literature.

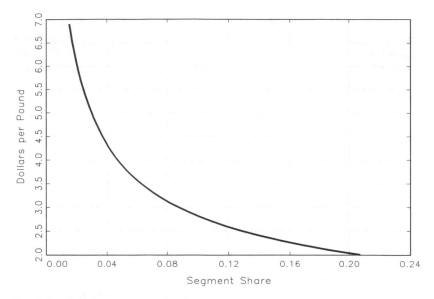

Fig. 5.3   CES demand curve for family-segment brands

Once imperfect competition is allowed, the possibility of different outcomes becomes quite large. I adopt the most widely used solution concept for my analysis, Nash-Bertrand pricing. Thus, a single-product firm is assumed to set the price for a given product according to the "marginal revenue equals marginal cost" rule:

$$(12) \qquad \frac{p_1 - mc_1}{p_1} = -\frac{1}{e_{11}}.$$

Equation (12) is the familiar equation in which the markup of price over marginal cost is set equal to the inverse of the magnitude of the demand elasticity. Now in a multiproduct-firm setting, when a firm changes the price of one good, it takes into account the effect on its other brands as well. Letting π be the firm's profit function, the first-order conditions for the multiproduct firm become

$$(13) \qquad \left[\frac{p_j}{\sum_{k=1}^{m} p_k q_k} \right] \frac{\partial \pi}{\partial p_j} = s_j + \sum_{k=1}^{m} \left[\frac{p_k - mc_k}{p_k} s_k \right] e_{kj} = 0$$

$$\text{for } j = 1, \ldots, m,$$

where q_k is the demand for brand k, s_k is its share, and e_{kj} are the cross-price elasticities. Thus equation (13) makes clear the dependence of a price change on how close a given multiproduct firm's brands are in terms of their cross-price elasticities.

I now express the first-order conditions of equation (13) as a system of linear equations:

$$(14) \qquad\qquad s + E'w = 0,$$

where s is the vector of revenues shares, E is the matrix of cross-price elasticities, and w is the vector of price/cost markups multiplied by the share (the term in brackets on the right-hand side of equation [13]) which arise under the Nash-Bertrand assumption in equation (12). I solve for these individual terms of the markup equation by inversion of the matrix of cross elasticities:

$$(15) \qquad\qquad w = -(E')^{-1}s.$$

I can then use the individual elements of w to determine the change in price after the new-brand introduction to the extent that marginal costs remain constant. Note that while I have derived the change in price under Nash-Bertrand assumptions, my analysis does not require this assumption. To the extent that pricing constraints will be decreased after the new brand is introduced, the analysis provides a lower bound on expected price changes, absent new entry by competitors.

I now apply the Nash-Bertrand model to the introduction of Apple-Cinnamon Cheerios. Remember that General Mills was already selling regular Cheerios and Honey-Nut Cheerios when it introduced Apple-Cinnamon Cheerios in 1989. Thus, when deciding on a possible new brand, General Mills had to take into account the negative effect ("cannibalization") that the introduction of Apple-Cinnamon Cheerios would have on the demand for its other brands. However, introduction of new brands also allows General Mills to price its existing brands higher because when it raises their prices part of the demand that it loses will go to the new brand, Apple-Cinnamon Cheerios. Thus, the welfare analysis must also be adjusted to take into account the imperfect competition which exists in the cereal market. Using the Nash-Bertrand assumption, this effect tends to lead to higher pricing for each of the other General Mills brands.

Using own and cross elasticities and pound shares for General Mills brands in the family segment given in table 5.3, I calculate table 5.7. These calculations are done using equations (12)–(15), which calculate the markups over marginal cost that are profit maximizing for General Mills under the Nash-

Table 5.7   **Nash-Bertrand Pricing of General Mills Family-Segment Brands**

	Cheerios	Honey-Nut Cheerios
Price-cost margin	.5268	.5203
Price-cost margin without Apple-Cinnamon Cheerios	.5251	.5096
Price-cost margin if brand were independent	.5193	.5050

Bertrand assumption that other firms, such as Kellogg, will not change their prices in response to the introduction of Apple-Cinnamon Cheerios. The values from the first two rows imply a hypothetical price change of $0.0095 for Cheerios and $0.0787 for Honey-Nut Cheerios. The increase in the markup for Cheerios is only 0.32 percent while the markup for Honey-Nut Cheerios increases by 3.0 percent, which is expected because Apple-Cinnamon Cheerios is a closer substitute for Honey-Nut Cheerios than for regular Cheerios.

I now account for the increase in price of the other two Cheerios brands when Apple-Cinnamon Cheerios are introduced by General Mills. The average (per city, weekly) pound sales for Cheerios and Honey-Nut Cheerios are 93,738 and 47,215, respectively. This effect implies a first-order decrease in consumer's surplus (per city, weekly) of $890 + $3,715 = $4,605 (as compared to the $32,000–44,000 consumer's surplus estimates). Therefore, the net gain in consumer's surplus is $32,000 − $4,605 = $27,395, or an amount 85.6 percent as high as the Hicksian calculation. On an annual basis the gain in consumer's surplus is $66.8 million (equivalently, $0.268 per person). Thus, while the gain from the new-brand introduction is still sizable, it must be adjusted downward. In terms of overall new-brand introduction, instead of the CPI for cereals being too high on the order of 25 percent under the perfect-competition assumption, the introduction of imperfect competition would reduce the overstatement of the cereal CPI to about 20 percent. This amount is still large enough to be important and demonstrates the importance of considering new-brand introduction in the calculation of economic welfare and consumer price indexes.

The introduction of imperfect competition in evaluating new goods is a marked departure from the classical Hicks-Rothbarth approach. Imperfect competition brings with it supply (cost) considerations that are typically absent from COL theory, which is typically concerned only with demand factors. The approach I have taken is to calculate the theoretical effect of imperfect competition under a particular model assumption, Nash-Bertrand competition. Another approach, left for future research, is to analyze the actual effect on prices of the introduction of a new brand. Data considerations do not permit the analysis here, because the Nielsen data I have does not cover the period prior to the introduction of Apple-Cinnamon Cheerios. However, now that detailed store-level microdata are available, such a study would be extremely interesting for the current subject of welfare effects of new-product introduction, as well as for the broader area of competitive interaction in industrial organization theory.

5.7   Conclusion

The correct economic approach to the evaluation of new goods has been known for over fifty years, since Hicks's pioneering contribution. However, it has not been implemented by government statistical agencies, perhaps because of its complications and data requirements. Data are now available. The impact of new goods on consumer welfare appears to be significant according to the demand estimates of this paper. According to the rough calculations in this paper, the CPI for cereal may be too high by about 25 percent because it does not account for new cereal brands. An estimate this large seems worth worrying about.

However, the classical theory propounded by Hicks leaves out an important potential element. In imperfect competition, which characterizes all differentiated-product industries, introduction of a new brand may permit a multiproduct firm to raise the prices of its other brands. The price increases for existing brands will decrease the welfare-increasing effects of the new brand. According to my estimate for the example of Apple-Cinnamon Cheerios, the imperfect-competition effect will reduce consumer welfare by about 15 percent compared to the perfect-competition situation. Nevertheless, the welfare effect of new-brand introduction under imperfect competition is still significant—about 20 percent according to my rough calculations. Thus, I find that new-brand introduction should often be considered favorable by most economists given its significant welfare-increasing effects.

Why do consumers spend their income on new brands? A classical reference may be in order: "The love of novelty manifests itself equally in those who are well off and in those who are not. For . . . men get tired of prosperity, just as they are afflicted by the reverse. . . . This love of change . . . opens the way to every one who takes the lead in any innovation in any country" (Machiavelli, *Discourses,* chap. 21, suggested to me by Stanley Lebergott). Alternatively, I include the following Calvin and Hobbes cartoon in which Calvin states, "A big part of life is boring routine. I need more excitement. So today, I'm going to have a new kind of cereal!" (suggested to me by my daughter Claire Hausman).

Calvin and Hobbes   by Bill Watterson

References

Anderson, S. P., A. de Palma, and J.-F. Thisse. 1992. *Discrete choice theory of product differentiation.* Cambridge: MIT Press.

Blackorby, C., D. A. Primont, and R. R. Russell. 1978. *Duality, separability, and functional structure.* New York: North-Holland.

Breusch, T. S., G. E. Mizon, and P. Schmidt. 1989. Efficient estimation using panel data. *Econometrica* 57:695–700.

Burtless, G., and J. Hausman. 1978. The effect of taxation on labor supply: Evaluating the Gary negative income tax experiment. *Journal of Political Economy* 86 (December): 1103–30.

Deaton, A., and J. Muellbauer. 1980a. An almost ideal demand system. *American Economic Review* 70:312–26.

———. 1980b. *Economics and consumer behavior.* Cambridge: Cambridge University Press.

Diewert, W. E. 1992. Essays in index number theory: An overview of volume 1. Discussion Paper no. 92-31, University of British Columbia, Vancouver.

Dixit, A., and J. E. Stiglitz. 1977. Monopolistic competition and optimum product diversity. *American Economic Review* 67:297–308.

Feenstra, R. C. 1994. New product varieties and the measurement of international prices. *American Economic Review* 84:157–77.

Fixler, D. 1993. The Consumer Price Index: Underlying concepts and caveats. *Monthly Labor Review* 116 (December): 3–12.

Gorman, W. 1971. Two stage budgeting. Nuffield College, Oxford. Mimeographed.

Hausman, J. 1975. Project independence report: A review of U.S. energy needs up to 1985. *Bell Journal of Economics* 6:517–51.

———. 1978. Specification tests in econometrics. *Econometrica* 46:1251–71.

———. 1980. The effect of wages, taxes, and fixed costs on women's labor force participation. *Journal of Public Economics* 14:161–94.

———. 1981. Exact consumer surplus and deadweight loss. *American Economic Review* 71:662–76.

Hausman, J., G. Leonard, and J. D. Zona. 1994. Competitive analysis with differentiated products. *Annales D'Economie et de Statistique* no. 34:159–80.

Hausman, J., and W. Newey. 1995. Nonparametric estimation of exact consumers surplus and deadweight loss. *Econometrica* 63:1445–76.

Hausman, J., and W. Taylor. 1981. Panel data and unobservable individual effects. *Econometrica* 49:1377–98.

Hausman, J., and D. Wise. 1978. A conditional probit model for qualitative choice. *Econometrica* 46:403–26.

Hicks, J. R. 1940. The valuation of the social income. *Economica* 7:105–24.

Judd, K. L. 1985. Credible spatial preemption. *Rand Journal of Economics* 16 (2): 153–66.

Konüs, A. A. 1939. The problem of the true index of the cost-of-living. *Econometrica* 7:10–29. First published (in Russian) in *The Economic Bulletin of the Institute of Economic Conjuncture* no. 9/10: 64–71 (Moscow, 1924).

Neary, J. P., and K. W. S. Roberts. 1980. The theory of household behavior under rationing. *European Economic Review* 13:25–42.

Pakes, A., S. Berry, and J. Levinsohn. 1993. Price indexes and the analysis of environmental change. *American Economic Review* 83:240–46.

Pollak, R. 1989. *The theory of the cost-of-living index.* Oxford: Oxford University Press.

Robinson, J. 1933. *The economics of imperfect competition.* London: Macmillan.

Rothbarth, E. 1941. The measurement of changes in real income under conditions of rationing. *Review of Economic Studies* 8:100–107.
Scherer, F. M. 1982. The breakfast cereal industry. In *The structure of American industry,* ed. W. Adams. 6th ed. New York: Macmillan.
Schmalensee, R. 1978. Entry deterrence in the ready-to-eat breakfast cereal industry. *Bell Journal of Economics* 9:305–27.
Sutton, J. 1991. *Sunk costs and market structure.* Cambridge: MIT Press.
Tirole, J. 1988. *The theory of industrial organization.* Cambridge: MIT Press.
Urban, G. L., G. M. Katz, T. E. Hatch, and A. J. Silk. 1983. The ASSESSOR pretest market evaluation system. *Interfaces* 13:38–59.

Comment   Timothy F. Bresnahan

It is easy to see that whole new industries and whole new product categories are economically important. They expand consumers' range of choice in a very substantial way. It is harder to be sure that the steadily increasing variety in many branded consumer product industries is equally important. There are a great many new brands, new varieties, and new packages available on the supermarket shelves. (*Brandweek* counted over 22,000 new-product introductions for 1994.) How important are these new goods individually? How large is their aggregate contribution to social welfare?

Existing research has not answered this question. There is a large and stimulating theoretical literature. It treats the question of whether the market, working through the free entry of new products, will supply too many marginal product varieties. The purely theoretical approach is ultimately inconclusive.[1] Empirical work has so far not pushed much further. For want of a better assumption, many policy and academic studies treat new goods as irrelevant or as perfect substitutes for existing goods. The official COL indexes, by linking in new goods only after they have been around for a while, treat them as irrelevant in their early stages.[2] Attempts to view new goods as quality improvements to existing goods, for example in hedonic pricing studies, involve the implicit assumption of perfect substitutability.

Each of these assumptions plausibly leads to an underestimate of the value

Timothy F. Bresnahan is professor of economics at Stanford University and a research associate of the National Bureau of Economic Research.

1. Eaton and Lipsey (1989) write that "in addition, the problem of optimal product diversity arises. . . . We showed in our discussion of that [address] model that there is no general relationship between product diversity in free-entry equilibrium and optimal product diversity. . . . The awkward problem is that we do not even know the nature of the bias—whether there is likely to be too much or too little diversity in equilibrium" (760).

2. The two problems are not unrelated. If a new good is a perfect substitute for existing goods, the law of one price is likely to hold. Then a delay in linking in a new good will not make an important difference to price indexes.

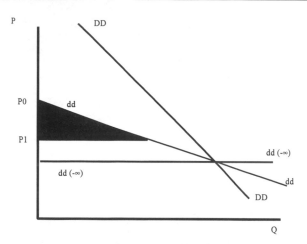

Fig. 5C.1   Consumers' gain from lowering one product's price

of new goods. The irrelevance assumption obviously understates the value of the new good, and the later the new good is incorporated, the worse the underestimate. The perfect substitutability assumption is less obvious. However, examine figure 5C.1, which I reproduce from the introduction to this volume. The assumption of perfect substitutability amounts, in the figure, to assuming that the demand curve for a new variety is flat, like $dd(-\infty)$. If the new good is in fact a less-than-perfect substitute for existing products, this ignores a consumer's surplus triangle. The worse the substitutability, the bigger the triangle and therefore the underestimate.

Following Trajtenberg (1989), Hausman takes on the question of the slope of dd and the consumer's surplus that results directly from a new good.[3] He estimates the demand system for the RTE breakfast cereals at the level of individual products. The estimated demand system is used to calculate the consumer's surplus of a single new good, Apple-Cinnamon Cheerios.

The analysis can serve as an example of the broader problem of variety-increasing new products in branded consumer product industries. Apple-Cinnamon Cheerios has some nice features for this purpose. Since there are other cereals available, and even others that are types of Cheerios, it is clear that the product represents only an incremental increase in the range of choice at breakfast. If, as Hausman reports, it has a large value of consumer's surplus, that is an important finding. In the absence of other systematic evidence about new product varieties (and of any particular reason to suspect RTE cereals are

---

3. Trajtenberg measured the improvement in buyer welfare for a whole new class of medical diagnostic products, computerized tomography scanners, and for fundamental improvements in them, such as the "body scanner." Trajtenberg used an "address" model of product differentiation like an important class in the Eaton-Lipsey survey. This led him to the conjecture that a new good's distance from existing products in the address space is an important determinant of the slope of dd and therefore of a product's consumer's surplus contribution to welfare.

much unlike other things sold in grocery stores) we should revise upward our assessment of the economic importance of incremental variety improvements. For example, existing methods for calculating price indexes for branded consumer products might be making a large error in assessing their rate of growth. At a minimum, accepting Hausman's finding means we should revise upward the potential value of research like that presented here for learning about branded consumer product valuation in general.

The introduction of new goods can also change the conditions of competition in an industry or, more simply, competitive outcomes. Existing products' market power may be reduced by competition from new goods. The transitory monopoly accruing to a new good may be an important incentive for inventors. A new good may complete the product-line strategy of an existing firm. All of these issues are related to imperfect competition, Hausman's second topic. Looking again at figure 5C.1, we see that a new product that generates considerable consumer's surplus is one that has a steep demand curve. Thus, if the new product is supplied by only one firm, it may be associated with considerable market power. The two topics of consumer's surplus and imperfect competition are closely linked.

Hausman offers two main substantive conclusions based on considerable econometric investigation. The consumer's surplus associated with the introduction of Apple-Cinnamon Cheerios was substantial. Second, imperfect competition considerations mean that the introduction tended to raise prices on other products, lowering the gain in consumer's surplus but not reversing it.

In this comment, I take up two general issues raised by Hausman's analysis. First, what is the evidence for substantial consumer's surplus gains from incremental product introductions in mature consumer-product industries? This question is largely econometric; the issue is the statistical finding of a steep single-product demand curve in figure 5C.1. Second, what role does imperfect competition play in determining the economic value of a new good? This is a question of economic interpretation of estimates.

Econometric Specification and Estimation Issues

It is natural to doubt the surprisingly large consumer's surplus values estimated by Hausman. How can it be true that Apple-Cinnamon Cheerios— surely a "me, too" product—is this poor a substitute for existing products?

Very Unrestricted Specification

In my opinion, Hausman's specification decisions are carefully made to overcome skepticism on this score. One might suspect that preexisting Cheerios products or other family-segment cereals already satisfy pretty much any palate. The result that there is large consumer's surplus must arise because this is empirically false. Hausman finds a steep *dd* for Apple-Cinnamon Cheerios because he finds relatively poor substitutability between Apple-Cinnamon

Cheerios and the other preexisting cereals in the family segment. What did the data do and what did the specification do in producing this result? Hausman is careful to impose very little structure on the pattern of own- and cross-price elasticities within segments. His estimates are very unrestrictive in this regard.[4]

To be sure, Hausman does assume that products within categories are closer substitutes than are products in different categories. But it is not interesting to question whether the elasticity of substitution between two children's cereals is higher than that between one of them and Special K. There is very little chance that the key assumptions are the segment separability (or "budgetability") ones. We and Hausman can trust the marketing people at the RTE cereal companies to have done that work already. Their research is not reported to us in any quantitative detail, but the origin of the segmentation assumptions is surely based on the analysis of much more detailed data than we have in this paper, including consumer microdata. Also, there is not a great deal of ambiguity in the segment structure.[5]

At the key juncture, which because of the special structure of the cereals market comes at the within-category level, the specification is unrestricted. Thus, the paper does a good job of convincing us that the finding of large consumer's surplus is not an artifact of specification.

Sources of Instruments

There is another set of econometric assumptions in this (or any other) analysis of product-differentiated demand. In measuring the degree of substitutability among products, the econometric treatment of the endogeneity of prices is very important (see Berry 1994 for a recent treatment). This is the other part of the econometric specification of the paper where the conclusions might have been accidentally assumed.

In this paper, the origins of the identifying assumptions are in a variance-components model of the errors. The analysis draws on the general theoretical results of Hausman and Taylor (1981) for estimation with variance-components identification assumptions. In the present analysis, Hausman assumes that the reduced-form equation for price (his equation [8]),

$$\log p_{jnt} = \delta_j \log c_{jt} + \alpha_{jn} + w_{jnt},$$

4. He also shows that a more restrictive functional form leads to a much larger estimated consumer's surplus.

5. In many industries, there are multiple, competing segmentation schemes that arise from the marketing studies. In automobiles, for example, there are segments (like "subcompact") that clearly matter for the structure of substitution elasticities. There is also evidence that brand names and even country product-quality reputations matter for the structure of elasticities of substitution. In many other branded consumer product markets, there is a natural question of "private label" products versus brand names as well as some named segments. Thus, several principles of differentiation, each with a distinct set of close-substitute products, compete for the analyst's attention in deciding what to cluster together a priori. The comparatively simple structure of RTE cereals is an exception in this regard.

has a particular structure. The cost error c_{jt} varies with time t and good j but not with city n. Thus, there are common cost shocks across cities. The city-related but time-independent effects α_{jn} could be differences either in demand or in cost (Hausman suggests cost), but their interpretation does not matter. The specific identifying assumption Hausman makes is that the error w_{jnt} is uncorrelated across cities. This means that all shocks to demand over time are assumed to be independent across cities.

Hausman has one and a half justifications for this assumption. First, it might really be true that there are no nationwide shocks to the demand for one brand of cereal relative to another. I don't know much about RTE breakfast cereals, but in branded consumer product industries in general I would be very doubtful of this assumption. It rules out too many important real-world phenomena. For example, for Hausman's assumption to be true, there can be no successful nationwide advertising campaigns which shift the demand for individual brands or products.[6] There can be no fads shifting demand temporarily to a particular product, or if there are fads, they must be geographically local. There can be no slow acceptance of new brands. And so on. Alternatively, such common demand shocks might not be incorporated in prices, because they are predetermined in the relevant run (cf. the last paragraph in section 5.3). Economically, this is the assumption that the common demand shocks cannot be foreseen when prices are set. This seems unlikely as well, given the nature of the nationwide demand shocks just mentioned.

If these assumptions fail, and if supply is upward sloping, the nationwide demand shock will mean that the error w_{jnt} is correlated across cities, counter to Hausman's identifying assumption.[7] The interesting question is, What happens to the finding of poor substitutability among products and therefore of a steep *dd* in figure 5C.1?

I examine this issue in a simple case: linear demand, Bertrand supply by single-product firms, and constant marginal cost.[8] The demand system is

$$Q_{jnt} = y\beta_j + P_{nt}\gamma_j + \varepsilon_{jnt},$$

where Q_{jnt} is the quantity of product j in market n at time t, y are regressors, and P_{nt} are the prices of all the different products in that market at that time. The demand error ε_{jnt} is assumed to have both a local and a national component. Finally, β_j and γ_j are the parameters of the jth product's demand system; I will use γ_{jj} to denote the own-price coefficient, and γ to denote the matrix of

6. Adding advertising stocks or flows to the demand system does not necessarily solve this problem. The issue of the econometrician not observing the success of competitive advertising campaigns remains.

7. Supply could be upward sloping in the one-week run either because inventories cannot adjust or because of market power. The pricing equations (13) later assumed by Hausman imply an upward-sloping supply, for example.

8. The extensions to Hausman's case of approximately log-linear demand and multiproduct firms do not change anything important in the analysis.

all price coefficients in all products' demand curves. The simplest possible supply curve with market power is the single-product Bertrand-equilibrium one, assumed by almost all authors studying this problem (including Hausman and, here, me):

$$P_{jnt} = Q_{jnt} (-\gamma_{jj})^{-1} + c_{jnt}.$$

In the appendix, I perform the simple algebra to get the formula for the asymptotic bias to Hausman's estimator. The sign and order of magnitude of the bias are determined by the matrix

$$\sigma_{\varepsilon-nat}[\text{diag}(-\gamma)-\gamma]^{-1}$$

Where $\sigma_{\varepsilon-nat}$ is the variance-covariance matrix of the national portion of the demand shock.

Hausman assumes $\sigma_{\varepsilon-nat}$ to be all zeros, in which case there is no bias. If there are nationwide demand shocks, the own-price coefficients are biased upward, toward zero. This is completely intuitive and familiar; with nationwide demand shocks, Hausman's estimator is like doing ordinary least squares on a supply and demand system; of course the estimates are biased toward too-steep demand curves.[9]

Unfortunately, this means that γ is biased in the direction of the finding reported by Hausman. The estimates will tend to report substitution patterns leading to a large consumer's surplus for new products, not because there are such substitution patterns, but because there are nationwide demand shocks not acknowledged in the estimation.

To believe Hausman's finding, then, one must be prepared to assume (1) that there are no nationwide shocks to demand which shift consumers among the products within segments, or (2) that shocks are not reflected in prices because they are unanticipated. That is a simple matter of econometric logic. It is a matter of scholarly taste whether one is prepared to make these assumptions. But assuming that there are no brand-specific advertising shocks in a consumer product category, or that these shocks are not communicated in advance to retailers, seems unwise without further investigation.

I do not mean to imply that the research program taken up here is impossible, only that the specific econometric methodology brought to the problem by Hausman seems particularly inappropriate to it. There is a wide variety of econometric models available for estimating the degree of substitutability in product-differentiated industries. I have reviewed some of them in Bresnahan (1989), and many different scholars are at work advancing the methods today.[10]

9. Similarly, if less familiarly, the cross-price coefficients are also likely to be biased upward, though this finding depends on the covariances of the shocks to demand across products. See equation A1 and following text.

10. This volume is not the place for a careful review of these methods. See Berry (1994) for a recent method contribution.

Imperfect Competition

Imperfect competition and new goods are linked through at least three major lines of causation. A new good in an imperfectly competitive environment can create market power for its inventor. It can destroy market power for competitive products. The equilibrium transitory market power these two forces imply contributes to the incentive to invent.

This is an interesting and important area of inquiry. In the paper at hand, "imperfect competition" means the analysis of a multiproduct firm with market power. In these remarks, I want first to point out some other useful and important implications of these estimates, and then turn to the question of how general Hausman's main analytical point might be.

Private Return to New Goods

A new product with a steep demand curve is involved with substantial consumer's surplus as Hausman in his paper and Trajtenberg (1989) point out. Let me point out that if the new product is proprietary to a single firm, it will also involve a monopoly rent to that firm. Exactly the same condition for large consumer's surplus—a not-too-flat *dd* in figure 5C.1—is the condition for a profitable single-product monopoly. Thus, demand measurement papers like this one are useful in assessing the private return to firms' introduction of new products as well as the social return that results from the introduction, Hausman's focus.

Of course, in the real world of multiproduct firms and competitive responses from other firms, more-complex calculations are needed. That is why, in this paper and others, it is valuable to estimate the entire demand system. Estimates of the supply system, not provided here, would obviously be needed as well.[11]

Prices in Imperfect Competition

Under imperfect competition among single-product firms, the impact of new-product introductions on pricing incentives is clear. The new product lowers the market power of existing products, lowering the overall level of prices.[12] This is one of the classical benefits of competition.

With multiproduct firms, the story changes slightly. Introduction of a new product by one firm lowers the market power of all other firms. This applies to all the other firms' products in varying degrees, depending on the demand

11. Assuming that the oligopoly solution concept is known, as here it is known to be Bertrand, and that the slope of marginal cost is known, here known to be flat, makes estimation of the supply system irrelevant. All the supply parameters which are not demand parameters are assumed to be known.

12. Peculiar values of the elasticities—as when the new good makes the demand curve for the old good steeper—can reverse this general theoretical finding.

elasticities and cross elasticities.[13] A new product in an imperfectly competitive industry makes demand curves at the single-product and single-firm levels flatter, thereby leading to a general lowering of prices.

Why, then, does Hausman find that the prices of other products rise in response to an introduction? There is a two-part answer. First, he assumes that the prices of other firms do not change, calculating "the markups over marginal cost that are profit maximizing for General Mills under the Nash-Bertrand assumption that other firms, such as Kellogg, will not change their prices in response to the introduction of Apple-Cinnamon Cheerios" (section 5.6). This is a common error among those who are new to models of imperfect competition, but an important one. The Bertrand solution concept has firms maximizing their postentry profits, taking one another's postentry prices as given.

For the analyst to calculate the equilibrium effect of entry, however, the other firms' postentry prices cannot be taken as given. The fact of entry changes the "game," and equilibrium prices will change in response. Typically, they will fall. What Hausman's analysis does is examine the price-discrimination problem for General Mills under the assertion that it is a monopoly, ruling out any equilibrium competitive response from the other firms. Hausman's assertion that he has a "lower bound" is wrong.

This observation also clarifies the calculations Hausman actually does make. By holding the prices of all other firms set, he examines the pricing problem of a multiproduct monopolist. Will a multiproduct monopolist raise prices on other goods? Hausman uses equation (13), the first-order condition for product j's prices:

$$\left[\frac{p_j}{\sum_{k=1}^{m} p_k q_k} \right] \frac{\partial \pi}{\partial p_j} = s_j + \sum_{k=1}^{m} \left[\frac{p_k - mc_k}{p_k} s_k \right] e_{kj} = 0.$$

The index k goes over all the firm's other products. What happens to this expression if we add a new product, $m + 1$? Two things: (1) the summation expression grows larger, by the term

$$\frac{(p_{m+1} - mc_{m+1}) \, s_{m+1}}{p_{m+1}} e_{m+1, j},$$

and (2) the firm has a higher marginal revenue for product j because it owns $m + 1$—shares are held constant. This is the effect emphasized by Hausman.

---

13. Furthermore, under the Bertrand (Nash equilibrium with prices as strategic variables) solution concept used by Hausman, the story does not stop there. If a product introduction by firm A causes firms B and C to lower prices in response, what is the impact of those lower prices in turn? They represent more competition, and lower firm-B prices will cause lower firm-C prices, etc. Thus, the indirect effects of a competitive product introduction reinforce the direct effects. Most other equilibrium product-differentiated competition theories have similar competitive equilibrium effects.

The offsetting effect is that the terms s_j and s_k are smaller, to the extent that the existing products lose share to the new product. Thus, there are three effects on the existing product j's price. First, there is a new, positive, term in the summation. Second, s_j has fallen because of cannibalization. Third, s_k falls for all the firms' existing products, lowering each term in the summation. The net effect is to either raise or lower equation (13), calling for a new price of product j that can be either higher or lower.

In general, it is not possible to tell which of these effects is larger. But Hausman's assertion that we should expect one effect to dominate the other is clearly wrong. For the case of linear demand and a two-product firm, for example, the two effects exactly offset. Thus, any tendency of one effect to dominate the other does not arise from the fundamental economics of the problem, but instead from higher-order derivatives. And the paper at hand contains no evidence that those are important.

Imperfect Competition's Implications

Let me summarize the logical possibilities for imperfectly competitive analysis of new goods in a simple diagram. In figure 5C.2, the columns represent the mechanism by which a new good has impacts on industry pricing more generally, through the prices of competitive products or through the prices of other products of the same firm. The rows represent the welfare impacts that the new good can have. I have shaded the box where Hausman focuses his effort.

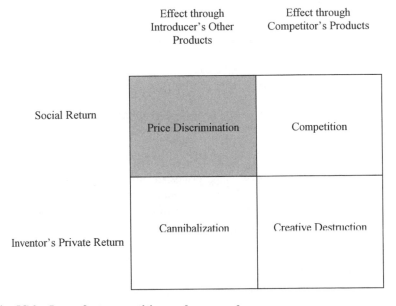

Fig. 5C.2   Imperfect competition and new goods

It seems to me that the focus is off. If we agree that the "social return" row is the interesting one, then Hausman has quantified the generally far less important effect. In general, the impact on pricing incentives for other imperfect competitors must be much more important. If we look at the overall picture, the problem involved in the conflict between incentives to introduce new goods and the value of those new goods looms large. And Hausman offers no analysis of this, though his estimates could easily be interpreted as having a bearing on it. The important topic of imperfect competition and new goods waits for analysis.

Conclusion

The topic of this paper is important for assessing the economic importance of new goods in mature, product-differentiated consumer goods industries. This reader was, unfortunately, left unconvinced by key econometric assumptions and found the imperfect-competition portion of the analysis off point. To remain unconvinced by the conclusion that single-product consumer's surplus was large may simply be to believe that there are nationwide brand-name demand shocks. The puzzle of the value of this incremental product introduction remains unsolved.

Appendix

The supply and demand system for each product in each city is

$$Q_{jnt} = y\beta_j + P_{nt}\gamma_j + \varepsilon_{jnt};$$
$$P_{jnt} = Q_{jnt}(-\gamma_{jj})^{-1} + c_{jnt}.$$

Solving out the quantities leaves

$$P_{jnt} = (y\beta_j + P_{nt}\gamma_j + \varepsilon_{jnt})(-\gamma_{jj})^{-1} + c_{jnt},$$

so that this equation system is the one solved by the prices of *all* the products in city n at time t:

$$P_{nt}[I - \gamma \operatorname{diag}(-\gamma)^{-1}] = (y\beta + \varepsilon_{nt})\operatorname{diag}(-\gamma)^{-1} + c_{nt}.$$

The instruments are functions of the prices in other cities. Assume that the vector ε_{nt} consists of a national variance component plus independent draws for each city. Then the matrix of correlations of the prices in any particular city to the errors, ε_{nt}, in any other city will be proportional to

$$\sigma_{\varepsilon-nat}[\operatorname{diag}(-\gamma) - \gamma]^{-1} = \sigma_{\varepsilon-nat}\begin{bmatrix} -\gamma_{11} - \gamma_{11} & -\gamma_{12} \\ -\gamma_{21} & -\gamma_{22} - \gamma_{22} \end{bmatrix}^{-1}.$$

It is easy to see the assertions in the text in the two-product case:

$$\sigma \begin{bmatrix} 1 & \rho \\ \rho & 1 \end{bmatrix} \begin{bmatrix} -2\gamma_{11} & -\gamma_{21} \\ -\gamma_{12} & -2\gamma_{22} \end{bmatrix}^{-1} =$$

$$\sigma \begin{bmatrix} 1 & \rho \\ \rho & 1 \end{bmatrix} \begin{bmatrix} -2\gamma_{22} & -\gamma_{21} \\ -\gamma_{12} & -2\gamma_{11} \end{bmatrix} \frac{1}{4\gamma_{11}\gamma_{22} - \gamma_{12}\gamma_{21}} =$$

$$\sigma \begin{bmatrix} -2\gamma_{22} + \rho\gamma_{21} & \gamma_{12} - 2\rho\gamma_{11} \\ -2\rho\gamma_{22} + \gamma_{21} & \rho\gamma_{12} - 2\gamma_{12} \end{bmatrix} \frac{1}{4\gamma_{11}\gamma_{22} - \gamma_{12}\gamma_{21}}.$$

This gives the following results:
   1. The on-diagonal bias has sign $(-2\gamma_{22} + \rho\gamma_{12})$, and
   2. The off-diagonal bias has sign $(\gamma_{12} - 2\rho\gamma_{11})$.
At $\rho = 0$, the on-diagonal bias has sign $(-\gamma_{22})$, that is, positive (toward zero), and the off-diagonal bias has sign (γ_{12}), that is, positive (away from zero).

References

Berry, Steven. 1994. Estimating discrete choice models of product differentiation. *Rand Journal of Economics* 25, no. 2 (summer): 242–62.

Bresnahan, Timothy. 1989. Empirical studies of industries of market power. In *Handbook of industrial organization,* ed. Richard Schmalensee and Robert Willig. Amsterdam: North-Holland.

Eaton, B. Curtis, and Robert G. Lipsey. 1989. Product differentiation. In *Handbook of industrial organization,* ed. Richard Schmalensee and Robert Willig. Amsterdam: North-Holland.

Hausman, Jerry, and William Taylor. 1981. Panel data and unobservable individual effects. *Econometrica* 49, no. 6 (November): 1377–98.

Trajtenberg, Manuel. 1989. The welfare analysis of product innovation, with an application to computed tomography scanners. *Journal of Political Economy* 97, no. 2 (April): 444–79.

6   Bias in U.S. Import Prices and Demand

Robert C. Feenstra and Clinton R. Shiells

6.1 Introduction

Since the work of Houthakker and Magee (1969), it has been known that estimates of the income elasticity of demand for imports to the United States (and to other industrialized countries) are substantially greater than unity. Since these estimates exceed foreign countries' income elasticities of demand for our products, the implication is that balanced world growth will lead to an automatic worsening in the U.S. trade balance. Dissatisfaction with this result has led a number of researchers to suggest that there is an upward bias in the import price indexes and income elasticity estimates, due to the omission of new product varieties or new foreign suppliers of existing products (see Sato 1977; Helkie and Hooper 1988; Hooper 1989; Krugman 1989; and Riedel 1991). According to this argument, over the past several decades the United States has experienced an expansion in the range of imports from rapidly growing, developing countries, but no corresponding decrease in import prices. As a result, the rising share of imports—which is correlated with rising U.S. income—is attributed to a high income elasticity in the import demand equation.

Helkie and Hooper (1988) attempt to correct the estimation of aggregate U.S. import demand by including a measure of foreign countries' capital stocks as a proxy that reflects their movement into new product lines. It would be preferable to incorporate these import varieties from new supplying countries directly into the import price index, and then to estimate the effect on the

Robert C. Feenstra is professor at the University of California, Davis, and director of the International Trade and Investment Program at the National Bureau of Economic Research. Clinton R. Shiells is an economist at the International Monetary Fund and was on the staff of the U.S. International Trade Commission during the preparation of this paper.

The authors thank Shunli Yao for research assistance and William Alterman, Lael Brainard, and William Helkie for providing data. The views expressed are the authors' and should not be attributed to either the International Monetary Fund or the U.S. International Trade Commission.

income elasticity. Drawing on the results in Feenstra (1994), we describe in section 6.2 how the appearance of new product varieties, or of new suppliers of existing products, could bias the import price indexes. The major purpose of the paper is to measure this bias over all U.S. imports, and then to determine the effect of this bias on the estimated income elasticity of import demand.

To obtain the import price indexes, the Division of International Prices of the Bureau of Labor Statistics (BLS) surveys importing firms, as described by Alterman (1991). For firms included in these surveys, interviews are conducted to determine the prices of imported goods whose quality characteristics are unchanged over time: we refer to these as "sampled products" and "sampled prices." These interviews necessarily exclude some products from sampled firms and exclude other importing firms entirely. In section 6.2, we argue that if the share of import expenditure on the sampled products is *falling* over time, this will lead to an *upward bias* in the measured index.

The entry of countries into new product lines is one reason to expect that the expenditure on sampled products may be falling, though this can also reflect a more rapid fall in prices from the new suppliers. Both of these hypotheses are consistent with the "product cycle" theory of international trade (Vernon 1966), whereby production of commodities will shift over time to the lowest-cost locations. Thus, the appearance of new suppliers can quite possibly lead to an upward bias in the import price index. This idea is related to the potential bias in the *consumer* price index due to the appearance of new retail outlets offering lower prices (Reinsdorf 1993). Our paper can be viewed as an international analogue to this domestic argument, with new foreign suppliers taking the place of new retail outlets.

In section 6.3, we discuss the sensitivity of our results to three issues: the functional form of the aggregator, the absence of multinational firms, and the availability of firm-level data. While the basic results are derived for a constant elasticity of substitution (CES) aggregator function, we show that similar results can be obtained for the translog case, so the choice of aggregator is not crucial. On the other hand, the results are very sensitive to the assumption that the international transactions being considered are at arm's length, that is, these are not transactions internal to a multinational firm. Since imports internal to the firm are prevalent in some industries, as we describe, the results concerning the bias are not expected to hold in these cases.

The third issue of concern is the availability of data: the correction to the BLS price index described in section 6.2 relies on having data for the expenditure on products sampled from *each importing firm*. This information is not currently collected on a continuous basis. Accordingly, we are forced to rely on country-level rather than on firm-level data. That is, instead of using the expenditure share on sampled products, we will be using the expenditure on *all products* from sampled countries. These import expenditures are obtained from the U.S. Bureau of the Census. Thus, we are relying on the census data to construct proxies for the theoretically correct adjustment to the BLS indexes, which would rely on firm-level data. The usefulness of these proxies will be judged by their statistical significance when included in import demand equations.

In section 6.4, we examine how the adjustments to the import price indexes affect the income elasticity of demand for aggregate U.S. imports. The inclusion of the foreign capital stock proposed by Helkie and Hooper lowers the income elasticity of import demand from about 2.5 to 2.2. In comparison, using the correction based on the falling expenditure share on sampled countries, we find that the income elasticity is reduced from 2.5 to 1.7, or about halfway to unity. Our estimates suggest that the aggregate import price index is upward biased by between 1 and 2 percentage points annually. We conclude our paper by making a simple recommendation on the collection of additional data by the BLS when it interviews firms.

6.2   Potential Bias in the Import Price Index

To motivate our analysis, we consider the case of new retail outlets for domestic goods. Reinsdorf (1993) argues that very similar products will sell at different prices across retail outlets, and cites Denison (1962) to suggest that these price differentials are due to the time lags needed for consumers to respond to the price information, rather than to quality differentials across retail outlets. These new retails outlets are linked into the consumer price index without the price differential being directly incorporated, which results in a potential upward bias in the index. In order to model this bias, it is essential to assume that the similar goods are imperfect substitutes across the retail outlets. This reflects the empirical observation that a lower price at one outlet does not eliminate demand for the same good at another outlet. Reinsdorf and Moulton (chap. 10 in this volume, sec. 10.5) put further structure on the imperfect-substitutes assumption by assuming that the good has a constant elasticity of substitution across the retail outlets.

We will be taking the same approach to modeling the choice of a U.S. firm to import a product from various possible foreign suppliers. That is, we will assume that the U.S. importer treats the different suppliers' products as imperfect substitutes, reflecting any quality differential across suppliers as well as differences in their time lag of delivery, ease of communication, reliability of supply, and so forth. That is, even when observed quality differentials are absent, we will suppose that the wholesale services provided by the various foreign suppliers are enough to differentiate them, from the buyer's point of view. We should stress that the "buyer" in our case is the U.S. *importer* rather than the U.S. *consumer,* since the latter may be entirely unaware of these differences in wholesale services by the various suppliers. We feel that this assumption of imperfect substitution across foreign suppliers is analogous to that made for domestic retail outlets, provided that the import in question is an arms-length transaction between two unrelated firms. In contrast, the import of a product by a multinational from its own production facility abroad would *not* fit into this framework and will have to be treated separately.

6.2.1   CES Index

Like Reinsdorf and Moulton (chap. 10 in this volume, sec. 10.5) we will also assume the buyer treats the product as having a constant elasticity of substitution across the various supplying firms. This assumption is made for tractability, though we will argue in the next section that similar results could be obtained under alternative specifications. With this assumption, the minimum cost of obtaining one unit of services from the foreign suppliers i of some product is given by

$$(1) \qquad c(p_t, I_t) = \left[\sum_{i \in I_t} b_i p_{it}^{(1-\sigma)} \right]^{1/(1-\sigma)}, \sigma > 1,$$

where σ denotes the elasticity of substitution, which we assume exceeds unity; $I_t \subset \{1, \ldots, N\}$ is the set of foreign suppliers in period t with prices $p_{it} > 0$, $i \in I_t$; p_t denotes the corresponding vectors of prices in period t; and $b_i > 0$ denotes a quality (or taste) parameter for the product from supplier i.

Several features of the CES function in equation (1) should be noted. First, we have treated each foreign firm as supplying a single variety i of the differentiated product. Multiproduct firms can be handled, however, by letting i index each variety supplied by each firm. Thus, we will sometimes refer to i as an index of product varieties, where it is understood that this can be across firms or across products within a firm. Second, we have treated the quality parameters b_i as constant over time. This is not essential, and we could alternatively allow these parameters to change. In that case, we would assume that the "quality-adjusted" price is correctly measured for products that the BLS samples: that is, movements in b_i are correctly evaluated for the sampled products. For the nonsampled products, movements in b_i will not affect our results below, because we will use the expenditure shares to evaluate the (unobserved) prices and these shares would also respond to any changes in quality (Feenstra 1994).

To briefly review known results, suppose that the same set of product varieties I are available in periods $t - 1$ and t, and that the amounts purchased of each variety, x_{t-1} and x_t, are cost-minimizing quantities for the prices p_{t-1} and p_t, respectively. Let $s_{t-1}(I)$ and $s_t(I)$ denote the corresponding expenditure shares:

$$(2) \qquad s_{it}(I) \equiv p_{it} x_{it} / \sum_{i \in I} p_{it} x_{it}.$$

As in Diewert (1976), the exact price index $P[p_{t-1}, p_t, s_{t-1}(I), s_t(I)]$ is defined as a function of observed prices and expenditure shares, such that

$$(3) \qquad c(p_t, I) / c(p_{t-1}, I) = P[p_{t-1}, p_t, s_{t-1}(I), s_t(I)].$$

The important feature of equation (3) is that the price index itself does not depend on the unknown parameters b_i, $i \in I$. From Sato (1976) and Vartia (1976), a formula for the exact price index corresponding to the CES unit-cost function is

(4a)
$$P[p_{t-1}, p_t, s_{t-1}(I), s_t(I)] \equiv \prod_{i \in I} (p_{it}/p_{it-1})^{w_{it}(I)}.$$

This is a geometric mean of the individual price changes, where the weights $w_{it}(I)$ are computed using the cost shares $s_{it}(I)$ in the two periods, as follows:

(4b)
$$w_{it}(I) \equiv \left[\frac{s_{it}(I) - s_{it-1}(I)}{\ln s_{it}(I) - \ln s_{it-1}(I)} \right] \Big/ \sum_{i \in I} \left[\frac{s_{it}(I) - s_{it-1}(I)}{\ln s_{it}(I) - \ln s_{it-1}(I)} \right].$$

The numerator on the right-hand side of equation (4b) is the logarithmic mean of $s_{it}(I)$ and $s_{it-1}(I)$, and lies between these cost shares. The weights $w_{it}(I)$, then, are a normalized version of the logarithmic means and add up to unity.[1]

The exact price index in equation (4a) requires that the same varieties are available in the two periods, and that the prices for all these products are sampled. We now show how the exact index can be computed when only a subset of the product varieties is sampled. To this end, suppose that I_{t-1} and I_t are the full sets of imported products and that $I \subseteq (I_t \cap I_{t-1})$, $I \neq \emptyset$, is sampled in *both* periods. We shall let $P[p_{t-1}, p_t, s_{t-1}(I), s_t(I)]$ denote the price index in equation (3) that is computed by using data on only this set. We shall refer to this as a "conventional" price index, in the sense that it is computed over a constant set of (sampled) products. The exact price index should equal the ratio $c(p_t, I_t)/c(p_{t-1}, I_{t-1})$. Our first result, proved in Feenstra (1994), shows how this can be measured with observed prices and quantities:

PROPOSITION 1.   *For any set of sampled products* $I \subseteq (I_t \cap I_{t-1})$, $I \neq \emptyset$, *the exact price index for the CES aggregator is*

(5)
$$c(p_t, I_t)/c(p_{t-1}, I_{t-1}) \equiv P[p_{t-1}, p_t, s_{t-1}(I), s_t(I)] \\ \times [\lambda(I)_t/\lambda(I)_{t-1}]^{1/(\sigma-1)},$$

where $\lambda(I)_r \equiv \sum_{i \in I} p_{ir} x_{ir} \Big/ \sum_{i \in I_r} p_{ir} x_{ir}$, for $r = t - 1, t$.

This result states that the *exact* price index equals the conventional index $P[p_{t-1}, p_t, s_{t-1}(I), s_t(I)]$ times an additional term that represents the bias in the conventional index. To interpret this term, note that $\lambda(I)_t$ equals the fraction of expenditure on sampled products in period t, relative to the entire set $i \in I_t$. Thus, $[\lambda(I)_t/\lambda(I)_{t-1}]$ is the ratio of expenditure on sampled products over the two periods. If this ratio is less than unity, reflecting a declining share of expenditure on the sampled products, then the exact price index will be

---

1. Using L'Hospital's Rule, it is readily shown that as $s_{it-1}(I) \rightarrow s_{it}(I)$ for all i, the weights $w_{it}(I)$ approach $s_{it}(I)$.

lower than the index $P[p_{t-1}, p_t, s_{t-1}(I), s_t(I)]$. In other words, the declining share of expenditure on the sampled products will lead to an upward bias in the conventional index.

A declining share of expenditure on the sampled products could be due to the appearance of new suppliers or, alternatively, to a fall in the relative price of products not included in the sample. Both of these hypotheses are consistent with the product-cycle theory of international trade (Vernon 1966), whereby the production of commodities will shift over time to the lowest-cost locations. Thus, the appearance of new suppliers can quite possibly lead to an upward bias in the import price index. The potential bias in the conventional index is measured by the change in the share of expenditure on the sampled products, raised to the power $1/(\sigma - 1)$. For example, if new suppliers are providing products that are perfect substitutes for existing products, so that σ approaches infinity, then there will be no bias in the existing index. Conversely, if σ is low (but still greater than unity), any given change in the relative expenditure on sampled products will indicate a greater bias in the conventional index.[2]

6.2.2 BLS Index

The BLS samples multiple varieties of a product within each ten-digit Harmonized System (HS) category and then constructs the index at that level. More precisely, given the ratio of prices in the two time periods for each sampled product, the BLS constructs an unweighted arithmetic mean of these prices in the ten-digit HS category; aggregation to broader industry levels then occurs with a Laspeyres formula. The use of an arithmetic rather than a geometric mean will result in some upward bias in the index, and the absence of weights in the index may also introduce some error. In addition to these, we can use proposition 1 to determine the potential upward bias in the BLS index if the sampled products have expenditure shares that are falling over time.

Note that proposition 1 holds even if the set we use to construct the conventional price index P contains only a single variety, so that $I = \{i\}$. In this case the conventional index is simply the price ratio for that single variety, $P = p_{it}/p_{it-1}$, while the term $\lambda_t(i) \equiv s_{it}$ measures the observed expenditure share on that variety. Then taking the geometric mean of equation (5) for all the sampled product varieties $i = 1, \ldots, N$, it follows that the exact price index equals

$$(6) \qquad c(p_t, I_t)/c(p_{t-1}, I_{t-1}) = \prod_{i=1}^{N} (p_{it}/p_{it-1})^{1/N} (s_{it}/s_{it-1})^{1/N(\sigma-1)}.$$

The unweighted arithmetic mean used by the BLS exceeds the simple geometric mean appearing in equation (6). We then obtain

---

2. The elasticity of substitution must exceed unity, because otherwise all product varieties are essential for consumption, so the set I_t cannot vary over time.

COROLLARY 1.   *The BLS index is related to the exact price index by*

(7)
$$\sum_{i=1}^{N} \frac{1}{N} (p_{it}/p_{it-1}) \geq \prod_{i=1}^{N} (p_{it}/p_{it-1})^{1/N} =$$
$$[c(p_t, I_t)/c(p_{t-1}, I_{t-1})] \prod_{i=1}^{N} (s_{it}/s_{it-1})^{-1/N(\sigma-1)}.$$

The final term on the right-hand side of equation (7) is the average decline in the expenditure shares on products sampled by the BLS. When these shares are declining, there is an upward bias in the measured index as compared to the exact index. This bias reflects either the inferred price decline of firms not sampled by the BLS, or the appearance of new product varieties. If we suppose that the newest suppliers—not yet in the BLS sample—also have the most rapidly rising shares, then this upward bias is a plausible outcome. The data used to measure this potential bias are discussed in the next section, after we review the sensitivity of our results to assumptions we have made.

6.3   Sensitivity of Results

6.3.1   Functional Form

The results above were derived under the assumption of a CES aggregator function, and it is important to determine how sensitive the results are to this choice. Suppose instead that the product varieties i enter into a translog aggregator function, so that the unit-cost function in equation (1) is rewritten as

(8)
$$\ln c(p_t, I) = \alpha_0 + \sum_{i \in I} \alpha_i \ln p_{it} + \frac{1}{2} \sum_{i \in I} \sum_{j \in I} \gamma_{ij} \ln p_{it} \ln p_{jt},$$

with $\alpha_i > 0$ and $\gamma_{ij} = \gamma_{ji}$. The set I in this definition refers to the universe of possible product varieties, and is not allowed to vary. For products that are not available in some period, reservation prices, which are generally finite (see below), must be used in the right-hand side of equation (8). This contrasts with the CES case in equation (1), where the reservation prices were infinite, and products that were not available would simply not appear in the unit-cost function. Summing over this universe of products, the unit-cost function is homogeneous of degree one in prices, provided that $\sum_i \alpha_i = 1$ and $\sum_i \sum_j \gamma_{ij} = 0$.

For the translog function, the share of expenditure devoted to variety i is

(9)
$$s_{it} = \alpha_i + \sum_{j \in I} \gamma_{ij} \ln p_{jt}.$$

If there is a variety n that is newly available in period t, then its reservation price in $t-1$ is calculated by setting $s_{nt-1} = 0$ in equation (9), obtaining

(10)
$$\ln \tilde{p}_{nt-1} = \frac{-1}{\gamma_{nn}} \left(\alpha_n + \sum_{\substack{i \in I \\ i \neq n}} \gamma_{ni} \ln p_{it-1} \right).$$

We assume that $\alpha_{nn} < 0$, so that the reservation price is positive and finite for some values of p_{it-1}. This reservation price is used in equations (9) and (10) when variety n is not available.

Our goal is to determine how the translog aggregator would affect the results in proposition 1. To this end, we suppose that variety n is not included in the set of sampled varieties in either period. This may be because variety n is new, or because it is available in both periods but not sampled. In either case, let $I/\{n\} \equiv \{i \mid i \in I \text{ and } i \neq n\}$ denote the set of sampled products. Then the change in the price of variety n between the two periods can be computed from equation (9) as

$$(11) \qquad \ln\left(\frac{p_{nt}}{p_{nt-1}}\right) = \left(\frac{s_{nt} - s_{nt-1}}{\gamma_{nn}}\right) - \sum_{i \in I/\{n\}} \left(\frac{\gamma_{ni}}{\gamma_{nn}}\right) \ln\left(\frac{p_{it}}{p_{it-1}}\right).$$

To interpret equation (11), recall that $\gamma_{nn} < 0$ and that $\sum_i \gamma_{ni} = 0$, so that $\sum_{i \in I/\{n\}}$ $\gamma_{ni}/\gamma_{nn} = -1$. Then the expression on the right-hand side of equation (11) is a weighted average of the change in prices of all goods $i \neq n$. So equation (11) states that the change in the price of good n, relative to a weighted average of the prices of other varieties, is proportional to the change in the expenditure share on variety n. Note that this expression continues to hold if variety n is not available in one (or both) of the periods, in which case its share is set at zero in equation (11).

To determine the impact of the nonsampled variety on unit costs, we use the result that the ratio of unit costs for the translog function equals a Divisia index of the changes in the individual prices (e.g., Diewert 1976):

$$(12) \qquad \ln[c(p_t, I_t)/c(p_{t-1}, I_{t-1})] \equiv \sum_{i \in I} \frac{1}{2}(s_{it-1} + s_{it})\ln(p_{it}/p_{it-1}).$$

When variety n is newly available in period t, then its reservation price (equation [10]) is used on the right-hand side of equation (12) in period $t - 1$. To determine the effect of omitting variety n from the price index in both periods, we substitute equation (11) into equation (12), obtaining

PROPOSITION 2.   *Letting* $I/\{n\} \equiv \{i \mid i \in I \text{ and } i \neq n\}$ *denote the set of sampled products, the exact price index for the translog aggregator function is*

$$\ln[c(p_t, I)/c(p_{t-1}, I)] =$$
$$\sum_{i \in I/\{n\}} \frac{1}{2}(\tilde{s}_{it-1} + \tilde{s}_{it})\ln(p_{it}/p_{it-1}) - \left(\frac{s_{nt} - s_{nt-1}}{\overline{\eta}_n - 1}\right),$$

where (a) $\overline{\eta}_n \equiv 1 - [2\gamma_{nn}/(s_{nt-1} + s_{nt})]$ *is the average elasticity of demand for variety n; and (b)* $\tilde{s}_{ir} \equiv s_{ir} - (s_{nr}\gamma_{ni}/\gamma_{nn})$ *equals the expenditure share of i if variety n was priced at its reservation level in period r, r = t - 1, t. If the varieties* $i \in I/\{n\}$ *are weakly separable from n, then* $\tilde{s}_{ir} = s_{ir}(I/\{n\})$ *as defined in equation (2).*

This result states that the exact index equals the sum of two terms: (i) a Divisia index constructed over the sampled products $i \in I/\{n\}$, where the shares $\tilde{s}_{ir}$ in this index reflect the optimal choice if variety n was not available; and (ii) a term reflecting the change in the expenditure share on variety n and its average elasticity of demand. As a proof, note that from equation (9) the elasticity of demand for variety n in period t is $\eta_{nt} = 1 - (\gamma_{nn}/s_{nt})$. Then the following term appears when equation (11) is substituted into equation (12):

$$\frac{1}{2}(s_{nt-1} + s_{nt})\left(\frac{s_{nt} - s_{nt-1}}{\gamma_{nn}}\right) = -\left(\frac{s_{nt} - s_{nt-1}}{\bar{\eta}_n - 1}\right),$$

where $\bar{\eta}_n \equiv 1 - [2\gamma_{nn}/(s_{nt-1} + s_{nt})]$ is the elasticity of demand computed with the *average* share between periods $t - 1$ and t. This establishes part (a) of proposition 2.

To establish part (b), let p_{nr} denote the observed price for variety n and $\tilde{p}_{nr}$ its reservation price. Holding all other prices fixed, it is immediately clear from equation (9) that $\ln(\tilde{p}_{nr}/p_{nr}) = -s_{nr}/\gamma_{nn}$. Substituting this change in prices into the share equation (9) for s_{ir}, it follows that $\tilde{s}_{ir}$ is the implied expenditure on variety i when n is not available. The shares $\tilde{s}_{ir}$ are not generally observed, which is a limitation of proposition 2. However, if the varieties $i \in I/\{n\}$ are weakly separable from n, then a change in the price of variety n (from its observed to its reservation level), should have no impact on the *relative* expenditure share for varieties $i \in I/\{n\}$. In that case, the formula for the shares in equation (2)—which simply omits variety n from the calculation—would equal $\tilde{s}_{ir}$, so that the Divisia index in proposition 2 can be readily measured.

The condition that the products $i \in I/\{n\}$ are weakly separable from n is rather special, more so because we have already assumed that $\gamma_{nn} < 0$ (so that the reservation price is finite). The latter condition means that the higher-level function defined over the aggregate $i \in I/\{n\}$ and variety n must be translog *but not* Cobb-Douglas. However, this implies that the lower-level function used to aggregate the varieties $i \in I/\{n\}$ *must be* Cobb-Douglas in order for the resulting unit-cost function to be translog.[3] Thus, the varieties $i \in I/\{n\}$ will have constant relative shares. The special nature of this separability assumption is perhaps no worse than the CES case, however, as it is the only function for which every subset of goods is weakly separable from every other. Indeed, it appears to be this separability property, rather than the infinite reservation prices, that makes the analysis of new and nonsampled goods so tractable in the CES case.

In order to compare the translog and CES cases, let us continue to assume that there is a single nonsampled variety n.[4] Then from proposition 1 the exact price index in the CES case is

---

3. The logic of this statement is that a translog function of translog functions is *not* translog in general: rather, it will involve terms of the form $\ln p_i \ln p_j \ln p_k \ln p_l$, which are ruled out by assuming that either the higher-order aggregator or the lower-order aggregates are Cobb-Douglas.

4. If there are *multiple* nonsampled goods, then we assume that this set of varieties $\{n\}$ is weakly separable from the set $i \in I/\{n\}$, and use the scalar n to denote the aggregate of the nonsampled goods. If these varieties $\{n\}$ originally entered the translog function in equation (8), then the aggregator over them must be Cobb-Douglas, for the reasons discussed in n. 3. Alternatively, we

(13) $\ln[c(p_t, I_t)/c(p_{t-1}, I_{t-1})] = \ln P[p_{t-1}, p_t, s_{t-1}(I), s_t(I)]$

$$+ \left(\frac{1}{\sigma - 1}\right) \ln \left(\frac{1 - s_{nt}}{1 - s_{nt-1}}\right)$$

$$\approx \ln P[p_{t-1}, p_t, s_{t-1}(I), s_t(I)] - \left(\frac{s_{nt} - s_{nt-1}}{\sigma - 1}\right),$$

where the final expression follows if the expenditure share on the nonsampled good is small, so that $\ln(1 - s_{nr}) \approx -s_{nr}$. Comparing equation (13) to proposition 2, we obtain

COROLLARY 2.   *If variety n is not sampled, then the ratio of the bias in the conventional index for the translog and CES cases is approximately*

$$\left(\frac{\sigma - 1}{\overline{\eta}_n - 1}\right) \begin{cases} = & 1 \text{ if } \overline{\eta}_n = \sigma, \\ = & 1/2 \text{ if } s_{nt-1} = 0 \text{ and } \eta_{nt} = \sigma, \\ \rightarrow & 0 \text{ as both } s_{nt-1} \text{ and } s_{nt} \rightarrow 0. \end{cases}$$

To interpret the first result above, note that the elasticity of demand for variety n in the CES case is $\sigma(1 - s_{nt}) + s_{nt}$. For small values of s_{nt} this is close to σ, so that if the average elasticity of demand in the translog case equals that in the CES case, then the bias terms are approximately equal. This comparison depends, however, on computing the elasticity of demand $\overline{\eta}_n$ using the average share $(s_{nt-1} + s_{nt})/2$. Alternatively, if variety n is newly available in period t so that $s_{nt-1} = 0$, then the bias term in proposition 2 is written as $s_{nt}/2(\eta_{nt} - 1)$ for $\eta_{nt} = 1 - (\gamma_{nn}/s_{nt})$. With $\eta_{nt} \approx \sigma$, this is about *one-half* the bias in the conventional index $s_{nt}/(\sigma - 1)$ obtained in the CES case. Since these bias terms can also be interpreted as the welfare gain due to the introduction of the new product variety, we have shown that this gain is approximately *twice* as large in the CES case (with $\eta_{nt} \approx \sigma$). Finally, the last result above indicates that these comparisons are quite sensitive to the share of the nonsampled good: if this share approaches zero, then the elasticity of demand $\overline{\eta}_n$ for the translog case approaches infinity and the ratio of the biases approaches zero.

While corollary 2 summarizes the quantitative relation between the biases, an immediate qualitative result from comparing equation (13) and proposition 2 is that for both the CES and translog unit-cost functions, a decrease (increase) in the share of the sampled products indicates an upward (downward) bias in the conventional price index. This result does not rely on the approximation in equation (13), but simply uses the facts that both $\sigma > 1$ and $\overline{\eta}_n > 1$ (since $\gamma_{nn} < 0$). Thus, the qualitative nature of the bias identified in corollary 1—that sampling from firms with a falling expenditure share on their products

could use any aggregator over the nonsampled varieties $\{n\}$ and then just assume that this aggregate enters the translog function in equation (8).

will lead to an upward bias in the index—is preserved across these two functional forms, though the magnitude of the bias will depend on the elasticities of substitution and demand as discussed in corollary 2.

6.3.2 Multinational Firms

An assumption maintained throughout our discussion is that the quantity purchased from foreign firms by the U.S. importer is cost minimizing at the observed prices. This assumption fails to hold, however, when the import is internal to a multinational firm, in which case the transfer price for the import may bear little relation to its economic value. Thus, for these "internal" imports we should not expect the bias we have identified in the conventional index to apply. This conclusion is reinforced by the observation that imports internal to a firm may *not* be differentiated across sources of supply: a U.S. multinational engaged in production abroad at two different plants may very well treat the products from these sources as perfect substitutes. Thus, our other maintained assumption—that imports are differentiated across foreign sources—also fails.

Data on intracompany imports are presented in tables 6.1 and 6.2. In table 6.1, we distinguish U.S. manufacturing imports that are internal to U.S. multinationals (shipped from nonbank U.S. affiliates abroad) from those that are internal to foreign multinationals (shipped to nonbank foreign affiliates in the United States). In addition, we distinguish imports that are intended for sale

Table 6.1   U.S. Imports by Source Companies and Countries, 1982 and 1987 ($ billion)

	1982	1987
Total U.S. nonpetroleum merchandise imports[a]	185.7	366.8
Manufacturing imports from nonbank U.S. affiliates abroad[b]	31.8	57.3
To nonbank U.S. parents	25.4	—
From Canada (transportation equipment)	13.4 (10.6)	—
From Japan	2.2	—
From Mexico	1.6	—
Wholesale trade from nonbank U.S. affiliates abroad[b]	2.7	6.7
To nonbank U.S. parents	2.3	—
Manufacturing imports to nonbank foreign affiliates in the United States[c]	13.8	24.5
From nonbank foreign parent group	—	17.6
From Japan	—	3.9
From Germany	—	3.2
From Canada	—	2.7
Wholesale trade to nonbank foreign affiliates in the United States[c]	58.7	107.3
From nonbank foreign parent group	—	85.1
From Japan (motor vehicles and equipment)	—	53.3 (26.1)
From Germany (motor vehicles and equipment)	—	11.6 (9.2)
From Canada (motor vehicles and equipment)	—	2.5 (—)

Sources: [a]Council of Economic Advisers (1993). [b]U.S. Department of Commerce (1982); Mataloni (1990). [c]Howenstine (1985); U.S. Department of Commerce (1987).
Note: A dash indicates that data were not available.

to consumers (wholesale trade) from those that are intended as inputs into further production (manufacturing imports). The most precise data—dealing with shipments from a company abroad to the same company in the United States—are available from a 1982 or a 1987 benchmark survey.

For U.S. multinationals, the intracompany manufacturing imports amounted to $25.4 billion in 1982, or 14 percent of total nonpetroleum merchandise imports.[5] Of this, $10.6 billion was accounted for by transportation imports from Canada, reflecting the Canada-U.S. auto pact. We have listed the three largest source countries, which were Canada, Japan, and Mexico. There was an additional $2.3 billion of intracompany imports classified as wholesale trade, bringing total intracompany trade from U.S. affiliates abroad to 15 percent of imports. Turning to the foreign multinationals with operations in the United States, the internal manufacturing imports of these firms amounted to $17.6 billion in 1987, or 5 percent of total imports. The three largest source countries are Japan, Germany, and Canada. A much larger amount of imports—$85.1 billion or 23 percent of the total—occurs in wholesale trade.[6] The bulk of this wholesale trade was from Japan, much of which is explained by wholesale trade in automobiles (such as Toyota Motor Corporation sending its vehicles to Toyota Motor Sales, U.S.A.). In total, the intracompany trade of U.S. and foreign affiliates is roughly one-half of total imports.

More detailed evidence for individual industries is provided in table 6.2, which covers only the U.S. affiliates of foreign multinationals and their internal imports in manufacturing.[7] The classification of industries is that used by the Bureau of Economic Analysis (BEA), and the industries are ranked according to the share of internal (i.e., intracompany) imports in total imports. At the top of the ranking are chemicals and primary metals, followed by industrial machinery, household audio equipment, and various food products. The average of the internal manufacturing imports for the entire sample is 8 percent.

The borderline industry in table 6.2 is motor vehicles and equipment, where the internal manufacturing imports are 7 percent of the total. Given the extremely large amount of wholesale internal imports in this industry, we ranked it as *above average* in internal imports, and the same is true for all industries listed above motor vehicles and equipment in table 6.2. Conversely, all industries listed below are treated as *below average* in their internal imports.[8] More specifically, for those industries with an internal-imports share exceeding 8

---

5. In both 1982 and 1987, imports from majority-owned U.S. affiliates abroad accounted for over 80 percent of the total intracompany imports of U.S. multinationals.

6. Zeile (1993) provides a general description of the merchandise trade of U.S. affiliates of foreign companies, including both manufacturing and wholesale trade.

7. These data are obtained directly from Brainard (1993), whom the authors thank for assistance. Ideally, it would be desirable to have the same data for the internal imports of U.S. multinationals, but this was not as readily available.

8. We judged that tobacco products (which are suppressed in table 6.2) would have above-average internal imports and so they were included in that group.

Table 6.2   **U.S. Affiliates of Foreign Companies: Internal Manufacturing Imports by Industry, 1989**

Classification Code[a]	Internal Imports[b]/Total Imports(%)	BEA Industry Definition
283	46	Drugs
281	28	Industrial chemicals and synthetics
102	22	Copper, lead, zinc, gold, silver
289	20	Chemical products, NEC
353	19	Construction, mining, and materials handling machinery
335	15	Primary metal products, nonferrous
356	15	General industrial machinery
366	14	Household audio, video, and communications equipment
284	12	Soap, cleaners, toilet goods
308	12	Miscellaneous plastics products
349	12	Metal services; ordnance; fabricated metal products, NEC
101	11	Iron ore
265	11	Other paper and allied products
202	10	Dairy products
205	10	Bakery products
208	10	Beverages
291	10	Integrated petroleum refining and extraction
321	10	Glass products
341	10	Metal cans, forgings, stampings
120	9	Coal
209	9	Other food and kindred
305	9	Rubber products
343	8	Heating equipment, plumbing, structural metal products
371	7[c]	Motor vehicles and equipment
355	7	Special industrial machinery
384	7	Medical and ophthalmic instruments and supplies
329	6	Stone, clay, concrete, gypsum, nonmetallic minerals
367	6	Electronic components and accessories
140	5	Nonmetallic minerals, except fuels
220	5	Textile mill products
357	5	Computer and office equipment
379	5	Aircraft, motorcycles, bikes, spacecraft, railroad
381	5	Measuring, scientific, and optical instruments
272	4	Miscellaneous publishing
331	4	Primary metal products, ferrous

(*continued*)

Table 6.2   (continued)

Classification Code[a]	Internal Imports[b]/Total Imports(%)	BEA Industry Definition
354	4	Metalworking machinery
358	4	Refrigeration and service industry machinery
107	3	Other metallic ores
262	3	Pulp, paper, board mill products
275	3	Commercial printing and services
271	2	Newspapers
342	2	Cutlery, hardware, screw products
352	2	Farm and garden machinery
390	2	Miscellaneous manufacturing
201	1	Meat products
230	1	Apparel and other textile products
250	1	Furniture and fixtures
386	1	Photographic equipment and supplies
010	0	Crops
020	0	Livestock, animal specialties
080	0	Forestry
090	0	Fishing, hunting, trapping
133	0	Crude petrol extraction, natural gas
240	0	Lumber and wood products
287	0	Agricultural chemicals
299	0	Petroleum and coal products, NEC
203	—[d]	Preserved fruits and vegetables
204	—[d]	Grain mill products
210	—[c,d]	Tobacco products
310	—[d]	Leather and leather products
351	—[d]	Engines, turbines
359	—[d]	Industrial and commercial machinery, NEC
363	—[d]	Household appliances
369	—[d]	Electrical machinery, NEC
Average	8	

Source: Brainard (1993).
Note: NEC stands for not elsewhere classified.
[a]Industry code from the Bureau of Economic Analysis.
[b]Includes imports by affiliates only from foreign parent group.
[c]Motor vehicles and tobacco products are treated as having above-average internal sales.
[d] Suppressed by the BEA for confidentiality of individual firms.

percent in table 6.2 (including motor vehicles and equipment), we identified the corresponding three-digit Standard International Trade Classification (SITC) numbers. Excluding petroleum products, there are roughly two hundred three-digit SITC categories, of which about one-half corresponded to those industries listed in table 6.2 with above-average internal imports; the other half are treated as having below-average internal imports. Given this crude division of our sample, our hypothesis is that the bias in the conventional import price index should be more prominent for the industries with below-average internal imports.

6.3.3 Availability of Data

The potential bias in the BLS import price index is measured by the last term appearing in corollary 1, that is, the change in expenditure shares on sampled products. An immediate difficulty with implementing this formula is that the expenditure shares on the sampled products are not collected on a continuous basis by the BLS. While expenditure information is used to form an initial sample, once a product has been selected for a price interview, the firm is no longer asked to report the expenditure on that product. For this reason, we have relied on certain proxies for this bias term, constructed from disaggregate import data available from the U.S. Bureau of the Census, over the period 1978–88. The census import data is reported according to the Tariff Schedule of the United States (TSUSA) classification, which includes over ten thousand categories annually. The extremely disaggregate nature of this data set makes it a useful source for constructing expenditure shares on imports.

We will consider two proxies for the bias term in corollary 1. The first replaces the *firm-level* expenditure shares with the corresponding *country-level* expenditure shares in the same product category. That is, for each three-digit SITC industry, we obtained from BLS a list of the countries from which price data was actually collected. This information was obtained for the interviews conducted at two times—September 1982 and March 1985. We also need to make some assumption about what interviews occurred in other years. In the absence of other information, we will assume that the country-product interviews used in 1982 remained constant over the period 1978–83, and that the country-product interviews used in 1985 remained constant over the (overlapping) period 1983–88.

To describe the first proxy, suppose that the BLS obtained information on product i imported from country $k(i)$, in years $t - 1$ and t. We have used s_{it} in corollary 1 to denote the share of expenditure on product i, relative to all imports in that product category.[9] We only have information on the countries sampled at the three-digit SITC level, so we construct the bias at that level. Letting $s_{k(i)}$ denote the import share of country $k(i)$ at the three-digit SITC level, our first proxy for the bias term appearing in corollary 1 is

$$(14) \qquad \text{SHARE1}_t = \prod_{i=1}^{N} [s_{k(i)t}/s_{k(i)t-1}]^{1/N} = \prod_{k=1}^{K} (s_{kt}/s_{kt-1})^{\omega_k},$$

where this term is constructed for each three-digit SITC industry.

To obtain equation (14), we simply replace the product share s_{it} in corollary 1 with the country shares $s_{k(i)t}$. We have also omitted the elasticity term

---

9. BLS will sample multiple products within each ten-digit HS category (which have replaced the TSUSA classifications since 1989), so in principle, s_{it} denotes the share within this category.

$1/(\sigma - 1)$ which appears as a power on the bias in corollary 1, since this will be estimated when we include equation (14) as a variable in an import demand equation (as described in the next section). Note that the share of country k is repeated each time an import product i (within the same three-digit SITC category) is interviewed from that country. Then, letting ω_k denote the share of interviews within each three-digit SITC for products coming from country k (which was provided to us by BLS), the second equality in equation (14) is obtained.

Our second measure of the potential bias is closely related to the first, but uses information on the detailed TSUSA-level products supplied by each country. In particular, a country that supplies in more TSUSA categories over time can be judged to have increasing product variety in its exports to the United States. The expected impact of greater product variety would be to reduce the expenditure share s_{it} on each variety supplied by individual firms. In the absence of firm-level data, we can evaluate these changes in product variety by computing the country share $s_{k(i)}$ over *only* those TSUSA categories that country k supplies continuously. That is, for each three-digit SITC category and for each source country, we identified the TSUSA products supplied *every year* in the subperiods 1978–83 and 1983–88. Then we calculated the expenditure on these TSUSA products relative to all U.S. imports in the same three-digit SITC industry: this expenditure share is denoted by s_{kt}^*, which is less than the country share s_{kt} by construction. Greater product variety from country k will mean that s_{kt}^* falls relative to s_{kt}. Our second measure of the potential bias is then

$$(15) \qquad \text{SHARE2}_t = \prod_{k=1}^{K} (s_{kt}^*/s_{kt-1}^*)^{\omega_k},$$

where $s_{kt}^* \leq s_{kt}$ denotes the expenditure on TSUSA products that country k supplies continuously over 1978–83 or 1983–88, relative to total U.S. imports in the same three-digit SITC category.

We expect that SHARE2 would be a better measure of the potential bias than SHARE1, because it takes into account changes in product variety from each country. A limitation of SHARE2 occurs, however, when the names of the TSUSA categories change over time, as they do in response to product innovations or changes in U.S. trade laws.[10] For example, as televisions of increased variety were imported into the United States, the TSUSA categories adjusted to reflect this (distinguishing color versus black and white, and different sizes of screen). If a TSUSA category is split during our sample period, then we count that product as not continuously supplied and ignore it in the calculation of s_{kt}^*. In principle, our calculation is robust to these changes in TSUSA names: if a product with a fixed percentage of country k's export sales (within some three-digit SITC industry) is omitted from the calculation of s_{kt}^*

---

10. The TSUSA numbers change very frequently, and for this reason, we ignore the numbers and use only the TSUSA names.

and s_{kt-1}^{*} because its TSUSA category split, this would have no impact on the ratio $(s_{kt}^{*}/s_{kt-1}^{*})$. However, when many of these changes in product names occur, then this ratio is calculated over a very small number of (continuously supplied) TSUSA products.[11] In that case, we might expect SHARE2 to display more erratic behavior than SHARE1. In general, we will judge the usefulness of these two proxies by their significance in regressions of import demand, as described in the next section.

6.4 U.S. Import Demand

We will follow Helkie and Hooper (1988) in specifying a log-linear equation for aggregate U.S. imports:

$$(16) \qquad \ln Q_{mt} = \beta_0 + \beta_1 \ln P_{mt} + \beta_2 \ln P_{dt} + \beta_3 \ln Y_t + \varepsilon_t,$$

where Q_{mt} is real nonpetroleum imports, P_{mt} is the aggregate import price index (based on the BLS interviews), P_{dt} is the U.S. gross national product (GNP) deflator, and Y_t is nominal GNP. Since demand should be homogeneous of degree zero in prices and income, we can impose the constraint $(\beta_1 + \beta_2 + \beta_3) = 0$ on equation (16) and rewrite it as

$$(17) \qquad \ln Q_{mt} = \beta_0 + \beta_1 \ln(P_{mt}/P_{dt}) + \beta_3 \ln(Y_t/P_{dt}) + \varepsilon_t,$$

which is the form usually estimated.

In the first row of table 6.3, we show the results of estimated equation (17) with quarterly data over the period 1979:1–1988:4. In addition to the variables in equation (17), Helkie and Hooper include a measure of capacity utilization (in the United States relative to that abroad). The coefficients of the relative import price follow a second-order polynomial with eight quarterly lags, real GNP includes one quarterly lag, and the equation is estimated with first-order autocorrelation. The long-run income elasticity is estimated at 2.5.[12] Helkie and Hooper use an average of foreign countries' capital stock (relative to the U.S. capital stock) as a determinant of their ability to move into new product lines. In the second regression in table 6.3, this relative foreign capital stock lowers the income elasticity to 2.15, though the coefficient of the capital stock is insignificant. Over the longer period 1969:1–1984:4 (used by Helkie and Hooper) this variable is more precisely estimated, though the income elasticity is nearly identical to that in table 6.3.

As an alternative to the capital-stock variable, we will use the bias terms

---

11. In an extreme case, there might be no TSUSA category within a three-digit SITC in which an interviewed country supplied continuously. When this happened (which was infrequently) we replaced the value of $(s_{kt}^{*}/s_{kt-1}^{*})$ for country k with (s_{kt}/s_{kt-1}) before computing equation (15).

12. If a (linear) time trend is introduced in this equation, its coefficient is 0.002, which is highly insignificant and reduces the income elasticity to 2.25. In contrast, for disaggregate import demand equations, Alterman (1993) argues that the inclusion of a time trend can significantly reduce the income elasticities.

Table 6.3   U.S. Import Demand

Relative Import Price	Real GNP	Relative Capacity Utilization	Relative Foreign Capital	SHAREA	SHAREB	ρ	$\bar{R}^2$
−1.147	2.491	−.030	—	—	—	.535	.993
(0.205)	(0.281)	(.175)				(.143)	
−0.979	2.154	−.157	−1.483	—	—	.476	.994
(0.216)	(0.332)	(.186)	(0.942)			(.151)	
−1.231	1.894	−.016	—	.662	−1.450	.312	.994
(0.175)	(0.475)	(.157)		(.204)	(0.795)	(.165)	
−1.149	1.733	−.105	—	.478	−0.926	.429	.991
(0.226)	(0.953)	(.284)		(.288)	(0.831)	(.169)	

Notes: Standard errors are in parentheses. The dependent variable is the log of the important quantity.

The sample range is 1978:1 to 1988:4. The coefficients of the relative import price follow a second-order polynomial with eight quarterly lags; real GNP includes one quarterly lag; and the relative foreign capital stock is entered as a lagged value.

The third regression uses SHARE1A and SHARE1B, while the fourth regression uses SHARE2A and SHARE2B; in both cases the instruments for this variable are t, t^2, t^3, and the other variables in the regression. Since the share variables are measured annually, quarterly dummies are included as instruments and are also included in the third and fourth regressions above (but not reported).

SHARE1 and SHARE2. We suppose that the correct price to include in the import demand equation (17) is the exact index, which is related to the conventional index by corollary 1.[13] Substituting this into equation (17), we obtain

$$(18) \qquad \ln Q_{mt} = \beta_0 + \beta_1 \ln \left(\frac{P_{mt}}{P_{dt}} \right) + \left(\frac{\beta_1}{\sigma - 1} \right) \ln(\text{SHARE1}_t)$$
$$+ \beta_3 \ln \left(\frac{Y_t}{P_{dt}} \right) + \varepsilon_t,$$

where SHARE2 is alternatively used. We take a weighted geometric mean over these variables at the three-digit SITC level to arrive at the aggregate value for SHARE1 or SHARE2, where we distinguish those industries with above-average and below-average intracompany imports (using table 6.2).[14] Thus, SHARE1A denotes the mean of SHARE1 over the industries with above-average imports, SHARE1B denotes the mean over the industries with below-average imports; for SHARE2A and SHARE2B are defined likewise. Using

13. It can be questioned whether using the exact price index in equation (17) also means that the exact quantity index should be used on the left-hand side. We will follow the usual practice of using the real imports obtained by deflating nominal imports by the BLS index, rather than deflating by an exact price index. Note that the issue of how to construct the quantity variable goes away if the share of imports in total expenditure is used on the left-hand side, as in Feenstra (1994), for example.

14. The weights in this geometric mean are the average export values in each three-digit SITC industry over the 1978–83 period or over the 1983–88 period.

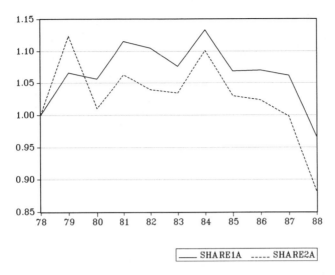

Fig. 6.1 Industries with above-average intracompany imports (shares, 1978–1988)

the aggregates for both groups of industries in equation (18), we arrive at the estimating equation

$$(19) \qquad \ln Q_{mt} = \beta_0 + \beta_1 \ln \left(\frac{P_{mt}}{P_{dt}} \right) + \alpha_1 \ln(\text{SHARE1A}_t)$$

$$+ \left(\frac{\beta_1}{\sigma - 1} \right) \ln(\text{SHARE1B}_t) + \beta_3 \ln \left(\frac{Y_t}{P_{dt}} \right) + \varepsilon_t,$$

where SHARE2A and SHARE2B are alternatively used.

In figure 6.1 we show the values for SHARE1A and SHARE2A, aggregated over industries with above-average intracompany imports, and in figure 6.2 we show SHARE1B and SHARE2B, for industries with below-average internal imports.[15] All the SHARE variables are normalized at 1.0 in 1978. In figure 6.1, the SHAREA variables are quite erratic, showing little trend aside from a decline in the last years of the sample. In figure 6.2, by contrast, the SHAREB variables for industries with below-average internal imports show a marked tendency to decline. SHARE1B reflects the import shares of countries with sampled products, and it declines to 0.88, or about 1 percent annually. A greater decline—to 0.75—is shown by SHARE2B, or about 2.5 percent annually. This fall indicates that the countries with sampled products were also moving into new product lines, so that the expenditure share on the products supplied continuously declined more rapidly.

15. The data for these aggregates are reported in the appendix, table 6A.1.

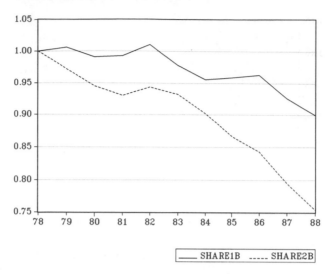

Fig. 6.2   Industries with below-average intracompany imports (shares, 1978–1988)

The results of including the SHARE variables in the import demand equations are reported in the third and fourth regressions in table 6.3, where the third uses SHARE1A and SHARE1B, while the fourth uses SHARE2A and SHARE2B. In both cases, we see that SHAREA enters with a positive sign and SHAREB with a negative sign. The sign on SHAREB is expected, since $\beta_1 < 0$ in equation (19) in the price elasticity of demand, so with $\sigma > 1$ the coefficient on SHAREB is negative. We have not offered any prediction about the sign on SHAREA, however.

One rationalization for the positive coefficient on SHAREA is that when a company decides to shift production offshore, rather than produce domestically, we will observe an increase in both quantity and share of imports from that foreign-country source. Conversely, when a foreign company decides to expand its U.S. manufacturing base, rather than to import, there will be a decline in both the quantity and the share of expenditure from that source country. It is entirely possible that the products internally imported by these companies are included in the BLS interviews, so that the positive correlation between SHAREA and imports is to be expected.[16]

This argument concerning the sign of SHAREA highlights the fact that all the SHARE variables are likely to be correlated with the error in equation (19), since any random change in the import quantity from the sampled countries will also affect their expenditure shares. To address this, the third and fourth regressions in table 6.3 use instrumental variables when including the SHARE

---

16. A product is excluded from the BLS interviews only if the company states that the import price for that product is not influenced by the market, which seldom occurs.

variables: the instruments are time, time^2, time^3, and the other variables on the right-hand side of equation (19). Since the SHARE variables are measured as annual values, quarterly dummies are also included in the instruments and the regression.

In the third regression in table 6.3, using SHARE1A and SHARE1B, the income elasticity falls from 2.5 to 1.9, and the coefficients of both SHARE variables are significant at the 10 percent level. The autocorrelation coefficient is also reduced. A slightly larger impact on the income elasticity is obtained when using SHARE2A and SHARE2B, calculated according to equation (15). In the fourth regression, the income elasticity falls to 1.7, though the standard errors of the SHARE coefficients are higher than before. The reduction in the income elasticity in either case is the principal result of our paper: the SHARE variables have a substantial effect on the income elasticity of aggregate import demand, moving it about halfway toward unity. This result supports the hypothesis that the high income elasticity of import demand is due, at least in part, to the inability of conventional indexes to account for the expansion of product varieties from new foreign suppliers.

Using the coefficient of SHARE2B in the fourth regression, along with the long-run price elasticity β_1, we can obtain an estimate of σ from equation (19) as $\hat{\sigma} = 1 + (1.149/0.926) = 2.24$ (with a standard error of 1.08). This estimate seems low for an elasticity of substitution between a product differentiated across suppliers, and it is smaller than the disaggregate estimates in Feenstra (1994). One reason for this might be that the SHARE variables are *proxies* for the true expenditure shares from interviewed firms, which could bias the elasticity estimate. For example, if SHARE2B measures only a fraction of the true expansion in product varieties, then this variable would fall too slowly, and the resulting elasticity estimate of $\beta_1/(\sigma - 1)$ in equation (19) will be upward biased—so $\hat{\sigma}$ will be downward biased. More generally, from our results in section 6.3.1, we need not assume that the true aggregator is CES, so that the coefficient of SHARE2B is open to interpretation.

Regardless of how we interpret the coefficients of the SHARE variables, we can combine these two terms with the relative import price and rewrite (19) as

$$\ln Q_{mt} = \beta_0 + \beta_1 \left[\ln\left(\frac{P_{mt}}{P_{dt}}\right) + \left(\frac{\alpha_1}{\beta_1}\right)\ln(\text{SHARE2A}_t) \right.$$
$$\left. + \left(\frac{1}{\sigma - 1}\right)\ln(\text{SHARE2B}_t) \right] + \beta_3 \ln\left(\frac{Y_t}{P_{dt}}\right) + \varepsilon_t.$$

The term in brackets is our estimate of the (relative) exact import price index. Then using the estimates from the fourth regression in table 6.3, we construct

$$\ln(\text{PRICEB}_t) = \ln(P_{mt}/P_{dt}) + \left(\frac{0.926}{1.149}\right) \ln(\text{SHARE2B}_t),$$

and

$$\ln(\text{PRICEAB}_t) = \ln(P_{mt}/P_{dt}) + \left(\frac{0.926}{1.149}\right)\ln(\text{SHARE2B}_t)$$
$$- \left(\frac{0.478}{1.149}\right)\ln(\text{SHARE2A}_t).$$

The first of these series only takes account of the industries with below-average intracompany imports, while the second series takes into account all industries. Also, let $\text{PRICE}_t = (P_{mt}/P_{dt})$ denote the (relative) BLS import price index.

In figure 6.3, we plot PRICE, PRICEB, and PRICEAB (with 1978:1 = 100). The fall in PRICE over the period 1980–85 reflects the appreciation of the dollar. Both of the other series lie below PRICE, indicating the upward bias of the conventional index, with PRICEAB lying below PRICEB in all years except 1987–88. The difference between PRICE and PRICEB in 1988 is 16.4, relative to their initial values of 100, while the difference between PRICE and PRICEAB in 1988 is 12.9. Since these differences develop over the decade 1978–88, we conclude that the conventional price index is upward biased by about *1.5 percentage points annually,* as compared to an exact index.

6.5   Conclusions

As a necessary result of the sampling procedure used by BLS to construct (domestic or international) price indexes, some products will be excluded from these indexes. In this paper, we have discussed the consequences of this exclusion. Our basic result is that the expenditure shares on the sampled products provided very useful information on the movement in prices of the nonsampled

Fig. 6.3   U.S. relative import price, 1978–1988 (1978:1 = 100)

goods. In particular, a falling expenditure share of the sampled products means that we infer a falling relative price for the nonsampled products. This inference is particularly useful when we consider that some of the nonsampled products may be new, with prices falling from their reservation to observed levels when they are first available. Since these reservation prices are never observed (and difficult to estimate when dealing with many goods simultaneously), the strategy of using the expenditure shares to infer the movements in prices seems quite attractive.

In figure 6.3, we have plotted the (relative) U.S. import price index along with two constructed indexes, to illustrate the upward bias in the former. It should be stressed that this diagram is *not* meant to demonstrate any limitation of the BLS procedures in collecting the import price data. Even with the best practice techniques, we would expect any price index constructed from interview data to be potentially biased from the exclusion of products. It would be futile (and prohibitively expensive) to attempt to collect a range of prices broad enough for this potential bias to be eliminated, since the (reservation) prices for new product varieties are simply not available.

Rather than expanding the scope of the price interviews, the recommendation of this paper is that the BLS collect *expenditure* data from firms at the same time as *price* data. Currently, the expenditure on sampled products is not collected on a continuous basis. While expenditure information is used to form an initial sample, once a product has been selected for a price interview, the firm is no longer asked to report the sales (for domestic price indexes) or purchases (for import price indexes) of that product. The collection of this information would impose some extra time costs on the reporting firms, but it would not require any new procedures for selecting the products to interview. That is, once a narrowly defined product has been identified for which to obtain price data, the firm could be asked to supply (quarterly or annual) value data on exactly that same product. These data could be reported at the same level of aggregation as the price indexes, so that the confidentiality of firms is maintained. We have argued that this expenditure data would be very useful for dealing with the potential bias in import prices, and it would undoubtedly be useful for domestic indexes, as well.

Appendix

Table 6A.1   Values of SHARE1 and SHARE2 for Aggregate U.S. Imports

Year	Industries with Above-Average Internal Imports[a]		Industries with Below-Average Internal Imports[b]	
	SHARE1A	SHARE2A	SHARE1B	SHARE2B
1978	1.0000	1.0000	1.0000	1.0000
1979	1.0658	1.1241	1.0060	0.9718
1980	1.0559	1.0098	0.9905	0.9451
1981	1.1155	1.0627	0.9923	0.9303
1982	1.1048	1.0393	1.0102	0.9437
1983	1.0760	1.0342	0.9779	0.9321
1984	1.1334	1.1012	0.9556	0.9018
1985	1.0684	1.0297	0.9586	0.8668
1986	1.0697	1.0230	0.9630	0.8429
1987	1.0615	0.9976	0.9261	0.7952
1988	0.9666	0.8803	0.8999	0.7538

[a]These industries have internal imports greater than 8 percent in table 6.2, including motor vehicle equipment and tobacco products and excluding petroleum products.

[b]These industries have internal imports less than 8 percent or suppressed in table 6.2, excluding motor vehicle equipment, tobacco products, and petroleum products.

References

Alterman, William. 1991. Price trends in U.S. trade: New data, new insights. In *International economic transactions,* ed. Peter Hooper and J. David Richardson, 109–39. NBER Studies in Income and Wealth, vol. 55. Chicago: University of Chicago Press.
———. 1993. Analyzing disaggregated U.S. trade flows in the 1980s. Division of International Prices, Bureau of Labor Statistics, Washington, D.C. Mimeographed.
Brainard, S. Lael. 1993. An empirical assessment of the proximity-concentration trade-off between multinational sales and trade. NBER Working Paper no. 4580. Cambridge, Mass.: National Bureau of Economic Research.
Council of Economic Advisers. 1993. *Economic report of the president.* Washington, D.C.: Government Printing Office.
Denison, Edward. 1962. *The sources of economic growth in the United States and the alternatives before us.* New York: Committee for Economic Development.
Diewert, W. Erwin. 1976. Exact and superlative index numbers. *Journal of Econometrics* 4:115–45.
Feenstra, Robert C. 1994. New product varieties and the measurement of international prices. *American Economic Review* 84, no. 1 (March): 157–77.
Helkie, William H., and Peter Hooper. 1988. The U.S. external deficit in the 1980s: An empirical analysis. In *External deficits and the dollar: The pit and the pendulum,* ed. R. C. Bryant, G. Holtham, and P. Hooper. Washington, D.C.: Brookings.
Hooper, Peter. 1989. Exchange rates and U.S. external adjustment in the short run and the long run. International Finance Discussion Paper no. 346, Board of Governors of the Federal Reserve Bank, Washington, D.C. March.

Houthakker, Hendrik S., and Stephen P. Magee. 1969. Income and price elasticities in world trade. *Review of Economics and Statistics* 51, no. 2 (May): 111–25.

Howenstine, Ned G. 1985. U.S. affiliates of foreign companies: Operations in 1983. *Survey of Current Business* November: 36–50.

Krugman, Paul. 1989. Differences in income elasticities and trends in real exchange rates. *European Economic Review* 33:1031–54.

Mataloni, Raymond J., Jr. 1990. U.S. multinational companies: Operations in 1988. *Survey of Current Business* June: 31–34.

Reinsdorf, Marshall B. 1993. The effect of outlet price differentials on the U.S. Consumer Price Index. In *Price measurements and their uses,* ed. Murray F. Foss, Marilyn E. Manser and Allan H. Young, 227–60. Chicago: University of Chicago Press.

Riedel, James. 1991. Export growth and the terms of trade: The case of the curious elasticities. Johns Hopkins University. Baltimore, Md. Mimeographed.

Sato, Kazuo. 1976. The ideal log-change index number. *Review of Economics and Statistics* 58 (May): 223–28.

———. 1977. The demand function for industrial exports. *Review of Economics and Statistics* 55:456–64.

Shiells, Clinton R. 1991. Errors in import-demand estimates based upon unit-value indexes. *Review of Economics and Statistics* 73, no. 2 (May): 378–82.

U.S. Bureau of the Census. Various years. *U.S. general imports for consumption, schedule A, FT135, commodity by country.* Washington, D.C.: U.S. Department of Commerce.

U.S. Department of Commerce. Bureau of Economic Analysis. 1982. *U.S. direct investment abroad: 1982 Benchmark survey data.* Washington, D.C.: Government Printing Office.

———. 1987. *Foreign direct investment in the United States: 1987 Benchmark survey, final results.* Washington, D.C.: Government Printing Office.

Vartia, Y. O. 1976. Ideal log-change index numbers. *Scandinavian Journal of Statistics* 3:121–26.

Vernon, Raymond. 1966. International investment and international trade in the product cycle. *Quarterly Journal of Economics* 80:190–207.

Zeile, William. 1993. Merchandise trade of U.S. affiliates of foreign companies. *Survey of Current Business* October: 52–65.

Comment   Zvi Griliches

This is an interesting and ambitious paper. It tries to use "share" data on priced commodities to infer the bias that arises from unpriced items. It also argues that import income elasticities are overestimated because of this omission.

There are two parts to the paper. First, the theoretical discussion shows that there is information in the movement of shares of new products about their unobserved "true" prices, *provided* we have or can estimate the relevant price elasticities. In the second part, they try to do just that, estimating the implied

Zvi Griliches is professor of economics at Harvard University and a research associate of the National Bureau of Economic Research.

substitution elasticities by including share data in an import demand equation to adjust for such a bias.

I have a number of comments about this methodology and the empirical results. I am especially interested in the former, since I have been trying to do something similar in my work on generic drug prices (see Griliches and Cockburn 1994). So I will discuss first the "generic" index problem tackled here, then complain about the particular functional form chosen, and then make a few comments on the empirical implementation.

There are two related topics, slightly confused in this literature: "missing prices" and "new distinct goods." The original hedonics literature arose out of the problem that the price of a new good was not available in the base period and looked for a method of retro- and inter-polation. In the spirit of what statistical agencies were doing, it tried to predict what the "market price" would have been for this product yesterday, had it been available, without asking the question whether this was a "demand" or a "supply" price. Once one asks that question, it is clear that the answers can differ, and that integrating the difference between them would yield a measure of consumer's surplus. The theory of exact price indexes and expenditure functions was a tool, developed later, to provide standard index numbers with such an interpretation.

Most of the earlier discussion of new goods was about the appearance of new varieties which were considered to be close substitutes for the previous items: more horsepower, higher speed, and so forth. When the qualitative-choice literature developed, it was natural to recast the problem as one of a distinct new good (choice) and this led to an explicit appearance of a discontinuity in consumer's surplus.

The basic insight used in Feenstra and Shiells's paper is the fact that new goods getting a significant product share implies that in some sense their "real" quality-adjusted price is lower. (This idea is also used in Trajtenberg 1990 and Berry 1994.) Feenstra and Shiells show that the "real" price of the new item must have fallen by

$$dp/p_n = s_n/(\eta - 1).$$

If we can observe the share change, "all" we need is an estimate of the relevant elasticity to find out by how much the price really changed.

So then we are led to the estimation of η (by Hausman, chap. 5 in this volume) or of σ by Feenstra and Shiells. I will come back to that.

The first part of Feenstra and Shiells's paper, as in Feenstra's earlier work, and the conclusions at the end are based on the assumption that the utility structure for varieties is CES. This is convenient computationally, but problematic in practice. First, theoretically, all versions have to be equally substitutable within a nest, and all nests have to be embedded in a Cobb-Douglas function, if there are other CES components. This issue was discussed by Hanoch (1971) twenty years ago in the production-function literature.

Both I (in the paper with Iain Cockburn) and Jerry Hausman, show that the CES calculations lead to implausibly large numbers. Feenstra and Shiells themselves show that assuming a translog term would cut their estimates by a factor of two.

Consider the generic drug (cephalexin) example discussed in Griliches and Cockburn. Roughly speaking the story is as follows: generics enter in at a 50 percent discount and after one year get 60 percent of the quantity market and 43 percent of the revenue share. In this world the incumbent does not change his price and the average price of all versions falls by 0.3. Using Feenstra and Shiells's formula, however, implies not only that the price of generics has declined by 0.5 but that their quality also "improved" (relative to the incumbent brand) by 29 percent! (See table 6C.1.)

Actually the elasticities estimates by Hausman for his functional form and the CES are about the same, but the estimates of consumer's surplus differ widely. My preferred assumption is outside this framework. It allows for heterogeneity of consumers, assumes that the taste for brandedness is distributed uniformly, and implies an average reservation price of $(p_b + p_g)/2$. The resulting total price index, labeled $P(u)$, falls by "only" 22 percent, versus the 40 percent that would be implied by Feenstra and Shiells's formula.

There are a number of problems with Feenstra and Shiells's application: The share of nonpriced items is growing. How nonsubstitutable are they? The implied estimate of $\sigma = 1.9$ is not credible for the average nonpriced item—seven-grain bread versus whole wheat or shirts from Mauritius versus shirts from Singapore.

It is also not well estimated, and the results are very sensitive to that. The approximate standard error for the estimated σ of 2.2 is 1.0. In the formula for the implicit price decline

$$\exp - ds/(\sigma - 1),$$

a difference of one standard deviation would shift the estimate for a 0.10 decline in the share of priced items, from the estimated -0.08, to either -0.50 or -0.05, a rise of 500 percent or a fall of 37 percent in the absolute value of the estimated price change.

There are at least two specification problems associated with the estimated equations: (1) The same excluded-prices story would also apply to domestic goods. I am not sure that the new-goods problem is worse for imports. Internationally traded goods may be *more* standardized than domestic goods. Also,

Table 6C.1   Branded versus Generics Example

Period	P_b	P_g	Q_b	Q_g	VS_b	P_{BLS}	P_a	$P(u)$	Feenstra ($\sigma = 2.1$)
1	1		1	0	1	1	1	1	1
2	1	0.5	0.4	0.6	0.57	1	0.7	0.78	0.6

Note: VS_b is the value share of the branded good.

(2) if price is mismeasured, so is the dependent variable, but then their formula for the coefficient becomes $(\beta + 1)(\sigma - 1)$, and the implied $\sigma = 1.2$ is even less credible.

"Aging of lines": Once popular restaurants lose customers over time. We could bring in new ones and make an adjustment for their superiority. But then, some time later, the chefs are hired away and the old restaurants regain their share. Will we come back to the same level? How?

A major finding is that if one allows for the changing mix of import goods this leads to lower estimates of their income elasticity. That makes sense, but how low "should" the import income elasticity be? Can one really explain rising world trade just by the reduction in transport costs and the rising quality of traded goods? I find the notion that traded goods have higher income elasticities quite plausible. The explicit "bias" adjustment to the price index that follows is, however, more problematic. But the advice to collect more data is surely right!

References

Berry, S. T. 1994. Estimating discrete-choice models of product differentiation. *Rand Journal of Economics* 25, no. 2 (summer): 242–62.

Griliches, Zvi, and Iain Cockburn. 1994. Generics and new goods in pharmaceutical price indexes. *American Economic Review* 84 (5): 1213–32.

Hanoch, Giora. 1971. CRESH production functions. *Econometrica* 39 (5): 695–712.

Trajtenberg, Manuel. 1990. Product innovation, price indices and the (mis-) measurement of economic performance. NBER Working Paper no. 3261. Cambridge, Mass.: National Bureau of Economic Research.

7

The Roles of Marketing, Product Quality, and Price Competition in the Growth and Composition of the U.S. Antiulcer Drug Industry

Ernst R. Berndt, Linda T. Bui, David H. Lucking-Reiley, and Glen L. Urban

7.1 Introduction

The introduction of Tagamet into the U.S. market in 1977 marked the beginning of a revolutionary treatment for ulcers and the emergence of a new industry. What distinguished the products of this new industry was their ability to heal ulcers and treat preulcer conditions pharmacologically on an outpatient basis, thereby substituting for traditional, and costly, hospital admissions and surgeries. Tagamet, known medically as an H_2-receptor antagonist, promotes the healing of ulcers by reducing the secretion of acid by the stomach.

A striking feature of the antiulcer market is that it has sustained growth in sales (quantity, not just revenue) for over fifteen years and still shows no sign of slowing. New prescribing habits have clearly diffused to an ever increasing number of physicians. Today there are a total of four H_2-receptor antagonists: Tagamet, Zantac, Pepcid, and Axid. Zantac is now the United States' (and the world's) largest-selling prescription drug, having estimated worldwide sales in 1992 of about $3.5 billion. Moreover, Tagamet is also among the ten top-selling prescription drugs in the United States.[1]

Ernst R. Berndt is professor of applied economics at the Sloan School of Management at the Massachusetts Institute of Technology. Linda T. Bui is assistant professor of economics at Boston University. David H. Lucking-Reiley is assistant professor of economics at Vanderbilt University. Glen L. Urban is professor of marketing and dean of the Sloan School of Management at the Massachusetts Institute of Technology.

Financial support from the Alfred P. Sloan Foundation is gratefully acknowledged, as is the data support of Stephen C. Chappell, Nancy Duckwitz, and Richard Fehring at IMS International, and Joan Curran, Marjorie Donnelly, Phyllis Rausch, Ditas Riad, Paul Snyderman, and Jeff Tarlowe at Merck & Co. The authors have also benefited from the research assistance of Adi Alon, Amit Alon, Ittai Harel, Michele Lombardi, and Bonnie Scouler, and from discussions with Tim Bresnahan, Stan Finkelstein, M.D., Valerie Suslow, and Stephen Wright, M.D.

1. One hundred powerhouse drugs (1993, S1). Incidentally, Tagamet ranks 7th, Pepcid 17th, Prilosec 25th, and Axid 61st in terms of U.S. sales. In terms of world sales, Tagamet is 7th, Pepcid 22d, Prilosec 49th, and Axid 67th.

In this paper we attempt to explain the growth and changing composition of the antiulcer drug market. Although we examine the impacts of pricing and product quality, we devote particular attention to the role of firms' marketing efforts. We distinguish between two types of marketing: (1) that which concentrates on bringing new consumers into the market ("industry-expanding" advertising), and (2) that which concentrates on competing for market shares from these consumers ("rivalrous" advertising). Note that of these two types, market-expanding advertising has particular economic importance in a new market, because no matter how potentially beneficial is the new product, it can generate no consumer's surplus until consumers have been informed about the new product and have been induced to experiment with it.

As others have done, we estimate the effects of industry-expanding advertising on sales. However, we also examine how the effectiveness of this socially beneficial type of advertising varies with market structure. We exploit two facts. First, in the earliest years of the market when Tagamet was a monopoly product all of the Tagamet advertising was, by definition, market-expanding. Second, the timing of entry is largely exogenous in this industry, for patent protection ensures that firms cannot enter until their research laboratories develop a new molecule that has the desired impact and until approval for use is given by the U.S. Food and Drug Administration (FDA).

We also analyze factors affecting the market shares earned by the limited number of firms in this market. A principal theme is that the patent and pioneer advantages to Tagamet were overcome by Zantac, the second entrant, through costly but effective marketing efforts, especially efforts that interacted with the apparent existence of more favorable side-effect profiles than Tagamet's. Moreover, Zantac's relative price, although higher than Tagamet's, declined substantially over time. Thus, evidence from this industry suggests that while the barriers to entry from patent and first-mover advantages are considerable, they are not insurmountable.

Our empirical analysis is based on an unusually rich and detailed data set. Beginning with the introduction of Tagamet in July 1977, we have obtained monthly data, for each of the products in this market, on quantity and average price of sales (separately for the retail drugstore and hospital markets); marketing efforts (minutes of detailing by sales representatives to physicians, and professional medical journal advertising); and product-quality information, including side-effect profiles, efficacy, dosage forms, and indications for which the product had received approval from the FDA.

We begin in section 7.2 by providing background information on ulcers and ulcer treatments. Then in section 7.3 we present an overview of data trends. We describe the growth of the antiulcer market, as well as the pricing and marketing behavior of the various market participants. We move on in section 7.4 to develop an econometric framework for modeling the growth of the antiulcer industry. In particular, we examine the effects of "informative" or market-expanding marketing efforts on industry sales. In section 7.5 we report findings from an analogous attempt to model factors affecting market shares earned by the various products in this industry. Here we examine in particular the roles of rivalrous marketing, product quality, order of entry, and price competition. Finally, in section 7.6 we offer some concluding observations and suggestions for future research. The paper also includes a data appendix.

7.2 Background on Ulcer Treatments

Peptic ulcer disease occurs in 10–15 percent of the U.S. population.[2] Ulcers located in the stomach proper are termed gastric ulcers, while those in the duodenum (the bulb connecting the stomach to the small intestine) are called duodenal ulcers. A related nonulcerous condition is gastroesophageal reflux disease (GERD), which occurs in the esophagus. What the three conditions have in common is that they involve inflammation of tissue in the digestive tract that is exacerbated by the presence of the body's naturally occurring gastric acid. GERD and duodenal ulcers have roughly the same rates of occurrence in the U.S. population, whereas gastric ulcers are about one-fourth as likely. The incidence of ulcers in adult males is about twice that in adult females and appears to be most common in individuals twenty to fifty years old.

Ulcers have a long history of clinical treatment. There is evidence that already in the first century A.D., coral powder (calcium carbonate, an antacid) was used to relieve symptoms of dyspepsia (see Fine, Dannenberg, and Zakim 1988). Early in the twentieth century, conventional medical wisdom conformed to the notion "no acid, no ulcer." As a result, until the 1970s recommended treatments sought to neutralize gastric acid and often consisted of hourly feedings of milk and/or antacids, as well as a dietary reduction of acidic food and drink. If ulcers persisted, surgery was undertaken. It is worth noting that while antacids such as Maalox and Mylanta neutralize gastric acid, they do not decrease the rate of gastric secretions (they may in fact increase them). Moreover, the required dosages of antacids are typically quite large, side effects can be considerable, and adverse interactions with other drugs are not uncommon. As a result, with antacids patient compliance can be problematic.

An alternative ulcer treatment involves acid suppression with anticholinergics, such as Pro-Banthine and atropine. Anticholinergic agents decrease acid secretion by inhibiting receptors for the hormone acetylcholine in the acid-producing cells of the stomach lining. However, these agents cause considerably unpleasant reactions, because acetylcholine is involved in a number of biochemical processes other than the secretion of gastric acid, and anticholinergics tend to be nonselective. The side effects of dry mouth, blurred vision, urinary retention, abnormally rapid heartbeat, and drying of bronchial secretions are particularly frequent.

---

2. The material in this section is taken in large part from Scouler (1993) and the references cited therein. Also see Fine, Dannenberg, and Zakim (1988) and McKenzie et al. (1990).

In 1977 a revolutionary form of antiulcer drug was introduced to the United States, known as an H_2-receptor antagonist.[3] H_2-receptor antagonists act by blocking the histamine-2 (H_2) receptor on parietal cells in the lining of the stomach—cells that produce gastric acid. Histamine-2 is one of three "messenger molecules" (along with gastrine and acetylcholine) that can stimulate the production of acid by the parietal cells. By blocking the receptor for H_2 (and, unlike the anticholinergic drugs, avoiding any interference with other biochemical processes), an H_2-antagonist can decrease overall acid concentration in the stomach. H_2-antagonist healing rates are very high. A four- to six-week treatment period, for example, is associated with a healing rate of 70–80 percent for patients suffering from duodenal ulcers.

SmithKline was the first pharmaceutical company to introduce an H_2-antagonist in the U.S. market (in August 1977), and they dubbed it Tagamet (its chemical name is cimetidine). Thereafter three companies followed suit— Glaxo with Zantac (ranitidine) in June 1983, Merck with Pepcid (famotidine) in October 1986, and Lilly with Axid (nizatidine) in April 1988. Each of these four H_2-antagonists is a slightly different chemical entity. Tagamet's patent protection could not prevent entry by such therapeutic substitutes.

Zantac was marketed very aggressively by Glaxo, in partnership with Hoffmann-LaRoche, and was also priced at a premium over Tagamet. Detailers (sales representatives who call on physicians) emphasized that unlike Tagamet, whose original dosage required it to be taken four times daily, Zantac needed to be taken only twice per day. Moreover, Zantac detailers highlighted side-effect profiles that had accumulated with Tagamet—nausea, diarrhea, drowsiness, decreased sperm count, gynecomastia (swelling of the breasts in males), and drug interactions.[4] Within eighteen months Tagamet responded to Zantac by introducing a twice-per-day version of its drug, but it continued to find itself on the defensive in terms of alleged side-effect and adverse-interaction profiles. A prolonged rivalry then ensued, first between Tagamet and Zantac in the form of new versions whose dosages were but once per day (thereby facilitating patient compliance even further), and later including additional competition from the newly entered Pepcid and Axid, each available with a once-daily dosage regimen.

In addition to side-effect profiles and frequency of dosage, another form of rivalry among the four H_2-antagonists involved FDA-approved treatments (indications). Since several distinct types of ulcerous conditions exist, similar drug products can compete on the basis of efficacy for different indications. In the United States, before a drug can be introduced into the market, the FDA must grant approval for at least one indication. When Tagamet was originally introduced into the U.S. market in August 1977, its approval was for duodenal

---

3. Tagamet was introduced into the United Kingdom one year earlier, in 1976.
4. By June 1983, Tagamet had registered ten adverse interactions at the FDA. Zantac recorded its first adverse interaction in January 1992.

ulcers; Tagamet was also the first to be approved for duodenal ulcer maintenance treatment (to prevent recurrence of a newly healed duodenal ulcer) in
April 1980, and gastric ulcers in December 1982. However, Zantac was the
first to obtain approval for the GERD indication (May 1986),[5] and it was not
until March 1991 that Tagamet obtained FDA approval for GERD. It is worth
noting that once FDA approval for an indication is granted, the manufacturer
is permitted to provide promotional and marketing material *only* for approved
indications. Thus, even though Tagamet had clinical effects very similar to
Zantac's, suggesting that it would probably be effective in the treatment of
GERD, Tagamet promotions were not permitted to mention GERD until 1991.
Although physicians often prescribe drugs for indications not approved by the
FDA (called off-label prescribing), not having FDA approval for an indication
which is held by a competitive product may constitute a signficant disadvantage in the marketplace. Hence, even though Tagamet pioneered in the three
antiulcer indications, the fact that it lagged behind Zantac in the relatively pop-
ulous GERD market was of considerable importance.

Today the four H_2-antagonist drugs are frequently viewed as being ". . .
equally efficacious in their ability to suppress acid secretion" (McKenzie et al.
1990, 58), but different in their pharmacological profiles. McKenzie et al. note
that Tagamet is "the H_2-antagonist implicated with the most side effects and
drug interactions," and that such adverse impacts occur "to a lesser extent"
with Zantac. The third and fourth entrants—Pepcid and Axid—appear to have
even fewer drug interactions and side effects. What is not yet clear, however,
is the extent to which apparent differences in side-effect profiles simply reflect
differential lengths of time over which the various drugs have been able to
accumulate medical experience.

Modern ulcer medicines are not restricted to H_2-antagonists. One alternative
therapy is Carafate (sucralfate), introduced into the United States by Marion
Labs in August 1981. Instead of inhibiting acid secretion, Carafate acts by
forming a protective coating over the ulcer that in turn promotes healing. While
it is relatively free from side effects, Carafate has problems of convenience
and compliance, since it must be taken four times per day, always on an empty
stomach (before meals). It also acts more slowly than the acid inhibitors in
relieving pain. For these reasons, Carafate serves a market niche, being used
predominantly for older patients and patients in intensive care.

Another entrant in the antiulcer market is Cytotec (misoprostol), introduced
in December 1988. Cytotec has been targeted at ulcers associated with the
use of nonsteroidal anti-inflammatory drugs (NSAIDs—pain relievers such as
Motrin). Its rather small market niche consists of patients who take NSAIDs
chronically and are at greater risk for the development of peptic ulcer disease
or complications from peptic ulcers—particularly the elderly, those with previ-

---

5. Discussions with industry officials suggest that Glaxo actually invented the GERD indication
at the FDA.

ous ulcers or concomitant debilitating diseases, and patients who smoke. A common side effect of Cytotec, however, is diarrhea, although it can often be mitigated by adjusting the dosage.

The most recent treatment innovation to enter the antiulcer market is Prilosec (omeprazole), introduced into the United States by Merck Sharp & Dohme in September 1989.[6] Prilosec is a powerful new drug known as a proton-pump inhibitor. It acts by directly blocking the action of the proton pump, which is the biochemical mechanism that actually produces the acid in the stomach. Initially approved for only the GERD indication, in June 1991 Prilosec was approved by the FDA for duodenal ulcer treatment. Originally approved only for short-term use, in 1995 the FDA gave approval for long-term maintenance usage. Dosing for Prilosec is unique in that it is supplied in a timed-release capsule, thus reducing dosage to once per day but yielding continuous levels of the drug within the body throughout the day.

With this brief overview on ulcer drugs and ulcer treatments as background, we now move on to a discussion of the pricing and marketing behavior of the manufacturers, the sales and market shares they attained, and the data sources underlying these statistics.

7.3   Overview of the Data

Most of the data used in this study originated with IMS America, a Philadelphia-based firm that independently collects data on the sales and marketing of pharmaceutical products. IMS sells its data to pharmaceutical manufacturers for their use in formulating marketing strategy.[7] IMS sales data track prescription pharmaceutical purchases made by hospitals and by retailers; market segments not monitored by IMS include food stores, dispensing physicians, HMOs, mail order, nursing homes, and clinics. IMS estimates that its drugstore audit covers 67 percent of the U.S. pharmaceutical market and that its hospital audit encompasses an additional 16 percent.[8]

The level of aggregation of the IMS purchase data is the presentational form, for example, bottles of 30 tablets of 150 mg strength. For each presentational form, we compute the average price as dollar purchases divided by number of units. We also convert these price and quantity measures into patient-days and price per patient-day, using the recommended daily dosage for duodenal ulcer treatment as the transformation factor. These monthly data series begin in August 1977 and continue through May 1993.

---

6. Merck obtained the rights to market Prilosec in the United States from AB Astra of Sweden. Prilosec was originally named Losec; however, its name was changed because of confusion surrounding the similarity of the name Losec to that of Lasix, a common diuretic.

7. IMS America, 660 W. Germantown Pike, Plymouth Meeting, Pennsylvania 19462 (215-834-5000).

8. Information on IMS is taken from the *IMS Pharmaceutical Database Manual.*

In addition to price and quantity data on drug purchases, we employ IMS data on marketing efforts from their Personal Selling Audit, earlier called the IMS National Detailing Audit. Based on a panel of about thirty-five hundred physicians who report the number of visits and minutes spent with detailers discussing particular drug products, IMS computes monthly detailing efforts by drug.[9] Using an estimated cost per detailing visit, IMS also estimates total detailing expenditures. Medical journal advertising expenditures are estimated by IMS in their National Journal Audit. Based on the number of square inches and pages of advertisements in about three hundred major medical journals, as well as features such as the number of colors in each advertisement, IMS uses standard rate sheets to estimate total dollars of journal advertising, monthly, by product. We convert these current-dollar expenditures into constant-dollar magnitudes using the Bureau of Labor Statistics' (BLS's) producer price index for "advertising in professional and institutional periodicals."

Discussions with industry personnel suggest that while these detailing and journal advertising expenditures likely understate total promotion costs (booths and promotions at conferences are not included, for example), there is no reason to suspect that the proportions differ across products, and thus we are led to believe that the relative expenditure data series are likely to be reasonably accurate. It is worth noting, incidentally, that according to one observer, in the early 1990s in the U.S. pharmaceutical industry, approximately $3.1 billion was spent on detailing, about $700 million was spent annually on journal advertising and direct-mail promotions, medical-education expenses accounted for about $400 million, and uses of other forms of media and communication amounted to approximately $300 million annually (Cearnal 1992, 23).

Finally, data on recommended daily dosages and product-specific attribute information are taken from *Physicians' Desk Reference,* annual issues from 1978 to 1993, and *U.S. Pharmacopeia Convention Dispensing Information.* Further details regarding data sources and transformations are presented in the data appendix.

With this background regarding data sources, we now present an overview of data trends. In figure 7.1 we plot the quantity of U.S. sales (number of patient-days of duodenal ulcer therapy) over time, separately for the retail drugstore and hospital markets, disaggregated into the H_2-antagonists (Tagamet, Zantac, Pepcid, and Axid) and all seven antiulcer drugs (the H_2-antagonists plus Carafate, Cytotec, and Prilosec). Starting from zero in August 1977, by May 1993 total monthly sales were almost 130 million patient-days; of this, approximately 93 percent was sold via retail drugstores. Broken down by drug type, the H_2-antagonist class accounted for approximately 84 percent of total sales, while the other antiulcer drugs made up the remaining 16 per-

---

9. This sample size has increased with time. The sample was thirty-five hundred in 1993. In the mid-1980s, the sample size was about twenty-eight hundred.

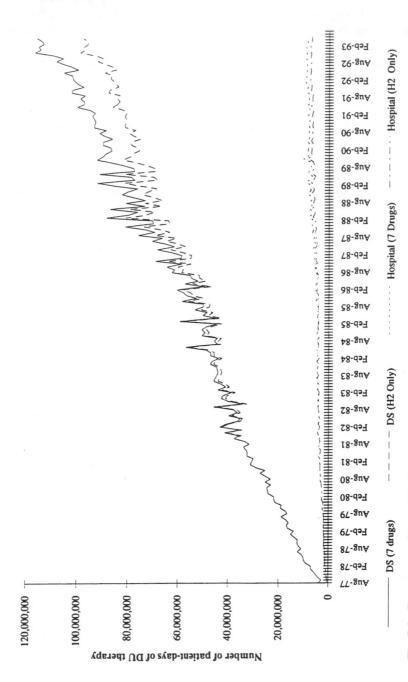

Fig. 7.1   Drugstore and hospital sales

cent. Hospital sales accounted for only 7 percent of total H_2-antagonist sales. Because of this market dominance, hereafter we confine our analysis to the H_2-antagonist drugstore market.

The growth of H_2-antagonist sales over time has been remarkably steady. For example, if one runs a simple regression of log sales on a constant and a monthly time counter, one obtains

$$\ln(Q_{H_2}) = 16.4 + 0.012t, \qquad R^2 = 0.82,$$

implying an average annual growth rate (AAGR) of about 15 percent.

In figure 7.2 we plot market shares of H_2-antagonist drugstore sales for the four H_2-antagonist drugs. Although Tagamet was the pioneer, Zantac entered in July 1983, and within one year it had already captured about 25 percent of the total Tagamet-Zantac market. Tagamet's share continued to decline when Pepcid entered in October 1986, but Pepcid was less successful than Zantac; one year after entry, Pepcid had a market share of only approximately 8 percent. The sales of Zantac grew remarkably quickly and steadily, and by January 1988 Zantac sales overtook those of Tagamet. At about the same time (April 1988), Axid entered the market; as fourth entrant, however, Axid faced considerable competition, and after one year, its sales accounted for only about a 4 percent market share. By the end of our sample in May 1993, Zantac had captured about 55 percent of the quantity market share, Tagamet 21 percent, Pepcid 15 percent, and Axid 9 percent.

Although the entry of Zantac into the H_2-antagonist market increased total market sales, the sales of Tagamet fell. As shown in figure 7.3, drugstore sales of Tagamet grew at a very rapid rate after entry in 1977, then began to level off a bit from 1981 to 1983, and although they peaked at about 46 million patient-days in April 1984, Tagamet's sales tended to decline after Zantac's entry in 1983. This general decline in sales continued until the end of our sample, when Tagamet's monthly sales were less than half their peak—about 21 million patient-days. By contrast, sales of Zantac generally increased over time, and by May 1993 Zantac accounted for about 54 million patient-days per month. Although Zantac's sales increased with time, as can be seen in figure 7.3, there was a modest decline in the growth slope beginning in early 1988, coinciding with a slight rebound in Tagamet sales and the effects of entry by the fourth entrant, Axid. Although both Pepcid and Axid recorded considerable growth in sales, they clearly were dominated by the two earliest entrants, Tagamet and Zantac.

An interesting phenomenon occurs in the pricing behavior of the four products over this tumultuous time period. Price per day of duodenal therapy (based on recommended dosages, and adjusted for inflation using the overall Consumer Price Index [CPI] with 1982–84 = 1.00) is displayed for the four products in figure 7.4. After original entry, until it faced competition from Zantac, Tagamet gradually decreased its real price from about $1.00 to about $0.80 per day. When Zantac entered in late 1983, it charged a substantial premium ($1.25

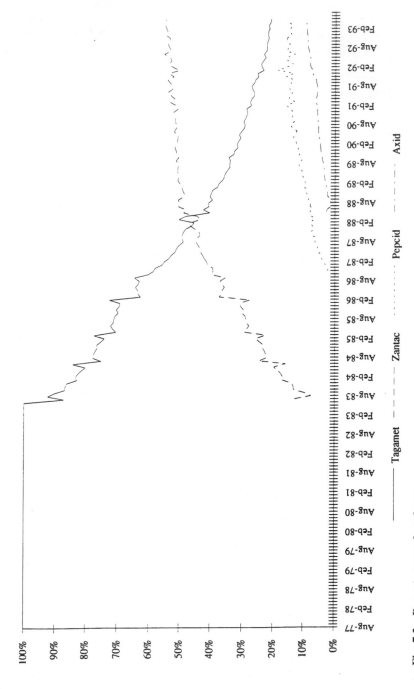

Fig. 7.2 Drugstore market shares

—— Tagamet   – – – Zantac   ········ Pepcid   –·–·– Axid

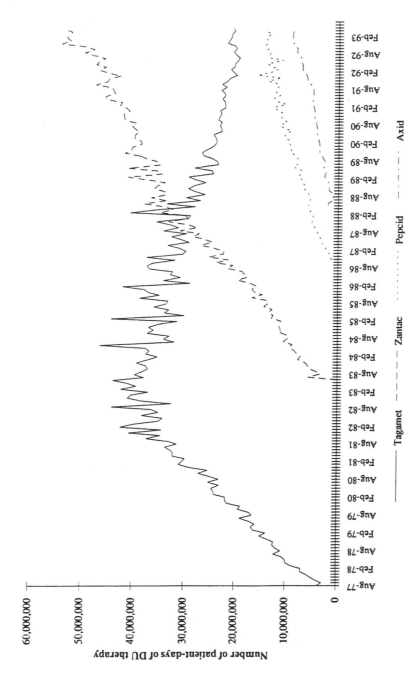

7.3 Drugstore sales

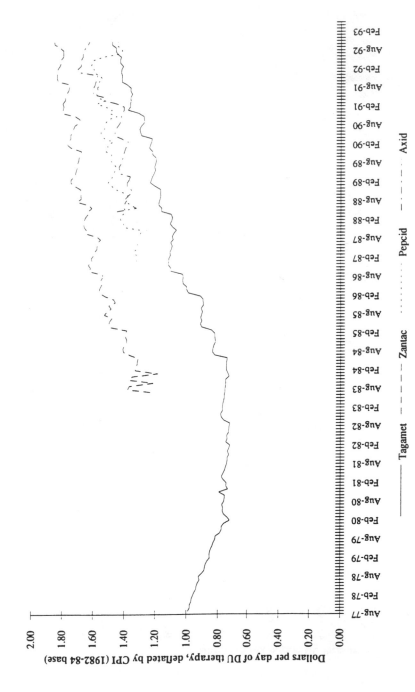

Fig. 7.4 Real drugstore prices

per day, a 56 percent premium). Thereafter, prices of *both* Zantac and Tagamet rose with time, although Tagamet's prices increased more rapidly. By the end of the sample, the Zantac price premium had narrowed from about 56 percent to 25 percent.

The third and fourth entrants, Pepcid and Axid, followed price policies that fell generally somewhere between those of Tagamet and Zantac. At the end of the sample period covered by our data, the price per day of therapy ranged from a low of about $1.41 per day for Pepcid to a high of $1.80 per day for Zantac. Prices for Tagamet and Axid fell between these amounts, at $1.44 and $1.62, respectively. An interesting recent development is that in November 1993 (after the end of our sample), Tagamet announced a major change in its pricing policy, offering rebates directly to consumers (see Freudenheim 1993).

Finally, as is seen in figure 7.4, there does not appear to be any substantial competitive pricing policy response by incumbents to the entry of new competitors into the H_2-antagonist market. Indeed, the only price-trend break that coincides with a new entry is that for Tagamet upon entry by Zantac, which resulted in the incumbent Tagamet increasing rather than decreasing its price.[10] Note also that price trends do not show breaks around the times of entry by Pepcid and Axid.

Pricing policy, however, is not the only instrument for competitive rivals. In the U.S. pharmaceutical industry, marketing plays a very significant role. In figure 7.5 we plot monthly minutes of detailing for the two principal rivals, Tagamet and Zantac; cumulative detailing minutes since the product's launch are plotted for each H_2-antagonist drug in figure 7.6.

As shown in figure 7.5, the launch of Tagamet coincided with a very substantial detailing effort—about 180,000 minutes in September 1977—which gradually diminished after entry. High levels of Tagamet detailing occurred in mid-1980 and early 1983, apparently in response to Tagamet's receiving FDA approval for the new indications of duodenal ulcer maintenance (April 1980) and gastric ulcer therapy (December 1982). When Zantac entered with a very aggressive detailing effort in July 1983 (over 350,000 minutes), Tagamet responded with about a 50 percent increase in its own detailing efforts. More detailing peaks for both Tagamet and Zantac occurred in 1986, a year in which Pepcid entered and Zantac obtained FDA approval for the treatment of GERD. Both Tagamet and Zantac appear to have anticipated the entry of Axid in April 1988 by increasing their detailing in February 1988 (substantially by Tagamet, more modestly by Zantac), but both detailing levels declined again after Axid's entry.

Although month-to-month variations are apparent in figure 7.5, there are definite trends in the intense Zantac-Tagamet detailing rivalry. As is seen in

10. For a discussion of the possible social-welfare impacts of a pioneer raising its price in response to the introduction of a competitive product by a second entrant, see Perloff and Suslow (1994). Related literature is found in Bresnahan and Reiss (1990), Cocks (1975), Cocks and Virts (1974), and Reekie (1978).

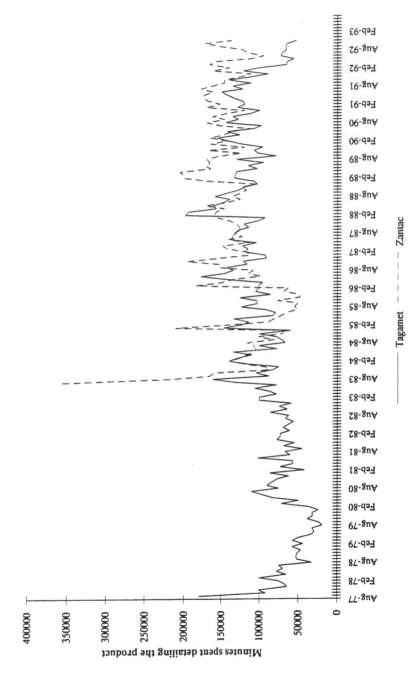

Fig. 7.5 Tagamet and Zantac minutes of detailing

figure 7.6, where cumulative detailing minutes are plotted for all four products, over its entire life Tagamet has out-detailed Zantac. However, in terms of detailing minutes per year, Zantac has considerably outpaced Tagamet. In part, Zantac has been able to do this because it has had two sales forces, as a result of Glaxo's comarketing agreement in the United States with Hoffmann-LaRoche. In terms of cumulative minutes of detailing through the end of our sample, the relative magnitudes are as follows: for every one minute of Axid detailing, there have been 3.21 minutes of detailing by Tagamet, 2.60 minutes by Zantac, and 0.88 minutes by Pepcid.

According to Bond and Lean (1977), one way in which pioneering advantages occur in the pharmaceutical industry is by the effectiveness of advertising. Bond and Lean argue that to convince physicians to switch from an existing drug to a new one and thereby to overcome advantages accruing to early entrants, the later entrant may be expected to offer either a lower price and/or a heavier promotion.[11] The Bond-Lean conjecture relates of course to the considerable theoretical and empirical literature in marketing and economics dealing with first-mover advantages.[12] It is therefore of interest to examine whether this conjecture is consistent with the data from the H_2-antagonist drug market. Although we present econometric evidence on order-of-entry effects in section 7.5, in figure 7.7 we display cumulative-detailing/cumulative-sales ratios as a function of order of entry after one, two, and three years in the marketplace. The results are striking. For these four products, given any duration of time, cumulative detailing-sales ratios are always lowest for the pioneer (Tagamet), are always larger for the second entrant (Zantac), always increase further for the third entrant (Pepcid), and are always highest for the final entrant (Axid). Moreover, since a disproportionate amount of detailing occurs immediately following product launch, for all four H_2-antagonist products the cumulative detailing-sales ratios decrease as the time interval since launch increases.

Detailing is not the only form of marketing rivalry, however. Another instrument for bringing product information to the attention of prescribing physicians is medical journal advertising. It is worth mentioning that relative to detailing, estimated expenditures on journal advertising are rather modest; as observed earlier, expenditures on detailing are approximately four to five times as great as expenditures on journal advertising in the overall U.S. pharmaceutical industry, although substantial variations occur across products.

It might be noted that to convert nominal to real dollars, one must employ a

11. As Bond and Lean (1977, vi) state, "Neither heavy promotion nor low price appears to have been sufficient to persuade prescribing physicians to select in great volume the substitute brand of late entrants. . . . When other things are equal, physicians appear to prefer the brands of existing sellers to those of new sellers."
12. On first-mover advantages, see, e.g., the surveys and references in Kalyanaram and Urban (1992), Robinson (1988), Robinson and Fornell (1985), Robinson, Kalyanaram, and Urban (1994), Samuelson and Zeckhauser (1988), Schmalensee (1982), and Urban et al. (1986). For an alternative interpretation, see Golder and Tellis (1992).

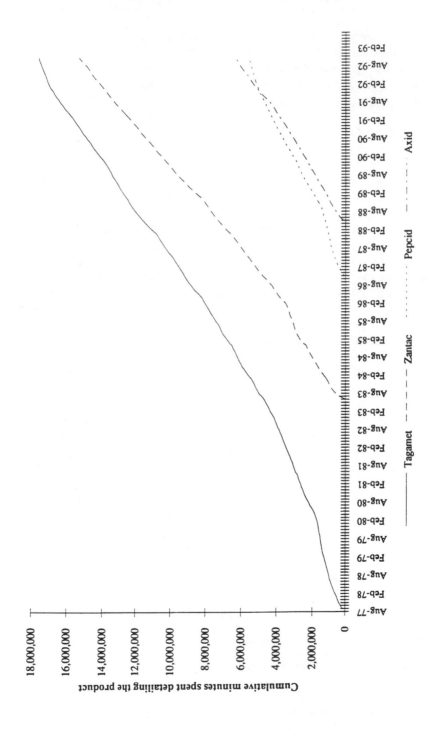

Fig. 7.6 Cumulative minutes of detailing

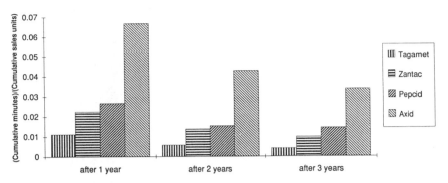

Fig. 7.7   Cumulative detailing-sales ratios

deflator. We use the BLS price index for scientific and professional journals. Based on a preliminary analysis of advertising rates charged by two major medical journals, the *New England Journal of Medicine* and the *Journal of the American Medical Association,* however, we found that the BLS deflator appeared to rise less rapidly in the 1980s than did advertising rates in these journals. An alternative measure of real medical journal advertising involves a simple page count. This measure does not account well, of course, for variations in copy quality or in journal circulation. Later in this paper we discuss these two measures further. For our current purposes, it is sufficient to note that the two measures are reasonably highly correlated. In figure 7.8 we plot cumulative journal advertising dollars spent for each of the four H_2-antagonist products, using the BLS deflator. Clearly the launch of Tagamet coincided with a considerable journal advertising campaign. Thereafter, until receiving FDA approval for duodenal ulcer maintenance in April 1980, Tagamet's journal advertising was relatively modest, with temporary increases around the time of FDA approval for gastric ulcer treatment (December 1982) and for GERD (March 1991). It is noteworthy that Tagamet's journal advertising increased only moderately after the entry of Zantac in August 1983, and it did not respond aggressively when Pepcid entered in late 1986. In terms of its response with journal advertising to entry by Pepcid and Axid, Zantac was roughly similar to Tagamet. Spurts in Zantac's journal advertising appear to follow closely the procurement of FDA approval for gastric ulcer treatment (June 1985), and the simultaneous approval for treatment of duodenal ulcer maintenance and GERD (May 1986). Finally, a comparison of figures 7.6 and 7.8 reveals that Pepcid and Axid differed considerably in their choice of marketing medium in the sense that Axid relied much more heavily than Pepcid on detailing and much less on medical journal advertising.[13]

13. Industry sources say that this is true not only for Axid, but for all of Lilly's products. Lilly's corporate strategy has been to use a much higher percentage of detailing over journal advertising in their marketing efforts. Lilly's mix of detailing to advertising is approximately 90 percent to 10 percent, whereas the industry average is 75 percent to 25 percent.

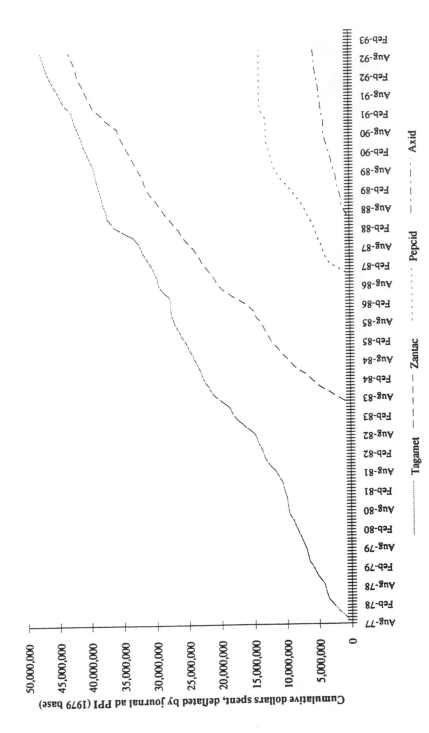

Fig. 7.8 Cumulative real journal advertising

With this overview of price, product quality, and marketing competition data trends in the H_2-antagonist market, we now turn our attention to modeling the growth in overall industry sales and to modeling changes in the shares earned by the various products. We begin in section 7.4 with an analysis of overall industry growth and then consider market shares in section 7.5.

7.4   Econometric Analysis of Growth in Industry Sales

In this paper we consider the four H_2-antagonist products as constituting a distinct market or industry. However, since Tagamet and Zantac so clearly dominate the H_2-antagonist market, we shall also consider a separate, simpler market—that consisting only of Tagamet and Zantac. We first digress to consider theory and measurement issues and then present econometric results.

7.4.1   Theoretical and Econometric Considerations

The traditional approach to modeling demand for a product involves calling upon the economic theory of consumer demand, in which consumers are assumed to maximize utility given prices of products and an overall budget constraint; additional assumptions are then employed to aggregate up from the individual consumer to an overall industry demand. In the context of pharmaceutical products, this approach is unlikely to be useful, for the typical decision maker (the physician) is not the consumer (the patient) who actually pays for the prescription drug product. Moreover the marginal price paid by the patient often differs considerably from the price received by the dispensing pharmacy, due to the existence of third-party insurance and various copayment schemes. While a discussion of such principal-agent problems is beyond the scope of this paper, we believe the existence of these institutional arrangements clearly suggests that rigid adherence to the traditional neoclassical approach of demand analysis is unlikely to be useful here.

Although we eschew the direct use of conventional utility-maximizing economic behavior, we still wish to incorporate the most important insights of demand analysis. Thus we specify that the quantity demanded depends on the price of the product, on product characteristics, and on marketing efforts. We now discuss these three factors affecting demand in further detail.

In terms of price, economic theory suggests that the quantity demanded depends on real rather than nominal price; since we employ time-series data, we deflate average product price by the CPI. Also, although product-specific price data are available, for examining overall industry demand one must construct an industry price index. The important point here is that since we wish later on in this paper to investigate the extent of price-substitutability among drugs, when we construct an aggregate price index for the industry we must not implicitly assume a value for such substitutability. In particular, if one simply summed up patient-days of therapy across drugs, then summed up total revenue across drugs, and finally, calculated price as total industry revenue divided by total industry patient-days, one would implicitly be assuming that the various drugs are perfectly substitutable. To circumvent this problem, we employ the economic theory of price indexes and calculate the industry price using the Fisher-Ideal price index.[14]

In terms of quality, to the extent that product-quality characteristics affect the size of the potential market, they should be included in an overall industry demand equation. We would expect that the size of the potential patient market would depend on the specific indications for which the FDA has granted approval. We shall concentrate on one particular indication, GERD, which represented an especially large potential new market, and for which the H_2-antagonists first received FDA approval relatively late in the sample. Specifically, when the FDA granted approval to Glaxo's Zantac for GERD, Zantac detailers were permitted to provide specific information to physicians concerning the treatment of GERD. This was significant, for instead of being confined to detailing to gastroenterologists who saw ulcer patients, now Zantac detailers also made calls on general practitioners who commonly saw patients having GERD symptoms. This undoubtedly expanded the potential market.

Such reasoning suggests that a dummy variable, say, GERD (taking the value of 1 following FDA approval), be employed in the overall industry demand equation. However, it is worth noting that information concerning the efficacy of drugs for different indications typically diffuses prior to formal FDA approval. The medical community is often aware of results of clinical trials prior to the FDA's reviewing the clinical-trial data and coming to a final decision concerning approval for a new indication. As a result, a great deal of prescribing is done off-label prior to the FDA's granting approval. Thus, it is not clear how reliable the GERD dummy variable will be in capturing major changes in the size of the potential patient base.

The third set of factors affecting industry demand involves marketing efforts. Earlier we noted that, in this industry, the two principal forms of marketing efforts are minutes of detailing and either pages or deflated dollars of medical journal advertising. There are several important issues concerning the measurement of marketing efforts. First, since drug marketing is largely a matter of providing information about the existence and usefulness of the product, we expect its impact to be long-lived; once a physician has been informed, it is hard to see how such information might be destroyed. Indeed, precisely because of this durability, firms typically expend a particularly large amount of marketing effort in the early stages of a new product's life. Hence the impact of marketing on sales is likely better measured by the cumulative stock of marketing efforts since product launch, rather than simply by the flow of cur-

14. Specifically, the Fisher-Ideal price index is the geometric mean of the Laspeyres and Paasche price indexes, where each of them is computed using updated weights. New products are incorporated as soon as is feasible (i.e., in the second period of their existence, so that their first difference is calculated). For further details concerning the Fisher-Ideal price index, see Diewert (1981, 1992).

rent monthly expenditures. We will also want to allow for the possibility that this stock of information depreciates or deteriorates over time, although we might expect the depreciation rate to be quite low.

We therefore employ the well-known perpetual-inventory method. Let M_t be the *stock* of marketing effort at the end of month t (as measured by the stocks of journal advertising and detailing minutes), let δ be the monthly rate of depreciation of this stock, and let m_t be the flow of marketing effort during time period t. Define M_t as the depreciation-adjusted stock of marketing effort carried over from the last month $(1 - \delta)M_{t-1}$, plus new marketing efforts during months t (m_t), that is

$$(1) \qquad M_t = (1 - \delta)\, M_{t-1} + m_t = \sum_{\tau = 1}^{t} (1 - \delta)^{t-\tau}\, m_\tau.$$

We construct separate stock measures for detailing and for journal advertising. Unlike the typical case for capital-stock accounting, we have no problem wth establishing benchmark or "starting values" since we know that prior to August 1977, the Tagamet journal (and detailing) stocks were zero. To implement equation (1), one must however assume rates of depreciation for each of these stocks. As discussed below, we will use the historical data on marketing and sales to estimate δ econometrically, rather than assume its value a priori.

The other major issue in measuring the effects of marketing efforts entails an innovation of this paper. Other authors have suggested that advertising be modeled as having two simultaneous effects in the market: overall advertising by all firms affecting overall market demand, and relative levels of advertising among firms affecting the individual firms' market shares.[15] We take this modeling one step further here by hypothesizing that firms may choose to direct their marketing efforts to emphasize one of the two effects more than the other. Although the degree to which firms' marketing efforts are directed, say, at overall market expansion cannot be directly observed from data on quantities of marketing done by firms, we now propose a method for estimating this effect econometrically.

To clarify this concept, we discuss it in the context of the antiulcer drug market. When SmithKline marketed Tagamet from its introduction in 1977 until the entry of Zantac in 1983, they did not worry about competing for market share in the H_2-antagonist market, for patent status conferred on them a temporary monopoly position. From this monopoly position, the goal of marketing for SmithKline was to convince more and more physicians of the utility of H_2-antagonists in treating ulcer patients. They, and no other firm, reaped the rewards of having expended efforts on diffusing information on H_2-antagonists to physicians, since they held 100 percent market share. However, once Zan-

---

15. See, for example, Schmalensee (1972). There is a considerable body of literature on a related, but distinct, approach that decomposes advertising into its "information" and "persuasive" components. For examples in the context of the pharmaceutical industry, see Leffler (1981) and Hurwitz and Caves (1988).

tac entered the market, another marketing goal appeared: to preserve market share against Zantac among those doctors who had already adopted the H_2-antagonist technology. Similarly, although Zantac detailers could benefit somewhat from continuing to reach out to new doctors and patients still not converted to the H_2-antagonist technology, Zantac detailers also had strong incentives to persuade physicians already in the H_2-antagonist market to begin prescribing Zantac instead of Tagamet, emphasizing the alleged Zantac advantages of lower-frequency dosing and more-favorable side-effect profiles. Unlike the monopoly case, in this duopoly situation the marketing efforts of firms may have both market-expanding and rivalrous (product-positioning) aspects.

Moreover, to the extent that Zantac would reap some of the benefits of Tagamet's market-expanding efforts to persuade physicians to adopt the H_2-antagonist drugs, and that Tagamet might similarly benefit somewhat from Zantac's market-expanding promotions, each firm's market-expanding promotional effort exerts a positive externality (spillover) on the other firm's sales. Similarly, we might consider rivalrous marketing to exert negative interfirm externalities. Furthermore, the magnitudes of both kinds of interfirm externalities should increase as the number of products on the market increases. Therefore, when the number of products in the market increases, ceteris paribus, we would expect a decrease in firms' incentives to engage in market-expanding promotional efforts, and correspondingly greater incentives to engage in marketing with a more rivalrous content.[16] The practical implication of this hypothesis is that in a duopoly, ceteris paribus, one would expect the product marketing of the two participants to have a smaller impact on industry demand than would be the case if this advertising had occurred in a monopoly market structure, for some of the duopolists' advertising would primarily impact market share, not overall industry demand; similarly, ceteris paribus, for a given amount of cumulative marketing stocks, one might plausibly expect that in a triopoly the effects of marketing on industry demand would be less than in a duopoly.

In this paper we examine this hypothesis empirically by inferring econometrically the proportionate impact (relative to a monopoly) that marketing efforts have under varying market structures. To this end, we distinguish cumulative marketing efforts according to the market structure in which such expenditures originally occurred. Let $M_{1,t}$ be the marketing stock at the end of month t that accumulated in the monopoly market environment, let $M_{2,t}$ be the marketing stock at the end of the month t that accumulated in the duopoly market environment, and let $M_{k,t}$ be the marketing stock at the end of month t that accumulated in a market environment consisting of K products. Define the

---

16. This also implies that incentives to advertise, and perhaps the content of advertising messages, can be expected to vary with industry structure. For further discussion of these issues, see Lucking-Reiley (1996).

"effective industry-marketing" stock M_t as the weighted sum of the cumulative marketing efforts distinguished by market structure, that is,

(2) $$\overline{M}_t = \mu_1 M_{1,t}\ \mu_2 M_{2,t} + \mu_3 M_{3,t} + \ldots + \mu_k M_{k,t},$$

where $M_{k,t}$, $k = 1, \ldots, K$, are each defined as in equation (1). Ceteris paribus, we therefore might plausibly expect that

(3) $$\mu_1 > \mu_2 > \mu_3 > \ldots > \mu_k,$$

reflecting the fact that in terms of affecting overall industry demand, participants' market-expanding effects decline as the number of products in the industry increases.[17] Since in a monopoly *all* marketing efforts affect industry demand, we normalize the μ_k's by setting $\mu_1 = 1$.

It is worth noting that two other hypotheses might be proposed involving the μ_k's. First, if the effects of firms' marketing on industry sales are independent of market structure, then $\mu_2 = \mu_3 = \mu_4 = 1$. Second and alternatively, if $\mu_2 = \mu_3 = \mu_4 = 0$, then in the presence of any competition all marketing efforts are rivalrous and affect only market shares. Note that in such a case of possibly but not necessarily socially "wasteful" marketing, firms' marketing efforts generate a zero-sum change in industry sales. In our empirical analysis, we will estimate the remaining μ_k's in equation (2) and assess whether the evidence is consistent with any of these hypotheses.

We begin with some definitions of variables. Let Q_t be total units of sales for all products (a Fisher-Ideal quantity index), let PR_t be the corresponding real price index (deflated by the CPI), let $D_{k,t}$ be the stock of minutes detailed by product k at the end of time period t, let $J_{k,t}$ be the stock of pages of advertising in medical journals by product k at time t, and let $GERD_t$ be the above-noted GERD dummy variable.

In terms of a mathematical formulation, we specify a traditional log-linear demand equation, where, however, the use of identities (1) and (2) necessitates estimation by nonlinear least squares (NLS) procedures. In particular, let

(4) $$\ln Q_t = \beta_0 + \beta_1 \ln PR_t + \beta_2 \ln \overline{D}_t + \beta_3 \ln \overline{J}_t + \beta_4 GERD_t + \varepsilon_t,$$

where ε is an identically normally distributed random error term, and where $\ln \overline{D}_t$ and $\ln \overline{J}_t$ are natural logarithms of the effective industry-marketing stocks of number of minutes detailed and pages of medical journal advertisements,[18] respectively, defined as

---

17. Note that the μ's do not deal at all with the effects of marketing stocks on the market *shares* garnered by the various firms in the market. We discuss determinants of market shares further in section 7.5 below.

18. Two possible measures of medical journal advertising are current-dollar expenditures divided by a BLS price index for advertising in professional journals, and the number of pages of medical journal advertising. Results from preliminary regression estimation suggested that the page measure provided more plausible parameter estimates.

(5) $$\overline{D}_t = D_{1,t} + \mu_2 D_{2,t} + \mu_3 D_{3,t} + \mu_4 D_{4,t},$$

and

(6) $$\overline{J}_t = J_{1,t} + \mu_2 J_{2,t} + \mu_3 J_{3,t} + \mu_4 J_{4,t}.$$

In turn, following equation (1), define the effective stock of minutes at the end of month t for a market structure consisting of K products as

(7) $$D_{k,t} = (1 - \delta_M)D_{k,t-1} + \text{MIN}_{k,t},$$

where δ_M is the constant rate of depreciation for the detailing-minutes stock, and MIN is the number of minutes detailed during month t, where month t was one in which the market structure consisted of k products. The construction of effective stocks of journal pages $J_{k,t}$ by type of market structure is analogous to that in equation (7). Since equations (4)–(7) are nonlinear in the μ's and δ's, for convenience we will constrain $\mu_k^M = \mu_k^J$, and $\delta_m = \delta_j$, but of course the μ_k (equal for minutes and journal pages) will still be permitted to differ with industry structure k in order that the hypothesized inequality in equation (1) might emerge.

There is one other issue that merits attention. At the industry level, one would expect price to be simultaneously determined with quantity. Moreover, as has been emphasized by, among others, Dorfman and Steiner (1954) and Schmalensee (1972), advertising efforts are also likely to be jointly determined with price and quantity. In terms of stochastic specification, therefore, it may well be the case that $\ln\text{PR}$, $\ln\overline{D}$, and $\ln\overline{J}$ are correlated with ε, in which case NLS estimation would provide inconsistent estimates of the parameters. In the next section, we therefore report results of a Hausman test for this possible endogeneity, and since we find the correlation to be significant, we also estimate and report results using the nonlinear two-stage least squares (NL-2SLS) estimator.

7.4.2   Results of Econometric Analysis

Our data set consists of 189 monthly observations beginning in September 1977. We proceed using two alternative definitions of the market, one comprising the two dominant products, Zantac and Tagamet, and the other comprising all four H_2-antagonists. In each case, we begin by setting the depreciation rate $\delta = 0$; we then examine and choose among several possible alternative specifications. Given reasonable regression equations, we perform a grid search for the best-fit value of δ by re-estimating the models assuming a variety of depreciation rates, where $0 \leq \delta \leq 1$. We choose as our final set of parameter estimates the values of δ and the other parameters for which the sum of squared residuals is minimized (the sample likelihood function is maximized). Our findings are summarized in table 7.1; the first two columns are estimates for the two-product market, while the last two columns are for the four-product market.

Table 7.1   **Parameter Estimates in the Two- and Four-Product Industry Models**

$$\ln Q_t = \beta_0 + \beta_1 \ln PR_t + \beta_2 \ln \overline{D}_t + \beta_3 \ln \overline{J}_t + \beta_4 GERD_t + \varepsilon_t, \text{ where}$$

$$\overline{D}_t = D_{1,t} + \mu_2 D_{2,t} + \mu_3 D_{3,t} + \ldots + \mu_k D_{k,t}, \text{ where}$$

$$D_{k,t} = (1 - \delta)D_{k,t-1} + MIN_{k,t}, \text{ and}$$

$$\overline{J}_t = J_{1,t} + \mu_2 J_{2,t} + \mu_3 J_{3,t} + \ldots + \mu_k J_{k,t}, \text{ where}$$

$$J_{k,t} = (1 - \delta)J_{k,t-1} + PJL_{k,t}.$$

	NLS T-Z (1)	NL-2SLS T-Z (2)	NLS T-Z-P-A (3)	NL-2SLS T-Z-P-A (4)
β_0	−6.574*	−5.165*	−7.291*	−7.110*
	(0.46)	(0.54)	(0.58)	(0.68)
β_1	−0.901*	−1.072*	−0.707*	−0.737*
	(0.11)	(0.14)	(0.14)	(0.20)
β_2	0.534*	0.413*	0.589*	0.574*
	(0.06)	(0.08)	(0.06)	(0.08)
β_3	0.210*	0.275*	0.166*	0.174*
	(0.06)	(0.08)	(0.06)	(0.06)
β_4	0.157*	0.164*	0.117*	0.118*
	(0.03)	(0.03)	(0.03)	(0.03)
μ_2	0.688*	0.892*	0.577*	0.600*
	(0.07)	(0.12)	(0.08)	(0.11)
μ_3			0.812*	0.848*
			(0.14)	(0.18)
μ_4			0.464*	0.491*
			(0.09)	(0.13)
δ	0.002	0.000	0.000	0.000
	(0.00)			
R^2	0.992	0.992	0.994	0.994
D-W	1.767	1.729	1.909	1.907
N	189	189	189	189

Notes: T-Z stands for Tagamet-Zantac. T-Z-P-A stands for Tagamet-Zantac-Pepcid-Axid. Standard errors are reported in parentheses.

*Significant at the 95 percent level.

First, as seen in column (1) of table 7.1, the iterative NLS procedure yields an optimum when δ is very small (0.2 percent per month) and is not significantly different from zero.[19] While we expected a low value for this depreciation rate since knowledge and information about a product is very durable, that we obtained such a very low rate of depreciation is somewhat surprising. It is worth noting, however, that in an interindustry productivity study estimating the depreciation rate of research and development (R&D) capital (another good whose use involves potential spillovers and for which information plays

19. The implicit standard error estimates in table 7.1 are conditional on the value of δ. The t-statistic for δ was computed by comparing the likelihood function at $\delta = 0$ with that at $\delta = 0.0020$, and then computing the implied test statistic.

a central role), Griliches and Lichtenberg (1984) reported an estimated depreciation rate of zero.

Second, the estimate of μ_2 is about 0.69, and with a standard error estimate of about 0.07, it is significantly different both from unity and from zero. Since μ_1 has been normalized to unity, this estimate of μ_2 implies that, ceteris paribus, observed marketing stocks of detailing minutes and journal pages are only about 70 percent as effective in changing *industry* sales when they occur in a duopoly (Tagamet and Zantac), relative to when they take place in a monopoly (Tagamet). This is a plausible result, for anecdotal evidence suggests to us that much of the Zantac-Tagamet duopoly was characterized by highly competitive marketing, aimed at securing market share rather than focused on increasing overall industry growth.[20] Nonetheless, as was shown in figure 7.1, during this duopoly industry sales grew rapidly.

Third, in terms of marketing effectiveness, as is seen in column (1) of table 7.1, the elasticity of sales with respect to effective cumulative industry detailing minutes ($\ln D$) is slightly greater than 0.5, which is about two and one-half times as large as the elasticity for effective cumulative industry journal pages ($\ln J$), whose value is about 0.2. Fourth, each of these two marketing elasticities is estimated to be considerably smaller in absolute magnitude than the market-price elasticity, which is slightly less than unity (-0.90). Finally, although we have some hesitations concerning its reliability in tracking physician awareness, the coefficient on GERD (a dummy variable equal to 1 during the time period in which the FDA approved an H_2-antagonist drug for the GERD indication) is positive and significant; the estimate implies that, ceteris paribus, FDA approval for GERD increased the market size by about 15 percent.

These NLS results are based on the assumption that the regressors are uncorrelated with the disturbance term (in our context, that the regressors are all exogenous). We have tested for this assumption using a Hausman specification test, using instruments that will be discussed below. We find that the joint null hypothesis of no correlation between ε and $\ln PR$, ε and $\ln D$, and ε and $\ln J$ is soundly rejected:[21] the likelihood-ratio test statistic is 49.2, while the 0.01 critical value for the five restrictions is 15.1.[22] This implies that NLS generates inconsistent parameter estimates and suggests that we instead employ the NL-2SLS estimator.

We utilize two groups of exogenous variables to form the instruments. One group is common to both firms: the log of the producer price index for intermediate materials, the log of the wage rate for production workers in the pharma-

20. For a journalist's account of Glaxo's marketing activities and their success in the marketplace, see Lynn (1991).

21. More precisely, the null hypothesis involves testing that the various component (monopoly, duopoly) stocks of MIN and PJL are uncorrelated with ε. Hence under the alternative hypothesis there are five endogenous variables, monopoly stocks of MIN and PJL, duopoly stocks of MIN and PJL, and price.

22. Coefficients on each of the marketing-stock variables, and on the price variable, were significantly different from zero as well.

ceutical industry, the GERD dummy variable, and a time counter. The other set incorporates firm-specific variations but aggregates them to the industry level: the number of detailing minutes by firms for their products other than those in the H_2-antagonist market and the number of real dollars of medical journal advertisements for the firms' non-H_2-antagonist products. To make these variables comparable to the components of the regressors $\ln D$ and $\ln J$ (see equations [5] and [6] above), we construct stocks separately by type of industry structure and then cumulate them assuming $\delta = 0$.

The results of the NL-2SLS estimation are presented in column (2) of table 7.1. Relative to the NLS findings, a number of results are worth noting. First, with NL-2SLS the criterion function is optimized when $\delta = 0$. This estimate is low, but as noted above, it is not without precedent in a related context. Second, under NL-2SLS estimation, the estimate of μ_2 increases from 0.69 to about 0.89 and is now no longer significantly different from unity. It is, however, significantly different from zero. Third, the price-elasticity estimate under NL-2SLS is slightly larger in absolute value (-1.07 vs. -0.90), but the detailing-minutes elasticity is smaller (0.41 vs. 0.53). Fourth, for the journal-page elasticity, under NL-2SLS estimation the estimate increases from 0.21 to 0.28. Hence with NL-2SLS as well as with NLS estimation, the estimates of the journal-page and detailing-minutes elasticities are much smaller in absolute value than is the price elasticity. Finally, under either estimation method, R^2 is above .99, and the Durbin-Watson test statistics are very close to 2.0.

We now turn to a discussion of findings obtained under a four-product market definition; results are given in columns (3) and (4) of table 7.1. As shown in the table, under either estimation method the goodness of fit is above .99, and the Durbin-Watson test statistic is again quite close to 2.0. For both NLS and NL-2SLS, the estimated δ at the optimum was 0.00. Hence the very low depreciation estimate results for marketing efforts of detailing minutes and pages of medical journals carries over from the two-product to the four-product market context. Also, the Hausman test for exogeneity is again clearly rejected, although not as decisively as in the two-product analysis; here the likelihood-ratio test statistic is 41.3, while the 0.01 critical value for the nine restrictions is 21.7. This suggests again that the NLS estimates may be inconsistent and that we should instead employ the NL-2SLS estimator.

The NL-2SLS estimate for the market-price elasticity in this four-product market is slightly smaller (in absolute value) than in the two-product case, around -0.74 versus -1.07. The estimate of the sales elasticity with respect to cumulative detailing minutes is somewhat larger here (0.57 vs. 0.41), while that with respect to journal pages is slightly smaller (0.17 vs. 0.28). Moreover, with the larger four-firm market definition the GERD coefficient declines slightly, from about 16 percent to 12 percent.

Of particular interest, however, are the estimates of μ_2, μ_3, and μ_4. Recall from the discussion surrounding equation (3) that we hypothesized that, ceteris paribus, $1 > \mu_2 > \mu_3 > \mu_4$. As is seen in the last two columns of table 7.1, this pattern is largely, but not completely, borne out; although less than unity, typical estimates of these three parameters are 0.6, 0.8, and 0.5, respectively. Why it is that marketing efforts in the triopoly epoch were more effective in generating industry sales than during the two- and four-product eras is an issue meriting further examination. Moreover, the joint null hypothesis that these μ's are all unity (that the effectiveness of marketing efforts on sales is independent of market structure) is decisively rejected, as is the joint hypothesis that $\mu_2 = \mu_3 = \mu_4 = 0$, the latter indicating that market-expansion spillovers do not entirely disappear when competition begins. While these spillovers are considerably lower in the duopoly period than would be the case in a monopoly and are lower when there are four products on the market than when there are two, in this market the relationship between μ_k and the number of products in the market is not completely monotonic.

7.5   Econometric Analysis of Factors Affecting Market Shares

Up to this point our analysis has focused on overall market demand, with alternative definitions of the market. We now report on an exploratory effort at modeling the factors that affect individual market shares earned by each of the products. The results reported here are those from our initial research; we intend to extend this analysis in future research. As in section 7.4, we begin with a discussion of considerations drawn from economic theory and then report on statistical findings.

7.5.1   Theoretical and Econometric Considerations

The specification of market-share or relative demand functions traditionally draws on the economic theory of consumer behavior. As noted earlier, however, principal-agent problems and wedges between marginal relative prices paid and received imply that one cannot directly employ the economic theory framework of consumers maximizing utility given prices and budget constraints.

Consistent with traditional economic specifications, however, we would expect that relative rather than level prices affect market shares. Moreover, within the marketing literature, there is ample precedent for specifying that relative values (ratios) of product characteristics, and relative marketing efforts, affect market shares. In addition, both the economic and marketing literatures suggest that order of entry can be expected to be a significant determinant of market shares (see, e.g., Schmalensee 1982; Kalyanaram and Urban 1992; and Urban et al. 1986). Following Urban et al. (1986), we employ a market-share specification of the general form

(8) $$\frac{Q_{jt}}{Q_{1t}} = f\left(\frac{P_{jt}}{P_{1t}}, \frac{\text{MIN}_{jt}}{\text{MIN}_{1t}}, \frac{\text{PJL}_{jt}}{\text{PJL}_{1t}}, X_{jst}, \text{ENT}_{jt}\right),$$

where Q_{jt}/Q_{1t} is the sales of product j relative to product 1 (the first or pioneer entrant, in this case, Tagamet) in month t, P_{jt}/P_{1t} are the corresponding relative prices per day of therapy, MIN_{jt}/MIN_{1t} and PJL_{jt}/PJL_{1t} are relative cumulative stocks of minutes of product detailing and cumulative pages of medical journal advertisements (defined as in eq. [1], X_{jst} are a set of s variables measuring the quality of product j relative to the pioneer (e.g., dosage frequency, number of [adverse] drug interactions reported to the FDA, whether product j has a GERD-indication advantage relative to the pioneer, etc.), and ENT_{jt} is the order of entry of product j (i.e., 2 for Zantac, 3 for Pepcid, and 4 for Axid).

In our context, the pioneer product is Tagamet, and thus all variables in equation (8) are measured for product j relative to Tagamet. Since market share is 100 percent for Tagamet during its monopoly epoch (September 1977–July 1983), the data set for which market-share analysis is appropriate commences in August 1983; data prior to this are not employed. In the case of a two-product market definition, the data therefore consist of Zantac-Tagamet relative quantities beginning with August 1983, a total of 118 observations. For the four-product (H_2-antagonist) market definition, however, the data set is expanded to incorporate relative Pepcid-Tagamet data points (December 1986 onward), as well as relative Axid-Tagamet observations (beginning with June 1988), giving us a total of 255 observations. Note that in this four-product model the data take the form of an unbalanced panel.

Finally, in terms of econometric considerations, one would expect that relative market shares, relative marketing efforts, and relative prices are jointly determined. For this reason, we compare the ordinary least squares (OLS) and NLS results with those based on 2SLS and NL-2SLS.

In terms of mathematical formulation, we specify a relative demand equation as in equation (8), where variables are logarithmically transformed:

$$(9) \ln\left(\frac{Q_{jt}}{Q_{1t}}\right) = \beta_1 ENTRY_{jt} + \beta_2 \ln\left(\frac{P_{jt}}{P_{1t}}\right) + \beta_3 \ln\left(\frac{MIN_{jt}}{MIN_{1t}}\right) + \beta_4 DGERD_{jt}$$
$$+ \beta_5 \ln\left(\frac{FREQ_{jt}}{FREQ_{1t}}\right) + \beta_6 \ln\left(\frac{INT_{jt}}{INT_{1t}}\right) + \beta_7 AGE_{jt} + \varepsilon_{jt},$$

where $ENTRY_{jt}$ takes on the value 2 for all Zantac observations, 3 for Pepcid, and 4 for Axid; $FREQ_{jt}$ is the recommended daily dosage frequency of drug j; INT_{jt} is the number of (adverse) drug interactions of drug j reported to the FDA as of time t;[23] $DGERD_{jt}$ is a variable indicating whether product j has a GERD-indication advantage relative to Tagamet (1 if an advantage, zero if no advantage, -1 if a disadvantage); and AGE_{jt} is the number of months product j has been in the marketplace. Notice that if the relative price, relative detailing minutes, relative adverse interaction, and relative dosing frequency variables

---

23. Data on INT_{jt} are taken from annual issues of the *Physicians' Desk Reference*.

were all unity, and if the products had no GERD advantage, then at age zero, the relative quantities would depend solely on the order-of-entry effects. Thus the coefficient on ENTRY reflects disadvantages confronting later entrants into the market, other things held equal. The coefficient on AGE reflects the impact of marketplace experience on sales, holding ENTRY (and other variables) fixed. A priori, we expect that $\beta_1 < 0$, $\beta_2 < 0$, $\beta_3 > 0$, $\beta_4 > 0$, $\beta_5 < 0$, $\beta_6 < 0$, and $\beta_7 > 0$.[24]

As noted earlier, the data set for this market-share model begins when the Tagamet monopoly period ends and Zantac enters. To implement the model empirically, we must make an assumption concerning the "starting value" of the Tagamet stock of detailing minutes. Since the results of our industry analysis suggested that depreciation rates for effective industry-marketing stocks were zero, we begin the duopoly era using Tagamet's end-of-monopoly-era value for MIN_t, assuming $\delta = 0$. However, we will permit δ, the depreciation rate for these stocks, to differ from zero now that competition has emerged, reflecting in part the fact that the content of marketing may now become more susceptible to counterclaims and therefore become less long-lived. Although we have not yet developed a formal model describing optimal behavior in this context, we would not be surprised if the depreciation rate, δ, in the rivalrous context were larger than it was in the industry-expanding environment.

7.5.2   Results of Econometric Analysis

We begin with a market-share analysis for the two-product market, Tagamet and Zantac. Conditional on any given rate of depreciation, the market-share model of equation (9) is linear in the parameters. We proceed by estimating parameters in equation (9) by OLS under different rates of depreciation and then choose as our preferred model that set of δ and the other parameters that minimizes the sum of squared residuals (maximizes the sample likelihood function). Results from preliminary analysis suggested that it was difficult to obtain precise estimates of both marketing instruments—minutes of detailing and pages of medical journal advertising—reflecting in part the fact that the simple correlation between MIN_{jt}/MIN_{1t} and PJL_{jt}/PJL_{1t} was .98. In the results presented in table 7.2, the lnPJL variable was therefore deleted. Several points are worth noting.

First, in the two-product industry equation, the likelihood function is maximized at the point where $\delta = 0$. A second, somewhat unexpected, result is that the coefficient on the relative frequency of dosage variable ($\ln RFRQ_t \equiv \ln(FREQ_{jt}/FREQ_{1t})$), though negative, is insignificantly different from zero. We therefore set this parameter to zero and re-estimate the model. As is seen in column (2) of table 7.2, the logarithm of the relative quantities of Zantac to

---

24. Note that if one insisted, this logarithmic functional form could be rationalized as deriving from the relative demand equations based on a constant elasticity of substitution (CES) indirect utility function augmented by marketing and product-characteristic variables.

Table 7.2   **Parameter Estimates in the Two- and Four-Product Market-Share Models**

$$\ln\left(\frac{Q_{jt}}{Q_{1t}}\right) = \beta_1 \, \text{ENTRY}_{jt} + \beta_2 \ln\left(\frac{p_{jt}}{p_{1t}}\right) + \beta_3 \ln\left(\frac{\text{MIN}_{jt}}{\text{MIN}_{1t}}\right)$$

$$+ \beta_4 \, \text{DGERD}_{jt} + \beta_5 \ln\left(\frac{\text{FREQ}_{jt}}{\text{FREQ}_{1t}}\right) + \beta_6 \ln\left(\frac{\text{INT}_{jt}}{\text{INT}_{1t}}\right) + \beta_7 \, \text{AGE}_{jt} + \varepsilon_{jt}$$

	OLS T-Z (1)	OLS T-Z (2)	2SLS T-Z (3)	2SLS T-Z (4)	OLS T-Z-P-A (5)	2SLS T-Z-P-A (6)
β_1	−0.054	−0.116	−0.147	−0.181	−0.492*	−0.507*
	(0.17)	(0.17)	(0.20)	(0.17)	(0.01)	(0.01)
β_2	−0.862*	−0.840*	−0.885*	−0.886*	−0.643*	−0.693*
	(0.24)	(0.24)	(0.24)	(0.24)	(0.06)	(0.07)
β_3	1.003*	0.950*	0.922*	0.893*	0.731*	0.673*
	(0.06)	(0.05)	(0.10)	(0.06)	(0.02)	(0.04)
β_4	0.087*	0.085*	0.093*	0.094*	0.032	0.046*
	(0.02)	(0.02)	(0.02)	(0.02)	(0.02)	(0.02)
β_5	−0.066		−0.023			
	(0.05)		(0.06)			
β_6	−0.090*	−0.093*	−0.097*	−0.099*	−0.251*	−0.232*
	(0.04)	(0.04)	(0.04)	(0.04)	(0.02)	(0.03)
β_7	0.010*	0.010*	0.011*	0.011*	0.012*	0.013*
	(0.00)	(0.00)	(0.00)	(0.00)	(0.00)	(0.00)
δ	0.000	0.000	0.000	0.000	0.039*	0.042*
					(0.00)	(0.01)
R^2	0.993	0.993	0.993	0.993	0.990	0.989
N	118	118	118	118	255	255

Notes: T-Z stands for Tagamet-Zantac. T-Z-P-A stands for Tagamet-Zantac-Pepcid-Axis. Standard errors are reported in parentheses.
*Significant at the 95 percent level.

Tagamet ($\ln(Q_{jt}/Q_{1t})$, the dependent variable) is significantly negatively affected by relative price ($\ln\text{RPR} \equiv \ln(P_{jt}/P_{1t})$)—the own-price elasticity is about -0.8 and is very substantially affected by the relative stocks of cumulative detailing minutes ($\ln\text{RMIN} \equiv \ln(\text{MIN}_{jt}/\text{MIN}_{1t})$), which have an elasticity estimate of about 1.0. As hypothesized, the coefficient on the GERD-advantage variable is positive (0.08) and significant, while that on $\ln\text{RINT} \equiv \ln[(\text{INT}_{jt} + 1)/(\text{INT}_{1t} + 1)]$, where INT is the number of (adverse) drug interactions reported to the FDA, is negative (-0.09) and significant. Finally, while the order-of-entry coefficient (in this two-product model, essentially just the intercept term) is negative, its standard error is quite large. By contrast, the coefficient on the AGE variable is positive and highly significant.

We then perform a Hausman test to check for possible endogeneity of $\ln\text{RPR}$ and $\ln\text{RMIN}$. The exogenous variables used here are the same as those noted in section 7.4 above, except now the firm-specific number of detailing minutes and dollars of medical journal advertising for products other than those in the H_2-antagonist market are employed, as are dummy variables for whether the product has received FDA approval for duodenal maintenance therapy, gastric ulcers, GERD and stress ulcer prevention. These latter variables are particularly useful as instruments, since they represent "shocks" and new information for marketing efforts. The results of the Hausman test are not as clear as in the overall market analysis; here the likelihood-ratio test for exogeneity of lnRPR and lnRMIN is 6.67, while the 0.01 chi-square critical value for the two restrictions is 6.63. As a sensitivity check, we proceed with 2SLS estimation. Our 2SLS results are presented in columns (3) and (4) of table 7.2.

With 2SLS estimation, the fitting optimum is again reached with the depreciation rate $\delta = 0$. Essentially, the results are the same as those obtained under OLS estimation. In particular, the own-price elasticity estimate is about -0.9, about the same in absolute value as the elasticity of sales with respect to cumulative detailing. The DGERD advantage is significant and equal to about 10 percent, AGE is significant and about 1 percent per month, while both ENTRY and lnRFRQ are negative but insignificantly different from zero. Finally, Zantac's relative market share is significantly negatively affected by its number of drug interactions relative to Tagamet. At the end of the sample, incidentally, values of INT are 12 for Tagamet and 1 for Zantac. Hence, the INT product-quality variable is particularly important in explaining the growth in Zantac's market share and the corresponding decline of Tagamet.

In summary, in the two-product market, relative Zantac-Tagamet quantities demanded are systematically related to relative product prices, relative cumulative detailing efforts, relative product quality (relative adverse interactions and GERD, but not, apparently, dosing frequency), and the length of time the product has been on the market. Moreover, for both OLS and 2SLS estimation, the goodness of fit is above .99.[25]

We now turn to the broader market definition, one encompassing all four H_2-antagonist products (Tagamet, Zantac, Pepcid, and Axid). The results of this analysis are given in the last two columns of table 7.2. First, we now uncover evidence suggesting that in the rivalrous-market context, depreciation rates on detailing minutes differ substantially from zero. Specifically, with OLS estimation, the sample log-likelihood function is maximized when $\delta = 0.039$; this monthly rate of 3.9 percent corresponds with an annual rate of about 38 percent. Second, with this expanded market definition, order-of-entry effects (no longer just an intercept term) become very large and significant; the -0.492 estimate corresponds with about a 39 percent disadvantage accruing to each later entrant, ceteris paribus, and is remarkably close to the "consensus" estimate of order-of-entry effects (-0.5) in numerous other markets surveyed by Robinson, Kalyanaram, and Urban (1994). Third, although the price-

---

25. Durbin-Watson test statistics in the two OLS equations are 1.646 and 1.624, while in the two 2SLS equations they equal 1.627 and 1.608.

elasticity estimate is slightly smaller in absolute value in this four-firm market than in the two-firm context (-0.7 vs -0.9), the standard error estimates are much smaller, and the t-statistics are therefore larger. Further, the elasticity of relative sales with respect to relative cumulative detailing minutes is slightly larger in absolute value than the price elasticity (0.73 vs. -0.64) and is also highly significant. Finally, as hypothesized, the coefficient on the variable for relative number of (adverse) drug interactions (lnRINT) is negative and significant (-0.25, t-statistic of 12), and the coefficient on DGERD is positive (0.03), but the latter coefficient is of only marginal statistical significance (t-statistic of 1.9). The AGE coefficient is again slightly greater than 1 percent, indicating that length of time in the marketplace affects relative sales in a positive manner. Goodness of fit is again about .99.[26]

To check on the possible endogeneity of relative prices and relative detailing stocks, we again perform a Hausman specification test. The null hypothesis of exogeneity of lnRPR and lnRMIN is decisively rejected; the likelihood-ratio test statistic is 8.53, while the 0.01 chi-square critical value for the two restrictions is 6.63.

Parameter estimates under 2SLS estimation are given in column (6) of table 7.2. Several findings are of particular interest. First, the estimate of δ at the fitting optimum is 0.042 and is significantly different from zero; this monthly depreciation rate of 4.2 percent implies an annual rate of about 40 percent. Hence, these results suggest that in the four-product antiulcer market, relative detailing efforts have a long-lived rivalrous impact that depreciates at about 40 percent per year. Second, order-of-entry effects are very substantial and statistically significant (-0.51, t-statistic of 59), and they again conform remarkably closely to the -0.5 consensus estimate reported by Robinson, Kalyanaram, and Urban (1994) for numerous other packaged-goods markets. Third, the absolute values of the price and advertising elasticities are roughly the same, 0.7, and each is significantly different from zero. Thus the evidence suggests that in the four-firm market, relative shares garnered by the four products vary systematically and significantly with order of entry, relative price, and relative cumulative detailing minutes. In terms of product-quality variables, increases in the relative number of adverse drug interactions reported to the FDA negatively impact relative sales, whereas having a GERD-approval advantage relative to Tagamet positively affects relative sales.

In summary, this exploratory four-firm market-share analysis suggests that order of entry, pricing behavior, marketing behavior, and product quality all affect relative sales quantities in the hypothesized manner. Moreover, rivalrous detailing appears to depreciate at about 40 percent per year.

Before leaving this discussion, however, we believe it is of interest to report estimates of total price elasticities. The price elasticity estimates reported in

---

26. Since the data set now consists of an unbalanced panel, the traditional Durbin-Watson test statistic is no longer appropriate.

table 7.2 focus only on relative quantities (market shares), but leave fixed the size of total industry demand at, say, $\overline{Q}$; denote these price elasticities by e_{jj}^*. A total-price elasticity also captures the impact of a product's price change on total industry demand; denote such a price elasticity by e_{jj} (no asterisk). As has been shown by, inter alia, Berndt and Wood (1979), the relationship between e_{jj}^* and e_{jj} is as follows:

$$(10) \qquad \varepsilon_{jj} = \varepsilon_{jj}^* \Big|_{Q=\overline{Q}} + \left(\frac{\partial \ln Q_j}{\partial \ln Q}\right)\left(\frac{\partial \ln Q}{\partial \ln P}\right)\left(\frac{\partial \ln P}{\partial \ln P_j}\right),$$

where Q_j is the quantity demanded of product j, Q is total industry demand, and P is industry price. The first partial derivative in equation (10) can be assumed to equal unity (other things being equal, demand for product j grows equiproportionally with market demand, i.e., according to its market share), while the second partial derivative is the industry- or market-price elasticity (estimated values of which are given in table 7.1). The last partial derivative in equation (10) indicates the impact of a change in product j's price on the overall industry price index; it can be approximated by the revenue share of product j in total industry revenues.

Alternative OLS and 2SLS estimates of e_{jj}^* are given in table 7.2, while NLS and NL-2SLS estimates of the industry-price elasticity are presented in table 7.1. For the two-product market, 1993 drugstore revenue shares for Tagamet and Zantac are approximately 0.25 and 0.75. For the four-product market, these shares are approximately 0.19 (Tagamet), 0.60 (Zantac), 0.12 (Pepcid), and 0.09 (Axid). Together, these relationships imply that in the two-product context, the 2SLS estimates of the total own-price demand elasticities for Tagamet and Zantac are approximately -1.154 and -1.690, respectively, while in the four-product market, the 2SLS estimated total own-price demand elasticity is -0.909 for Tagamet, -1.153 for Zantac, -0.820 for Pepcid, and -0.799 for Axid. Note that while these point estimates imply that some of the demand elasticities are less than one in absolute magnitude, the associated standard errors may well imply that reasonable confidence intervals include values of one and above (in absolute value).

7.6   Concluding Remarks

In this paper we have attempted to explain the phenomenal growth of the H_2-antagonist antiulcer drug industry in the United States, as well as changes in the market shares garnered by the various products over time. Although we have examined the roles of product quality, order of entry, and price, we have focused particular attention on the role of various marketing efforts. Our framework and results can be summarized as follows.

First, marketing efforts such as detailing and medical journal advertising have long-lived impacts. Thus, in explaining current-period sales, a stock of cumulative detailing or cumulative medical journal advertising is a more appropriate measure of marketing impacts than are current monthly expenditures. In the context of industry demand, we distinguish investments of firms in these marketing activities by the industry structure prevailing when the expenditures originally occurred. In a monopoly market structure, all marketing expenditures are market-expanding, for the monopolist has 100 percent market share. In a market structure with k products, however, marketing activities become more rivalrous, and as k becomes large, we expect relatively little "spillover" of a firm's marketing efforts in affecting industry demand. We have hypothesized, therefore, that in terms of affecting *industry* demand, the relative effects of marketing expenditures originally made when k products were in the market will tend to decline as k increases. In other words, we hypothesize that the effectiveness of marketing in generating industry sales depends on market structure in a systematic manner.

In our empirical analysis of the antiulcer drug market, we obtained considerable but not quite unanimous support for this hypothesis. In particular, normalizing the impact of a monopolist's marketing investments on current sales to unity, we estimated the impact in a duopoly to be 0.6, in a three-product industry to be 0.8, and in a four-product market to be 0.5; these last three numbers are all statistically significantly different from unity (implying that we reject the hypothesis that the effectiveness of marketing efforts is independent of market structure), and from zero (indicating that we reject the hypothesis that once there is competition, the only impact of marketing is on market share, and there is none on overall market size). Thus our results suggest that in the antiulcer drug market there is clear evidence of spillovers, and that these spillovers are considerably less than 100 percent effective. Moreover, for the most part, these spillovers decline as the number of products in the industry increases.

Second, we find that at the industry level, both cumulative minutes of detailing and cumulative pages of medical journal advertising affect sales; typical estimates of these elasticities are 0.5 and 0.2, respectively. At the market-share level, relative sales of products are also positively related to relative cumulative minutes of detailing; this elasticity is typically in the range of 0.7 to 0.9. Together these results imply that the marketing efforts of firms in the antiulcer drug market had substantial effects, in terms of affecting both market shares and the size of the overall industry.

Third, a somewhat unexpected result we obtained is that at the industry level, the rate of depreciation of stocks of both minutes of detailing and medical journal advertising was estimated to be zero. We believe that this result reflects the fact that market-expanding marketing primarily involves informing physicians about the usefulness of this class of drugs, and that once a physician begins prescribing these drugs, he or she is not likely to forget about their existence and stop prescribing them. By contrast, at the level of market shares a rather different picture emerges. In particular, in the four-product market

(Tagamet, Zantac, Pepcid, and Axid), we find that the market-share impact of the stock of detailing minutes deteriorated at an annual rate of around 40 percent, reflecting perhaps a more rivalrous content of marketing efforts.

The remarkable growth in the market share of Zantac over time can be partially explained, then, by the very substantial marketing efforts undertaken by Glaxo. However, pricing policies also had an impact. Zantac gained share over Tagamet in part because the price premium commanded by Zantac declined from about 56 percent in 1983 to only 25 percent in 1993. Our estimates of industry-price elasticities range from about -0.7 to -0.9, while estimates of cross-price elasticities between any pair of the four products are about 0.7.

Another set of important factors affecting sales of antiulcer drugs concerns product-quality attributes. At the industry level, the evidence suggests that the size of the market was enlarged considerably when the FDA granted approval for the GERD indication—a condition that occurs in a relatively large population. At the market-share level, we find that when a product had a GERD-approval advantage relative to other products, its market share increased. Thus another reason why Zantac fared so well in the marketplace is that for quite some time it was the only product that had received FDA approval for the treatment of GERD. Another variable affecting market share significantly is the number of adverse interactions with other drugs reported to the FDA. On this account Tagamet fared relatively badly (by 1993, Tagamet had twelve drug interactions, Zantac and Axid had only one, and Pepcid had none). Thus Zantac also enjoyed advantages from this product-quality characteristic. An unexpected result we obtained, however, was that dosing frequency did not appear to affect market shares in a statistically significant manner.

Finally, we found that, as in many other markets, order-of-entry effects are very substantial. In particular, holding constant price, marketing efforts, and product quality relative to the nth product, the $(n + 1)$th entrant can expect about forty percent lower sales.

The results of this paper are of considerable interest in the current health-care reform debate. Critics of the pharmaceutical industry have argued that much detailing is merely aimed at market share and is socially wasteful. Some have suggested placing ceilings on the marketing activities of pharmaceutical firms, but our findings demonstrate that this could have negative social welfare impacts. The findings in this paper suggest that marketing efforts also play a very important role in the diffusion of information to physicians, although the degree to which this is true probably declines somewhat as the number of products in a market increases. Moreover, our results suggest that in order to overcome pioneer-product advantages, later entrants have found it necessary to advertise more intensively. An implication of these results is that if all pharmaceutical firms were constrained in their marketing activities, it is possible that the benefits would accrue primarily to the pioneer firms, at the expense of later entrants who would be prevented from trying to overcome pioneer-product advantages. Thus, such a policy could have anticompetitive impacts, although it would be consistent with a patent system that rewards innovation.

The research reported in this paper should be extended in a number of ways. First, although the industry and market-share equations are plausible and provide important initial evidence on the roles of marketing, price, and product-quality competition in the antiulcer market, the underlying models could be modified in a number of useful ways. The most obvious extension is to reformulate the models within an explicitly dynamic diffusion framework, such as those involving the Gompertz, logistic, or other more general diffusion-curve formulations. In such a framework, marketing and pricing policies might not only affect the long-run or equilibrium level of demand, but they might also affect the speed at which a long-run equilibrium level is approached.

As second useful extension would involve incorporating data on direct-to-consumer marketing. In 1988 SmithKline experimented with a "Tommy Tummy" television advertising campaign that was aimed directly at consumers but did not mention Tagamet by name. More recently, Glaxo has advertised in magazines and on television, suggesting that patients with heartburn and acid discomfort should see their physicians. These ads are sponsored by the Glaxo Research Institute and, consistent with FDA regulations on direct-to-consumer advertising, do not mention the Zantac product by name unless the requisite warning and other product information is also fully disclosed. Since these advertisements typically do not mention products' names, their impact is more likely to be on industry demand than on market share. Moreover, direct-to-consumer advertising may change the physician-patient information-sharing relationship, and therefore could modify the diffusion process. It would be useful to examine whether such effects have actually occurred, and by extension, how effective is direct-to-consumer marketing in the antiulcer marketplace.

Third, and perhaps most importantly, the findings of this paper suggest interesting topics in the theory of industrial organization. What is the optimal marketing strategy for firms when there are spillovers and marketing activities have long-lived impacts? What is the correspondingly optimal pricing behavior? How does this optimal behavior vary with market structure? How is the optimal behavior affected by federal tax provisions that allow the expensing (rather than amortizing) of long-lived marketing investments? What are the implications for social welfare?

Obviously, much remains to be done. We believe we have demonstrated quite clearly that marketing efforts are very important in understanding the diffusion and economic success of new products. Product quality and pricing behavior have also been shown to play important roles in the diffusion process. We hope the results of this paper contribute to this and other related research projects that enrich our understanding of the economics of new products.

Appendix
Data Sources from IMS America

We hope that this discussion will serve as a useful reference for economists who will be using IMS sales data on pharmaceuticals in the future, as there are a number of important issues and quirks to the data which are not well documented in IMS literature.

U.S. Drugstore Audit and U.S. Hospital Audit

A panel of pharmaceutical wholesalers reports to IMS each month on the sales of each presentational form (unit-dose syringes, bottles of 100 tablets, etc.) of each drug product (Tagamet, Zantac, etc.) to drugstores and hospitals in the United States. From the sales reports they obtain in this audit, IMS computes national projections of the number of units and the dollars of revenue of each presentational form of each product sold each month in the United States, separately for drugstores and for hospitals. In recent years, the panel has grown to encompass nearly the entire universe of pharmaceutical wholesalers, according to IMS, making the audit nearly a full census and the projections therefore quite accurate.

One interesting feature of all of the IMS data used in this study is that although IMS has been collecting such data for decades, the company keeps computer records of only the immediate past six years, on a rolling basis. In order to have the opportunity to study the antiulcer market since its very inception, which dates back over fifteen years, we chose to type in numbers from archived monthly IMS publications. The sales data from January 1986 through December 1991 come directly from IMS computer records, but all other IMS data used in this study were retyped.

Because the sales data contained so many different numbers (quantities and revenues each month for each presentational form of each drug, for a total of over 5,200 retyped numbers in the fifteen-year sample, above and beyond the 8,000 numbers provided by IMS in computer format), and because the original copies of the published data were often very difficult to read (often the numbers were available only on poor-quality microfilm, where a 3 was indistinguishable from an 8), we deemed the possibility for error to be very high. We therefore chose to invest several months in ensuring the integrity of the retyped data by carefully checking it for typographical errors. It turns out that there is a reasonable degree of variation from month to month in the sales quantities and revenues for each individual drug presentation (variation often on the order of 10 percent or more), but the prices of the drug presentations (IMS-reported revenues divided by IMS-reported units) are relatively stable. Therefore, our method of error correction was to sort the data by presentational form of each drug and then print separate graphs of the drugstore and hospital prices of each presentation as a function of time. We were easily able to spot potential typographical errors as outliers on these graphs, at which point we were able to correct the errors by checking them against copies of the original published data. (Unfortunately, we had to make more than one trip back to Philadelphia in order to obtain copies of data pages which were missing from our collection! It was easy to lose a page, or miss it in the first place, because our data were obtained from dozens of three-inch-thick monthly volumes of printed data, or their microfilm equivalents, in which the data of interest were contained on just a page or three in the middle of each hefty tome.) In all, we corrected a few dozen serious errors on the approximately one hundred graphs printed, but as a result we are now quite confident of the reliability of the data, to the extent that they accurately match the data collected by IMS.

Nevertheless, additional manipulations remained to be performed on this data set in order to put it into a form that would be useful for this study. First, as noted earlier, there were multiple presentational forms of each drug sold. To obtain a single number describing the quantity of each brand of drug (e.g., Tagamet) sold in a given month, we summed the total number of milligrams of the chemical sold that month. For example, if in August 1979 SmithKline sold 6,200 bottles of 100 Tagamet 300 mg tablets and 1,600 packages of 10 unit-dose containers of 10 ml of Tagamet syrup at 5 mg/ml concentration, then we would compute the total number of milligrams of Tagamet sold that month as

$$(6,200)(100)(300 \text{ mg}) + (1,600)(10)(10 \text{ ml})(5 \text{ mg/ml}) = 186,800,000 \text{ mg}.$$

An alternative approach to constructing a single monthly-sales series for each drug, and one which a number of other studies have adopted, would be merely to proxy a drug's total sales (units and revenues) by the sales of a single leading presentation. The advantage of this alternative approach is its computational simplicity; by contrast, our method required dozens of additional hours of data manipulation. However, there is a serious disadvantage to the simpler approach, especially in this ulcer market, which is that the leading presentation changes over time. For example, see figure 7A.1, which displays the sales of Tagamet over time, broken down by its four major product forms (note that even this is a simplification of the full sales data set, as for example, the portion of the graph corresponding to Tagamet 800 mg tablets represents a sum of two different presentational forms: bottles of 30 tablets and unit-dose packages of 100 tablets). From this graph, we see that although originally Tagamet was sold only in the 300 mg form, by 1992 the 400 mg form had become the leading form, considerably overtaking the 300 mg sales. Other drugs in the sample present similar problems, having more than one presentation which hold significant shares of the drug's total sales.

Also, we chose to include only those presentational forms which were intended to be taken orally by patients: tablets, capsules, and oral liquids. Excluded were those forms packaged in vials, minibags, syringes, and so forth, for injection or intravenous administration. One reason for this decision is that

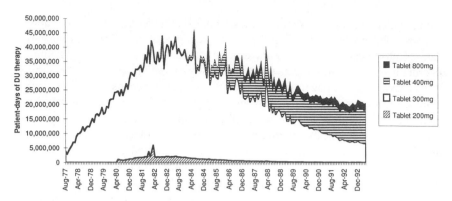

Fig. 7A.1   Tagamet drugstore sales

we intended to concentrate our study mainly on the drugstore market, where the bulk of the antiulcer sales occur and where detailing to physicians is most salient. By contrast, the non-oral preparations are developed mainly for hospitals, although some non-oral sales also show up in the drugstore market, presumably for patients either in nursing homes or under hospice care. (For the twelve-month period ending in May 1993, drugstore sales revenues for non-oral presentations of H_2-antagonists were less than one-thousandth of the values of revenues for oral presentations. Even in the hospital market, non-oral presentations brought in less than half as much revenue as the oral presentations during that time period.) A second, very substantive reason for including only the oral preparations is that we learned, from conversations with doctors and pharmaceutical marketing professionals, that the non-oral preparations are generally used for very different purposes: instead of healing painful ulcers in otherwise healthy people, as the tablets and capsules are intended to do, the intravenous administration of antiulcer medication is used mainly for the prevention of ulcers in emergency-room patients at risk for ulcers due to the increased acid secretion brought on by trauma, for example, and in patients who are at risk for ulcers due to regimens of large doses of nonsteroidal painkillers. Antiulcer medication may also be injected as part of a complete anesthesiology for surgery. These uses require very different numbers of milligrams of a drug than do the standard therapies (duodenal ulcers, gastric ulcers, duodenal ulcer maintenance, and GERD) that are usually administered orally, and the price per milligram of drug tends to be an order of magnitude higher for the intravenous preparations (this is likely a combination of two effects: price discrimination and the more complicated packaging and storage requirements of the intravenous preparations). So rather than confound the two types of uses, we have chosen to define our market of interest to be the orally administered antiulcer drugs.

Next, we had to find a way to make the quantity units comparable across drugs. Milligrams were not an appropriate unit for comparison, because, for example, treatment of an active duodenal ulcer with Tagamet requires 800 mg of drug to be ingested per day, but an equivalent therapy with Pepcid requires only 40 mg of drug. Each drug is a different chemical entity, with a different molecular weight, a different rate of absorption, and a different rate of binding to bioactive sites in the body, which combine to cause wide variations in the amount of each drug that must be consumed to achieve the same desired effect. Because marginal manufacturing costs in the pharmaceutical industry are generally much lower than prices, we have chosen to concentrate on the demand side of the market in our choice of quantity units: patient-days of therapy. (This may have some concordance with the producer side as well, for although the different chemicals may not have the exact same marginal costs of synthesis, it is at least plausible to assume that packaging the drug into tablets, and the tablets into bottles, should have approximately the same marginal cost per tablet, regardless of the chemical being so packaged.) This choice of quantity units considers 800 mg of Tagamet to be the same amount of drug as 40 mg of Pepcid, for purposes of computing sales levels and market shares, since these quantities are therapeutically equivalent.

The quantity of patient-days of therapy of a drug sold in a given month is equal to the total number of milligrams sold divided by the number of milligrams per day of active duodenal ulcer therapy for that particular drug (in the case of Cytotec, which is not indicated for active duodenal ulcer therapy, we instead used the daily recommended dosage for NSAID-induced ulcer prevention). Thus, continuing our earlier example of Tagamet, we would find that in our hypothetical month, there were sold

$$(186,800,000 \text{ mg})/(800 \text{ mg/day}) = 233,500 \text{ patient-days of therapy.}$$

The numbers of milligrams per day of therapy used for our quantity conversions are shown in table 7A.1.

Defining our quantity unit to be the total number of milligrams divided by the standard dosage in milligrams per day is, unfortunately, not without problems. First, the same drug may be used for slightly different therapies, and it may be taken in different dosages for the different purposes. For example,

Table 7A.1   **Number of Milligrams per Day of Therapy Used for Quantity Conversions**

Drug	Milligrams per Day of Therapy
Tagamet	800
Zantac	300
Pepcid	40
Axid	300
Prilosec	20
Carafate	400
Cytotec	0.2

Zantac may be prescribed at a dosage of 300 mg per day (either 300 mg once daily or 150 mg twice daily) for active duodenal ulcer, gastric ulcer, or GERD therapies, but its recommended dosage for duodenal maintenance therapy is only 150 mg per day, half of that required for the other therapies. Each of the H_2-antagonists has a similar prescribing regimen for those four different indications. Therefore, our quantity measures are not literally the number of patient-days of therapy being consumed, but rather the number of patient-days of therapy which would be consumed if all of the sales were for treatment of active duodenal ulcers. Second, while we have assumed that the milligram dosage required for duodenal ulcer therapy remained constant over time, this was not the case for Tagamet. At the time of its introduction in 1977, the recommended dosage for duodenal ulcer therapy was 1,200 mg per day (300 mg four times daily), but subsequent experimentation showed that lower doses could be just as effective for ulcer healing, and by 1988 the recommended dosage was only 800 mg per day (either 800 mg once daily or 400 mg twice daily). We have taken the approach that a milligram of Tagamet in 1977 is the same quantity as a milligram of Tagamet in 1990, despite the fact that people may have been consuming fewer milligrams on average in the later years for the same length of treatment. Since we have no way of knowing how many duodenal ulcer patients were taking 1,200 mg of Tagamet rather than 800 mg at any point in time (the choice between the two depended upon the vagaries of individual doctors' prescribing habits), we feel that we have chosen the most appropriate way to proceed.

A final modification which needed to be made to the sales data concerns the fact that the data collection from pharmaceutical warehouse invoices has, at different times during the sample, been rather lumpy. This problem introduces seasonal noise into the data, which can be eliminated by rescaling the sales and revenue figures. For purposes of rescaling, there are three distinct periods in our sample. Until December 1980, the sales audit was actually conducted at a sample of pharmacies rather than at warehouses, and there was no lumpiness to the data, so no rescaling was required. From January 1981 to December 1989, the data were apparently (according to the best information we could obtain from IMS, whose data specialists are not accustomed to answering questions about historical data) reported from warehouses on the basis of full weeks, so some months could contain four weeks of data, while others contained five. This causes large month-to-month variations in the sales data, which is obviously inappropriate for a detailed monthly analysis of the competitive effects of price and advertising on sales. A lengthy investigation has failed to reveal an appropriate way to rescale the data to correct for these fluctuations. (Based on conversations with IMS representatives, we tried several possibilities, such as rescaling the data by the number of Wednesdays in each month, but none turned out to be correct.) Thus our best approximation to the truth is that the sales data for this period of time contain a component of stochastic measurement error. In the third period of the sample, from January

1990 to the present, the number of reporting weeks per month were standard-ized so that the first four weeks of the year were designated as January, the next four weeks as February, the next five weeks as March, and so on in a 4-4-5 pattern for each quarter. (The single exception is December 1991, which for accounting purposes—there are not exactly fifty-two weeks in each year—was designated as a month of six weeks rather than of five). To rescale the data for our purposes, we divided the IMS sales figures in each month from January 1990 to the end of the sample by the number of reporting weeks in that month, and then multiplied by 4.33 in order to retain the same normalization of physi-cal units as in the original IMS data.

Finally, in order to transform the nominal prices from the IMS data into real prices, we deflated by the CPI (1982–84 base years).

National Detailing Audit

The National Detailing Audit (which as of 1993 has been subsumed by the Office Contact Report of IMS's Integrated Promotional Services) is a service that collects data from a nationwide panel of doctors about the visits which have been paid to them by pharmaceutical sales representatives. The doctors participating in the panel keep a log of the number of minutes they spend talk-ing to detailers on each detail visit. If the detailer talks to the doctor about more than one product (for example, a Lilly detailer might discuss both Axid, an ulcer drug, and Ceclor, an antibiotic, with a family doctor), the physician makes an estimate of how many minutes were devoted to each product. From this panel, IMS then reports nationally projected estimates of the number of details and the number of minutes spent detailing each product, each month.

The detailing data series, unlike the sales data series, consist of only one observation per month, since detailing is performed at the level of the drug brand, rather than at the level of the presentational form. This fact made typo-graphical errors a much smaller problem than they were in the sales data, de-spite the fact that we had to enter manually the detailing data for every month in the more than fifteen years of our sample. We collected monthly data on details and minutes for our seven drugs of interest, as well as for the total number of details and minutes done by each of the manufacturers producing these drugs (across all of their products) and for the total number of details and minutes in the entire U.S. pharmaceutical industry. These last two types of data are intended to be used as instruments for brand detailing, which is a potentially endogenous variable.

Beyond typographical errors, there were still some corrections to be made. In 1986, IMS expanded its panel of doctors from fourteen hundred physicians reporting two weeks of every month to twenty-eight hundred physicians re-porting full months. Concurrently, they changed their projection methodology, and it turns out that a scaling factor of 0.74 must be applied to the data for all months prior to January 1986 in order to make them comparable to the data for January 1986 through December 1992. (In suggesting this scaling factor,

IMS cautions that it is much more confident in its ability to measure the relative shares of detailing by different products than in its ability to measure absolute levels. Nevertheless, we assume that after applying the recommended transformations, we can make reasonably accurate comparisons of the levels of detailing in different periods.)

A second change occurred in January 1993, when IMS significantly increased the breadth of coverage of detailing data. Under the newly created Integrated Promotional Services, there exists a wide variety of reports, including the Office Contact Report, which is the most directly related to the now-defunct National Detailing Audit. In the Office Contact Report, there are now reported many more *types* of details, including sample drops, educational visits, service visits, and telephone calls, than were reported before, so the data on details and minutes are not easily comparable.

We were able to construct a measure of the number of details for 1993 which would be comparable to the pre-1993 years by looking at the new breakdown of details into the various new IMS categories, and counting as details only those visits which were either "full discussion" details or "brief mention" details, which is what IMS considers to be the "traditional" details that doctors were intended to include in their reports for the National Detailing Audit prior to 1993. Although similarly disaggregated information on *minutes* of detailing are not readily available from IMS's printed reports, we were able to match up minutes of detailing from 1993 on with the pre-1993 data on minutes before 1993 by special arrangement with IMS, who provided us with computer-generated reports from their database on the number of minutes of detailing in 1993 devoted to full discussions and brief mentions.

National Journal Audit

In this audit, IMS performs a complete census of advertising in medical journals. They subscribe to every known medical journal and examine every advertisement in every issue of each journal. They note the number of whole and partial pages, the number of colors used in printing the ads, the location of the advertisement in the journal (e.g., if it was found at the very front or printed on the back cover, in either case getting more exposure than an ad buried in the middle of the publication), and other attributes that affect the cost of placing an advertisement. Then, using standard rate sheets, they compute the cost of each of the advertisements placed. Reported in the National Journal Audit monthly report are the total number of pages of advertising published for each product in that month (weighting all journals equally, regardless of circulation or professional influence), as well as the total estimated cost of all medical journal ads for that product.

We consider the cost figure to be the most accurate single measure of the amount of medical journal advertising done for a particular product, because (assuming that medical journal advertising is close to being a competitive industry) the prices of the ads reflect the reach of the advertisements, in terms of number of doctors reached, visual impact of the advertisement (through color, for example), and so forth. These cost figures are reported in nominal dollars, so to obtain a real measure of medical journal advertising effort, we deflate these series by the producer price index for "advertising in professional and institutional periodicals" (BLS product code 2721-415).

As with the detailing data, the series we collected from the National Journal Audit include monthly series for each drug product in our sample, as well as monthly series on total monthly advertising for each manufacturer producing one of the products in our sample on total monthly advertising by the pharmaceutical industry as a whole.

References

Berndt, Ernst R., and David O. Wood. 1979. Engineering and econometric interpretations of energy-capital complementarity. *American Economic Review* 69, no. 3 (June): 342–54.

Bond, Ronald S., and David F. Lean. 1977. *Sales, promotion and product differentiation in two prescription drug markets.* Staff report of the Bureau of Economics of the Federal Trade Commission. Washington, D.C. February.

Bresnahan, Timothy F., and Peter C. Reiss. 1990. Entry in monopoly markets. *Review of Economic Studies* 57 (October): 531–53.

Cearnal, Martin E. 1992. Medical marketing communications today: Use and abuse. In *Promotion of pharmaceuticals: Issues, trends, options,* ed. Dev S. Pathak, Alan Escovitz, and Suzan Kucukaslan, 23–32. Binghamton, N.Y.: Haworth Press.

Cocks, Douglas L. 1975. Product innovation and the dynamic elements of competition in the ethical pharmaceutical industry. In *Drug development and marketing,* ed. Robert B. Helms. Washington, D.C.: American Enterprise Institute.

Cocks, Douglas L., and John R. Virts. 1974. Pricing behavior of the ethical pharmaceutical industry. *Journal of Business* 47 (July): 349–62.

Diewert, W. Erwin. 1981. The economic theory of index numbers: A survey. In *Essays in the theory and measurement of consumer behavior in honor of Sir Richard Stone,* ed. Angus Deaton, 163–208. Cambridge: Cambridge University Press.

———. 1992. Fisher Ideal output, input, and productivity indexes revisited. *Journal of Productivity Analysis* 3:211–48.

Dorfman, Robert, and Peter O. Steiner. 1954. Optimal advertising and optimal quality. *American Economic Review* 44, no. 5 (December): 826–36.

Fine, Steven N., Andrew J. Dannenberg, and David Zakim. 1988. The impact of medical therapy on peptic ulcer disease. In *Peptic ulcer disease and other acid-related disorders,* ed. David Zakim and Andrew J. Dannenberg, 1–13. New York: Academic Research Associates.

Freudenheim, Milt. 1993. A drug promotion based on price breaks the prescription tradition. *New York Times,* 9 November, D2, col. 1.

Golder, Peter N., and Gerard J. Tellis. 1992. Do pioneers really have long-term advantages? A historical analysis. Report no. 92-124. Cambridge, Mass.: Marketing Science Institute. September.

Griliches, Zvi, and Frank Lichtenberg. 1984. R&D and productivity growth at the industry level: Is there still a relationship? In *R&D, patents, and productivity,* ed. Zvi Griliches, 465–502. Chicago: University of Chicago Press.

Hurwitz, Mark A., and Richard E. Caves. 1988. Persuasion or information? Promotion and the shares of brand name and generic pharmaceuticals. *Journal of Law and Economics* 31 (October): 299–320.

Kalyanaram, Gurumurthy, and Glen L. Urban. 1992. Dynamic effects of the order of entry on market share, trial penetration, and repeat purchases for frequently purchased consumer goods. *Marketing Science* 11, no. 3 (summer): 235–50.

Leffler, Keith B. 1981. Persuasion or information? The economics of prescription drug advertising. *Journal of Law and Economics* 24 (April): 45–74.

Lucking-Reiley, David H., Jr. 1996. The effects of market structure on firm advertising behavior. Department of Economics, Massachusetts Institute of Technology. Unpublished, April.

Lynn, Matthew. 1991. *The billion dollar battle: Merck v. Glaxo.* London: Mandarin.

McKenzie, Constance A., Ellen S. Underwood, Kim Poinsett-Holmes, and Lynn Graham. 1990. Peptic ulcer disease: Therapeutic options. *U.S. Pharmacist* 15 (10): 53–64.

One hundred powerhouse drugs. 1993. Special supplement, *MedAdNews* 12, no. 6, May.

Perloff, Jeff, and Valerie Y. Suslow. 1994. Higher prices from entry: Pricing of brand-name drugs. School of Business Administration, University of Michigan, Ann Arbor. Unpublished.

Reekie, W. D. 1978. Price and quality competition in the United States drug industry. *Journal of Industrial Economics* 26 (March): 223–37.

Robinson, William T. 1988. Sources of market pioneer advantages: The case of industrial goods industries. *Journal of Marketing Research* 25 (February): 87–94.

Robinson, William T., and Claes Fornell. 1985. The sources of market pioneer advantages in consumer goods industries. *Journal of Marketing Research* 22, no. 2 (August): 297–304.

Robinson, William T., Gurumurthy Kalyanaram, and Glen L. Urban. 1994. First mover advantages for pioneering new products: A survey of empirical evidence. *Review of Industrial Organization* 9 (1): 1–23.

Samuelson, William, and Richard Zeckhauser. 1988. Status quo bias in decision making. *Journal of Risk and Uncertainty* 1 (March): 349–65.

Schmalensee, Richard L. 1972. *The economics of advertising.* Amsterdam: North-Holland.

———. 1982. Product differentiation advantages of pioneering brands. *American Economic Review* 27:349–65.

Scouler, Bonnie Jean. 1993. A segmentation analysis of the ulcer drug market. S.M. Thesis, Alfred P. Sloan School of Management, Massachusetts Institute of Technology. May.

Urban, Glen L., Theresa Carter, Steve Gaskin, and Zofia Mucha. 1986. Market share rewards to pioneering brands: An empirical analysis and strategic implications. *Management Science* 32 (June): 645–59.

Comment   Valerie Y. Suslow

The story of the antiulcer market, although rich with complications, is primarily a tale of an established monopolist being overthrown by a new entrant.

Valerie Y. Suslow is associate professor of business economics and public policy at the University of Michigan Business School and a faculty research fellow of the National Bureau of Economic Research.

Zantac, the entrant, brought new growth to the market, due to its lower dosage frequency and friendlier side-effect profile, but it also clearly stole customers from the incumbent, Tagamet, with its aggressive marketing campaign. Thus, the antiulcer drug market is a fascinating arena within which to study, as Berndt, Bui, Lucking-Reiley, and Urban do so well in their paper, the effects of marketing on the growth of industry sales and individual market shares.

Theoretically, there are several ways that oligopolistic rivalry could manifest itself in pharmaceutical markets. Naturally, there could be intense price competition. As the authors point out, Zantac's price premium over Tagamet decreased from 56 percent to 25 percent over their sample period. Still, the evidence presented does not point to price as the primary competitive tool. The second potential form of rivalry is the race to win FDA approval for various treatments (the most important in this market being GERD). The third form that competition could take is a battle to offer the most attractive package of nonprice attributes, such as dosage frequency and side-effect profile, among others. The fourth form is advertising, both persuasive and informative.

SmithKline did, in fact, move to match Zantac's more favorable dosing frequency by eventually coming out with a twice-a-day and then a once-a-day version of Tagamet. There was, however, little that they could do to alter the side-effect profile of Tagamet, the aspect of Tagamet perceived by doctors to be its weakest in head-to-head competition with Zantac. SmithKline's strongest weapon was to match Glaxo's aggressive advertising campaign with its own, making counterclaims about the side-effect profile and general effectiveness of Tagamet. Advertising is thus an important, if not the most important, strategic variable in this market.

In this paper, the authors analyze the factors affecting market shares and present evidence on the strength of first-mover advantages in this industry. However, the notable empirical contribution of the paper is their effort to separate empirically the strength of industry-expanding advertising from rivalrous advertising, and further, to investigate whether the strength of these effects varies with changes in market structure. I will therefore focus my comments on their contribution to this latter line of research.

Analysis of Industry Demand

The authors begin with an analysis of the growth of industry sales and specify the "effective industry-marketing stock" (M_t) as

$$M_t = (1 - \delta)M_{t-1} + m_t = \sum_{\tau=1}^{t}(1 - \delta)^{t-\tau}m_{\tau}.$$

The assumption, long standard in advertising literature, is that advertising is long-lived and that the stock of advertising, rather than the monthly flow, is the primary force driving industry sales.

The next step, however, is not standard. The authors go on to specify the effective industry stock of advertising as a weighted sum of the cumulative marketing effort, where the weights reflect changes in market structure as entry occurs:

$$\overline{M}_t = \mu_1 M_{1,t} + \mu_2 M_{2,t} + \mu_3 M_{3,t} + \ldots + \mu_k M_{k,t}.$$

That is, marketing efforts are posited to have a differential effect on industry sales as the market structure changes. The specific hypothesis to be tested is that $\mu_2 > \mu_3 > \ldots > \mu_k$, where μ_1 has been normalized to one. This hypothesis is based on the premise that industry efforts directed at market expansion will decline as the number of products in the industry increases. In other words, with an increasing number of products, ceteris paribus, a decreasing fraction of each advertising dollar will have a market-expanding impact (e.g., total advertising dollars expended in a duopoly market will have a smaller impact on industry demand than the same advertising dollars spent in a monopoly). The authors specify their hypotheses in terms of the number of products on the market, which is equal to the number of firms in this case. Presumably, in the general case, both the number of firms and the number of brands in existence will affect the outcome.

The next step is to specify the industry sales regression, which is a function of a real price index, the stock of detailing minutes, the stock of pages of advertising in medical journals, and a dummy variable which indicates FDA approval for GERD. Both detailing stock and journal pages stock are functions of the μ's. The μ parameters are constrained to be the same across detailing and journal advertising, but they are permitted to differ as the number of products in the industry grows.

For the Tagamet-Zantac model, using NL-2SLS, δ is estimated as near zero. Note that, econometrically, the spike in Zantac detailing in 1983 may be the driving force behind the δ estimate of zero. However, the zero depreciation rate may, in fact, be an accurate reflection of the patterns of depreciation in the stock of knowledge in prescription drug markets. There is evidence in the literature that doctors tend to stay with what they know, that is, the drugs that they became familiar with during their medical residency. Leffler (1981) discusses this issue in the context of what he calls uninformative reminder ads. He finds that "advertisers tend to focus their advertisements on the physician age group that was in medical school when the product was introduced" (63).

Scouler (1993) also presents survey evidence that there is a high retention rate of knowledge created by advertising and physician education. Table 7C.1 shows how doctors' perceptions of a drug might differ from the medical "facts" as published in the *Physicians' Desk Reference* (PDR) and also how these perceptions tend to persist through time. Tagamet is clearly perceived as an inferior product compared to Zantac for "adverse reactions" and "heal rate," despite a reasonably close ranking between the two drugs in the PDR. In fact, table 7C.1 shows that the PDR actually ranks Tagamet as superior in terms of adverse reactions. If one (reasonably) assumes that these perceptions of supe-

Table 7C.1   **Physicians' Ranking of Tagamet and Zantac among Eight Antiulcer Drugs**

	Adverse Reactions	Drug Interactions	Heal Rate
Tagamet			
Physicians	6	8	5
PDR	3	7	3
Zantac			
Physicians	2	4	2
PDR	5	3.5	4

Source: Excerpted from table 4.14 of Scouler (1993, 68–70).

Note: The eight drugs included in the ranking are Reglan, Tagamet, Carafate, Axid, Zantac, Pepcid, Cytotec, and Prilosec.

rior safety were formed as a result of Zantac's initial marketing campaign, then physicians' perceptions are clearly difficult to sway.

The Tagamet-Zantac model's estimate for the value of μ_2 (0.89) implies that, relative to a monopoly, marketing stocks are roughly 90 percent as effective in changing industry sales when they occur in a duopoly. There seems, then, to be little change in the effectiveness of market-enhancing advertising when the market becomes a duopoly. One wonders whether the authors were expecting a bigger drop in advertising effectiveness when moving from one to two firms. In future research, it would be interesting to learn whether this is a common result across other pharmaceutical markets.

For the four-product model, the depreciation rate is again near zero, with $\mu_2 = 0.6$, $\mu_3 = 0.8$, and $\mu_4 = 0.5$. This is not quite the monotonic pattern that the authors expected. One plausible explanation for this pattern is that the dynamics of competition are potentially very different in an unbalanced three-firm industry from that in a balanced (equal market share) four-firm industry. For example, when the third drug, Axid, came onto the market, there was a highly skewed distribution of firm sizes: SmithKline and Glaxo may have been relatively unconcerned about competition from Axid. Similarly, when the number of firms increases from three to four, the nature of competition can change in a variety of ways. In the antiulcer market, there might not have been a four-firm rivalry, but rather one battle between firms one and two and another battle between firms three and four. It is not at all clear that we can assume the relationship among the μ's to be monotonically declining without knowing more about the structural interpretation of the estimates.

Sutton (1991) also discusses in detail the relationship between setup costs, advertising outlays, and the equilibrium structure of the industry. He maintains that there is an initial outlay to create a brand image and then a defensive flow of advertising to maintain that image. Several of the examples he presents in the first few chapters of his book show that the relationship between market size and concentration (in the presence of advertising) is nonmonotonic. While this is not the same as the relationship studied by Berndt et al., it does have implications for the interpretation of their empirical results, given that they measure market structure by the number of firms in the industry. Again, if concentration is not perfectly correlated with the number of firms or the size of the market, then it is hard to say what the relationship between the μ's should be.

The authors appropriately note that the model should be extended to incorporate a dynamic diffusion process. Advertising, for example, may have a smaller impact on industry sales as the number of products increases because the market is saturated with advertising messages. Or, the cost of advertising may rise over time as firms experiment with less-profitable ways of reaching physicians (such as periodicals with lower circulation levels or television advertisements that tell consumers to talk to their doctors).

Finally, there is a natural experiment looming on the horizon for testing developments in market-enhancing advertising for the antiulcer market. With the recent news over the last couple of years about the role of *Helicobacter pylori* bacteria in causing peptic ulcers, we should see an increase in market-enhancing advertising by the H_2-antagonist manufacturers. This highlights the more general point that the level of market-enhancing advertising, in addition to being a function of market structure within the H_2-antagonist industry, is also a function of the stock of advertising goodwill generated by competing classes of drugs (such as antacids, and, in the future, the treatment for *H. pylori*).

Analysis of Market Shares

The model used to analyze those factors effecting market shares is as follows (where all variables are defined relative to Tagamet):

Relative Share $= f(ENTRY, P, MIN, DGERD, FREQ, INT, AGE)$.

The main finding is that for the two-product submarket, the estimated depreciation rate of rivalrous advertising is again roughly zero. However, for the four-product market the authors estimate an annual depreciation rate of the relative detailing stock of approximately 38 percent (or 40 percent under 2SLS estimation). Also, as has been found in many other industries, the order-of-entry effects are large and significant.

There are several modifications that could be made to the specification of the effective marketing stock that would be interesting to pursue. First, the stock variable could be broadened to include significant positive and negative reports in scientific journals about a particular product. Second, it is worth noting that by the time Zantac was being sold in the United States, it had already achieved a thirty percent market share in the European market (Dell'Osso 1990). Thus, the stock of knowledge in the rivalrous context in the United States did not start from zero. Finally, there might be important spillovers within a firm if a firm's stock of advertising goodwill carries over from one product to another.

Connection with the Literature

Traditional literature on advertising has focused on the relationship between advertising and profits, concentration, and market share. Recent theoretical literature has moved on to examine the dynamic nature of equilibrium advertising strategies. One open empirical question which relates directly to the Berndt et al. paper is whether firms use open-loop strategies (where advertising is a function only of time), or closed-loop strategies (where advertising is a function of time and some measure of the state of the system, such as market share).

Roberts and Samuelson (1988) develop a general open-loop model and estimate it using data for U.S. cigarette producers. Their analysis of advertising includes the theoretical modeling and empirical estimation of both the rivalrous effects of advertising and the market-expanding effects. The durable nature of advertising implies that the current sales of a firm will depend on the past history of its own and its rivals' advertising expenditures. A firm with a "naive" strategy will choose the optimal level of goodwill stocks, given the stocks of other firms. A firm with a "sophisticated" strategy recognizes that its choice of advertising stock may alter its rivals' choices of future advertising stocks.

Their empirical model includes estimating equations for firm demand, production cost, and optimal advertising choice. Cost functions and factor demands are estimated first and are used to construct estimates of marginal cost. The market-share equations and first-order conditions for advertising choice are then estimated as a simultaneous system. As with Berndt et al., the depreciation rate (specified in Roberts and Samuelson as a retention rate) can differ across submarkets (in this case, the low-tar and high-tar cigarette markets) but does not differ across firms.

Roberts and Samuelson find that (1) advertising does not have a significant effect on firm's market shares; (2) a firm can increase its market share by increasing the number of brands it offers; (3) advertising by one firm may increase total market demand; (4) the estimated retention rates of advertising stock are approximately 0.8 for the low-tar market and 0.9 for the high-tar market; (5) naive behavior by firms can be rejected; and (6) strategies differ across firms within a market. Specifically, they find that for the two largest firms, demand is increased for each by the advertising of their rivals, while for the three smaller firms, the rivalrous aspects of rivals' advertising dominate and the demand for their product falls as rival-firm advertising is increased. Finally, in the same spirit as the Berndt et al. paper, they find that as the market increases in size, ceteris paribus, market-enhancing advertising diminishes in importance.

In a paper along similar lines, Gasmi, Laffont, and Vuong (1990) decompose advertising elasticities into the sum of what they call a "predatory elasticity" and a "global elasticity." Estimating their model on data from the soft drink industry, they find that both elasticities are significant (and with the expected signs, so that advertising by one firm decreases the market share of its rival but also has a positive effect on total market demand). As with the Roberts and Samuelson paper, the estimated elasticities vary across firms.

These results raise several interesting questions for research on the role of advertising within pharmaceutical markets. First, an intriguing conclusion of Roberts and Samuelson is that "[t]he market-share aspects of oligopolistic rivalry are better captured through changes in the number of brands sold by the firms, rather than by changes in advertising" (1988, 215). This makes one wonder whether a similar effect would be found in pharmaceutical markets, where the equivalent measure of the number of brands might be the number of presentations of a drug (e.g., 30 mg tablets, 100 mg tablets, and liquid forms). Second, the results suggest that *aggregate* rival advertising goodwill may belong in the market-share equation, rather than simply the stock relative to the first entrant, as in the Berndt et al. paper. Finally, it would be interesting to investigate whether firms in the antiulcer market chose different advertising strategies in the duodenal ulcer submarket versus the GERD submarket and, if so, whether those differences can be tied to a structural explanation.

Conclusion

This paper raises important industrial organization questions about advertising and market structure and, through meticulous handling of the data and careful econometric work, gives us insights into the important question of advertising and market structure. As the authors point out, there is room for future work. Some of the most interesting questions deal with differences across firms and the explicit modeling of the intertemporal dependence of a firm's choice of advertising strategy. Overall, there is much to be gained from a continued detailed study of advertising in this industry.

References

Dell'Osso, Filippo. 1990. When leaders become followers: The market for anti-ulcer drugs. Case series no. 12. London Business School. February.
Gasmi, F., J. J. Laffont, and Q. H. Vuong. 1990. A structural approach to empirical analysis of collusive behavior. *European Economic Review* 34:513–23.
Leffler, Keith B. 1981. Persuasion or information? The economics of prescription drug advertising. *Journal of Law and Economics* 24 (April): 45–74.
Roberts, Mark J., and Larry Samuelson. 1988. An empirical analysis of dynamic, non-price competition in an oligopolistic industry. *Rand Journal of Economics* 19 (2): 200–220.
Scouler, Bonnie Jean. 1993. A segmentation analysis of the ulcer drug market. S. M. thesis, Alfred P. Sloan of Management, Massachusetts Institute of Technology. May.
Sutton, John. 1991. *Sunk costs and market structure.* Cambridge: MIT Press.

8 From Superminis to Supercomputers: Estimating Surplus in the Computing Market

Shane M. Greenstein

8.1 Introduction

Innovation is rampant in adolescent industries. Old products die or evolve and new products replace them. Each new generation of products offers new features, extends the range of existing features, or lowers the cost of obtaining old features. Vendors imitate one another's products, so that what had been a novelty becomes a standard feature in all subsequent generations. Depending on the competitive environment and the type of innovation, prices may or may not reflect design changes.

The computer industry of the late 1960s and 1970s experienced remarkable growth and learning. At the start of the period several technological uncertainties defied easy resolution. Most knowledgeable observers could predict the direction of technical change, but not its rate. Vendors marketed hundreds of new product designs throughout the 1970s, and a fraction of those products became commercially successful. In time the industry took on a certain maturity and predictability. By the late 1970s, both buyers and sellers understood the technical trajectory of the industry's products. Even the least experienced

Shane Greenstein is professor of economics at the University of Illinois, Urbana/Champaign, and a faculty research fellow in the productivity program at the National Bureau of Economic Research.

Thanks to Steve Berry, Tim Bresnahan, Ken Brown, Erik Brynjolfsson, Ellen Dulberger, Bob Gordon, Zvi Griliches, Bronwyn Hall, Roger Koenker, Pablo Spiller, and Frank Wolak for useful discussion. Conference participants and individuals at the NBER, the University of Illinois, the University of West Virginia, and the Econometric Society meetings also provided many useful comments. Julie Lee and Jennifer Howitt entered data. Sandra Ospina and Ken Brown provided excellent research assistance. The author gratefully acknowledges funding from the Center for Economic Policy Research at Stanford University and from the Arnold O. Beckman Endowment at the University of Illinois. He also thanks the Charles Babbage Institute for their help with assembling the data used herein. The author is responsible for the errors contained in this paper.

users understood the capabilities and limits of the most popular commercial systems.

This paper attempts to measure the economic benefits that accrued to buyers from technological innovation in the computer industry. Its thesis is that many innovations that created economic value in this period are associated with extensions in computing capabilities, as distinguished from declines in prices which occurred at the same time as the extensions. This paper does not argue that price decreases were unimportant to buyers, but that price decreases alone tell an incomplete story about the welfare improvements realized by buyers.

This thesis goes to the heart of the relationship between rapid "constant-quality" price declines and the inferred improvement in economic welfare. The open issue concerns whether constant-quality price indexes provide the same information about the experience of a buyer who continues to buy computer systems with a similar set of characteristics as about that of a buyer who takes advantage of the availability of characteristics that did not previously exist. There are reasons to think constant-quality price indexes do not provide the same information on both types of buyers. The correspondence between constant-quality price indexes and economic welfare will be weaker when product characteristics cannot be repackaged (e.g., see Trajtenberg 1990). For example, one large computer system may provide more services to a buyer than two systems with exactly half the measurable characteristics. The appropriate welfare issue concerns buyer satisfaction with the extension of product space—that is, the extension of the range of quality available. If a set of adopters of new products could be accurately surveyed, how much would they be willing to pay not to give up the new capability associated with extensions of computers? A large body of work on cost-of-living indexes suggests that the "willingness to pay" for product extensions may have a nonlinear relationship to constant-quality price decreases.[1]

The problem considered here does not lend itself to a single statistical test or experiment. To reach a convincing conclusion, it would be better to see if a variety of information sources point in a similar direction. This paper addresses several related questions. First, what innovations in this period are associated with extensions of capabilities? Second, do buyers adopt products that embody extensions of capabilities? Third, how could a measurement framework represent that action? Are extensions embodied only in increases in capacity or other measurable features of a computer system?

Many of these questions require an explicit supply and demand framework.

---

1. It is well known that there are problems with using price indexes to measure the benefits associated with new goods. The same problems arise if extensions of product space (e.g., inventing a system with computing capacity that is twice as high as any previous system's) are associated with new services. In either event, there is an important issue regarding the procedures for incorporating new goods into price indexes. As Triplett (1989) argues, the central issue in developing appropriate procedures revolves around the goals of the index: whether it intends to reflect changes in the "costs of producing" or changes in the "costs of living." This paper focuses primarily on issues regarding the measurement of changes accruing to buyers.

The difficulty here concerns the fit of a framework to a differentiated-product industry; inevitably, some features of reality are sacrificed to a model. This paper modifies a Bresnahan-Berry model of vertical quality differentiation, which differentiates products along only one dimension, here, computing power.[2] While simple, this specification captures much of the difference in demand for systems with different computing capacities, that is, measurable changes in demand for systems with higher speed and more memory. The paper argues that changes in capacity provide information about the introduction of new capabilities and services. Thus, the model quantifies important extensions in product space over time and the contribution to surplus from these extensions. In addition, the model estimates the decline in the cost function of computer vendors over time, which serves a secondary goal, namely to estimate a fully specified model of the computing market in which changes to the costs of producing quality alters market outcomes. Finally, though the model predicts intersystem competitive outcomes with only limited success, it provides a rough measure of the importance of new-product entry for buyer's surplus.

8.2 Technological Changes in Computing, 1968–1981

This section briefly describes important features of technological change in the mainframe computing market from 1968 to 1981. During this period the industry witnessed a rapid decline in prices, a dramatic extension of capabilities, and a notable change in the quality of alternatives to mainframes. For some buyers the economic benefit associated with technological change in mainframes was declines in prices, for others it was extensions of capabilities. Each is discussed in turn.

Over the long run, mainframe products underwent a rapid decline in prices per measurable unit of computing, usually measured by central processing unit (CPU) speed and memory capacity. The important open debate concerns the association of dramatic change in price per computing unit with the introduction of particular products and other market events.[3] For example, there is no

---

2. All previous research investigates automobile-producer and -buyer behavior (Bresnahan 1981, 1987b; Feenstra and Levinsohn 1989; Berry, Levinsohn, and Pakes 1993). Previous use of these methods required a complete census of the price, quantity, and characteristics of every product in the market. The methods developed in this paper can be used when a complete census of product characteristics is not known, which suits data typically available to a computer-industry researcher.

3. Construction of constant-quality price indexes has received much attention because of its importance for gross national product (GNP) measurement. There is much disagreement about the proper methods to use and the proper data to employ to measure this phenomenon. See Gordon (1989, 1990); Dulberger (1989); Cole et al. (1986); Triplett (1986, 1989); Berndt and Griliches (1993); Berndt, Showalter, and Woolridge (1991); and Oliner (1993). Related research on the welfare benefits from technical change uses similar price indexes to recover surplus generated from declines in the price of aggregate computing capital. Sometimes this approach also requires measurement of willingness to pay for new capabilities, which is often difficult to obtain (e.g., see Bresnahan 1987b; Flamm 1987a, 1987b; Brynolfsson 1993).

agreement about the improvement over previous generations associated with the introduction of the IBM system 370. This disagreement is important for any calculation of economic welfare because the system 370 replaced the system 360, and each was the most popular system in the United States in its day. Second, and more generally, the prices of old and new generations of systems, which may be substitutes, do not follow a simple pattern. Some observers argue that "disequilibrium" influenced the pricing of mainframes, though there is much disagreement about its root causes (Fisher, McGowan, and Greenwood 1983; Dulberger 1989; Gordon 1989). This debate influences the interpretation of the technical improvements embodied in new and old models. Both issues are discussed below.

The industry also experienced extensions in capabilities in many dimensions. Some improvements are reflected in the easily measurable features of a system, particularly those extensions associated with increases in computing capacity. Larger computing memory and faster CPU speeds permitted users to address increasingly complex problems and to perform regularly tasks that could not previously be attempted, let alone accomplished. Scientists and engineers were the first to take advantage of faster computing speeds and larger memories. Internal and external storage capacity also expanded, and input/output speeds increased. These innovations made large databases easier to use and broadened their potential applicability. Hardware architecture and operating-system software underwent many refinements associated with multiuser systems, a development crucial to all timesharing applications and applications that require many users to perform quick queries of centralized databases. Service bureaus, insurance and banking users, and many large organizations employed these developments in new inventory and reservation systems. Later refinements required quick access to large databases in real time. These applications were diffused widely in the 1960s, and the refinements began to be diffused in the mid-1970s (Fisher, McGowan, and Greenwood 1983; Flamm 1987a, 1987b).

Other extensions were also very important but are not so easily associated with measurable features of a system. Solid-state circuitry, improved air-conditioning units, and more-compact designs also made systems more reliable and lowered servicing costs, which resulted in the expansion of computing into ever more essential enterprise functions. New and better programming languages also diffused across many systems. By the end of the 1970s a third-party software industry had begun to mushroom, further diffusing refined application software across many computing platforms. Other peripherals also improved, such as printers, terminals, and countless other minor components. The relevant point is that these innovations and many others were important to buyers but are not easy to measure.

As the computer industry matured, users came to expect change—that is, extensions of capabilities or entirely new products—and plan for it. Buyers modified the memory and speed of their CPUs but kept other durable investments in software or peripherals. Or buyers enhanced particular software programs or peripheral components, but not other parts of their systems. As buyers learned about their needs and discovered technological opportunities, as new products were introduced, and as old products became obsolete, buyers had to continually reevaluate their situations. A regular cycle began to emerge: peripheral and software upgrading induced bottlenecks in CPUs, which induced further CPU upgrading, which induced further peripheral and software enhancements. The introduction of timesharing and techniques for querying central databases further accelerated these regular cycles.

Three important points follow from this cycle: first, upgrading to a larger CPU capacity became associated with taking advantage of technical improvements in other parts of the system. Thus, the invention, and reduction in price, of large computing capacity enabled many users to take advantage of technical change in complementary components. For many buyers, demand for greater computing capacity reflected demand for complementary peripherals and software. Second, the extension of capabilities in peripheral components, software, and CPUs interacted with enhancements in other parts of the system. The economic value created by the extension of computing capacity, while obviously important, does not relate in any linear fashion to the decline in prices in constant-quality CPUs. Value creation must also relate to the prices and functions of other parts of the system.

Third, the rate of value creation to a buyer could be much different than the rate of price decline in computing capacity. It could be faster if declines in prices enabled a user to realize local economies of scale in the distribution of computing services and in the employment of computing capital investments. Localized economies of scale could produce the repackaging problem in CPU product characteristics, that is, buyers valued the increase in computing capacity embodied in CPUs. Since researchers of centralized management of computing facilities (e.g., Inmon 1985; Friedman and Cornford 1989) emphasize the replacement cycle, this factor was probably very important for many buyers. On the other hand, the rate of value creation to a buyer could be slower if the bottlenecks underlying the replacement cycle choked off the ability to realize much advance. Since researchers of centralized management of computing facilities also emphasize increasing buyer dissatisfaction with translating enterprise needs into feasible technical solutions, particularly by the early 1980s, many buyers may not have realize localized economies of scale.

Notable changes to nonmainframes partially determined the relative value buyers placed on the changes to large systems. If some buyers do not have a repackaging problem, declines in prices may simply induce purchases of cheaper computing power, but not necessarily purchases of bigger CPUs. That is, the choice between a large or a small CPU depends on the relative price per characteristic for small and large systems as each is introduced. This is important because there were many changes in these choices over the period. Few general-purpose computing substitutes for mainframes were available in 1968, but over the 1970s minicomputer hardware along with general-purpose software was developed, so that users could perform some small tasks that previously required mainframes. These minicomputers were especially attractive for a decentralized computing environment. By 1981 minicomputer vendors were also beginning to offer users viable growth paths for their systems if the users' needs outgrew large superminis.[4] In principle, buyers could (and many did) break up their computing needs into smaller units, taking advantage of decentralized management. Most importantly for empirical purposes, the costs and capabilities of smaller systems shifted over the period, and their purchase is outside the view provided by the data in this paper.

This brief history suggests that it may not make sense to conceive of technological change as equivalent to a simple fall in price levels. Price declines enabled many events that took place. Yet, important episodes of value creation were associated with specific inventions that extended buyer capabilities into new areas—for example, the invention of reliable real-time database querying or the invention of interruption-free multiuser computing. Value creation was not associated solely (or even primarily) with the decline in costs of the delivery of these services. The willingness to take advantage of new capabilities in any period became associated with a willingness to adopt computing capacity of higher and higher levels. The importance of the willingness to pay for new capabilities will ultimately be an empirical issue. Is there evidence of much adoption of systems with increases in capabilities?

8.3   The Model

A supply-side model and a demand-side model constitute this paper's measurement framework. The model focuses attention on the demand for computing capacity. The model is flexible enough to allow underlying demand preferences to vary over difference capacities and sizes and to change over time. It also permits the costs of supplying computing capacity to decline over time. Finally, it provides a rough test of whether vendors compete solely in measurable features of computing capacity.

8.3.1   Demand-Side Considerations

Consider a market in a given year. As in Bresnahan's (1981, 1987a) model of the automobile market, this study makes five assumptions: (1) All users evaluate all mainframe computers in terms of the same (vertical) index of quality, that is, computing power. (2) Users differ in their willingness to pay for computing power. (3) There are many "uses" for computer systems, each requiring one computer system. (4) Each potential user compares N possible

---

4. Note that personal computers (PCs) were only beginning to diffuse by 1981 and were largely employed as sophisticated terminals. PCs were not viewed as substitutes for mainframes except for very small problems.

different models. The net benefit from each model j in use i is $U_{ij} = e_i d_j - P_j$. Here, e is the marginal utility of quality, which varies across users i, d is quality, and p is the price of the product. (5) There is a composite good of "lower" quality, which is not part of the focus product group but is a potential option for purchase by users. This will be good zero, the "outside good." It sells for price P_0 and has quality d_0. In this study, the outside good is equivalent to a small IBM mainframe or general-purpose superminicomputer. Its price and quality change each year.

Equilibrium in the market concerns the demand for computing power. The system chosen satisfies $U_{ij} > U_{ik}$ for all j, $k \neq j$. Thus, an optimal choice implies that $e_i > b_{jk} = (P_j - P_k)/(d_j - d_k)$ for all j, $k \neq j$. In equilibrium, users will find that they can rank systems (see Bresnahan 1981 for elaboration) according to their computing power. All j models are ranked according to d_j or P_j; either ranking is equivalent in equilibrium.[5] Some systems will provide considerable computing power but will be expensive, while others will provide little computing power but will be inexpensive. The data in this study appear consistent with this structural assumption for two reasons: (1) a spread exists between the capabilities (and prices) of the least and most powerful mainframes, and (2) most measures of computing performance and prices are highly correlated.

Let the willingness to pay for computing power, e_i, be distributed according to some function $F(z)$. This function represents the cumulative distribution of purchasers with a marginal utility of purchase less that z. Let S_j measure the market share of product j. Model $j = N$ is the highest quality available, and b_j measures a choice between j and $j - 1$. This implies $b_j = F^{-1}[1 - (\sum_{k=j}^{N} S_k)]$, $j = 1, \ldots, N$, where $S_j = Q_j/M$, Q_j is the quantity sold of product j, and M is the total potential size of the number of uses. If M is a parameter to be estimated and Q is data, then by design $0 < \sum_{j=1}^{N} S_j \leq 1$, so $M > \sum_{j=1}^{N} Q_j$, since the outside good is not observed. That is, estimates of M, the total size of the market, must exceed the total number of observed purchases.[6] As in Bresnahan (1981, 1987a), this paper also employs a uniform distribution, $b_j = [1 - (\sum_{k=j}^{N} S_k)]$. Thus, estimating the density is essentially the same as estimating M.[7] This is illustrated in figure 8.1. The above implies a relationship

---

5. In this model $d_j > d_{j-1}$ implies $P_j > P_{j-1}$ for all observed j systems, since a system violating this inequality would not be chosen at all. Thus, prices must rise faster than quality as quality improves. Increasing the marginal costs of quality can yield this outcome. See Bresnahan (1981, 1987a) and Berry (1994) for further elaboration.

6. Previous authors have assumed that M was known, so estimating M is one novelty here (Berry 1994).

7. Berry (1994) suggests using distributions other than the uniform. With an exponential distribution we get $b_j = -\Theta \ln[S_j + \exp(-b_{j+1}/\Theta)] = -\Theta \ln(\sum_{k=j}^{N} S_k)$, where Θ is the mean of the exponential distribution. This must be set equal to one, since it is not identified. Preliminary research also used an exponential distribution and found no change in the essential results, so this paper will only show results for the uniform distribution. For the price and quantity data used in this paper, estimates of implied quality with the two distributions were highly correlated in every year of this sample (around .9).

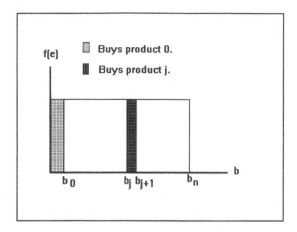

Fig. 8.1   Determination of market share in a vertical model

between market share and quality, that is, $d_j = d_{j-1} + (P_j - P_{j-1})/b_j, j = 1, \ldots,$ N. To adapt to an incomplete data set (explained below), take the definition for b and substitute recursively to get

$$(1) \qquad d_j - d_0 = \sum_{k=1}^{j} \left\{ (P_k - P_{k-1})/\left[1 - \left(\sum_{h=k}^{N} S_h \right) \right] \right\}.$$

The model has several noteworthy features. First, equivalent prices between models j and $j + 1$ imply equivalent qualities. Second, the value of $d_j - d_0$ is the net quality of a system compared with an outside good. Without a measure of the quality of the outside good, it is only possible to directly compute an index of a system's quality compared with an (unobserved) outside good. This makes for careful interpretation because the price and quality of the outside good are changing over time. Third, computing $d_j - d_0$ does not require any data on system characteristics, only data on prices and quantities. It is entirely a function of the total estimated users and the data about the prices and market shares. This will suit available data well, because there is acceptable information on prices and quantities but not on every system's characteristics.

8.3.2   Supply-Side Considerations

There are many optional forms for describing supply-side behavior. The simplest is the case of independent pricing. This model assumes that the economic actor who prices a system only considers the effect of a system's price on the profitability of that system and does not internalize the effect of that system's price on the profitability of any other system. Marginal revenue equals

$$(2) \qquad MR_j = P_j - S_j / \left\{ \left[1 - \left(\sum_{h=j}^{N} S_h \right) \right] / (P_j - P_{j-1}) \right.$$
$$\left. + \left[1 - \left(\sum_{h=j+1}^{N} S_h \right) \right] / (P_{j+1} - P_j) \right\},$$

where this expression takes advantage of the definition of b_j in terms of prices and implied qualities.[8]

The independent-pricing model easily generalizes to a conjectural-variation model (Bresnahan 1989), an approach widely used in empirical applications for testing behavioral assumptions.[9] The conjectural-variation parameter tests the assumption of Bertrand pricing, which is roughly equivalent to testing whether some unobserved factor other than demand for computing capacity influences prices. Marginal revenue is

$$(3) \qquad MR_j = P_j - \exp(\delta)Q_j/M[(d_j - d_{j-1})^{-1} + (d_{j+1} - d_j)^{-1}].$$

It is easier to estimate $\exp(\delta)$ than v, because it prevents accidental division by zero in a maximum-likelihood algorithm. Testing Bertrand behavior amounts to testing $H:\delta = 0$. If δ is large, then v is close to 1 and Bertrand pricing is rejected. The demand elasticity for system j is $e_{QP}^j = -P_j g(P,Q,M)/\exp(\delta)S_j$. Notice that M and $\exp(\delta)$ are the only estimated parameters in MR and e_{QP}^j, which means many factors influence the estimate of M. This is important because the bounds on the estimate of M, $M > \sum_{j=1}^{N} Q_j$, limits the elasticity. Since $\exp(\delta)$ acts in inverse relation to M, estimates of δ may offset limits associated with estimating M.

This model of vendor behavior has several obvious drawbacks. Independent pricing violates the spirit of multiproduct competition in the mainframe computer industry.[10] Moreover, the above specification is not ideal for modeling the pricing of older systems, where the used market constrains pricing (Oliner 1993). Finally, the above specifications do not treat vendors asymmetrically, which violates industry folklore about IBM's dominance. These are important issues for the estimation of vendor behavior, though not necessarily important for the estimation of buyer's surplus, nor necessarily for quantifying extensions in product space. The discussion of results will highlight the points at which these issues pertain to this study's analysis.

8.4   Estimation

Berry (1994) compares the computed implied quality with measured quality and the implied marginal revenue with measured marginal cost, which is the strategy used here with modifications to match available data. The measures of quality are the vector x_j for product j. Then

$$(4) \qquad \begin{aligned} d_j - d_0 &= \exp(x_j\beta + \varepsilon d_j), \text{ and} \\ MR_j &= \exp(x_j\alpha + \varepsilon s_j), \end{aligned}$$

8. Note that marginal revenue must be suitably adjusted when $P_j = P_{j-1}$, which is a rare event in this data. This paper adopts the convention that both systems compete against their nearest neighbors. Thus, the marginal benefit from changing a price is from cutting into that neighbor's market share.

9. See the discussion in Bresnahan (1987a) for more on this point.

10. This experiment cannot employ Bresnahan's (1981) approach to this issue because in this paper's data it is very uncommon for the same firm to market two "neighboring" products.

where εd_j and εs_j are error terms. The multiplicative form for the quality index is for convenience. The multiplicative form for marginal cost, following previous research (e.g., Bresnahan 1981, 1987a), assumes that marginal costs are convex in characteristics. It also guarantees positive estimated marginal costs. It is necessary to instrument for x_j since the cost of designing systems with x_j characteristics determines the observed characteristics and their prices (and quantities and implied quality), leading to simultaneous-equations bias.

Note that d_j is an implicit function of M and P_0. This analysis assumes M is unknown and P_0 is known, with one exception described below.[11] Let $M = TQ(1 + r)$, where $TQ = \sum_{j=1}^{N} Q_j$ is the total number of observed purchases. This analysis assumes $r_t = r_{t+1}$ for all t, but otherwise there will be separate supply and demand equations for each year in the initial estimates.[12] As described below, the data are arranged to determine P_0 in each year. This benefits the simulations later and does not significantly change estimation results.[13]

When M and the other parameters are not known, they can be estimated using nonlinear three-stage least squares (Amemiya 1985). Minimize

$$(5) \qquad\qquad f = \varepsilon'(\sigma \otimes P_z)\varepsilon,$$

where $\varepsilon = Y - (X'P_zX)^{-1}X'P_zY$, $P_z = Z(Z'Z)^{-1}Z$, $Y' = (d', MR')$, d and MR are vectors of the left-hand-side variables, x is the matrix of regressors, X is a block diagonal matrix of regressors x, z is a matrix of the set of instruments for x, and Z is a block diagonal matrix of instruments z. The choice of x and z will be discussed below. Note, however, that this system can be estimated since there exists a complete set of data on prices and quantities. There is no need for x variables for every system's characteristics. The σ term is a two-by-two matrix of consistent estimates for the variance and covariance of ε. These estimates are found from the nonlinear two-stage least squares errors and are equal to $\sigma = \sum(\varepsilon'\varepsilon)/T$, where T is the number of observations. Minimizing the above equation yields estimates for α, β, and M, which then yelds estimates of $d_j - d_0$ and elasticities.[14]

There is a subtle tradeoff between guaranteeing positive estimates of mar-

---

11. If M is known, then it is easy to estimate the independent-pricing model. P_0 can be left unidentified within a constant term. Thus, one can estimate $\ln(d_j - d_0 - x_j\beta = \varepsilon d_j$ and $\ln(MR_j) - x_j\alpha = \varepsilon s_j$ using a standard minimum-distance estimator.

12. Other parameterizations of the size of the market did not produce qualitatively different results, so this paper only presents the simplest specification.

13. Without further economic modeling of the outside good and its quality, d_0, the structural form for P_0 will necessarily be ad hoc. Bresnahan (1981, 1987a) deals with this issue by positing a hedonic relationship between the quality of the outside good and its price.

14. In practice, minimizing f can be very time consuming. Effort is saved by recognizing that the optimized estimated β and α will be $[\alpha,\beta]' = [X'(\sigma\otimes P_z)X]^{-1}[X'(\sigma\otimes P_z)Y]$. Setting β and α equal to optimized values and substituting into f yields a concentrated function determined solely by the value of M and market-power parameters. It is then straightforward to find the optimal α and β (as functions of the optimal d and MR). The final step is to find the standard errors for all the estimates by computing the variance-covariance matrix with all the (already optimized) parameters.

ginal costs and guaranteeing plausible elasticity estimates for every product. If marginal costs are positive by design, marginal revenue may be negative for a few observations where parameter estimates are "far away" from their respective optimums. This is problematic because it destroys any maximum-likelihood algorithm (i.e., $\ln[MR]$ does not exist for $MR < 0$). The more general point is that the functional form cannot guarantee that all product elasticities are less than -1 at nonoptimized parameters. This is related, since $MR_j = [P_j(1 + 1/e_j)]$.

The approximation $\ln[P_j(1 + 1/e_j)] \approx \ln(P_j) + 1/e_j$ eliminates both problems and results in positive marginal costs everywhere. This works well with this paper's data because $1/e_j$ is much less than -1 for all but a few observations in the final estimates. The alternative solution to the above problems, which is not presented, is to not guarantee that marginal costs are positive. This alternative lets elasticities attain both plausible and implausible values without stopping the whole estimation, but it sometimes results in negative predicted marginal costs. Since a few implausible elasticities are inevitable under either specification, at least the approximation above guarantees positive marginal costs. As it turned out, all but a few elasticities were much smaller than -1 at optimized parameters, so the cost of using the approximation was small.[15]

8.5   Surplus Measurement

The total buyer's surplus net of the outside good is

$$(6) \qquad \sum_{j=1}^{N} [(b_j + b_{j+1})(d_j - d_0)/2 - (P_j - P_0)]Q_j.$$

Since d_0 is not identified, d_j alone cannot be identified. The $d_j - d_0$ can come from two possible sources. If there is characteristic data for all systems, then it is possible to use the estimate of β and x_j. Since this paper does not have data for all systems, $d_j - d_0$ come directly from the estimate of M and from the data on prices and quantities.

This method does not measure the benefits from buying a system in terms of its characteristics. Nor does it measure the average benefits from buying a system, or the total benefits to buyers from computerization. There are two reasons for this. First, this model of each year's competition presumes to measure the benefits associated with the last bit of computing power purchased, not the surplus associated with buying the first fractional unit of computer

---

15. One other alternative is to use an error structure like the one found in Bresnahan (1981, 1987a). He solves for the optimal price and quantity under the assumption that the model is correct and compares those computed numbers against the actual observed data. Bresnahan's alternative requires a complete data set, i.e., characteristics for all models. While this exists for new automobiles, such data do not exist for the historical computer market, rendering this alternative infeasible.

power. Second, the method does not anchor the estimates of the quality of a system over time. That is, the absolute level of quality of a particular model is not constrained to be similar over time. Thus, surplus estimates may change over time due to changing units of comparison. In particular, the outside good changes each year, altering the relative benefits of being in the mainframe market.

These limitations make the method well suited to two unit-free estimates of the importance of new entry. One is to estimate the percentage of surplus in a given year attributable to systems with certain features, such as young age or large computing power. The main advantage of this measure is that the percentage of surplus is unit-free and easily compared over time. If extension of capabilities matters in this market, then it must at least hold in the single capability extended here, computing power. If the percentage of surplus associated with large systems falls over time, then we reject the view that this factor matters.

A second experiment involves removing systems with particular characteristics and comparing surplus generated with and without those systems. This comparison is in the spirit of welfare calculations that hold population and demand characteristics constant but change the choice set available to consumers. As before, the percentage difference in surplus is unit-free and easily compared over time. If buyers adopt new systems because they embody unobservable, but valuable, extensions of capabilities, then removing new systems could result in large losses in surplus.

8.6   The Data

This paper's data on computer prices, quantities, and vintages come from industry censuses from International Data Corporation's (IDC's) Electronic Data Processing Industry Reports (EDP/IR).[16] IDC estimated the number of installations of each type of computer system and, until 1981, estimated the monthly rental at which an average type of system leased.[17] The data in this paper begin with the 31 December 1968 report and end with the 1 January 1981 report. The first year in which IDC distinguished between the number of installations inside and outside the United States was 1968. Over the entire fourteen-year period, these data concern the installed base of over 350 different

---

16. Patrick McGovern began compiling this census in 1962 in *Computers and Automation* magazine. It continued in modified form under IDC auspices from the mid-1960s onward. The archives of the Charles Babbage Institute at the University of Minnesota contains a collection. This paper also makes use of a set of EDP Industry Reports contained at the Library for the Graduate School of Business at Stanford University.

17. Phister identifies several years in which IDC revised the reported number of installations in previous years, particularly for IBM models in 1967–72. In those cases, Phister's reported updates were used. This makes this paper's estimates comparable with Phister's (1979) and Flamm's (1987a, 1987b) descriptions of the diffusion of computing equipment, which used more-aggregate IDC data. It also makes this paper's results comparable to Oliner's (1993) analysis of the retirement patterns among IBM mainframes, which uses similar IDC data for IBM systems.

computer systems (see the appendix of Greenstein 1994). These are clearly the best data available on the size of installed base and rental prices.[18]

8.6.1 The Sample

Without modification, two biases arise from maintaining exclusive use of IDC's definition of a mainframe. First, the 1968–69 definition of a mainframe is too broad. It includes some systems that IDC reclassified as "digital dedicated applications" in 1970. These systems are actually minicomputers, like the Digital Equipment Corporation's (DEC's) PDP-8, not general-purpose systems. Second, more redefinition problems arise on a smaller scale because IDC established several on going databases for systems other than mainframes (i.e., minicomputers, small business systems, desktop systems). Its researchers occasionally move a system into the mainframe category that was not previously there. Its researchers also move a system out of the mainframe category that previously was there.[19]

The best solution to this problem defines the outside good consistently across different years of the sample. This paper's outside good is the smallest mainframe offered by IBM, a system 360/20 (introduced in September 1965). The system 360/20 has the virtue that it is very close to the smallest mainframe in IDC's census, but it provides a more consistent definition of the lower bound on this market over time than that used by IDC. Moreover, its price changes throughout the sample period, reflecting real changes in the quality and market price of systems that performed small decentralized computing tasks. Finally, it eliminates only a few useful potential observations in each year.[20] Table 8.1 shows the results of this selection. Consistently defining the outside good does not impose a large loss. The systems used by more than twenty thousand buyers typically are sampled. The greatest losses occur in the most recent years, when this procedure eliminates 12 of the 178 potential observations from IDC's census.

Even with a consistently defined outside good, two potential problems remain. First, IDC revised its survey scope twice, once between 1969 and 1970, and once between 1976 and 1977. In both cases, IDC consolidated the number of models it covered.[21] Second, by the end of the sample, the difference between mainframes and some large general-purpose minicomputers ("su-

---

18. No other comparable data source exists for this period. Remarkably, only a few studies of the computing market (e.g., Michaels 1979; Phister 1979; Flamm 1987a, 1987b; Dulberger 1989; Oliner 1993; Khanna 1994) have used parts of this data and none has ever exploited all facets of it (e.g., see Greenstein 1994 for an examination of diffusion).

19. The most important case is IDC's decision to include the IBM system 36 in the sample in 1976 (estimated installed base at five thousand units) and exclude it from mainframes after that (but include it in "small business systems"). Early experiments showed that this particular flip-flop makes 1976 estimates inconsistent with those of other years.

20. Part of the reason is that there are fewer characteristics data available for the small systems. In addition, the vast majority of eliminated systems were commercial failures.

21. For example, the number of models covered in 1969 was 176, while only 147 were covered in 1970. In 1976 there were 205 models covered, but only 188 in 1977. See table 8.1.

Table 8.1   **Matching Industry Data with Characteristics Data**

Year	Sample of Installed Bases	Original Number of Models	Models with Characteristics Data	
			All	Included in the Sample
1968	19,361	166	59	53
1969	21,470	176	66	60
1970	25,233	147	72	64
1971	19,008	154	81	67
1972	21,909	171	95	77
1973	21,541	173	103	88
1974	22,253	181	113	96
1975	23,351	189	119	101
1976	23,673	205	133	113
1977	23,436	188	134	122
1978	25,124	205	148	136
1979	25,261	218	150	138
1980	24,723	244	167	155
1981	28,116	257	178	166

perminis") becomes blurred, which raises questions about the survey's completeness. The main issue is whether IDC included in the mainframe category all the superminicomputer systems that were close substitutes for general-purpose mainframes. A reasonable case could be made that IDC included most relevant systems,[22] but a reasonable case could also be made that it did not.[23] Ending the sample in 1981 holds this problem to a minimum.

8.6.2 Definition of Market Share and Price

The paper uses the installed base of systems in a given year as a measure of quantity and market share. This is justified because most buyers leased their

---

22. It is not clear whether the money spent on superminis ever amounted to more than a small fraction of the amount of money spent on mainframes. According to the 1983 IDC census for minicomputers and mainframes, the value of installed base associated with superminicomputers came to roughly half the value of all minicomputers, or roughly 15 percent of the value of the installed base of mainframes. IDC's census differs from the other censuses, particularly that of the Computer Business Equipment Manufacturing Association (CBEMA), because IDC includes several systems as mainframes (i.e., those from IBM) which others classify as superminicomputers. This makes IDC's census more "complete," which matters by the early 1980s. For example, according to CBEMA (1992), in 1976 mainframe shipments reached over $5 billion, while the total spent on all minicomputers was $1.8 billion. By 1982, CBEMA estimates that mainframe shipments reached $10.6 billion and minicomputer shipments reached $7.7 billion. CBEMA does not state what fraction went to superminicomputers, but $7.7 billion clearly overstates the size of the competition between mainframe and minicomputers.

23. The most questionable omissions in IDC's mainframe tables are those regarding the VAX models from DEC, and similar competitive models from other firms such as Wang, Prime, and Data General.

equipment in the late 1960s and 1970s. Moreover, many mainframe computers are not subject to frequent mechanical breakdowns, so the services delivered do not physically depreciate rapidly after sale, if at all (though market value may depreciate due to technological obsolescence). The drawback is that this definition overstates the popularity of an old system (and the general competitiveness of the market) by showing that old and new systems are in competition.

While Phister (1979) clearly believes that IDC's estimates of installed base are the best among the available alternatives, he nevertheless warns about several potential problems that could influence calculations using these data.[24] Dulberger (1989) also questions the accuracy of IDC's estimates of installed base, while conceding that they are the best publicly available.[25] Given these concerns, the data were tested for internal consistency, which they readily met.[26] In any event, no alternative is satisfactory. Sales data are not available, and it is not possible to estimate sales from the change in installed base from year to year, because it becomes an increasingly poor estimate of shipments of systems when systems become more than a few years old.

IDC estimated the price of a typical system configuration, which is the price used in this study. IDC's estimates are probably of the right order of magnitude, but they are also subject to measurement error. Phister uses these prices for estimates of the value of installed base. However, he believes that the prices for obsolete systems are too high, since IDC would use the last offered price for a system lacking any recent transaction, but that the bias in old prices influences only a few of the systems in the United States. Flamm (1987b) reaches a similar conclusion before using Phister's estimates for a few calculations.[27] Thus, no strong conclusions should rely exclusively on one price.

8.6.3 System Characteristics

The characteristics that make up x_j partially overlap those used in Gordon's (1989, 1990), Dulberger's (1989), and Oliner's (1993) analyses of computer-system hedonic regressions (see Triplett 1989 for a complete summary of the relevant issues). MIPS, or millions of instructions per second, is an estimate

24. He states, "It is my opinion that IDC's staff, files, and data sources make that organization's published statistics the best available" (250). Yet, due to occasional revisions of previous EDP/IR reports, Phister is not convinced that IDC's estimates of the size of installed base are precise. However, many of his uses of these data reveal his belief that IDC got the order of magnitude correct. Where available, this paper uses Phister's corrections.

25. One especially difficult problem is that IDC may underestimate the number of users who upgrade their systems (Dulberger, personal communication, July 1991).

26. The history of each new system was examined. Did the development of its installed base follow a reasonable pattern of growth, i.e., several years of growth followed by several years of decline? The absence of such a pattern would have called into question the plausibility of the data.

27. In addition, using these prices is not without precedent in the hedonic literature. The prices for new systems used by Gordon (1989, 1990), as well as by many others, are very similar to those used here. Gordon's prices for his sample after 1977 were taken from *Computerworld,* which is published by IDC.

of speed. The maximum memory in megabytes (MB) included in a system is an estimate of memory size.[28]

MIPS and memory-size data are not available for every system in every year. Computer Intelligence Corporation (CIC) provides information about the features of systems extant in 1991 and other important historical systems.[29] CIC's characteristics data cover roughly three-quarters of the most important mainframe and superminicomputer systems (used primarily in business applications) in 1981, or more than 90 percent of the installed base, which makes it more comprehensive than any other single data source. Table 8.1 shows that CIC characteristics data match an increasing fraction of the total number of models IDC surveyed. The sample size begins at 59 for 1968 and grows to 178 by 1981.

IDC provides a measure of the technical generation of a system. Dulberger (1989) warns that hedonic techniques may be mismeasuring the factors deciding prices when the data are taken from a cross section of systems in a market undergoing rapid technological "leap frogging" by successive new systems. Dulberger argues that this "disequilibrium" requires an explicit treatment in a hedonic framework. The simplest means of testing Dulberger's argument, as found in Berndt and Griliches (1993) and Oliner (1993), is to measure the time that has elapsed since the introduction of a system. This variable is labeled "techage." Systems that had more experience in the marketplace should have more software and other complementary system enhancements, which increased the system's quality for the user.

IDC's censuses categorize every system by size, with size ranging from two to seven. This measure is of limited usefulness for a regressor because it is categorical, not continuous, and is highly correlated with MIPS and memory. However, it will be useful for the simulations, because it is available for all systems, and therefore it provides a means for testing important differences between entry behavior on the highest and lowest ends of the computing-power spectrum.

Instruments (the z matrix) for each system are all of the characteristics data from the nearest lower and higher neighboring systems (for which there is characteristics data). These characteristics are typically exogenous, since they are designed by another firm. Yet they are also correlated with the characteristics of the neighboring system, so they make good instruments.[30]

---

28. Because minimum and maximum memory are highly correlated (between .6 and .7 in a year), only one could be used. Because there are many reasons to think that maximum memory is more relevant to buyers than minimum (Bresnahan and Greenstein 1992), maximum memory is used throughout the estimation.

29. The measures of these variables come from CIC's 1991 Computer System Report, which has many virtues relative to the alternatives. The *Computerworld* data, which Professor Gordon kindly lent, begin in 1977. They cover too few systems up to 1981 to be useful. The Auerbach data, which Professor Michaels lent, cover the early part of the 1970s. Unfortunately, they also only cover a small number of years. While the Phister (1979) data cover a longer period, they generally only record the system characteristics for the most popular systems and not for the whole market. In fact, Phister's data cover only about 20–30 percent of the system models surveyed by IDC. CIC's data cover the same systems, plus many more.

30. Thanks to Steve Berry and Frank Wolak for this suggestion.

Table 8.2 shows how the typical system in the sample changes over time. The average price of a system (deflated by a producer price index) and the average size of a system's installations included in the sample decline over most of the years of the sample. The typical system contains more memory (from 1,099 or 5,592 MB maximum memory on average) and performs more instructions per second (from 0.326 to 2.22). These statistics about MIPS and memory suggest that the product space was extended over the sample period, but they are insufficient for conclusions about the economic importance of the extension. The most dramatic changes in the average occur in the last three years of the sample upon the entry of some large supercomputers. Despite the addition of new systems to the sample, the average technical age grows (from 4.1 to 9.0); the inclusion of some very old systems in the sample of later years is to blame for this increase in the average.

Figure 8.2 provides an illustration of the diffusion of large systems and foreshadows results from the estimation. The figure shows a box plot of the distribution of MIPS in the computer systems used in each year.[31] The dark areas indicate the range between the first and third quartiles, while the white line shows the median. Every line above it represents a particular system until the maximum. While this is a coarse measure of computing capacity, the figure shows a gradual extension of the product space. It also shows a gradual buyer adoption of those extensions and a gradual shifting of revenues to systems with higher computing capacity. For example, the MIPS of the 95th percentile of 1968 is the median of the MIPS of systems in use by 1981. In addition, the product space between the maximum and the 95th percentile becomes progressively filled in over time with new products, even as these points vary. Yet many years must pass before the extensions of product space are widely adopted. The 95th percentile stays roughly the same between 1968 and 1973 and between 1974 and 1976, and it only begins to grow after 1977.

8.7   Results

This section presents estimates of the model and various tests of those estimates. The discussion also presents calculations of buyer's surplus and the rate of decline in the cost function. These estimates and calculations quantify the dramatic changes in the computer industry that took place over this period.

8.7.1   The Estimates

Table 8.3 presents estimates of the conjectural-variation model. With a few exceptions, most of the estimates of α and β are of the predicted sign and are significant. Systems with more computing power possess higher quality and

---

31. The figure shows only the MIPS ratings for the systems that were used in the estimation. While this is an incomplete sample of the systems in use, the coverage tends to be almost complete for the largest systems and the most popular systems. Hence, this provides a pretty accurate reflection of changes for the larger systems.

Table 8.2   **Sample Statistics**

Year	Mean	Standard Deviation	Variance	Minimum	Maximum	Sample Size
			Maximum Memory (1,000 MB)			
1968	1.0993	1.7273	2.9836	0.0080	9.9200	53
1969	1.0962	1.7267	2.9816	0.0080	9.9200	60
1970	1.1426	1.7301	2.9933	0.0080	9.9200	64
1971	1.3489	1.8013	3.2445	0.0080	9.9200	67
1972	1.3197	1.5546	2.4168	0.0160	8.1920	77
1973	1.3984	1.6770	2.8123	0.0080	8.1920	88
1974	1.4783	1.8317	3.3550	0.0080	8.1920	96
1975	1.4520	1.7939	3.2182	0.0080	8.1920	101
1976	1.7331	2.3720	5.6264	0.0080	16.3840	113
1977	1.7934	2.5271	6.3861	0.0080	16.3840	122
1978	2.2391	3.9123	15.3063	0.0080	32.7680	136
1979	3.3615	6.1622	37.9726	0.0080	32.7680	138
1980	3.7290	6.4303	41.3483	0.0080	32.7680	155
1981	5.5925	11.7506	138.0776	0.0080	65.5360	166
			MIPS			
1968	0.3264	0.2654	0.0704	0.1000	1.2000	53
1969	0.3983	0.6560	0.4303	0.1000	5.0000	60
1970	0.4203	0.6626	0.4391	0.1000	5.0000	64
1971	0.5060	0.7800	0.6084	0.1000	5.000	67
1972	0.5636	0.8637	0.7460	0.1000	5.0000	77
1973	0.5886	0.8647	0.7477	0.1000	5.0000	88
1974	0.5865	0.8571	0.7347	0.1000	5.0000	96
1975	0.5644	0.8413	0.7077	0.1000	5.0000	101
1976	0.6434	0.9436	0.8903	0.1000	5.2000	113
1977	0.6311	0.9163	0.8395	0.1000	5.2000	122
1978	0.6816	0.9593	0.9202	0.1000	5.2000	136
1979	0.9942	1.7482	3.0563	0.1000	15.0000	138
1980	1.0903	1.8502	3.4231	0.1000	15.0000	155
1981	2.2235	9.9076	98.1608	0.1000	99.0000	166
			Monthly Rental Price (millions of 1982 $)			
1968	0.0801	0.0828	0.0069	0.0074	0.3844	53
1969	0.0840	0.1050	0.0110	0.0097	0.6434	60
1970	0.0939	0.1083	0.0117	0.0078	0.6210	64
1971	0.1134	0.1137	0.0129	0.0128	0.5815	67
1972	0.1104	0.1047	0.0110	0.0109	0.5103	77
1973	0.0987	0.0926	0.0086	0.0092	0.4302	88
1974	0.0859	0.0824	0.0068	0.0075	0.3963	96
1975	0.0767	0.0746	0.0056	0.0068	0.3583	101
1976	0.0694	0.0676	0.0046	0.0063	0.3336	113
1977	0.0720	0.0763	0.0058	0.0049	0.4143	122
1978	0.0687	0.0720	0.0052	0.0048	0.4089	136
1979	0.0731	0.0750	0.0056	0.0045	0.3731	138
1980	0.0638	0.0671	0.0045	0.0040	0.3575	155
1981	0.0584	0.0617	0.0038	0.0037	0.3379	166

Table 8.2   (continued)

Year	Mean	Standard Deviation	Variance	Minimum	Maximum	Sample Size
		Number of Installations per System				
1968	362.3019	874.8564	765,373.6763	2.0000	4,550.0000	53
1969	357.8333	920.8783	848,016.8531	1.0000	6,000.0000	60
1970	394.2656	1,124.194	1,263,813.9442	3.0000	8,200.0000	64
1971	283.7015	908.7735	825,869.2429	1.0000	6,700.0000	67
1972	284.5325	798.1648	637,067.0154	1.0000	5,720.0000	77
1973	244.7841	603.0341	363,650.1482	1.0000	4,360.0000	88
1974	231.8021	489.3544	239,467.7604	1.0000	3,104.0000	96
1975	231.1980	485.6864	235,891.2604	2.0000	2,750.0000	101
1976	209.4956	457.7657	209,549.4129	2.0000	2,685.0000	113
1977	192.0984	399.0211	159,217.8580	1.0000	2,460.0000	122
1978	184.7353	354.0059	125,320.1516	1.0000	1,820.0000	136
1979	183.0507	352.5604	124,298.8368	1.0000	1,910.0000	138
1980	159.5032	306.8748	94,172.1477	1.0000	1,930.0000	155
1981	169.3735	391.1079	152,965.3991	1.0000	3,600.0000	166
		Technical Age (years)				
1968	4.0758	1.9413	3.7686	0.3340	8.8340	53
1969	4.6989	2.1969	4.8262	1.0000	9.8340	60
1970	5.1931	2.5382	6.4426	0.9170	10.8340	64
1971	5.4792	2.9625	8.7765	0.2500	11.8340	67
1972	5.3781	3.2988	10.8823	0.8340	12.8340	77
1973	5.8166	3.4082	11.6161	0.4170	13.8340	88
1974	6.5785	3.7091	13.7573	1.1670	14.8340	96
1975	7.2281	3.8218	14.6060	1.1670	15.8340	101
1976	7.1648	4.2318	17.9084	1.3340	16.8340	113
1977	7.8173	4.2723	18.2525	1.1670	17.8340	122
1978	8.2595	4.6783	21.8868	1.1670	19.0000	136
1979	8.6930	5.0657	25.6615	1.0840	20.0000	138
1980	8.8090	5.4082	29.2483	1.0840	21.0000	155
1981	8.9833	5.7038	32.5337	1.1670	22.0000	166

have higher marginal cost. More memory contributes to the perceived quality of a product and to its increasing cost in all but the 1968 sample. Faster systems have higher quality and higher marginal costs in all of the estimates except the 1972, 1973, and 1980 samples, when the coefficients are not significant. Older systems usually possess higher quality and have higher marginal cost, but the coefficient is insignificant half the time on the supply side. Estimates for the size of the potential market are small, at 1 percent. For inapparent reasons, the model appears to fit badly in 1968, 1974, and 1980.

The variables measuring computing power are often quantitatively important on both the demand and the supply sides. These results are consistent with the basic assumption of this model, that computing power alone explains most of the cross-sectional variation in demand for computing. The varying

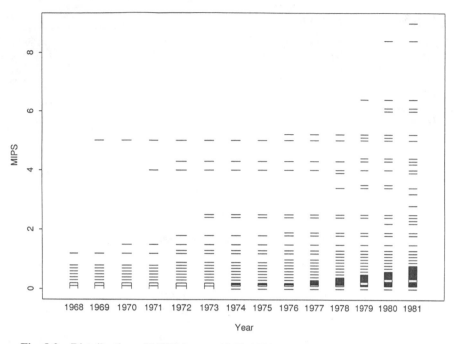

Fig. 8.2   Distribution of MIPS in use, 1968–1981

size of the technical-age variable does not support the view that disequilibrium pricing matters much for the model and data, which is also consistent with the methodological approach of this paper.

A curiosity of these first estimates is that coefficients on the supply side do not seem to show a large reduction in the costs of supplying characteristics over time. At most, there is a small (and erratic) downward shift in the costs of characteristics. This seems at odds with well-known declines in the costs of memory and processors. Later estimates showed that this pattern was an artifact of too much econometric freedom. A more constrained cost-function specification, more typical of the literature, will measure some anticipated decline below.

One other feature of these estimates has to do with the model's econometrics. The estimate of the implied quality of a system in one year has almost no econometric relationship to that estimate in another year. The model in each year requires that systems "price discriminate" between users with different willingness to pay for computing power, but it does not require similar quality estimates for a given system from year to year. Thus, nothing inherently ties down the estimates of the implied quality of a system from year to year and the estimates of surplus generated from those estimates of implied quality. Given this econometric freedom, it is remarkable that the coefficient estimates do tend to have the same sign and roughly the same order of magnitude from

Table 8.3   Parameter Estimates: Conjectural-Variation Model

	1968	1969	1970	1971	1972	1973	1974	1975	1976	1977	1978	1979	1980	1981
						Demand								
Constant	-2.54*	-2.41*	-2.56*	-1.46*	-2.02*	-0.59	-4.13*	-3.61*	-3.82*	-2.85*	-2.66*	-2.14*	-6.14*	-3.43*
Memory	-0.26	0.31*	0.25*	0.10*	0.33*	1.21	0.37*	0.41*	0.16*	0.05*	0.12*	0.07*	0.30	0.07*
MIPS	3.33*	0.08	0.21*	0.25*	-0.03	-0.94	0.18*	0.08	0.47*	0.58*	0.28*	0.18*	-0.20	0.08*
Age	0.04*	0.11*	0.13*	0.01	0.06*	-0.39	0.21*	0.11*	0.13*	0.05*	0.02	-0.03	0.32	0.04
						Supply								
Constant	-5.20*	-5.58*	-5.39*	-3.54*	-5.05*	-0.56	-6.73*	-5.96*	-5.39*	-5.30*	-4.26*	-3.90*	-9.02	-4.76*
Memory	-1.17*	0.75*	0.59*	0.50*	1.08*	3.36	0.59*	0.66*	0.27*	0.22*	0.27*	0.15*	0.46	0.11*
MIPS	12.4*	0.15	0.38*	0.35*	-0.37*	-2.90	0.33*	0.16	0.71*	0.97*	0.49*	0.38*	-0.32	0.13*
Tech-age	-0.15*	0.36*	0.34*	0.01	0.218*	-1.19	0.41*	0.24*	0.18*	0.13*	0.01	-0.01	0.50	0.05
exp (r)	0.015*													
exp (k)	90.04													
Weighted sum of squares	32.41													

*Significant at the 5 percent level.

year to year and roughly make sense. At the same time, the demand parameters are not close to constant across all years. These changes support the view that there are frequent changes to the basic relationship between the underlying valuation of computing capacity and the measurable features of computing capacity.

8.7.2   Testing the Model

The null hypothesis is that the conjecture parameter is zero, which is rejected. The value of the conjectural parameter rejects Bertrand pricing. The benefit to undercutting rivals is small, that is, price increases are closely matched. All specifications and experiments with this data, many not shown here, could not eliminate this result.

There are two fundamental reasons for this estimate. First, many products are priced close together, especially at the low end where many older systems are found.[32] The model must interpret these systems as close substitutes, especially when each system has such low market share. While this is probably the right inference for most systems with small market share, it underemphasizes the importance of systems that have significantly higher market share. Second, there is not enough flexibility in the marginal revenue equation to adapt to the wide dispersion of market shares in this data. The only free parameter is M, but M is constrained to be greater than the number of systems sold. While the model does attribute less-competitive elasticities to the high–market share systems, it may scale all the elasticity estimates incorrectly. M would have to become much smaller to generate elasticity estimates that are sensible for the high–market share systems. The conjectural-variation parameter provides more flexibility because it rescales the elasticities while retaining more-inelastic elasticities for systems with higher market share. Systems with large market share display elasticities consistent with large differences between marginal cost and price and high markups over marginal cost.[33]

This result suggests one of two things: First, if the model correctly describes product differentiation, then the firms behave quite differently from Bertrand pricing (i.e., they are much less aggressive). Second, using a hypothesis that is more plausible, the parameter may show that some factors outside the model— that is, factors other than the pricing and product differentiation modeled here—largely decide competition between vendors. This is plausible if vendors are competing by embodying unmeasured new features in each generation of their products. This possibility raises the same fundamental issues with

32. The difference between neighboring systems averages around 3 percent of the price of the lower-priced system, but grows for the higher-priced systems.
33. Only a subset of the total number of systems available displays high markups over cost, which seems plausible. Inspection of the data reveals that these systems are almost always the systems with large market share and they almost always come from IBM. There is also a slight tendency for more-expensive systems to have larger markups in absolute value, but smaller markups as a percentage of price. This is because these systems are not as closely priced (in absolute value terms) to their neighbors as the lower-priced systems and they also have lower market share.

Table 8.4   **Estimated Surplus (millions of 1982 $)**

Year	Net Surplus per System	Net Expenditure Less Outside Good	Total Installed Base	Net Surplus per Dollar of Net Expenditure	Total Net Surplus
1968	.0701	649.53	25,641	2.76	1,796.84
1969	.0742	783.69	27,386	2.59	2,033.79
1970	.0694	892.01	29,283	2.28	2,033.82
1971	.1153	859.85	24,603	3.29	2,837.05
1972	.0938	923.13	26,920	2.73	2,525.84
1973	.0553	889.75	27,301	1.69	1,511.44
1974	.0334	864.14	27,787	1.07	929.47
1975	.0346	880.13	29,510	1.16	1,022.11
1976	.0287	866.50	31,583	1.04	909.08
1977	.0417	1,070.93	33,201	1.29	1,385.83
1978	.0388	1,163.21	36,209	1.20	1,407.28
1979	.0380	1,267.32	38,386	1.15	1,461.10
1980	.0187	1,337.63	43,798	0.61	820.33
1981	.0219	1,457.85	49,538	0.74	1,086.45

Notes: Net surplus measures the surplus generated net of the outside good. Net expenditure less outside good represents the expenditures on systems in the sample ($\sum P_j Q_j$) less the expenditure on the outside good ($\sum P_0 Q_j$).

which this paper began—that is, about the proper means for modeling product differentiation and behavior in this industry.

8.7.3   Buyer's Surplus

Table 8.4 summarizes the simulation of the consumer's surplus for each year for the conjectural-variation model. The estimates of net total surplus are large, roughly one to two billion dollars a month (these are net of the potential benefits of purchasing the outside good).[34] However, the estimates are also erratic, moving around by more than 50 percent from one period to the next. The average surplus per system, which controls for the changes in the number of systems in use in a year, makes more sense. These estimates also fluctuate, but less so than those that estimate the amount of total surplus. These estimates show an irregular but steady decline in the consumer's surplus per system after 1971. Table 8.4 also shows the net total surplus per net dollar of expenditure (net of potential expenditure on the outside good). This too shows a slow but steady decline after 1971.

There are several possible explanations for the decline in net surplus per system and net surplus per dollar. First, the model may increasingly fail to properly explain buyer exit from the mainframe market in the late 1970s. The availability of superminicomputers, which show up as devalued mainframe

---

34. Strictly speaking, this restriction makes these estimates of surplus incomparable with previous surplus estimates in this market (e.g., Bresnahan 1987b; Flamm 1987b; Brynjolfsson 1993).

computers in this model, could lie behind the trend. This solution is possible, but only partially successful. The rise in the net expenditure after 1977 is due to a large discrete change in the nominal price of the outside good (from $3,675 to $2,800) and to inflation in the late 1970s, which produces the decline in the surplus per expenditure after 1977. Yet no such simple explanation can account for trends between 1971 and 1976. The increase in the number of systems, which can explain the decline in net surplus per system, did not cause a corresponding increase in the total net surplus. The lack of increase in net surplus is still the mystery.

A second possibility, the most plausible one, is that the reduction of product differentiation to one dimension oversimplifies substitution possibilities. The model implausibly shows a crowded product space as new systems enter, as if all new entry occurs on intensive margins. In practice, many new systems may enter on extensive margins that this model cannot measure. This new entry generates gains in true, yet unmeasured, consumer's surplus. Therefore, the estimate in table 8.4 is too low, particularly in later years as systems get many new capabilities. This explanation suggest that, at best, these estimates can only do a good job of estimating surplus generated at the extensive margin (more computing capacity).

8.7.4   Importance of Entry on Extensive Margins

Table 8.5 displays estimates of entry on the only extensive margin in this model, more computing capacity. The table shows the amount of surplus attrib-

Table 8.5   **Percentage of Surplus Associated with Different Vintages and Sizes**

Year	Techage ≤ 4 Years Old		Techage ≤ 6 Years Old		Medium (size 5)		Large (size 6)		Very Large (size 7)	
	A	B	A	B	A	B	A	B	A	B
1968	.48	.37	.70	.62	.13	.06	.07	.03	.01	.01
1969	.08	.11	.73	.63	.15	.08	.08	.03	.02	.01
1970	.10	.14	.82	.71	.16	.08	.09	.04	.03	.01
1971	.06	.10	.16	.22	.19	.10	.11	.05	.03	.01
1972	.15	.15	.25	.29	.20	.11	.15	.07	.04	.02
1973	.29	.24	.36	.36	.23	.12	.17	.08	.05	.02
1974	.44	.32	.49	.41	.24	.13	.21	.09	.06	.02
1975	.27	.30	.53	.48	.25	.13	.19	.08	.06	.02
1976	.20	.29	.58	.53	.24	.13	.20	.08	.07	.02
1977	.10	.24	.44	.52	.21	.12	.20	.09	.08	.03
1978	.14	.23	.41	.50	.22	.13	.20	.09	.09	.03
1979	.23	.28	.35	.46	.22	.14	.21	.10	.11	.04
1980	.23	.15	.38	.34	.19	.11	.25	.10	.14	.04
1981	.31	.27	.49	.47	.17	.10	.23	.10	.14	.05

Notes: A: Surplus associated with types of systems as a percentage of total surplus. B: Percentage of installed base associated with the same type of system.

utable to systems in IDC's size-five, -six, and -seven categories, the top three categories in its ordinal ranking of system size. The percentage of surplus attributable to systems with high capacities grows over time. Roughly 21 percent of total surplus in 1968 is attributable to systems of sizes five, six, and seven, and only 8 percent to systems of sizes six and seven. This grows to as much as 54 percent for all, and 23 and 14 percent for sizes six and seven, respectively, in 1981. Much of the growth in size six comes before 1976, while growth occurs almost every year for size-seven systems. This reflects a general trend and is not an artifact of any arbitrary data definition of size by IDC.[35]

The table highlights two other factors about growth on the extensive margin. First, the fraction of the installed base of systems attributable to the high-capacity systems is small, never amounting to more than 10 percent of the total number of systems in 1968 and 25 percent in 1981. Yet this small fraction of systems accounts for a disproportionate amount of consumer's surplus—21 percent in 1968 and 54 percent in 1981. Part of this occurs because larger systems cost the customer more. Even though there are fewer of them, the expenditure per system is greater. Extending the product space a bit results in a huge increase of expenditure, though not nearly as many new units. This estimate supports the argument that growth on the extensive margin may have large influences on buyer's surplus.

However, the same estimates quantify a new aspect to extensive margin growth. Note how long it took for this market to register much growth on the extensive margin. Surplus in size seven undergoes steady but slow growth. Surplus in size six grows rapidly in the first half of the sample and slowly, but unevenly, in the second half. A close examination of the data illustrates why. The most popular size-six system, IBM 360/65, was first installed in late 1965. By 1968 users had installed over three hundred 360/65 models and over five hundred other more expensive systems. The IBM 370/155 then supplanted the 360/65 as the most popular system of size six in the early 1970s, but the diffusion took several years to reach its peak. By the late 1970s, however, no single system dominated the large-system-size category any longer. There was only gradual change on the extensive margin in the mid- to late 1970s as new systems only slowly became widely used. The slow but steady entry of many different new systems accounts for most of the growth in the late 1970s.

Table 8.5 also presents estimates of the percentage of surplus in each year attributable to systems of different vintages, principally those less than or equal to four and six years old. This partially addresses the concern that new products not only are cheaper, but embody new unmeasured features not reflected in the price. First, as expected, young vintages tend to generate the most surplus, averaging 22–47 percent of surplus, depending on the measure. This

---

35. For example, IDC's censuses show a perceptible decline in the entry of size-two systems after 1976 (Greenstein 1994). Yet this bias does not explain the time trend in table 8.5 because most size-two systems were not included in this sample as a result of the adoption of a consistent definition for the outside good.

result, combined with the inability of technical age to predict system demand, suggests that buyers purchase systems for more than just capacity, but this quality is not measurable in a simple manner. Second, the importance of young vintages differs dramatically from year to year. A few specific vintages influence surplus estimates. The technical vintage introduced in 1965–66 dominates the surplus calculations until the mid-1970s, which unquestionably reflects the popularity of the IBM system 360. The next major wave of surplus is associated with IBM system 370 (mostly from 1971 and 1973). These two vintage effects do not work themselves out until virtually the end of the sample, when the entry of many new systems begins to influence the surplus simulations.

No other family of systems generates so much surplus as the systems 360 and 370 because no other family of systems has such a large market share. While this qualitative result is not surprising (see Greenstein 1994), it raises important issues. First, it suggests that estimates of the benefits from technical change in the early years of computing are determined by estimates of the benefits associated with the technical improvements in a few of the dominant systems of that era. Only in the later years are the benefits spread across more models. Second, it highlights the importance of properly measuring the benefits associated with the system 360/370. In any quantity-weighted measurement exercise, such as the above, small changes in estimates of the benefits associated with the system 360/370 lead to large changes in estimates of the benefits to society from technical changes in computing. This observation adds importance to the debate about the (measured) economic benefits associated with the system 370 (e.g., see Dulberger 1989; Gordon 1989; and Triplett 1989) and about whether most of the benefits from technical change accrued to buyers. Finally, these results again raise the unresolved question about the proper method for weighting a popular system relative to less commercially successful systems in a hedonic regression.

Table 8.6 puts the pattern of entry into final perspective. It computes the counterfactual surplus generated if all new systems were absent (those less than four and six years old). It displays this counterfactual surplus as a fraction of buyer's surplus measured with all the systems. This is in the spirit of welfare calculations that keep the demand characteristics fixed but alter the choices available to buyers. Removing young systems simulates demand in the absence of any technical change.[36] Not surprisingly, surplus declines without new systems. However, in any given year it does not decline by more than a few percentage points. The largest declines are associated with the counterfactual elimination of the system 360 in the early years of the sample. In the mid-

36. It seems less plausible to estimate the counterfactual surplus in the absence of a system of a particular size. In that counterfactual world, there would be a large supplier response in short-run pricing behavior and long-run design behavior. Simulating that counterfactual behavior does not make any point that cannot already be made with the results in table 8.6.

Table 8.6   **Size of Counterfactual Surplus as a Percentage of Observed Surplus**

Year	Techage ≤ 4 Years Old Removed	Techage ≤ 6 Years Old Removed
1968	.961	.938
1969	.997	.919
1970	.994	.875
1971	.991	.990
1972	.994	.982
1973	.986	.979
1974	.973	.970
1975	.977	.963
1976	.982	.958
1977	.986	.965
1978	.985	.965
1979	.982	.972
1980	.990	.980
1981	.984	.975

1970s the decline is less than 1 percent and less than 3 percent by the late 1970s, especially for young systems.

Table 8.6 displays a well-known characteristic of counterfactual welfare measures of technical change: a new technology is only as good as the alternatives to it are bad. Even if no new systems were invented, buyers would continue to use old technology. In this model, old systems are very close substitutes, and switching between substitutes is assumed to be costless. The product space is "crowded" as a result, so that the absence of a new technology sends buyers to a worse, but lower-priced, system. Since entry on the intensive margins can only generate large gains when the product space is not crowded, the biggest gains to such entry in this model are recorded early in the sample, when the industry is still young. Since this crowding is probably an artifact of not measuring all the dimensions that buyers value, and table 8.5 shows that a substantial number of buyers continue to purchase young systems, table 8.6 represents a (potentially severe) underestimate of the true surplus losses.

Table 8.6 echoes the observation that innovation takes a long time to achieve its full effect (only here it is about the entry of new systems). Though the net benefit from new systems is small in any given year, the cumulative effect over many years is quite large. That is, if all technical change had ceased in 1968, by 1981 the cumulative losses in each year would have been enormous. However, not to belabor the point, the long-run estimate of loss is surely an underestimate. Much evidence suggests that important product characteristics are not being measured here. The amount of mismeasurement must increase as the time periods in comparison become further apart.

Tables 8.5 and 8.6 embody both the strengths and weaknesses of the approach taken in this paper. On the one hand, standard hedonic methods could not lead to these tables or to the conclusions reached from them. Table 8.6 quantifies the benefits from new technology in use, while hedonic price methods stop at estimating improvements in what is available. Though this paper's conclusions require structural assumptions about the nature of demand, this is par for the course in using data on both quantities and prices. Any other structural model that incorporates more dimensions will necessarily show the same effects highlighted in this paper and possibly more. On the downside, tables 8.5 and 8.6 are only as good as the structural assumptions that generated them. Parts of this paper (and other analyses of this market, e.g., Bresnahan and Greenstein 1992) suggest that product differentiation is incompletely modeled here and potentially correlated with age. Entry probably also occurred on more extensive margins than are modeled. If that is so, tables 8.5 and 8.6 provide a lower bound on the welfare losses from the absence of innovation.

8.7.5   Cost Function Decline

Table 8.7 estimates cost functions on exactly the same data as were used in table 8.3. The two equations use something akin to standard hedonic specifications but supplement them with a market-power correction, as found in a vertical model with conjectural variations. The first specification takes the form

$$(7) \qquad \ln(P_j) = \Gamma Q_j / [P_j Mg(P,Q,M)] + x_j \alpha + e_j.$$

The next specification is similar, but specifies a different Γ over time. The market size, M, is assumed to be about 1 percent larger than the observed market, taken from the previous conjectural-variation estimates in table 8.3.[37] All the data are pooled such that α has one coefficient for MIPS, memory, and age, but different year-dummy coefficients, which captures the change in the level of the cost function of firms.[38] This assumes that all firms draw from the same cost function in a given year. Rather than explicitly model the demand size, which is of little interest here, the estimates employ a reduced form for demand. Demand is a function of the same set of regressors and instruments as used previously, plus time dummies. This treats MIPS, memory, age, and market power as endogenous and the time dummies as exogenous.

The cost function estimates have the following three features: First, coefficients for memory, MIPS, and age all have the correct sign. Second, none of

37. The above results suggest that little is lost by estimating a conjectural-variation model as if M is known (even when it is not). In any event, in a conjectural-variation model, the conjectural parameter would scale any estimate, effectively acting in the opposite direction of any estimate of the market size. Hence, it is must easier, and no less insightful, to simply assume a given size of a market, compute the implied product elasticities, and then estimate a conjecture parameter to scale the elasticity estimates properly.

38. Though the dummy coefficients are unbiased estimates, the index will not be. It is a nonlinear function of an unbiased estimate. To correct for this bias, the estimated standard errors use an approximation suggested by Triplett (1989). This involves adding one-half of the standard error to the coefficient before computing the index.

Table 8.7   **Cost-Function Estimates**

		Sample Statistics			
Variable	Mean	Standard Deviation	Variance	Minimum	Maximum
Year	1975.8816	3.8561	14.8696	1968	1981
Memory	2.4305	5.4442	29.6394	0.0080	65.5360
MIPS	0.8553	3.5653	12.7110	0.1000	99.0000
Techage	7.2617	4.5623	20.8143	0.2500	22.0000
ln(price)	−3.0553	1.0447	1.0913	−5.6011	−0.4409

	Correlation of Variables		
Variable	Memory	MIPS	Age
MIPS	0.24271562		
Techage	−0.25643255	−0.12986814	
ln(price)	0.26571416	0.22847909	−0.14177210

Specification 1

Valid cases = 1,436
$R^2 = 0.218$
Residual SS = 4,315.12
Dependent variable = ln(price)
$\bar{R}^2 = 0.209$
Standard error of estimates = 1.744

Variable	Estimate	Standard Error	Real Cost Index
Memory	0.276	0.0471**	
MIPS	0.166	0.0763*	
Techage	0.155	0.0771*	
Γ(CV parameter)	−655.9	128.8**	
1968	−3.602	0.41**	100.0
1969	−3.678	0.45**	94.6
1970	−3.435	0.49**	123.1
1971	−3.457	0.50**	121.6
1972	−3.426	0.49**	124.2
1973	−3.771	0.51**	88.8
1974	−4.013	0.57**	71.8
1975	−4.425	0.61**	48.5
1976	−4.693	0.60**	37.1
1977	−4.658	0.65**	39.2
1978	−5.061	0.69**	26.7
1979	−5.448	0.74**	18.4
1980	−5.806	0.75**	13.1
1981	−6.615	0.81**	6.0

(*continued*)

Table 8.7   (continued)

	Specification 2
	Valid cases = 1,436
	$R^2 = 0.193$
	Residual SS = 6,367.5
	Dependent variable = ln(price)
	$\bar{R}^2 = 0.182$
	Standard error of estimates = 2.120

Variable	Estimate	Standard Error	Real Cost Index
Memory	0.234	0.0707**	
MIPS	0.127	0.106	
Techage	0.066	0.120	
Γ (1968–69)	−132.7	252.3	
Γ (1970–76)	−983.5	204.6**	
Γ (1977–81)	−1,470.3	603.0*	
1968	−3.479	0.52**	100.0
1969	−3.511	0.56**	98.8
1970	−2.586	0.67**	261.9
1971	−2.668	0.68**	243.7
1972	−2.635	0.67**	249.4
1973	−3.000	0.69**	174.9
1974	−3.141	0.77**	158.1
1975	−3.598	0.81**	102.1
1976	−3.897	0.80**	75.7
1977	−3.470	0.99**	127.0
1978	−4.023	0.96**	72.3
1979	−4.313	1.04**	56.3
1980	−4.751	1.02**	36.0
1981	−5.419	1.12**	19.4

*t = value exceeds 1.96.
**t = value exceeds 2.56.

the estimates shows a monotonically declining rate of technical change. The most problematic of all the estimates are those for 1968 through 1970, which may be due to changes in IDC's sampling frame in those years. This problem does not seem to be a manifestation of the movement from the IBM 360 to the IBM 370, which was first introduced in 1971. Third, all the estimates measure rapid rates of technical change over the long run. The first equation, which estimates only one conjecture parameter for the entire sample, finds a decline in the cost function of 20.0 percent over fourteen years and 30.3 percent from 1971 to 1981. The second equation, which estimates a different conjecture parameter for each of the three IDC sampling periods, estimates declines of 11.7 percent over fourteen years and 25.5 percent from 1971 to 1981.[39] The

39. Interacting a time trend with the conjecture parameter did not result in qualitatively different conclusions. The first equation is presented because it is easier to read and interpret.

differences in the estimates suggest that functional form influences the precise estimate of change in market power and the change in the cost function. In both cases, decreases in the prices to consumers were due partly to changes in market power and partly to declines in the cost function.[40]

8.8 Conclusion

This paper measures the economic benefits that accrued to buyers from technical innovation in mainframe computers. The thesis is that many innovations that created economic value in this period are associated with extensions in computing capabilities. Answers to the questions raised in the introduction provide a suitable summary of this analysis.

What valuable innovations in this period are associated with extensions of capabilities? It was argued that technical change in the computing market involved much more than rapid declines in the price of existing capabilities. While price declines enabled many of the events that took place, important episodes of value creation were associated with specific inventions that extended buyer capabilities into new areas—for example, the invention of reliable real-time database querying and the invention of interruption-free multiuser computing. Value creation was not associated solely with the decline in costs of the delivery of these services.

Do buyers adopt products that embody extensions of capabilities? The economic history and the econometric results show that adoption decisions were not solely the result of buyers taking advantage of lower prices for existing capabilities. The data and estimates show that many buyers purchased larger computing capacity embodied in products that came into existence in the 1970s.

How does a measurement framework represent that action? This study argued that some fraction of the new capabilities associated with new systems is not measurable but is complementary with increases in computing capacity. Therefore, a model of the supply and demand for products with different computing capacity will capture some demand for new capabilities. Such a model has several interesting features: (1) buyers slowly adopt higher-capacity systems, suggesting that greater attention needs to be paid to the diffusion of new technology in this market (Greenstein 1994); (2) decreases in prices to consumers were due partly to changes in market power and partly to declines in cost. All the estimates measure rapid rates of decline in the costs of providing computer capacity over the long run.

---

40. Finally, it is not correct to infer that market power increased over time just because Γ increased. Instead, one must examine changes in the distribution of product-specific elasticities. Close examination of these elasticities, not shown here, reveals a more competitive market over time—in the sense that the median product-specific elasticity is more elastic, as is every other order statistic of the elasticity. This is not surprising in this model since the product space becomes increasingly crowded over time.

Are most extensions only embodied in capacity or other features of the products? Competition in computing is partially represented by extensions in computing capacity and by the technological age of systems, but not entirely. The conjectural-variation estimates and the demand-parameter estimates suggest that there was not a stable relationship over time between measurable features of products and revealed buyer choice. This is not surprising because of the well-known changing value of outside goods. It is also not surprising because of the likely changing valuation of computing capacity that resulted from innovation of complementary components. Therefore, constant-quality indexes of price decline potentially omit the factors that influence changes to economic welfare for many buyers.

In sum, much significant innovation in this industry was associated with extending capabilities to new levels. This is not an argument that price decreases were unimportant to buyers, only that price decreases do not tell the whole story about the welfare improvements realized by buyers—perhaps they even tell a deceptive story. There are many implications from this conclusion for understanding competition and value creation in this industry (e.g., see Bresnahan and Greenstein 1992). This study focuses on whether constant-quality price indexes provide good information about welfare benefits from technological change. They do for the buyers who continue to buy products with similar sets of characteristics, but not necessarily for the buyers who take advantage of the availability of characteristics that did not previously exist. Many buyers fall into this latter camp. It is time that these observations about extension of capabilities became a central part of the discussion about the creation of economic benefits from technological change in computing.

References

Amemiya, Takeshi. 1985. *Advanced econometrics.* Cambridge, Mass.: Harvard University Press.

Berndt, Ernst, and Zvi Griliches. 1993. Price indexes for microcomputers: An exploratory study. In *Price measurements and their uses,* ed. M. Foss, M. Manser, and A. Young, 63–89. Chicago: University of Chicago Press.

Berndt, E. R., M. H. Showalter, and J. M. Woolridge. 1991. On the sensitivity of hedonic price indexes for computers to the choice of functional form. Massachusetts Institute of Technology, Cambridge. Mimeographed.

Berry, Steven T. 1994. Discrete choice models of oligopoly product differentiation. *Rand Journal of Economics* 25, no. 2 (summer): 242–62.

Berry, Steven T., James Levinsohn, and Ariel Pakes. 1993. Automobile prices in market equilibrium: Part I and II. NBER Working Paper no. 4264. Cambridge, Mass.: National Bureau of Economic Research. January.

Bresnahan, Timothy F. 1981. Departures from marginal cost pricing in the American automobile industry. *Journal of Econometrics* 17:201–27.

———. 1987a. Competition and collusion in the American automobile oligopoly: The 1955 price war. *Journal of Industrial Economics* 35(4): 457–82.

———. 1987b. Measuring the spillover from technical advance: Mainframe computers in financial services. *American Economic Review* 77, no. 1 (March): 742–55.

————. 1989. Empirical studies of industries with market power. In *The handbook of industrial organization,* ed. Richard Schmalensee and Robert Willig. Amsterdam: North-Holland.

Bresnahan, Timothy F., and Shane M. Greenstein. 1992. Technological competition and the structure of the computing industry. Center for Economic Policy Research Working Paper no. 315. Stanford, Calif.: Stanford University. June.

Brynjolfsson, Eric. 1993. Some estimates of the contribution of information technology to consumer welfare. Sloan School of Management, Massachusetts Institute of Technology, Cambridge. Mimeographed, August.

CBEMA (Computer Business Equipment Manufacturing Association). 1992. *Information technology industry databook, 1992.* Washington, D.C.: CBEMA.

CIC (Computer Intelligence Corporation). 1991. *Computer system report.* La Jolla, Calif.: CIC.

Cole, Rosanne, Y. C. Chen, Joan A. Barquin-Stolleman, Ellen Dulberger, Hurhan Helvacian, and James H. Hodge. 1986. Quality-adjusted price indexes for computer processors and selected peripheral equipment. *Survey of Current Business* 66 (January): 41–50.

Dulberger, Ellen R. 1989. The application of a hedonic model to a quality-adjusted price index for computer processors. In *Technology and capital formation,* ed. Dale W. Jorgenson and Ralph Landau, 37–76. Cambridge: MIT Press.

Feenstra, Robert, and James Levinsohn. 1989. The characteristics approach and oligopoly pricing. University of Michigan, Ann Arbor. Mimeographed.

Fisher, Franklin M., John J. McGowan, and Joen E. Greenwood. 1983. *Folded, spindled, and mutilated: Economic analysis and U.S. vs. IBM.* Cambridge: MIT Press.

Flamm, Kenneth. 1987a. *Targeting the computer: Government support and international competition.* Washington, D.C.: Brookings.

————. 1987b. *Creating the Computer: Government, industry, and high technology.* Washington, D.C.: Brookings.

Friedman, Andrew, and Dominic Cornford. 1989. *Computer systems development: History, organization, and implementation.* New York: John Wiley and Sons.

Gordon, Robert J. 1989. The postwar evolution of computer prices. In *Technology and capital formation,* ed. Dale W. Jorgenson and Ralph Landau, 77–126. Cambridge: MIT Press.

————. 1990. *The measurement of durable goods prices.* Chicago: University of Chicago Press.

Greenstein, Shane. 1994. The diffusion of multiple vintages in a differentiated product market: Best and average practice in mainframe computers, 1968–1983. NBER Working Paper no. 4647. Cambridge, Mass.: National Bureau of Economic Research.

Inmon, William M. 1985. *Technomics: The economics of technology and the computer industry.* Homewood, Ill.: Dow Jones-Irwin.

Khanna, Tarun. 1994. Racing behavior: Technological evolution in the high-end computing industry. Working Paper no. 94–009. Harvard Business School, Cambridge, Mass.

Michaels, Robert. 1979. Hedonic prices and the structure of the digital computer industry. *Journal of Industrial Economics* 27(3): 263–75.

Oliner, Steve. 1993. Constant quality price changes, depreciation, and retirement of mainframe computers." In *Price measurements and their uses,* ed. M. Foss, M. Manser, and A. Young, 19–62. Chicago: University of Chicago Press.

Phister, Montgomery, Jr. 1979. *Data processing technology and economics.* Santa Monica, Calif.: Digital Press.

Trajtenberg, Manuel. 1990. *Economic analysis of product innovation, the case of CT scanners.* Cambridge, Mass.: Harvard University Press.

Triplett, Jack E. 1986. The economic interpretation of hedonic methods. *Survey of Current Business* 66 (January): 36–40.

———. 1989. Price and technological change in a capital good: A survey of research on computers. In *Technology and capital formation,* ed. Dale W. Jorgenson and Ralph Landau. Cambridge: MIT Press.

Comment   Erik Brynjolfsson

The proliferation of new goods in the economy over the past several decades has been indirectly enabled by a ten-thousand-fold improvement in the performance of computer technology. Computers give companies the capability to manage the complexity of developing, producing, marketing, and servicing ever more products. They are new goods which enable even more new goods. Of course, in addition to this indirect effect, the unprecedented improvement in the underlying technology has had a direct impact on the computer industry itself, where new generations of products arrive at a pace measured in months.

Shane Greenstein has undertaken the important job of estimating the contribution that new mainframes made to welfare in the 1970s, when they were the dominant class of computers. This is not an easy task. The evolution of this paper through three revisions and three presentations reflects substantial effort.

This paper reflects state-of-the-art research, and the basic thesis, that growth on the extensive margin is a major source of surplus in the mainframe computing market, is sensible. Nonetheless, one of the lessons I take from this paper is that the methods applied must be used with great care. We do not yet have a "silver bullet" for evaluating the value of new goods. This point can be best illustrated by stepping back and putting the reported results in perspective. Accordingly, after summarizing some of the main contributions of Greenstein's paper, I will contrast them to the inferences that could be made from a somewhat simpler look at the data.

This paper has a number of strengths. First, Greenstein has chosen a critically important topic. Computers are an increasingly large contributor to economic welfare, and the main hypothesis of the paper, that extending the capabilities of computers is important, is clearly on target.

Second, the paper makes use of a very promising, underexploited data set which provides broad coverage of the rental prices of mainframes and their installed base. Identifying and working with this kind of detailed data is not easy and needs to be commended whenever it is done. Often, a great deal can be learned by even a first pass through such data. Indeed, the simple plot in figure 8.2 makes the key point that mainframe capabilities have grown over time nearly as effectively as the tables derived from more detailed calculations.

Erik Brynjolfsson is the Douglas Drane Career Development Associate Professor of Information Technology and Management at the Sloan School of Management of the Massachusetts Institute of Technology.

Third, this paper represents the first use outside of the automobile industry of some of the tools developed by Bresnahan (1987) and Berry (1994). The mainframe market seems as though it might be fertile ground for these tools insofar as vertical differentiation is an important characteristic of this market. There is a large spread in the power of systems, whether measured by the speed of the CPU, the amount of random access memory, or the storage capacity, and that power is highly correlated with the price of the systems. Of course, horizontal differentiation is also important in this industry; how much this will affect the results is difficult to know in advance.

Fourth, Greenstein demonstrates some technical innovations which overcome a number of difficulties with the data and help account for some important features of the mainframe market. For example, by including a conjectural-variation parameter to account for competitive response to price changes, Greenstein's model is an improvement over the hedonic approach which typically assumes a constant markup. As a result, he is able to present evidence that some of the decline in prices in mainframes may have been due either to an erosion of IBM's monopoly power or to the diminution of network externalities associated with the value of the IBM standard. Another technical innovation is adapting the Bresnahan-Berry model to a data set with some missing observations. Greenstein also had to do some work to derive reasonable-looking cost functions. By judiciously adding some additional constraints to the model, cost declines became evident on an order of magnitude that is comparable to that found in hedonic models.

With all these strengths, the ingredients are in place for some important results. The reported results can be grouped into three sets. The main finding was that entry on the extensive margin was economically significant. A careful reading of the last column of table 8.4 indicates that mainframes generated over one thousand million (i.e., one billion) dollars of surplus per *month* in 1981, or about $13 billion per year. Table 8.5 shows that the larger mainframes accounted for an increasing share of this amount: the surplus due to class seven mainframes, IDC's largest category, rose from 1 to 14 percent.

Second, while Greenstein finds evidence that the extensive margin was growing in importance, his results also imply that neither consumers nor producers benefited much overall. Table 8.4 suggests that the total surplus in this market has declined over time, despite a rapid increase in spending and the installed base. This finding is particularly striking given the increases in product quality which we know to have occurred in this industry and which are confirmed in table 8.7. Interestingly, note 40 reports that the decline in surplus cannot be attributed to more-monopolistic pricing. Indeed, producers also lost out: competition increased in this market as measured by median product elasticity.[1]

---

1. For IBM, by far the biggest mainframe producer, the worst was yet to come. See Bresnahan and Greenstein (1994).

The final set of results suggests that diffusion was slow and the new systems added little to surplus. Amazingly, the model predicts that if all systems less than four years old were removed from the market in 1981, surplus would have been reduced only by 1.6 percent!

While each of these results was derived by the careful application of state-of-the-art theory to the best available data, they are subject to important qualifications. In particular, several of these results call for closer scrutiny because they are not consistent with some of the conventional wisdom regarding the market for mainframe computers. For example, the welfare estimates, while large, may still be too low; the reported decline in surplus over time is suspect; and the small welfare contribution of new goods (less than four years old) is almost certainly incorrect, or at least misleading, given the blazing technological advances in this industry. While it is always interesting to see long-held beliefs challenged, in this match, I think the weight of the evidence will still be found to be on the side of the conventional wisdom.

Let's begin by looking more closely at the estimates of total surplus. It is useful to compare Greenstein's analysis with a simpler benchmark estimate based on the demand curve implied by the decline in the price of computer power and the concurrent increase in the quantity of computer power purchased. This approach will make some different assumptions which highlight the role of price declines in creating welfare benefits (as opposed to extensions in the product space).

To simplify the analysis, suppose that the computer power that can be purchased for a dollar has similar welfare characteristics, regardless of where that dollar is spent. In other words, a key departure from Greenstein's approach is that we now make the assumption that the ratio of surplus to spending is unaffected by the mix of big systems and smaller systems in a given year.[2] We shall see below that this assumption does not appear to be far from the truth. The resulting welfare estimates will not be strictly comparable to Greenstein's but can be used to put his estimates in perspective.[3]

Over the past several years, one well-documented feature in the computing sector has been dramatic decline in the cost of computing: on the order of 20 percent per year (e.g., see Gordon 1993). In theory, price declines can be caused by shifts in either supply or demand, but there can be little doubt that this magnitude of decline must be due almost entirely to one thing: technical change in the production function. In fact, technical change in the computer industry is relatively well-understood and is remarkably predictable (Grove 1990). A rather fortuitous combination of physics, geometry, and materials science has enabled microchip performance to double every eighteen months for the past three decades.

2. This is not the same as the stronger assumptions that surplus per computer or surplus per unit of computer power are constant.
3. The results will be more comparable to those of Bresnahan (1986) and Brynjolfsson (1993, 1996), who undertake similar, if more detailed, exercises.

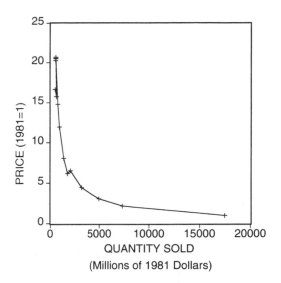

Fig. 8C.1   Mainframe price versus quantity, 1968–1981

Given this knowledge of the underlying dynamics of price change, there is less need for the traditional agnosticism of economists regarding the source of the price changes derived from hedonic estimates (e.g., Griliches 1990, 189). Clearly, the steady decline in the price of computer power is due mainly to a shift of the supply curve, and this is consistent with Greenstein's cost function estimates for the mainframe market.

This knowledge enables us to identify a benchmark demand curve, as suggested by figures 8C.1 and 8C.2, using the values for price and quantity based on Greenstein's tables 8.7 and 8.4, respectively. Indeed, demand appears to be well fit by the traditional log-linear specification:

$$q = e^{\gamma}p^{\alpha}y^{\delta},$$

where q is quantity (based on Greenstein's table 8.4), p is price (based on Greenstein's table 8.7), y is income (from real gross domestic product reported by the Council of Economic Advisers 1992) and γ, α, and δ are parameters. The parameter estimates, based on a simple regression, are reported in table 8C.1.

Given such an estimate of demand it is easy to generate a straightforward estimate of exact consumer's surplus (Hausman 1981).[4] This back-of-the-envelope calculation suggests that the increase in consumer's surplus attribut-

---

4. The increase in exact consumer's surplus from a price change from p_0 to p_1 is given by

$$\{(1-\delta)[e^{\gamma}(p_1^{1+\alpha} - p_0^{1+\alpha})/(1 + \alpha)] + y(1 - \delta)\}/(1 - \delta - y).$$

In principle, this approach should capture some of the benefits of new goods through the increase in quantity sold, but it will be an underestimate if these new goods contribute disproportionately to welfare.

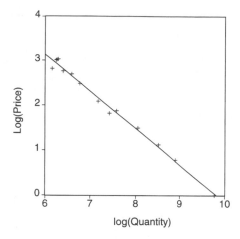

Fig. 8C.2   Log (price) versus log (quantity), with regression line

Table 8C.1   **Regression Estimates for the Demand for Mainframe Computers as a Function of Price**

Dependent variable = LQUANT81
Sample range = 1968–1981
$N = 14$
$R^2 = 0.994$
Adjusted $R^2 = 0.993$
Standard error of regression = 0.0963
F-statistic = 912
Mean of dependent = 7.29
Standard deviation of dependent = 1.14
Sum of squared residuals = 0.102

Variable	Coefficient	Standard Error	t-statistic	2-Tail Significance
C	−11.9	8.63	−1.38	0.194
LPRICE81	−1.05	0.0677	−15.6	0.000
LGDP	1.44	0.573	2.52	0.029

able to the price decline in mainframe computer power between 1968 and 1981 was about $43.9 billion in 1981.[5] This is likely to be an underestimate of surplus, since, inter alia, some allowance should be made for the fact that, due to diffusion, the demand curve probably shifted outward somewhat over this period, beyond the increase in GNP.

5. Log-linear demand is also consistent with the application of the index number method used by Bresnahan (1986), which gives a slightly higher estimate of about $49.2 billion. Either figure is consistent with the finding in Brynjolfsson (1993) that consumer's surplus in the overall computer market amounts to three to four times expenditures. Another interesting point of reference is IBM's 1981 net income of $4.4 billion and 60.2 percent gross margins.

What can we learn from such a benchmark estimate? In comparison, Greenstein estimates that surplus from advances in the extensive margin of computing was $13 billion for 1981. This benchmark exercise supports his contention that the extensive margin was an important component of mainframes' contributions to economic welfare, although perhaps less important than I would previously have guessed.[6] Because Greenstein's surplus estimates are based on a changing definition of the "outside good" over time, it is difficult to interpret the figures much further.

However, as Greenstein notes, his method should lend itself more fruitfully to relative comparisons, such as the proportion of welfare generated by computers of various sizes. In particular, he reports that 14 percent of surplus is generated by the 5 percent of units in the highest size class in 1981. This appears to suggest that large systems contribute disproportionately to welfare. However, this statistic must be interpreted carefully. Since large units are much costlier, a more relevant comparison would be the amount of welfare generated versus the dollars spent on these units. Greenstein has stated that the largest computers also account for about 14 percent of spending in 1981, so ironically, this suggests that, in terms of surplus, perhaps large systems *can* be modeled as "clumps" of small systems. If this is the case generally, then the benchmark surplus estimates derived above may not be far from the truth.

It is important to note, however, that without Greenstein's analysis, the assumption that welfare was proportional to spending for large systems could not have been tested. It is certainly not true that mainframes are technologically equal to collections of smaller machines in cost per unit of computer power. Since we know that mainframe users pay a higher unit price for their computer power, they must also be getting greater benefits. These benefits need not necessarily scale up proportionately, since, because of indivisibilities in many computational tasks, one cannot fully arbitrage processing power on PCs for processing on mainframes, client-server architectures notwithstanding.

If the amount of surplus attributable to large systems seems broadly consistent with what we know about the mainframe market, the reported decline in measured surplus over time is more difficult to explain, especially given the rising expenditures on mainframes and their growing capabilities. One possibility is that because the measured benefit is net of outside good, this result could be a function of the powerful minicomputers encroaching on the mainframe market. It is true that mainframe software was ported to many minicomputers in the 1970s and the data set is missing many of these machines, particularly in DEC's VAX line. However, total expenditure on mainframes continued

---

6. My spoken comments on the two previous versions of his paper were much less supportive of his main result. Based on a similar benchmark analysis, I then argued that his estimates were probably off by at least an order of magnitude. However, in the latest version of the paper, Greenstein's original estimates of $1–2 billion *per year* have been updated to be $1–2 billion *per month*. Since his original calculations were internally consistent, this fact might never have been noticed without the "reality check" provided by the benchmark method.

to rise over this period, leading Greenstein to discount the role of increasing capabilities of the "outside good" as an explanation.

Nonetheless, a slightly more complex story may be viable. Begin by noting that the Greenstein model measures the *marginal* surplus associated with the last bit of computing power, not the average or total surplus. As the portion of the vertically differentiated product space occupied by mainframes moved "up," it is possible that the marginal surplus from mainframe computing declined, although the total benefits of computers might have been increasing. A related story could be told in which increasingly less-valuable niches in the mainframe market were gradually filled over time, leading to lower marginal benefit but increasing total surplus.[7]

However, I agree with Greenstein that the most compelling explanation for the decline in measured surplus is the growing importance of horizontal differentiation. The rise of the horizontal differential suggests that there are many extensive margins to the computing market and that a one-dimensional vertical-differentiation model is too simple in this application. In fact, much of the value to consumers probably came from the new uses of *low end* computers that were enabled by complementary innovations in software and other products. In the 1970s, this meant dedicated word-processing systems and special-purpose minicomputer packages. In the 1980s, personal computers were made valuable by dozens of new applications and markets. In the 1990s, it appears that game machines and "smart" cable-television boxes may create some of the biggest fortunes and consumer benefits.[8]

As suggested by figure 8C.3, marketing experts in the computer industry, such as former Apple CEO John Sculley, do not tend to think of the product space as being most meaningfully described by a single vertical dimension. While there are numerous extensive margins in "Sculley space," mainframes don't appear to be on any of them. To put it another way, given the general-purpose nature of computer power, it seems unlikely that vendors and users would soon exhaust its potential for new applications and new markets even if there were *no* further advances in the power delivered at the high end of the market.

Because the product space may be getting more crowded in the horizontal dimension as different products address different markets but do so with comparable amounts of computing power, the vertical-differentiation model may

---

7. If the definition of the outside good had remained fixed in absolute terms, instead of changing each year, the increase in total surplus would have been more evident. This is apparent in figure 8.2.

8. The term "low end" is only relative: Nintendo's 64 video game player, scheduled for release in early 1996 at a price of $300, is aimed at providing three-dimensional "virtual reality" gaming for young teenage boys. To address this new application, the machine uses a 64-bit microprocessor running at 100 Megahertz which delivers 125 MIPS of raw computing power. In contrast, the most powerful mainframe available in 1980 (in Greenstein's sample), delivered 15 MIPS for a rental price of about $350,000 a month. (Of course, MIPS is only one measure of a computer's power.)

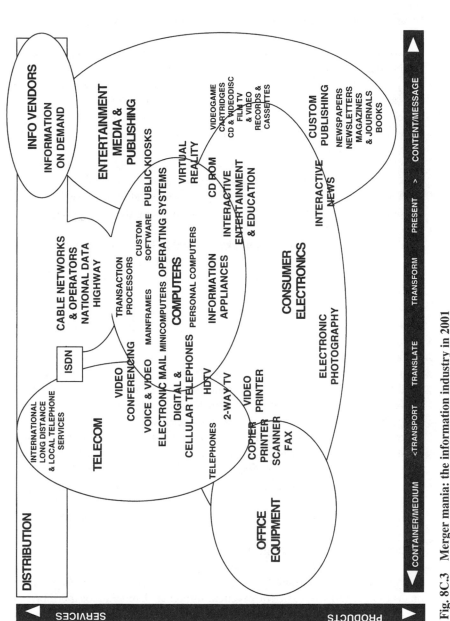

Fig. 8C.3 Merger mania: the information industry in 2001

Source: Survey of the Computer Industry, 27 February 1993, 59. © 1993 The Economist Newspaper Group, Inc. Reprinted with permission. Further reproduction prohibited.

not be valid even for relative comparisons over time. For instance, Greenstein's finding that the market appears to be growing more competitive may simply be an artifact of neighbors in the vertical dimension looking like substitutes even when they are not.

Growing horizontal differentiation can also account for the counterintuitive finding that new systems (less than four years old) added so little to surplus in any given year. A vertical-differentiation model will underestimate the contribution of new goods when it assumes that a new Wang word-processing system merely substitutes for an old IBM transaction-processing system with comparable processing power. This makes it look like eliminating Wang would not have affected welfare much.

In comparison, the benchmark welfare contribution of the price declines embodied in new technologies are apparently much larger. For instance, a 20 percent decline in prices between 1980 and 1981 would have increased exact consumer welfare by $3 billion, or 7.5 percent, using the demand-curve estimates presented above.

What can we learn from this work? Certainly Greenstein has addressed an important problem and valuable insights spring from his data and analyses. Perhaps most importantly, Greenstein's paper underscores both the strengths and the weaknesses of the vertical-differentiation models and will set future work on a firmer foundation. While the interpretation of the absolute value of the surplus estimates derived is difficult, it appears that relative comparisons can be more meaningful. For instance, one of Greenstein's most important contributions is in establishing that the welfare contributions of very large classes of mainframes are significant, although not necessarily disproportionate to expenditures on them. On the other hand, the counterfactual estimates of the welfare losses from eliminating machines of recent vintages are almost certainly too low. This highlights the fact that a vertical-differentiation model will underestimate the surplus contribution of new goods when horizontal differentiation is important. Unfortunately, it seems as though this will become an increasingly important weakness as more new goods appear in the economy which cannot be differentiated solely by a one-dimensional quality metric.

The somewhat humbling message is that our tools are still fairly blunt. Estimating the value of new goods may still be an area in which economics is a one-digit science. Accordingly, whenever possible we will need to use multiple methods to triangulate on an answer. My own bias is that a simple pass through new detailed data may often be one of the most informative approaches. For example, Greenstein's figure 8.2 told most of the story of his paper and struck me as a more reliable basis for practical inference than some of the more sophisticated analytical results he also presented. A related point is that reasonableness checks based on knowledge of the specific domain being analyzed can tell us whether our estimates are at least in the right order of magnitude. Insights flow not only from models to our knowledge of the world, but also in the reverse direction.

The economy is evolving in directions that make this type of analysis increasingly critical and I certainly expect that it will be successfully applied again in future empirical work. For most goods, looking only at price declines may miss most of the welfare benefits. Perhaps the computer market is one place where the simple price-decline approach does not do too much injustice. More likely, a focus solely on either price declines or vertical differentiation will miss important features of the market: future work will need to look at margins in other dimensions. In any case, Greenstein's paper unquestionably advances the extensive margin of economic research on the value of new goods.

References

Berry, S. T. 1994. Estimating discrete choice models of product differentiation. *Rand Journal of Economics* 25:242–62.
Bresnahan, T. F. 1986. Measuring the spillovers from technical advance: Mainframe computers in financial services. *American Economic Review* 76(4): 742–55.
———. 1987. Competition and collusion in the American auto industry: The 1955 price war. *Journal of Industrial Economics* 35:457–82.
Bresnahan, T., and S. Greenstein. 1994. The competitive crash in large-scale commercial computing. Paper presented at the Conference on Growth and Development: The Economics of the Twenty-first Century, June. Stanford, Calif.: Stanford University.
Brynjolfsson, E. 1993. Some estimates of the contribution of information technology to consumer welfare. Working paper no. 3647–94. Sloan School of Management, Massachusetts Institute of Technology, Cambridge.
———. 1996. The contribution of information technology to consumer welfare. *Information Systems Research* 7 (September).
Council of Economic Advisers. 1992. *Economic report of the president and the council of economic advisers.* Washington, D.C.: Government Printing Office.
Gordon, R. J. 1993. *The measurement of durable goods prices.* Chicago: University of Chicago Press.
Griliches, Z. 1990. Hedonic price indexes and the measurement of capital and productivity: Some historical reflections. *Fifty years of economic measurement,* ed. E. Berndt and J. Triplett, 185–206. Chicago: University of Chicago Press.
Grove, A. S. 1990. The future of the computer industry. *California Management Review* 33 (1): 148–60.
Hausman, J. 1981. Exact consumer's surplus and deadweight loss. *American Economic Review* 71 (4): 662–76.

III   Measurement Practice in Official Price Indexes

9   New Products and the U.S. Consumer Price Index

Paul A. Armknecht, Walter F. Lane, and Kenneth J. Stewart

The U.S. Consumer Price Index (CPI), which the Bureau of Labor Statistics (BLS) publishes, measures the average change in the price of consumer goods and services from a base period to subsequent periods. BLS publishes a CPI for each month; consequently, the CPI is frequently used to measure price change between periods other than the base period; most commonly, the change in price level from one month to the previous month or to the same month one year earlier. By linking together historic CPIs (with earlier base periods), BLS has created a series of monthly price indexes that begins in January 1913. Although it is hoped that users recognize that this use is less precise, the CPI is also used to measure price change over longer periods that may span one or more of these linkings.

New items—items that did not exist in the CPI's base period—pose some distinct problems for the CPI. How well the CPI deals with the problems new consumer goods and services pose is critical to how well it measures consumer price change. Diewert notes that "ignoring new goods could lead to a substantial overestimation of price inflation and a corresponding underestimation of real growth rates, especially in advanced market economies where millions of new goods are introduced each year" (1987, 779).

The problem of new goods and services is potentially acute for the U.S. CPI because we at BLS revise it, and thereby reestablish its base period, so rarely.

Paul A. Armknecht is assistant commissioner for prices and price indexes at the Bureau of Labor Statistics and a member of the Conference on Research in Income and Wealth of the National Bureau of Economic Research. Walter F. Lane is chief of the Branch of Consumer Prices and Kenneth J. Stewart is chief of the Information and Analysis Section in the Division of Consumer Prices and Price Indexes of the Bureau of Labor Statistics.

The authors thank several members of the Consumer Price Index program staff for their assistance. In particular, Joe Chelena researched the data on the introduction of videocassette recorders into the index.

We set a new base period only once every ten years. To minimize the variance of the expenditures that form the basis of the base-period weights and to minimize any cyclical effects, we use a three-year period for the base. In addition, lags in obtaining the expenditure data mean that we cannot use a new base period until two years after it has ended. For example, the CPI for January 1987 was the first using the current base period, which is 1982–84; our current plans are for 1993–95 to be the next base period starting with the index for January 1998.

We compute and publish the CPI every month. As a result, a given base period is in effect for a very long time, perhaps as long as fourteen years after its midpoint—ample time for many new goods and services to come along. In addition, the base period is the reference point for many indexes, perhaps 120 months' worth, so there are many intermediate comparisons (month to month or year to year) which mishandled new products can affect.

In our dynamic economy new items come into the consumer marketplace virtually continuously. We distinguish three cases of new products according to our response to them:

- *Replacement items* are new models are previously available items that are or soon will be discontinued, such as the current year's automobile models.
- *Supplemental items* include newly added brands of currently available goods such as cereal and new ways to sell a service like airline travel.
- *Entirely new items* are those not closely tied to any previously available item. Although they may satisfy a long-standing consumer need in a novel way, they do not fit into any established CPI item category.

The examples of entirely new products that most readily come to mind are new technologies in home electronics or perhaps medicine. However, the new items that are likely to be much more important in their potential effect on the CPI are in the more mundane areas such as food, apparel, housing, and transportation, where the vast majority of consumption expenditures occur. These include new forms of outlets such as fast-food restaurants, new types of packaging such as microwave meals, apparel made of new fabrics, new housing features such as air-conditioning, and new transportation products such as minivans.

9.1   Problems New Products Pose for the CPI

The handling of replacement items gives rise to the first problem new products pose for the CPI. When manufacturers of old items discontinue them and replace them with new versions or models, the index must replace the old items with their new versions. However, such a replacement may differ from its predecessor in some respects and likely will sell for a different price. Consequently, it is important that the CPI capture any price change occurring simultaneously with the replacement while avoiding any changes attributable to change in quality. When, for example, automobile or apparel manufacturers introduce new models and thereby create new versions of their old items, they may change the style or add features to items. One reason for introducing new versions is to create novelty, and manufacturers often take this opportunity to raise prices. To the extent that it is possible, we in the U.S. CPI program decompose these price changes. We break each one into a "quality change" component and a "pure price change" component and then remove the change due to changes in item quality so as to reflect only the "pure" price change in the CPI. Since the CPI will reflect any subsequent price declines that occur as the new product versions age, it must show any initial price jump that occurred when they were born. As described below, BLS has methods to capture the price change that accompanies the introduction of new models and styles, and it is fairly successful in applying them. When we are not able to separate the price change from the quality change, we treat the observation as a special type of nonresponse and estimate the true price change by a sophisticated imputation process.

The second problem relates to supplemental goods. These are new goods or services that are similar to ones already available; however, unlike replacement goods, their arrival is not coincident with the discontinuation of previously available goods. Examples of these items include new types of discount airline fares and generic drugs. In the replacement case, the disappearance of the old version of an item forces us to find the best substitute; the disappearing item provides a point of comparison for the new item. In the case of supplemental items, lower prices and/or higher quality—often in the form of new features or other considerations—may cause many consumers to shift to the new version of the item. As long as the old item remains in the marketplace, there is no external factor forcing us to shift with them. Supplemental items usually enter the index as we refresh our samples through our sample rotation process. When extreme marketplace changes force us to act, we use our best judgment and direct a reinitiation of a proportion of the sample to the new versions. However we bring in a supplemental item, either through sample rotation or through directed reinitiation, we do not compare it to an old item and attempt to gauge the value of the quality differential with an old product; this can lead to the CPI missing a price decrease.

The third problem that new items pose for the CPI results from the arrival of entirely new products in the consumer marketplace. The U.S. CPI covers many time periods between base-period revisions. It must introduce new items and begin reflecting their price movements as soon as possible after their debuts. Since it is likely that the prices of new products move differently from those of established ones, not finding a way to bring new items promptly into the index will diminish its accuracy. Typically, new items, because of their initial scarcity or novelty, enter the marketplace at relatively high prices; then, as they become established and competing sources enter the marketplace and increase their supply, their novelty diminishes and their prices fall. Again, as described below, the BLS has ways to bring new goods into the CPI market basket and to account for their price changes from that time forward.

The final and most intractable problem results from the fact that the arrival of new products allows consumers to satisfy their needs and desires more efficiently. New products displace the roles older ones played in consumers' consumption patterns. Consumers may cut back or even eliminate their consumption of some older items and still be as well-off as they were in the base period. They do this by purchasing, possibly at the same or lower cost, some of the new items-perhaps some that are quite different from the old ones—because the new items provide consumer satisfaction much more efficiently. In addition, the reality is that consumers combine the products they purchase to satisfy the basic needs and desires that result in their standard of living. For example, at one time a consumer may have combined a shirt and the services of a professional laundry to obtain a level of dress; the arrival of easy-care fabric shirts has for some consumers replaced the need for professional laundry services with the need for home laundry service at a lower marginal cost. Many consumers have shifted to the easy-care fabric shirts laundered at home and away from the older shirts laundered professionally. Arguably, just the presence of additional items, because they provide a greater range of consumer choice, is a form of price decrease. Unfortunately, the U.S. CPI has no way to show the price decreases that consumers experience as they take advantage of the new items to maintain or increase their living standards, and, consequently, the CPI fails to take account of the decline in the cost of living that new items bring.

9.2   CPI Sampling Frames and CPI Samples

To understand how these new products are introduced into the U.S. CPI, one needs to know a little more about how the CPI structures the consumer marketplace and selects items to represent it. The first sample we drew for the 1987 CPI revision was a geographic sample of eighty-five urban areas, which we call *primary sampling units* (PSUs). The BLS uses a 44-strata geographic sampling frame, which represents all urban consumers in the United States. We sometimes refer to these 44 geostrata as *market baskets*. We assigned each urban area in the United States to a unique geostrata.The geographic universe consists of all U.S. urban areas, both officially defined metropolitan areas and CPI-defined nonmetropolitan urban places. Thirty-two large metropolitan areas are *self-representing areas* because they are the only members of their strata, and consequently, they represent their entire geostrata. In the remaining 12 strata we probability-selected another fifty-six areas to represent medium- and smaller-sized metropolitan areas and nonmetropolitan urban places.

The item structure for the CPI consists of 207 item strata for commodity groups such as white bread, carbonated drinks, boys' apparel, and so forth. The cross of the 44 geostrata with the 207 item strata creates the 9,108 basic strata, which is the level of index calculation at which the weights are fixed. Within each item strata we defined one or more substrata, called *entry-level items* (ELIs). There are 364 ELIs which are the first stage of item selection. ELIs are also the level of item definition at which BLS data collectors begin item sampling within each outlet.

9.2.1   Consumer Expenditure Survey

The CPI uses three surveys to conduct item/outlet sampling. The first is the Consumer Expenditure Survey (CES), which provides the weights for the basic strata and sample weights for ELI selection within the strata. The CES consists of an interview survey and a diary survey. The interview survey collects inventories of items held by the respondent and his or her expenditures for a full year on major consumer purchases (vehicles, durable goods, insurance policies). The diary survey records every purchase made during a two-week period to any member of the family. Each expenditure recorded is mapped to one of the 364 ELIs. Estimates of annual expenditures for each ELI and item strata by area are then produced. The average of these estimated annual expenditures for the 1982–84 period compose the expenditure weights used in the U.S. CPI.

To enable the CPI to reflect changes in the marketplace, item and outlet samples are reselected on a rotating basis. Each year, we select a new sample of ELIs and outlets for 20 percent of the areas (about seventeen cities). Each year, four regional universes are tabulated at the ELI level from the two most recent years of CES data. An independent sample of ELIs is selected for each items stratum with the probability of selection determined by the relative importance of the ELI within the strata. The sample-selection example (table 9.1) demonstrates the way this allows new items to enter in the information-processing item stratum. For the areas that had their samples rotated in 1984, the 1982–83 CES data were used. The "typewriters and calculators" ELI had the highest relative importance within the item stratum, followed by home computers. For the 1987 sample-rotation cities, these ELIs reversed positions, with home computers having the highest probability of selection, Thus, the ELIs selected for area samples will change based on their importance in the ongoing CESs.

9.2.2   Outlet Samples

The second survey used for the U.S. CPI is the Point-of-Purchase Survey (POPS), which determines the retail outlets from which consumers purchased goods and services. In the areas scheduled for sample rotation in the following year, the Census Bureau, under contract with BLS, conducts a POPS. The POPS is a household survey conducted over a four- to six-week period, usually beginning in April. It asks respondents whether or not cetain categories of items were purchased within a specified recall period. The recall period varies depending on the type of items purchased. ELIs are grouped into sampling categories (called *POPS categories*). Some POPS categories consist of only

Table 9.1   **Example of Sample Selection: Information-Processing Equipment for Southern Region**

	Probability of Selection	
ELI	1984	1987
Home computers	.25055	.34792[a]
Home computer software	.13491	.18734
Telephones	.13326	.19619
Typewriters, calculators	.27819[a]	.21018
Other processing equipment	.20308	.05825

Notes: Probability of selection is calculated as the ELI total expenditure divided by the item stratum total expenditure. The 1984 probabilities are computed from 1982–83 CES data; the 1987 probabilities are computed from 1984–85 CES data.

[a]Most important ELI in the item stratum

one ELI; other POPS categories contain several ELIs when certain types of commodities or services are generally sold in the same retail outlets. For example, the "meat and poultry" POPS category consists of eight beef ELIs, six pork ELIs, four ELIs for other meats, and three poultry ELIs. These are combined because an outlet that sells beef also tends to sell other meats. For each category the respondent in the household is asked about purchases made within the stated recall period, the names and locations of places of purchase, and the expenditure amounts. After this information is tabulated for the city, a sample of outlets is drawn for each selected ELI.

Since the item and outlet samples are selected in separate processes for each geographic area, they must be merged before data collection. A concordance maps each ELI to a POPS category. Each sample ELI is assigned for price collection to the outlet selected for the corresponding POPS category. The number of price quotes collected for an ELI in each outlet is equivalent to the number of times the ELI was selected for the area in the item-sampling process.

The number of price quotes assigned for collection in a sample outlet is determined through the item- and outlet-sample merge. In the outlet-sample process, an outlet may be selected more than once for a given POPS category, provided the expenditures reported for the outlet are large. The outlet may also be selected for more than one POPS category. If an outlet is selected multiple times for a given POPS category, the same multiple of price quotes will be assigned for collection for each sample ELI matching the category. If an outlet is selected for more than one POPS category, price quotes will be assigned for collection for all sample ELIs matching the categories.

9.2.3   Selection Procedures within Outlets

The third survey—the Commodities and Services (C&S) survey—is the main data-collection vehicle for the CPI program. It consists of the combined sample from the item- and outlet-sample merge. For each ELI assigned for price collection in a sample outlet, a BLS field representative selects a specific store item using multistage probability-selection techniques. The field representative first identifies all of the items included in the ELI definition and offered for sale by the outlet. Items are grouped by common characteristics, such as brand, style, size, or type of packing. With the assistance of the respondent for the outlet, probabilities of selection are assigned to each group based on sales information.

After assigning probabilities of selection, the field representative uses a random-number table to select a group. All items included in the selected group are identified. Further groups are formed based on the common characteristics of the items. Probabilities are assigned to each group in the second stage, and a random-number table is used for selection. The process is repeated through successive stages until a unique item is identified. The field representative describes the selected item on a checklist which contains the descriptive characteristics necessary to identify the item and to determine or explain differences in characteristics that determine an item's price for all items defined within the ELI.

These procedures produce an objective, unbiased probability sampling of items throughout the CPI. They also allow broad definitions of ELIs so that the same tight specification need not be priced everywhere, as was the case prior to the 1978 revision of the CPI. An important benefit from the broader ELIs is a significantly higher probability of finding an item to price within the sample outlet that is included in the definition of the ELI and finding items that represent what the stores and other outlets often sell.

BLS agents complete the selection process at their initial visit to the outlet. Subsequently, either monthly or bimonthly, they revisit (or, less commonly, telephone) the outlet to obtain the price for the selected item.

9.3   Introducing New Items through Substitution

When a BLS field representative attempts to collect the price of an item in the CPI sample and discovers that the outlet no longer sells it, he or she follows our *substitution* procedures. Each month about 3 percent of the nonshelter observations in our sample are replacements of this kind, which we refer to as substitutions. Under the substitution procedures the field representative finds the item for sale in the outlet that is closest in quality to the discontinued item; this will be a new or updated version of it if one is there. The difference between the price of the old version of the item, observed the previous time, and the price of the substitute version this time, may represent

- pure price change that occurred during the time between the two observations,
- quality differences between the two versions, or
- some of both.

As a constant-quality price index, the CPI must isolate, measure, and remove any quality changes between the discontinued and replacement versions, while retaining any pure price change between the previous and current periods. Professional economists, called *commodity analysts,* make what are known as *comparability decisions* on how to handle substitute items. In the U.S. CPI, the treatment of substitutions can be broadly divided into three categories:

- those considered to be directly comparable to the discontinued variety,
- those where a direct quality adjustment is applied, and
- those where price-change imputation occurs.

In contrast to other ways of bringing in new items, all three categories of substitution compare, in some fashion, the price of a new item to that of the one it is replacing. We give a cursory review of the directly comparable and the direct quality-adjustment methods for treating substitutions; these have already been well documented elsewhere in Armknecht and Weyback (1989) and Kokoski (1993). We have recently improved the methods the CPI uses to impute price change for commodities and services, and these will be discussed in greater detail.

9.3.1 Direct Comparison

Long-in-place CPI procedures ensure that, when a specific item included in the CPI sample is no longer available, our field representatives select a replacement item that is as comparable in quality as possible to the discontinued variety. If the CPI commodity analyst deems the replacement version to be of the same or similar quality as its predecessor, we compare the price of the new item directly to the price of the discontinued variety—and we use that price change in index calculations. In this case we assume that there are no changes in quality between the two versions. To the extent that the replacement version of an item deemed to be of comparable quality is in fact of higher quality than the discontinued variety, the estimate of constant-quality price change for that item will be biased upward. For example, televisions often fall in price while they improve their features; in that case, we treat the replacement as comparable to show the decline in the market price of the television, but we miss the additional decline due to the improved quality, unless we can put a value on the improved features.

9.3.2 Direct Quality Adjustment

If a commodity analyst deems a replacement item to be qualitatively different from its predecessor, we attempt to isolate and remove the quality differences between the two versions. Direct quality adjustments are particularly common in the automobile and apparel components of the CPI.

Since the early 1960s, the new car and truck price indexes have used production-cost differences, marked up to retail, to adjust new vehicles for changes in quality between model years. Automobile manufacturers supply

BLS with production-cost data. We then adjust them upward by wholesale and retail markup rates to derive retail equivalent values for the quality changes. Quality changes for new vehicles in the CPI are made for changes which affect the performance and efficiency of the car. In addition, BLS treats all federally mandated safety and pollution requirements as quality changes.

Many new varieties of apparel are directly adjusted for changes in quality. Apparel analysts have developed regression models for specific apparel item strata (e.g., women's dresses). The model parameter estimates serve as implicit prices for the item characteristics. We use these implicit prices to isolate and remove the quality change that occurs with the introduction of replacement apparel items (Liegey 1993). We implemented this improvement into most CPI apparel categories in January 1991. Over time we hope to extend it to other goods and services.

9.3.3   Imputation of Price Change

If a new version of an item is of dissimilar quality to the discontinued version, and we cannot identify and factor out those quality differences either by the use of marked-up production costs or by hedonic regression techniques, we impute an estimate of constant-quality price change. In effect, we are assuming that in this case the price of the original version of the item would have gone up at that same rate as that for some other items. We are assuming further that the price difference between the old and the new version in excess of this assumed increase is due to quality differences between the versions.

Before 1993, when a version of an item in the CPI sample was discontinued, and the replacement item was of dissimilar quality and could not be directly compared or quality-adjusted, the price change imputed to that item was the change for its item stratum in its index area. Effectively, the price change between versions of dissimilar quality was imputed by the average price change of all other similar items in the same period and in the same geographic area. This method, which is known as *overall-mean imputation,* is the same method we use to impute a price change for a nonresponse; it is appropriate for imputing a price change when there is no reason to believe anything special is occurring. This is the case in most food and service CPI item strata.

However, we can see in many categories of items, when comparing the price change of comparable substitutes to the price change for nonsubstitutes, that there is a significant relationship between price change and the introduction of replacement lines or models. For other items, such as most types of nonfood commodities, price change is closely associated with the annual or periodic introduction of replacement lines or models. Typically, many replacement versions (e.g., new car models, new apparel lines) initially sell at relatively high prices. The prices of these new versions often fall over time, until they, in turn, are discontinued in favor of even newer and often higher-priced replacement versions. For these types of items, the imputation procedures within the CPI have recently been improved; these changes are detailed below.

The overall-mean imputation method estimates price change for replacement versions from the price change of all other items in the same item stratum and index area. These include price changes for continuously priced (same) versions, as well as price changes for replacement versions of directly comparable quality (or those adjusted for changes in quality). Since price change for most types of nonfood commodities is associated with the introduction of new varieties, imputing price change for new varieties of dissimilar quality by price changes for both same and replacement versions was an improper estimate of price change (Armknecht and Weyback 1989). The continuously priced items showed little change and dampened the changes of the relatively few substitutes.

For example, automobile prices within a given model year often remain unchanged, or fall, as the model year progresses. On the other hand, price increases often accompany replacement new-model-year cars, even those of comparable quality to the discontinued models. Consequently, the average price change of comparable model changeover automobiles can be seen as a better approximation of price change for new models with dissimilar quality.

Since October 1989 we have imputed price changes for new-model-year cars and trucks using only the constant-quality price change of other model-year changeovers. In other words, price changes for cars and trucks *within* the same model year are no longer used to impute price changes *between* model years. This type of imputation, which is called *class-mean imputation* (Kalton and Kasprzyk 1986), is a more appropriate strategy for imputing price changes within the CPI.

Prior to its implementation, we tested class-mean imputation for the new car index for the twelve-month period ending February 1988. Over that study period, the test index (under the proposed new imputation strategy) rose 2.76 percent, compared to 2.42 percent for the published index. This occurred because, as expected, the average price change for model-year changeovers of comparable quality was usually higher than the average price change for automobiles within the same model year.

Subsequently, we simulated indexes using class-mean imputation for other types of nonfood commodities. Apparel items were obvious choices. Not only are apparel price changes associated with the introduction of new lines, but substitution is common for apparel items. While apparel represented only about 7 percent of all prices the CPI collected in 1993, over 31 percent of all replacement versions we encountered are in apparel (see table 9.2). Taken together, apparel and new vehicles make up around three-quarters of all direct quality adjustments in the CPI.

As with new vehicles, the price change associated with the introduction of new apparel lines, even after adjusting for changes in quality, was different from price changes for apparel lines within the same version. We began phasing in class-mean imputation for most other nonfood commodities in December 1992. Again, the sources of imputation of price change for replacement nonfood commodities of dissimilar quality are price changes for other, constant-quality replacement items.

Table 9.2   **Prices Collected for the Consumer Price Index for Replacement Versions, 1993**

CPI Major Groups and Selected Components	Total Prices Collected	Replacement Versions Priced	Replacement Versions Coded Directly Comparable	Replacement Versions Coded Directly Quality Adjusted	Replacement Versions Imputed by Overall Mean	Replacement Versions Imputed by Class Mean[a]
Food and beverages	467,396	7,854	3,200	41	4,299	314
Bananas	6,810	5	5	0	0	0
Housing (excluding shelter)[b]	123,876	4,164	2,479	149	1,008	528
Apparel and upkeep	58,739	8,558	6,307	912	775	564
Women's apparel	18,068	4,328	3,117	718	291	202
Transportation[c]	67,635	4,204	2,216	1,036	431	521
New cars and trucks	12,738	2,187	576	1,016	114	451
Medical care	50,490	876	254	317	281	24
Entertainment	27,403	1,196	673	68	356	99
Other goods and services	17,535	452	216	55	150	31
Total[d]	813,074	27,304	15,345	2,578	7,300	2,081

Source: Bureau of Labor Statistics.

[a]Includes some replacement versions of an imputation method that is being phased out.

[b]Treated here as a major group; "shelter" uses a different source of price data.

[c]Excludes used cars.

[d]Excludes selected components.

Table 9.2 shows the frequency of substitution within the various CPI major groups in 1993, that is, how many times during 1993 versions of items in our samples were discontinued and replaced by new varieties. The table also shows how the price change for those replacement versions was estimated.

9.4   Introducing New Items through Sample Rotation

The substitution and imputation procedures described above provide several ways for new products to join the CPI. A process we call *sample rotation* also provides several ways for the CPI to bring new products promptly into the index. Although the items entering through sample rotation do not get compared to those exiting at the same time, sample rotation enables the CPI to capture the movement of their prices soon after their arrival in the marketplace; this is important because the prices of new items are likely to move differently from the prices of established items.

Sample rotation is the annual reselection of the item and outlet samples for 20 percent of the geographic areas, which is about seventeen geographic areas. Consequently, all the samples turn over every five years. We link the new outlets and items that enter during rotation into the index by *overlap pricing*. This means that we price the old samples for the last time we use them in the CPI in the same month that we collect the new samples for the first time. In contrast to the situation in substitution, in sample rotation the prices of the two versions refer to the same time period. Consequently, we regard price differences between the old and new samples as quality differences. However, if the items in the new sample provide consumer satisfaction more efficiently, the index misses that effect, which is a form of price decrease. Since the items and outlets in the new sample are randomly selected, there is no way to compare the new items coming in during rotation to the old ones exiting.

As previously discussed, the Bureau of the Census conducts a new POPS for us in each CPI geographic area slated for rotation. This permits us to draw new outlet samples based on current information. As a result, the postrotation outlet samples contain new types of outlets, such as specialty boutiques or discount stores. Of course, we make no comparisons cross outlets or outlet types; again, if the new outlets in some way provide the items (or the consumer satisfaction embodied in them) more efficiently, we miss this form of price decline.

As mentioned earlier, for each of the 207 item strata in the CPI structure we select an independent sample of lower-level items (called entry-level items because they are defined at the level at which within-outlet sampling begins) with the probability of selection determined by the relative importance of the ELI within its stratum. At each rotation we reselect the ELIs in each stratum. Because the probabilities of selection come from the most recently available CES, ELIs with growing importance, which may contain emerging new items, have an opportunity to be selected based on recent consumer behavior. Recall from table 9.1 that home computers now receive a higher probability of selection than typewriters and calculators. Thus, the ELIs in the CPI change following their changing importance in consumer spending patterns.

Some new items that appear in the market do not fit into existing ELI definitions but are close substitutes for products in an existing ELI. Such products emerge in the CES interviews and are coded separately so that expenditure data are available. For example, compact-disc players and compact discs are new substitute sound-equipment products for phonographs/tape players and records/tapes. The current ELI definition includes these items along with their expenditures, and the entire ELI could be initiated in all existing areas to reflect the current product mix. These situations occur infrequently, but CPI procedures can accommodate them. However, because of the time lapse associated with the CES and POPS surveys, unless special efforts are made to reinitiate an item stratum, it will be three to four years from the time the product appears in the marketplace to the time the product appears in the CPI.

At rotation, in addition to reselecting outlets and ELIs, we reinitiate all the ELI samples in the newly selected outlets. This gives supplementary new items (those that are similar to old items such as new brands or generics) a proper chance of selection and no doubt brings many into our samples in a fairly prompt manner. For the new products to enter through sample rotation they generally must fall within the definition of items eligible for price collection in an established ELI. Most new products in areas such as packaged foods, toys and hobbies, toilet goods and personal care products, new cars and trucks, and so forth, are eligible for pricing as their market penetration expands because of the broad ELI definition and/or their close similarity to existing products, and therefore they fall into established ELIs.

9.5   New Items That Cannot Be Introduced through Substitution or Rotation

In some instances, new products emerge that we cannot assimilate into any existing ELI, but that do fit within the item stratum definitions. In these cases we can define a new ELI and select sample items in accordance with the item's importance within the stratum. The product would then be introduced gradually through the five-year sample-rotation process. This process could take five to seven years for full implementation due to the lag in the CES and POPS surveys although samples would probably be somewhat representative after three to four years. The new series for midgrade unleaded gasoline is an example of this.

Finally, a new class of products may be introduced that cannot readily be defined within the existing item-strata structure. Such products would not be introduced until all item strata are redefined and the new stratum can be introduced within the CPI classification structure. This reclassification only occurs when major revisions of the CPI are introduced about every ten years. Examples of such products are videocassette recorders (VCRs) and home computers, which were introduced into the CPI classification with the 1987 revision.

For example VCRs first entered the consumer marketplace in significant volume in 1977 (see table 9.3). During the 1983–85 period the number of VCR manufacturers grew rapidly, resulting in rapidly falling prices and even more rapidly growing sales. In 1987, when the CPI began measuring the price changes of VCRs, they represented about 0.1 percent of consumer expenditures. During the ten years between their effective marketplace introduction in 1977 and their 1987 introduction into the CPI, their price had fallen by approximately 60 percent and their quality had increased considerably. Unfortunately, the CPI did not reflect these developments.

9.6   The U.S. CPI as a Cost-of-Living Index

We view the U.S. CPI as an approximation of a true cost-of-living (COL) index (Fixler 1993). A COL index measures the change in the minimum cost of the base-period standard of living, that is, the standard of living that consumers in aggregate experienced in the base period. The U.S. CPI is actually a Laspeyres index. A Laspeyres index measures the change in the prices of the set of goods and services actually purchased in the base period. We call this set the CPI market basket. Although the market basket in any period should always yield the same standard of living as in the base period, it is not likely always to be the cheapest way to get that standard of living.

The COL index, with its reference to consumer satisfaction grounded in the economic theory of consumer behavior, can indicate how to handle some difficult questions or suggest the theoretically correct if practically difficult approach. Diewert (1987, 779), following a path he attributes to Hicks, suggests that, for new products, we should impute to a new good a base-period price that is just high enough to make its base-period quantity of demand equal to zero. Of course, it would be quite an econometric challenge to estimate the demand equations for even a few new items, and realistically, such an approach is not feasible for us in the U.S. CPI.

The COL index can also guide us in determining what items to include in the CPI and how to stratify them. As a COL index approximation, the CPI should be an index of all—and limited to only—goods and services that contribute to consumers' well-being. Organizing the universe of consumer goods and services into item strata and higher-level groups provides both a means of sampling them and a way of analyzing changes in the CPI. In economic theory the consumer needs the requirements of life and desires the pleasures of life. His or her satisfaction increases continuously with the increasing of the quantity of the items that satisfy those needs and desires. These items are usually grouped into broad categories such as "food and beverages," "shelter," "apparel," "entertainment," "medical care," and so forth. In the United States we call these categories *major groups*. Presumably the consumer has some hierar-

Table 9.3   **VCR Sales and Estimated Retail Prices, 1978–1987**

Year	Unit Sales (thousands)	Value ($ millions)	Estimated Retail Price per Unit ($)
1978	402	299	1,240
1979	475	362	1,269
1980	805	498	1,032
1981	1,471	1,000	1,132
1982	1,599	1,300	1,355
1983	3,354	1,575	728
1984	6,731	2,898	717
1985	10,750	3,771	587
1986	11,810	3,893	549
1987	11,720	3,442	486

Source: Consumer Electronics Annual Review, Consumer Electronics Group, Electronic Industries Association, Washington, D.C., various issues.

Notes: Unit sales are total factory sales to dealers. Value is wholesale value of units sold to dealers. The estimated retail price is the wholesale value marked up to retail by estimated typical whole-sale-to-retail markup ratios.

chy of needs and desires and seeks to satisfy them incrementally. For example, he or she will not consume greater and greater quantities and qualities of food before acquiring any shelter or clothing. In other words, at any standard of living—except perhaps the lowest—consumers will consume items in several categories. In this gross sense, we can view the categories as gross *complements.*

Similarly, the items within the categories are gross *substitutes.* Each category is the means to satisfy some broad need or desire. "Food" satisfies the need for nourishment; "shelter," the need for protection from the elements; "entertainment," the desire for mental stimulation; "medical care," the need for relief from an ailment. In this sense, virtually any new item that comes along should find a home in one of the categories and be at least a partial substitute for an older item. To cite some examples from the past few decades:

fast food has replaced some home cooking;

microwave meals, some lunches in restaurants;

margarine, butter;

trucks and vans, some automobiles;

television-watching, some movie-going or reading;

airline travel, most train travel;

polio vaccine, treatment in an iron lung;

word processors, paper and pencil;

dental sealants, oral surgery;

contact lenses, eye glasses;

high-tech athletic shoes, sneakers;

air-conditioning, fans;

drugs, ultrasound, and microsurgery, much more invasive procedures.

In all of these examples, and in many, many more, consumer choice increased as the new items provided new ways to achieve the same or a higher level of satisfaction. For some new items, such as flying as a potential replacement for train travel, it is not unequivocally clear that consumers could achieve the same level of satisfaction for the same or a lower price. For others, such as the polio vaccine, there really can be no question that the new product is superior as well as cheaper.

The principle of the COL index that only the items that contribute to consumer utility belong in a consumer price index implies that we should model consumers' utility functions. Some utility-function models imply that what yields utility are not the individual items that consumers buy but combinations of them that they create through household or consumer production. For example, Nordhaus's provocative thesis in chapter 1 in this volume implies that consumers get utility from light, which they produce by combining several consumer goods and services, such as candles, matches, whale oil, kerosene, lanterns, batteries, flashlights, electricity, lightbulbs, light fixtures, and so on. The CPI can follow the prices of consumer items such as these but, so far at least, it has not tried to price the cost of light, which consumers in various eras have produced by combining some of them. Yet it seems that it is light and not the lightbulbs or the electricity that directly yields utility or a level of living to consumers. Another example might be the cost of an evening at the movies: in one era, consumers obtained this by combining the services of a movie theater, an automobile, and perhaps a baby-sitter; now perhaps they obtain equivalent entertainment from a VCR, a television, and a video rental. The CPI tends to limit its efforts to following the cost of items sold in the marketplace. To measure accurately the change in the cost of a standard of living we perhaps should follow the change in the cost of obtaining or producing a level of light or entertainment or other immediate contributors to consumer satisfaction.

The CPI has ways to add new products to its market basket and it adds them in a reasonably prompt manner. Unfortunately, except for replacement items that are new versions of older goods, it has no way to show the price decreases that consumers experience as they take advantage of the new items to maintain or increase their living standards. Consequently, the CPI fails to measure the decline in the cost of living that new items and new technology bring. Of course, over short periods of a year or so, this effect is not likely to be significant. New products initially have limited importance in the market. In the long term, we incorporate new products into the CPI, but we will still face the problems of adjusting for quality change and reflecting how the new items replace quite different older ones in the satisfaction of human wants and needs.

9.7   Summary

From the preceding discussion it should be clear that most new products that emerge are gradually introduced into the CPI for measuring price movement. In some cases we at the BLS are able to compare the new item to a previous item and make some form of quality adjustment. In other cases the new products are linked into the index and the CPI may miss any improvements to living standards associated with their arrival. Some items are introduced much more quickly than others depending on their rate of market penetration as measured in the CES and on research BLS economists perform to make sure the structure accommodates them easily. When a new genre of item appears in the marketplace and does not fit within the existing CPI structure, the new products can only be introduced when the classification structure is redefined during major revisions. To the extent that ELI and item-stratum definitions can be kept very broad, new products do get representation in the CPI. However, the broader questions—whether new products get sufficient representation, whether they are brought in soon enough, and perhaps most importantly, how they come in and get compared with older items—remain.

References

Armknecht, Paul A., and Donald Weyback. 1989. Adjustments for quality change in the U.S. Consumer Price Index. *Journal of Official Statistics* 5 (2): 107–23.

Diewert, W. E. 1987. Index numbers. In *The new Palgrave: A dictionary of economics,* vol. 2, ed. John Eatwell, Murray Milgate, and Peter Newman, 767–80. London: Macmillan.

Fixler, Dennis. 1993. The Consumer Price Index: Underlying concepts and caveats. *Monthly Labor Review* 116 (December): 3–12.

Kalton, Graham, and Daniel Kasprzyk. 1986. The treatment of missing survey data. *Survey Methodology* 12, no. 1 (June): 1–16.

Kokoski, Mary. 1993. Quality adjustment of price indexes. *Monthly Labor Review* 116 (December): 34–46.

Liegey, Paul R., Jr. 1993. Adjusting apparel indexes in the Consumer Price Index for quality differences. In *Price measurements and their uses,* ed. Murray F. Foss, Marilyn Manser, and Allan Young, 209–26. NBER Studies in Income and Wealth, vol. 57. Chicago: University of Chicago Press.

Comment   Frank C. Wykoff

The CPI, perhaps the most important single price statistic produced by the government, is used to calculate changes in many indexed public benefits and private contracts. It is a major indicator of economic and political performance;

Frank C. Wykoff is the Eldon Smith Professor of Economics at Pomona College.
The author thanks Chuck Hulten and Jack Triplett for comments on an earlier draft. The author is responsible, of course, for all errors of commission or omission.

some analysts even argue that the CPI alone should guide Federal Reserve Board policy. For these reasons, design and construction of the CPI is important.

Nonetheless, many academic and business economists have shown remarkable neglect of the actual construction of the CPI by the BLS. An occasional call by a Simon Kuznets or a Zvi Griliches for "better data" tends to fall on deaf ears among those in the profession. This neglect may have been abetted by some institutional inertia, a (perfectly understandable) bureaucratic tendency to avoid clear explanations of actual practice and a possible reluctance to change. But the BLS does produce a detailed *BLS Handbook of Methods* that includes a chapter on the CPI, and much effort does go into correcting the various biases.

In fact, collection of raw price data, compilation of various subaggregates, and the final design of the CPI are quite complex, involving hundreds of individuals and thousands of observations drawn from a large and highly dynamic economic system over time. This measurement process requires theoretical and practical decisions at various levels by many different people. The CPI does not, and indeed cannot, reflect the design of a simple, fixed rule. The world presents the BLS with too many vagaries to allow this. Instead, field agents must make pragmatic decisions in implementing their instructions, and the instructions themselves must be simple enough to follow and yet complex enough to allow for the changing nature of the marketplace.

Paul Armknecht, Walter Lane, and Kenneth Stewart (ALS) have made a major contribution in this paper by explaining, as carefully as they can, the architecture and construction of the index. They explain the concepts that drive the equation structure and the pragmatic decisions that drive the sampling procedures. Finally, they point out some practical problems with implementation that result from changes in the nature of goods and in the mode of marketing. Some of these decisions are bound to be controversial; some are not exactly clear, and some are unresolved, but now, thanks to ALS, we know enough to start working on how best to allow, in designing price series, for the types of rapid changes that are taking place in today's markets, one of the most difficult of which is the introduction of entirely new goods, like VCRs and magnetic resonance imagers.

One can think of the CPI as an economic statistic, intended to summarize changes over time in prices of goods purchased by consumers, that is a compromise between two competing sets of influences. On the one hand, economic theory, reflecting which questions economists think the CPI is supposed to answer, drives the architecture. On the other hand, the actual object under study, the economy, confronts field agents who are collecting data with practical problems that are often difficult to anticipate and resolve—design changes, production changes, model changes, marketing changes, shopping pattern changes, and so forth. The index itself is a product of attempts to reconcile these two influences, one theoretical and the other practical. The CPI also is complex because it is used to give a simple one-number description of so much that is going on.

In the BLS view, the CPI is designed as a "cost-of-living index," that is, an index that measures changes in the cost of living over time relative to a base period for which the index value is set to one. In principle, this means that if the period-t CPI equals 1.33, then the same standard of living costs a representative consumer 33 percent more than it did in the base period. Even within the confining framework of classical, representative-consumer economic theory, there are many different ways to measure changes in the cost of living, so more must be said about the theoretical underpinnings of the CPI than that it is a COL index.

The CPI is based on a Laspeyres price index model, which is to say that it is intended to be a measure of the period-t cost of a fixed bundle of goods relative to the cost of the exact same bundle in the base period. By construction the CPI value for period-t is supposed to be a weighted average of the period-t prices of the original bundle in which the weight assigned to each good in the bundle is the period-t quantity of the good consumed divided by the value spent on the good in the base period, which is the product of the base-period price and quantity. This formula yields one for the base period. If the original bundle costs 33 percent more in period-t, then the CPI will be 1.33.

Many other COL indexes, for instance Paasche, Fisher-Ideal, or Törnqvist, could be produced from similar data (though some collection aspects could be harder) but would be based on slightly different economic theories—different perspectives, specific utility functions, different mathematical bases, and so on. Why has BLS chosen the Laspeyres? Two obvious virtues of the Laspeyres formula are its simplicity and its familiarity. It is easy to explain a measure to compare the price of a fixed market basket of goods over time, and anyone who has studied a bit of economics has learned about a Laspeyres index, though perhaps without the title.

The Laspeyres also has the convenient and practical feature that once the weights are determined from the base year(s), only prices need to be collected in order to update the index monthly. Thus its ease of construction and its intuitive simplicity, that you simply multiply each good's price by the relative importance of that good in the basket and that the basket does not change, surely explain its popularity. Were BLS to abandon the Laspeyres formula, someone else would construct one, and everyone would probably use it instead of whatever newfangled index BLS produced in its place.

Nonetheless, two points need to be made. First, the Laspeyres price index comes from a very static, rigid, and limited economic model, and one certainly must question its effectiveness in describing the very complex, dynamic economy it is intended to reflect. Second, the CPI is not, in fact, a Laspeyres index: it only purports to be for ease of explanation. The actual numbers reflect a more subtle compromise with reality than Mr. Laspeyres's formula would suggest. The exact nature of these compromises is what the ALS paper is all about, and it is a very constructive discussion of how BLS solves practical problems not anticipated by those of us who describe Laspeyres indexes to our students.

Briefly, the CPI is a Laspeyres index over 207 *strata* where a strata is not an actual individual good but a category of goods such as apparel, gasoline, or cereal. The weight associated with each strata is a constant determined by the average quantity of total expenditures devoted to this strata during a three-year interval centering on the base year. However, each strata price is itself an aggregate index of the prices of the many goods in that strata. It is not exactly clear to me from the paper how the price of a strata is compiled, however. Field agents do alter their sampling procedures from year to year in compiling the data that lead into these strata prices; thus, sample variations and therefore sampling error do take place within the price of each strata every year. Only in the crudest sense, then (i.e., at the most aggregated level), is the CPI a Laspeyres index. The sampling variations include changes in the geographical regions from which data is actually drawn each year. Of a total of eighty-five regions, 20 percent are rotated in or out each year. Again it is not exactly clear what goes on in these rotations.

To illustrate the nature of the difficulties faced by field agents who collect the actual raw data that lead to the price of each strata, let us consider the problems caused by the two facts that the vintage characteristics of products frequently change and that the nature of retail outlets frequently changes. Boutiques, mail order catalogues, department stores, discount houses, and specialty shops are all different retail modes of transaction. Thus, if we let v index the vintage style or model, o the outlet type, and t the date the price of a good is observed, then the difference between what price is reported from the field between period t and period $t + 1$ for a given good in any one strata is

$$p(v + 1, o + 1, t + 1) - p(v, o, t).$$

In period $t + 1$, a possibly new (in a characteristics sense) product, $v + 1$, is sold by a possibly new outlet type, $o + 1$. Just resampling this new price can overstate a pure price increase, in the sense of pricing a fixed bundle of goods within a strata, because either $v + 1$, $o + 1$, or both may differ, representing quality improvements. Here BLS has two options. One, they can either observe or estimate, with hedonics or cost estimates, $p(v, o, t + 1)$ or $p(v + 1, o + 1, t)$, which can then be used to strip out the percentage of price change attributable to quality change. Estimation of these new-old vintages or old-new vintages with hedonic techniques is well known. See Gordon (1990) for an extensive application to a variety of assets, and see Triplett (1990) for an analysis of hedonics in statistical agencies. For a subtle analysis of difficulties encountered in trying to observe new-old vintage or old-new vintage assets, see Berndt and Griliches (1993).

If one does not have these prices, due to either time or cost constraints, then the second option is to compute some average of the prices of stuff in the strata that did not change. This latter procedure in effect amounts to excluding possible quality improvements embodied in new goods. This could bias the price index upward by excluding improvements in variety and quality that may have accompanied price increases of all products. It could also bias the index downward by excluding the very goods whose prices rose because they were better. To some extent the second option, leaving out new or improved goods, is driven by resource limitations at BLS. They simply do not have the resources to allow for every change that occurs. All they can do is try to correct for really big changes once they have clearly been a factor, but not until such evidence is obvious. Unfortunately, as Diewert (1987) has pointed out this will lead to substantial upward bias in price indexes; a bias that Triplett (1993) refers to as *new introductions bias.*

Of course, in some sense, if they are really trying to produce a Laspeyres index, then perhaps BLS should simply ignore such changes anyway. If one is trying to price the cost of a fixed bundle of goods purchased by a given consumer with the same utility function in each period, then perhaps new goods and new outlets should be left out altogether. On the other hand, though, perhaps economists, in and out of BLS, ought to study ways we could abandon this static framework altogether and build an index that reflects the very dynamic world in which we are trying to price the cost of what ever it is *contemporary* consumers are trying to buy compared to what they would have had to pay for this lifestyle years before. In other words, perhaps BLS should abandon the fiction that the world is simple enough to be captured by a Laspeyres formula at all.

It does seem evident to me that the CPI, as it is actually compiled by BLS, is not in fact a Laspeyres index. As a practical matter, BLS cannot construct a Laspeyres index because too many changes are occurring over time for such an index to reflect the economy after just a few years. Thus, BLS staff are trying to allow sensibly for some of these changes in demographics, shopping habits, quality change, new goods, and so forth, but all this work is still embedded in a Laspeyres framework. Perhaps the only solution to this conundrum is the ever fashionable 1990s warning-label solution to bring truth in advertising:

WARNING: The CPI is not a Laspeyres index*

*But we thought you would like to think it is. Have a nice day.

References

Berndt, Ernst, and Zvi Griliches. 1993. Price indexes for microcomputers: An exploratory study. In *Price measurements and their uses,* ed. Murray F. Foss, Marilyn E. Manser, and Allan H. Young, 63–93. NBER Studies in Income and Wealth, vol. 57. Chicago: University of Chicago Press.

Diewert, W. Erwin. 1987. Index numbers. *The new Palgrave: A dictionary of economics,* vol. 2, ed. J. Eatwell, M. Milgate, and P. Newman, 767–80. London: Macmillan.

Gordon, Robert J. 1990. *The measurement of durable goods prices.* Chicago: University of Chicago Press.
Triplett, Jack E. 1990. Hedonic methods in statistical agency environments: An intellectual biopsy. In *Fifty years of economic measurement: The jubilee of the Conference on Research in Income and Wealth,* ed. Ernst R. Berndt and Jack E. Triplett, 207–33. NBER Studies in Income and Wealth, vol. 54. Chicago: University of Chicago Press.
———. 1993. Comment. In *Price measurements and their uses,* ed. Murray F. Foss, Marilyn E. Manser, and Allan H. Young, 197–206. NBER Studies in Income and Wealth, vol. 57. Chicago: University of Chicago Press.

10 The Construction of Basic Components of Cost-of-Living Indexes

Marshall B. Reinsdorf and Brent R. Moulton

New products pose a difficult problem in the construction of price indexes. In 1887, in one of the earliest discussions of new products and price-change measurement, Alfred Marshall suggested the use of chaining to incorporate new products into price indexes. More than a hundred years later, this solution remains the most common method of handling new products.

The possibility that chaining could lead to bias was also understood quite early. Although Pigou argued that chaining is necessary to keep the index from becoming unrepresentative due to the exclusion of new products, he warned: "It must, indeed, be conceded that, if the successive individual comparisons embodied in the chain method, each of which admittedly suffers from a small error, are for the most part to suffer from errors *in the same direction,* the cumulative error as between distant years may be large. Were people equally likely to forget how to make things now in use as to invent new things, a large cumulative error would be unlikely. But, in fact, we know that the great march of inventive progress is not offset in this way. Hence the errors introduced by the chain method are likely to be predominantly in one direction" (1932, 71–72).

The basic component indexes investigated in this paper aggregate prices for a single good or a narrow category of goods. New manufacturers, outlets, and product designs pose a problem in these indexes parallel to that posed by new goods at a higher level of aggregation. Indeed, flux in the population of outlets and varieties in which goods are offered is frequently greater than the flux in the population of consumer goods. Furthermore, since new products are often

Marshall B. Reinsdorf and Brent R. Moulton are economists at the Bureau of Labor Statistics.

The views expressed in this paper are those of the authors and do not represent views of the Bureau of Labor Statistics. The authors are grateful to Marilyn Manser, Jack Triplett, and Andy Baldwin for helpful comments.

similar in function to products that already exist, they generally enter the U.S. Consumer Price Index (CPI) by being chained into an existing component index. (For example, compact-disc players entered the CPI by being chained into one of the audio component indexes, where they may have partly replaced analog phonographs.) Reinsdorf (1993) discusses how chaining basic component indexes may prevent the CPI from crediting progress embodied in new outlets, new brands, or new varieties of goods.

The present paper examines a bias of a different type. It arises when a statistical estimator of a Laspeyres index is used for a basic component of a chained index. If competition rules out large discrepancies between the prices offered in a market, all the sellers who continuously participate in a market will tend to have similar long-run average rates of price change. Absent turnover in the population of sellers, convergence of all rates of price change to a common trend value (in effect, fulfilling the conditions for a Hicksian composite commodity) would tend to make the bias negligible in any long-run component index that passes the proportionality test.[1] In contrast, we show below that when sample estimates of short-run Laspeyres component indexes are chained to measure long-run price change, trend reversion of sellers' prices exacerbates, rather than eliminates, the bias. Prices that start out low tend to have excessive weights in these indexes, but trend reversion means that these initially low prices tend subsequently to have high growth rates. This makes prices' weights positively correlated with their rates of change, resulting in upward bias.

In exploring this effect theoretically, it is convenient to adopt the abstraction that the economy contains just two levels of aggregation, goods and sellers of goods. Goods make up a consumer's market basket, while sellers make up the supply side of a market in which a good is sold. In practice, of course, a single good may be offered by many manufacturers in many versions at many outlets. Hence, depending on the context, our "sellers" paradigm may refer to either the competing outlets that stock a good or the competing varieties of a good in a market. A tendency to follow a common price trend may be expected across outlets and varieties. This tendency arises because consumers may be apt to substitute between outlets or between varieties and, also, because the sellers in a market may use similar inputs and technologies, which would lead to common cost trends.

An overview of the body of this paper is as follows. In section 10.1 we introduce the Laspeyres approach to the construction of the basic component indexes for a good. In section 10.2 we describe the way in which this approach is implemented in practice in the U.S. CPI. In section 10.3 we discuss how consumers' tendency to substitute products whose relative price has fallen for

---

1. The proportionality test requires that the index comparing price vector p_t to price vector p_0 equal λ whenever $p_t = \lambda p_0$.

products whose relative price has risen can cause upward bias in true Laspeyres component indexes. In section 10.4 we explain why chaining CPI or true Laspeyres component indexes may exacerbate rather than ameliorate their upward bias. In section 10.5 we derive simple formulas for the bias of several types of component indexes using a model of price and consumer behavior. In section 10.6 we discuss a possible solution to the bias problem, the use of geometric-mean component indexes. In section 10.7 we provide empirical evidence on how geometric mean indexes would affect the CPI. Finally, in section 10.8 we discuss additional empirical evidence on the performance of CPI component indexes.

10.1 Laspeyres Component Indexes

Laspeyres price indexes measure the comparative cost of purchasing, in a later time period, the basket of items that consumers originally purchased in a "base" period. They are widely used (at least at higher levels of aggregation) because they can be calculated with greater timeliness and at a lower cost than price indexes that require both current- and base-period quantity data.

Another advantage of Laspeyres indexes is that they have the property of consistency in aggregation. This means that repeated application of the Laspeyres formula at any number of stages of aggregation yields the same result as combining the multitude of prices into a comprehensive index number in a single step. In particular, a Laspeyres price index may be constructed in one step as a weighted average of the ratio of each seller's comparison- and base-period prices, where the weights are the sellers' shares of aggregate expenditure in the base period. It may also be constructed in two steps by calculating Laspeyres component indexes combining sellers' prices for each good, and then finding the weighted average of goods-level indexes, with each good's weight proportional to the amount that consumers spent on it in the base period. The Laspeyres component indexes may themselves be constructed as weighted averages of the ratios of sellers' comparison- and base-period prices for the particular good in question, where the weights are proportional to consumers' base-period expenditures on that good at each of its sellers. Sample estimates of such indexes of this type are the basic building blocks of the U.S. CPI.

To see explicitly how an aggregate-level Laspeyres index may be constructed from Laspeyres indexes for individual goods, let G denote the market basket of goods, let S_g denote the universe of sellers of good $g \in G$, and let K denote the population of consumers. Also, let p_{gst} be the price for good g from seller $s \in S_g$ at time t, and let q_{gskt} denote the quantity that consumer $k \in K$ buys of good g from seller s at time t. Finally, in order to guarantee that at any time t any particular consumer pays a single price for a given good, assume that q_{gskt} is positive for exactly one seller for any particular g,k,t combination. Combining all consumers' purchases of a good from all the sellers selling that good gives the quantity of that good in the aggregate market basket. The aggregate Laspeyres index is thus defined as

(1)
$$I_t = \frac{\sum_{g \in G} \sum_{s \in S_g} \sum_{k \in K} p_{gst} q_{gsk0}}{\sum_{g \in G} \sum_{s \in S_g} \sum_{k \in K} p_{gs0} q_{gsk0}}.$$

Let w_{g0} be the proportion of aggregate expenditures devoted to good g in period 0:

(2)
$$w_{g0} = \frac{\sum_{s \in S_g} \sum_{k \in K} p_{gst} q_{gsk0}}{\sum_{\gamma \in G} \sum_{s \in S_g} \sum_{k \in K} p_{\gamma s0} q_{\gamma sk0}}$$

Also, let L_{gt} be the Laspeyres component index for good g:

(3)
$$L_{gt} = \frac{\sum_{s \in S_g} \sum_k p_{gst} q_{gsk0}}{\sum_{s \in S_g} \sum_k p_{gs0} q_{gsk0}}.$$

Then equation (1) can be written in terms of w_{g0} and L_{gt} as

(4)
$$I_t = \sum_{g \in G} w_{g0} L_{gt}.$$

As a Laspeyres index, L_{gt} can itself be constructed as a weighted average of sellers' price ratios. Let σ_{gs0} be seller s's base-period share of consumers' expenditures on good g. Then,

(5)
$$L_{gt} = \sum_{s \in S_g} \sigma_{gs0} (p_{gst}/p_{gs0}).$$

10.2   CPI Component Indexes

Directly applying equation (2) or equation (4) to calculate the components of a Laspeyres price index is impossible because the large number of sellers precludes taking a census of their prices. In addition, collecting base-period quantity (or expenditure) data at the seller level can be difficult and expensive. Consequently, prior to 1978 no country attempted to use the Laspeyres index concept consistently at all levels of aggregation. At that time, the Bureau of Labor Statistics (BLS) introduced a sample-based estimator of a Laspeyres component index for the lowest-level aggregates in the CPI. This approach offers three important advantages: (1) it makes possible a unified approach at all levels of aggregation; (2) it incorporates scientific sampling of sellers based on consumers' recent buying patterns; and (3) it allows calculation of reliable index standard errors that include the effects of seller sampling.

Giving small and large sellers equal sample-selection probabilities is inefficient.[2] Consequently, in most cases other than housing, BLS uses probability-proportional-to-size (PPS) sampling, where a seller's "size" is measured by the expenditures it receives in the base period. Thus, the sampling probabilities are—in theory, at least—equal to the weights that equation (4) uses to average price ratios to obtain L_t.

A simple illustration of the PPS estimator of the population value of equation (4) is as follows. Suppose that the population contains three sellers that charge prices of $3, $4, and $5 in time period 0 and that consumers buy the same quantity from each seller. The three sellers' base-period expenditure shares are 3/12, 4/12, and 5/12. Hence, if at time t the sellers charge $5, $4, and $3, equation (4) is

$$L_t = \frac{3}{12} \times \frac{5}{3} + \frac{4}{12} \times \frac{4}{4} + \frac{5}{12} \times \frac{3}{5} = 1.$$

Assuming that a PPS sample of size two is used to estimate L_t, the first seller should have probability of selection 1/2, the second seller should have probability of selection 2/3, and the third seller should have probability of selection 5/6. Given sampling without replacement, a sample consisting of sellers one and two must then have a 1/6 probability, selection of sellers one and three must have a 1/3 probability, and selection of sellers two and three must have a 1/2 probability. The expected value of the PPS estimator of L_t is therefore

$$\left(\text{sample selection probability of } \frac{1}{6} \right)$$
$$\times \left(\text{sample index estimate of } \frac{1}{2} \times \frac{5}{3} + \frac{1}{2} \times \frac{4}{4} \right)$$
$$+ \left(\frac{1}{3} \right) \times \left(\frac{1}{2} \times \frac{5}{3} + \frac{1}{2} \times \frac{3}{5} \right) + \left(\frac{1}{2} \right) \times \left(\frac{1}{2} \times \frac{4}{4} + \frac{1}{2} \times \frac{3}{5} \right) = 1.$$

Note that equal sampling probabilities would have implied a higher expected value of 49/45 for the index estimator. Such equal sampling probabilities could occur if consumer substitution of lower-priced items made quantities inversely proportional to prices, or if the sellers' expenditure shares had identi-

---

2. It is noteworthy that estimating a Laspeyres component index by drawing a small simple random sample of sellers and then treating that sample as though it were the whole population in equation (2) or equation (4) leads to upwardly biased estimates of the population Laspeyres index. This occurs because the total base-period expenditures in the sample, which is the denominator when equation (2) is applied to a sample of sellers, would be a random variable. Randomness of the denominator raises the expected value of the sample estimator of L_{gt} because Jensen's inequality implies that $E(y/x) > E(y)/E(x)$ if x has a positive variance, where x and y are arbitrary random variables that are not perfectly correlated; see Mood, Graybill, and Boes (1974, 72). In the example immediately below, the population Laspeyres index equals 1 but the simple random sample Laspeyres index estimator has an expected value of 193/189.

cal long-run averages and those averages were used as measures of size in lieu of the actual shares occurring at the base prices.

In practice, BLS estimates the σ_{gs0} of equation (4) in two stages. First, BLS uses results from a household Point-of-Purchase Survey (POPS) to estimate outlets' shares of the expenditures on the good in question by the consumers covered by the index. These expenditure shares furnish a measure of size for PPS sampling of the outlets selling the good in question. Second, each outlet selected to be in the sample is asked to furnish a revenue breakdown for the varieties of the good that it sells. BLS then uses these revenue shares to select a PPS sample of one or more detailed varieties whose price at the outlet can be tracked over time. (For example, if the good in question is white pan bread, a selected variety might be a twenty-four-ounce loaf of white Wonder Bread.) Each year this process occurs in one-fifth of the cities furnishing CPI data, so any given city gets an updated sample of sellers every five years.

Let M_1 denote such a sample. Then if the elements of M_1 are selected with probabilities proportional to consumers' expenditures at time 0, the unbiased and efficient Horvitz-Thompson estimator of L_{gt} for the city and good in question is[3]

$$(6) \qquad \hat{L}_{gt} = (1/n) \sum_{s \in M_1} (p_{gst}/p_{gs0}).$$

Processing seller-level expenditure-share data and drawing a sample reflecting those data takes time. Consequently, the sampling probabilities must necessarily reflect an earlier period of time than the initial price data from the sampled sellers. Unless expenditure shares are constant, this timing difference precludes sample-based estimation of a true Laspeyres index of sellers' prices. Assuming constancy of expenditure shares is not a solution to this dilemma because it implies that elasticities of substitution equal 1 rather than 0, as would be required for the Laspeyres index to equal a cost-of-living (COL) index.

In the case of the CPI, the POPS has long recall periods for purchases of some types of goods, and six months to two years may pass before POPS responses are used to draw an outlet sample. Furthermore, once BLS selects an outlet to be in the sample and conducts PPS sampling of its varieties, several months pass before it begins collecting prices for the new index, and outlets' estimates of their revenue breakdowns are also based on lagged (and, often, approximate) averages. In addition, both POPS expenditures and outlet revenues are generally aggregated over periods of time long enough for prices to vary. Consequently, the sampling probabilities for M_1 reflect approximate aver-

---

3. Horvitz-Thompson estimators and their efficiency property are discussed in Cochran (1977, 258–61). Equation (6) is not precisely the estimator used for the CPI because PPS sampling does not completely obviate the need for seller weighting in practice. Also, equation (6) presumes that the entire outlet sample has a single base period, but some CPI outlet samples consist of two or more segments that have different base periods. The details of seller weighting in the CPI are quite complex; for a more thorough description, see U.S. Department of Labor (1992).

age expenditure shares over some interval of time that precedes the beginning of price data collection by months or even years. The correlation between CPI sampling probabilities and sellers' initial prices is thus likely to be closer to zero than the correlation between contemporaneous expenditures and prices implied by Leontief behavior. Consequently, sellers with low initial prices tend to receive too much weight in the CPI, but these sellers also tend to have unusually high rates of price growth as their prices revert to more normal levels. The result is an upward bias due to positive correlation between sellers' price growth rates and errors in their weights. This bias differs from the substitution bias that textbook discussions of Laspeyres price indexes cover because it is not caused by consumer behavior. Instead, it resembles the functional form bias that Irving Fisher emphasized in his discussion of the simple arithmetic averages of price ratios that Sauerbeck used for his indexes.[4]

CPI component indexes can be expected to behave similarly to true Laspeyres component indexes if all seller-level demand elasticities equal 1. Under this circumstance, expenditure shares would be uncorrelated with base-period prices regardless of when each was measured. Consequently, both L_{gt} and $E(L_{gt})$ would equal $\sum_{s \in S_g} (p_{gst}/p_{gs0})$, where $E(\cdot)$ denotes an expected value. On the other hand, if seller-specific demand elasticities exceed 1, the use of lagged expenditure shares to calculate sampling probabilities for the CPI component indexes may actually reduce their bias compared with a COL index.

10.3   Substitution Bias in Laspeyres Component Indexes

Although the estimation of a true Laspeyres component index is infeasible, the use of this concept as an estimation goal makes it important to understand its properties. Laspeyres price indexes have the disadvantage that as relative prices depart from their initial values, the relative quantities in consumers' initial market baskets may become suboptimal. At the level of goods, it has long been known that the resulting product substitution causes a Laspeyres price index to exceed the corresponding Konüs ("true") COL index. Nevertheless, U.S. consumption data indicate that Laspeyres indexes suffer less bias from substitution between goods that many economists had suspected: using 53 categories of goods Braithwait (1980) finds an average commodity-substitution bias of just 0.1 percent per year; using 101 goods categories Manser and McDonald (1988) find an average bias of under 0.2 percent per year; and, finally, using over 200 categories of goods in forty-four localities, Aizcorbe and Jackman (1993) find an average bias of slightly over 0.2 percent per year.

---

4. Fisher ([1927] 1967, 29–30, 86–91, and 527) discusses Sauerbeck indexes and how, in practice, sample-based estimation of a Laspeyres index is likely to entail an upward bias similar to that of the Sauerbeck index. Pigou (1932, 79) and Törnqvist (1936, 28) also discuss the upward bias of the Sauerbeck or "arithmetic average" index.

Laspeyres indexes may perform less well below the goods level of aggregation, however. For many goods, outlets and varieties often have large price changes due to sale pricing. Moreover, consumers probably substitute more readily between different sellers of the same good than between different goods. In fact, since any monopolistic competitor choosing a price on the inelastic portion of its demand curve is not maximizing profits, seller behavior alone may often guarantee that seller-level price elasticities of demand remain above 1. In the short term, therefore, bias may accumulate rapidly in a Laspeyres component index.

A formal analysis of seller-substitution bias requires a comparison between a Laspeyres component index and a COL index benchmark. In this benchmark, an explicit treatment of aggregation across consumers is necessary because price dispersion causes consumers to have different COL indexes even if they have the same homothetic utility function.

Aggregate Laspeyres price indexes have been called "plutocratic" because they can be constructed as averages that weight individual consumers' Laspeyres price indexes in proportion to their base-period expenditures (see Pollak 1980). Similarly, a Laspeyres component index can be expressed as a plutocratic average of the ratios of the time t and time 0 prices at the sellers that consumer chose in the base period. In this case, however, consumers' weights depend on their expenditures on the good in question rather than on all goods.

Since a population Laspeyres index uses plutocratic aggregation across consumers, its COL index counterpart is a plutocratic average of consumers' Konüs COL indexes:

$$(7) \qquad K_t = \sum_k s_{k0} \frac{e(\boldsymbol{P}_t^{kt}, u_{k0})}{e(\boldsymbol{P}_0^{k0}, u_{k0})} = \frac{\sum_k e(\boldsymbol{P}_t^{kt}, u_{k0})}{\sum_k e(\boldsymbol{P}_0^{k0}, u_{k0})}.$$

Here, s_{k0} is consumer k's share of aggregate expenditures in period 0, $e(\cdot)$ is the expenditure function giving the minimum cost of achieving utility u_0, and $\boldsymbol{P}_t^{kt}$ is the vector of prices paid for the goods in G by consumer k at time t. Dividing the numerator and the denominator by the number of consumers in K shows that the dispersed-price COL index K_t can be interpreted as the ratio of consumers' expected expenditure functions in periods 0 and t.[5]

To avoid the added complexity of separating out commodity-substitution effects from problems arising in aggregation over sellers, we assume that consumers have Leontief preferences over goods. We further assume that consumers regard sellers as perfect substitutes. This requires the presence of search costs to explain how higher-priced sellers can make positive sales. Nevertheless, we do not include search costs in the price index because a model that

---

5. This dispersed-price COL index is discussed in Reinsdorf (1994a). It resembles Pollak's (1981, 328) Laspeyres-Scitovsky social COL index.

incorporated them would be very complicated and might give only limited practical guidance on how to construct a component index.[6]

If preferences over goods are Leontief, but sellers are perfectly substitutable, then $e(\boldsymbol{P}_t^{kt}, u_0) = \sum_g P_{gt}^{kt} q_g^{k0}$, where P_{gt}^{kt} is the price that consumer k pays at time t, and q_g^{k0} is k's quantity of good g in the market basket yielding utility u_0. Let q_g^0 denote the combined quantity of all consumers' purchases of good g at time 0, and let $\tilde{p}_{g\tau} = \sum_s \sum_k p_{gs\tau} q_{gsk\tau}/q_g^0$, the average price paid for good g at time τ. As a ratio of total expenditures on the good to the total quantity of the good that is sold, $\tilde{p}_{g\tau}$ is, in fact, a unit value. Aggregating over consumers shows that the ratio of expected expenditure functions equals $\sum_g \tilde{p}_{gt} q_g^0/\sum_g \tilde{p}_{g0} q_g^0$. Using the fact that $w_{g0} = \tilde{p}_{g0} q_g^0/\sum_\gamma \tilde{p}_{\gamma 0} q_\gamma^0$, this index can also be expressed as

$$(8) \qquad K_t = \sum_{g \in G} w_{g0} \left(\tilde{p}_{gt}/\tilde{p}_{g0} \right)$$

Comparing equations (3) and (8) reveals that the COL index differs from the Laspeyres price index only in the way it measures price change for each good. The COL index's components are ratios of the average prices paid in the comparison and base periods. In contrast, the Laspeyres component indexes compare the average price that consumers would have paid if they repeated their base-period seller choices to the average price that they paid in the base period. Under the assumption of no quality differences between sellers, the difference between a Laspeyres component index and the ratio of the average prices paid by consumers is a measure of seller-substitution bias.

10.4 Trend Reversion of Sellers' Prices and Bias in Chained Component Indexes

Forsyth and Fowler (1981, 241) report that oscillating prices are commonly observed in constructing basic component indexes. One reason for this is that sellers' prices tend to exhibit trend reversion.[7] Although competition rarely acts quickly enough to make retail market obey Jevons's law of one price, it does prevent sellers from deviating indefinitely from their market's overall price trend. Consumers' propensity to buy from low-priced sellers rather than high-priced sellers puts downward pressure on prices that are comparatively high, and it may also put upward pressure on prices that are unusually low by making them attract high sales. Moreover, consumers' willingness to substitute

6. Reinsdorf (1994a) discusses implications of commodity substitution for dispersed-price COL indexes. Anglin and Baye (1987) develop a COL index that does include search costs.

7. Assuming independence of sellers' prices and their subsequent rates of change implies that these prices follow a random walk and hence have a nonstationary distribution whose variance grows over time without bound. Thus, at least in a linear time-series framework, the weak assumption that competing sellers' price discrepancies are bounded is sufficient for prices' changes to be negatively correlated with their starting levels. Friedman (1992) offers an interesting perspective on the ubiquity of trend reversion in time series.

an outlet or variety offering a low price sometimes makes it profitable for sellers to run off-price specials to build customer traffic, to introduce new consumers to a product, or simply to sell large quantities to price-sensitive consumers who would otherwise not buy. Consequently, prices that are low compared to the average price in a market tend to rise, while comparatively high prices tend to fall or to remain stable.

In the absence of new sellers, such reversion-to-trend behavior would cause the average yearly bias of any type of index of sellers' prices to tend toward zero in the long run as every seller's average rate of price change asymptotically approached a common value. In the short run, however, trend reversion can exacerbate the bias of a Laspeyres, Sauerbeck, or CPI component index. For example, suppose that sellers sometimes offer highly discounted "sale" prices. A Sauerbeck or CPI component index will implicitly give large quantity weights to those sellers offering sale prices in the base period, and a true Laspeyres component index will also assign them large quantities if consumers readily substitute between sellers. Such a weighting pattern makes the index rise rapidly as the sale prices revert to their regular values.

The compounding of such high short-run biases could severely affect a long-run component index calculated by linking together a succession of short-run indexes. Yet unfortunately, flux in populations of sellers makes it necessary to update the market basket periodically to reflect changes in consumers' purchasing patterns. Otherwise, the fixed market basket represented by the index might become quite unrepresentative as entry and exit of sellers caused large permanent changes in consumers' purchasing patterns.

Although it may seem paradoxical that chaining exacerbates a Laspeyres component index's substitution bias, Christensen and Manser (1976, 442) report empirical evidence of this in their index for meat. Szulc (1983) demonstrates theoretically that in a Laspeyres or a Sauerbeck index, the effect of chaining depends on the pattern of price changes. Different price-change patterns may tend to emerge at different levels of aggregation. Broadly defined goods may often be subject to price trends that persist for many months or years, causing positive autocorrelation in their changes. In contrast, at the seller level, prices' reversion to trend can be expected to cause negative autocorrelation of price changes. As Frisch (1936, 9) observes, under this circumstance, chaining a Laspeyres or a Sauerbeck index causes it to drift upward compared to its unchained counterpart.

The mathematical explanation of how negatively autocorrelated price changes lead to spurious increases when indexes that arithmetically average price ratios are chained relies on the fact that the expected value of a product of two variables equals the product of their expected values plus their covariance—see Mood, Graybill, and Boes (1974, 180). When component indexes are chained, products of variables with zero covariances tend to replace products of variables with negative covariances. In particular, a price's change from period 0 to period t equals the product of two subinterval price changes:

(9) $$p_{gst}/p_{gs0} = (p_{gst-1}/p_{gs0})(p_{gst}/p_{gst-1}).$$

Suppose that price changes are negatively autocorrelated and that the second term in the above product is replaced by a new term, p_{gzt}/p_{gzt-1}, that is independent of p_{gst-1}/p_{gs0}. Then even if the expected value of the new term equals the *unconditional* expected value of the term it replaces, the new product will have a higher expected value than the original product.

10.5 A Statistical Approach to Evaluating Bias in Basic Component Indexes

The presumption that the prices offered by competing sellers in a market tend to have stationary (inflation-adjusted) distributions suggests the use of a statistical model for evaluating alternative component index formulas. Another advantage of considering statistical properties along with COL indexation properties is that tracking changes in consumers' cost of living—though the goal of the CPI—is only one of its uses. For example, the CPI is sometimes used as an indicator of the effectiveness of monetary policy or of general price trends in the economy.

Suppose that prices are generated by the following model:

(10) $$\log p_{gst} = \pi_{gt} + u_{gs} + e_{gst},$$

where π_{gt} is the log of the true price trend for good g; u_{gs} is a stochastic permanent component of a seller s's price, e_{gst} is a stochastic transitory component; u_{gs} and e_{gst} are independent; and e_{gst} is normal with mean zero, variance σ_g^2, and $\text{Corr}(e_{gst}, e_{gs\tau}) = \rho_{t-\tau}(t > \tau)$. The e_{gst} represent sellers' temporary deviations from the market trend such as could be caused by special sale pricing or by differences among sellers in the timing of price increases. They play a critical role in the results below, whereas the other disturbances end up having no effect on the value to which the index converges as the seller sample grows large.

For sellers' quantities $q_{gst} = \Sigma_k q_{gskt}$, assume the following constant demand elasticity model:

(11) $$\log q_{gst} = -\eta_g \log p_{gst} + \delta_{gt} + \nu_{gs} + \omega_{gst}.$$

Here η_g is the elasticity of demand for the item, δ_{gt} is a time-period effect, ν_{gs} is a stochastic permanent component of an item's quantity demanded, ω_{gst} is a stochastic transitory component, and ν_{gs} and ω_{gst} are independent of e_{gst}. The constant elasticity specification is chosen for tractability, and other specifications that also imply an inverse relation between quantities and prices can be expected to imply qualitatively similar results.

Henceforth we omit the g subscripts for convenience. Note that although normality is assumed for e_{st}, no distributional assumption is required for u_s,

v_s, or ω_{s0}. We do assume, however, that $\exp[(1 - \eta)(u_s + e_{s0}) + v_s + \omega_{s0}]$ and $\exp[(1 - \eta)u_s + e_{st} - \eta e_{s0} + v_s + \omega_{s0}]$ have constant, finite variances.

Consider first the Laspeyres component index of equation (3). The appendix uses the properties of the log-normal distribution to show that, as the number of sellers becomes large, the true Laspeyres component index converges in probability to

$$(12) \qquad \text{plim } L_t = \exp(\pi_t - \pi_0) \times \exp[\eta(1 - \rho_t)\sigma^2].$$

After t periods, the upward bias of the logarithm of the Laspeyres component index is $\eta(1 - \rho_t)\sigma^2$. Large demand elasticities raise the bias by causing transitory disturbances in time 0 prices to have a large effect on time 0 quantities. On the other hand, high correlations between time 0 and time t prices reduce the bias by weakening the inverse relation between sellers' price levels at time 0 and their rates of price change from time 0 to time t.

If BLS could obtain sellers' price histories back to the period covered by the POPS, it could consistently estimate the Laspeyres index with a market basket from that time period. Since this index would be linked into the CPI at a much later time, the Laspeyres index would, in effect, be aged before it is used. The assumption in the present model that sellers' prices are stationary around a common trend implies that such an aged Laspeyres index would have almost no bias. In particular, suppose that a Laspeyres index with base period 0 were linked into a chained index at time l and used to measure price change from time l to time t. The probability limit of the index from time l to time t would be

$$(13) \qquad \text{plim } L_t/L_l = \exp(\pi_t - \pi_0) \times \exp[\eta(\rho_l - \rho_t)\sigma^2].$$

Unless time l is very close to time 0, $\rho_l - \rho_t$ is likely to be close to zero. This will make the bias factor in equation (13) approach 1 even if η and σ^2 are large.

Next, consider an average-of-ratios or Sauerbeck index. Since this index does not use weights that depend on consumers' behavior, it should not depend on η. In fact, its probability limit is simply $E(p_{st}/p_{s0})$, which is the Laspeyres index's probability limit when $\eta = 1$. The Sauerbeck index is biased by a factor whose logarithm equals half the variance of sellers' rates of price change from time 0 to time t. This follows from the properties of the log-normal distribution and from equation (10), which implies that

$$(14) \qquad \text{Var}(\log p_{st} - \log p_{s0}) = 2(1 - \rho_t)\sigma^2.$$

The CPI component index probably lies somewhere between a true Laspeyres index and a Sauerbeck index. Its seller sampling probabilities approximately reflect the average shares that outlets, and varieties within outlets, had of consumers' expenditures during some historical time period, which we denote as period h. Also, denote by l (for "link month") the time when BLS begins to collect prices for use in the new component index that is linked into the CPI. The CPI measure of price change from link month l to period t for an index area whose entire seller sample rotates simultaneously is

$$(15) \qquad R_{t,l} = \frac{\sum_s W_{s0} \times p_{st}/\hat{p}_{s0}}{\sum_s W_{s0} \times p_{sl}/\hat{p}_{s0}},$$

where $\hat{p}_{s0} = p_{sl}/(\hat{L}_l/\hat{L}_0)$ and $W_{s0} \propto p_{sh}q_{sh}$ by assumption. Equation (15) can be rewritten as

$$(16) \qquad R_{t,l} = \frac{\sum_s p_{sh}q_{sh} \times p_{st}/p_{sl}}{\sum_s p_{sh}q_{sh}}.$$

Assuming that no changes in sample composition occur between period l and period t, and that $\exp[(1 - \eta)(u_s + e_{sh}) + v_s + \omega_{sh}]$ and $\exp[(1 - \eta)(u_s + e_{sh}) + e_{st} - e_{sl} + v_s + \omega_{sh}]$ have constant, finite variances, the appendix shows that equation (16) converges in probability to

$$(17) \qquad \text{plim } R_{t,l} = \exp(\pi_t - \pi_l) \\ \times \exp\{[1 - \rho_{t-l} + (\eta - 1)(\rho_{l-h} - \rho_{t-h})]\sigma^2\}.$$

Note that if time l = time h = time 0, then equation (17) equals the probability limit for the true Laspeyres index. Also, if $\rho_{l-h} = \rho_{t-h}$ or if $\eta = 1$, then equation (17) equals the probability limit of a Sauerbeck index with base month l. The remoteness of time l from time h makes near equality between ρ_{l-h} and ρ_{t-h} quite plausible.

As a numerical example, suppose that $\eta = 1.5$, $\sigma^2 = 0.02$, and $\rho_t = 0.6^t$. Then for the first period ($t = 1$), the Laspeyres index overstates inflation by $e^{0.012} - 1$, or 1.21 percent. In this example, the index continues to overestimate inflation during subsequent periods, but the magnitude of the overestimate declines. For the first six periods, the cumulative asymptotic seller-substitution bias in the example amounts to 2.90 percent. After the sixth period, very little additional overstatement of inflation occurs, and the index eventually converges to a value that is too large by 3.05 percent. By contrast, the asymptotic bias of the CPI component index in equation (17), assuming that $l - h = 5$ months, is 0.83 percent the first month. The cumulative expected overestimate for the first six periods is 2 percent, and the CPI would eventually converge to a value that is too large by 2.10 percent. We find that the cumulative overstatement of price change in the CPI formula is relatively insensitive to η and usually is close to σ^2.

10.6 The Use of Geometric Means in Basic Component Indexes

Empirical results in Reinsdorf (1993) and (1994b) suggest that in food at home and gasoline portions of the U.S. CPI, the bias of the chained Laspeyres component index estimator could be substantial. Forsyth and Fowler (1981), Szulc (1989), and Turvey (1989) suggest that using geometric means of sellers' prices or price relatives may prevent upward bias from price oscillations in component price indexes. In 1987 the International Labour Organisation adopted a motion calling on its member countries to consider the use of geometric means for constructing basic component indexes, though no European or North American country had done so by 1994.

We now consider the limiting properties of the geometric mean estimator under the statistical model of the last section. Assume again that sellers' weights (or probabilities of selection) are proportional to expenditures during initiation period h, that no changes in sample composition occur between link period l and period t, and that $\exp[(1 - \eta)(u_s + e_{sh}) + v_s + \omega_{sh}]$ and $\exp[(1 - \eta)(u_s + e_{sh}) + e_{st} - e_{sl} + v_s + \omega_{sh}]$ have constant, finite variances. The geometric mean measure of price change from link month l to period t for an index area whose entire seller sample rotates at once can then be written as

$$
(18) \qquad G_{t,l} = \exp\left[\frac{\sum_s p_{sh}q_{sh} \times \log(p_{st}/p_{sl})}{\sum_s p_{sh}q_{sh}}\right].
$$

The appendix shows that this expresion converges in probability to

$$
(19) \qquad \text{plim } G_{t,l} = \exp(\pi_t - \pi_l) \times \exp[(\eta - 1)(\rho_{l-h} - \rho_{t-h})\sigma^2].
$$

If expenditure shares are unaffected by sellers' prices because seller-level price elasticities of demand equal 1, the geometric mean index is unbiased. At the seller level, however, η may often exceed 1. In this case, the gap between time h and time l (which, when $\eta = 0$, leads to bias in the CPI component index) becomes an advantage as ρ_{t-h} and ρ_{l-h} largely offset each other. For the numerical example in the preceding section, the weighted geometric mean formula converges to a value that is too large by 0.08 percent. Furthermore, the expenditure-share measures used for CPI sample selection may often reflect average behavior over an interval of time. Such average expenditure shares, which are analogous to estimates of a fixed effect in a panel data regression, may have very little correlation with prices at times l and t. If so, ρ_{t-h} and ρ_{l-h} in equation (19) should be replaced with correlation coefficients that are close to zero. In this case, equation (19) suggests that using geometric means would virtually eliminate the bias in the CPI components.

An analysis of how geometric mean component indexes perform in the context of the economic theory of the COL index is also important. We are currently pursuing research on this topic.

10.7   The Effects of Geometric Mean Component Indexes on the CPI

This section empirically compares the Laspeyres and geometric mean formulas for basic CPI components. The basic component indexes that have been recomputed cover those strata of goods that use the POPS/outlet-rotation sampling method (which carry approximately 70 percent of the weight, or relative importance, of the CPI), over the period from June 1992 to June 1993. The

CPI database was reconstituted from archived data, and two sets of basic component indexes were calculated using exactly the same price quotes.[8] One set simulates the CPI's Laspeyres-type component indexes, though it occasionally differs slightly from the published indexes because the computer program used to simulate the CPI is not identical to the program used in actual CPI production. The other set uses the alternative geometric mean formula. In aggregating both sets of basic components to higher levels, we have used the usual CPI Laspeyres formula and Consumer Expenditure Survey–based aggregation weights. There is a difference in formulas only at the lowest level of aggregation.

Table 10.1 compares the annual percentage changes for the two sets of indexes for various items over the period. Note that the geometric mean component indexes almost always exhibit lower rates of price growth than the Laspeyres component indexes do, a result that is not surprising in view of the known properties of the two types of averages.[9] More importantly, the size of the difference between the two indexes varies substantially between classes of items. For fresh fruits and vegetables and apparel, the Laspeyres indexes showed rates of change 2 to 3 percentage points higher than the geometric mean indexes. These differences are comparable in magnitude to the large differences in rates of change between CPI and average price series for food that have been noted by Reinsdorf (1993, 1994b). The large differences in annual rates of change for these expenditure classes are consistent with the model sketched out above, as fresh fruits and vegetables and apparel tend to have highly variable prices, due either to the perishability of food items or to the use of frequent sales with substantial discounting.

For other expenditure categories, however, the differences tend to be smaller, in most cases less than 1 percent a year. For some expenditure categories where sale pricing is rare, such as automobile parts and equipment and apparel services, there is little difference between the Laspeyres and geometric mean indexes.

Another implication of the model sketched out above is that the largest differences in measured rates of change between the Laspeyres and geometric mean indexes should occur immediately following sample rotation. Table 10.2 compares the rates of change of local area indexes based on the simulated Laspeyres and geometric mean estimators for the basic components.

8. Ken Stewart, Claire Gallagher, and Karin Smedley of the Division of Consumer Prices and Price Indexes of the BLS developed the computer programs and estimates for the two sets of indexes. Most of these empirical results have appeared in Moulton (1993), though in this paper we correct and extend the sample used in table 10.3.

9. A well-known mathematical result is that the geometric mean of a set of positive numbers having a positive variance must be less than the corresponding arithmetic mean. This result applies to the geometric mean index number formula in equation (18) and the Laspeyres-like index number formula in equation (15) only if the period whose inflation rate is measured begins with the link month. During subsequent periods it is possible for the geometric mean index to imply higher inflation than the Laspeyres index, although this seldom seems to occur in practice.

Table 10.1   **Rates of Change of Simulated Consumer Price Index for All Urban Consumers, U.S. City Average, June 1992–June 1993 (%)**

Expenditure Category	Laspeyres Index	Geometric Mean Index	Difference
All available items (70.3% of all items)	*2.95*	*2.48*	*0.47*
Food and beverages	*2.11*	*1.56*	*0.55*
Food	2.18	1.59	0.59
Food at home	2.37	1.52	0.85
Cereals and bakery products	3.36	2.78	0.58
Meat, poultry, fish, and eggs	3.90	3.28	0.62
Dairy products	1.61	1.29	0.33
Fruits and vegetables	1.58	−0.70	2.28
Fresh fruits and vegetables	4.09	1.09	3.00
Processed fruits and vegetables	−3.03	−3.98	0.96
Other food at home	0.86	0.39	0.48
Sugar and sweets	−0.09	−0.59	0.50
Fats and oils	−0.02	−0.46	0.44
Nonalcoholic beverages	−0.27	−0.64	0.38
Other prepared foods	2.22	1.67	0.55
Food away from home	1.85	1.70	0.14
Alcoholic beverages	1.48	1.32	0.16
Housing	—	—	—
Shelter	—	—	—
Renters' costs	—	—	—
Homeowners' costs	—	—	—
Maintenance and repairs	1.90	1.84	0.06
Fuel and other utilities	—	—	—
Fuels	3.55	3.54	0.01
Fuel oil and other household fuel commodities	0.38	0.31	0.07
Gas (piped) and electricity (energy services)	3.88	3.87	0.01
Other utilities and public services	—	—	—
Household furnishings and operation	—	—	—
House furnishings	0.14	−0.53	0.67
Housekeeping supplies	1.22	0.59	0.63
Housekeeping services	—	—	—
Apparel and upkeep	*0.59*	*−1.21*	*1.80*
Apparel commodities	0.47	−1.52	1.98
Men's and boys' apparel	0.19	−1.31	1.50
Women's and girls' apparel	0.44	−2.43	2.87
Infants' and toddlers' apparel	−0.13	−0.01	−0.13
Footwear	0.21	0.03	0.17
Other apparel commodities	1.83	−0.84	2.67
Apparel services	1.79	1.71	0.08
Transportation	—	—	—
Private transportation	—	—	—
New vehicles	2.46	2.30	0.16
New cars	2.23	2.09	0.15

Table 10.1   (continued)

Expenditure Category	Laspeyres Index	Geometric Mean Index	Difference
Used cars	—	—	—
Motor fuel	−3.03	−3.04	0.01
Maintenance and repairs	1.90	1.84	0.06
Other private transportation	—	—	—
Other private transportation commodities	−1.75	−1.85	0.10
Other private transportation services	—	—	—
Automobile insurance	5.39	5.33	0.06
Automobile finance charges	—	—	—
Automobile fees	5.21	5.19	0.02
Public transportation	13.19	12.86	0.33
Medical care	—	—	—
Medical care commodities	3.58	3.19	0.38
Medical care services	—	—	—
Professional medical services	5.37	4.99	0.38
Hospital and related services	8.74	8.24	0.49
Entertainment	—	—	—
Entertainment commodities	—	—	—
Reading materials	3.60	3.22	0.38
Sporting goods and equipment	—	—	—
Toys, hobbies, and other entertainment	1.07	0.37	0.70
Entertainment services	3.32	2.57	0.74
Other goods and services	*6.41*	*6.05*	*0.35*
Tobacco and smoking products	7.80	7.20	0.60
Personal care	2.43	2.05	0.38
Toilet goods and personal care appliances	2.40	1.89	0.51
Personal care services	2.48	2.24	0.24
Personal and educational expenses	7.06	6.83	0.23
School books and supplies	3.76	3.79	−0.03
Personal and educational services	7.27	7.03	0.24

Notes: A dash indicates that data are not available (usually because the index includes some strata that are not part of the POPS survey and sample rotation). Rates of change of the simulated Laspeyres indexes are not identical to the published rates of change of the CPI, because of differences between the index simulation and the actual index calculation and because the simulated indexes were not rounded prior to computing rates of change. For both indexes, aggregation above the level of the basic components (i.e., indexes of strata of items and areas) was based on the usual Laspeyres formula and weights that were in turn based on the Consumer Expenditure Survey.

Table 10.2   **Rates of Change of Simulated Consumer Price Index for All Urban Consumers, Selected Local Areas, June 1992–June 1993 (%)**

Local Area	Laspeyres Index	Geometric Mean Index	Difference
All available items (70.3% of all items)			
Chicago/Gary/Lake County, IL/ IN/WI	3.57	2.81	0.76
Los Angeles/Anaheim/Riverside, CA	2.83	2.34	0.49
New York/Northern New Jersey/ Long Island, NY/NJ/CT	3.11	2.54	0.57
Philadelphia/Wilmington/ Trenton, PA/NJ/DE/MD	2.22	1.78	0.44
San Francisco/Oakland/San Jose, CA	2.66	1.77	0.89
Baltimore, MD[a]	2.02	1.63	0.40
Cleveland/Akron/Lorain, OH[a]	2.17	1.66	0.51
Miami/Fort Lauderdale, FL[a]	4.22	3.95	0.27
St. Louis/East St. Louis, MO/IL[a]	0.56	0.45	0.11
Washington, DC/MD/VA[a]	3.52	3.16	0.36
Dallas/Fort Worth, TX	1.96	1.32	0.64
Detroit/Ann Arbor, MI	2.95	2.37	0.58
Houston/Galveston/Brazoria, TX	2.18	2.35	−0.17
Pittsburgh/Beaver Valley, PA	3.21	2.66	0.55
Food at home			
Chicago/Gary/Lake County, IL/ IN/WI	2.62	2.00	0.62
Los Angeles/Anaheim/Riverside, CA	4.21	3.61	0.60
New York/Northern New Jersey/ Long Island, NY/NJ/CT	1.65	0.35	1.30
Philadelphia/Wilmington/ Trenton, PA/NJ/DE/MD	1.69	2.13	−0.44
San Francisco/Oakland/San Jose, CA	2.62	0.06	2.56
Baltimore, MD	2.12	2.05	0.06
Boston/Lawrence/Salem, MA/ NH	3.55	3.46	0.09
Cleveland/Akron/Lorain, OH	2.81	2.47	0.34
Miami/Fort Lauderdale, FL	5.81	5.34	0.47
St. Louis/East St. Louis, MO/IL	−2.55	−2.69	0.14
Washington, DC/MD/VA	1.86	2.03	−0.17
Dallas/Fort Worth, TX	2.32	1.81	0.51
Detroit/Ann Arbor, MI	1.32	1.04	0.28
Houston/Galveston/Brazoria, TX	−0.59	−1.68	1.09
Pittsburgh/Beaver Valley, PA	3.38	2.72	0.66

Notes: Rates of change of these simulated Laspeyres indexes are not identical to the published rates of change of the CPI, because of differences between the index simulation and the actual index calculation and because the simulated indexes were not rounded prior to computing rates of change. For both indexes, aggregation above the level of the basic components (i.e., indexes of strata of items and areas) was based on the usual Laspeyres formula and weights that were in turn based on the Consumer Expenditure Survey.

[a]Because of the bimonthly sampling for nonfood items, the period for these indexes is July 1992– May 1993.

From June 1992 to June 1993, only one of the local areas listed in table 10.2 had its sample replaced: San Francisco. San Francisco had the largest difference in rates of change for the Laspeyres and geometric mean component indexes for both all available items and food at home. Another local area, New York, had part of its sample replaced during this period. New York has the second largest difference for food at home. In the other areas that did not introduce a new sample during the June 1992–June 1993 period, the Laspeyres component indexes also showed a larger rate of change than the geometric mean component indexes did, but the differences were smaller than those for the cities that rotated their samples. The effect of rotation is particularly noticeable when one examines the month-to-month differences. For San Francisco, the Laspeyres component index for food at home produced a rate of change 1.11 percentage points larger than the geometric mean component index during the month after the new sample was introduced. For New York, the difference during the month following the introduction of the partial new sample was 1.49 percentage points.

10.8 Other Empirical Evidence

If using a Laspeyres type of formula causes an index to overstate significantly the inflation rate immediately following sample rotation, evidence of the effect should appear in the historical behavior of the indexes. Because the samples in the smaller urban areas do not all rotate at the same time, we examined the price changes for large urban areas (A-size primary sampling units) immediately following rotation. Rotation schedules designating the link month for the two samples were obtained for the years 1980–85 and 1988–93. The link months are listed in the note to table 10.3.

Table 10.3 presents the mean difference between the measured inflation rate for the rotated area a and the U.S. average inflation rate during two separate periods: the two-month period and the six-month period after the rotated samples are introduced. If introducing the new sample induces a positive shock to the inflation rate, it should result in positive values for the mean difference.

The results shown in the table are generally consistent with this prediction of the model. There are significant positive differences between the area inflation rates and the U.S. average inflation rates for food, especially fruits and vegetables and meat. The numerical magnitude of these differences, however, appears to be too small to explain the entire difference between the geometric mean indexes and the Laspeyres indexes. For example, if the Laspeyres index overstates the inflation rate for fruits and vegetables by about 2 percent a year, as suggested by the comparison with the geometric-mean index, and if most of the overstatement occurs shortly after each five-year rotation, then we might expect a 10 percentage point differential in the inflation rate immediately following each rotation. The observed differentials for fruits and vegetables in table 10.3 are 2.6 percent for the two-month period and 3.1 percent for the six-

Table 10.3   **Mean Differences in Measured Inflation between Consumer Price Indexes for A-Size Primary Sampling Units and U.S. Average Consumer Price Indexes**

Expenditure Category	Two Months after Sample Rotation	Six Months after Sample Rotation
All items	*0.07 (0.10)*	*−0.00 (−0.16)*
All items less shelter	0.04 (0.10)	−0.04 (0.15)
Food and beverages	0.58[a] (0.13)	0.59[a] (0.23)
Food	0.62[a] (0.14)	0.61[a] (0.24)
Food at home	0.96[a] (0.20)	1.02[a] (0.34)
Cereals and bakery products	0.60[a] (0.29)	−0.06 (0.32)
Meats, poultry, fish, and eggs	1.25[a] (0.25)	1.40[a] (0.45)
Dairy products	−0.32 (0.29)	−0.14 (0.48)
Fruits and vegetables	2.57[a] (0.58)	3.11[a] (0.96)
Other food at home	0.45 (0.29)	0.53 (0.34)
Food away from home	−0.02 (0.11)	−0.12 (0.19)
Alcoholic beverages	−0.04 (0.21)	−0.05 (0.32)
Transportation	0.05 (0.14)	−0.27 (0.23)
Motor fuels	−0.28 (0.40)	−0.66 (0.48)
Medical care	0.01 (0.20)	0.14 (0.32)
Entertainment	−0.40 (0.27)	−0.27 (0.50)
Other goods and services	0.19 (0.19)	0.10 (0.27)

Notes: Numbers in parentheses are standard errors of the means. The sample sizes are $N = 37$ for the two-month comparisons and $N = 36$ for the six-month comparisons. The indexes come from the BLS LABSTAT program. The rotation link months for A-size primary sampling units used in the analysis are as follows: Philadelphia—January 1980, January 1985, February 1989; Boston—July 1983, January 1989; Pittsburgh—October 1982, October 1991; Buffalo—August 1980, February 1985; Detroit—February 1981, August 1991; St. Louis—July 1980, September 1990; Cleveland—October 1982, July 1993; Minneapolis—October 1983; Milwaukee—January 1984; Cincinnati—September 1984; Kansas City—August 1984; Washington—January 1981, July 1991; Dallas—June 1981, October 1990; Baltimore—September 1983, July 1989, November 1993; Houston—June 1982, June 1993; Atlanta—August 1982; Miami—July 1983, July 1993; San Francisco—August 1982, November 1992; Seattle—July 1981; San Diego—September 1983; Honolulu—August 1984; Anchorage—January 1980.

[a]Significance at the 5 percent level in a one-sided test of H_0: Diff = 0 versus H_a: Diff > 0, where Diff is defined as $\text{Diff}_2 = 100 \times (R^a_{l+2,l} - R^{US}_{l+2,l})$ and $\text{Diff}_6 = 100 \times (R^a_{l+6,l} - R^{US}_{l+6,l})$, in which $R^a_{l+2,l}$ is the CPI change in prices for area a in the first two months after link month l, and $R^{US}_{l+2,l}$ is the same period's change in the U.S. average CPI.

month period after new samples are introduced. One possible explanation is that the autocorrelation of the individual transitory component of prices may diminish slowly, rather than rapidly as has been assumed.[10] Another possible explanation is that sample-initiation effects also occur between sample rotations as items drop out of the sample and are replaced with substitutes.

Another prediction of the theoretical model is that the Laspeyres index will have the greatest tendency to overstate inflation when price oscillation is

10. For example, the autocorrelations would die down slowly if the transitory component followed a fractionally integrated time-series process. See, for instance, Beran (1992).

Table 10.4   **Rates of Change of Simulated Consumer Price Index, Selected Items, June 1992–June 1993**

Item	Laspeyres Index (%)	Geometric Mean Index (%)	Difference	$\mathrm{Var}\left[\log\left(\dfrac{p_{\mathrm{Jun\,93}}}{p_{\mathrm{Jun\,92}}}\right)\right]$
White bread	2.70	1.86	0.84	.0290
Round roast	4.40	4.48	−0.08	.0624
Round steak	4.49	4.12	0.37	.0523
Bacon	7.36	7.43	−0.06	.0403
Pork chops	3.79	3.45	0.34	.0397
Fresh whole chicken	5.82	5.00	0.82	.0497
Bananas	−3.22	−3.89	0.67	.0976
Oranges	−4.82	−7.82	3.00	.1108
Lettuce	3.84	2.12	1.72	.1509
Tomatoes	60.00	55.69	4.31	.1603

Notes: Rates of change of the simulated Laspeyres indexes are not identical to the published rates of change of the CPI because of differences between the index simulation and the actual index calculation and because the simulated indexes were not rounded prior to computing rates of change. For both indexes, aggregation above the level of the basic components (i.e., indexes of strata of items and areas) was based on the usual Laspeyres formula and weights that were in turn based on the Consumer Expenditure Survey.

largest. Equation (14) implies that we can measure the degree of price oscillation by $\mathrm{Var}(\log p_{st} - \log p_{s0})$, the variance of the logarithms of the price relatives.

To test this model prediction, we selected ten strata of food-at-home items that, in our opinion, are likely to be nearly homogeneous. Table 10.4 presents a comparison of the Laspeyres and geometric mean indexes, as well as Var $(\log p_{\mathrm{Jun93}} - \log p_{\mathrm{Jun92}})$, for these items. The three strata with the largest variances—oranges, lettuce, and tomatoes—also have the largest differences between the Laspeyres and geometric mean indexes, more than 1 percentage point in each case. The Laspeyres index does indeed have the greatest tendency to overstate inflation when the variance in the logarithm of the price differences is largest.

10.9   Conclusion

Since 1978, the basic components of the CPI have been sample estimators of Laspeyres indexes which weight outlets and varieties by their base-period quantities. To estimate these base-period quantities, BLS divides base-period expenditure estimates by link-month prices that have been deflated back to the base period.[11] Unfortunately, this way of imputing base-period prices results in

---

11. Between the time that this paper was originally written and when it went to press, BLS changed to a new method of imputing base-period prices that avoids the use of link-month prices. BLS chose not to adopt the geometric mean index solution because it would have entailed a fundamental change in the index concept. A discussion of the new method of imputing base prices and its likely effect on the CPI may be found in Moulton (1996).

a positive correlation between errors in weights and price changes subsequent to the link month. In other words, the CPI component index estimator tends to give too much weight to prices that increase, and too little weight to prices that decline.

The bias from this positive correlation between weighting errors and price changes may explain much of the growth rate discrepancies between CPI component indexes and matched Average Price series reported by Reinsdorf (1993). In particular, this bias probably raised the growth rates of the CPI components by more than consumers' substitution of lower priced outlets and varieties lowered the growth rates of BLS's Average Price series. A substantial effect of this type would be consistent with Dalén's (1992, 144) finding that calculating the basic component indexes of the Swedish CPI as averages of price ratios raised their growth rates considerably.

A possible solution to the functional form bias problem may be to use geometric mean indexes. Geometric means are especially suitable for use with lagged and averaged expenditure-share data, which are generally the only data available for weighting purposes. Empirical tests of the effect of using geometric mean indexes suggest that their adoption for items other than shelter might reduce the inflation rate of the "all items" CPI by about 0.4 percent per year.

Appendix
Probability Limits under the Statistical Model of Section 10.5

Derivation of Equation (12)

In large samples, $(1/n) \sum p_{st}q_{s0}$ converges in probability to $E(p_{st}q_{s0})$ and $(1/n) \sum p_{s0}q_{s0}$ converges in probability to $E(p_{s0}q_{s0})$, so L_t converges in probability to $E(p_{st}q_{s0})/E(p_{s0}q_{s0})$ (see White 1984, 22–24).

Under the model set out in equations (10) and (11), the two expectations are

$$
\text{(A1)} \quad \frac{E(p_{st}q_{s0})}{E(p_{s0}q_{s0})} = \frac{E\left\{ \exp\left[\begin{array}{c} \pi_t - \eta\pi_0 + (1 - \eta)u_s \\ + e_{st} - \eta e_{s0} + \delta_0 + v_s + \omega_{s0} \end{array} \right]\right\}}{E\{\exp[(1 - \eta)(\pi_0 + u_s + e_{s0}) + \delta_0 + v_s + \omega_{s0}]\}}
$$

$$
= \exp(\pi_t - \pi_0) \frac{E[\exp(e_{st} - \eta e_{s0})]}{E\{\exp[(1 - \eta)e_{s0}]\}}.
$$

This result is derived by taking the expectation of the antilog of the sum of the right-hand sides of equations (10) and (11) for the appropriate time periods, substituting the expression in equation (10) for $\log p_{st}$ in equation (11), and noting that if two random variables x and y are independent, then $E[f(x)g(y)] = E[f(x)]E[g(y)]$. This allows $E\{\exp[(1 - \eta)u_s + \delta_0 + v_s + \omega_{s0}]\}$ to be factored out of both the numerator and denominator and cancelled. (Factorization of expectations of independent variables is discussed in Mood, Graybill, and Boes 1974, 160.)

We now use properties of the log-normal distribution to solve for the expectations. If z is normally distributed with mean μ and variance σ_z^2, then $x = e^z$ has a log-normal distribution and $E(x) = e^{\mu + \sigma_z^2/2}$ (see Mood, Graybill, and Boes 1974, 117). Thus,

$$E(e_{st} - \eta e_{s0}) = E[(1 - \eta)e_{s0}] = 0,$$

$$\text{Var}(e_{st} - \eta e_{s0}) = (1 - 2\eta\rho_t + \eta^2)\sigma^2,$$

(A2) $\quad\quad$ $$\text{Var}[(1 - \eta)e_{s0}] = (1 - \eta)^2\sigma^2,$$

$$\frac{E[\exp(e_{st} - \eta e_{s0})]}{E\{\exp[(1 - \eta)e_{s0}]\}} = \frac{\exp[(1 - 2\eta\rho_t + \eta^2)\sigma^2/2]}{\exp[(1 - \eta)^2\sigma^2/2]}$$

$$= \exp[\eta(1 - \rho_t)\sigma^2].$$

Derivation of Equation (17)

By the same argument given above, equation (16) converges in probability to $E(p_{sh}q_{sh}P_{st}/P_{sl})/E(p_{sh}q_{sh})$. Under the model of equations (10) and (11), this ratio is

(A3) $\quad$ $$\frac{E(p_{sh}q_{sh}P_{st}/P_{sl})}{E(p_{sh}q_{sh})} = \frac{E\left\{\exp\left[\begin{array}{c}(1 - \eta)(\pi_h + u_s + e_{sh}) \\ + \pi_t + e_{st} - \pi_l - e_{sl} + \delta_h + v_s + \omega_{sh}\end{array}\right]\right\}}{E\{\exp[(1 - \eta)(\pi_h + u_s + e_{sh}) + \delta_h + v_s + \omega_{sh}]\}}$$

$$= \exp(\pi_t - \pi_l)\frac{E\{\exp[(1 - \eta)e_{sh} + e_{st} - e_{sl}]\}}{E\{\exp[(1 - \eta)e_{sh}]\}},$$

where independence again permits $E\{\exp[(1 - \eta)u_s + \delta_h + v_s + \omega_{sh}]\}$ to be factored out of the numerator and denominator and cancelled.

Using the properties of the log-normal distribution to solve the expectations, we obtain

$$E[(1 - \eta)e_{sh} + e_{st} - e_{sl}] = E[(1 - \eta)e_{sh}] = 0,$$

$$\text{Var}[(1 - \eta)e_{sh} + e_{st} - e_{sl}] = [2 + (1 - \eta)^2 + 2(1 - \eta)(\rho_{t-h} - \rho_{l-h}) - 2\rho_{t-l}]\sigma^2,$$

(A4) $\quad\quad$ $$\text{Var}[(1 - \eta)e_{sh}] = (1 - \eta)^2\sigma^2,$$

$$\frac{E\left\{\exp\left[\begin{array}{c}(1 - \eta)e_{sh} \\ + e_{st} - e_{sl}\end{array}\right]\right\}}{E\{\exp[1 - \eta)e_{sh}]\}} = \frac{\exp\left\{\left[\begin{array}{c}2 + (1 - \eta)^2 \\ + 2(1 - \eta)(\rho_{t-h} - \rho_{l-h}) - 2\rho_{t-l}\end{array}\right]\sigma^2/2\right\}}{\exp[(1 - \eta)^2\sigma^2/2]}$$

$$= \exp\{[1 - \rho_{t-l} + (1 - \eta)(\rho_{t-h} - \rho_{l-h})]\sigma^2\}.$$

Derivation of Equation (19)

To derive equation (19), we begin with the following result about the expected value of the product of a normal and a log-normal random variable.

LEMMA.   *Suppose x and y are bivariate normal with means μ_x and μ_y, variances σ_x^2 and σ_y^2, and correlation ρ. Let $z = xe^y$. Then $E(z) = (\sigma_x\sigma_y\,\rho + \mu_x)$ $e^{\mu_y+\sigma_y^2/2}$ where $\sigma_x\sigma_y\rho$ is the covariance of x and y.*

PROOF.   Write out the expectation:

$$E(xe^y) = \int_{-\infty}^{\infty} \int_{-\infty}^{\infty} \frac{xe^y}{2\pi\sigma_x\sigma_y\sqrt{1-\rho^2}} \times \exp\left\{-\frac{1}{2(1-\rho^2)}\right.$$

$$\left.\times \left[\left(\frac{x-\mu_x}{\sigma_x}\right)^2 - 2\rho\left(\frac{x-\mu_x}{\sigma_x}\right)\left(\frac{y-\mu_y}{\sigma_y}\right) + \left(\frac{y-\mu_y}{\sigma_y}\right)^2\right]\right\} dx\, dy.$$

Make the simplifying transformations $u = (x - \mu_x)/\sigma_x$ and $v = (y - \mu_y)/\sigma_y$, with Jacobian of transformation $|J| = \sigma_x\sigma_y$:

$$= \frac{e^{\mu_y}}{2\pi\sqrt{1-\rho^2}} \int_{-\infty}^{\infty} \int_{-\infty}^{\infty} (\sigma_x u + \mu_x)$$

$$\times \exp\left[\sigma_y v - \frac{1}{2(1-\rho^2)}(u^2 - 2\rho uv + v^2)\right] dv\, du.$$

Next, complete the square on u in the exponent:

$$= \frac{e^{\mu_y}}{2\pi\sqrt{1-\rho^2}} \int_{-\infty}^{\infty} \int_{-\infty}^{\infty} (\sigma_x u + \mu_x)$$

$$\times \exp\left\{\sigma_y v - \frac{1}{2(1-\rho^2)}[(u - \rho v)^2 + (1 - \rho^2)v^2]\right\} dv\, du,$$

then substitute $w = (u - \rho v)/\sqrt{1 - \rho^2}$, with Jacobian $\sqrt{1 - \rho^2}$.

$$= \frac{e^{\mu_y}}{\sqrt{2\pi}} \int_{-\infty}^{\infty} e^{-v^2/2+\sigma_y v}\left(\int_{-\infty}^{\infty} \frac{\sigma_x\sqrt{1 - \rho^2}\,w + \sigma_x\rho v + \mu_x}{\sqrt{2\pi}} e^{-w^2/2}\, dw\right) dv.$$

Since $\int_{-\infty}^{\infty} e^{-x^2/2}/\sqrt{2\pi}\, dx = 1$, and $\int_{-\infty}^{\infty} xe^{-x^2/2}/\sqrt{2\pi}\, dx = 0$, integration of the expression in parentheses produces

$$= \frac{e^{\mu_y}}{\sqrt{2\pi}} \int_{-\infty}^{\infty} (\sigma_x\rho v + \mu_x)e^{-v^2/2+\sigma_y v}\, dv.$$

Complete the square on v in the exponential, substitute $t = v - \sigma_y$, and solve:

$$= e^{\mu_y + \sigma_y^2/2} \int_{-\infty}^{\infty} \frac{[\sigma_x \rho(t + \sigma_y) + \mu_x]}{\sqrt{2\pi}} e^{-t^2/2} \, dt$$

$$= (\sigma_x \sigma_y \rho + \mu_x) e^{\mu_y + \sigma_y^2/2}.$$

To continue the derivation of equation (19), by the same argument given above, equation (18) converges in probability to $\exp\{E[p_{sh}q_{sh} \log(p_{st}/p_{sl})]/E(p_{sh}q_{sh})\}$. Under the model of equations (10) and (11), the ratio of expectations is

$$(A5) \quad \frac{E[p_{sh}q_{sh}\log(p_{st}/p_{sl})]}{E(p_{sh}q_{sh})} = \frac{E\left\{ \begin{array}{l} (\pi_t - \pi_l + e_{st} - e_{sl}) \times \\ \exp[(1-\eta)(\pi_h + u_s + e_{sh}) + \delta_h + v_s + \omega_{sh}] \end{array} \right\}}{E\{\exp[(1-\eta)(\pi_h + u_s + e_{sh}) + \delta_h + v_s + \omega_{sh}]\}}$$

$$= (\pi_t - \pi_l) \frac{E\{(e_{st} - e_{sl})\exp[(1-\eta)e_{sh}]\}}{E\{\exp[(1-\eta)e_{sh}]\}},$$

where independence again permits $E\{\exp[(1-\eta)u_s + \delta_h + v_s + \omega_{sh}]\}$ to be factored out and canceled.

To apply the above lemma, we need to know the means of $e_{sh} - e_{sh}$ and $(1-\eta)e_{sh}$, the variance of $(1-\eta)e_{sh}$, and the covariance of $e_{sh} - e_{sh}$ and $(1-\eta)e_{sh}$. These are

$$(A6) \quad \begin{array}{l} E(e_{st} - e_{sl}) = E[(1-\eta)e_{sh}] = 0, \\ \text{Var}[(1-\eta)e_{sh}] = (1-\eta)^2\sigma^2, \\ \text{Cov}[(e_{st} - e_{sl}), (1-\eta)e_{sh}] = (1-\eta)(\rho_{t-h} - \rho_{l-h})\sigma^2. \end{array}$$

(The expression for the covariance follows from a formula for the covariance of a linear function of random variables in Mood, Graybill, and Boes 1974, 179.) Using the above lemma about the expectation of the product of normal and log-normal random variables,

$$\frac{E\{(e_{st} - e_{sl})\exp[(1-\eta)e_{sh}]\}}{E\{\exp[(1-\eta)e_{sh}]\}} = \frac{(1-\eta)(\rho_{t-h} - \rho_{l-h})\sigma^2\exp[(1-\eta)^2\sigma^2/2]}{\exp[(1-\eta)^2\sigma^2/2]}$$

$$= (1-\eta)(\rho_{t-h} - \rho_{l-h})\sigma^2,$$

from which equation (19) immediately follows.

References

Aizcorbe, Ana, and Patrick Jackman. 1993. Commodity substitution bias in Laspeyres indexes: Analysis using CPI source data for 1982–91. *Monthly Labor Review* 116 (December): 25–33.

Anglin, Paul M., and Michael R. Baye. 1987. Information, multiprice search, and cost-of-living index theory. *Journal of Political Economy* 95 (December): 1179–95.

Beran, Jan. 1992. Statistical methods for data with long-range dependence. *Statistical Science* 7 (4): 404–27.

Braithwait, Steve D. 1980. The substitution bias of the Laspeyres price index. *American Economic Review* 70 (March): 64–77.

Christensen, Laurits R., and Marilyn E. Manser. 1976. Cost of living indexes and price indexes for U.S. meat and produce, 1947–71. In *Household production and consumption,* ed. Nestor E. Terleckyj, 399–446. NBER Studies in Income and Wealth, vol. 40. New York: Columbia University Press.

Cochran, William G. 1977. *Sampling techniques.* 3d ed. New York: John Wiley and Sons.

Dalén, Jörgen. 1992. Computing elementary aggregates in the Swedish consumer price index. *Journal of Official Statistics* 8 (2): 129–47.

Fisher, Irving. [1927] 1967. *The making of index numbers: A study of their varieties, tests and reliability.* 3d ed. Reprint, New York: Augustus M. Kelly.

Forsyth, F. G., and R. F. Fowler. 1981. The theory and practice of chain price index numbers. *Journal of the Royal Statistical Society* ser. A, 144 (2): 224–46.

Friedman, Milton. 1992. Do old fallacies ever die? *Journal of Economic Literature* 30 (December): 2129–32.

Frisch, Ragnar. 1936. Annual survey of general economic theory: The problem of index numbers. *Econometrica* 4 (January): 1–38.

Manser, Marilyn, and Richard McDonald. 1988. An analysis of the substitution bias in measuring inflation, 1959–1985. *Econometrica* 56 (July): 909–30.

Marshall, Alfred. [1887] 1925. Remedies for fluctuations of general prices. *Contemporary Review* 51:355–75. Reprinted in *Memorials of Alfred Marshall,* ed. A. C. Pigou, chap. 8. London: Macmillan.

Mood, Alexander M., Franklin A. Graybill, and Duane C. Boes. 1974. *Introduction to the theory of statistics.* 3d ed. New York: McGraw-Hill.

Moulton, Brent R. 1993. Basic components of the CPI: Estimation of price changes. *Monthly Labor Review* 116, no. 12 (December): 13–24.

———. 1996. Estimation of elementary indexes of the Consumer Price Index. Bureau of Labor Statistics, Washington, D.C. Unpublished, May.

Pigou, Arthur C. 1932. *The economics of welfare.* 4th ed. London: Macmillan.

Pollak, Robert A. 1980. Group cost-of-living indexes. *American Economic Review* 70 (May): 273–8.

———. 1981. The social cost-of-living index. *Journal of Public Economics* 15 (June): 311–36.

Reinsdorf, Marshall B. 1993. The effect of outlet price differentials on the U.S. Consumer Price Index. In *Price measurements and their uses,* ed. Murray F. Foss, Marilyn E. Manser, and Allan H. Young, 227–60. NBER Studies in Income and Wealth, vol. 57. Chicago: University of Chicago Press.

———. 1994a. The effect of price dispersion on cost of living indexes. *International Economic Review* 35, no. 1 (February): 137–49.

———. 1994b. Price dispersion, seller substitution and the U.S. CPI. Working Paper no. 252, Bureau of Labor Statistics, Washington, D.C. April.

Szulc, Bohdan J. 1983. Linking price index numbers. In *Price level measurement: Proceedings from a conference sponsored by Statistics Canada,* ed. W. Erwin Diewert and Claude Montmarquette, 537–66. Ottawa: Ministry of Supply and Services.

———. 1989. Price indices below the basic aggregation level. In *Consumer price indices: An ILO manual,* ed. Ralph Turvey, 167–77. Geneva: International Labour Office.

Törnqvist, Leo. 1936. The Bank of Finland's consumption price index. *The Bank of Finland Monthly Bulletin* October, 27–34.

Turvey, Ralph, et al. 1989. *Consumer price indices: An ILO manual.* Geneva: International Labour Office.
U.S. Department of Labor. 1992. *BLS handbook of methods.* Bureau of Labor Statistics Bulletin 2414. Washington, D.C.: Government Printing Office.
White, Halbert. 1984. *Asymptotic theory for econometricians.* San Diego, Calif.: Academic Press.

Comment   W. E. Diewert

Introduction

> Though the problem might appear very simple, this is far from the case.
> Surprisingly little work appears to have been done on it.
>   A. G. Carruthers, D. J. Sellwood, and P. W. Ward (1980, 16)

> There is an abundant literature, both theoretical and descriptive, on the computation of consumer price indexes above the basic aggregation level, but little is written about their derivation below that level. In this respect, the index makers resemble those chefs who only allow their dishes to be presented to patrons at a certain stage of preparation, without sharing how they have been mixed and simmered in the kitchen.
>   B. J. Szulc (1987, 11)

In an important paper, Marshall Reinsdorf (1993) used BLS data to compare the growth of average prices in the United States with corresponding official CPI growth rates. He found that the official index for food showed average annual increases during the 1980s of 4.2 percent while the weighted mean of average prices grew at only 2.1 percent. For gasoline, Reinsdorf found that average prices fell during the 1980s about 1 percent per year more than the official CPI components for gasoline. Thus it appeared that the CPI components for food and gas were biased upward by about 2 percent and 1 percent per year, respectively, during the 1980s.

Reinsdorf (1993, 246) attributed the above results to outlet-substitution bias; that is, consumers switched from traditional high-cost retailers to new discount stores in the case of food and to self-serve gas stations from full-service stations in the case of gasoline. The existing methodology used by statistical

W. E. Diewert is professor of economics at the University of British Columbia and a research associate of the National Bureau of Economic Research.

This research was supported by a Strategic Grant from the Social Sciences and Humanities Research Council of Canada. A longer version of this comment which reviews and extends the literature on elementary price indexes is available as Diewert (1995). The author thanks Paul Armknecht, John Astin, Bert Balk, John Bossons, Jörgen Dalén, Melvyn Fuss, Robert Gordon, Marta Haworth, Peter Hill, Brent Moulton, Alice Nakamura, Marshall Reinsdorf, Jacob Ryten, Alain Saglio, Bohdan Szulc, Don Sellwood, Jack Triplett, Ralph Turvey, and Keith Woolford for valuable discussions and Louise Hebert for careful typing of a difficult manuscript.

agencies in compiling price indexes does not pick up this shift of purchasers from high- to low-cost suppliers.[1]

The more recent paper under discussion by Reinsdorf and Moulton presents an alternative explanation for Reinsdorf's earlier results:[2] when the BLS moved to probability sampling of prices in 1978, the micro price quotations were aggregated using an index number formula that generates an upward bias. In the second section of this comment, I discuss index number formulas that are used to aggregate prices at the finest level of disaggregation, and I provide Irving Fisher's (1922, 383) intuitive explanation for the Reinsdorf-Moulton empirical results. In the third section, I briefly review the recent literature on sources of bias in consumer price indexes. The fourth section concludes with a number of recommenations to statistical agencies.

The Problem of Aggregating Price Quotes at the Lowest Level

Who ever heard, for instance, of Carli and of Dutot as authorities on the subject?
F. Y. Edgeworth (1901, 404) commenting on C. M. Walsh (1901)

In order to provide an intuitive explanation for the empirical results of Reinsdorf and Moulton, it is necessary to introduce a bit of notation and define a few index number formulas. I assume that the statistical agency is collecting price quotations on a commodity at the lowest level of aggregation where information on quantities purchased is not available.[3] Assume that the physical and economic characteristics of the good are homogeneous and that N price quotes on it are collected in periods 0 and 1 respectively. Denote the period t vector of price quotes as $p^t \equiv (p_1^t, p_2^t, \ldots, p_N^t)$ for $t = 0, 1$. Define an *elementary price index* as a function of the $2N$ prices $(p_1^0, \ldots, p_N^0; p_1^1, \ldots, p_N^1) = (p^0; p^1)$. Examples of specific functional forms for elementary price indexes are

(1) $$P_{CA}(p^0, p^1) \equiv \Sigma_{n=1}^N (1/N)(p_n^1/p_n^0);$$

(2) $$P_{JE}(p^0, p^1) \equiv \Pi_{n=1}^N (p_n^1/p_n^0)^{1/N};$$

(3) $$P_{DU}(p^0, p^1) \equiv \Sigma_{n=1}^N (1/N)p_n^1 / \Sigma_{i=1}^N (1/N)p_i^0.$$

P_{CA} is the arithmetic mean of the price ratios p_n^1/p_n^0 (first suggested by Carli

---

1. When an outlet supplying a price quote disappears and is replaced by a new outlet, the new outlet's price quote does not immediately replace the missing price quote. Usually, price quotes are obtained from the new outlet for at least two periods, and then a price ratio using only new-outlet prices is linked into the index at the end of the second period. Thus any absolute change in prices going from the old outlet to the new outlet is ignored.

2. See also Moulton (1993); Reinsdorf (1994a); and Armknecht, Moulton, and Stewart (1994).

3. Turvey (1989, chap. 3) and Dalén (1992) refer to this situation as computing elementary aggregates while Szulc (1987) refers to it as constructing a price index below the basic aggregation level. Additional references which deal with this situation are Forsyth (1978, 352–55); Carruthers, Sellwood, and Ward (1980); Forsyth and Fowler (1981, 241); and Balk (1994).

[1804] in 1764); P_{JE} is the geometric mean of the price ratios (first suggested by Jevons [1884] in 1863), and P_{DU} is the arithmetic mean of period 1 prices divided by the arithmetic mean of period 0 prices (first suggested by Dutot [1738]).[4]

Reinsdorf and Moulton point out that the starting point for the BLS method of aggregating elementary price quotes resembles the Carli price index P_{CA} defined by equation (1).[5] In actual BLS practice, a more complicated formula than equation (1) is used (which Reinsdorf and Moulton describe; see also Armknecht, Moulton, and Stewart 1994), but as a very rough approximation, we can say that the elementary components of the U.S. CPI are computed using equation (1).

Reinsdorf and Moulton used official U.S. BLS aggregation techniques to construct consumer price index components for June 1992–June 1993, and they compared these simulated components to corresponding indexes that aggregated the elementary-level price quotes using the geometric mean formula in equation (2). Omitting housing, they found that their simulated "official" index exceeded the corresponding geometric mean index by about 0.5 percent for the year.[6]

Of course, if precisely equations (1) and (2) were being compared, we would always have

$$(4) \qquad P_{CA}(p^0,p^1) \geq P_{JE}(p^0,p^1),$$

since an arithmetic mean is always equal to or greater than the corresponding geometric mean.[7] Moreover, the less proportional that prices are in the two periods (i.e., the more variable are prices), the greater the inequality in equation (4) will be.

It is likely that the inequality in equation (4) explains a large portion of the empirical results in Reinsdorf and Moulton's paper. However, at this stage, it is not clear why we should prefer the geometric average of the price relatives to the corresponding arithmetic average.

4. Unweighted price indexes of the forms in equations (1)–(3) were among the first to appear in the index number literature; see Walsh (1901, 553–58), Fisher (1922, 458–520), and Diewert (1993) for references to the early history of price indexes. Pigou (1924, 59), Frisch (1936), Szulc (1987, 13), and Dalén (1992, 139) refer to equation (1) as the Sauerbeck (1895) index.

5. Reinsdorf and Moulton note that equation (1) is called the unbiased and efficient Horvitz-Thompson estimator in the statistical literature, provided that the outlets in the statistical agency's sample were selected with probabilities proportional to their sales to consumers in the base period (period 0).

6. Armknecht, Moulton, and Stewart (1994) found that the U.S. "owners' equivalent rent" component of the U.S. CPI exceeded the corresponding geometric mean index by about 0.5 percent per year over the period March 1992–June 1994. They attributed this difference to the use of equation (1) as the elementary price index formula rather than equation (2). This upward "bias" in the owners' equivalent rent component of the CPI is likely to be present since the current implicit rent formula was introduced in January 1987.

7. Price index theorists who have used or derived the inequality in equation (4) include Walsh (1901, 517), Fisher (1922, 375–76), Szulc (1987, 12), and Dalén (1992, 142).

An explanation for our preference can be found in the work of Dalén (1992) who adapted the traditional bilateral test approach to index number theory (see Fisher 1911, 1922 and Eichhorn and Voeller 1976) to the present situation where information on quantities is missing. Dalén (138) suggested that a reasonable functional form P for an elementary price index should satisfy the following *time reversal test:*

$$(5) \qquad P(p^0, p^1)P(p^1, p^0) = 1;$$

that is, if prices in period 2 are identical to prices in period 0, then the price change going from period 0 to 1 should be exactly offset by the price change going from period 1 to 2.[8] It can be verified that the geometric mean price index P_{JE} defined by equation (2) satisfies equation (5) but the arithmetic mean price index P_{CA} defined by equation (1) will be biased upward, that is,

$$(6) \qquad P_{CA}(p^0, p^1) \, P_{CA}(p^1, p^0) \geq 1,$$

with a strict inequality if p^0 is not proportional to p^1.[9] Fisher (1922, 66, 383) seems to have been the first to establish the upward bias of the Carli price index P_{CA}[10] and he made the following observations on its use: "In fields other than index numbers it is often the best form of average to use. But we shall see that the simple arithmetic average produces one of the very worst of index numbers. And if this book has no other effect than to lead to the total abandonment of the simple arithmetic type of index number, it will have served a useful purpose" (29–30).

Unfortunately, Fisher's warning about the use of the arithmetic mean of price ratios as a functional form for an elementary price index was forgotten, not only by the compilers of the U.S. CPI, as the work of Reinsdorf and Moulton shows, but also by the compilers of the Swedish CPI for a short period in 1990, as was noted by Dalén (1992; 139).[11] Thus in view of its upward bias, the use of the Carli price index P_{CA} for aggregating elementary price quotes is definitely not recommended; the use of the geometric index P_{JE} defined by equa-

---

8. Fisher (1922, 82) credited the time reversal test to the Dutch economist Pierson (1896, 128). Letting P denote the index number formula, Pierson's test was $P(\mathbf{1}_N, p_1, p_2, \ldots, p_N) = P(p_1^{-1}, p_2^{-1}, \ldots, p_N^{-1}, \mathbf{1}_N)$ where $\mathbf{1}_N$ is a vector of ones. This can be interpreted as an invariance to changes in the units-of-measurement test. However, Pierson (130) later gave a simple example which showed that the Carli price index did not satisfy the time reversal property. Walsh (1901, 389) and Fisher (1911, 401) gave the first formal statements of the time reversal test.

9. Note that $1/P_{CA}(p^1, p^0)$ is the harmonic mean of the price ratios $p_1^1/p_1^0, \ldots, p_N^1/p_N^0$. The inequality in equation (6) now follows from the fact that the arithmetic mean of N positive numbers is always equal to or greater than the corresponding harmonic mean; see Walsh (1901, 517) and Fisher (1922, 383–84).

10. See also Pierson (1896, 130), Pigou (1924, 59 and 70), Szulc (1987, 12), and Dalén (1992, 139).

11. This bias problem is probably much more widespread; e.g., Allen (1975, 92) and Carruthers, Sellwood, and Ward (1980, 15) mentioned that the U.K. retail price index used the Carli formula at the elementary level, as well as the Dutot formula. Woolford (1994) reported that the Australian Bureau of Statistics also uses the Carli formula. Flux (1907, 619) reported that the early U.S. Bureau of Labor price index was a Sauerbeck (or Carli) index.

tion (2) or the average price index P_{DU} defined by equation (3) is definitely preferable since they both satisfy the time reversal test in equation (5).

Sources of Bias in Consumer Price Indexes

Retail markets furnish many examples of the Schumpeterian process of "creative destruction" in which more efficient producers enter and displace less efficient incumbents. The displacement of various classes of small, independent retailers by large mail order supply houses, department stores and chain grocery stores furnish historical examples of this. Recent times have seen phenomenal growth of a variety of large discount chains such as Wal-mart, Home Depot, Staples and Food Lion, as well as various "warehouse" style food stores and wholesale clubs.

M. Reinsdorf (1994b, 18)

Numerical computation of alternative methods based on detailed firm data on individual prices and quantities where new goods are carefully distinguished would cast light on the size of the new good bias.

W. E. Diewert (1993, 63)

Before we can discuss sources of bias in the computation of consumer price indexes, it is necessary to note that "bias" is a relative concept. Thus when we speak of bias, we have in mind some specific conceptual framework or purpose for the price index and if we had complete information, this underlying "truth" could be measured and "bias" would be relative to this "true index."

Economists and statisticians have been debating the question of the appropriate conceptual basis for a price index for over a hundred years.[12] The conceptual framework that I shall adopt in order to discuss bias is the COL framework due originally to Konüs (1939). More specifically, I adopt Pollak's (1981, 328) social COL index as the underlying "correct" concept.[13] This concept assumes utility maximizing (or expenditure minimizing) behavior on the part of consumers and thus is open to the criticism that it is unrealistic. However, as Pierson (1895, 332) observed one hundred years ago, consumers do purchase less in response to higher prices; that is, substitution effects do exist. The existing economic theory of COL indexes can be viewed as a way of incorporating these substitution effects into the measurement of price change (as opposed to the traditional statistical agency fixed-basket approach[14] which holds quantities fixed as prices change).

12. The debate started with Edgeworth (1888, 347), as the following quotation indicates: "The answer to the question what is the *Mean* of a given set of magnitudes cannot in general be found, unless there is given also the object for the sake of which a mean value is required." Other papers discussing different purposes and alternative conceptual frameworks include Edgeworth (1901, 409; 1923, 343–45; 1925), Flux (1907, 620), Bowley (1919, 345–53), March (1921), Mudgett (1929, 249), Ferger (1936), Mills et al. (1943, 398), Triplett (1983), Turvey (1989, 9–27), and Sellwood (1994).

13. This concept excludes the newer economic approaches to COL indexes that incorporate consumer search; see Anglin and Baye (1987) and Reinsdorf (1993, 1994a).

14. This traditional Laspeyres approach to measuring price change is comprehensively discussed in Turvey (1989). For earlier discussions, see Flux (1907, 621), Bowley (1919, 347), and Mills et al. (1943).

Instead of using the economic theory of the consumer as the theoretical basis for the construction of price indexes, it is possible to use instead a producer-theory approach to the measurement of price change; see Court and Lewis (1942–43); Fisher and Shell (1972); Samuelson and Swamy (1974); Archibald (1977); and Diewert (1983, 1054–77).[15] I will not pursue this approach here.

Once a theoretically ideal price index has been chosen, bias can be defined as a systematic difference between an actual statistical agency index and the theoretically ideal index. Instead of the term "bias," Fixler (1993, 7) and other BLS economists use the term "effect." Since most academic economists use the term "bias," I will follow in this tradition.[16]

In addition to the *elementary index functional form bias* considered in the previous section, I shall follow the examples of Gordon (1993) and Fixler (1993) and consider commodity-substitution bias, outlet-substitution bias, linking bias and new-goods bias.

The Laspeyres fixed-basket price index suffers from *commodity-substitution bias;* that is, it is biased upward compared to a COL index because it ignores changes in quantities demanded that are induced by changes in relative prices. Estimates of the size of this bias (at levels of aggregation above the elementary level) can be obtained by comparing statistical agencies' Laspeyres-type indexes with superlative index numbers such as the Fisher-Ideal index P_F^* defined as the geometric mean of the Paasche and Laspeyres indexes. Superlative indexes provide good approximations to the unobservable COL indexes.[17] Using this methodology, Manser and McDonald (1988), using 101 categories of goods and services, and Aizcorbe and Jackman (1993), using 207 categories in forty-four U.S. locations, found an average substitution bias in the U.S. CPI of about 0.2 percent per year. Using the same methodology, Généreux (1983) found the same substitution bias in the Canadian CPI over the years 1957–78. Using a different methodology, Balk (1990, 82) obtained estimates for the substitution bias in the Dutch CPI in the 0.2–0.3 percent per year range using 106 commodity groups over the years 1952–81.[18]

In the first section, I defined *outlet-substitution bias* in the context of disappearing high-cost outlets. I now want to broaden the above preliminary defini-

---

15. Diewert (1983, 1051–52) also compared the consumer- and producer-theory approaches.

16. Fisher (1922, 86) called an index number formula "erratic" if it did not satisfy the time reversal test and "biased" if it were "subject to a foreseeable tendency to err in *one particular direction*." Thus, using Fisher's terminology, the arithmetic and harmonic elementary price indexes, P_{CA} and P_H, are *biased,* while the Laspeyres price index, $P_L^*(p^0,p^1,q^0,q^1) \equiv p^1 \cdot q^0/p^0 \cdot q^0$, is merely *erratic.* Note that Lovitt (1928, 11) seems to have been the first to show that P_L^* was "erratic" and not "biased" in the sense of Fisher.

17. See Diewert (1976, 1978). Hill (1988, 134) assumed that superlative price indexes are essentially weighted averages of price relatives which have quantity or expenditure weights that treat the two periods under consideration in a symmetric manner.

18. A topic closely related to substitution bias is the sensitivity of the Laspeyres index to the choice of the base year or to the choice of expenditure weights for the price relatives; see Hogg (1931, 56), Mudgett (1933, 30), Saulnier (1990), Schmidt (1993), and Dalén (1994).

tion to encompass the possibility that consumers may shift their purchases from high-cost to low-cost outlets over time. Thus instead of calculating outlet-specific unit values for a commodity, a unit value could be calculated over all outlets in the market area. The difference between this market-area unit-value price relative and the corresponding Laspeyres component for the commodity in the official CPI can be defined as outlet-substitution bias.[19] This definition of outlet-substitution bias assumes that commodities should not be distinguished by their point of purchase; that is, a particular make of a video camera yields the same utility to a consumer whether it is bought in Dan's Discount Den or Regal Imports Boutique. This assumption may not be appropriate in other situations.[20] Turning to empirical evidence on the size of the outlet-substitution bias, in his direct statistical method, Reinsdorf (1993, 239–40) found that the outlet-substitution bias in the "food at home" and "motor fuel" components of the U.S. CPI was about 0.25 percent per year during the 1980s (although he regarded this as an upper bound due to possible quality differences). Saglio (1994), using Nielsen data for 915 French outlets over the years 1988–90, found that the outlet-substitution bias for milk chocolate bars averaged 0.8 percent per years; that is, the market unit value for chocolate bars of the same size and brand averaged 0.8 percent per year lower than the corresponding Laspeyres index which treated chocolate bars of the same size and brand in each outlet as separate commodities. Saglio (1994), using INSEE (Institut National de la Statistique et des Études Économiques) data on twenty-nine food groups over twelve years, also found an outlet-substitution bias of approximately 0.4 percent per year below the corresponding Laspeyres price index.

The outlet-substitution bias is formallly identical to what might be termed the *linking bias,* that is, a new good appears which is more efficient in some dimension than an existing good. After two or more periods, the statistical agency places a price relative for the new good into the relevant elementary price index, but the absolute decline in price going from the old to the new variety is never reflected in the relevant elementary price index. This source of bias was recognized by Griliches and by Gordon (1981, 130–33; 1990) as the following quotations indicate: "By and large they [statistical agencies] do not make such quality adjustments. Instead, the new product is 'linked in' at its introductory (or subsequent) price with the price indices left unchanged" (Griliches 1979, 97); "An even more dramatic case largely involving a producer durable involved the supplanting of the old rotary electric calculator by the electronic calculator; all of us can purchase for $10 or so a calculator that can perform all the functions (in a fraction of the elapsed time) of an old 1970-

19. This definition of outlet-substitution bias coincides with Reinsdorf's (1993, 228) original definition and includes both of Fixler's (1993, 7) seller- and outlet-substitution biases. It also corresponds to Saglio's (1994) point-of-purchase effect.

20. This ambiguity creates difficulties for statistical agencies; i.e., the decision whether to aggregate over outlets in a market area or not is clearly a matter of judgment.

vintage $1000 rotary electric calculator. Yet in the U.S. the electronic calculator was treated as a new product, and the decline in price from the obsolete rotary electric model to the early models of the electronic calculator was 'linked out' in the official indexes" (Gordon 1993, 239).

A more appropriate treatment of the above situation would be to calculate an average price or unit value per the relevant characteristic over the old and repackaged goods. A similar bias was recognized by Griliches and Cockburn (1994) in the context of generic drugs which are chemically identical to brand-name drugs (it should be noted that the BLS changed its procedures in January 1995 to fix this problem). An analogous bias in the statistical agency treatment of illumination was pointed out by Nordhaus (chap. 1 in this volume). These last two papers obtain very large linking biases.[21]

The *new-goods bias* results from the inability of bilateral price indexes to take into account the fact that the number of commodities from which consumers can choose is growing rapidly over time.[22] Hill makes the following comment on this situation: "In general, it may be concluded that in the real world, price indices which are inevitably restricted to commodities found in both situations will fail to capture the improvement of welfare associated with an enlargement of the set of consumption possibilities. The benefits brought by the introduction of new goods are not generally taken into account in price indices in the period in which the goods first make their appearance" (1988, 138).

Diewert (1980, 498–505; 1987, 779; 1993, 59–63), following Marshall (1887, 373) and Hicks (1940, 114), discussed the new-goods bias and suggested along with Griliches (1979, 97) and Gordon (1981, 130) that this bias could be substantially reduced by simply introducing new goods into the pricing basket in a timely fashion (this would not eliminate the bias in the period when the good makes its first appearance). Triplett (1993, 200) termed the subset of the new-goods bias caused by delays in introducing new products into an index as the *new-introductions bias*.[23] Turning now to empirical estimates of the new-goods bias, Gordon (1990) estimated that the U.S. consumer durables price index had a new-goods or quality-change bias of 1.5 percent per year over the period 1947–83. Berndt, Griliches, and Rosett (1993) provided evi-

21. Again, this source of bias creates problems for statistical agencies; i.e., when should a new product be treated as a genuinely new good rather than as a superficially repackaged old product? It should also be noted that linking bias could go in the opposite direction if firms simply repackage their products to disguise price increases.

22. Actually, what is relevant is the number of commodities that are available in the consumer's market area. Thus the growth of cities and urbanization leads to more specialized goods and services being offered by producers and hence will lead to a growth in the number of commodities that are effectively available to the consumer. Transportation and communication improvements also lead to larger choice sets, a point already noticed by Marshall (1887, 373–74).

23. Mudgett (1933, 32) noted that in 1930, the BLS had not yet added such important items of expenditure to its basket as automobile expenditures, meals outside the home, and life insurance. Gordon (1993) noted that automobiles entered the U.S. CPI in 1940, penicillin in 1951 after it had experienced a 99 percent decline from its initial price, and the pocket calculator in 1978 after it had declined in price about 90 percent since 1970. Mudgett (1929, 250) also noted that only forty commodities were comparable between 1870 and 1920 out of five hundred commodities whose prices were collected by the BLS in 1920.

dence that the BLS did not sample the prices of new drug products in a sufficiently timely fashion. They found that from January 1984 through December 1989, the BLS producer price index for prescription pharmaceutical preparations (drugs) grew at a rate of 3 percent per year higher than a superlative price index that used the monthly price and quantity sales data for 2,090 drug products sold by four major pharmaceutical manufacturers in the United States, accounting for about 29 percent of total domestic industry sales in 1989. Thus they found a combined drug-substitution and new-introductions bias of about 3 percent per year. Hausman (chap. 5 in this volume) used Nielsen scanner data from January 1990 to August 1992 on cereal consumption for seven major metropolitan areas in the United States. He used econometric techniques to estimate consumer preferences over cereals and thus he was able to estimate the Hicksian (1940, 114) reservation prices that would cause consumers to demand zero units of a new cereal. His conclusion was that an overall price index for cereals, which excluded the effects of new brands, would overstate the true COL subindex for cereals by about 25 percent over a ten-year period.[24] Finally, Trajtenberg (1990) attempted to measure reservation prices for computerized tomography (CT) scanners over the decade 1973–82. His nominal price index went from 100 to 259 but his quality-adjusted price index went from 100 to 7, implying a 55 percent drop in prices per year on average.

Summarizing the empirical evidence reviewed in this section and the previous one, we see that it is likely that in recent years, a typical official consumer price index has a 0.2 percent per year commodity-substitution bias, a 0.25 percent per year outlet-substitution bias, a linking bias of perhaps 0.1 percent per year, and a new-goods bias of at least 0.25 percent per year; that is, an upward bias of at least 0.8 percent per year. If the statistical agency is also making use of a biased elementary price index formula, this will add an additional upward bias to the official index. The reader will note that all five sources of bias were regarded as being additive, an assumption which is probably approximately correct.[25]

I conclude this section with a detailed discussion of the possible biases in the U.S. CPI. Marshall Reinsdorf and Brent Moulton have provided important empirical evidence of upward bias in the U.S. CPI due to an inappropriate choice of the functional form used to aggregate price quotations at the lowest level of aggregation. Reinsdorf and Moulton found that their geometric mean index (which used the elementary price index P_{JE} defined by equation (2) at the lowest level of aggregation) grew by 2.48 percent from June 1992 to June 1993, compared to a simulated U.S. consumer price index growth rate of 2.95 percent. Their simulations excluded housing and hence covered 70.3 percent of

24. This bias is the "pure" new-goods bias (the bias that occurs in the period when the new good is introduced) as opposed to the new-introductions bias (the bias that occurs in the second and subsequent periods after the good is introduced). Hausman found that his estimated reservation prices were approximately double the first-appearance prices of the new cereals.

25. Sellwood (1994) discussed the question of additivity. He also noted that estimates of bias have standard errors attached to them.

the U.S. CPI universe. Thus their simulated U.S. consumer price index (which largely uses the Carli-Sauerbeck price index P_{CA} defined by equation [1] at the elementary level) appears to have an upward bias of about 0.5 percent per year. Furthermore, Armknecht, Moulton, and Stewart (1994) noted that since 1987, the owner's implicit rent component of the CPI has used a Carli elementary price index, which has led to a 0.5 percent per year upward bias in that component. Thus the choice of index number formula at the elementary level is not a trivial matter.

Reinsdorf (1993, 242–47) compared the behavior of official U.S. rates of inflation for food and gasoline with corresponding rates obtained using average prices; that is, he compared CPI rates of inflation for food and gas with those obtained by using the elementary price index P_{DU} defined by equation (3). Over the 1980s, he found that means of the U.S. CPI food indexes weighted according to their importance in the CPI showed an average annual increase of 4.2 percent, while the corresponding weighted mean of the average prices grew at a rate of 2.1 percent per year. For gasoline, he found that average prices fell faster than the corresponding CPI prices at about 1 percent per year during the 1980s. Reinsdorf (242) attributed these results to outlet-substitution bias but it now seems clear that some of this upward bias in food and gas was due to the inappropriate method used by the BLS to aggregate price quotes at the elementary level. However, it is also clear that not all of Reinsdorf's results can be explained away as being elementary-level functional form bias: a substantial portion of the bias that he found must be outlet-substitution bias.

The results of Reinsdorf and Reinsdorf and Moulton suggest that outlet-substitution bias in the U.S. CPI as a whole was somewhere between 0.1 and 0.5 percent per year in the 1980s and the elementary functional form bias was somewhere between 0.35 and 0.5 percent per year in the 1990s. In addition to the above two sources of bias, we have commodity-substitution bias at levels above the elementary level, linking bias, and new-goods bias. These three sources of bias probably add an additional 0.3 to 0.7 percent per year of upward bias to traditional fixed-basket-type indexes. Adding up all of these sources of bias for the U.S. CPI leads to a total upward bias in the region of 0.75 to 1.7 percent per year in the 1990s. This is a substantial bias.[26]

Recommendations and Conclusions

[E]very person in the room would have realized after hearing his Paper that the measurement of the cost of living was by no means a simple conception. Nobody would expect that a difficult question of engineering or a nice point of art could be put in the Press and explained in words of one syllable and in a single sentence.

A. L. Bowley (1919, 371) commentary on his own paper

26. Similar sources of bias apply to the producer price index; see Gordon (1990, 1993) and Triplett (1993). Recent surveys of sources of bias in the CPI are Gordon (1993), Crawford (1993), and Wynne and Sigalla (1994).

Would it not be well if statisticians and economists should again come together and decide authoritatively on the proper method of constructing index-numbers?

C. M. Walsh (1921, 138)

A number of recommendations seem to follow from the empirical work of Reinsdorf and Moulton:

1. Statistical agencies should follow the emphatic advice of Irving Fisher (1922, 29–30) and avoid the use of the Carli arithmetic mean of price relatives formula in equation (1) to form elementary price aggregates.

2. If information on quantities is not available at the elementary or basic level, either the geometric price index in equation (2) advocated by Jevons (1884) or the average price index in equation (3) suggested by Dutot (1738) should be used.

3. At the level of the individual outlet, the best elementary average price for a homogeneous commodity would seem to be its unit value: the value of units sold during the sample period divided by the total quantity sold. If outlet unit values are available, then in aggregating over outlets there is no need to restrict ourselves to using the Jevons or Dutot formulas to construct elementary prices. From the viewpoint of economic theory, it seems preferable to use the Fisher-Ideal price index in this second stage of elementary aggregation.

4. Values and quantities should be sampled rather than just prices. Sampling values and quantities will greatly reduce the new-introductions bias.

5. Statistical agencies should consider either purchasing electronic point-of-sale data from firms currently processing these data, or the agencies should set up divisions which would compete in this area.

6. Recent economic history will have to be rewritten in view of the substantial outlet-substitution and elementary price index biases that Reinsdorf and Moulton have uncovered in U.S. price indexes. Since the United States is so large in the world economy, world inflation was lower in the 1980s than was officially recorded and world output growth (and hence productivity growth) was higher. It is very likely that many of the sources of bias in price indexes documented for the U.S. economy are also applicable to other economies.

References

Aizcorbe, A. M., and P. C. Jackman. 1993. The commodity substitution effect in CPI data, 1982–91. *Monthly Labor Review* 116 (December): 25–33.
Allen, R. G. D. 1975. *Index numbers in theory and practice.* London: Macmillan.
Anglin, P. M., and M. R. Baye. 1987. Information, multiprice search, and cost-of-living index theory. *Journal of Political Economy* 95:1179–95.
Archibald, R. B. 1977. On the theory of industrial price measurement: Output price indexes. *Annals of Economic and Social Measurement* 6:57–72.
Armknecht, P. A., B. R. Moulton, and K. J. Stewart. 1994. Improvements to the food at home, shelter and prescription drug indexes in the U.S. Consumer Price Index. Paper presented at the International Conference on Price Indices, 31 October–2 November, at Statistics Canada, Ottawa, Ontario.

Balk, B. M. 1990. On calculating cost-of-living index numbers for arbitrary income levels. *Econometrica* 58:75–92.

———. 1994. On the first step in the calculation of a consumer price index. Paper presented at the International Conference on Price Indices, 31 October–2 November, at Statistics Canada, Ottawa, Ontario.

Berndt, E. R., Z. Griliches, and J. G. Rosett. 1993. Auditing the producer price index: Micro evidence from prescription pharmaceutical preparations. *Journal of Business and Economic Statistics* 11:251–64.

Bowley, A. L. 1919. The measurement of changes in the cost of living. *Journal of the Royal Statistical Society* 82:343–72.

Carli, G. R. [1764] 1804. Del valore e della proporzione de' metalli monetati. Reprinted in *Scrittori classici italiani di economia politica.* Volume 13, 297–366. Milan: G. G. Destefanis.

Carruthers, A. G., D. J. Sellwood, and P. W. Ward. 1980. Recent developments in the retail prices index. *The Statistician* 29:1–32.

Court, L. M., and H. E. Lewis. 1942–43. Production cost indices. *Review of Economic Studies* 10:28–42.

Crawford, A. 1993. Measurement biases in the Canadian CPI: A technical note. *Bank of Canada Review,* summer, 21–36.

Dalén, J. 1992. Computing elementary aggregates in the Swedish Consumer Price Index. *Journal of Official Statistics* 8:129–47.

———. 1994. Sensitivity analysis for harmonising European consumer price indices. Paper presented at the International Conference on Price Indices, 31 October–November 2, at Statistics Canada, Ottawa, Ontario.

Diewert, W. E. 1976. Exact and superlative index numbers. *Journal of Econometrics* 4:115–45.

———. 1978. Superlative index numbers and consistency in aggregation. *Econometrica* 46:883–900.

———. 1980. Aggregation problems in the measurement of capital. In *The measurement of capital,* ed. Dan Usher, 433–528. Chicago: University of Chicago Press.

———. 1983. The theory of the output price index and the measurement of real output change. In *Price level measurement,* ed. W. E. Diewert and C. Montmarquette, 1049–1113. Ottawa: Statistics Canada.

———. 1987. Index numbers. In *The new Palgrave: A dictionary of economics.* Vol. 2, ed. J. Eatwell, M. Milgate, and P. Newman, 767–80. London: Macmillan.

———. 1993. The early history of price index research. In *Essays in index number theory.* Vol. 1, ed. W. E. Diewert and A. O. Nakamura, 33–65. Amsterdam: North-Holland.

———. 1995. Axiomatic and economic approaches to elementary price indexes. Discussion Paper no. 95-01, University of British Columbia, Vancouver.

Dutot, C. 1738. *Réflexions politiques sur les finances et le commerce.* Vol. 1. La Haye: Les frères Vaillant et N. Prevost.

Edgeworth, F. Y. 1888. Some new methods of measuring variation in general prices. *Journal of the Royal Statistical Society* 51:346–368.

———. 1901. Mr. Walsh on the measurement of general exchange value. *Economic Journal* 11:404–16.

———. 1923. The doctrine of index-numbers according to Mr. Correa Walsh. *Economic Journal* 33:343–51.

———. 1925. The plurality of index-numbers. *Economic Journal* 35:379–88.

Eichhorn, W., and J. Voeller. 1976. *Theory of the price index.* Lecture Notes in Economics and Mathematical Systems, vol. 140. Berlin: Springer-Verlag.

Ferger, W. F. 1936. Distinctive concepts of price and purchasing-power index numbers. *Journal of the American Statistical Association* 31:258–72.

Fisher, F. M., and K. Shell. 1972. The pure theory of the national output deflator. In *The economic theory of price indices*, 49–113. New York: Academic Press.

Fisher, I. 1911. *The purchasing power of money.* London: Macmillan.

———. 1922. *The making of index numbers.* 1st ed. Boston: Houghton Mifflin.

Fixler, D. 1993. The Consumer Price Index: Underlying concepts and caveats. *Monthly Labor Review* 116 (December): 3–12.

Flux, A. W. 1907. Modes of constructing index-numbers. *Quarterly Journal of Economics* 21:613–31.

Forsyth, F. G. 1978. The practical construction of a chain price index number. *Journal of the Royal Statistical Society* ser. A, 141:348–358.

Forsyth, F. G., and R. F. Fowler. 1981. The theory and practice of chain price index numbers. *Journal of the Royal Statistical Society* ser. A, 144:224–46.

Frisch, R. 1936. Annual survey of general economic theory: The problem of index numbers. *Econometrica* 4:1–39

Généreux, P. 1983. Impact of the choice of formulae on the Canadian Consumer Price Index. In *Price level measurement*, ed. W. E. Diewert and C. Montmarquette, 489–511. Ottawa: Statistics Canada.

Gordon, R. J. 1981. The Consumer Price Index: Measuring inflation and causing it. *Public Interest* 63 (spring): 112–34.

———. 1990. *The measurement of durable goods prices.* Chicago: University of Chicago Press.

———. 1993. Measuring the aggregate price level: Implications for economic performance and policy. In *Price stabilization in the 1990s*, ed. K. Shigehara, 233–76. London: Macmillan.

Griliches, Z. 1979. Issues in assessing the contribution of research and development to productivity growth. *Bell Journal of Economics* 10 (spring): 92–116.

Griliches, Z., and I. Cockburn. 1994. Generics and new goods in pharmaceutical price indexes. *American Economic Review* 84:1213–32.

Hicks, J. R. 1940. The valuation of the social income. *Economica* 7:105–40.

Hill, P. 1988. Recent developments in index number theory and practice. *OECD Economic Studies* 10 (spring): 123–48.

Hogg, M. H. 1931. A distortion in the cost of living index. *Journal of the American Statistical Association* 26:52–57.

Jevons, W. S. 1884. A serious fall in the value of gold ascertained and its social effects set forth. In *Investigations in currency and finance*, 13–118. London: Macmillan.

Konüs, A. A. 1939. The problem of the true cost of living. *Econometrica* 7:10–29. First published (in Russian) in *Economic Bulletin of the Institute of Economic Conjuncture* (Moscow, 1924) 3, no. 9–10 (September-October): 64–71.

Lovitt, W. V. 1928. Index number bias. *Journal of the American Statistical Association* 23:10–17.

Manser, M. E., and R. J. McDonald. 1988. An analysis of substitution bias in measuring inflation, 1959–85. *Econometrica* 56:909–30.

March, L. 1921. Les modes de mesure du mouvement général des prix. *Metron* 1: 57–91.

Marshall, A. 1887. Remedies for fluctuations of general prices. *Contemporary Review* 51:355–75.

Mills, F. C., E. W. Bakke, R. Cox, M. G. Reid, T. W. Schultz, and S. Stratton. 1943. An appraisal of the U.S. Bureau of Labor Statistics cost of living index. *Journal of the American Statistical Association* 38:387–405.

Moulton, B. R. 1993. Basic components of the CPI: Estimation of price changes. *Monthly Labor Review* 116 (December): 13–24.

Mudgett, B. D. 1929. Some unsettled questions in the theory of index numbers. *Journal of the American Statistical Association* 24:249–51.

———. 1933. The problem of the representative budget in a cost of living index. *Journal of the American Statistical Association* 28:26–32.

Pierson, N. G. 1895. Index numbers and appreciation of gold. *Economic Journal* 5:329–35.

———. 1896. Further considerations on index-numbers. *Economic Journal* 6:127–31.

Pigou, A. C. 1924. *The economics of welfare.* 2d ed. London: Macmillan.

Pollak, R. A. 1981. The social cost-of-living index. *Journal of Public Economics* 15:311–36.

Reinsdorf, M. 1993. The effect of outlet price differentials in the U.S. Consumer Price Index. In *Price measurements and their uses,* ed. M. F. Foss, M. E. Manser, and A. H. Young, 227–54. NBER Studies in Income and Wealth, vol. 57. Chicago: University of Chicago Press.

———. 1994a. The effect of price dispersion on cost of living indexes. *International Economic Review* 35:137–49.

———. 1994b. Price dispersion, seller substitution and the U.S. CPI. Working Paper no. 252, Bureau of Labor Statistics, Washington, D.C. March.

Saglio, A. 1994. Comparative changes in average price and a price index: Two case studies. Paper presented at the International Conference on Price Indices. 31 October–2 November, at Statistics Canada, Ottawa, Ontario.

Samuelson, P. A., and J. Swamy. 1974. Invariant economic index numbers and canonical duality: Survey and synthesis. *American Economic Review* 64:566–93.

Sauerbeck, A. 1895. Index numbers of prices. *Economic Journal* 5:161–74.

Saulnier, M. 1990. Real gross domestic product: Sensitivity to the choice of base year. *Canadian Economic Observer* 3, no. 5 (May): 1–19.

Schmidt, M. L. 1993. Effects of updating the CPI market basket. *Monthly Labor Review* 116 (December): 59–62.

Sellwood, D. 1994. Constrained macro effects of the use of different methods at the basic level in the project to harmonize consumer price indices in the European Union. Paper presented at the International Conference on Price Indices, 31 October–2 November, at Statistics Canada, Ottawa, Ontario.

Szulc, B. J. 1987. Price indices below the basic aggregation level. *Bulletin of Labour Statistics* 2:9–16. Reprinted in *Consumer price indices: An ILO manual,* ed. R. Turvey, 167–78, Geneva: International Labour Office, 1989.

Trajtenberg, M. 1990. Product innovations, price indices and the (mis)measurement of economic performance. NBER Working Paper no. 3261. Cambridge, Mass.: National Bureau of Economic Research.

Triplett, J. E. 1983. Escalation measures: What is the answer? What is the question? In *Price level measurement,* ed. W. E. Diewert and C. Montmarquette, 457–82. Ottawa: Statistics Canada.

———. 1993. Comment. In *Price measurements and their uses,* ed. M. F. Foss, M. E. Manser, and A. H. Young, 197–206. NBER Studies in Income and Wealth, vol. 57. Chicago: University of Chicago Press.

Turvey, R. 1989. *Consumer price indices: An ILO manual.* Geneva: International Labour Office.

Walsh, C. M. 1901. *The measurement of general exchange value.* New York: Macmillan.

———. 1921. *The problem of estimation.* London: P. S. King and Son.

Woolford, K. 1994. A pragmatic approach to the selection of appropriate index formula. Paper presented at the International Conference on Price Indices, 31 October–2 November, at Statistics Canada, Ottawa, Ontario.

Wynne, M. A., and F. D. Sigalla. 1994. The Consumer Price Index. *Economic Review Federal Reserve Bank of Dallas,* second quarter, 1–22.

11 New Goods from the Perspective of Price Index Making in Canada and Japan

Andrew Baldwin, Pierre Després, Alice Nakamura, and
Masao Nakamura

11.1 Introduction

This paper takes a fresh look at the treatment of new goods in official index number making. It is a paper about a project that changed directions as the research progressed. We set out to document the treatment of new goods in the price statistics of Canada and Japan. We saw this as an incremental effort, building on common knowledge concerning the construction of national price indexes. We also had a preconceived notion of what new goods are: goods that have come into being recently because of technological advances. One reason we were interested in the project is that productivity growth is measured at the national and regional levels using price indexes to control for price-related changes in the values of output and input goods. To the extent that price inflation is overestimated because of the failure to account for new goods appropriately in the construction of price statistics, the estimates of productivity growth will be downward biased. The extent of the bias could differ over time and among countries owing to differences in the treatment of new goods.

As the project progressed, we found that, on the whole, the new goods in the price indexes for Canada and Japan are not the sorts of goods we had had

Andrew Baldwin is head of Machinery and Equipment Price Indexes of Statistics Canada. Pierre Després is a researcher in the Prices Division of Statistics Canada. Alice Nakamura is professor in the Faculty of Business at the University of Alberta. Masao Nakamura is professor in the Faculty of Commerce, the Faculty of Applied Science, and the Institute of Asian Research at the University of British Columbia.

An earlier version of this paper was presented at the Calgary meeting of the Canadian Economics Association, 10–13 June 1994. The research was supported in part by a Strategic Grant from the Social Sciences and Humanities Research Council of Canada. The authors thank Teruki Oba of the Research and Statistics Department of the Bank of Japan for extensive help in preparing this paper, and Erwin Diewert, Robert Gordon, Peter Lawrence, Alan Russell, Christine Schwab, Robert Summers, and Jack Triplett for helpful comments. The authors are solely responsible for the views expressed in this paper and for any factual or interpretive errors.

in mind. We came to recognize also that the nature and treatment of new goods in official statistics is bound up with specific aspects of the selection of the goods to be priced, and that these selection processes are less known and less documented than we had expected. Nor are they standardized for all of the price indexes of a given country. For this reason, we narrowed our investigation to the main producer price indexes for Canada and Japan. Our notions about the measurement of productivity growth and how this relates to the treatment of new goods in price statistics also changed.

We begin in section 11.2 with an overview of some of the different ways of defining new goods that have been suggested in the economics index number literature, by national statistical agencies, and by those interested in using price indexes to measure economic productivity. We go on to examine the operational treatment of new goods in the Canadian Industrial Product Price Index (sections 11.3–11.5) and the Japanese Domestic Wholesale Price Index (sections 11.6–11.8). There has been relatively little published about the price statistics of either Canada or Japan. Thus this descriptive material is important in its own right as well as in the context it provides for considering the treatment of new goods in national price statistics. Concluding remarks are presented in section 11.9.

11.2   Alternative Definitions and Treatments of New Goods in National Price Statistics

Economists have made ongoing representations to their national statistical agencies concerning the need for more rapid inclusion of new goods in official price statistics. New goods are a common topic as well in the reports of national statistical agencies. But is the term "new goods" being used in the same way in these different circles? It seems important to address this question before going on to examine operational aspects of the treatment of new goods in the producer price statistics of Canada and Japan.

What we see as alternative definitions of new goods used by economists and index makers are summarized in subsections 11.2.1 and 11.2.2. Subsections 11.2.3–11.2.5 deal with the conceptual relationships of new goods, evolving goods, and new and evolving processes for producing goods and services.

11.2.1   New Goods in the Economics Index Number Literature

Like several other economists who have written on this topic, Diewert sums up the new-goods problem as one of missing prices: "Obviously, the quantity of a 'new' good produced or consumed in the period before its introduction is zero. However, the economic theory of index numbers requires a price to go along with this zero quantity—what should this price be?" (1993a, 25). The suggested solutions that Diewert reviews provide further clarification of the underlying definition of a new good in much of the economics literature. One solution is to ignore a new good in the first pricing period in which it is introduced and to bring it into the market basket in the second period using the chain approach. Marshall (1887) is credited with suggesting this. A second approach involves imputing the missing price for a new good for the period prior to when it first appeared. To do this, a conceptual characterization of the missing price must be developed. Diewert sums up Hicks's (1940) characterization of the unobservable price of a new good before its introduction: "(i) from the viewpoint of a consumer or producer buying units of the 'new' good in the first period that it makes its appearance, the price in the previous period should be that price which would have been just high enough to have driven the purchaser's demand down to zero and (ii) from the viewpoint of the producer of the 'new' good, the price in the previous period should be that price which would have been just low enough to have induced the producer to supply zero units" (1993a, 25). In sketching out the stream of research that Hicks's insights inspired, Diewert (1993b, 62) notes that Hofsten (1952) used Hicks's approach, and adapted it for dealing with disappearing goods; Fisher and Shell (1972) laid out the formal algebra for the construction of Hicksian "demand reservation prices"; and Diewert (1980, 498–503) used the Fisher price index as a context for exploring the consequences of incorrectly setting the demand reservation prices to zero versus the alternative of ignoring the existence of new goods in the first period in which they are introduced (Marshall's method).

The imputed prices approach recommended by economists such as Hicks and Diewert implies the following *market behavior* definition of new goods:

DEFINITION 1. *A new good is a good that is available in the present period for which there was no demand in the previous period because potential customers believed it could not be supplied at any price they would be willing to pay and for which there was no supply because potential producers believed it could not be sold at any price for which they would be willing to produce the good.*

Marshall's suggested approach to the missing prices problem of ignoring new goods in the first period of their existence suggests a simpler definition of new goods based on *availability*:

DEFINITION 2. *A new good is a good that is available in the present period and that was not available in the previous period.*

Definition 2, which encompasses definition 1, would allow for goods that no one had thought of prior to their appearance, so that potential purchasers and suppliers had given no thought to their reservation prices.

However, both definitions 1 and 2 are incomplete without clarification of what is meant by a good being "available" and what a "good" is. For example, is a good available in the present period if producers could, or perhaps did, produce it and could, or would, sell it for a price consumers would pay, but consumers have not yet discovered this due to a lack of advertising? Is a good available if it could be purchased elsewhere and transported at a cost that local customers would pay, but no business is bringing it into the local market? Is a new model of an old good a new good?

11.2.2   A Traditional Index Maker's Definition of a New Good

Our research suggests that the *de facto operational definition* of a new good for many agencies producing official statistics is fundamentally simpler than definition 1 or even definition 2:

DEFINITION 3.   *A new good is a good that is included (or being considered for inclusion) in an index number basket in the current period for this index but that was not included in previous periods, or a previously included good for which the pricing status has been, is going to be, or some feel should be, upgraded.*

Using definition 3, questions like those posed above must then be answered. In many situations, the "answers" are an outcome of case-by-case operational choices made by those responsible for the production of price indexes. Notice that definition 3 in some respects encompasses definitions 1 and 2.

11.2.3   Quality Change as a Source of New Goods

The treatment of quality change for successive varieties of a good is inextricably interrelated with the treatment of new goods even though, to most of us, new models of cars and new styles of clothes and shoes are not "new" goods. There are a number of established methods used by statistical agencies for relating new varieties of goods to ones they were previously pricing.

Direct comparison is used when the new variety is viewed as the same, in terms of quality, as the old one. The entire price difference is treated as a pure price increase or decrease. The other methods allow for changes in quality. If both the new good or variety and the old one were available in the same pricing period and if the price difference between them can be viewed as solely reflecting the quality difference, then relative prices for the goods at a point in time can be used in *linking* the price for the new good or variety to the price for the old one. A second method makes use of *cost evaluation* information for stated quality changes. Usually the cost information comes from the reports of manufacturers on the quality changes instituted in their products and the costs of making these changes. A third approach is to use available prices for different models of the good of interest and information about the characteristics of these models deemed to affect prices to estimate the values of the characteristics. In this *hedonic approach,* the estimates of characteristic values are then used to allow for quality differences in relating the price for a new model to the price for the old one.

All of the above approaches involve relating new varieties of goods to old goods. A different type of approach is to treat new varieties as distinct goods: in particular, as new goods. Triplett comments on this approach in the context of the old Wholesale Price Index (WPI) for the United States:

A traditional method for handling the quality problem in index numbers has been to convert it into the (supposedly) more tractable product-mix problem: different varieties are treated as if they were different products and carried along in the index separately. In the WPI, for example, prices may be collected for several varieties of an item of machinery and separate components published for each of them. Then, when the quality of machines improves, it may be possible to allow for the change by shifting the weights attached to each of the separate subcomponents. (1971, 199)

The choices about when to quality-adjust, when to ignore changes in goods for pricing purposes, and when to treat changed goods as new goods are the operational reasons that the treatment of new goods is interrelated with the treatment of quality change in official price statistics.

New varieties of old goods that are treated as new goods may be new either in the sense of market behavior or availability, as in definitions 1 or 2, or in the operational sense of definition 3.

11.2.4   The New-Goods Problem in the Context of Hedonic Pricing

In the hedonic approach to pricing, sellers and buyers are viewed as transacting characteristics of goods. That is, goods are viewed as bundles of marketable characteristics. Theoretically at least, this approach makes it possible to deal with many more goods that are new in an operational sense—and perhaps in market or availability respects as well—as quality-adjusted varieties of goods that were already included in the index. Nevertheless, there are at least two ways in which a new-goods problem can arise in this context. The first is the appearance of goods with new characteristics. These characteristics could be new in a market or availability or in a de facto operational sense in the terms of definitions 1, 2, and 3, respectively. The second is the combination of old characteristics in a new way that cannot be represented using a hedonic equation estimated with data for the previously available goods and their characteristics.

The growing use of the hedonic approach to quality-adjust vehicles and electronic goods (but very little else), and the greater flexibility of this approach compared to the more traditional ones for dealing with quality change, have been further blurring the boundary between how quality change and new goods are dealt with. This complicates price comparisons over time within individual countries and among countries.

11.2.5   New Ways of Producing Goods and Services

Remarks in the preface of Robert Gordon's 1990 book, *The Measurement of Durable Goods Prices,* suggest yet another possible way of thinking about new goods. Gordon writes about the production process for his own book and how it changed over time:

Since this is a book about quality change and technological progress in durable goods, a word is in order about the change in the production technology of this book between the 1974 and 1988 versions. The draft of the first version was typed on a Smith-Corona portable typewriter and retyped in its entirety, often several times, by a secretary using an IBM [S]electric typewriter. Any change that I might have contemplated, particularly an extra paragraph early in a chapter, required extensive retyping by the secretary and a difficult cost-benefit calculation as to whether it was really worth it. Technology was a barrier to improvements in substance. In contrast, the new chapters written in 1988 were composed and printed at the level of professional typesetting inside my home by a 386 "clone" personal computer, a Hewlett-Packard laser printer, and WordPerfect 5.0. Revisions could be made instantly and chapters reprinted at the rate of eight pages per minute, all without any involvement of a secretary. (xvi)

In the case study laid out in the above quotation, there are two processes for producing printed manuscript pages: a typewriter-based "process A," and a personal computer–based "process B." Each process involves a specified input collection. Input collection A for process A consists of a Smith-Corona portable typewriter, an IBM Selectric typewriter, and a secretary to operate the IBM Selectric typewriter. Input collection B consists of a 386 "clone" personal computer, a Hewlett-Packard laser printer of a given vintage, and WordPerfect 5.0. (For convenience, Professor Gordon's typing time is ignored as a free input good.)

Suppose that each of the inputs to the above production processes for printed pages could be priced over the entire 1974–88 period, and that a price index was computed over these years using some but not all of this information. Suppose, in particular, that the personal computers were omitted until the early 1980s because the models were constantly changing and furthermore the quantities transacted were fairly small until then. If price movements for personal computers were proxied in the index by the price movements for the typewriters until the early 1980s, and if prices fell much more dramatically for the personal computers, then there would be a new-goods bias in the price index relative to the true price movements for all of these inputs considered together because of the omission of the personal computers. This bias problem could have been lessened by adopting hedonic methods to cope with the frequent model changes for the personal computers, and introducing the price information for them into the price index sooner. (This is essentially what statistical agencies in countries like Canada and Japan are striving to do now with goods like this.) But this still might not properly account for the impact of the new good—the personal computer—on the cost of the printed pages.

Printed pages are not a new good at any point over the 1974–88 period, by any of our above definitions. Rather, they are an "old" good for which, like light (for which Nordhaus studies price movements over time in chap. 1 in this volume), the price has been falling because of the declines in price and related spreading adoption of new machinery. The impacts of the new machines on prices might be sorted out more appropriately if the personal computer were treated as a quality-adjusted typewriter, perhaps using printed pages as the basis for making this adjustment, much as MIPS (millions of instructions per second) are sometimes used in quality-adjusting new models of computers. However, quality adjustment between dissimilar goods like typewriters and personal computers would place a much heavier burden on statistical agencies, and it is not being attempted for any of the price index systems examined in this paper.

Alternatively, statistical agencies might go further in making available price information for individual categories of goods. This information, together with information on the alternative technologies in use for producing the outputs of interest and on the prevalence of the various technologies, could then be used by other researchers to compute and explain price movements for particular output goods, much as Nordhaus traces changes over time in the price of light. This would be an output-good-specific, microsimulation sort of an approach to studying price changes and their sources. At present, however, this is not being done either, except in Nordhaus's chapter.

11.3   The Canadian Industrial Product Price Index

In order to understand details of how new goods are dealt with in any given official price statistics system, it is first necessary to know the basics of the production of those price statistics. Some of these details have important implications for the sorts of goods that end up being treated as new for the construction of specific price indexes.

11.3.1   Origins of the Industrial Product Price Index

The Canadian Industrial Product Price Index (IPPI) is a product-based aggregative index that is produced by Statistics Canada and is intended to measure price changes for the universe of commodities sold by Canadian manufacturers. This index (with 1981 = 100) replaced Statistics Canada's Industry Selling Price Index (ISPI).

The initial 1956-based ISPI covered only a limited set of industries and excluded most machinery manufacturing. For example, office-machinery and -equipment production was not covered. In the 1961 update of the ISPI, basket shares were assigned to all industries in manufacturing, though some of the categories were very broad. For instance, office machinery and equipment was in a general category called "other machinery industries." Moreover, many product classes within the designated industry categories were not directly surveyed, and, in aggregating up, price changes for the nonsurveyed product classes were treated as being the same as the subindexes for the respective industries in which the nonsurveyed goods were included.

11.3.2   The IPPI Today

At present, the Canadian IPPI is constructed from price indexes for 1,314 principal commodity groups (PCGs) of outputs defined in the 1986 input-output tables. About 50 PCGs are further split into two or more elemental indexes, defined by destination of shipments (domestic market or export), finer detail on commodities, region of manufacture, or some combination of these criteria. In the remaining cases, the PCG indexes are the elemental indexes.

The weights used to aggregate the elemental indexes are taken from the output of the Make matrix for the input-output system, which provides an integrated set of commodity values for all manufacturing industries. The Make matrix in turn is derived from the 1986 values of the Canadian Annual Survey of Manufactures.

For the IPPI, which is a product-based aggregative index, the entire universe of manufacturing products is conceptually covered. Contrary to the practice that was in use in the old ISPI, where prices of goods not directly surveyed were assumed to change with those of the industry to which they were assigned, the current IPPI assigns specifically chosen proxy indexes to all elemental groups not directly surveyed.

Directly surveyed commodities are supported by either a formal probability sampling or an incomplete judgmental sampling procedure, and a quality rating is presented for the pricing results. If a formal probability sampling procedure is used, then certain important producers are identified as "must-take" respondents and a random selection is taken from the smaller producers. Such samples are redrawn on a regular cycle as dictated by changes in the market. The normal cycle varies between three and four years.

About 700 of the 1,314 PCGs in the manufacturing sector are accommodated by direct survey and these account for about 85 percent of the value of manufacturing output in 1986. The price movements for the remaining 600 PCGs are estimated indirectly either from other directly priced PCGs or through borrowing price movement from other price series.

11.3.3   The Treatment of New Goods in the IPPI

In terms of the weighting of the IPPI, a new good is either a new product class within an existing elemental index or a new elemental index. All manufacturing shipments reported in the Survey of Manufactures data on which the weights are based are represented in the IPPI weights. In this sense, weighting gaps in the IPPI due to new goods are taken care of as rapidly as the information is picked up in the Survey of Manufactures and the weights are updated. However, for many new goods, they would at first simply be included in the weights for existing elemental indexes.

In terms of pricing coverage, a new good can be viewed as one for which direct pricing has been, or is considered to be, instituted; for which there has been a change from incomplete to full probability sampling of prices; or for which proxy or direct pricing has just begun. For example, a product class was assigned to integrated circuits and crystals within PCG 6365, "electronic equipment and components," when the initial price sample for that PCG was drawn. There had been no commodity index for integrated circuits in the ISPI. They were represented in the overall ISPI by the series for electrical products industries. Optical fiber cables are being considered for this sort of upgrading of status in the IPPI. They were represented in the overall ISPI by the series for nonmetallic mineral products industries. They are now part of PCG 4750, "glass products, not elsewhere specified." At present, the IPPI elemental index is a proxy; there is no direct pricing for fiber-optic cables. Along with the switch to a 1992 base period in 1994, a new elemental index for PCGA 4758, "optical fiber cable," will be defined. (The PCGAs [Principle Commodity Group Aggregates] will be the successors to the PCGs as of 1994. These will be based on the new Standard Classification of Goods, Statistics Canada's elaboration on the international Harmonized System.)

There are gaps in the pricing of manufacturing goods for the IPPI. There are several reasons for these gaps. One is that a prices census for all transactions between Canadian manufacturers and their clients would obviously be prohibitively expensive, in terms of both operational costs for Statistics Canada and response burden for the manufacturers. Even pricing all of the PCGs would be hard to justify in cost-benefit terms. Within an elemental index, once a sample of manufacturers is drawn for pricing, the probability of drawing a price quote from a given product class is proportional to its share of the manufacturer's shipments. If there is no pricing in a product class for a PCG, then its share of manufacturing shipments is probably small. This is consistent with the IPPI sampling procedures of excluding the smallest firms, which together account for less than 10 percent of shipments for an elemental group. (But there can be a problem if a good, say a new good, is produced mainly or exclusively by manufacturers below the 90 percent cutoff, so that the good has almost no weight in the sample grid above the cutoff, even though it represents a substantial share of shipments for the elemental group.)

Another cause of pricing gaps is related to the technical complexity of some of the products included in the IPPI and to the difficulty of pricing high-technology items which have substantial research and development embedded in them or short life cycles. The response burden on the manufacturer of supplying quotes for these sorts of items is substantially greater than for most products. Also, a high-tech manufacturer is more likely to regard prices and production-cost information for its products as proprietary and to be unwilling to provide this information to statistical agencies, even with stringent guarantees in place against disclosure of such information to third parties. This is the principal reason that the IPPI for telephone and telegraph apparatus and equipment is still a proxy series, although it represents about a sixth of the IPPI basket for electrical and communications products and is in fact one of the ten largest PCGs in the IPPI. Prices for digital switching equipment and other high-tech telephone equipment that are used in the deflation of the Canadian System of National Accounts estimates of investment in machinery and equipment come not from the Industry Price Survey, but from purchase price indexes compiled by the telephone carriers themselves. Some of the pricing gaps of this second sort involve products and producers for which production values have become quite large. In the early 1980s, this was the case for micro-computers.

11.3.4   Goods Changing Pricing Status from 1981 to 1986

A better understanding of the sorts of pricing gaps that there have been, and the nature of the new and emerging versus the old and declining goods in the IPPI, can be gained by examining the elemental indexes that changed pricing status from the 1981 to the 1986 index basket. Such a comparison is shown in table 11.1. In the table, an E stands for directly surveyed with a full probability sample, an S for directly surveyed from an incomplete judgmental sample, a P for proxied, and a — for not priced at all and not covered by the index. The indexes are organized by the change in their pricing status. For example, changing from an E or an S for 1981 to a P or a — for 1986 represents a downgrading of pricing status. These are the disappearing goods for the IPPI (1986 = 100). On the other hand, from a — for 1981 to a P for 1986, or from a P for 1981 to an S or an E for 1986 represents an upgrading of pricing status. Those goods for which the pricing status has been upgraded are the new and emerging goods in the IPPI from a pricing perspective. For example, from panel A of table 11.1, we see that umbrellas and walking sticks are "new goods" in the sense that the pricing status was upgraded from — (for not in-cluded) to P (for proxied). Similarly, we find that the pricing status of lawn and garden tractors has also been upgraded from — to P. Of course, these goods are not new in a market (definition 1) or an availability (definition 2) sense. They do not represent the cutting edge of technological change. And certainly they are not new in the sense in which we had thought of new goods before beginning this project. They are only new, or recently new, in the operational sense of definition 3.

11.4   Computers in the Canadian IPPI

Of course, there *are* high-tech and other newly invented goods in the IPPI, of the sort that are the focus of most of the economics literature on the treat-ment of new goods in price statistics. Some of these have been introduced into the IPPI as new elemental indexes, but others have been treated as quality-adjusted versions of goods already included. Computers are an example of a family of high-tech goods for which quality adjustments have been important.

Actual pricing development at Statistics Canada for electronic computing equipment did not begin until the early 1980s, concurrent with the develop-ment of the IPPI. As already noted, the ISPI which the IPPI replaced had virtu-ally no pricing for computing equipment. At that point, other countries, includ-ing the United States, also largely ignored electronic computing equipment in the construction of their national price statistics.

Table 11.1   **Principal Commodity Groups Whose Pricing Status Changed from 1981 to 1986**

PCG Number	PCG Title
A. PCGs for which the pricing status was upgraded from — to P	
4389	Coal and coal briquettes
5511	Lawn and garden tractors
4453	Oil-drill pipe, steel
3914	Corn oil, crude
7064	Optical lenses and parts
7859	Umbrellas and walking sticks
6855	Globes and reflectors for lighting fixtures
2554	Nickel (nickel-copper) matte
4194	Heterocyclic compounds, NES
3419	Wood pulp, NES
2450	Natural fibers
B. PCGs for which the pricing status was upgraded from P to S	
3944	Soybean oil, deodorized
5250	Parts, chain saws
7865	Other apparel, knitted, not knitted
3378	Wooden fruit and vegetable boxes
634	Corn starch
631-14	Whole wheat and graham flour, domestic
5296	Chemical and pharmaceutical products machinery
4796	Sand lime bricks and blocks
4743	Laminated glass
4473	Plates, steel, fabricated
7866	Apparel accessories, NES
5219	Parts, petroleum refining machinery
4914	Artificial abrasive grains
5218	Petroleum refining machinery
4675	Solder-type pipe fittings
5092	Parts, packaging machinery
5193	Miscellaneous material-handling equipment
4073	Sodium phosphates
C. PCGs for which the pricing status was upgraded from P to E	
4791	Gypsum plasters
4311	Aviation gasoline
4732	Refractory cements, mortars
D. PCGs for which the pricing status was upgraded from S to E	
5112	Parts, conveyors and conveying systems
7314	Commercial dishwashers
3652	Thread, of man-made fabrics
2563	Refined gold bullion
5414	Soil preparation machinery
4535	Copper wire and cable, not insulated
7853	Gloves and mittens
4279	Compound catalysts

(*continued*)

Table 11.1 (continued)

PCG Number	PCG Title
8543	Tableware, plastic
8114	Hollow-ware, flatware, and cutlery
4092	Heavy water
5421	Farm dairy machinery and equipment

E. PCGs for which the pricing status was downgraded from E to S

8311	Sporting equipment
4015	Sulfuric acid
7312	Vending machines
4114	Ethylene
5247	Veneer and plywood forming equipment
4382	Creosote, carbolic
6876	Wiring devices
7715	Accounting machines
4722	Glazed floor and tiles, clay
4744	Glass in basic shapes
4723	Sewer pipes, drain tile, and fittings
5235	Metal-cutting machine tools
9411	Brushes excluding personal care
4068	Sodium carbonate (soda ash)
5121	Elevators and escalators, excluding conveying and mining
4751	Asbestos linings and facings
5813-12	Trucks, domestic, medium
5216	Oil and gas field equipment
4711	Natural stone, basic products, structural
5811-21	Automobiles, export, station wagons
5813-32	Trucks, goods purchased for resale, medium
5023	Hydraulic turbines
4132	Methyl alcohol
4171	Adipic acid
4163	Acetic anhydride
6865	Power circuit breakers
6316	Radio and TV broadcasting equipment
4794	Thermal insulation, NES
6873	Switchgear cutouts and protective equipment
6812	Magnet wire, insulated
4812	Film and sheet, cellulosic plastic
6822	Electrical conduit and tubing
6517	Air heaters, electric, fixed, permanent
4859-20	Hard plastic automobile parts
5712	Railway rolling stock, railway service
4837	Tracks for snowmobiles
5711	Locomotives, railway service
5916	Pleasure and sporting craft sold
5721	Self-propelled cars
4122	Vinyl chloride monomer
5935	Subassemblies, parts, etc., for ships
7061	Medical and related instruments

Table 11.1   (continued)

PCG Number	PCG Title
5241	Welding machinery and equipment
8511	Kitchenware, metal or metal enamel
5417	Combines, self-propelled and pull
3655	Baler and binder twine
3013	Glove and garment leather
3019	Leather other than upper
3051	Leather shoe findings
3635	Filament yarn, excluding nylon polyester
3673	Broadwoven fabric, cotton/polyester
3684	Double-knit fabrics
3657	Twine, NES
8413	Curtains and draperies, textile
4899-10	Rubber products
8416	Textile bedding, NES
7837	Knit dresses, suits, shirts, slacks
7831	Coats, textile, women's
7833	Dresses and blouses, not knitted
7835	Skirts, not knitted
7862	Uniforms, occupational clothing
5513	Wheel tractors, excluding lawn and garden, agricultural
4899-30	Rubber and plastics products, NES
4820-30	Foamed and expanded plastics, other
3311-20	Lumber and ties, hardwood, export
3915	Soybean oil, crude
320-22	Fish fillets, steak, export, other
330-12	Fish canned, export, salmon
920-10	Potato products, frozen
1591-40	Complete feeds, farm domesticated animals, NES
631-20	Wheat flour, export
642-10	Pies, cakes, and pastries, fresh baked or unbaked frozen
1049	Sugar preparations, NES
636	Malt
4820-20	Foamed & expanded plastics, polyurethane
637	Rice, milled
1450	Food preparations, NES
4819	Rubber, chemically blown, sponge
4822-30	Plastic pipe, ABS
4822-40	Pipe pipe, other
4834-20	Pipe fittings, other than ABS
4814	Plastic film, sheet and layflat
7860	Belts
7863	Beachwear
3312-42	Lumber, softwood, other, Prairies
3345	Veneer, softwood
2569	Cobalt
4420	Blooms, billets, slabs, alloy steel

(continued)

Table 11.1 (continued)

PCG Number	PCG Title
4432	Plate, alloy steel, not fabricated
4497	Engine-block castings, cast iron
4531	Copper wire rods
2565	Platinum-group metals
2567	Magnesium
2570	Refined metals, NES
3416	Wood pulp, mechanical
6511	Heating boilers, steam generation
4611-30	Hermetically sealed window units, metal
4625	Bottle caps, metal
4661	Rods, wire, and electrodes, metal
320-21	Fish fillets, steaks, domestic, other
8512	Kitchenware, plastic
9018	Office supplies, NES
4419	Blooms, billets, slabs, carbon steel
3415	Wood pulp, sulfite, unbleached
2325-60	Pulpwood, chips, B.C. coast
3365	Roof trusses, wooden
3371-10	Prefabricated wood buildings, Atlantic
3371-20	Prefabricated wood buildings, Quebec
3371-30	Prefabricated wood buildings, Ontario
3371-40	Prefabricated wood buildings, Prairies
2325-20	Pulpwood chips, Quebec
2325-50	Pulpwood chips, B.C. interior
528	Milk, evaporated
7423-20	Furniture components, NES
3377	Pallets, wooden
3391	Shingles

F. PCGs for which the pricing status was downgraded from E to P

4390	Petrochemical feed stocks
7818	Sleepwear, men's, youths', and boys'
5233	Metalworking machine tools
7711	Typewriters
5813-22	Trucks, export, medium

G. PCGs for which the pricing status was downgraded from S to P

9428	Gaskets, NES
4145	Phenol
6917	Personal care appliances
6918	Heating pads and electric blankets
4222	Reclaimed rubber
6311	Domestic TV and other receiving sets
6840	Lamps, residential type, incandescent
6312	Radio receiving sets, automotive type
3665	Broadwoven fabric, wool mix, apparel
4118-20	Other hydrocarbons, NES
6844	Automotive-type lighting fixtures
3692	Tire fabrics, other

Table 11.1   (continued)

PCG Number	PCG Title
4753	Asbestos products, NES
6615	Heating elements for electric appliances
635	Starches, cereal, NES
3946	Peanut oil, deodorized
7712	Parts, typewriters
6314	Phonograph records
8112	Costume jewelry
6515	Air heaters, electric, portable
3664	Broadwoven fabric, wool, apparel
7065	Optical instruments
8810	Medical and surgical apparatus
6913	Sewing machines, domestic type
8214	Timers, NES

H. PCGs for which the pricing status was downgraded from E to N

6912	Flatirons, domestic type

Source: Statistics Canada (1986, 1991).

Notes: E stands for directly estimated from a full probability sample of prices. S stands for directly estimated from an incomplete (nonprobability) sample of prices. P stands for proxied. — stands for not priced and not included in the IPPI. NES stands for not elsewhere specified.

11.4.1   The Use by Statistics Canada of U.S. Price Indexes for Computing Equipment

In early 1986, the U.S. Bureau of Economic Analysis (BEA) released price indexes for computing equipment extending back in time to 1969 and made the decision to use these in the revision of the U.S. national accounts system. This spurred developmental work within Statistics Canada on a quality-adjusted indicator for electronic computing equipment that could be used for the Canadian system of national accounts.

New deflators were produced by Statistics Canada for domestic production, exports, imports, and the final demand categories of electronic computing equipment using the original BEA historical figures as proxies for price movements in Canada. In particular, the composition of domestic Canadian production at that time led Statistics Canada to choose as a price indicator for domestic production and exports for the period 1971–81 the BEA index for video displays. From 1981 to 1990, the BEA figures for price movements for various types of electronic computing equipment were used together with weights reflecting the composition of domestic Canadian production. On the import side from 1971 on, because of the broad mix of products being imported into Canada, Statistics Canada used the BEA index figures for various types of electronic computing equipment weighted according to import data and also adjusted for exchange rate fluctuations, tariffs, and federal sales tax (and more recently for the Goods and Services Tax).

11.4.2   The Move to Actual Pricing of Computing Equipment

The selection of manufacturers for the first Statistics Canada pricing sample for computing equipment was based on the Census of Manufactures data for 1979. As noted above, at that time the bulk of Canadian production was concentrated in video displays and, to a lesser extent, communication-interface equipment. Pricing development at Statistics Canada reflected that situation. Microcomputers were still of minute value in the overall scheme and, as such, were not part of the first pricing sample for electronic computing equipment.

A second sample was developed using 1981 Census of Manufactures data. It included microcomputer pricing with mostly 286-type machines. A third sample was developed using 1985 Census of Manufactures data. By then, major changes had occurred in the composition of the product mix: printers had become the dominant computing-equipment product produced in Canada, with video displays having become relatively less important. Microcomputers were also beginning to be a significant portion of the production mix, as well as communication-interface computing equipment. The question of quality adjustment for these products was viewed as a critical issue by Statistics Canada.

11.4.3   The Move to Hedonic Pricing

In 1990 and 1991, Statistics Canada embarked on the development of hedonic pricing for computers. This step was taken because several national statistical agencies around the world had become concerned about the need to publish reliable measures of price change for microcomputers as well as for larger members of the computer family. Leading the way was the U.S. BEA. The BEA commenced publication of price indexes for mainframes, minicomputers, and peripherals in 1986. Shortly after the release of the BEA indexes, the Bureau of Labor Statistics (BLS) launched a research and development program to tackle the measurement of price change for microcomputers and related peripherals. A series of experimental price indexes based on alternative quality-adjustment methods was developed. The version known as the "composite," which combines hedonic and conventional quality-adjustment techniques, was selected as the official measure. Statistics Canada is one of the national statistical agencies now following in the footsteps of the United States. (See MacDonald 1991.)

11.5   Consequences of the Late Inclusion of Computers in Canadian Producer Price Indexes

As has already been noted, prices for electronic computing equipment are included in the IPPI but were not included in the ISPI. It would be interesting to know how the producer price movements measured using the old ISPI would have been affected if computing equipment had been included earlier with proxy pricing.

11.5.1   The Impact of Excluding Computing Equipment over 1956–1970

In the IPPI, computing equipment is incorporated into the office- and store-machines group. From this perspective, the inclusion of computing equipment in the IPPI could be viewed as an extension of earlier efforts to include machinery produced for offices and stores in the ISPI. We noted previously that machinery production of this sort was not covered at all in the initial ISPI (base 1956 = 100). The 1961 = 100 ISPI series assigned basket shares to all industries in the manufacturing sector, though office machinery and equipment was treated as part of a general category, "other machinery industries," and pricing was by proxy.

For the 1956–70 period, the lack of coverage, and then the pricing by proxy only, for machinery for offices and stores probably was a serious gap in the coverage of producer prices in Canada. However, at least in the earlier part of this period, the lack of coverage for the electronic computing equipment portion of office and store machinery may not have been important. For the ISPI as a whole, using 1961 shipments data, the production of electronic computing equipment would have constituted less than 0.1 percent of the index basket. In 1953, the basket share would have been even smaller.

It is true that, just confining attention to the aggregate for machinery industries (except electrical), computers would have had more than five times their weight in the total ISPI. But even within this aggregate, electronic computing equipment would have accounted for no more than 0.5 percent of the relevant portion of the index basket in 1961.

However, the following decade witnessed a rapid expansion of the production of electronic computing equipment in Canada. In fact, as discussed below, Canadian production was sufficiently important that Japan was pricing Canadian-made electronic memory for computers over the period 1965–70 as part of its efforts to track the movements of import pricing for electronic computing equipment. (See subsection 11.7.1.) This suggests that, even over the course of the 1960s, the failure to include electronic computing equipment in the ISPI may have become a more serious problem. In the following subsection, we examine this problem empirically for the decade that followed.

11.5.2   The Impact of Excluding Computing Equipment over 1971–1980

From 1971 to 1980, the ISPI series pertaining to computers was the index for office and store machinery (D535601, see Statistics Canada 1978). This index did not include electronic computing equipment in its pricing even though this equipment accounted for 7.5 percent of the office- and store-machinery basket according to 1971 manufacturing shipment values. At that time, the office- and store-machinery series was based on pricing for typewriters, accounting machines, and cash registers. There was substantial production of typewriters and cash registers in Canada in the 1970s which faded away by the mid-1980s. Thus, price movements for computing equipment sales, which were characterized by rapid growth, were being proxied by price movements for other types of office and store machinery, some of which were declining in sales. This makes the 1971–80 period a particularly interesting one for more carefully examining the impact on the old ISPI of the exclusion of computing equipment, as is done in the following subsection.

Recomputing the ISPI with Computing Equipment Included

For the 1971–81 period, the Canadian domestic production of computer equipment was geared heavily toward display units: particularly dumb terminals. (A dumb terminal lacks an internal microprocessor and cannot perform even rudimentary data processing without resort to its host computer.) For this reason, we use the BEA series for display units adjusted for U.S. exchange rates as a proxy series for domestic production over this period. Except for the years 1972–73, the BEA series declines steadily from 1972 to 1981, falling on average by 5.9 percent per year. Over the same period, the American dollar gained relative to the Canadian dollar, so that the exchange rate–adjusted series drops on average by only 4.3 percent per year. From the results displayed in table 11.2, we conclude that if this BEA series had been used to represent price movements for the production of computing equipment and parts in the ISPI, the index for office and store machinery would have risen on average by 1.6 percent per year from 1971 to 1981 rather than by 1.9 percent as the official series does.

At higher levels of aggregation, the difference resulting from using the BEA series as a proxy for computing-equipment price movements becomes negligible. The machinery industries index recomputed to include computers is only 0.6 index points lower by 1981 than the official index, and the total ISPI recomputed with computers included is the same as the official index to one decimal point of accuracy. Perhaps this result is not surprising given that, in 1971, electronic computing equipment still constituted only 0.8 percent of the output of the machinery industries and less than 0.05 percent of total manufacturing shipments.

Taking Account of Changing Basket Shares

There is a caveat concerning the table 11.2 results on which the above conclusions are based. The differences between the official series and the series computed using the BEA proxy are so small partly because the same 1971 basket-share weights are used for the entire period even though this was a period of rapid growth in the volume of production for computing equipment in Canada. This is in line with actual practice for the production of the ISPI, but not with current practices for the IPPI.

The current policy at Statistics Canada for the IPPI is to update the basket weights every five years. This policy was instituted with the 1991 updating of

Table 11.2   Industry Selling Price Indexes for Canada

	Computers[a]	Computers: Exchange Adjusted	Office & Store Machinery Including Computers	Office & Store Machinery: Official	Office & Store Machinery: Chain Index	Machinery Industries: Official	Machinery Industries Excluding Office & Store Machinery: Official	Machinery Industries Including Computers	Machinery Industries Including Computers: Chain Index	Total ISPI: Official	Total ISPI Excluding Office & Store Machinery	Total ISPI Excluding Computers	Total ISPI Including Computers: Chain Index
Adjustment of official series to include computer indexes in 1971 basket													
Industry share	7.5		100.0		92.5								
Total share		0.042		0.553		4.162	3.609	4.162		100.000	99.447	100	
1971	100.0	100.0	100.0	100.0	100.0	100.0	100.0	100.0	100.0	100.0	100.0	100.0	100.0
1972	101.7	99.8	102.1	102.3	102.1	103.2	103.3	103.2	103.2	104.4	104.4	104.4	104.4
1973	101.9	100.9	109.4	110.1	109.4	108.5	108.3	108.4	108.4	116.1	116.1	116.1	116.1
1974	98.9	95.8	113.5	114.9	113.5	123.9	125.3	123.7	123.7	138.1	138.2	138.1	138.1
1975	91.3	92.0	118.5	120.7	118.5	142.7	146.1	142.4	142.4	153.7	153.9	153.7	153.7
1976	83.4	81.4	117.2	120.1	117.2	151.3	156.1	150.9	150.9	161.6	161.8	161.6	161.6
1977	82.5	86.9	112.4	114.5	112.9	158.9	165.7	158.6	158.0	174.3	174.6	174.3	174.2
1978	73.4	82.9	112.7	115.1	112.9	168.8	177.0	168.5	167.3	190.4	190.8	190.4	190.3
1979	63.9	74.2	114.7	118.0	114.4	186.7	197.2	186.3	184.1	217.9	218.5	217.9	217.8
1980	56.6	65.6	115.3	119.4	114.6	207.9	221.5	207.4	204.0	247.2	247.9	247.2	247.0
1981	54.6	64.8	116.9	121.2	116.1	233.1	250.2	232.5	228.0	272.4	273.2	272.4	272.1
Annual rate of price change	−5.9	−4.3	1.6	1.9	1.5	8.8	9.6	8.8	8.6	10.5	10.6	10.5	10.5
Adjustment of series to include computer indexes in hypothetical 1976 basket													
Industry share	8.7		100.0		91.3								
Share of machinery industries		15.1				100.0	84.9	100.0					
Total share		0.052		0.598		3.953	3.355	3.953			99.402		
1976		100.0	100.0	100.0		100.0	100.0	100.0			100.0	100.0	
1977		106.7	96.3	95.3		105.0	106.2	104.7			107.9	107.8	
1978		101.8	96.4	95.8		111.6	113.4	110.8			117.9	117.8	
1979		91.1	97.6	98.3		123.4	126.4	122.0			135.0	134.8	
1980		80.5	97.8	99.4		137.4	141.9	135.2			153.2	152.9	
1981		79.5	99.0	100.9		154.1	160.3	151.1			168.8	168.4	

Source: Statistics Canada (1978 and various issues).

[a]This is the BEA index for displays reexpressed in Canadian dollars with 1971 = 100.

Table 11.3   Relative Importance of Electronic Computer Equipment in an Office- and Store-Machinery Manufacturers Aggregate

	Value of Shipments of Goods of Own Manufacture				
	1971 (1971 prices)	1976 (1976 prices)	1971 (1976 prices)	1976 (1971 prices)	1976 index (1971 = 100)
Electronic computer equipment	14,163	36,017	11,529	44,247	81.4
Total office and store machinery	187,911	412,017	220,023	351,550	117.2
Percentage share	7.5	8.7	5.2	12.6	

Sources: Statistics Canada (1971, 1976).

the IPPI to a 1986 basket (see Statistics Canada 1991). Consistent with that policy, table 11.2 also shows what the chain index for the office- and store-machinery category, with computers included, would look like with a 1976-based Laspeyres series linked to the 1971-based Laspeyres series at 1976. (Only the basket shares of computers within the office and store ISPI and of the office and store ISPI within the machinery and total ISPIs were adjusted for in this exercise.) The chain index for machinery industries and for the total ISPI were similarly calculated as weighted averages of the office- and store-machinery series and the remainder of each given aggregate.

The impact of the chain calculation is to lower the 1981 value of the office- and store-machinery aggregate by 0.8 index points, changing the average annual growth rate for 1971–81 to 1.5 percent. The 1981 value for the chain index for machinery industries is 4.5 index points lower than the direct index, so that it shows an 8.6 percent average annual increase from 1971–81: 0.2 percentage points lower than for the official index. For the total ISPI, the recomputed index numbers from 1977 forward until the index ceased to be produced now differ at the first decimal place from the official series, although the average annual increase is still 10.5 percent.

For all manufacturing shipments, the 1971 share of computing equipment was 7.5 percent versus 8.7 percent for 1976 (see table 11.3). It may at first seem surprising that such a modest increase in basket share should have an appreciable impact, but the two percentages are not properly comparable since they are based on different price structures. The relative importance of computers in the direct index in 1976 (that is, its basket share evaluated at 1976 prices) is only 5.2 percent. This is significantly lower than the corresponding 1971 basket share because computer prices fell between 1971 and 1976, though prices of other office and store machines rose. In fact, at 1971 prices, the output of computing equipment in 1976 accounts for better than an eighth of production by office- and store-machinery manufacturers, which is much above its 1971 output share.

One would expect most new goods to follow a similar pattern, falling in price while established goods increase in price and showing a much higher rate of output growth than established goods. An interesting consequence of this is that even if a Laspeyres index does contain pricing for a new good from the time of its introduction, the relative importance of that good will tend to decline after the base period. By the same token, in a Laspeyres volume series the relative importance of a new good will tend to increase with time.

Changing Production Processes

Even if ignoring computing equipment in the Canadian producer price indexes had little impact on their values, this does not mean that the effects of the price declines for computing had little impact on the prices of consumer and producer goods, in subsequent time periods at least. The early price declines for computing equipment, when sales volumes were small, undoubtedly led many producers to shift in *subsequent* time periods to labor-saving and materials-saving computer-based technologies.

11.6   The Japanese Domestic Wholesale Price Index

It is interesting to compare the Canadian treatment of new goods, including electronic computing equipment, in the IPPI with the Japanese official producer price statistics. The Japanese Domestic Wholesale Price Index (DWPI) is one of a family of producer price indexes put out by the Bank of Japan. These include four wholesale prices indexes: the domestic WPI (DWPI), the export WPI (EWPI), the import WPI (IWPI), and the overall WPI (WPI). In addition, the Bank of Japan prepares indexes for input-output prices for the manufacturing sector. We focus on the DWPI in this and the following sections. However, there is considerable similarity in the methods of construction for this whole family of price indexes produced by the Bank of Japan.

The DWPI covers goods transacted at the interfirm level, *excluding* services, fresh produce, fish, shellfish, weapons and munitions, ships, and land and buildings. The reasons given for the exclusions come down to pricing difficulties. For example, it is stated that fresh produce (fruits and vegetables), fish, and shellfish are excluded because the seasonal price and quantity changes are volatile and hard to measure on a national basis. There are other indexes covering fresh produce, fish, and shellfish. In the case of services purchased by firms, many of these are now covered by the separate Corporate Service Price Index (CSPI), which starts in January 1985 and is also produced by the Bank of Japan. There appears to be a preference for monitoring price movements for goods viewed as hard to price with separate indexes as opposed to bringing these into the DWPI.

Basic details of the construction of the DWPI are provided in the following subsection. We review the choice of goods to be priced, the selection of firms from which price quotes are obtained, and the calculation of index weights. The market basket that is priced and the weights for the DWPI are updated every five years using the chain method. The updating discussed here is for 1990. Concerns about potential new-goods bias problems are one of the reasons given for the regular updating process. The new goods introduced in the 1990 updating are the topic of subsection 11.6.2. Subsection 11.6.3 focuses on the weight changes that took place in 1990. The treatment of evolving goods in the Japanese DWPI is briefly discussed in subsection 11.6.4.

11.6.1   Basic Features

The basic pricing principle for the DWPI is essentially the same as for the Canadian IPPI. It is to collect continuing price series for goods, controlling for any changes in transacting conditions, quality, brands, or other attributes of goods that appear to affect their prices. The stated objective is to measure pure price movements over time for unchanged goods.

The basic criterion for choosing goods for the DWPI market basket is that the transaction values are at least 0.01 percent of the total value of covered goods transacted at the interfirm level. The threshold level for the 1990 updating was 26.7 billion yen. This threshold rule for bringing "new" goods into the Japanese DWPI essentially means that none of these new goods are new in the market or availability senses (definitions 1 or 2 in section 11.2). Almost any good with a large transaction value in the present period would have existed in the previous period: these are new goods only in the operational sense of definition 3.

Basic transaction figures are computed as shipment values minus exports. The shipment values are based on survey information from the Ministry of International Trade and Industry (MITI) for manufactured goods and on a variety of other government and industry sources for the nonmanufactured goods. Goods which are not explicitly excluded from the DWPI, and for which the transaction values exceed the threshold but which are not priced due to various problems, are termed "goods not adopted for WPI." Imputed weights for the goods not adopted are added to the weights for similar sorts of goods that are adopted.

An effort is made to measure "customary prices" at the level where interfirm transactions are most intensive. This is usually the first-tier wholesale level. For most of the goods shipped directly from manufacturers to users, shipment prices are measured taking account of usual pricing practices. Rebates and other discounts are incorporated where these can be identified with specific goods. For each good adopted, prices are measured in at least two firms.

For the 1990 updating of the DWPI, there were 945 adopted goods, accounting, in terms of value, for 77.3 percent of all of the goods covered by (i.e., all of the goods not excluded by definition from) the DWPI market basket. A total of 3,164 price quotes are collected trimonthly for the adopted goods from 1,284 firms. About 80 percent of the prices are measured in the Tokyo area.

The selected brands of goods and specified transaction conditions, including the form of payment, are based on transaction-volume data and industry consultations. The intent is to select the brands that are most prevalent and to price these for the most common transaction conditions at the selected measurement sites.

The weights for the DWPI are also based on transaction-share estimates. When new goods are added or goods are deleted in the updating process, the weights for the remaining old goods are adjusted accordingly.

11.6.2   New Goods Introduced in 1990

In the 1990 updating, 69 goods were deleted and 102 new goods were added. The 102 new goods represent 10.8 percent of the 945 adopted goods. One of the added goods is computer peripherals, with a 1990 weight of 11.6 (out of a total for the DWPI of 1,000). In addition, the 1985 specification of "computers (main parts)" which only included personal computers was changed in the 1990 updating to include mainframe computers as well. Table 11.4 summarizes these changes and lists the new goods together with their 1990 weights. The category of "computers (main parts)" is also included in this list because of the important change in specification.

The information in table 11.4 on new goods in the DWPI illustrates the observation made in the previous subsection that none of the new goods in the DWPI are new as economists have defined new goods. Not only were the quantities consumed of all of these goods nonzero in the pricing period prior to their introduction in 1990, due to the threshold selection criteria, but in general, the quantities were also nonzero in 1985, the next most recent point at which the DWPI was updated and rebased. Products such as corn oil, roasted pork, and hamburgers have been used in Japan for a very long time, and mochi is a traditional rice product used in the manufacture of a wide variety of foodstuffs. Even for electrical machinery, much of which has probably been subject to technological change, it is obvious that items such as clothes dryers and halogen lamps have long been available in Japan.

Recall also that a relatively substantial number of goods were deleted in 1990. There were 69 deleted goods versus 102 added goods. However, the deleted goods are not disappearing goods in the sense of theoretical discussions. These goods were still available, and prices could still be observed for them, in the period after they were dropped from the DWPI market basket. In fact, many of the new goods are modifications of deleted goods, which is one reason why we include the deleted goods in this paper. It is simply that no quality-adjustment linkage was made between these old and new goods. Again we see that the treatment of quality change is an essential determinant of how new goods are defined in index number making. The threshold transaction criterion for the inclusion of a good in the DWPI market basket ensures that the new goods added will not be very new and the goods dropped will still be commercially available.

Table 11.4 **New Goods Added in the 1990 Updating and Their 1990 Weights**

Added New Goods (1985 weight = 0)	Weights
Food, manufactured (17 added with total weight of 6.5)	
Corn oil	0.2
Roasted pork	0.1
Hamburgers	0.2
Milk drinks (not including milk)	0.3
Smoked seafood products	0.5
Pickled seafood	0.3
Sauce for meat	0.3
Sauce for soba or udon	0.3
Chazuke, furikake	0.3
Macaroni, spaghetti	0.2
Deep-fried food	0.5
Mochi (rice cake)	0.2
Bread crumbs	0.2
Nonfat coffee cream powder	0.1
U-ron cha, u-ron cha in container	0.3
Coffee, coffee in container (excluding instant coffee)	2.0
Sport drink	0.5
Textile products (8 added with total weight of 3.3)	
Towel material	0.7
Blouse	0.3
T-shirt	0.2
Women's suits	0.6
Skirt	0.6
Ready-made kimonos, obis	0.2
Floor mat	0.5
Textile-based footwear	0.2
Pulp/paper products (2 added with total weight of 0.4)	
Raw paper for building material	0.1
Paper products for ceremonial purposes	0.3
Lumber/wood products (4 added with total weight of 1.3)	
Northern pine flat board	0.4
Spruce board	0.5
U.S. hemlock spruce board	0.3
U.S. pine board	0.1
Chemical products (14 added with total weight of 5.1)	
Dioxidized hydrogen	0.2
Potash salt	0.3
Oxidized propylene	0.5
Aniline	0.2
Polycarbonate	0.3
Saturated polyester resin	0.3
Medicine for animals	0.5
Live medicine	0.8
Surface active agent	1.1
Detergent for industrial use	0.1
Mud pack	0.1

Table 11.4   (continued)

Added New Goods (1985 weight = 0)	Weights
Hair rinse	0.3
Hair dye	0.2
Chemicals for photography	0.2
Electrical machinery (24 added with total weight of 36.0)	
Control instruments	4.3
Power distributor	0.5
Relay equipment	0.4
Industrial heating equipment	0.3
Circuit breaker	0.9
Ignition coil	0.4
Computer peripherals	11.6
Computers (main parts)[a]	8.3
Fixed-station communication equipment	1.0
Videodisc player	0.4
Speaker	0.9
Electric carpet	1.1
Electric jar (pot)	0.4
Clothes dryer	0.2
Magnetic disks	0.2
thermostat	0.1
Relays for communication equipment	0.7
Magnetic heads	2.1
Crystal oscillator	0.4
Halogen lamp	0.1
High-intensity discharge lamp	0.3
High-voltage discharge lamp equipment	0.1
Traffic signal maintenance system	0.7
Lead frames for integrated circuits	0.5
Precision equipment (5 added with total weight of 2.2)	
Industrial length scale	0.2
Precision measurement device	0.8
Measurement equipment	0.3
Separation/distillation device	0.5
Optical lens (excluding lenses for cameras and glasses)	0.4
General machinery (12 added with total weight of 10.3)	
Gas welding equipment	0.4
Ultrahard steel tools	1.4
Industrial robots	2.4
Rough-terrain crane	1.1
Asphalt paving equipment	0.2
Chemical fiber producing equipment	0.3
In-water pump	0.9
Toothed wheel	1.0
Washing machine for industrial use	0.3
Wrapping equipment	1.4
Packaging equipment	0.3
Pipe products	0.6

(continued)

Table 11.4   (continued)

Added New Goods (1985 weight = 0)	Weights
Iron/steel products (2 added with total weight of 0.4)	
Bar in coil	0.2
Carbon steel wire for ordinary steel cold press	0.2
Metal products (3 added with total weight of 1.6)	
Material for piping	0.8
Metal nameplate	0.5
Metal heat-processing equipment	0.3
Nonferrous metal (4 added with total weight of 1.2)	
Copper for copper alloy	0.1
Zinc for zinc alloy	0.4
Aluminum casting	0.2
Copper rough wires	0.5
Agriculture, seafood (1 added with weight of 0.2)	
Dried horse mackerel	0.2
Other manufactured goods (7 added with total weight of 4.3)	
Wooden-frame kitchen sink set	1.5
Religious ceremony tools	0.7
Lacquerware furniture	0.4
Lacquerware kitchen and dinner sets	0.4
Metal shelf	0.3
Video records	0.6
Room unit	0.4

Source: Bank of Japan (1992, 96–100, 111, app. table 2).

Note: Weights do not sum to totals due to rounding error.

[a]The 1985 weight for computers (main parts), which included only personal computers, was 2.1.

11.6.3   The 1990 Weight Changes

For Japan, we were able to get weight information by product group. Based on this information, shown in table 11.5, it can be seen that the weight changes at the time of the 1990 updating were substantial. A "Paasche check" was carried out by the statistical agency. The percentage difference was computed between a Paasche-type index for 1990 evaluated with the 1990 weights and a Laspeyres-type index for 1990 evaluated using the old 1985 weights, with the difference standardized by the Laspeyres index value. This percentage figure was −2.0 percent. This figure is compared with the value of −1.7 percent for the Paasche check for the 1985 updating from 1980 weights. These are small-percentage figures.

It is interesting to examine some of the goods for which the 1990 weights did, and did not, change from the 1985 weights. For example, the price of Japanese word processors, which are personal computers specifically designed for Japanese word processing, fell by 48.4 percent between 1985 and 1990, while the number of units produced in 1990 was 8.3 times the number pro-

Table 11.5   **Changes in Weights from 1985 to 1990**

	1990 Weights	1985 Weights	Change from 1985 to 1990
Manufactured goods	919.1	893.8	+25.3
Food, manufactured	97.5	102.1	−4.6
Textile products	35.8	42.6	−6.8
Pulp/paper products	30.0	32.7	−2.7
Lumber/wood products	17.1	18.3	−1.2
Chemical products	73.7	78.9	−5.2
Electrical machinery	148.1	118.5	+29.6
Precision equipment	12.1	11.5	+0.6
General machinery	113.9	97.9	+16.0
Iron/steel products	54.8	59.8	−5.0
Metal products	46.5	40.4	+6.1
Nonferrous metal	25.5	25.2	+0.3
Other manfuactured goods	83.2	79.1	+4.1
Plastic products	38.3	36.0	+2.3
Ceramics products	36.0	35.8	+0.2
Petroleum/coal products	30.3	59.1	−28.8
Transport	76.3	55.9	+20.4
Agricultural/forestry products	30.9	40.0	−9.1
Agriculture; seafood	27.7	35.9	−8.2
Nonfood	3.2	4.1	−0.9
Mineral products	9.3	8.9	+0.4
Electricity, city gas, and water	37.1	52.0	−14.9
Scrapped materials	3.6	5.3	−1.7
Total	1,000.0	1,000.0	0.0

Source: Bank of Japan (1992, 13, table 3).

duced in 1985. The weight for Japanese word processors increased from 1.2 in 1985 to 3.9 in 1990. Another example is video cameras. While the number of video cameras produced in 1990 was 2.6 times that for 1985, their price fell by 40.2 percent between 1985 and 1990. Because of these offsetting changes, the weight for video cameras changed little: from 0.5 in 1985 to 0.6 in 1990.

11.6.4   Dealing with Evolving Goods

In the construction of the DWPI for Japan, when new goods are recognized as modifications of old adopted goods, the direct-comparison pricing approach is used as long as the difference between the new and the old good are not thought to relate materially to the quality of what is being purchased.

For some of the cases where the direct-comparison approach is deemed to be inappropriate, quality adjustments are carried out. When the decision is made that the observed price difference between a new good and an old good is entirely due to changes in quality, a method which the Japanese call *consistency processing* is used. An imputed unit price for the new good is related to the unit price for the old good using the ratio of the observed prices for the new and old goods in the linking period. This is the method of quality adjustment called linking by statistical agencies in other countries such as the United States and Canada.

The Japanese also make use of cost-evaluation quality adjustments in the DWPI. In fact, this is probably the main quality-adjustment method used. However, it is stated that the agency has been relying less on this method in recent years, in part because, with rapid technological change and new and more flexible design and production methods, it is believed that producers are often unable to isolate the costs of production associated with quality changes. Instead, the Bank of Japan is making more use of the hedonic method for valuation of quality differences. Use of the hedonic approach is the stated reason that computer peripherals could be brought into the DWPI and the "computer (main parts)" specification could be broadened in the 1990 updating, as is discussed in the following section. An apparent implication of the shift to greater use of hedonic quality adjustment is that more goods will probably be brought into the DWPI as new variants of older goods included in the index rather than as new DWPI goods.

11.7   Computers in the Japanese DWPI

11.7.1   General History

The first Bank of Japan price index in which computers were included was an import price index, but not the modern day IWPI.[1] Electronic computers were introduced into that index in the 1965 revision as a separate commodity in the "office equipment" category, which also included other commodity groups such as electric calculators and accounting machines. Two types of electronic computing equipment were priced for the old import price index, with the type specifications changing in 1970. Up through June 1970 these two types were (1) U.S.-made small digital computers, and (2) Canadian-made electronic memory. After June 1970, they were (1) U.S.-made medium-sized digital computers, and (2) West German–made electronic memory.

The supply of Japanese-made computers rose rapidly over the 1965–75 period, and foreign import sales fell. Because of this, computers were dropped from the old import price index in the 1975 revision. After that, it was a decade before electronic computing equipment was again introduced into Bank of Japan price indexes. The pattern of reintroduction reflected the revision cycle for the main price indexes produced by the Bank of Japan.

Every five years, the Bank of Japan first revises its wholesale price indexes and then its input-output price indexes (IOPI). Electronic computing equip-

---

1. Note that the WPI system during this period included imported and exported goods but did not cover computers. The import price index mentioned here was not part of the WPI system.

Table 11.6   **The "Standard" Personal Computer**

Characteristics	No. of Notebook Types	No. of Desktop Types
Display	2 (monochrome liquid crystal and STN color liquid crystal)	1 (color CRT)
CPU	2 (386 and 486)	1 (486)
RAM	5 (1MB, 1.6MB, 2MB, 4MB, 11.6MB)	2 (1.6MB, 4MB)
Hard-disk drive	4 (0, 20MB, 40MB, 80MB)	3 (100MB, 170MB, 340MB)
Floppy-disk drive	2 (1 drive and 2 drives)	2 (1 drive and 2 drives)
Total types	$2 \times 2 \times 5 \times 4 \times 2 = 160$	$1 \times 1 \times 2 \times 3 \times 2 = 12$

Source: Bank of Japan, internal memorandum.

ment was first brought into the WPI system with the 1985 revision (published beginning in December 1987). The only type of computing equipment covered in the WPI system at that time was personal computers. Computers were first included in the IOPI in the 1985 revision also (published beginning in December 1989). For the IOPI, the type of computing equipment covered was specified to be general-purpose computers.

Coverage of different types of computing equipment was expanded for the WPI in the 1990 revision, published in December 1992. It was also expanded in the 1990 revision of the IOPI.

11.7.2 Pricing Methods

Standard-Model Pricing in the DWPI

When personal computers were first included in the DWPI in 1985, a standard-model pricing approach was used. The "standard" personal computer was represented by 160 types of notebook computers and 12 types of desktop computers with combinations of characteristics as shown in table 11.6. As for mainframe computers, at the time of the 1985 revision it was decided that more research was needed on possible pricing methods that could account for changing model types and optional special features included as part of purchase agreements. Until 1990, mainframe computers were not even included in the sample of goods used in determining weight values. The shipment value of mainframe computers was *not* allocated to other commodities or commodity groups adopted for the DWPI.

Hedonic Pricing in the DWPI

The Bank of Japan adopted hedonic pricing methods for computers in the 1990 revision of the DWPI, and the types of computers being priced were expanded to include mainframe computers. A double-log functional form is used for the hedonic equation. The characteristics included are processing speed, memory size, the number of channels, size dummies (large, medium, small), and year dummies.

In general, for all other categories of goods, the Bank of Japan has had a policy of trying to collect transaction prices. When the computer category was broadened and hedonic pricing was adopted in 1990, a decision was also made to use list (or catalogue) prices for this commodity category as the basic price information. Thus, it is the log of the list price that is the dependent variable for the computer hedonic equation. There are several reasons this decision was made. One is that computers and their accessories, and also associated software, are often transacted as parts of a system. It is difficult to collect data on and to allow fully for system differences, even using a hedonic approach to adjust for quality differences. A second reason is that producers of computers often provide discounts based on guesses about customers' future purchases of related equipment and services. Information on these discounts is difficult to obtain. Moreover, the grounds for these discounts are not *product* characteristics; rather, they are characteristics of the purchasing enterprise.

The Determination of Weights in the DWPI

Another important issue is the determination of weights to be assigned to specific items (products) which represent individual commodities. We are grateful to the Bank of Japan for outlining for us the procedures used for determining weights for computer products. First, the values of domestic shipments for various computer products are calculated by subtracting export figures from the values of production for seven types of goods: (1) analog computers, (2) digital computers, (3) external memory, (4) input/output (I/O) devices, (5) business remote terminals, (6) other peripheral support devices, and (7) parts and attachments (see table 11.7).

After calculating the values of domestic shipments, shipment values of goods in each category are calculated or allocated to the goods listed on the right-hand side of table 11.8. For example, the value of domestic shipments for external memory is 751 billion yen and includes magnetic tape units, magnetic drum units, magnetic disk units, and other devices. In table 11.8, the values for these goods are allocated to the following three goods categories: "magnetic disk units," "flexible disk units," and "other goods." Similar allocations of shipment values are carried out for other categories.

In table 11.9, the value for "other" categories of goods are allocated to specific product types. For example, 133 and 195 billion yen of other computers in category (2) are allocated to "general-purpose computers" and "personal computers," respectively. (The reason for this particular division of the 328 billion yen is not known to us.) A similar allocation of the shipment values of "other goods" in categories (3) and (4) is carried out, as indicated in table 11.9. The goods for which prices are monitored for DWPI are general-purpose computers and personal computers, magnetic disk units and flexible disk units, printers and displays, remote terminals, and other goods in category (7).

One difference in the sampling frame used for computer products between

Table 11.7   **Calculating Domestic Shipment Values for Computer-Related Products: Detailed Calculation for 1990**

Six-Digit Code	Goods Group	Total Shipments (billion yen)[a]	Included Goods
(1) 305111	Analog computers (incl. hybrid type)	0 (0)	
(2) 305112	Digital computers (CPU)	2,252 (389)	General purpose, large General purpose, medium General purpose, small Personal computers Work stations
(3) 305113	External memory	1,253 (502)	Magnetic tape unit Magnetic drum unit Magnetic disk unit, etc.
(4) 305114	I/O devices	1,320 (803)	Keyboards Line printers Optical readers and scanners
(5) 305115	Business remote terminals	1,313 (0)	Point-of-sale terminals Automated teller machines
(6) 305119	Other peripheral support devices	271 (64)	
(7) 305121	Parts and attachments	1,473 (965)	
Total[b]		7,883 (2,724)	

Source: Bank of Japan, internal memorandum and personal communication.

[a]Numbers in parentheses are export values.

[b]Shipment values do not sum to total due to rounding error.

Japan and the U.S./Canada is that, for Japan, computers and their accessories are mostly in the electronic and communication machinery subgroup, which in turn is part of the electric machinery group. The general machinery group contains the office and household machinery subgroup which includes the office machines class (DWPI 1990 weight = 11.6), which in turn includes table-top electronic calculating machines (1.3), copying machines (6.2), cash registers (0.2), and Japanese word processors (3.9). Given that the 1990 DWPI combined weight for computers and their accessories is about 20, the office machines commodity class is small relative to computers. Japanese word processors, which are microcomputers specifically tailored for Japanese word processing, would likely be called computers in North America. As with personal computers, the DWPI started to include Japanese word processors in 1985. In Canada, as in the United States, computers are part of a broad office, computing, and accounting machinery group (the office machines and equipment group for Canada).

Table 11.8   **First-Stage Inputting by Goods Group (1990)**

Six-Digit Code	Goods Group	Domestic Shipments (billion yen)	Included Goods	Allocated Production Value
(1) 305111	Analog computers (incl. hybrid type)[a]			
(2) 305112	Digital computers (CPU)	1,863	General-purpose computers	902
			Personal computers	633
			Work stations	328
(3) 305113	External memory	751	Magnetic disk unit	486
			Flexible disk unit	101
			Other goods (imputed)	164
(4) 305114	I/O devices	516	Printers	376
			Displays	102
			Other goods (imputed)	39
(5) 305115	Business remote terminals	1,313	Remote terminals	1,313
(6) 305119	Other peripheral support devices[b]	206	Auxiliary devices	
			Other goods (imputed)	
(7) 305121	Parts and attachments	509	Programs	715
			Other goods (imputed)	
Total[c]		5,160		5,160

Source: See table 11.7.
[a]Imputed into category (2).
[b]Imputed into category (7).
[c]Shipment values do not sum to totals due to rounding error.

Representative-Model Pricing in the IOPI

As stated above, the Bank of Japan introduced computing equipment into their IOPI system as well as into their WPI system in the 1985 revision cycle. For the IOPI, both producers' buying and selling prices must be measured. Some goods cannot be adopted for the IOPI because of a lack of either input- or output-price information. Also, the selection criteria for adopting a good into a commodity group for the IOPI are somewhat different from those for the WPI. Price information for about 750 goods is collected specifically for the IOPI, and is used in conjunction with price information for approximately 1,240 more goods from the Bank of Japan's WPI production operation.

When electronic computing equipment was first introduced into the IOPI, three types of items were priced: (1) a large general-purpose mainframe computer, (2) a medium-sized general-purpose mainframe computer, and (3) a personal computer. With the cooperation of industry, representative models were selected for these three types of electronic computing equipment. When one of the representative models had to be changed, a linking procedure was used. This linking procedure focuses on the unit price per million instructions per second (MIPS) before and after a representative model change. It could be

Table 11.9 Second-Stage Inputting by Goods Group (1990)

Six-Digit Code	Goods Group	Domestic Shipments (billion yen)	Included Goods	Plus Imputed Value for Other Goods	Total[a]
(1) 305111	Analog computers (incl. hybrid type)[b]				
(2) 305112	Digital computers (CPU)	1,863	General-purpose computers	902[c]+133	1,035 (3.9)
			Personal computers	633[c]+195	828 (3.1)
			Other	328[d]	
(3) 305113	External memory	751	Magnetic disk unit	486[c]+136	622 (2.3)
			Flexible disk unit	101[c]+28	129 (0.5)
			Other goods (imputed)	164[d]	
(4) 305114	I/O devices	516	Printers	376[c]+30	406 (1.5)
			Displays	102[c]+9	111 (0.4)
			Other goods (imputed)	39[d]	
(5) 305115	Business remote terminals	1,313	Remote terminals	1,313[c]	1,313 (4.9)
(6) 305119	Other peripheral support devices[e]	206			
(7) 305121	Parts and attachments	509	Other goods (imputed)	715[c]	715 (2.7)
	Total[f]	5,160			5,160 (19.4)

Source: See table 11.7.

[a]Numbers in parentheses are 1990 DWPI weights, where 1 point = 267 billion yen.

[b]Imputed into category (2).

[c]Prices for the goods are monitored.

[d]Allocated to other goods in this category.

[e]Imputed into category (7).

[f]Values do not sum to totals due to rounding error.

viewed as a hedonic adjustment taking into account only one product characteristic (MIPS).

The 1990 revision of the IOPI also makes use of hedonic pricing for computing equipment. However, we could not obtain details of the hedonic equations used.

11.8   Consequences of the Delayed Inclusion of Computers in the Japanese DWPI

The relative share of the value of shipments of computer products in the category "all commodities" (for which the 1990 DWPI weight is 1,000) or in the category "manufacturing industry products" (for which the 1990 DWPI weight is 919.1) is negligible, given the 1990 DWPI weight of about 20 for computer products. This is consistent with the Canadian case discussed in section 11.5.

The share of computer products in the category "electrical machinery," for which the 1990 DWPI weight is 148.1, is 13.5 percent. That is, the value of domestic shipments of computer products was 13.5 percent of the domestic production of electrical machinery. This ratio of the shipment value of computer products to that of electrical machinery increased gradually from a plateau of about 5 percent throughout the 1970s to about 6 percent in the early 1980s, to above 10 percent by the late 1980s, and to 13.5 percent in 1990.

Computers were not included in the Japanese WPI system until 1985, but subindexes for semiconductors and integrated circuits (produced by all the computer producers in Japan) were included prior to 1985. Table 11.10 shows the substantial price declines for transistors and integrated circuits in Japan over the last two decades. Since transistors and other semiconductors, and also integrated circuits, are used widely in many manufactured goods, it is not possible to relate computer prices directly to the prices of these components. (The combined 1990 weight for semiconductor devices and integrated circuits was 16.3 compared to about 19.9 for computers and related accessories.) It seems likely, however, that the downward movements in the prices of semiconductors and integrated circuits partially explain the downward price movements for Japanese computers, for which we have price information only since 1985.[2] (See table 11.11.)

In Japan, superiority in the production of semiconductors and integrated circuits was viewed as vital to the longer-run success of the domestic computer industry, and many of the computer manufacturers also produced semiconductors and integrated circuits. Like computers, the production of semiconductors and integrated circuits became increasingly large relative to the total value of shipments for electrical machinery: 3.3 percent in 1975, 7.3 percent in 1980,

---

2. It is well known that semiconductors, integrated circuits, and computers were among a number of technology-based projects supported by the Japanese industry and government.

Table 11.10   DWPI Subindexes for Electrical Machinery, Transistors, and
                         Integrated Circuits

	Electrical Machinery	Transistors	Integrated Circuits
1970	100.0	100.0	100.0
1971	96.8	93.7	59.8
1972	95.0	88.7	47.0
1973	96.7	81.7	44.8
1974	114.8	84.0	47.1
1975	118.0	73.7	36.7
1976	116.3	72.2	32.5
1977	115.7	70.2	29.3
1978	112.7	65.8	25.9
1979	113.0	62.1	23.5
1980	116.1	61.8	23.7
1981	117.4	60.9	22.3
1982	115.5	57.7	20.6
1983	113.7	54.7	19.2
1984	112.5	56.0	19.5
1985	110.3	53.8	14.2
1986	103.5	49.1	10.7
1987	97.4	40.5	9.7
1988	93.4	37.0	10.0
1989	91.9	37.7	10.1
1990	89.6	37.1	8.8
1991	86.5	36.7	7.7
1992	85.0	36.7	6.9
1993	83.0	36.7	6.5

Source: Bank of Japan, *Price Index Annual,* various years.

12.0 percent in 1985, and 11.0 percent in 1990 for semiconductors; and 2.6 percent in 1975, 4.2 percent in 1980, 9.3 percent in 1985 and 9.1 percent in 1990 for integrated circuits.

Suppose that the Japanese subindexes for transistors or for integrated circuits had been used as a proxy for computer prices over the 1970–89 period. Our calculations show that using the prices of transistors as the proxy series for computing equipment, the price index for electrical machinery (1970 = 100) would have been lower than the official value by 4.7 percent in 1989. Using the prices of integrated circuits as the proxy series, the price index for electrical machinery (1970 = 100) would have been lower by 7 percent.

11.9   Conclusions

We have examined the treatment of new goods in both the Canadian Industrial Product Price Index (IPPI) and the Japanese Domestic Wholesale Price Index (DWPI). For both indexes, most of the new goods introduced in recent

Table 11.11   **Price Indexes for Computer Products and Electronic Parts (1985 = 100): Japan, 1985–1992**

	Domestic Wholesale Price Index			Input/Output Price Index[a]		
	Personal Computers	Semiconductors	Integrated Circuits	Computers[b] (main parts)	Computer Accessory Devices	Japanese Word Processors
Weight (1985 base)[c]	2.1	14.2	11.0	15.00	27.70	5.94
1985	100.0	100.0	100.0	100.0	100.0	100.0
1986	83.8	78.0	74.6	94.1	98.7	90.3
1987	72.1	69.9	68.5	79.1	97.9	75.2
1988	70.1	70.3	70.7	74.5	84.5	56.2
1989	71.8	71.1	71.5	74.5	82.7	53.4
1990	71.5	63.8	62.3	73.7	81.9	51.6
1991	65.1	60.1	57.8	63.6	81.9	48.9
1992	—	—	—	52.9	81.9	48.6

Source: Bank of Japan, *Price Index Annual,* various years.

[a]The input and output price indexes for 1985–92 are identical for the commodity groups reported here. These indexes are gross-weight based.

[b]The basket for this commodity group consists of large- and medium-sized general-purpose computers and personal computers.

[c]Component weights for the DWPI sum to 1,000.

revisions are not new in a market or an availability sense. They are simply goods that were not included before because of the basket selection procedures. These selection procedures make it unlikely for goods to be included that had low transaction values in the previous period, and people rarely begin to buy large amounts of goods with which they have had no previous experience. Most of the exceptions that come to mind are goods that, in fact, are related closely enough to older goods that people feel familiar with them and their uses.

There *are* some high-tech goods like computers that were ignored, even after their transaction values were quite high. But this is because these goods are difficult to price; not because there were no prices for previous periods. These are goods which have many different variants because of technological improvements over time, or which are commonly sold as part of customer-specific package deals. Both Canada and Japan are using hedonic quality-adjustment methods to try to deal with these problems. This is lessening the gaps in pricing coverage. One undesirable consequence, however, is that the pricing treatment of computing equipment is qualitatively different than that for most of the other included goods, which are still being priced using a matched-models approach. Also, since many details of the hedonic pricing are not public, this further complicates the problem of making comparisons of price changes over time or among countries.

Despite the delay in introducing computing equipment into the producer price indexes for Canada and Japan, we find that these omissions had small effects on the overall values of the Canadian and Japanese producer price indexes. This is in contrast to others' findings for U.S. indexes, where production values for computing equipment were much larger over the period for which computers were excluded from the Canadian and Japanese price statistics. It is important to note that this finding does not mean that downward movements in the producer prices for computing equipment were economically unimportant. These declines undoubtedly led many producers to begin efforts to shift to computer-based technologies in *subsequent* time periods that, in turn, led to downward movements in the costs of production and prices for large numbers of goods and services.

References

Bank of Japan. 1992. *Explanation of the Wholesale Price Indexes: 1990 Base* (in Japanese). Tokyo: Bank of Japan.

Diewert, W. E. 1980. Aggregation problems in the measurement of capital. In *The measurement of capital,* ed. D. Usher, 433–528. NBER Studies in Income and Wealth, vol. 45. Chicago: University of Chicago Press.

————. 1993a. Overview of volume 1. In *Essays in index number theory,* ed. W. E. Diewert and A. O. Nakamura, 1–31. Amsterdam: North-Holland.

————. 1993b. The early history of price index research. In *Essays in index number theory,* ed. W. E. Diewert and A. O. Nakamura, 33–65. Amsterdam: North-Holland.

Diewert, W. E., and A. O. Nakamura, eds. 1993. *Essays in index number theory.* Amsterdam: North-Holland.

Fisher, F., and K. Shell. 1972. *The economic theory of price indexes.* New York: Academic Press.

Fisher, I. 1922. *The making of index numbers.* Boston: Houghton Mifflin.

Gordon, R. J. 1990. *The measurement of durable goods prices.* Chicago: University of Chicago Press.

Hicks, J. R. 1940. The valuation of the social income. *Economica* 7:105–24.

Hofsten, E. von. 1952. *Price indexes and quality change.* London: Allen and Unwin.

MacDonald, L. 1991. Appendix: Development of hedonic models for microcomputer price index project. Prices Division, Statistics Canada, Ottawa. Unpublished memorandum.

Marshall, A. [1887] 1925. Remedies for fluctuations of general prices. *Contemporary Review* 51:355–75. Reprinted in *Memorials of Alfred Marshall,* ed. A. C. Pigou, chap. 8. London: Macmillan.

Statistics Canada. 1971. *General review of the manufacturing industry of Canada, vol. 1.* Catalogue no. 31-203, annual. Ottawa: Statistics Canada.

————. 1976. *Products shipped by Canadian manufacturers.* Catalogue no. 31-211, annual. Ottawa: Statistics Canada.

————. 1978. *Industry selling price indexes: Manufacturing, 1971 = 100, 1956–1976.* Catalogue no. 62-543, occasional. Ottawa: Statistics Canada.

————. 1986. *Industrial product price indexes, 1981 = 100: Concepts and methods.* Catalogue no. 62-556, occasional. Ottawa: Statistics Canada.

————. 1991. *Industry price indexes, 1986 = 100: User's guide.* Catalogue no. 62-558, occasional. Ottawa: Statistics Canada.

————. Various issues. *Industry price indexes.* Catalogue no. 62-011. Ottawa: Statistics Canada.

Triplett, J. E. 1971. Quality bias in price indexes and new methods of quality measurement. In *Price indexes and quality change,* ed. Z. Griliches, 180–214. Cambridge, Mass.: Harvard University Press.

Comment   Robert Summers

This paper focuses on a spatial dimension of the new-goods price index problem, and my remarks about it flow from a particular United Nations International Comparison Programme (ICP) point of view about interspatial comparisons. (Generically, ICP refers to the set of organizations and individuals worldwide concerned with national-accounts comparisons across countries.) In a dynamic world in which new goods are constantly being introduced, the construction of a price index that takes account of their availability is thought of primarily in one-dimensional, *temporal* terms. For most purposes, the concentration is on a particular political subdivision—say, a country or region or city—and a way to take into account the utility changes there that result from both changes in the availability of new goods and changes in prices. All of the emphasis is on the price index *time series.*

In recent years various kinds of economic comparisons across political subdivisions have become more common. Greater interdependence of national economies and globalization of financial markets has increased the need for international comparisons of prices and price changes. Clearly, the new-goods problem arises in this area also, but with a small subtlety. In the construction of a space-time system of national accounts (SNA) covering most of the countries of the world, an endeavor in which I am involved, differences in the availability of goods across countries is a problem not unrelated to the new-goods problem. A good not present in one country but present in another at an identifiable price is like a good not available in one period but available subsequently. Making price-level comparisons for particular goods categories, across countries at a point in time, may be straightforward even if particular goods in the category vary in vintage from country to country. However, estimating differential price changes across countries escapes none of the new-goods headaches.

A vexing problem encountered almost immediately in a thoughtful construction of a space-time SNA is the reconciliation of estimates of countries' relative gross domestic products at different dates that are derived from successive ICP benchmark studies with estimates of their relative intervening growth rates

Robert Summers is professor of economics at the University of Pennsylvania.

as measured by the countries' own price statisticians. Because of the difficulty of matching goods of identical quality across dissimilar countries, interspatial price comparisons are generally thought to be less accurate than intertemporal ones. Full consideration of the intertemporal new-goods problem makes this less obviously true. By matching types of new investment goods in the various countries, it is at least arguable that at a point of time some kinds of goods are valued more accurately than are changes in goods over time.

It should be clear that my somewhat parochial national-account viewpoint is by no means the only one for thinking about spatial comparisons. An example: international macroeconomists attempting to make unemployment and potential-output comparisons across countries would be frustrated by significant differences in the way the countries measure their unemployment rates. Similarly, they would find it difficult if not impossible to describe, much less understand, the international dynamics of price movements and resulting estimated quantity changes if countries do not use a fairly uniform price index methodology. Do they?

If I were drafted to begin a research effort to understand better the new-good impact on the ICP numbers or more generally the macroeconomic issues, I would start by asking what reporting countries do in this area, and I would check on what organizations that have a stake in this investigation are already doing. (The European Union Statistical Office has been concerned for some time with harmonizing the statistical activities of the European Union countries.) I would want to know whether the countries do the right things, of course, but almost as significant would be, right or wrong, whether they all do the same things. I would probably first look at the actual practices of a couple of important countries. The statistical offices of developing countries are not likely to be at the methodological cutting edge, so I would pick advanced countries, preferably not closely related culturally. I would start by writing down what I thought the countries *ought* to do and then see what they *in fact* do. In the course of this I would pay particular attention to some product area where the new-good problem is most prevalent. Being painfully aware of the impact of obsolescence, as distinct from wear-and-tear, on my computer budget, I probably would choose some part of the electronics industry as the basis of a case study. In the end I would call the resulting paper something like "The New-Goods Problem from the Perspective of Price Index Making in Countries X and Y," after trying to get, say, Canada and Japan to serve as X and Y. How nice that I've been spared the need to defect to Canada to avoid this draft. To run the metaphor into the ground, how ironic that Canadians have done my work for me already.

There is so much ground to cover in seeing how countries handle the new goods problem that it would be mean-spirited to complain if the authors did something different from what I would have done. Since consumption is considerably larger than investment, I probably would have started with the Consumer Price Index. (That would have the advantage of enabling me to apply my favorite index number test that really goes with improved rather than new goods but it comes to much the same thing: If it costs no more to produce yellow tennis balls than white ones but playing with yellow ones is universally regarded to be better than playing with white ones, does the price index calculation properly reflect the reduction in cost of playing enjoyable tennis?) Since working with producers' goods is necessary before the whole job is done, perhaps which is taken up first is only a matter of taste and ease.

As I look at the whole paper, I see many questions left open, but that is exactly what should be expected at the beginning of a long-term effort. Beginnings excite less attention than endings, but in fact may be harder to carry out. Long journeys begin with many small steps, and Rome wasn't built in a day.

Contributors

Paul A. Armknecht
Bureau of Labor Statistics
2 Massachusetts Avenue NE
Room 3211 BC
Washington, DC 20212

Andrew Baldwin
Prices Division, Statistics Canada
D2, Jean Talon Building, 13th floor
Tunney's Pasture
Ottawa, ON K1A 0T6, Canada

Ernst R. Berndt
Sloan School of Management
Massachusetts Institute of Technology
50 Memorial Drive, E52-452
Cambridge, MA 02139

Timothy F. Bresnahan
Department of Economics
Landau Center
Stanford University
Stanford, CA 94305

John C. Brown
Department of Economics
Clark University
950 Main Street
Worcester, MA 01610

Erik Brynjolfsson
Sloan School of Management
Massachusetts Institute of Technology
50 Memorial Drive, E53-313
Cambridge, MA 02139

Linda T. Bui
Department of Economics
Boston University
270 Bay State Road
Boston, MA 02215

Pierre Després
Prices Division, Statistics Canada
Jean Talon Building, 13th floor
Tunney's Pasture
Ottawa, ON K1A 0T6, Canada

W. E. Diewert
Department of Economics
University of British Columbia
Vancouver, BC V6T 1Z1, Canada

Robert C. Feenstra
Department of Economics
University of California
Davis, CA 95616

Robert J. Gordon
Department of Economics
Northwestern University
2003 Sheridan Road, Room G-174
Evanston, IL 60208

Shane M. Greenstein
Department of Economics
University of Illinois
1206 South Sixth Street
Champaign, IL 61820

477

Zvi Griliches
National Bureau of Economic Research
1050 Massachusetts Avenue
Cambridge, MA 02138

Jerry A. Hausman
Department of Economics
Massachusetts Institute of Technology
Room E52-271A
Cambridge, MA 02138

Charles R. Hulten
Department of Economics
University of Maryland
Tydings Hall, Room 3105
College Park, MD 20742

Walter F. Lane
Bureau of Labor Statistics
2 Massachusetts Avenue NE
Room 3615 PSB
Washington, DC 21202

Joel Mokyr
Department of Economics
Northwestern University
2003 Sheridan Road
Evanston, IL 60208

Brent R. Moulton
Bureau of Labor Statistics
2 Massachusetts Avenue NE
Room 3105
Washington, DC 20212

Alice Nakamura
Faculty of Business
University of Alberta
3-23 Business Building
Edmonton, AB T6G 2R6, Canada

Masao Nakamura
Faculty of Commerce, Institute of Asian
    Research, and Faculty of Applied
    Science
University of British Columbia
2053 Main Mall
Vancouver, BC V6T 1Z2, Canada

William D. Nordhaus
Department of Economics
Yale University
28 Hillhouse Avenue
New Haven, CT 06511

Walter Y. Oi
Department of Economics
University of Rochester
Rochester, NY 14627

Daniel M. G. Raff
Department of Management
The Wharton School
University of Pennsylvania
Philadelphia, PA 19104

David H. Lucking-Reiley
Department of Economics and Business
    Administration
Box 1819, Station B
Vanderbilt University
Nashville, TN 37235

Marshall B. Reinsdorf
Division of Price and Index Number
    Research
Bureau of Labor Statistics
2 Massachusetts Avenue NE
Room 3105
Washington, DC 20212

Clinton R. Shiells
International Monetary Fund
700 Nineteenth Street NW
Room 5-218
Washington, DC 20431

Rebecca Stein
Department of Economics
Northwestern University
2003 Sheridan Road
Evanston, IL 60208

Kenneth J. Stewart
Bureau of Labor Statistics
2 Massachusetts Avenue NE
Washington, DC 20212

Robert Summers
Department of Economics
University of Pennsylvania
3718 Locust Walk
Philadelphia, PA 19104

Valerie Y. Suslow
University of Michigan Business School
701 Tappan Street
Ann Arbor, MI 48109

Manuel Trajtenberg
Department of Economics
Tel Aviv University
Tel Aviv 69978, Israel

Jack E. Triplett
Bureau of Economic Analysis
Department of Commerce
1401 K Street NW
Washington, DC 20230

Glen L. Urban
Sloan School of Management
Massachusetts Institute of Technology
50 Memorial Drive, E52-473
Cambridge, MA 02139

Frank C. Wykoff
Pomona College
645 N. College Avenue
109 Seaver North
Claremont, CA 91711

Name Index

Ackerknecht, Erwin H., 181
Aizcorbe, Ana, 403, 428
Alchian, Armen A., 119n14
Allen, R. G. D., 426n11
Alterman, William, 250, 265n12
Amemiya, Takeshi, 338
Anderson, S. P., 230n29
Anglin, Paul M., 405n6, 427n13
Appert, Benjamin N., 160
Apple, Rima D., 162n34, 163
Archibald, R. B., 428
Armknecht, Paul A., 382, 384, 424n2, 425,
    432
Arrow, K. J., 132
Arsenault, Raymond, 128n27, 131
Asher, Harold, 119n14

Bailey, N. T. J., 119n12
Baily, Martin N., 16, 55n9
Baker, Russell, 124
Balk, B. M., 424n3, 428
Bastiat, Frédéric, 33
Baye, Michael R., 405n6, 427n13
Beaver, M. W., 163
Becker, Gary S., 5, 14, 133, 144n1
Beebe, Alfred, 158
Behring, Emil, 158, 185
Beran, Jan, 416n10
Berndt, E. R., 88, 310, 331n3, 344, 394, 430
Berry, Steven, 76–77n13, 229n27, 240,
    242n10, 274, 331n2, 335nn5,6,7, 337,
    363
Bezanson, Anne, 49t

Blackorby, C., 218n17
Boes, Duane C., 401n2, 406, 419, 421
Bond, Ronald S., 291
Bonomo, Giovanni, 159n30
Booz, Allen, and Hamilton, Inc., 116n7
Borden, Gail, 160
Bowley, A. L., 427nn12,14, 432
Brainard, S. Lael, 260n7, 261–62t
Braithwait, Steve D., 403
Bresnahan, Timothy, 8, 79, 87n25, 242,
    289n10, 331nn2,3, 334, 335, 337, 338,
    339n15, 344n28, 351n34, 356, 360, 363,
    364n3, 366n5
Breusch, T. S., 219n20
Broussais, François, 181n63
Brown, John C., 144, 151n14, 184, 185
Brown, R. K., 161, 178n60, 180
Brynjolfsson, Eric, 331n3, 351n34, 364n3,
    366n5
Buchanan, Ian, 163, 165n37
Budd, William, 154n21
Burnett, John, 61t, 62n11
Burtless, Gary, 211n4

Cain, Louis, 184
Carli, G. R., 424–25
Carlson, Chester, 117n10
Carrier, Willis H., 122
Carruthers, A. G., 423, 424n3, 426n11
Cautley, Edmond, 162, 163n35
Caves, Richard E., 297n15
Cearnal, Martin E., 283
Chaney, Paul K., 118

Subject Index